SELLING **TODAY**

creating customer value

FOURTH CANADIAN EDITION

GERALD L. MANNING
Des Moines Area Community College

BARRY L. REECE
Virginia Polytechnic Institute and State University

H.F. (HERB) MacKENZIE
Brock University

Toronto

Library and Archives Canada Cataloguing in Publication

Manning, Gerald L
Selling today : creating customer value / Gerald L. Manning, Barry L. Reece, H.F. (Herb) MacKenzie. – 4th Canadian ed.

Includes bibliographical references and index.
ISBN 0-13-127599-2

1. Selling—Textbooks. I. Reece, Barry L. II. MacKenzie, H. F. III. Title.

HF5438.25.M35 2006 658.85 C2005-907526-0

ISBN 0-127599-2

Vice President, Editorial Director: Michael J. Young
Editor-in-Chief, Business, Finance and Economics: Gary Bennett
Acquisitions Editor: Laura Paterson Forbes
Marketing Manager: Eileen Lasswell
Senior Marketing Coordinator: Kathie Kirchsteiger
Senior Developmental Editor: Pamela Voves
Production Editor: Avivah Wargon
Copy Editor: Susan Quirk
Production Coordinator: Deborah Starks
Page Layout: Jansom
Permissions and Photo Research: Terri Rothman
Art Director: Julia Hall
Cover and Interior Design: Miguel Angel Acevedo
Cover Image: Getty / Photodisc Red / Manchan

1 2 3 4 5 11 10 09 08 07

Printed and bound in the United States of America.

Brief Contents

Contents

Preface

Today, and in the years ahead, salespeople will be guided by a new principle: **Buyer–seller partnerships are established and maintained only when the salesperson creates customer value.** Value-added selling is the theme and force behind *Selling Today: Creating Customer Value,* Fourth Canadian Edition. Customers are changing their expectations. They want to partner with salespeople who can create value, not just communicate it. Value creation involves a series of improvements in the sales process that enhance the customer experience. As customers and the field of selling have evolved, so has our text, to meet the expectations and needs of our customers.

The new age of personal selling requires that we build on past improvements and adjust to the changes that have accompanied the age of information. Learning how to manage and communicate information to customers within an effective relationship based on trust is one of the major challenges facing salespeople today. Personal selling in the age of information also involves fulfilling customer expectations through "partnering" relationships. These alliances, which represent the highest-quality selling relationships, are growing in importance. They have created a new selling environment that requires the use of advanced customer relationship management (CRM) technology. The fundamentals of CRM represent an important feature of the fourth Canadian edition of *Selling Today: Creating Customer Value.* Important components have been retained from earlier Canadian editions. ACT! contact management software, for example, is again included on CD-ROM within the text.

Creating Customer Value

1. The four broad strategic areas of personal selling, introduced in Chapter 1, serve as a catalyst for skill development and professional growth throughout the text. Success in selling depends heavily on the student's ability to develop strategies for relationships, products, customers, and presentations. Salespeople who have achieved long-term success in personal selling have mastered the skills needed in each of these four strategic areas.
2. Value-added selling strategies are presented throughout the text. Customers are increasingly seeking a cluster of satisfactions that include a quality product, a salesperson who is truly a partner, and outstanding service after the sale. The successful salesperson discovers what the customer deems as added value, then determines ways to create the desired value.
3. Real-world examples—a hallmark of our previous editions that is continued in this edition—build interest and promote understanding

of major topics and concepts. Examples have been obtained from a range of progressive organizations, large and small, such as Xerox, Janssen-Ortho, and Windsor Factory Supply. We have also increased references to many of North America's most prominent sales trainers and consultants.

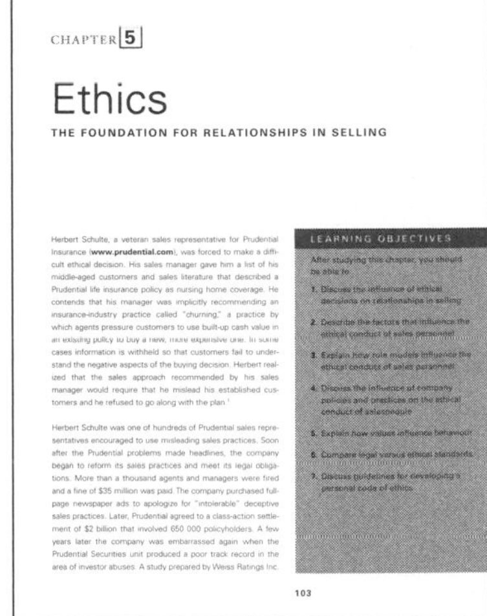

4. A full chapter on ethics and an exciting ethics game provide students with both knowledge of ethics in selling and several ways to make ethical selling decisions. Chapter 5 "Ethics: The Foundation for Relationships in Selling" provides information on ethical issues in selling along with application exercises, a role-play exercise, and a case where you can experience ethical issues first-hand. An exciting business game, entitled *Grey Issues—Ethical Decision Making in Personal Selling* is available in the Instructor's Resource Manual. Participation in this game introduces students to a range of real-life ethical conflicts. It stimulates deep thinking about the ethical consequences of your decisions and actions. You can play the game to learn without having to pay actual consequences.

Staying on the Cutting Edge—New to the Fourth Canadian Edition

Today, business as usual is not an option. The restructuring of the industrial economy to an information economy has hastened the transformation of personal selling. The fourth Canadian edition of *Selling Today: Creating Customer Value* describes how sales professionals must cope with new forces shaping the world of sales and marketing.

This edition includes several significant changes and additions.

1. This edition has been rewritten to include key concepts from the three major sales training programs used by the world's top-performing companies—Keith Eades's *The New Solution Selling*, Neil Rackham's *SPIN Selling*, and Miller Heiman's *The New Conceptual Selling*.

2. A completely revised chapter (11) explains the strategic use of questions to help customers better understand the nature of their buying situation and the potential solutions available to them. This chapter will have a new video support package—***the first one of its kind available with a text***—including three separate professional videos produced by one of the world's leading video-training personalities. This new package will include a professional narrator explaining the use of the questions; professional actors demonstrating, in typical selling situations, how to ask the questions; and specific role-play exercises designed to help you to learn these important skills.

3. A completely revised chapter (8), on the buying process and buyer behaviour, aligns the material more closely with the customer's buying process. This revision focuses on a *Buying-Decision Process* model, new

to this edition. The model features five steps the typical buyer goes through when making a buying decision: need awareness, evaluation of solutions, resolution of problems, purchase, and implementation. These steps are carefully aligned with the steps in the *selling process* presented later in the book.

4. This edition expands your understanding of when the customer is in need of consultative assistance rather than a low-price transactional solution. New models and key concepts improve your insight into what kind of buying strategy the customer is using in the buying-decision process. New information and models throughout the book explain how to interact with each of these types of customers from a sales process standpoint. The book also provides new insights and models on understanding and meeting the needs of the relationship buyer.

5. New to the fourth edition are five additional role-play exercises, one for each of the first five parts. These brief yet comprehensive exercises reinforce the key concepts of each part. As well, there is an additional new role-play exercise at the end of each chapter.

6. We have revised Chapter 15, "Servicing the Sale and Building the Partnership." This revision places more emphasis on the important steps of follow-through and follow-up after a sale is made. New information on *expansion selling* will help students to more effectively meet the needs of the customer.

7. This edition improves coverage of the partnering process and of how to add value within the sales process. Carefully researched techniques from Tom Reilly's new book *Value Added Selling* and from *Value Added Selling* magazine have been integrated throughout the text.

8. We offer new coverage on the impact of *specific benefits* versus what is sometimes called the "product dump" using *general benefits.* Well-documented and well-researched coverage shows the effectiveness of linking *specific benefits* with expressed customer needs. Detailed techniques are presented for integrating them into the sales process.

9. Many new boxed features have been added to focus on new, important aspects for selling today. There are now boxed features under the following six titles: "Everyone Sells," "Selling Mentor," "Selling in the Global Economy," "The Customer's Perspective," "Customer Relationship Management with Technology," and "Selling in Action." At least three boxed features appear in each chapter.

Organization of This Book

The material in *Selling Today* continues to be organized around the four pillars of personal selling: relationship strategy, product strategy, customer strategy, and presentation strategy.

Part I. The two chapters that make up Part I set the stage for a detailed study of the four major selling strategies. The first chapter describes the evolution of personal selling to the present day and introduces the four strategies. The second chapter gives students an opportunity to explore specific career opportunities in four major employment areas: service, retail, wholesale, and manufacturing.

Part II. Research indicates that high-performance salespeople can build and maintain relationships better than moderate performers can. Part II, "Developing a Relationship Strategy," focuses on several important person-to-person relationship-building practices that contribute to success in personal selling. Chapter 3 provides suggestions for creating value with a relationship strategy. Chapter 4 examines the influence of communication styles on relationships between customers and salespeople. Chapter 5 focuses on sales ethics and the importance of ethical behaviour by salespeople for establishing and building customer relationships.

Part III. In Part III, "Developing a Product Strategy," we examine the importance of complete and accurate product, company, and competitive knowledge in personal selling. A well-informed salesperson is in a strong position to apply the fundamentals of consultative selling.

Part IV. In Part IV, "Developing a Customer Strategy," we present information on why and how customers buy, and explain how to identify prospects. With increased knowledge of the customer, salespeople are in a better position to achieve their sales goals.

Part V. The concept of a salesperson as adviser, consultant, and partner to buyers is stressed in Part V, "Developing a Presentation Strategy." Rather than the traditional sales presentation that emphasizes closing as the primary objective of personal selling, we focus on the importance of proper questioning skills to identify buyer needs. Here, the salesperson is viewed as a counsellor and consultant.

Part VI. In the final Part, "Management of Self and Others," we include two chapters: "Management of Self: The Key to Greater Sales Productivity" and "Management of the Sales Force."

Learning Tools That Enhance Instruction

The fourth Canadian edition of *Selling Today* includes several learning tools that will aid both teaching and learning. The design and development of these learning activities were influenced by experiences acquired by the authors during more than a thousand seminars, workshops, and conferences.

1. *Role Play and Simulation.* An optional role play and simulation provides a realistic opportunity to apply major concepts presented in selected chapters. You are given information about a selling position in the service industry and required to make several critical decisions and

complete a number of tasks. All materials needed for both salesperson and customer roles are provided in this easy-to-use exercise. Instructions are provided in the text at the end of chapters 1, 6, 10, 11, 12, 13, 14, and 15. These instructions refer to "Partnership Selling: A Role Play/Simulation for Selling Today" on the CD-ROM that is provided with each text. The role play and simulation provides a bridge between classroom instruction and the real world of personal selling.

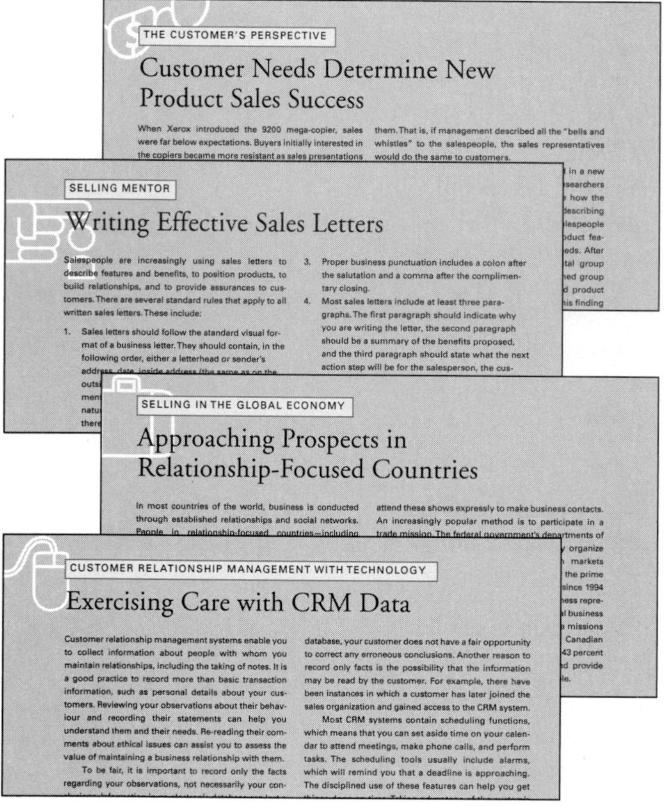

THE CUSTOMER'S PERSPECTIVE
Customer Needs Determine New Product Sales Success
SELLING MENTOR
Writing Effective Sales Letters
SELLING IN THE GLOBAL ECONOMY
Approaching Prospects in Relationship-Focused Countries
CUSTOMER RELATIONSHIP MANAGEMENT WITH TECHNOLOGY
Exercising Care with CRM Data

2. *Boxed Features.* Most chapters include three or four boxed features focusing on the themes "The Customer's Perspective," "Selling Mentor," "Selling in the Global Economy," "Everyone Sells," "Customer Relationship Management with Technology," and "Selling in Action." These explore current real-world examples of what the student is learning throughout the text. These features give a contemporary look at personal selling.

3. *Learning Features.* Each chapter includes the following special features that aid the teaching and learning process:

   - a list of learning objectives to help the student focus on the important concepts
   - definitions of key terms in the margin next to where they appear in the text
   - a summary that provides a brief review of the most important ideas presented
   - a list of key terms, following the chapter summary
   - a set of review questions to reinforce understanding of the major concepts presented in the chapter
   - a role-play exercise and a series of field-based application exercises that will provide opportunities to apply concepts and practices presented (each chapter includes at least one Internet exercise)
   - a case problem that permits students to analyze and interpret actual selling situations. Each case problem is based on a real-life situation.

4. *CRM Application Exercises and Case Studies.* Every chapter features an insight on the use of sales force automation, now referred to as Customer Relationship Management (CRM) with Technology. The trend toward greater use of technology to improve personal selling effectiveness has grown extensively and will continue to expand in the years ahead. The fourth Canadian edition contains 17 features entitled

"Building Relationships with Technology." Each insight explains how salespeople use sales force automation to improve quality in the selling process. Optional, easy-to-complete Customer Relationship Management (CRM) Application Exercises have been expanded in this edition to 16 chapters, and CRM Case Studies now appear at the end of 8 chapters. These interactive exercises give students the opportunity to use the Windows® version of the highly acclaimed ACT! Contact Management Software program developed by Pat Sullivan and Mike Muhney, leaders in the field of sales force automation.

The software is included on the CD-ROM that accompanies the text. Please read the instructions in the Appendix for installing and using this customer relationship management software.

The ACT! Contact Management System features a prospect database and other information you can use to make a range of decisions regarding qualifying prospects, approaching prospects, the sales presentation, demonstration, negotiation, closing, and servicing the sale. You can print prospect profiles, sales letters, and telephone contact lists; conduct key-word searches to find important references in the database; and do many other things. Simple single-stroke instructions are provided that enable students to experience the many advances in sales force automation.

Supplements

Selling Today: Creating Customer Value, Fourth Canadian Edition is accompanied by a complete supplements package. Instructor's Resource CD-ROM (0-13-198341-5) includes the following instructor supplements:

Instructor's Manual. The comprehensive Instructor's Manual includes detailed presentation outlines, answers to review questions, a trainer's guide for the *Grey Issues* selling ethics game, suggested responses to learning activities, copies of printouts for CRM Application Exercises, detailed instructions for using the case problems, and a complete trainer's guide for using the role play and simulation.

Pearson TestGen. More than 1000 test questions—including multiple-choice, true/false, and essay questions—are provided in TestGen format. Each question is rated by level of difficulty and includes a text page reference. TestGen is a testing software that enables instructors to view and edit the existing questions, add questions, generate tests, and distribute the tests in a variety of formats. Powerful search and sort functions make it easy to locate questions and arrange them in any order desired. TestGen also enables instructors to administer tests on a local area network, have the tests graded electronically, and have the results prepared in electronic or printed reports. TestGen is compatible with Windows and Macintosh operating systems, and can be downloaded from the

TestGen website located at **www.pearsoned.com/testgen**. Contact your local sales representative for details and access.

PowerPoints. A collection of more than 200 transparencies—culled from the textbook or specifically designed to complement chapter content—is also available electronically in PowerPoint software on the Instructor's Resource CD-ROM.

Role-Play Videos. VHS Format (0-13-196278-7), DVD Format (0-13-221290-0) This custom set of videos, produced by one of the world's leading video training personalities, features professional actors engaged in multi-call sales situations. A completely revised Chapter 11 on the strategic use of questions focuses on the importance of questioning—asking survey, probing, confirmation, and need-satisfaction questions—to enable customers to better understand the nature of their buying situation and the potential solutions available to them. A professional narrator explains the use of the questions, and actors role-playing typical selling situations illustrate how to ask the questions. Specific role-play exercises are also provided to reinforce development of these sales skills.

Most of these instructor supplements are also available for download from a password-protected section of Pearson Education Canada's online catalogue (**vig.pearsoned.ca**). Navigate to your book's catalogue page to view a list of those supplements that are available. See your local sales representative for details and access.

COMPANION WEBSITE

The Companion Website at **www.pearsoned.ca/manning** is a handy reference for students. The site provides an online study guide that includes chapter quizzes and application and Internet exercises. A Virtual Library lists annotated Weblinks organized by key areas of personal selling, providing a great source of valuable information at the user's fingertips. The module "Finding Employment: A Personalized Marketing Plan for the Age of Information" on the Companion Website provides career-minded students with additional employment strategies.

COMPANION TECHNOLOGY TEXT

Selling Today: Using Technology to Add Value (0-13-140560-8) is a 70-page companion text available for instructors to use in class or for students to study on their own. This supplement introduces the technology that is available to sales and marketing personnel, including Customer Relationship Management software, Web-based prospect lists, product configuration software, presentation software, electronic data interchange software, and travel-planning software. Written as a self-study guide, *Selling Today: Using Technology to Add Value* can be used in the classroom with 36 application exercises or as an out-of-class personal enrichment activity.

PEARSON CUSTOM PUBLISHING

Pearson Custom Publishing (**www.prenhall.com/custombusiness**) can provide texts, cases, and articles to enhance courses. Choose material from Darden, Ivey, Harvard Business School Publishing, NACRA, and Thunderbird to create your own custom casebook. Contact your Pearson sales representative for details.

ONLINE LEARNING SOLUTIONS

Pearson Education Canada supports instructors interested in using online course management systems. We provide text-related content in WebCT and Blackboard. To find out more about creating an online course using Pearson content in one of these platforms, contact your Pearson sales representative.

INSTRUCTOR'S ASSET

Pearson Education is proud to introduce Instructor's ASSET: Academic Support and Service for Educational Technologies. ASSET is the first integrated Canadian service program committed to meeting the customization, training, and support needs for your course. Ask your Pearson sales representative for details.

YOUR PEARSON SALES REPRESENTATIVE

Your Pearson sales representative is always available to ensure that instructors have everything they need to teach a winning course. Armed with experience, training, and product knowledge, your Pearson representative will support an instructor's assessment and adoption of any of the products, services, and technology outlined here, to ensure that Pearson's offerings are tailored to suit individual needs of instructors and students. Whether it's getting instructions on TestGen software or specific content files for a new online course, your Pearson sales representative is there to help.

Acknowledgments

Many people have made contributions to the fourth Canadian edition of *Selling Today: Creating Customer Value.* We are very grateful to Jack W. Linge, who contributed significantly to the development of the sales force automation case study, which is an important addition to this text. Special recognition is also extended to Cadalyst Resources and Contact Software International for assistance in developing materials used in conjunction with the fourth Canadian edition. The text has been improved as a result of numerous helpful comments and recommendations. We extend special appreciation to the following reviewers: Steve Janisse, St. Clair College; Frank Maloney, George Brown College; Lesley J. Moffitt, Assiniboine Community College; Kayrod Niamir, Dawson College; Allen Richert, Confederation College; Randal Singer, British Columbia Institute of Technology; and Padma Vipat, Douglas College.

The Search for Wisdom in the Age of Information

The search for the fundamentals of personal selling has become more difficult in the age of information. The glut of information—or information explosion—threatens our ability to identify what is true, right, or lasting. The search for knowledge begins with a review of information, and wisdom is gleaned from knowledge (see model in margin). Books continue to be one of the best sources of wisdom. Many new books, and several classics, were used as references for the fourth Canadian edition of *Selling Today.* A sampling of the more than 80 books used to prepare this edition follows.

Blur: The Speed of Change in the Connected Economy by Stan Davis and Christopher Meyer
Data Smog: Surviving the Information Glut by David Shenk
Strategic Selling by Robert B. Miller and Stephen E. Heiman
Selling the Invisible by Harry Beckwith
Working with Emotional Intelligence by Daniel Goleman
Psycho-Cybernetics by Maxwell Maltz
The Double Win by Denis Waitley
Zero-Resistance Selling by Maxwell Maltz, Dan S. Kennedy, William T. Brooks, Matt Oechsli, Jeff Paul, and Pamela Yellen
Messages: The Communication Skills Book by Matthew McKay, Martha Davis, and Patrick Fanning
SPIN Selling by Neil Rackham
The Power of 5 by Harold H. Bloomfield and Robert K. Cooper
Sales Magic by Kerry L. Johnson
The New Professional Image by Susan Bixler and Nancy Nix-Rice
Complete Business Etiquette Handbook by Barbara Pachter and Marjorie Brody
The 7 Habits of Highly Effective People by Stephen R. Covey
Integrity Selling by Ron Willingham
Selling with Integrity by Sharon Drew Morgan
Thriving on Chaos by Tom Peters
Changing the Game: The New Way to Sell by Larry Wilson
Business @ the Speed of Thought by Bill Gates
Consultative Selling by Mack Hanan
The 10 Natural Laws of Successful Time and Life Management by Hyrum W. Smith
Personal Styles and Effective Performance by David W. Merrill and Roger H. Reid
The Versatile Salesperson by Roger Wenschlag
Management Information Systems for the Information Age by Stephen Hagg, Maeve Cummings, and James Dawkins
Megatrends and *Megatrends 2000* by John Naisbitt
Rethinking the Sales Force by Neil Rackham
The Agenda by Michael Hammer
Hope Is Not a Strategy by Rick Page

The Butterfly Customer by Susan M. O'Dell and Joan A. Pajunen
Making Contact by Barry Siskind
Seminars to Build Your Business by Barbara Siskind
Secrets of Power Presentations by Peter Urs Bender
Secrets of Customer Relationship Management by James G. Barnes
The Salesperson's Handbook by Cy Charney
Stop, Ask, and Listen by Kelley Robertson
How to Make Hot Cold Calls by Steven J. Schwartz
If You Were Arrested for Selling, Would There Be Enough Evidence to Convict You? by Ian Selbie
Up Your Bottom Line by Bob Urichuck
No B.S. Sales Success by Dan Kennedy
The EQ Edge by Steven J. Stein and Howard E. Book

An Investment in the Future

Charles Schwab, the great industrialist and entrepreneur, said, "We are all salespeople every day of our lives, selling our ideas and enthusiasm to those with whom we come in contact." As authors, we suggest that you retain this book for future reference. Periodic review of the ideas in this text will help you daily in such areas as:

- interviewing for new jobs in the future
- understanding and training salespeople who work for you or with you
- selling new ideas to senior management, co-workers, or employees you might be supervising
- selling products or services that you represent as a salesperson

We wish you much success and happiness in applying your knowledge of personal selling.

About the Authors

Dr. Barry L. Reece, *Professor, Virginia Polytechnic Institute and State University* Dr. Reece has devoted more than three decades to teaching, research, consulting, and developing training programs in the areas of sales, supervision, human relations, and management. He has conducted more than 600 seminars and workshops for public- and private-sector organizations. He has written extensively in the areas of sales, supervision, communications, and management. Dr. Reece was named "Trainer of the Year" by the Valleys of Virginia Chapter of the American Society for Training and Development, and was awarded the "Excellence in Teaching Award" by the College of Human Sciences and Education at Virginia Polytechnic Institute and State University. Dr. Reece has contributed to numerous journals and is author or co-author of 30 books, including *Business, Human Relations—Principles and Practices, Supervision and Leadership in Action,* and *Effective Human Relations—Personal and Organizational Applications.* He has served as a consultant to numerous profit and not-for-profit organizations.

Gerald L. Manning, *Chair, Marketing/Management Department, Des Moines Area Community College* Mr. Manning has served as a chair of the Marketing/Management Department for more than 30 years. In addition to his administrative duties, he has served as lead instructor in sales and sales management. The classroom has provided him with an opportunity to study the merits of various experimental learning approaches such as role plays, simulations, games, and interactive demonstrations. "Partnership Selling: A Role Play/Simulation," included in this text, was developed and tested in the classroom by Mr. Manning. He has also applied numerous personal selling principles and practices in the real world as owner of a real estate development and management company. Mr. Manning has served as a sales and marketing consultant to senior management and owners of more than 500 businesses, including several national companies. He appears regularly as a speaker at national sales conferences. Mr. Manning has received the "Outstanding Instructor of the Year" award given annually by his college.

Dr. H.F. (Herb) MacKenzie, *Associate Professor, Brock University, St. Catharines, Ontario* Dr. MacKenzie has taught in the undergraduate, graduate, and executive education programs at universities in Canada, Europe, and the Middle East, and has been recognized with teaching awards for four consecutive teaching years: "Marketing Professor of the Year," "Professor of the Year," and "Faculty Award of Excellence" (twice). He has more than 15 years of business-to-business sales and sales management experience, and has been consulting to both private- and public-sector businesses since 1985. Dr. MacKenzie has co-authored Canadian editions of textbooks on selling and marketing, has edited two editions of a Canadian marketing casebook, and has published many cases, conference proceedings, and articles in the areas of sales management, buyer–seller relationships, and distribution channel management. Dr. MacKenzie has conducted many professional selling and sales management seminars with both public and private organizations.

Keeping Current in a Changing World

Throughout the past decade, professors Manning, Reece, and MacKenzie have relied on three strategies to keep current in the dynamic field of personal selling. First, they are actively involved in sales training and consulting. Their frequent interaction with salespeople and sales managers provides valuable insights into contemporary issues and developments in the field of personal selling. A second major strategy involves extensive research and development activities, the major focus of which has been factors that contribute to high-performance salespeople. The third major strategy involves completion of training and development programs offered by many respected sales training companies. Among them, professors Manning, Reece, and MacKenzie have completed seminars and workshops offered by, among others, Learning International, Wilson Learning Corporation, Forum Corporation, and Franklin Covey.

Every employee at Federal Express
must be sales oriented and each
manager must be an outstanding
individual salesperson. —*Federal Express*

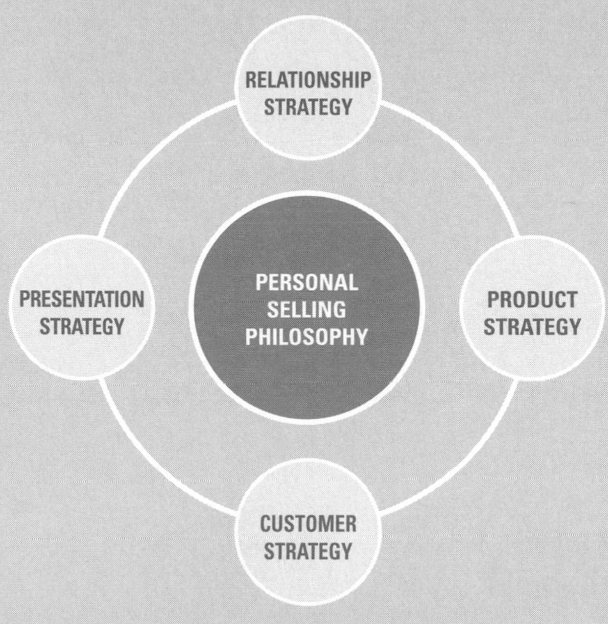

Creating Customer Value

PART I

Developing a Personal Selling Philosophy for the New Economy

The two chapters that make up Part I establish a foundation for the entire textbook. Chapter 1 introduces the major themes that connect all of the chapters. Chapter 2 describes personal selling career opportunities in the new economy.

CHAPTER 1

Personal Selling Today

INTRODUCTION AND OVERVIEW

LEARNING OBJECTIVES

After studying this chapter, you should be able to

1. Describe the contributions of personal selling to the information economy
2. Define *personal selling* and discuss personal selling as an extension of the marketing concept
3. Describe the evolution of consultative selling from the marketing era to the present
4. Define *strategic selling* and name the four broad strategic areas in the Strategic/Consultative Selling Model
5. Define *relationship selling* and name three things that enhance it
6. Explain how value-added selling strategies enhance personal selling

When Kevin Francis was a sales manager at Xerox Canada **www.xerox.ca**, he convinced his friend Joe Murphy, a classmate at Saint Francis Xavier University, to join the company. Kevin Francis went on to become president and CEO, and Joe Murphy went on to enjoy an outstanding sales career and became affectionately known by many of his customers as "Joe Xerox." Joe began his career making cold calls on smaller accounts and eventually got to manage only a few major accounts, including Memorial University and government accounts.

Reflecting on his personal selling philosophy, Joe says, "You can't see people without a purpose. If you waste their time, they soon get tired of seeing you. I planned my call cycles so that I would regularly see everyone, and so I would keep current with everyone's needs. Managing customer satisfaction is critical when you have only a few accounts. One dissatisfied person could result in lost sales throughout the entire organization."

When Joe Murphy decided to retire from Xerox, Memorial University held a retirement party for him and invited people from across the university who dealt with Joe over his career. Memorial's president honoured Joe by signing a "retirement" certificate for him, recognizing the outstanding service he provided to the university over the 21 years he managed the account.

Joe Murphy's success can be attributed to his personal selling philosophy: he valued personal selling as a career; he adopted the marketing concept, focusing on customer satisfaction; and he was a problem solver/partner for his customers. Joe Murphy practised consultative selling, strategic selling, and relationship selling—three approaches to personal selling that we will introduce in this chapter.[1]

Xerox sales professionals are experiencing changes in selling that are common to salespeople around the world. Today, a highly competitive one-world market exists for products ranging from document-handling equipment to consulting services. Salespeople need to adopt a global perspective. A Xerox salesperson must compete with salespeople who sell products manufactured in many areas of the world. Salespeople must also develop the skills needed to sell intangibles. A majority of today's salespeople sell services. Salespeople employed by ADT Security Services, Manulife Financial, Dun & Bradstreet, Ernst & Young, and Marriott Hotels sell services, not physical products. As our service economy continues to expand, so will employment opportunities for salespeople in the service sector. Another area of commonality is the need for all sales professionals, regardless of employer, to adjust to the changes that accompany the transition from the industrial age to the age of information. These changes have created a new economy that offers salespeople many opportunities and exciting employment openings. Learning how to manage and communicate information to customers within a working relationship that thrives on trust is one of the major challenges facing today's salesperson.

Personal Selling in the Age of Information

Restructuring from an industrial economy to an information economy began in the 1950s (see Fig. 1.1). John Naisbitt, author of the popular book *Megatrends*, noted that, during this period, our economy began shifting from an emphasis on industrial activity to an emphasis on the processing of information. He recognized that, in this new economy, most of us would work with information rather than produce goods.[2] We now live in an age in which the effective exchange of information is the foundation of most economic transactions. The implications for personal selling are profound. We will describe four major developments that have shaped the information economy and discuss the implications for personal selling.

Major advances in information technology. The information age has spawned an information technology revolution. Salespeople and other

Industrial Economy 1860–1960	Information Economy 1960–2020
Major advances in manufacturing and transportation	Major advances in information technology
Strategic resources are capital and natural resources	Strategic resource is information
Business is defined by its products and factories	Business is defined by customer relationships
Sales success depends on meeting sales quotas	Sales success depends on creating value for customers

INCREASES IN RELATIONSHIP SELLING AND RELATIONSHIP MARKETING

Figure 1.1 The age of information has greatly influenced personal selling. Salespeople today use a variety of technological tools to gather and process information to create customer value. They recognize that information is a strategic resource and that relationship skills are needed to build trust for information acceptance.

players in the information age use personal computers, electronic mail, faxes, mobile phones, and other forms of technology to obtain and process information. Explosive growth in electronic commerce and other Internet activities has changed the way we use computers. Stan Davis, futurist and co-author of *Blur: The Speed of Change in the Connected Economy,* says we now use the computer less for data crunching and more for connecting, for example, people to people, machine to machine, product to service, organization to organization, and combinations of all of these.[3] Without these connections, workers in the information age cannot do their jobs. People who work extensively with information, such as salespeople, need these connections to carry out their information gathering and information management responsibilities.

Information is a strategic resource. Advances in information technology have increased the speed by which we acquire, process, and disseminate information. David Shenk, author of *Data Smog: Surviving the Information Glut,* notes that we have moved from a state of information scarcity to one of information overload.[4] The information age is dynamic, but it can also be disorienting. In an era of limitless data, informed salespeople will be expected to help us decide which information has value and which information should be ignored. Customers who have less time to adjust to new products and circumstances will value this assistance.

Business is defined by customer relationships. Michael Hammer, consultant and author of *The Agenda,* says the *real* new economy is the customer economy. As scarcity gave way to abundance, as supply exceeded demand, and as customers became better informed, we have seen a power shift. Customers have taken more control of their own destinies.[5] On the surface, the major focus of the age of information seems to be the accumulation of more and more information and the never-ending search for new forms of information technology. It's easy to overlook the importance of the human element. Humans, not computers, have the ability to think, feel, and create ideas. It is no coincidence that relationship selling and relationship marketing, which emphasize long-term, mutually satisfying buyer–seller relationships, began to gain support at the beginning of the age of information. Personal selling provides a human response that counterbalances the impersonal nature of technology.

"One question: If this is the Information Age, how come nobody knows anything?"

Sales Success Depends on Adding Value. Value-added selling can be defined as a series of creative improvements in the sales process that enhance the customer experience. Salespeople can add value by developing a quality relationship, carefully identifying the customer's needs, and then configuring and presenting the best possible product solution. Value is also added when the salesperson provides excellent service after the sale. Neil Rackman, author of *Rethinking the Sales Force*, agrees with other experts in sales and marketing that success no longer depends merely on communicating the value of products and services. Success in personal selling rests on the critical ability to create value for customers. The value added by salespeople today is increasingly derived by such intangibles as the quality of the advice offered and the level of trust that underlies the relationship with the customer. However, the value of these intangibles can erode with shocking speed when the customer feels deceived or discovers that the competition is able to add more value to the sales process.[6]

value-added selling Improving the sales process to create value for the customer. Salespeople add value when they offer better advice and product solutions, carefully manage customer relationships, and provide better service after the sale.

Personal Selling—a Definition and a Philosophy

Personal selling involves person-to-person communication with a prospective customer, or **prospect.** It is a process of developing relationships, discovering needs, matching appropriate products with these needs, and communicating benefits through informing, reminding, or persuading. Increasingly, personal selling is viewed as a process that adds value for customers. In an ideal situation the salesperson diagnoses the customer's needs and custom fits the product solution to meet these needs. The term **product** should be broadly interpreted to encompass physical goods, services, and ideas.

Preparation for a career in personal selling begins with the development of a personal philosophy or set of beliefs that provides guidance. To some degree this philosophy is like the rudder that steers a ship. Without a rudder the ship's direction is unpredictable. Without a personal philosophy the salesperson's behaviour is also unpredictable. The development of a **personal selling philosophy** requires a commitment to value personal selling, adopt the marketing concept, and become a problem solver and partner to help customers make better buying decisions (see Fig. 1.2). These three prescriptions for success in personal selling are presented here as part of the Strategic/Consultative Selling Model. In later chapters, this model will be expanded to include additional strategic steps in the selling process.

personal selling Involves person-to-person communication with a prospect. It is a process of developing relationships; discovering customer needs; matching appropriate products with these needs; and communicating benefits through informing, reminding, or persuading.

prospect A potential customer, someone who meets the qualification criteria established by you or your company.

product Should be broadly interpreted to encompass physical goods, services, and ideas.

personal selling philosophy A salesperson's commitment to value personal selling, adopt the marketing concept, and become a problem solver and partner to help customers make better buying decisions.

Strategic/Consultative Selling Model	
Strategic step	**Prescription**
Develop a Personal Selling Philosophy	• Value Personal Selling • Adopt Marketing Concept • Become a Problem Solver/Partner

Figure 1.2 Today, salespeople use a strategic plan based on a personal philosophy that emphasizes valuing personal selling, adopting the marketing concept, and becoming a problem solver/partner.

Value Personal Selling

Firms make large investments in personal selling in response to several major trends:

- products and services are becoming increasingly sophisticated and complex;
- competition, including from global sources, has greatly increased; and
- customers are demanding greater value from their suppliers.

In response to these trends, personal selling has evolved to a new level of professionalism. Today's professional salesperson works more closely than ever with customers. Many salespeople get tremendous personal satisfaction from helping customers solve buying problems and from the close working relationships they develop with their customers. Salespeople also increasingly recognize that the success of their firm depends on their own sales success. Nothing can happen inside the firm unless the sales force has success outside the firm.

Firms are developing new, more efficient methods to communicate with customers, but personal selling will continue to be the most important sales method. The selling process has always been, and always will be, driven by personal contact and interpersonal relationships. Harold Jarche of Moncton, N.B.–based E-com Inc. says, "Even though we are a Net-based company, in order to close a sale or really understand the client, [we] need face-to-face."[7]

Personal Selling and the Marketing Concept

marketing concept A philosophy that the firm should co-ordinate all its activities to satisfy its customers while achieving its own goals.

The marketing concept has influenced personal selling since it was first formulated in the 1950s (see Table 1.1). There are three aspects to the **marketing concept**: the co-ordination of marketing activities throughout the company, focused to create customer satisfaction, while achieving the firm's goals. The importance of the marketing concept is that it focuses companies away from pushing or peddling products to customers and toward understanding customer needs. For most sales firms, the primary goal is profitability. Without satisfactory profits, the firm would not survive and it would be unable to create value for its customers. Stated more simply, everyone must focus on profitably creating customer value.

www.ups.ca

The foundation of the marketing concept is a business philosophy that leaves no doubt in the mind of every employee that customer satisfaction is of primary importance. UPS founder Jim Casey adopted the marketing concept when the company was first established. He described the firm's customer focus this way: "Our real, primary objective is to serve—to render perfect service to our stores and their customers. If we keep that objective constantly in mind, our reward in money can be beyond our fondest dreams."[8]

Marriott Hotels uses a blend of "high tech" and "high touch" to build customer goodwill and repeat business. Each of the 5500 sales representatives can sell the services of 10 motel brands in Marriott's portfolio. The customer

Table 1.1

Evolution of Personal Selling (1950 to Present)

Sales and Marketing Eras		Selling Emphasis
Marketing Era *Organizations determine needs and wants of target markets and adapt themselves to delivering desired satisfaction. Product orientation is replaced by a customer orientation.*	*Middle 1950s—1960s*	• *More organizations recognize that the salesperson is in a position to collect product, market, and service information regarding the buyer's needs.*
Consultative Selling Era *Salespeople are becoming diagnosticians of customers' needs as well as consultants offering well-considered recommendations. Mass markets are breaking into target markets.*	*Late 1960s—1970s*	• *Buyer needs are identified through two-way communication.* • *Information-giving and negotiation tactics replace manipulation.*
Strategic Selling Era *The evolution of a more complex selling environment and greater emphasis on market niches creates the need for greater structure and more emphasis on planning.*	*1980s*	• *Strategy is given as much attention as selling tactics.* • *Product positioning is given more attention.*
Relationship Selling Era *Salespeople are encouraged to think of everything they say or do in the context of their long-term, high-quality partnership with individual customers. Sales force automation provides specific customer information.*	*1990s—present*	• *Customer supplants the product as the driving force in sales.* • *Greater emphasis is placed on strategies that create customer value.*

with a small meeting budget might be encouraged to consider a Fairfield Inn property. The customer seeking luxury accommodations might be introduced to a Ritz-Carlton hotel. All reservations go through the same system, so that, if one Marriott hotel is full, the sales representative can cross-sell rooms in another Marriott hotel in the same city.[9]

Salespeople today are placing a greater emphasis on consulting with customers to identify their needs, on strategically planning their selling activities, and on building closer longer-term relationships with specific customers. These new thinking patterns—which have all evolved since the marketing concept was first proposed—have had an impact on every aspect of personal selling and sales management. They come from three distinct approaches to personal selling that developed over the past six decades: consultative selling, strategic selling, and relationship selling. We will examine each of these approaches.

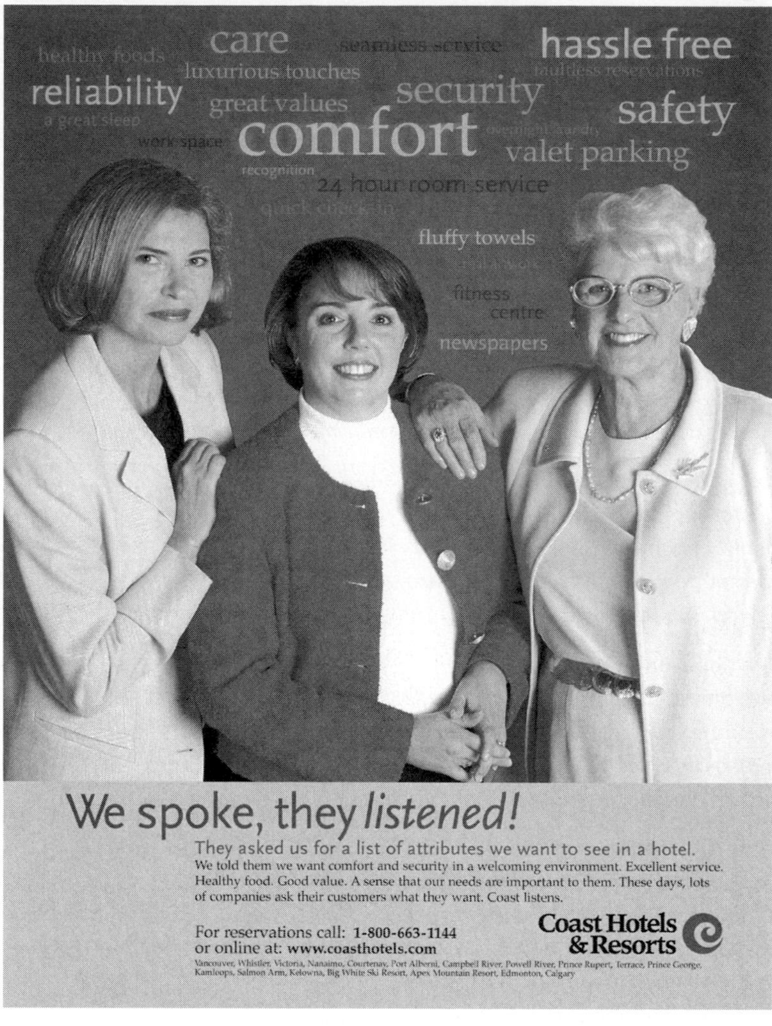

Coast Hotels & Resorts understands that its success depends on understanding and satisfying its customers—creating value for them.

The Evolution of Consultative Selling

consultative selling An approach to personal selling that is an extension of the marketing concept. Emphasis is placed on need identification, need satisfaction, and the building of a relationship that results in repeat business.

Consultative selling, which emerged in the late 1960s and early 1970s, is an extension of the marketing concept (see Table 1.1). This approach emphasizes identification of a buyer's need, which is achieved through effective communication between the salesperson and the customer. The salesperson establishes two-way communication by asking appropriate questions and listening carefully to the customer's responses. The salesperson assumes the role of consultant and offers well-considered recommendations to satisfy the identified need. Negotiation replaces manipulation as the salesperson sets the stage for a long-term partnership. Salespeople who have adopted consultative selling possess a keen ability to listen, define the customer's need or problem, and offer one or more solutions.[10]

Service, retail, wholesale, and manufacturing firms that embrace the marketing concept have already adopted or are currently adopting consultative selling practices. The major features of consultative selling are as follows:

1. The customer is seen as *a person to be served*, not a prospect to be sold. Consultative salespeople believe their function is to help the buyer make an intelligent decision. They use a four-step process that includes need discovery, selection of the solution, a need-satisfaction presentation, and servicing the sale (see Fig. 1.3). These customer-centred strategies will be explained in chapters 10 to 15.
2. The consultative salesperson, unlike the peddler of an earlier era, does not try to overpower the customer with a high-pressure sales presentation. Instead, the buyer's needs are identified through *two-way* communication. The salesperson asks questions in an attempt to learn as much as possible about the customer's needs and perceptions.
3. Consultative selling emphasizes *information giving, problem solving,* and *negotiation* rather than manipulation. This approach leads to a more trusting relationship between buyer and seller. Helping the buyer make an informed and intelligent buying decision adds value to the sales process.
4. Consultative selling emphasizes service after the sale. Author and consultant Ted Levitt recognizes that the relationship between a seller and a buyer seldom ends when a sale is made. As the number of buying transactions increases, the relationship actually intensifies, because the customer has higher expectations after the sale. Personalized service after the sale may include supervising product delivery and installation, servicing warranties, and following up on complaints.

At first glance, it may appear that consultative selling practices can be easily mastered. The truth is, consultative selling is a complex process that puts great demands on sales personnel.[11] This approach to personal selling requires an understanding of concepts and principles borrowed from the fields of psychology, communications, and sociology. It takes a great deal of personal commitment and self-discipline to become a sales consultant/adviser.

THE EVOLUTION OF STRATEGIC SELLING

Strategic selling began to receive considerable attention during the 1980s (see Table 1.1). During this period we witnessed the beginning of several trends that resulted in a more complex selling environment, owing to increased global competition, broader and more diverse product lines, more decision makers involved in major purchases, and greater demand for specific custom-made solutions. These trends will continue to influence personal selling and sales training.

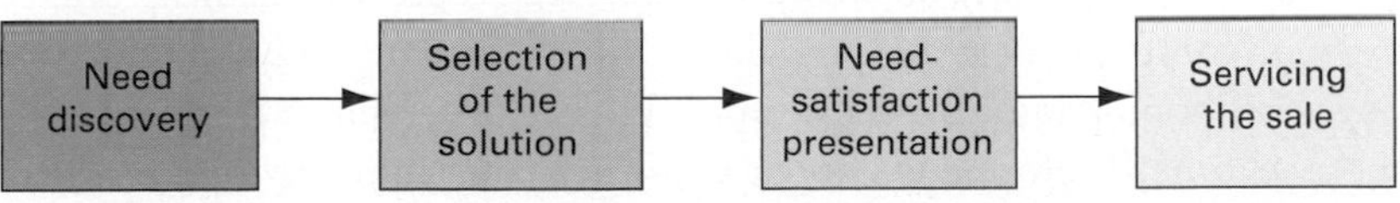

Figure 1.3 The Consultative Sales Presentation Guide. This contemporary presentation guide emphasizes the customer as a person to be served.

Sales success in the new economy requires us to think of ourselves as a problem solver/partner throughout the sales process.

As companies face increased levels of complexity in the marketplace, they must give more attention to strategic planning. The strategic planning done by salespeople is often influenced by the information included in their company's **strategic market plan**, which is an outline of the methods and resources required to achieve an organization's goals within a specific target market. It takes into consideration all of the major functional areas of the business that must be co-ordinated, such as production, marketing, finance, and human resources management.[12] Almost every aspect of the plan directly or indirectly influences the sale of products.

strategic market plan An outline of the methods and resources required to achieve an organization's goals within a specific target market, taking into consideration all the major functional areas of the business that must be co-ordinated, such as production, marketing, finance, and human resources management.

strategic selling plan A plan that includes strategies that a salesperson uses to position him- or herself with the customer before beginning a sales call.

tactic Technique, practice, or method that a salesperson uses during face-to-face interactions with customers.

strategy What a salesperson does as the result of precall planning to ensure that they call on the right people, at the right time, and with the right tactics to achieve positive results.

The strategic market plan should be a guide for a **strategic selling plan**. This plan includes strategies that you use to position yourself with the customer before the sales call even begins. Robert Miller and Stephen Heiman, the authors of *Strategic Selling*, point out that there is a difference between a *tactic* and a *strategy*.[13] A **tactic** is a technique, practice, or method you use when you are face to face with a customer, for example, the use of questions to identify needs, presentation skills, and various types of closes. These and other tactics will be discussed in chapters 10 to 15. A **strategy**, on the other hand, is a prerequisite to tactical success. If you develop effective strategies, you are more likely to make your sales presentation to the right person, at the right time, in a manner most likely to achieve positive results.

A selling strategy is a carefully conceived plan that is needed to accomplish a sales objective. Let's assume you are a sales representative employed by a pharmaceutical company. In an ideal situation, you want to establish a dialogue with the physician and learn about the types of patients she sees, diseases she treats, and challenges she faces in her practice. However, you do not want to call on busy doctors who may have no use for the drugs offered by your company. A strategy might include a careful study of the entire physician population in your territory. This analysis will help you identify those who need information about the drugs your company offers.[14] With

Today's customer wants a quality product and a quality relationship. Salespeople who create customer value will be rewarded with repeat business and referrals.

this information you can select the most appropriate selling tactic, or method, which might be to present samples to doctors who are not currently prescribing your drug.

Strategic planning sets the stage for a value-added form of consultative selling that is more structured, more focused, and more efficient. Andrew Parsons, director of consumer marketing for McKinsey and Company, points out in general terms that personal selling has become more strategic and has moved from "a game of checkers to a game of chess."

www.mckinsey.com

For many salespeople, strategic planning is not an option, but the key to survival. It results in better time allocation, more precise problem solving, and a greater chance of matching product solutions to customer needs. It creates value for customers and helps build better buyer–seller relationships.

The Evolution of Relationship Selling

The term **relationship selling** recognizes the growing importance of relationships in selling. Its increasing popularity is being driven by several factors. One is the demise of the product solution, as products among competitors in some industries become increasingly similar. When products of one company are nearly identical to those of the competition, the product strategy becomes less important than the relationship strategy. In *Secrets of Customer Relationship Management*, author James Barnes says, "It is my view that a company's ability to set itself apart from its competitors increases as we move away from focusing on the core product (which in many industries today is virtually nondifferentiable) and pay greater attention to the effect on the customer of the interaction with employees."[15] By contrast, some relationships grow out of the need for customized products or services:

relationship selling Salespeople who have adopted relationship selling work hard to build and nourish long-term partnerships. They rely on a personal, customized approach to each customer.

flexibility in terms of product configuration, scheduling of deliveries, or some other factor. Salespeople who have adopted relationship selling work hard to build and nourish long-term relationships. They rely on a personal, customized approach to each customer.[16]

Relationship selling stands in stark contrast to the more traditional transactional selling. While we emphasize relationship selling throughout this text, we accept that it is helpful to understand the role of transactional selling in our economy. **Transactional selling** is a sales process that most effectively matches the needs of the value-conscious buyer who is primarily interested in price and convenience. Because the buyer focused on transactions tends to focus primarily on low price, some marketers are adopting such lower-cost selling strategies as telesales, direct mail, and the Internet. Transactional selling is usually used by marketers who do not see the need to create customer value by carefully assessing customer needs, problem solving, relationship building, or sales follow-up.[17] It is not recommended as an alternative to relationship selling in situations that involve more complex decision-making processes.

transactional selling A sales process that most effectively matches the needs of the value-conscious buyer, who is primarily interested in price and convenience.

Today's customer wants a quality product *and* a quality relationship. Salespeople willing to abandon short-term thinking and invest the time and energy needed to develop a high-quality, long-term relationship with customers will be strongly rewarded. A sound relationship serves as a barrier to competing salespeople who want to sell to your accounts. Salespeople with durable customer relationships enjoy more referrals and repeat business (see Fig. 1.4). Keeping existing customers happy makes a great deal of sense from an economic point of view. Experts in the field of sales and marketing know that it costs four to five times more to get a new customer than to keep an existing one. Therefore, even small increases in customer retention can result in major increases in profits.[18]

INTEGRATED MARKETING COMMUNICATIONS ENHANCES RELATIONSHIP SELLING

Personal selling is only one method companies use to communicate with customers. However, because of the interpersonal dimension, it is the one

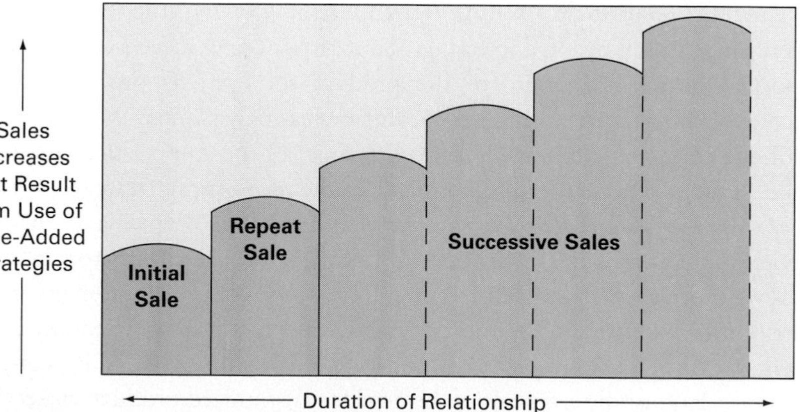

Figure 1.4 Relationship selling focuses on building closer, longer-term relationships with customers. Successful relationship selling results in repeat sales and referrals that expand the prospect base. The strength of the relationship increases each time the salesperson uses value-added selling strategies.

that is "closest" to the customer and, by many measures, it is the most important. Companies spend more money on personal selling than on any other form of marketing communications.[19] There is a recent trend to provide a consistent, persuasive message to customers through all forms of marketing communications, including personal selling, advertising, sales promotion, public relations, and direct marketing. This is referred to as **integrated marketing communications** (see Fig. 1.5). It improves effectiveness by giving target customers consistent messages across communications media. These messages will then have a greater impact and will help promote brand loyalty as they are continually reinforced. It also improves cost efficiency. For example, a customer may acquire information from an advertisement or an Internet site prior to the salesperson's call; as a result, the customer may be more receptive to seeing the salesperson and may be better informed so that it is easier to persuade the customer to buy. Integrated marketing communications is a practice increasingly used by larger companies to promote a consistent image to global markets, and by smaller companies that are attracted by the possibility of stretching their communications budget.

integrated marketing communications An attempt to provide a consistent, persuasive message to customers through all forms of marketing communications, including personal selling, advertising, sales promotion, public relations, and direct marketing.

HIGH ETHICAL STANDARDS ENHANCE RELATIONSHIP SELLING

In the field of selling, salespeople are frequently exposed to pressures that can influence their ethical conduct. However, poor ethical decisions can weaken or destroy relationships. To illustrate, let us assume a competitor makes

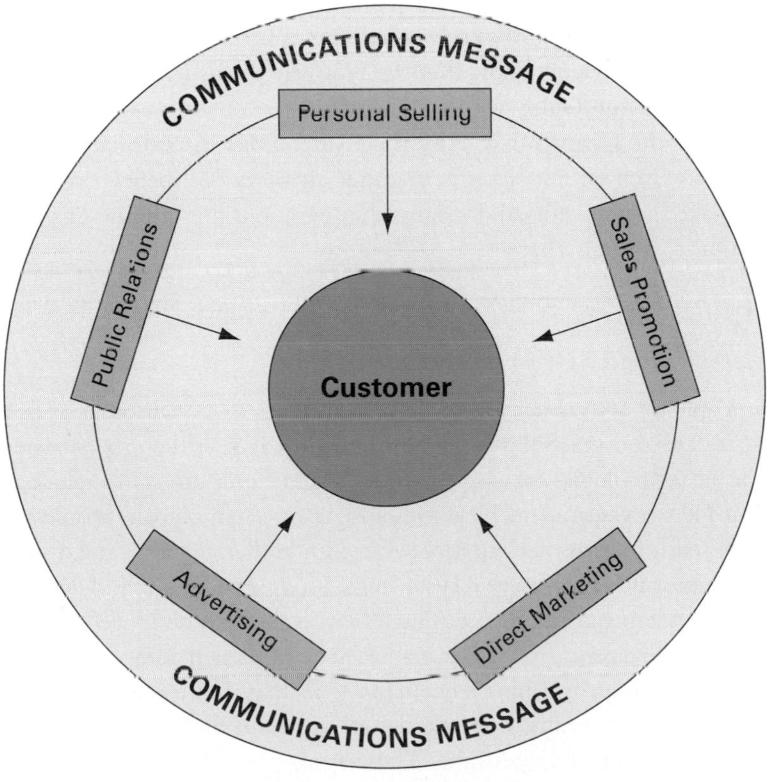

COMMUNICATIONS MESSAGE
Personal Selling
Public Relations
Sales Promotion
Customer
Advertising
Direct Marketing
COMMUNICATIONS MESSAGE

Figure 1.5 Integrated marketing communications to customers tries to ensure that all messages, regardless of their source, are consistent and persuasive.

CUSTOMER RELATIONSHIP MANAGEMENT WITH TECHNOLOGY

Introducing Customer Relationship Management

Today, many sales professionals use computers to help them better perform the tasks associated with successful personal selling. Various software programs are used, including e-mail, electronic spreadsheets, word processors, configuration systems, presentation packages, fax managers, and customer relationship management (CRM) systems. A basic CRM system consists of a database containing information about the people with whom a salesperson maintains relationships, such as customers, prospects, co-workers, and suppliers. For your use with the CRM studies in this text, a basic Windows-based CRM system is available on the CD-ROM that comes with this book for you to install on your computer (see the exercise Installing CRM Software on page 26 for more information). You can learn the fundamentals of CRM with this software, including searching for customer and product-related information, managing time and priorities, communicating, forecasting sales, and estimating your commissions.

exaggerated claims about a product. Do you counter by promising more than your product can deliver? What action do you take when time is tight and you must choose between servicing past sales and making new sales? What if a superior urges you to use a tactic that you consider unethical? These and other pressures must be dealt with every day. While pressures exist in every selling position, most salespeople are able to draw the line between ethical and unethical behaviour. This is especially true of those who have taken a long-range view of sales work that emphasizes building strong relationships. These people know that the best way to ensure repeat business is to deal honestly and fairly with every customer.

We devote Chapter 5 to ethical considerations in personal selling but have interwoven ethics throughout other chapters. We believe salespeople must make so many ethical decisions that we could not confine this important topic to a single chapter.

SALES FORCE AUTOMATION ENHANCES RELATIONSHIP SELLING

sales force automation (SFA) The process whereby electronic technologies are used to improve customer responsiveness and the efficiency of the sales force and sales support personnel.

Salespeople are increasingly using some form of sales force automation as part of their daily routine. **Sales force automation (SFA)** is the process whereby electronic technologies are used to improve communications in a sales organization and with customers. New technologies are enabling salespeople to add value for customers as they can more efficiently gather, manage, and distribute information, and can manage relationships, internal processes, and daily tasks. SFA is so widespread among today's sales forces that it is no longer a source of competitive advantage; instead, it is a necessity to remain competitive.

Today's salespeople now have many tools they can use to enhance proposals and presentations, improve demonstrations, and help manage their time and customer relationships. These tools, described in later chapters, include electronic product catalogues, product configurators, and sales proposal writers (Chapter 6); customer relationship management systems (see ACT! references throughout the book); presentation and spreadsheet software (Chapter 12); Internet and extranet applications (Chapter 15); electronic mapping software, and personal digital assistants (Chapter 16).

Increasingly, companies are moving beyond simple sales force automation to implement **customer relationship management (CRM)** solutions. CRM systems try to ensure that customers get a seamless and consistent experience with the company, regardless of whether they are dealing with a sales representative or with any other person in the company who has responsibility for contacting customers. Good CRM systems improve efficiency as well, but their main focus is to improve effectiveness; they ensure that customers get timely, consistent, and valued information. Although salespeople involved in transactional selling may disappear, salespeople who effectively use sales force automation tools and who are supported by effective CRM systems will continue to build strong customer relationships.

customer relationship management (CRM) Systems designed to provide a seamless and consistent experience with the company, regardless of whether a customer is communicating directly with a salesperson or with any other person in the company.

NATIONAL ACCOUNT PROGRAMS AND RELATIONSHIP SELLING

Some organizations rely on a few customers for a very high percentage of their sales. A common response is to develop a national account program—also called a strategic, key, major, or global account program—to manage relationships with these important customers. A **national account program** is designed to provide increased attention and customized solutions, and it requires a considerable resource commitment by both the seller and buyer to co-ordinate strategies and increase profits for both companies. It is the highest form of relationship selling, requiring very close working relationships. Wal-Mart Canada, for example, is such an important account that some manufacturers, including Procter & Gamble, have several salespeople who are responsible for only this one customer.

national account program A program developed to provide increased attention and customized solutions for very important customers.

Value Creation—The New Selling Imperative

We have defined value-added selling as a series of creative improvements that enhance the customer experience. The customer economy will reward those salespeople who have the skills, the knowledge, and the motivation to determine how to add value at every step of the sales process. To better understand value-added selling, you might reflect on the approaches by other professionals such as management consultants, fee-based financial planners, doctors, dentists, lawyers, and psychologists. The value they bring to a relationship with a client or patient is based on the intangible information they possess. They create value by establishing a dialogue with the patient or client and becoming thoroughly familiar with his or her problem.

Traditional selling has too often emphasized the value that lies in the product or service. The focus of the sales call has too often been the product,

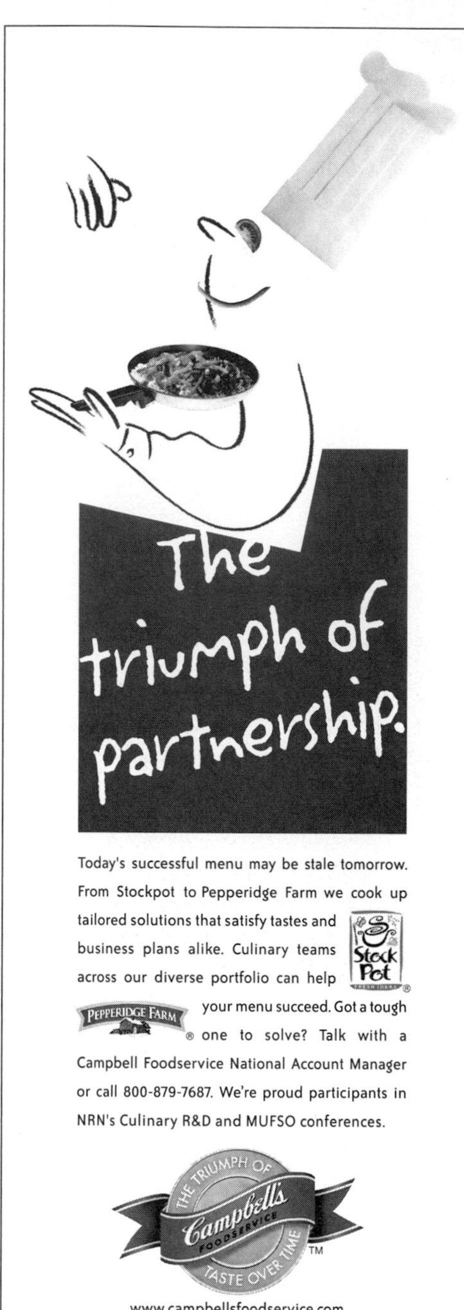

National account managers at Campbell's work closely with sales teams that call on culinary accounts. They add value by helping these customers improve their menu. These improvements add value and help build long-term partnerships.

not the customer.[20] When the customer is not aware of the value added by the salesperson, the focus of the sale may shift to price. Successful salespeople determine what drives a customer's behaviour beyond price. In today's rapidly changing marketplace the perception of value shifts often: low price may be what's valuable today, but tomorrow it may be fast delivery or a different packaging configuration. Sensing value shifts is one of the major benefits of staying close to the customer. Salespeople who can effectively solve the customer's current buying problems will prosper and be in great demand.

Value-added selling does not replace consultative selling, nor strategic selling, nor relationship selling—it encompasses them all. Early consultative sales training programs emphasized the development of face-to-face selling skills. These skills continue to be important today, but they must be enhanced with strategic planning and a strong commitment to building strong buyer–seller relationships. Customers want to buy from a salesperson who is well organized, well informed, and able to use strategic thinking to help them meet their buying needs.

The Strategic/Consultative Selling Model

A value-added approach to personal selling combines strategic planning, consultative selling practices, and relationship selling principles. It is similar to solving a jigsaw puzzle. As the salesperson, you are given many pieces of information that must form a complete picture. Putting the parts together isn't nearly as difficult if you can see the total picture before you start. To offer you a picture of value-added selling, we present a single model to serve as a reference throughout the text. Figure 1.6 shows the Strategic/Consultative Selling Model. This model features five strategic steps, each based on three prescriptions. The first step involves the development of a personal selling philosophy. Each of the remaining steps relates to a broad strategic area of personal selling. Each makes an important and unique contribution to the selling process, and salespeople can add customer value at each of these steps. A brief introduction to each of these remaining strategic steps follows.

DEVELOPING A RELATIONSHIP STRATEGY

Success in selling depends heavily on the salesperson's ability to develop, manage, and enhance interpersonal relations with the customer. People seldom buy products or services from someone they dislike or distrust. Harvey B. Mackay, founder of Mackay Envelope Corporation, says, "People don't care how much you know until they know how much you care." Most customers are more apt to openly discuss their needs and wants with a salesperson with whom they feel comfortable. It's essential, then, for a salesperson to develop a **relationship strategy**, a thorough plan for establishing, building, and maintaining quality relationships with customers. This type of plan is essential for success in today's marketplace, which is characterized by vigorous competition, look-alike products, and customer loyalty dependent on quality relationships as well as quality products. The relationship strategy must encompass every aspect of selling, from the first contact with a prospect to servicing the sale once this prospect becomes an established customer. The primary goal of the relationship strategy is to create rapport, trust, and mutual respect, which will ensure a long-term partnership. To establish this type of relationship, salespeople must project a positive, professional image; practise communication-style flexing; and behave ethically (see Fig. 1.6). These topics will be discussed in detail in chapters 3 to 5.

relationship strategy A well-thought-out plan for establishing, building, and maintaining quality relationships with customers.

www.mackayenvelope.com/

Some people think that *relationships* is too soft and too emotional a concept for a business application; these people think that it's too difficult to think about relationships in strategic terms. In fact this is not the case at all. Every salesperson can and should formulate a strategic plan that will build and enhance relationships with customers.

DEVELOPING A PRODUCT STRATEGY

Products and services represent tools for solving customer problems. The **product strategy** is a plan that helps salespeople make correct decisions concerning the selection and positioning of products to meet identified customer needs or to solve customer problems (see Fig. 1.6). The development of a product strategy begins with a thorough study of one's product using a feature–benefit analysis. Such product features as technical superiority, reliability, fashionableness, design integrity, or guaranteed availability should be converted to benefits that will appeal to the customer. Today's high-performance salespeople strive to become product experts. Chapter 6 focuses on company, product, and competition knowledge needed by salespeople.

product strategy A well conceived plan that emphasizes acquiring extensive product knowledge, learning to select and communicate appropriate product benefits that will appeal to the customer, and positioning the product.

A well-conceived product strategy for the age of information also requires that decisions be made concerning **product positioning**. The positioning of a product refers to the decisions, activities, and communications that establish and maintain the concept of a firm's intended product in the customer's mind. The goal of salespeople at a Lexus dealership, for example, is to create the perception that their automobiles are the best in the high-performance luxury category and that the company will stand behind its products with an excellent customer service program. The brokers at BMO Nesbitt Burns strive to create the perception that they are well-informed consultants and that the company is able to service its accounts to maximum customer satisfaction. The positioning of products and other product-related sales strategies is the major focus of Chapter 7.

product positioning The decisions, activities, and communications that establish and maintain the concept of a firm's intended product in the customer's mind.

The development of a product strategy often requires thoughtful decision making. Today's more knowledgeable customers seek a cluster of satisfactions that arise from the product itself, from the manufacturer or distributor of the product, and from the salesperson. The "new" product that customers are buying today is the sum total of the satisfactions that emerge from all three sources. This "cluster of satisfactions" concept is discussed in more detail in Chapter 7.

DEVELOPING A CUSTOMER STRATEGY

Patricia Seybold, author of *The Customer Revolution*, says we are in the midst of a profound revolution—the customer revolution. And it's bigger than the Internet revolution:

> "Customers have taken control of our companies' destinies. Customers are transforming our industries. And customers' loyalty—or lack thereof—has become increasingly important"[21]

Figure 1.6 The Strategic/Consultative Selling Model. This model of the value-added approach to personal selling is an extension of the marketing concept.

Strategic/Consultative Selling Model*	
Strategic step	**Prescription**
Develop a Personal Selling Philosophy	• Value Personal Selling • Adopt Marketing Concept • Become a Problem Solver/Partner
Develop a Relationship Strategy	• Project positive, professional image • Practise communication-style flexing • Behave ethically
Develop a Product Strategy	• Become a product expert • Sell specific benefits • Configure value-added solutions
Develop a Customer Strategy	• Understand customer behaviour • Discover customer needs • Develop prospect base
Develop a Presentation Strategy	• Understand buying process • Prepare objectives • Provide outstanding service

* Strategic/consulative selling evolved in response to increased competition, more complex products, increased emphasis on customer needs, and growing importance of long-term relationships.

Marketing Concept:

- co-ordinate all activities
- to create satisfied customers
- and achieve company goals.

SELLING IN THE GLOBAL ECONOMY

Strategies for Building Global Relationships

The authors of *Complete Business Etiquette Handbook* state that "The key to being successful in international business revolves around knowing where you've come from as well as where you are headed." Keep in mind these tips when hosting an international visitor or visiting another country.

- Be respectful and nonjudgmental about the cultural differences you encounter. Try to react positively to unusual experiences.
- Understand your own viewpoint. International travel provides an opportunity to examine your own beliefs, values, and habits.
- Be flexible and patient. If you are too rigid or set in your ways, international travel will be difficult.
- Know enough about the etiquette in the country you plan to visit so you do not unwittingly offend its customs. If you need additional information on doing business in a specific country, visit **www.executiveplanet.com**.[a]

Customers have become more and more sophisticated in their buying strategies. They have come to expect value-added products and services, and long-term commitments. Selling to today's customer starts with getting on the customer's agenda and carefully identifying his or her needs, wants, and buying conditions.

A **customer strategy** is a carefully conceived plan that will result in maximum responsiveness to the customer's needs. This strategy is based on the fact that success in personal selling depends, in no small measure, on the salesperson's ability to learn as much as possible about the prospect.[22] It involves the collection and analysis of specific information for each customer. When developing a customer strategy, the salesperson should develop a broad understanding of buying behaviours, discover individual customer needs, and build a strong prospect base (see Fig. 1.6). The first two parts of the customer strategy will be introduced in Chapter 8. Suggestions regarding ways to build a solid prospect base will be discussed in Chapter 9.

customer strategy A carefully conceived plan that will result in maximum responsiveness to the customer's needs.

Many of the most progressive companies in Canada have well-established customer strategies. Windsor Factory Supply, with seven locations in Ontario, provides a good example of a marketer that has developed product management programs for many of its customers. Windsor Factory Supply salespeople encourage large customers, particularly ones with multiple locations, to source all of their maintenance, repair, and operating (MRO) supplies from them. When successful, product management contracts result in stable long-term relationships between suppliers and customers, to the benefit of both parties. These contracts require salespeople to collect and analyze information on the specific needs of each customer, and to make frequent inventory adjustments, custom fitting their inventory to guarantee delivery requirements and meet the needs of these important customers (see Fig. 1.7 on page 22).[23]

www.wfsltd.com

Figure 1.7 Windsor Factory Supply's customer strategy loop illustrates how salespeople obtain information on ways to better serve their customer.

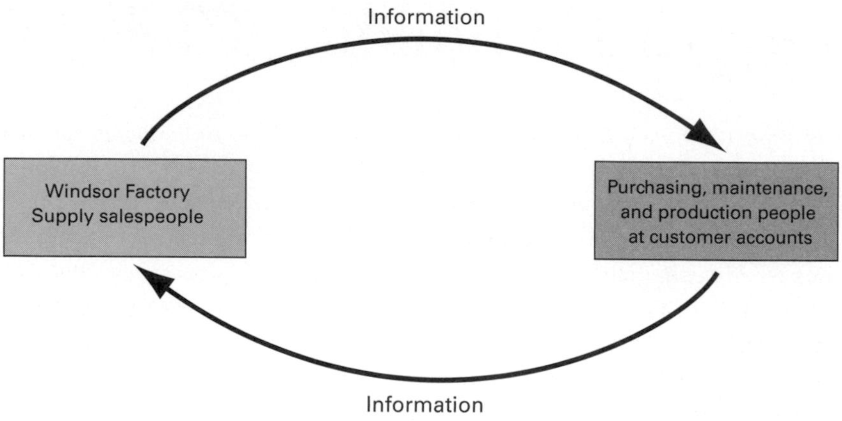

Information

Windsor Factory Supply salespeople

Purchasing, maintenance, and production people at customer accounts

Information

presentation strategy A well-conceived plan that includes three prescriptions: establishing objectives for the sales presentation; preparing the presentation plan needed to meet these objectives; and renewing one's commitment to providing outstanding customer service.

Figure 1.8 The major strategies that form the Strategic/Consultative Selling Model are by no means independent of one another. The focus of each strategy is to satisfy customer needs and create customer value.

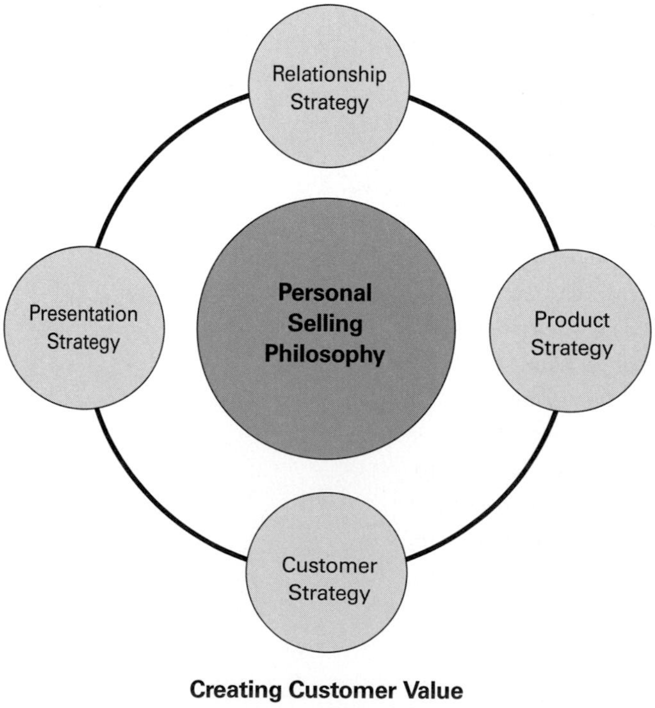

Relationship Strategy

Presentation Strategy

Personal Selling Philosophy

Product Strategy

Customer Strategy

Creating Customer Value

DEVELOPING A PRESENTATION STRATEGY

Typical salespeople spend about 30 percent of their time in actual face-to-face selling. However, the sales presentation is a critical part of the selling process. The **presentation strategy** is a well-developed plan that includes preparing the sales presentation objectives, preparing a presentation plan that is needed to meet these objectives, and renewing one's commitment to provide outstanding customer service (see Fig. 1.6).

The presentation strategy usually involves developing one or more objectives for each sales call. For example, a salesperson might update personal information about the customer, provide information on a new product, and close a sale during one sales call. Multiple-objective sales presentations, which are becoming more common, will be discussed in Chapter 10. Presale presentation plans give salespeople the opportunity to consider those activities that will take place during the sales presentation. For example, a salesperson might preplan a demonstration of product features to use when meeting with the customer. Presale planning ensures that salespeople will be well organized during the sales presentation and prepared to offer outstanding service.

INTERRELATIONSHIP OF BASIC STRATEGIES

The major strategies that form the Strategic/Consultative Selling Model are by no means independent. The relationship, product, and customer strategies all influence development of the presentation strategy (see Fig. 1.8). For example, a salesperson might develop one relationship-building tactic for use during the initial face-to-face meet-

SELLING IN ACTION

The Six-Hat Salesperson

Dave Kahle, author of *The Six-Hat Salesperson*, identifies four forces that characterize the age of information. First, there is rapid discontinuous change. New technologies bring new products and new competitors, as well as new customers with changing needs. Second, there is relentlessly growing complexity. Salespeople need more knowledge to keep abreast of changes among their product offerings and their competitors, and to manage increased customer demands. Third, there are constantly growing competition and choices. New forms of competitors and an increase in global competition both bring competitors that did not exist just a short time ago. Fourth, salespeople are facing increased time pressure. Their working environment is more complex and competitive, and salespeople need to work harder to keep up. These four forces compel today's successful salesperson to wear six hats—that is, to build competencies in six main areas to effectively manage a sales career. A salesperson must be

- **An Astute Planner.** Effective salespeople must be able to plan. Time for a salesperson is a scarce resource so it's important to allocate time appropriately across accounts for effective management of his or her territory. Salespeople must be able to organize and manage information, and to plan whom to see, when to see them, and what to say to them, long before they make an initial customer approach.
- **A Trusted Friend.** This hat emphasizes the importance of establishing, building, and maintaining trusting relationships with customers. In a high-tech world, customers value relationships with competent, ethical salespeople.
- **An Effective Consultant.** A salesperson wearing this hat is a valuable resource to customers and assists them to solve buying problems. These salespeople are more adept at identifying opportunities, and are then better able to match products, programs, and services to specific customer needs.
- **A Skillful Influencer.** This hat emphasizes the strategies and tactics that salespeople use during the sales process: approach, presentation, demonstration, handling buyer resistance, closing, and servicing the sale.
- **An Adept Human Resources Manager.** Salespeople must be able to manage themselves. Since they frequently work in an environment without daily supervision, they need to be self-motivated, and take responsibility for their accounts and their actions. They need—more than most employees—an ability to handle rejection and stress.
- **A Master Learner.** With constant changes to products, programs, and services, as well as changing customer needs and more intense competition, today's salesperson must be a dedicated lifelong learner. Salespeople who wish to stay at the top of their profession must constantly seek ways to upgrade their skills and knowledge.[b]

ing with the customer, another for use during the presentation, and another for use after the sale is closed. The discovery of customer needs (part of the customer strategy) will greatly influence planning for the sales presentation.

SUMMARY

There are exciting employment opportunities today in personal selling, particularly for those who know how to manage and communicate information to customers within a high-trust working relationship. *Personal selling* is the process of developing customer relationships, discovering customer needs, matching appropriate products or services with those needs, and communicating benefits through informing, reminding, or persuading.

The *marketing concept* is the belief that a firm should co-ordinate all activities to create satisfied customers while achieving its own goals. The marketing concept has grown in popularity throughout the age of information. The marketing era that began in the 1950s looked first at customer needs and wants, and then created goods and services to meet those needs and wants. (Previously, during the industrial age, the emphasis had been on creating products and then building customer interest in those products.) Consultative selling emerged in the late 1960s as an approach that emphasizes identification of customer needs through effective communication between the salesperson and the customer. Strategic selling evolved in the 1980s and involved the preparation of a carefully conceived strategic market plan, taking into consideration the co-ordination of all of the major functional areas of the business—production, marketing, finance, and human resources—to accomplish the firm's sales objectives. In the 1990s, the development of relationship selling involved providing customers with a quality product *and* quality service. Relationship selling is focused on the creation of long-term relationships with customers and requires salespeople to continuously search for ways to create customer value. Relationship selling is enhanced by integrated marketing communications, ethical behaviour, and sales force automation. Some organizations have developed strategic account programs to deal specifically with important accounts.

Salespeople who can effectively integrate all these approaches to selling can create value for their customers by focusing on one or more of the four broad strategic areas in the Strategic/Consultative Selling Model after developing a personal selling philosophy: relationship strategy, product strategy, customer strategy, and presentation strategy.

Key Terms

Consultative Selling **10**
Customer Relationship Management (CRM) **17**
Customer Strategy **21**
Integrated Marketing Communications **15**
Marketing Concept **8**
National Account Program **17**
Personal Selling **7**
Personal Selling Philosophy **7**
Presentation Strategy **22**
Product **7**
Product Positioning **19**
Product Strategy **19**
Prospect **7**
Relationship Selling **13**
Relationship Strategy **19**
Sales Force Automation (SFA) **16**
Strategic Market Plan **12**
Strategic Selling Plan **12**
Strategy **12**
Tactic **12**
Transactional Selling **14**
Value-Added Selling **7**

Review Questions

1. Explain how personal selling can help solve the problem of information overload.
2. According to the Strategic/Consultative Selling Model (Fig. 1.2), what are the three prescriptions for developing a successful personal selling philosophy?
3. How is peddling or "pushing" products inconsistent with the marketing concept?
4. Identify a local company that you believe has adopted the marketing concept and explain what makes you believe it has done so.
5. What is "consultative" selling? Give examples.
6. Diagram and label the four-step consultative sales presentation guide.
7. List and briefly explain the four broad strategic areas that make up the selling process.
8. Briefly describe the evolution of relationship selling. Discuss the forces that contributed to this approach to selling.
9. What is meant by *integrated marketing communications*? Why is it important?
10. Explain why the ethical conduct of salespeople has become so important.
11. Define *sales force automation* and explain why it is important for today's salesperson.
12. What are strategic account programs? Why do companies develop these programs?

Application Exercises

1. Assume that you are an experienced professional salesperson. A professor who teaches at a nearby university has asked you to speak to a consumer economics class about the social and economic benefits of personal selling. Make an outline of what you will say.
2. A friend of yours has invented a unique and useful new product. This friend, an engineer by profession, understands little about marketing and selling this new product. She does understand, however, that "nothing happens until somebody sells something." She has asked you to describe the general factors that need to be considered when you market a product. Prepare an answer to her question.
3. When Brenda Fisher received her B.Ed., she thought she would like to teach. However, a pharmaceutical firm offered her a sales position that would require her to call on doctors and pharmacists to explain her firm's product line. Describe the similarities and the differences between teaching and selling.
4. Go to **www.google.ca** (or another search engine if you prefer) and hit "advanced search." Type "consultative selling" under "Find results with exact phrase." Limit your search by typing ".ca" under "domain." Do the same for the terms "strategic selling" and "relationship selling." Be prepared to discuss some of what you find in class.

ROLE-PLAY EXERCISE

The purpose of this role play is to provide you with an opportunity to engage in needs identification. You will be meeting with someone (a class member) who is preparing for an important job interview and needs a pen and/or pencil. Prior to the meeting, make a list of the questions you will ask. Then ask your questions to another class member. Be sure to take notes. At the end of the interview, be prepared to recommend the most appropriate pen and/or pencil.

CRM Application Exercise **INSTALLING CRM SOFTWARE**

The CRM system that is available for you to install is a demonstration version of the best-selling software called ACT!, a product of SalesLogix. This version of ACT! includes a database of information about prospective customers for a company that sells network systems. In the case study and exercises ahead, you will assume the role of a salesperson who is selling these network systems. To install the software, please turn to Appendix A and follow the instructions.

ACT! is a database program, which means that it uses records and fields. *Records* are the screens that contain information about each person. *Fields* are the boxes on the records for entering and displaying data, such as the name of the person, Bradley Able. ACT! is also known as a contact management program because it maintains a record for each contact (person). Some CRM systems offer a separate record for each organization.

You can experiment with ACT! without concern about damaging the program. If you inadvertently delete information in the database, you can simply download the software again. As you experiment with ACT!, you can obtain help at any time by pressing the F1 function key. (See the exercise Learning CRM Software on page 48 for more information.)

To get acquainted with the ACT! version of CRM, click on the various menu items and icons and observe the functions that are available to you. Experimenting with this software will give you a feel for the potential power of using technology to enhance your sales career. Test ACT!'s reporting capabilities by printing a phone list: select Report and Phone; in the Prepare Report box choose Active Group and Printer; then print the list.

Case Problem

Windsor Factory Supply Limited (WFS) is a large general-line industrial distributor that started as a two-man operation in Windsor, Ontario, in 1955. It now has 174 employees, including 32 outside salespeople across its seven branches. Many customers remain loyal to WFS because they want good service, a broad range of general industrial products, and a supplier that will help them solve their buying problems. The success of WFS can be traced to a number of factors:

- *A company philosophy that is based on the belief that being able to service existing accounts is more important than gaining new accounts.* According to Wes Delnea, president of WFS, "Growth is important, but sometimes you have to keep your desire to grow in check if you do not have the ability to maintain superior service to your existing accounts."
- *A desire to build as many relationships and the strongest relationships possible with all customers.* WFS frequently moves people to new positions within the company: a warehouse person may become an outside salesperson and, later, be transferred to inside sales; an outside salesperson may be transferred to purchasing or back to inside sales. This creates maximum flexibility within the company but, more importantly, means that inside salespeople know the difficulties that outside salespeople face, and they often have personal contacts within customer firms. It also means that outside salespeople have had the benefit of training and learning while in the warehouse and on the inside sales desk. As a result, customers frequently have strong relationships with and trust in several WFS employees who they know can help them.
- *A strong belief that work should be rewarding for all employees.* "Happy employees help make happy customers," says Wes Delnea. Employees share many experiences, from going to major sporting events, to having company parties and picnics, to going together to Las Vegas. Twice, all of the employees shared an expense-paid trip to Las Vegas, with about 25 percent of them going per weekend on consecutive weekends. Employees have an excellent benefits package, which also includes education and recreation allowances. This employee investment has been rewarded many times over. At one point, the company had gone four years without a single absentee day. Employees even provide important input on management. In fact, a nine-member management committee, including the president, is elected each year. Confidence in the committee is high; six members have been on the committee since it was formed several years ago.
- *An investment in customer service and a strong service culture.* The company has invested in computer equipment and programming, and is able to tell customers immediately how much inventory it has and where that inventory is located. Purchasing, payables, invoicing, receivables, account profiles, sales and other financial reports, and vehicle maintenance schedules are all computerized. Employees are empowered to make decisions whenever customer service is an issue. On one occasion, two employees took a company van and left Windsor to get some material in Pittsburgh, Pennsylvania, for a customer who urgently needed it, and they returned immediately with the material. If a customer calls to order something that is urgently needed but the delivery truck has left for the day, the customer is never told to wait for the next delivery. Wes Delnea says, "We will get it to them. If the salesperson can't deliver it, someone will."
- *An investment and improvement in service processes.* Many large accounts have online order capabilities as they are connected to WFS through an electronic data interface. For example, Ford Motor Company of Canada can order from WFS directly via computer. WFS has also established a program of commodity management whereby it manages all of the general supply items for companies with multiple locations. WFS is always willing to add items to its inventory for customers who will buy them, and an increasing number of customers are taking advantage of this service.[24]

Questions

1. Does it appear that the management and members of the sales force at Windsor Factory Supply Limited have adopted the three prescriptions of a personal selling philosophy (see Fig. 1.2)? Explain your answer.
2. What are the characteristics of the product strategy adopted by Windsor Factory Supply Limited? How will this strategy contribute to the company's long-term success?
3. How would you describe the customer strategy developed by Windsor Factory Supply Limited? How does this strategy contribute to long-term success?
4. Windsor Factory Supply Limited salespeople are paid by straight salary and do not get a commission. Why has the company decided on this compensation plan? What would be the advantages and disadvantages of salary versus commissions for Windsor Factory Supply Limited?
5. Does it appear that Windsor Factory Supply Limited has adopted the four broad strategic areas that are part of the Strategic/Consultative Selling Model? Explain.

Partnership Selling

A ROLE PLAY/SIMULATION (see Appendix B, on CD-ROM)

If your instructor has chosen to use the Partnering Role Play/Simulation exercise that accompanies this text, these boxes will alert you to your Role Play/Simulation assignments. Your instructor will also provide you with needed information.

Preview the role-play simulation materials on the CD-ROM that accompanies this book. These materials are also provided in the Student Resources section of your Companion Website at **www.pearsoned.ca/manning**.

These materials are produced by the Park Inn International Hotel and Convention Centre, and you will be using them in your role as a new sales trainee—and, at times, as the customer—for the hotel and its convention services.

The Role Play/Simulation exercises start in Chapter 6, as you begin to create your product strategy. However, in anticipation of the role play, you can begin to imagine yourself in the role of an actual salesperson. Start to think about how you will develop your personal selling philosophy. What are some ethical guidelines that you may wish to adopt for yourself? What skills will you need to develop to become a partner with your prospective customers?

The Park Inn has implemented a quality improvement process. How will this affect your role as a sales representative?

CHAPTER 2

Personal Selling Opportunities

IN THE AGE OF INFORMATION

Personal selling attracts people from many different professions. Susan Green received her B.A. and B.Ed. from Acadia University and spent 10 years as a teacher before joining her mother in the real estate business. When her mother became ill, Susan was faced with a decision to take over the business or let it close down. Her office now has 10 agents, and she doesn't regret her decision. She says, "I have more freedom to be creative and I'm financially much better off. I love this business. Many people think that real estate is about selling houses, but it's really about providing a service to clients, both buyers and sellers. That may explain why so many successful real estate agents come from teaching and nursing careers."[1]

Laura Wood studied culinary management at George Brown College in Toronto, worked as a pastry chef after graduation, and eventually opened her own pastry bakery in London, Ontario. Laura describes herself as a very social creature who was always curious about selling. Since applying for a sales position with Red Carpet Vending and Refreshment Services, she has become a very successful sales professional. Laura's responsibility is to find new business for the company. Once she closes a sale, the account is turned over to a route driver who must provide the client with regular service. Laura does, however, maintain contact with each new account for some time after a sale is made to ensure that a healthy relationship develops.[2]

LEARNING OBJECTIVES

After studying this chapter, you should be able to

1. Describe how personal selling skills contribute to work performed by knowledge workers
2. Discuss the rewarding aspects of personal selling careers
3. Describe the opportunities for women and minorities in the field of personal selling
4. Discuss the characteristics of selling positions in four major employment settings: service, retail, wholesale, and manufacturing
5. Identify the four major sources of sales training

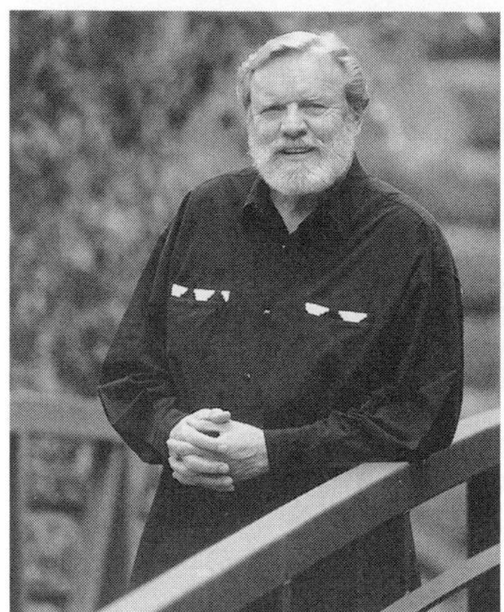

John Naisbitt, well-known author of *Megatrends* and *Megatrends 2000*, says, "The game of life in the information age is people interacting with people." Today's personal selling skills contribute to the successful interaction with people in business.

Personal Selling Opportunities in the Age of Information

Many people have predicted that, in the age of information, "the death of the salesman" is imminent. They predict that new technologies will replace salespeople who are too costly and will no longer be needed to make sales. Canadian Internet guru Jim Carroll (**www.jacc.com**), author or co-author of 34 books—including *Surviving the Information Age, Selling Online*, and *Light Bulbs to Yattabits*—disagrees. He says, "I shudder every time I hear one of the 'experts' suggest we are about to see a lot less human contact in the world of work, particularly when it comes to the sales process. . . . Give me two sales professionals. Lock one in the room with all the hi-tech gear we can throw at them. Send the other out to see the customer. And I'll guarantee you that 9.9 times out of 10, the latter will win the deal."[3]

As noted in Chapter 1, relationships began to become more important for selling at the beginning of the information age. In many cases information does not have value unless people interact effectively. A salesperson may possess information concerning an important new technology, but that information has no value until it is communicated effectively to an investor, a customer, or someone else who can benefit from knowing more about his or her product. A bank loan officer may have the resources needed to assist a prospective homeowner reach a personal dream, but, in the absence of a good relationship, communications may break down. John Naisbitt was right on target when he noted that, in the age of information, "[t]he game... is people interacting with people."[4]

Today personal selling skills contribute in a major way to four groups of knowledge workers who often do not consider themselves salespeople:

- Customer service representatives
- Professionals (accountants, consultants, financial planners, lawyers, etc.)
- Entrepreneurs
- Managerial personnel

CUSTOMER SERVICE REPRESENTATIVES

customer service representative A person who processes reservations, accepts orders by phone or other means, delivers products, handles customer complaints, provides technical assistance, and assists full-time sales representatives.

Assigning selling duties to employees with customer service responsibilities has become quite common. The term **customer service representative** (CSR) is used to describe people who process reservations, accept orders by phone or other means, deliver products, handle customer complaints, provide technical assistance, and assist full-time sales representatives. Some companies are teaming CSRs and salespeople. After the sale is closed, the CSR helps process paperwork, checks on delivery of the product, and engages in other customer follow-up duties. Some examples of how companies are moving customer service representatives into the proactive role of selling follow.

- A growing number of employees in the financial services industry are completing sales training and certification programs. These include not just personal and corporate financial planners but tellers, commercial lenders, and any other people who have customer contact responsibility. Kathy Gilkey, vice-president of sales and marketing at one bank that is encouraging sales training, says, "If you don't have a strong sales and service program in place, you're not as effective in helping your clients."[5]

- The CEO of a large recycling and waste-management company provided sales training for all of his staff members. To illustrate how sales training has made a difference for his company, he points to a member of his accounting staff who received a call from a customer concerning an overbilling problem. In the process of clarifying the problem, the staff member identified an opportunity to expand business with the client through extending service to more locations.[6]

Assigning sales duties to customer service representatives makes sense when you consider the number of contacts customers have with CSRs. When a customer seeks assistance with a problem or makes a reservation, the CSR learns more about the customer and often provides the customer with needed information. Customer needs often surface as both parties exchange information. It is important to keep in mind advice offered by Henry Beckwith, the author of *Selling the Invisible*: "Every act is a marketing act. Make every employee a marketing person."[7]

PROFESSIONALS

Today's professional workers include accountants, computer programmers, consultants, dentists, doctors, engineers, financial planners, lawyers, teachers, and many other specialized knowledge workers. Our labour force includes nearly two million professional service providers, persons who need

C Barsotti
"WILSON, WHAT EXACTLY IS A KNOWLEDGE WORKER AND DO WE HAVE ANY ON THE STAFF?"

Courtesy of Charles Barsotti.

The new economy's workforce is made up of millions of knowledge workers who succeed only when they add value to information. Today's salesperson collects information, organizes it, clarifies it, and presents it in a convincing manner, thereby adding value.

many of the skills used by professional salespeople. Clients who purchase professional services are usually more interested in the person who delivers the service than the firm that employs the professional. They seek expert diagnosticians who are truly interested in their needs. The professional must display good communication skills and be able to establish a relationship built on trust.

Technical skills are not enough in the information age. Many employers expect the professional to bring in new business in addition to keeping current customers satisfied.[8] Employers often screen professional applicants to determine their customer focus and ability to interact well with people. Many firms are providing their professional staff with sales training. The accounting firm Ernst & Young sets aside several days each year to train its professional staff in personal selling. Faced with increased competition and more cost-conscious customers, law, accounting, engineering, and architectural firms are increasingly discovering the merits of personal selling as an auxiliary activity.[9]

While many professional service firms are trying to train their employees to sell, others have been hiring professional salespeople to assist or team up with their service professionals. A common approach is to use a team-selling approach that involves a salesperson and a service professional who has received training in the area of team selling.[10]

ENTREPRENEURS

A recent survey of current and prospective entrepreneurs conducted for the Canadian Professional Sales Association (CPSA) found that 38 percent of

EVERYONE SELLS

Selling Is a Life Skill

Many business students who have no intention of pursuing a career in sales will eventually have successful sales careers. Some students will begin their careers in sales and then move on—sometimes to management positions in their company. Some students will begin their careers in other areas and will find that the opportunities and benefits of being in sales will motivate them to switch to sales careers. Many students will spend their whole lives in non-sales careers, but most will find that the skills they learn from selling will benefit them throughout their careers. As we point out in this chapter, selling skills are needed by management personnel, entrepreneurs, and professionals.

Eddie Greenspan, Canada's best-known criminal lawyer, has been practising law for more than 30 years. He has many of the personal characteristics of superior salespeople: he loves what he does, and he hates to lose. While salesmanship is not a word he would ascribe to as solemn a situation as a jury trial, he says, "In a court of law, you're in the business of selling the truth. . . . You have to make the listeners believe that you believe what you are selling."[a]

respondents believed developing relationships was the key to their success. However, a mere 4 percent thought good salesmanship—critical to developing good customer relationships—important to corporate performance. Terry Ruffell, president of CPSA, says, "Entrepreneurs clearly understand that moving their product or service is critical. But when you call these skills 'sales,' entrepreneurs simply don't identify with them."[11]

www.cpsa.com

This misperception is unfortunate because entrepreneurs who start a new business frequently need to sell their plan to investors and others who can help get their firm established. To grow and remain healthy, many new businesses rely on personal selling by the owners. Some entrepreneurs, such as Harry McWatters, co-founder of Sumac Ridge Estate Winery Ltd. in British Columbia, do recognize that they really are salespeople. McWatters started to develop his selling skills very early in his life. He sold light bulbs door-to-door and newspapers on the Vancouver docks; eventually, he got a job selling produce in a supermarket and then as a booking agent for a moving and storage company. While learning how to sell, Harry continued to improve himself as well. He practised public speaking and took a two-year course in merchandising and marketing sponsored by the Vancouver Board of Trade. The selling skills he learned over his career he uses now as an entrepreneur, and he sums up the lessons he learned by the following piece of wisdom: ENTREPRENEUR = SALESPERSON.[12]

MANAGERIAL PERSONNEL

People working in managerial occupations represent another large group of knowledge workers. They are given such titles as executive, manager, or administrator. Leaders are constantly involved in capturing, processing, and communicating information. That some of the most valuable information is acquired from customers helps to explain the rapid growth in what is being described as "executive selling." Chief executive officers and other executives often accompany salespeople on sales calls to learn more about customer needs and in some cases assist with presentations. Manny Fernandez of the Gartner Group, a technology consulting firm, spends more than half his time travelling on sales calls.[13] Leaders also must articulate their ideas in a persuasive manner and win support for their vision. Brian Tracy, author of *The 100 Absolutely Unbreakable Laws of Business Success*, says, "People who cannot present their ideas or sell themselves effectively have very little influence and are not highly respected."[14]

Increasingly, work in the information economy is understood as an expression of thought. At a time when people change their careers eight times during their lives, selling skills represent important transferable employment skills.[15]

Your Future in Personal Selling

There are more than a million people employed in sales positions across Canada—nearly 10 percent of the Canadian workforce. In addition, the number of sales positions is increasing in most industrialized countries. A

Salespeople who call on supermarkets make 8 to 10 calls during a single day.

close examination of these positions reveals that there is no single "selling" occupation. Our labour force includes hundreds of different selling careers, and chances are there are positions that match your interests, talents, and ambitions. The diversity within selling will become apparent as you study the career options discussed in this chapter.

While many college and university students will ultimately become salespeople, it's often not their first career choice. Students tend to view sales as dynamic and active but feel that a selling career will require them to engage in deceitful or dishonest practices. The good news is that old stereotypes about sales are gradually going by the wayside.[16] Students who study the careers of highly successful salespeople discover that ethical sales practices represent the key to long-term success.

A professional selling position encompasses a wide range of tasks (see Fig. 2.1), and therefore salespeople must possess a variety of skills. A salesperson representing Federal Express (FedEx) will make numerous sales calls each day in an attempt to establish new accounts and provide service to established accounts. There is a wide range of potential customers who can use FedEx delivery services. A salesperson working for a Caterpillar construction equipment dealer may make only two or three sales calls per day. The products offered by the dealer are expensive and are not purchased frequently.

Just as selling occupations differ, so do the titles by which salespeople are known. Their titles reflect, in part, the variety of duties they perform. A survey of current job announcements indicates that fewer and fewer companies are using the word "salesperson" to refer to the people they employ to sell their products. Instead they are using such titles as these:

Account Executive	Sales Consultant
Account Representative	Relationship Manager
Sales Account Manager	Sales Associate
Business Development Manager	Marketing Representative
District Representative	Territory Manager

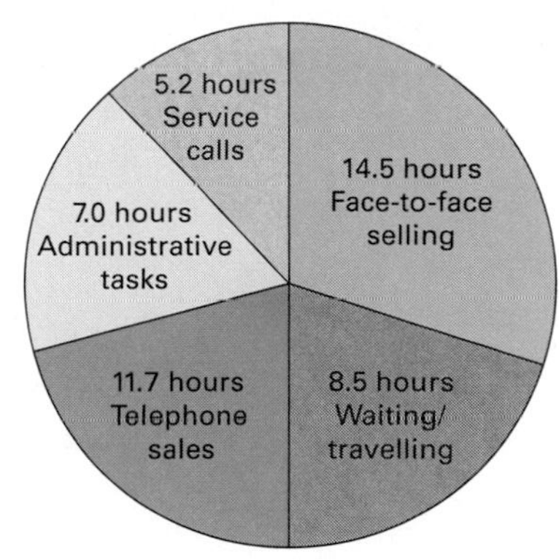

Figure 2.1 How salespeople spend their time during an average 46.9–hour workweek (*Selling*, February 1997, p. 4).

Two factors have contributed to the creation of new titles. First, we have seen a shift from "selling" to "consulting." When salespeople assume a consulting role, the value of the relationship exceeds the value of the transaction. Second, the new titles reflect a difference in education and skill sets needed for sales positions.[17]

Salespeople, regardless of title, play an important role in sustaining the growth and profitability of organizations of all sizes. They also support the employment of many non-selling employees. A recent study indicates that, in service and manufacturing firms, one salesperson creates enough sales revenue to pay for nine other jobs within the company.[18]

REWARDING ASPECTS OF SELLING CAREERS

Gene Fay, account manager for Avid Sports, sells digital video and software systems to professional and college sports teams in Canada and the United States. His successes to date include a large sale to the Vancouver Canucks; his largest sale, US$370 000, was to the Orlando Magic.[19] His job offers him many rewards. Not only does he sell a very innovative product that improves team play, he gets to meet well-known sports executives he has admired for years.

From a personal and an economic standpoint, selling can be a rewarding career. Careers in selling offer financial rewards, recognition, security, and opportunities for advancement to a degree that is unique compared with other occupations.

ABOVE-AVERAGE INCOME

Studies dealing with incomes in the business community indicate that salespeople earn significantly higher incomes than most other workers. Some salespeople actually earn more than their sales managers and other executives within the organization. The high level of compensation—whether from base salary, bonus, or incentives—is justified for good performance. Three major definitions for sales position categories and the compensation (salary plus incentives) earned by each type of salesperson follow.

- **Junior Salesperson.** Junior salespeople often sell a limited variety of non-technical products or services within a limited area and may have one or two years of experience. They solicit additional sales from existing clients or may solicit new clients by mail or telephone. Compensation range is $32 400 to $58 700 annually.[20]
- **Intermediate Salesperson.** Intermediate salespeople often sell to medium or larger customers in an assigned territory and typically have three to four years of experience. They are fully qualified salespeople who work under general supervision and are accountable for achieving

specific sales objectives. They solicit additional sales from existing clients or may solicit new clients by mail, by telephone, or in person. Compensation range is $41 200 to $79 600 annually.[21]

- **Senior Salesperson.** Senior salespeople often sell to larger and more complex accounts, possibly even key accounts. They typically have many years of sales experience and they may even supervise more junior sales representatives. They are often accountable for achieving specific sales objectives in major territories. Compensation range is $52 000 to $100 600 annually.[22]

The lower compensation figure for each category represents entry-level earnings and the higher figure represents compensation for experienced, high-performance salespeople. The amount earned by a salesperson is clearly tied to individual selling skill and the amount of effort.

ABOVE-AVERAGE PSYCHIC INCOME

psychic income Consists of factors that provide psychological rewards; it helps to satisfy the need for recognition and security, and motivates us to achieve higher levels of performance.

Two major psychological needs common to all people are recognition and security. **Psychic income**, which consists of factors that provide psychological rewards, helps satisfy these important needs and motivates us to achieve higher levels of performance. The need for recognition has been established in numerous studies that have examined human motivation. Workers from all employment areas indicate that recognition for work well done is an important morale-building factor.

In selling, recognition will come more frequently and with greater intensity than in most other occupations. Because selling contributes so visibly to the success of most business firms, the accomplishments of sales personnel will seldom go unrecognized.

Most people want to achieve some measure of security in their work. Selling is one of those occupations that usually provides job security during both good and bad times. A recent survey of more than 1100 human resources managers revealed that sales professionals and marketers are among the most sought-after employees.[23]

OPPORTUNITY FOR ADVANCEMENT

Each year, thousands of openings appear in the ranks of supervision and management. Because salespeople work in positions of high visibility, they are in an excellent position to be chosen for advancement to positions of greater responsibility. The presidents of many of today's companies began their careers in the ranks of the sales force. Of course, not every salesperson can become president of a large corporation, but, in the middle-management ranks there are numerous interesting and high-paying positions in which experience in selling is a prime requisite for advancement. Information on careers in sales management will be presented in Chapter 17.

OPPORTUNITIES FOR WOMEN

Prodded by a growing awareness that gender is not a barrier to success in selling, business firms are recruiting qualified women in growing numbers. The

Brenda Fisher, a sales representative with Janssen-Ortho Inc. (see page 224), loves her work and loves her family. She must make regular sales trips away from home. However, she has considerable flexibility with her schedule and she enjoys the freedom she has while at home to manage family obligations and to bond with her young son, Matthew.

percentage of women in the sales force has increased considerably. Women are turning to sales employment because it offers excellent economic rewards and in many cases a flexible work schedule. Flexible schedules are very appealing to women who want to balance career and family.

Although women are relative newcomers to industrial sales, they are enjoying expanded career opportunities in such areas as real estate, insurance, financial planning, advertising, and consulting. Ron Burke, professor of organizational behaviour at York University adds, "Obviously, all men aren't the same, nor are all women, but men are more task-oriented and women are more people-oriented."[24] This distinction makes women particularly suited to sales careers where building and maintaining long-term relationships is important.

SELLING IN THE GLOBAL ECONOMY

Major Faux Pas Results in Lost Sale

Selling overseas or to foreigners who visit Canada demands a high degree of cultural sensitivity. Steve Waterhouse, affiliated with Waterhouse Group, learned this lesson the hard way. For six months, he had been courting a Tokyo-based meeting planning company. Finally, he arranged a meeting with the company's representative who was visiting North America to attend a national convention. She handed her business card to him in the traditional Japanese way, extending the card while holding onto both corners. Waterhouse says, "I took the card and scribbled a note on the back of it." This behaviour shocked the woman. "I might as well have spit in her face," Waterhouse says. He hadn't realized that, in Japan, the business card is examined carefully at the time it is offered because it provides all of the information needed to assess the person's status (title, position, etc.) in the business community. Even though he quickly offered a sincere apology, the damage was done. His breach of etiquette resulted in the loss of a $100 000 sale.[b]

Opportunities for people who belong to a minority exist in a variety of selling careers.

OPPORTUNITIES FOR MINORITIES

From a historical perspective, the field of selling has not provided equal opportunity to minorities. In the past it was not easy for a member of a minority to obtain a sales position. Today the picture has changed, and more firms are actively recruiting employees from minorities. While equal opportunity legislation can be credited, in part, for bringing about changes in hiring practices, many firms now view the recruitment and training of employees who represent minorities simply as good business. Many organizations now have top-producing salespeople who belong to minorities.

In recent years, several trade journal reports have highlighted the underrepresentation in sales of employees who represent minorities. Many companies recognized that shifting population demographics—where women, minorities, and immigrants have made the biggest gains—required a re-examination of hiring practices. Many companies realize the need for a diverse sales force that can gain access to the diverse clientele that make up certain market segments.[25] This philosophical shift should continue to open doors for Canada's growing population of minorities.

Employment Settings in Selling Today

Careers in the field of selling may be classified in several ways. One of the broadest differentiations is based on whether the product is a tangible or an intangible. Tangibles are physical goods such as furniture, homes, and data processing equipment. Intangibles are non-physical products or services such as stocks and bonds, insurance, and consulting services. This chapter will classify selling careers according to employment setting. We will explore the following four major employment settings and identify some of the unique characteristics of each:

Selling a service
Selling for a retailer
Selling for a wholesaler
Selling for a manufacturer

SELLING A SERVICE

What do KPMG Canada, Bell Sympatico, Holiday Inn, Purolator Courier, and London Life Insurance Company have in common? Each of these companies is selling services. In recent years the number of consumer and business dollars spent on services in our society has steadily increased. The great majority of the Canadian labour force is now employed in the service sector. Customers feel the need for assistance from a knowledgeable salesperson when making purchases of many types of services.

www.arnoldworldwide.ca

Michael Davidson is vice-president, marketing and business development, at Arnold Worldwide Canada, a full-service marketing communications agency. He is responsible for leading new business initiatives for the agency. In a typical week, Michael spends time cultivating relationships with prospects and introducing them to the agency. He spends considerable time with prospects, getting a solid sense of their needs, assessing the opportunity, and then assembling and leading the right agency team for the client. Michael Davidson says, "Successful selling comes down to your ability to truly understand client needs and building trust and respect. Ultimately, people hire people that they want to work with in this business."[26]

Here's a brief look at some opportunities in the service field.

- **Banks and financial services.** This is one of the hottest areas of sales growth. There are more than 3000 firms that provide financial services in Canada, directly employing more than 550 000 people.[27] Banks, brokerage firms, and other businesses are branching out, selling a broader range of financial planning and investment services. More and more bank employees are involved in personal selling activities, developing new accounts and servicing existing ones. Bank personnel are completing sales training courses in record numbers these days.
- **Radio and television advertising.** Revenue from advertising supports the radio and television broadcasting industry. Every station must employ salespeople whose job is to call on current and prospective advertisers. Each client's needs are unique, and meeting them makes the work of a media sales representative interesting. In addition, there is a creative side to media sales, for members of the sales staff often help develop commercials.
- **Newspaper advertising.** There are more than one thousand daily and weekly newspapers in Canada. Each newspaper is supported by both local and national advertisers and must sell advertising space to stay in business. Many business firms rely heavily on media sales personnel for help in developing effective advertising campaigns.
- **Hotel, motel, and convention centre services**. Each year, thousands of seminars, conferences, and business meetings are held throughout Canada. Most of these events are hosted by hotels, motels, or convention centres. By diversifying their markets and upscaling their services these marketers are catering to business clients in many new and exciting ways. The salespeople employed by these firms play an important role in attracting meetings. They sell room space, food, beverages, and other services needed for a successful meeting. (See the job description of a convention centre salesperson in Appendix B, on the CD-ROM.)
- **Real estate.** Buying a home is a monumental undertaking. It is usually the single largest expenditure in the average consumer's lifetime. The purchase of commercial property by individual investors or business firms is also a major economic decision. Therefore, the people who sell real estate assume an important responsibility. Busy real estate salespeople often hire assistants who help hold open houses or perform other duties.
- **Insurance.** Selling insurance has always been one of the most rewarding careers in sales. Common forms of insurance sold include fire, liability, life, health, automobile, casualty, and homeowner's. There are

two broad groups of insurance salespeople. Employees of major companies such as Manulife Financial or Clarica Life Insurance make up one group. Independent insurance agents who serve as representatives for a number of companies make up the second group. The typical independent agency will offer a broad line of personal and business insurance services.

- **Business services.** The heavy volume of business mergers and corporate downsizing has increased demand for business services provided by outside contractors. Some of the business services purchased today include computer programming, recruiting, training, printing, credit reporting, and payroll.

The list of careers involving the sale of services is much longer. We have not explored the expanding fields of home and business security, travel and

Financial services is one of the hottest areas of sales growth. Edward Jones has earned the number 1 ranking on *Fortune*'s list of "100 Best Companies to Work for."

Grow with a leader.

As one of the nation's fastest growing financial-services firms, Edward Jones recognizes that the surest way to deliver outstanding service to our customers is to continually develop and reward our associates who provide that service. That simple formula has helped us to attract and retain the very best people and is key to our leadership in the financial-services industry. Recently, it has earned us the No. 1 ranking for the second straight year in FORTUNE® magazine's list of the "100 Best Companies to Work For."

To learn more about opportunities with Edward Jones, call 1-800-999-5650 or to complete our online application, visit **www.edwardjones.com/careers**

EdwardJones®

Serving Individual Investors Since 1871

EOE

recreation, pest control, landscaping and lawn care, pool maintenance, and transportation. As the demand for services increases, so will the employment opportunities for salespeople.

SELLING FOR A RETAILER

At age 26, Ruth Bell Steinhauer received the Business Development Bank of Canada Young Entrepreneur Award, recognizing her as one of Canada's outstanding young business people. Her store Bellissima sold more than a million dollars' worth of women's fashions in its first 11 months. Bell Steinhauer credits her success to customer service. Bellissima is a retailer that visits stroke patients and other shut-ins in their homes, allows people to take items home "on approval," will open its doors after hours for people who cannot get in during the regular store hours, and guarantees in-store alterations within 24 hours. The customer database keeps track of all customers, what they purchased, and important information about their preferences. "When customers come in the store," she says, "we greet them quickly and in a friendly manner. We try to have several of our salespeople develop relationships with each customer. That way, whenever a customer visits the store, they can find someone who is familiar with them and how best to serve them."[28]

The **retail salesperson** usually engages in full-time professional selling and is paid well for his or her contributions to the business. Products sold at the retail level range from exotic foreign automobiles to fine furniture. Here is a partial list of retail products that usually require a high degree of personal selling:

retail salesperson A salesperson who is employed at the retail level to help prospects solve buying problems. This person is usually involved in selling higher priced, technical, and specialty retail products.

Automobiles	Recreational vehicles
Musical instruments	Television and electronic products
Photographic equipment	Furniture/Decorating supplies
Fashion apparel	Tires and related accessories
Major household appliances	Computers

Today, traditional retailers are facing new competition from online retailers. Canadian consumers are spending millions of dollars on Internet purchases, a clear sign that electronic commerce is here to stay. Traditional retailers must offer customers more than products. Robert Plant, a retail expert and chairman of Toronto–based Karabus Consulting Management Inc., says that today's biggest spenders are tired of humdrum shopping. Retailers must win them over by delivering more in-store thrills.[29] Customers today are looking for more. They want a combination of product, value, and experience. Well-trained salespeople can add value to the traditional shopping experience.

SELLING FOR A WHOLESALER

Canadian wholesalers generate more than $450 billion in sales annually and employ about 600 000 people.[30] Wholesalers play an important role in making channels of distribution efficient. A full-service wholesaler offers a wide variety of services to its customers, including maintaining inventories, gathering and interpreting market information, extending credit, distributing goods, and providing promotional activities. Wholesalers employ two kinds of salespeople: inside and outside.

The Inside Salesperson

inside salesperson A salesperson who relies almost totally on telephone orders, and who follows a strict timetable of customer contact. Inside sales is a cost-efficient method of selling, but one that still requires a thorough understanding of the selling process and how to manage customer relations.

The **inside salesperson** relies almost totally on telephone orders and follows a strict timetable of customer contact. Jim Domanski, Canada's most quoted telemanagement consultant, estimates that contacting a customer by telephone costs one-tenth what it costs to make the same contact in person, and that a telemarketer can make as many sales calls in a day as a field salesperson can make in a week.[31] Because of the escalating cost of personal selling, selling by telephone is growing in popularity. This selling method has become so popular that some companies are taking their salespeople off the road and bringing them back to headquarters, where they are retrained to sell by telephone. The Internet is increasingly being used to support the work of inside salespeople.

The Outside Salesperson

outside salesperson A salesperson who must have knowledge of many products and be able to serve as a consultant to the customer on product or service applications. This position usually requires detailed understanding of the customer's operation.

The duties of an **outside salesperson** vary from one wholesale firm to another. Some specialize in a single area, such as electronics or small appliances, while others sell a wide range of product lines. The typical outside salesperson must have knowledge of many products and be able to serve as a consultant to the customer. For example, a sales representative for a pharmaceutical wholesaler calling on retail stores will need to be familiar with advertising and display techniques, store layout, and other merchandising strategies. Most importantly, this person must be completely familiar with the customer's operation.

SELLING FOR A MANUFACTURER

www.ibm.ca

David Vokey is a senior client manager in the higher-education industry group of IBM Canada. While selling in Nova Scotia and Prince Edward Island, he grew IBM's sales from $1.5 million to $11 million in only four years.[32] David Vokey led the sales team that helped Acadia University become Canada's first "ThinkPad University." In his role as senior client manager, David Vokey manages IBM's relationships with many of its most important customers.

Manufacturers employ sales and sales support personnel in many different capacities. Field salespeople, sales engineers, and detail salespeople are outside salespeople who interact face to face with prospects and customers. Inside salespeople rely primarily on the telephone to identify prospects and engage in other selling activities.

The Field Salesperson

field salesperson A salesperson employed by a manufacturer who handles well-established products that require a minimum of creative selling. The position usually does not require a high degree of technical knowledge.

The **field salesperson** sells to new customers and increases sales to current ones. These salespeople must be able to recognize buyer needs and prescribe the best product or service to meet these needs. Field salespeople who provide excellent service find their customers to be a good source of leads for new prospects.

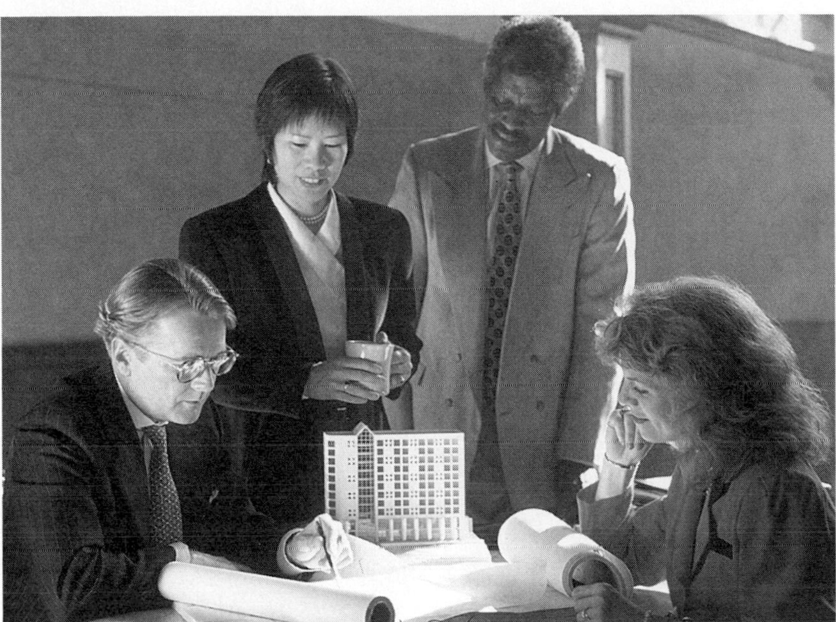

Sales engineers must have detailed and precise technical knowledge.

The Sales Engineer

The **sales engineer** must have detailed and precise technical knowledge, and the ability to discuss the technical aspects of his or her products. Expertise in identifying, analyzing, and solving customer problems is of critical importance. While their primary responsibility is selling, they must be technically proficient in product applications.

sales engineer A person who must have detailed and precise technical knowledge, and the ability to discuss the technical aspects of his or her products.

The Detail Salesperson

The primary goal of a **detail salesperson** is to develop goodwill and stimulate demand for the manufacturer's products. This person is usually not compensated on the basis of the orders obtained, but receives recognition for increasing the sale of goods indirectly. The detail salesperson calls on wholesale, retail, and other customers to help improve their marketing. In a typical day this salesperson may help train a sales staff or offer advice to a firm that is planning an advertising campaign. Detail salespeople also collect valuable information regarding customer acceptance of products. They must be able to offer sound advice in such diverse areas as credit policies, pricing, display, store layout, and storage. The detail salesperson is sometimes referred to as a missionary salesperson.

detail salesperson A salesperson representing a manufacturer, whose primary goal is to develop goodwill and stimulate demand for a product or product line. This person usually assists the customer by improving the customer's ability to sell the product.

The Inside Salesperson

As face-to-face sales costs increase, many manufacturers have developed an inside sales force. At IBM, about 15 percent of members of the sales force never leave the office. They make calls to smaller customers, take orders, and in some cases provide support to field salespeople.[33] Some marketers are finding that only the initial sale of the product requires face-to-face contact. Inside salespeople can handle repeat contacts.

SELLING MENTOR

Are You Ready for the Sales Interview?

The personal interview is an important part of the selection process when filling sales positions. When companies use a series of interviews, the first one is often used to eliminate unacceptable candidates—those who lack maturity, lack enthusiasm, or display poor appearance. Subsequent interviews are used to match people to job qualifications. At Hewlett-Packard, candidates may have as many as six interviews with various people. At Smith Kline, a team approach is used so candidates do not learn the "right" answers from one interview to the next.

While interviews will vary from one company or interviewer to another, there are some popular questions and requests that you should be prepared to handle:

- Tell me about yourself.
- Describe the sales process as you understand it.
- What books have you read recently on selling or for personal development?
- What is your greatest weakness? strength?
- What was the most boring job you ever had, and how did you handle it?
- How do you feel about your present (or previous) employer?
- What was the biggest contribution you made to your last employer?
- Sell me this pen (laptop computer, lamp).
- Why should we hire you?

Some employers will also ask you to complete a test to demonstrate your written communication skills or your numeracy skills—important skills for a sales professional.[c]

Learning to Sell

"Are salespeople made or are they born?" This classic question seems to imply that some people are born with certain qualities that give them a special advantage in the selling field. This is not true. The principles of selling can be learned and applied by people whose personal characteristics are quite different. In the past few decades, sales training has expanded on four fronts: corporate-sponsored training, training provided by commercial vendors, certification studies, and courses provided by colleges and universities.

www.pb.com

Some companies have developed their own sales training certification programs. These companies spend millions of dollars each year to develop their sales personnel. Salespeople at Pitney Bowes can earn the designation of Certified Postal Consultant following successful completion of its demanding training program. David Munro, the first successful Canadian graduate, credits the program with giving him greater confidence, improved earnings, and national recognition.[34] *Training* magazine, which conducts an annual analysis of employer-provided training, indicates that salespeople are among the most intensively trained employee groups. The typical salesperson completes 38 hours of training a year, which is 10 hours more than senior executives receive.[35]

David Munro is the first Canadian graduate of Pitney Bowes' Certified Postal Consultant program.

The programs designed by firms specializing in the development of sales personnel are a second source of sales training. Wilson Learning Corporation, The Forum Corporation, Dale Carnegie Training, Learning International, Zig Ziglar Corporation, and AchieveGlobal offer some of the most popular

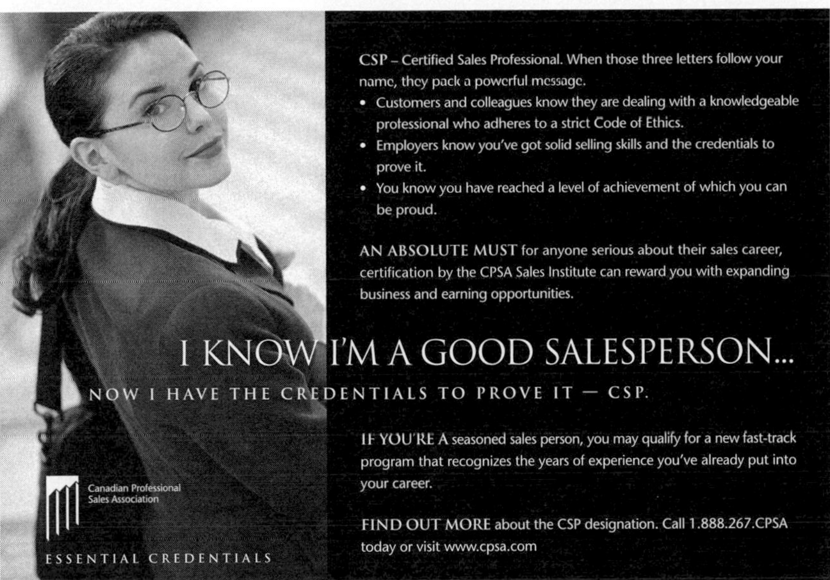

CSP – Certified Sales Professional. When those three letters follow your name, they pack a powerful message.
• Customers and colleagues know they are dealing with a knowledgeable professional who adheres to a strict Code of Ethics.
• Employers know you've got solid selling skills and the credentials to prove it.
• You know you have reached a level of achievement of which you can be proud.
AN ABSOLUTE MUST for anyone serious about their sales career, certification by the CPSA Sales Institute can reward you with expanding business and earning opportunities.
I KNOW I'M A GOOD SALESPERSON...
NOW I HAVE THE CREDENTIALS TO PROVE IT — CSP.
IF YOU'RE A seasoned sales person, you may qualify for a new fast-track program that recognizes the years of experience you've already put into your career.
Canadian Professional Sales Association
FIND OUT MORE about the CSP designation. Call 1.888.267.CPSA today or visit www.cpsa.com
ESSENTIAL CREDENTIALS

The Canadian Professional Sales Association provides professional accreditation for salespeople who complete its Certified Sales Professional program.

courses. The legendary Professional Selling Skills (PSS) course developed in the late 1960s by Gene Keluche is still offered by AchieveGlobal. This carefully designed course, once owned by Xerox, has been completed by millions of salespeople.[36]

The trend toward increased professionalism in personal selling has been the stimulus for a third type of training and education initiative. Many salespeople are returning to the classroom to earn certification in a sales or sales-related area. In real estate, financial planning, and life insurance sales, there are professional designations for salespeople. The Canadian Professional Sales Association (CPSA) provides professional accreditation as a Certified Sales Professional for salespeople who complete a certification program offered through the CPSA Sales Institute. The CPSA also offers a number of professional development seminars in selling and sales management, and has recently launched eight online selling courses that can be credited toward earning the designation as a Certified Sales Professional.

www.consilient.net

Universities and colleges throughout Canada offer the fourth source of sales training. These courses are attracting an increasing number of students interested in careers in accounting, entrepreneurship, and finance, as well as sales and marketing. The business community, in general, is increasingly asking for more selling skills from graduates of business programs. Trevor Adey, president of Consilient Technologies, a wireless technologies solutions provider based in St. John's, Newfoundland and Labrador, notes

> It is unfortunate that more university business students do not get any sales training in their undergraduate business programs. They study a lot of marketing. When I think about opportunities now, I see many small- and medium-sized organizations that need good salespeople who understand marketing, more than they need good marketing people who might be able to sell.[37]

CUSTOMER RELATIONSHIP MANAGEMENT WITH TECHNOLOGY

Learning CRM Software

Many salespeople are at first apprehensive about using a computer, yet research shows a high degree of acceptance. Salespeople are often heard remarking, "I don't know how I got along without it."

Following the instructions in this text's CRM application exercises and case problems will give you a good understanding of basic CRM. This knowledge can be valuable as you enter today's selling environment. Many sales organizations are using CRM, and your understanding of the basics will help you learn the particular system that is used by your potential employer. Some people, after following these instructions, list their use of CRM on their résumé.

Many users of CRM enter information about friends and family into their database and use it to enhance all of their relationships. CRM helps people remember the status of relationships, steps to take, and pending events, such as anniversaries and birthdays. (See the application exercise on learning CRM software on page 48 for more information.)

SUMMARY

Today's workforce is made up of millions of knowledge workers who succeed only when they add value to information. The new economy rewards salespeople and other knowledge workers who collect, organize, clarify, and present information in a convincing manner. Selling skills contribute in a major way to four groups of knowledge workers who usually do not consider themselves to be salespeople: customer service representatives, professionals (e.g., accountants, consultants, lawyers), entrepreneurs, and managerial personnel.

Selling careers offer many rewards not found in other occupations. Income, both monetary and psychic, is above average, and there are many opportunities for advancement. Salespeople enjoy job security, mobility, and independence. Opportunities in selling for members of minorities and for women are growing. In addition, selling is very interesting work, because a salesperson is constantly in contact with people. The adage "No two people are alike" suggests that sales work will never be dull or routine.

The text described each of the four major employment settings in the field of personal selling. We have provided a brief introduction to the variety of employment opportunities in service, retail, wholesale, and manufacturers' sales. Keep in mind that each category features a wide range of selling positions, which vary in terms of educational requirements, earning potential, and type of customer served. The discussion and examples should help you see which kind of sales career best suits your talents and interests.

Key Terms

Customer Service Representative **30**

Detail Salesperson **43**

Field Salesperson **42**

Inside Salesperson **42**

Outside Salesperson **42**

Psychic Income **36**

Retail Salesperson **41**

Sales Engineer **43**

Review Questions

1. List and describe the four employment settings for people who are considering a selling career.
2. Explain the meaning of *psychic income.*
3. Explain why personal selling is an important auxiliary skill needed by lawyers, engineers, accountants, and other professionals.
4. Why are opportunities for women and minorities in sales improving?
5. Develop a list of retail products that require well-developed personal selling skills.
6. Some salespeople have an opportunity to earn certification in a sales or sales-related area. How might a salesperson benefit from certification?
7. Describe the two types of wholesale sales jobs.
8. List four titles commonly used to describe salespeople in manufacturing. Describe the duties of each.
9. Develop a list of eight selling career opportunities in the service field.
10. List and briefly describe the four major sources of sales training.

Application Exercises

1. Examine a magazine or newspaper ad for a product or service that you have never seen before. Evaluate its chances for receiving wide customer acceptance. Will this product require a large amount of personal selling effort? What kind of salespeople (service, manufacturing, wholesale, or retail) would be involved in selling this product?
2. Ten indicators that have been proposed as important for sales aptitude include:

highly persuasive	honest
reliable	sociable
enthusiastic	obviously ambitious
high verbal skills	well organized
general sales experience	specific sales experience

   Rank the three indicators that you think are most important (1 = most important). Rank the three that you think are least important (1 = least important). Be prepared to defend your answer.
3. Interview a salesperson from one of the four major employment settings (service, retail, wholesale, manufacturing), and ask the following questions:
   a. Why did you decide on a sales career?
   b. What do you like most about your job?
   c. What do you like least about your job?
   d. What is a typical sales day like?
   e. What are the most important things for sales success?
4. When Shelly Jones, a vice-president and partner in the consulting firm Korn/Ferry International, looks into the future, he sees some new challenges for salespeople. He recently shared the following predictions with *Selling* magazine:
   a. Salespeople will spend more time extending the range of applications or finding new markets for the products they sell.
   b. The selling function will be less pitching your product and more integrating your product into the business equation of your client. Understanding the business environment in which your client operates will be critical.
   c. You will have to be a financial engineer for your client. You need to understand how your client makes money and be able to explain how your product or service contributes to profitable operation of the client's firm.

   Interview a salesperson who is involved in business-to-business selling (e.g., a manufacturer's representative) and determine if this person agrees with the views of Shelly Jones.
5. Go to **www.google.ca** (or another search engine if you prefer) and hit "advanced search." Find career information on a pharmaceutical salesperson (or representative), a sales engineer, and a retail salesperson by typing each of these terms under "Find results with exact phrase." Limit your search by typing ".ca" under "domain." Be prepared to discuss some of what you find in class.

ROLE-PLAY EXERCISE

This role play will give you experience in selling your knowledge, skills, and experience to a prospective employer. You will be meeting with a class member who will assume the role of an employer who is developing a new sales team. Prior to this interview, reflect on the courses you have competed, work experience, and other life experiences that may have value in the eyes of the employer. You may also want to reflect on any volunteer work you have completed and leadership roles you have held. Be prepared to discuss the personal selling skills you are developing in this course.

CRM Application Exercise **LEARNING CRM SOFTWARE**

Launch the CRM software that you have downloaded from your CD-ROM to become acquainted with the layout and features of the ACT! program. Start by pressing the F1 function key, which displays the contents of the help file. Clicking on the first entry, ACT! Screens, shows information about the program's three main screens: contact screens (records with information about people), word processing screens, and the query screen. Print the ACT! Screens page by selecting File, Print Topic. At the bottom of this page is a row of icons, essentially a small version of the toolbar icons found on the main contact screen. Click on each of these icons for an explanation of its function.

Next, select the underlined link The Contact Screens to learn about the two screens where you can view information about a contact (person). At the top of this screen, click on the link labelled Status Area to read a description of the information found along the side of the contact screens. Here you will learn to determine the number of records in the database, how to use the card index icon to navigate, and how to discover whether there are notes, historic information, or activities scheduled for this contact.

Browse through the help screens to learn more about the structure and functions of this CRM software.

Case Problem

TFI Food Equipment Solutions is a privately owned specialty food service equipment distributor. (Visit **www.tficanada.com**.) It has been providing complete food service equipment packages and programs to Canadian customers since 1954. Among the best known manufacturers that TFI represents are Taylor, Henny Penny, Flavor Burst, Smokeroma, and Power Soak. TFI is one of the largest Taylor distributors in North America and the number one Henny Penny distributor in the world. TFI was the Taylor distributor of the year in 2004, and the Henny Penny distributor of the year in 2003.

Alex Pettes, vice-president sales and marketing, is responsible for three national account managers and twelve retail sales managers. National account managers service a number of high-profile national and international customers, including McDonald's, Burger King, Wendy's, KFC, Imperial Oil, and Mac's Convenience Stores. Because their main responsibility is to manage existing customer relationships through providing superior service, these salespeople are paid high salaries with smaller commission incentives. Retail sales managers, on the other hand, are responsible to sell mainly to smaller independent business owners and are paid exclusively by commission.

People who are new to sales should normally be wary of companies that pay strictly by commission. Frequently, these are smaller companies that have limited financial resources, and they limit their risk by committing to pay salespeople only after they have produced sales for the company. These companies also frequently hire too many salespeople and create situations where salespeople compete for sales within territories because, regardless of which salesperson wins or loses, the company still wins. This, however, is not the situation at TFI. Alex Pettes negotiates individual agreements with each salesperson because there are differences among sales territories. However, sales territories are protected for each salesperson. Even though salespeople are paid strictly by commission, they get a bi-weekly draw against their commissions based on an agreed annual target income, typically in the $35 000 to $40 000 range. For the first eight weeks, however, it is considered a training allowance. If salespeople do not sell enough to cover their draw, there is no penalty. The draw really comes into effect after this period.

TFI also supplies a company vehicle to its salespeople, and pays for gas, insurance, and maintenance for this vehicle. Normal expenses incurred for business purposes are also paid by TFI, on submission of receipts. After 90 days of employment, salespeople are enrolled in a health insurance plan, and after one year, they become eligible for a retirement savings plan. Alex Pettes provides some of the important sales statistics to potential new recruits. In a recent year, commissions paid to salespeople ranged from 12 to 20 percent, with the overall average of 14 percent. Salespeople closed between 28 and more than 100 deals, the average being 45 deals. Individual deals ranged from $4000 to more than $50 000 for a complete package. The average deal was approximately $7500.

As part of the recruitment process, Alex Pettes asks potential recruits to prepare a territory plan and present it formally. The territory plan outlines what the candidate expects to do in the territory, and how he or she intends to do it. It usually indicates the number and types of potential customers in the territory and outlines how many sales calls the person thinks he or she will make each day and each week, and how he or she will cover the territory. Alex also suggests that, when preparing a territory plan, the potential recruit also includes a plan for personal development what he or she intends to do to become a better salesperson.

Speaking of the requirement to present a territory plan, Alex says, "It is one of the best things we do. It forces potential recruits to consider what they want and what they have to do to be a success. If we decide to hire them, we can help them fine-tune it. The territory plan also helps weed out some candidates who don't have what it takes to be a success in this selling environment. We don't want salespeople who are happy making their minimum targets; we want salespeople who are willing to stretch to achieve their personal financial success. We want them to succeed."

When new recruits are hired, Alex Pettes hands them a pen to sign the formal contract between TFI and the salesperson. It is a Cross pen, personally engraved with the salesperson's name: the company's first gift to the salesperson.[38]

Questions

1. What do you consider is positive about this sales job?
2. What do you consider is negative about this sales job?
3. If you were applying for a TFI sales position, what questions would you ask Alex Pettes during your interview?

ROLE-PLAY EXERCISE

RELATIONSHIP STRATEGY
PRESENTATION STRATEGY
PERSONAL SELLING PHILOSOPHY
PRODUCT STRATEGY
CUSTOMER STRATEGY

Developing a Personal Selling Philosophy

SCENARIO

You are currently working part time at the Dell Direct Store located in Three Rivers Mall. You are a full-time student majoring in marketing at Red River College. The manager of your store wants you to identify potential customers on your campus and sell Dell notebook computers to those persons who have a need for this product.

CUSTOMER PROFILE

Theresa Feng is a full-time commuter student who lives with her parents and shares the family's one computer with her mom. Each morning she drives about 32 kilometres (20 miles) to the campus and spends most of the day attending classes, working in the library, and visiting with friends. She currently spends about two hours each evening on the computer at home.

SALESPERSON PROFILE

Paul Windom started working at the Dell Direct Store shortly after graduating from high school. The store manager was impressed with Paul's computer expertise and his friendly manner. Although Paul is able to sell any type of computer, he tends to specialize in notebook computers, which are ideal for college students who have mobile computing needs. Paul's personal computer is a new Dell notebook, which replaced his desktop computer.

PRODUCT

Paul Windom sells several different notebook computers that vary in price from $795 to $1649. Each notebook is equipped with specific, easily accessible ports to interact with a variety of external components. All of his notebooks offer both productivity and entertainment applications. Services offered by Dell include helpful assistance via telephone or online tutorials at *support.dell.com.* Dell's warranty provides service and support at no extra charge.

INSTRUCTIONS

For this role play activity you will assume the role of Paul Windom. You will meet with Theresa Feng, played by another student, and determine her interest in and need for a notebook computer. Prior to meeting with Theresa, preplan your relationship strategy, product strategy, customer strategy, and presentation strategy. Chapter 1 provides a description of each strategic area. Be prepared to close the sale if you feel that the customer will benefit from this purchase.

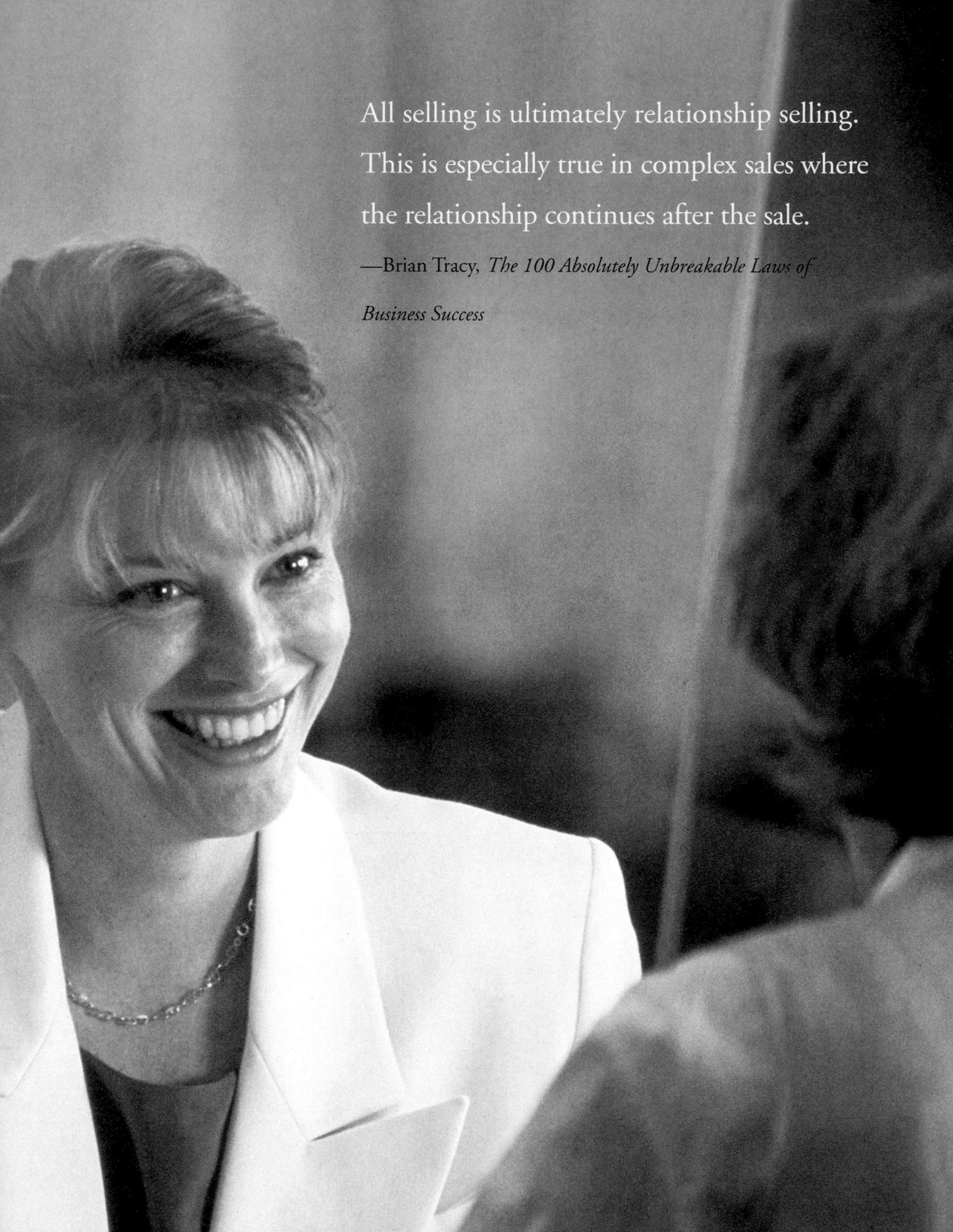
All selling is ultimately relationship selling. This is especially true in complex sales where the relationship continues after the sale.
—Brian Tracy, *The 100 Absolutely Unbreakable Laws of Business Success*

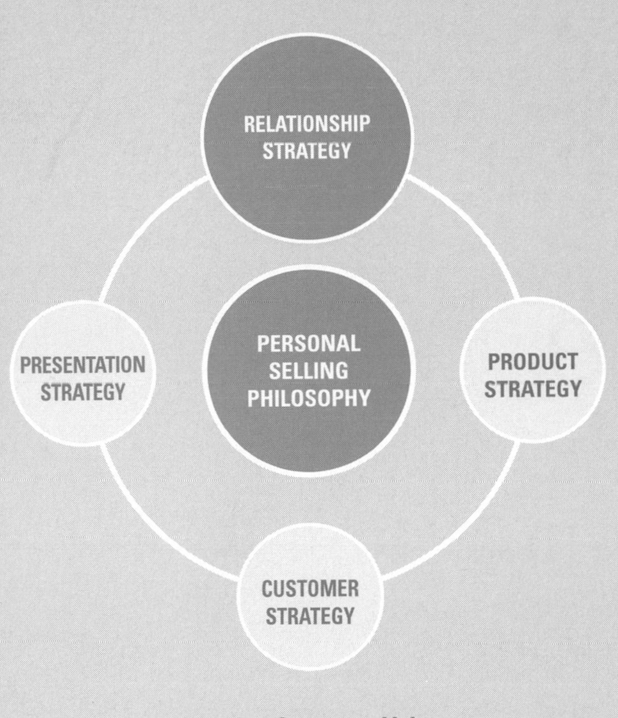

Creating Customer Value

PART II

Developing a Relationship Strategy

High-performance salespeople are generally better able to build and maintain relationships than moderate performers. Part II focuses on the person-to-person relationship-building strategies that are the foundation for personal development and for relationships with customers that result in long-term, value-added partnerships. The influence of ethical decisions on relationships in selling is also discussed in Part II.

CHAPTER 3

Creating Value

WITH A RELATIONSHIP STRATEGY

LEARNING OBJECTIVES

After studying this chapter, you should be able to

1. Explain the importance of developing a relationship strategy
2. Define partnering and describe the partnering relationship
3. List the four key groups with which the salesperson needs to develop relationship strategies
4. Discuss how self-image forms the foundation for building long-term selling relationships
5. Describe the importance of a win-win relationship
6. Identify and describe the major nonverbal factors that shape our sales image
7. Describe conversational strategies that help us establish relationships
8. Explain how to establish a self-improvement plan based on personal development strategies

The salespeople who work for Masonite International **www.masonite.com** (formerly Premdor Inc.) understand the importance of developing relationship strategies to build long-term partnerships with their customers. The Mississauga-based manufacturer produces more than 100 000 doors per day in its plants in five countries and sells them in more than 40 countries through a well-established wholesale and retail distribution system.

To demonstrate their commitment to service, salespeople develop "relationship plans" in consultation with their customers. Philip Orsino, president and CEO, says that the process of developing and committing these plans to paper ensures that sales personnel understand each customer's needs and have clearly defined objectives for serving each customer. The customized plans also outline how the salespeople will meet their objectives for each customer and how their performance will be measured. According to Orsino, the number one comment from customers who have been presented with a written relationship plan has been "No one has ever done this with us before."

Masonite International is creating value with its relationship strategy.[1]

Developing a Relationship Strategy

Developing and applying the wide range of interpersonal skills needed in today's complex sales environment can be challenging. Daniel Goleman, author of the best-selling books *Emotional Intelligence* and *Working with Emotional Intelligence*, notes that there are many forms of intelligence that influence our actions throughout life. One of these, **emotional intelligence**, refers to the capacity for monitoring our own feelings and those of others, for motivating ourselves, and for managing emotions effectively in ourselves and in our relationships. People with a high level of emotional intelligence display many of the qualities needed in sales work: self-confidence, trustworthiness, adaptability, initiative, optimism, empathy, and well-developed social skills.[2]

emotional intelligence The capacity for recognizing our own feelings and those of others, for motivating ourselves, and for managing emotions effectively in ourselves and our relationships.

Daniel Goleman and other researchers state that there are widespread exceptions to the rule that a high intelligence quotient (IQ) predicts success. In the field of personal selling and most other business occupations, emotional intelligence is a much greater predictor of success.[3] The good news is that emotional intelligence can be enhanced with a variety of self-development activities. We discuss many of these activities in this chapter.

Selling in the information age involves three major relationship challenges:

Building new relationships. Salespeople who can quickly build rapport with new prospects have a much greater chance of achieving success in personal selling.[4]

Transforming relationships from the personal level to the business level. Once rapport is established, the salesperson is in a stronger position to begin the need-identification process.

Management of relationships. Dr. Charles Parker—a noted consultant and sales trainer—says, "In order to achieve a high level of success salespeople have to manage a multitude of different relationships."[5] Salespeople must develop relationship management strategies that focus on four key groups. These groups are discussed later in this chapter.

In this chapter we introduce the win-win philosophy and discuss the importance of projecting a professional image. Chapter 4 explains how an understanding of communication styles can help us better manage the relationship process. Chapter 5 focuses on the importance of maintaining high ethical standards in order to build long-term relationships with the customer. (See Fig. 3.1.)

RELATIONSHIPS ADD VALUE

Denis Waitley, in his book *Empires of the Mind*, describes developments in the business community, noting especially that "yesterday value was extra. Today value is everything."[6] The manner in which salespeople establish, build, and manage relationships is not an incidental aspect of personal selling; in the information age it is the key to success. In the information economy, business is defined by customer relationships, and sales success depends on adding

www.deniswaitley.com

Figure 3.1 Every salesperson should have an ongoing goal of developing a relationship strategy that adds value to the sale.

Strategic/Consultative Selling Model	
Strategic step	Prescription
Develop a Personal Selling Philosophy	✓ Value Personal Selling ✓ Adopt Marketing Concept ✓ Become a Problem Solver/Partner
Develop a Relationship Strategy	• Project positive, professional image • Practise communication-style flexing • Behave ethically

SELLING IN ACTION

The Importance of EQ

Steven J. Stein and Howard E. Book, both at the University ofToronto, have been actively researching emotional intelligence (EQ). In their book, *The EQ Edge* www.eqedge.com, they argue that, while IQ can predict on average 6 percent success in a given job, EQ can predict between 27 and 45 percent success, depending on the job.

What is emotional intelligence? Two terms that loosely describe at least part of it are "street smarts" and "common sense." Stein and Book measure it as five dimensions, comprising a total of 15 sub-dimensions:

1. The Intrapersonal Realm: Self-Awareness, Assertiveness, Independence, Self-Regard, and Self-Actualization
2. The Interpersonal Realm: Empathy, Social Responsibility, Interpersonal Relationships
3. The Adaptability Realm: Reality Testing, Flexibility, Problem Solving
4. The Stress Management Realm: Stress Tolerance, Control
5. The General Mood Realm: Optimism, Happiness

The good news about EQ is that it can be reliably measured and, unlike your IQ, you can improve it throughout your life. Men and women achieved roughly the same scores overall, although there were a few differences on sub-scale scores. Women everywhere scored higher on social responsibility and empathy, and men scored higher on stress tolerance. In North America, there were a few additional differences. Women scored higher on interpersonal relationships, and men on self-regard. There were no noted differences on EQ scores across races.

Stein and Book report the five most important subdimensions that distinguish low from high performers in a number of sales-related occupations. The following is a list for some selected positions.

General Sales
Self-Actualization
Assertiveness
Happiness
Optimism
Self-Regard

Business Services Sales
Self-Regard
Reality Testing
Assertiveness
Stress Tolerance
Optimism

Insurance Sales
Assertiveness
Self-Regard
Happiness
Stress Tolerance
Self-Actualization

Customer Service Representatives
Stress Tolerance
Assertiveness
Happiness
Interpersonal Relationships
Self-Actualization[a]

value (see Fig. 3.1). We have defined value-added selling as a series of creative improvements in the sales process that enhance the customer experience.

Customers perceive that value is added to a sale when they feel good about the relationship they have with a salesperson. A good relationship encourages customers to feel that, if a problem arises, they will get prompt service and fair treatment. A good relationship creates a clear channel of communication about issues that might surface during each step of the sales process. Len Rodman, CEO of a large engineering and construction company, recalls a problem in one particular region: earnings were minimal and the person in charge could not sell to high-tier clients. Len put a different salesperson in charge whose strength was building relationships and, within an 18-month period, that region became one of the most profitable.[7]

It's about relationships

Our benefits solutions start with one simple ingredient – clear dialogue with our customers.

Through dialogue we learn and understand our customers' needs. And our customers get to know and understand what we can deliver.

It's all about relationships. Relationships built on listening, understanding each other, and working closely together.

Together we'll find solutions to your benefits needs. Contact Jeff Kinch, National Marketing, at 1-888-588-5650 or e-mail jeff.kinch@clarica.com

Clarica. Your clear choice for group benefits.

Investment and insurance solutions - Since 1870

Clarica understands the importance of clear dialogue with its customers to help build good relationships.

The salesperson who is honest, accountable, and sincerely concerned about the customer's welfare adds value to the sale. These characteristics give the salesperson a competitive advantage—an advantage that is becoming increasingly important in a world of look-alike products and similar prices.

PARTNERING—THE HIGHEST-QUALITY SELLING RELATIONSHIP

Salespeople today are encouraged to think of everything they say or do in the context of their relationship with the customer. They should constantly strive to build a long-term partnership. In a marketplace characterized by increased levels of competition and greater product complexity, we see the need to adopt a relationship strategy that emphasizes the "lifetime" customer. High-quality relationships result in repeat business and important referrals. Many salespeople recognize that the quality of the partnerships they create is as important as the quality of the products they sell. Today's customer wants a quality product *and* a quality relationship. One example of this trend is the J. D. Power and Associates' customer satisfaction studies. J. D. Power conducts customer satisfaction research in several different industries; for example, the Domestic Hotel Guest Satisfaction Study measures guest satisfaction among frequent business travellers.[8]

www.jdpower.com

partnering A strategically developed, high-quality relationship that focuses on solving each customer's buying problem.

Partnering can be defined as a strategically developed, high-quality, long-term relationship that focuses on solving each customer's buying problem.[9] Traditional industrial-age sales training programs emphasized the importance of creating a good first impression and then pushing your product. Partnering emphasizes building a strong relationship during every aspect of the sale and working hard to maintain a quality relationship with the customer after the sale. Today, personal selling must be viewed as a process, not an event.[10]

Larry Wilson, a noted author and sales consultant, identifies partnering as one of the most important aspects of strategic thought processes needed by salespeople. He points out that the salesperson who is selling a one-shot solution cannot compete against the one who has developed and nurtured a long-term, mutually beneficial partnership. Wilson believes there are three keys to a partnering relationship:

- *The relationship is built on shared values.* When your client feels that you both share the same ideas and values, this impression goes a long way toward creating a powerful relationship.
- *Everyone needs to clearly understand the purpose of the partnership and be committed to the vision.* Both the salesperson and the client must agree on what they are trying to do together.
- *The role of the salesperson must move from selling to supporting.* The salesperson in a partnership is actively concerned with the growth, health, and satisfaction of the company to which he or she is selling.[11]

Salespeople willing to abandon short-term thinking and invest the time and energy needed to develop a high-quality, long-term relationship with

Partnering is a strategically developed, high-quality, long-term relationship that focuses on solving the customer's buying problem. Partnering involves establishing, re-establishing, and maintaining relationships with customers.

customers are rewarded with greater earnings and the satisfaction of working with repeat customers. Sales resulting from referrals also increase.

RELATIONSHIP STRATEGIES FOCUS ON FOUR KEY GROUPS

Establishing and maintaining partnering relationships internally as well as with customers is a vital aspect of selling. High-performance sales personnel build strong relationships with for four groups (see Fig. 3.2):

1. *With customers.* As noted previously, a major key to success in selling is the ability to establish working relationships with customers in which mutual support, trust, and goals are nurtured over time. Salespeople who maintain regular contact with their customers and develop sound business relationships based on mutual trust are able to drive up sales productivity.[12] Cisco Systems is one of many companies that now measures itself by the quality of its relationships with its customers. Salespeople earn their bonuses in large part on customer satisfaction instead of gross sales or profit.[13]
2. *With secondary decision makers.* High-performance salespeople understand the importance of building relationships with the people who work with customers. In many selling situations the first person the salesperson meets is a receptionist, a secretary, or an assistant to the primary decision maker. These persons often can facilitate a meeting with the prospect. Also, the prospect may involve other people in making the buying decision. For example, the decision to buy new

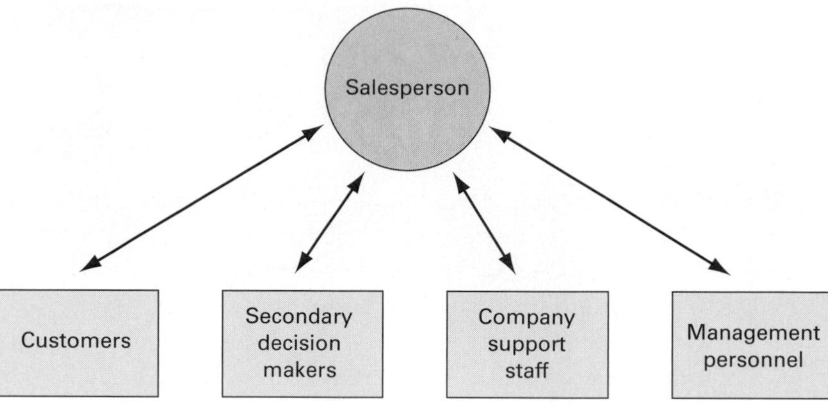

Figure 3.2 An effective relationship strategy helps high-performing salespeople to build and maintain win-win relationships with four key groups.

office furniture may be made by a team of persons including the buyer and persons who will actually use the furniture.

3. *With company support staff.* The maintenance of relationships internally is a vital aspect of selling. Support staff may include persons working in the areas of market research, product service, credit, training, or shipping. Influencing these people to change their priorities, interrupt their schedules, accept new responsibilities, or fulfill any other request for special attention is a major part of the salesperson's job. At UPS, the drivers are the eyes and ears of the sales force, so the most successful UPS salespeople nurture a relationship with the drivers in their territory.[14]

4. *With management personnel.* Sales personnel usually work under the direct supervision of a sales manager, a department head, or some other member of the firm's management team. Maintaining a good relationship with this person is important.

CUSTOMER RELATIONSHIP MANAGEMENT WITH TECHNOLOGY

Communicating Using CRM

Customer relationship management (CRM) software can be used to enhance the quality of your relationships. A good example is the software's ability to enhance communications between you and your contacts. With the ACT! software, for example, you can quickly prepare and send a letter, fax, or e-mail to one or more people who have records in the database. Recipients of your appointment confirmations, information verifications, company or product news, or brief personal notes will recognize and appreciate your effort to keep them informed. The written word conveys consideration and helps avoid misunderstandings and miscommunications. CRM empowers you to easily use the written word to advance your relationship building. (See the exercise Preparing Letters with CRM on page 76 for more information.)

TAILORING THE RELATIONSHIP STRATEGY

Ideally, the relationship strategy should be tailored to the type of customer you are working with. Chapter 1 provided a description of the three most common types of selling situations: transactional selling, consultative selling, and relationship selling.

Transactional buyers are usually aware of their needs and often stay focused on such issues as price, convenience, and delivery schedules. They often know a great deal about the products or services they wish to purchase. In the transactional sale, the relationship strategy is often of secondary importance.

In the consultative sale, however, the impact of relationships on the sale is quite important. A consultative sale emphasizes need identification which is achieved through effective communication and a relationship built on mutual trust and respect. The consultative salesperson must display a keen ability to listen, define the customer's problem, and offer one or more solutions. The opportunity to uncover hidden needs and create custom solutions is greatly enhanced by a well-conceived relationship strategy.[15]

In terms of relationship building, relationship selling is often the most challenging. Very often the salesperson is working with a company team made up of persons from such areas as research and development, finance, and distribution. The salesperson must build a good working relationship with each team member. Forming a partnership with another company involves building relationships with several representatives of that buying organization.

We will revisit these three types of selling situations later in this chapter when we discuss the trust factor. In the meantime, keep in mind that customers almost never buy products from someone whom they dislike. A salesperson who is not viewed as helpful and trustworthy will not succeed in any type of selling.

Thought Processes That Enhance Your Relationship Strategy

Industrial-age folklore created the myth of the "born" salesperson—a dynamic, outgoing, highly assertive individual. Experience acquired during the age of information has taught us that many other factors determine sales success. Key among these factors are a positive self-image and the ability to relate to others in effective and productive ways. With the aid of knowledge drawn from the behavioural sciences, you can develop the relationship strategies needed in a wide range of selling situations.

SELF-IMAGE—AN IMPORTANT DIMENSION OF THE RELATIONSHIP STRATEGY

self-image A set of ideas, attitudes, and feelings you have about yourself that influences the way you relate to others.

Self-image is shaped by the ideas, attitudes, feelings, and other thoughts each of us has about ourselves that influence the way we relate to others. Psychologists have found that, once we form a thought process about ourselves, it serves to edit all incoming information and influence our actions. It can set the limits of our accomplishments, defining what we can and cannot do. Realizing the power of self-image is an important breakthrough in our understanding of the factors that influence us.

www.psycho-cybernetics.com

A pioneer in the area of self-image psychology was the late Dr. Maxwell Maltz, author of *Psycho-Cybernetics* and other books devoted to this topic. We are indebted to him for two important discoveries that help us understand better the "why" of human behaviour:

1. *Feelings and behaviour are consistent with the self-image.* The individual who feels like a failure will likely find some way to fail. There is a definite relationship between self-image and accomplishments at work. A positive self-image helps generate the energy needed to get things done.
2. *The self-image can be changed.* Numerous case histories show that we are never too young or too old to change our self-image and thereby achieve new accomplishments.[16]

Phillip McGraw, author of *Self-Matters*, says we often sabotage our own success by adopting limiting beliefs. These are the specific things we think about that cause us to conclude that we are not capable of achieving success. These beliefs restrict our thinking and our actions.[17] Low self-esteem, according to Nathaniel Branden, author of *Self-Esteem at Work*, correlates with resistance to change and with clinging to the known and familiar. He notes that low self-esteem is economically disadvantageous in an information economy where knowledge and new ideas count for almost everything.[18]

How can you develop a more positive self-image? How can you get rid of self-destructive ways of thinking? Bringing your present self-image out into the open is the first step in understanding who you are, what you can do, and where you are going. Improving your self-image will not happen overnight, but it can happen. A few practical approaches are summarized as follows:

1. *Focus on the future and stop being overly concerned with past mistakes or failures.* You should learn from past errors, but they should not immobilize you.
2. *Develop expertise in selected areas.* By developing "expert power" you not only improve your self-image but also increase the value of your contributions to your employer and your customers.
3. *Learn to develop a positive personal attitude.* To develop a more positive outlook, read books or listen to audio presentations that describe ways to develop a positive personal attitude—and try them. Consider materials developed by Denis Waitley, Stephen Covey, Brian Tracy, Dale Carnegie, Zig Ziglar, and Phillip McGraw.

Later in this chapter you will learn how to develop and initiate a plan for self-improvement. If you want to improve your self-image, consider adopting this plan.

EVERYONE SELLS

Relationships Are Important for Fund Development

Brenda Lockyer is the director of fund development at the Dr. H. Bliss Murphy Cancer Care Foundation, a not-for-profit organization that depends partly on public and private donations for its support. Brenda recently completed a university course in professional selling and sales management and was surprised how much of the course was applicable to her job.

Brenda Lockyer says, "A key to our success is how we approach, engage, and steward our donors. Many donors start with small donations but continue to support charities with increasing commitment. We have stewardship plans in place for different giving levels and monitor increased gifts from one appeal to the next. When a donor is identified as a major gift prospect, he or she is visited personally by a volunteer or staff person. Once a donor has donated cumulatively to a major gift level ($5000 or more), the next obvious giving vehicle is through a planned gift—the most popular being a bequest from the donor's estate. We value and foster our relationships with these donors because they are so important to us. The cost of losing such donors and having to replace them can be very significant, just like losing a major customer [is] for a sales organization."[b]

THE WIN-WIN PHILOSOPHY

As noted in Chapter 1, the win-win marketing concept is a philosophy that leaves no doubt in the mind of every employee that customer satisfaction is of primary importance. Salespeople who work closely with customers are in a position to monitor customer satisfaction. Adopting the win-win philosophy is the first step in developing a relationship strategy. One author described the win-win approach as follows:

> "You both come out of the sale feeling satisfied, knowing that neither of you has taken advantage of the other and that both of you have profited, personally and professionally, from the transaction. In the simplest terms, you know you have a win-win sales encounter when both you and the buyer come out of it feeling positive."[19]

The win-win strategy is based on such irrefutable logic that it is difficult to understand why any other approach would be used. However, some salespeople still have not accepted the merits of the win-win approach. They have adopted a win-lose approach, which means that the salesperson wins at the buyer's expense. When a salesperson sells a product that is not the best solution to the buyer's problem, the win-lose strategy has been used.

You can adopt the win-win attitude that is one of the principles of partnering-style selling. The starting point to development of a win-win philosophy is to compare the behaviours of persons who have adopted the win-lose approach with the behaviours of persons who have adopted the win-win approach (see Fig. 3.3).

Figure 3.3 The starting point to developing a win-win philosophy is to compare behaviours of win-lose salespeople with those of win-win salespeople. (Adapted from a list of losers, winners, and double winners in *The Double Win* by Denis Waitley.)

Win-lose people	Win-win people
• See a problem in every solution	• Help others solve their problem
• Fix the blame	• Fix what caused the problem
• Let life happen to them	• Make life a joyous happening for others and themselves
• Live in the past	• Learn from the past, live in the present, and set goals for the future
• Make promises they never keep	• Make commitments to themselves and to others and keep them both

CHARACTER AND INTEGRITY

The first years of the twenty-first century may be remembered for major ethical lapses by several large Canadian and U.S. corporations. It was a period when many business leaders focused more on short-term profits than their long-term reputation. Employees at Arthur Anderson LLP, Enron Corporation, and Merrill Lynch Company, to name three, engaged in white-collar crime.[20] Most white-collar crime is committed by persons who lack character. **Character** is composed of personal standards, including honesty, integrity, and moral strength. It is a quality that is highly respected in the field of personal selling. **Integrity**, the basic ingredient of character, is exhibited when you achieve congruence between what you know, what you say, and what you do.[21] In a world of uncertainty and rapid change, integrity has become a valuable character trait. Salespeople with integrity can be trusted to do what they say they will do. One way to achieve trustworthiness in personal selling is to avoid deceiving or misleading the customer. More will be said about this topic in Chapter 5, which examines the ethical conduct of salespeople.

character Your personal standards of behaviour, including your honesty and integrity. Your character is based on your internal values and the resulting judgments you make about what is right and what is wrong.

integrity Part of your character; what you have when your behaviour is in accordance with your professed standards and personal code of moral values.

Nonverbal Strategies That Add Value to Your Relationships

The first contact between a salesperson and a prospect is very important. During the first few minutes—or seconds in some cases—the prospect and the salesperson form impressions of each other that will either facilitate or detract from the sales call.[22] It is very difficult to rebound from a poor first impression.

Every salesperson projects an image to prospective customers, and this image influences how a customer feels about the sales representative. The image you project is the sum total of many verbal and nonverbal factors. The quality of your voice, the clothing you wear, your posture, your manners, and your communication style represent some of the factors that contribute to the formation of your image. We discuss body language, voice quality, and manners in this chapter. Communication style is examined in Chapter 4.

This salesperson's clothing and facial expression project a professional image. A pleasant smile and eye contact convey friendliness to the customer.

NONVERBAL MESSAGES

When we attempt to communicate with another person, we use both verbal and nonverbal communications. A **nonverbal message** is a "message without words" or "silent message." These are the messages—other than spoken or written words—that we communicate through facial expressions, voice tone, gestures, appearance, posture, and other nonverbal means.[23]

nonverbal message A form of communication that has been defined as a "message without words" or a "silent message."

Research indicates that, when two people communicate, nonverbal messages convey much more impact than verbal messages. Words play a surprisingly small part in the communication process. Studies indicate that, in a typical two-person conversation, only about 7 percent of our understanding comes from words spoken by the other person. About 38 percent of our understanding comes from what we hear. Does the other person sound sincere, credible, and knowledgeable? Every spoken message has a vocal element, coming not from what we say, but from how we say it. The voice communicates in many ways: through its tone, volume, and speed of delivery. A salesperson wishing to communicate enthusiasm needs to use a voice that is charged with energy.

About 55 percent of the meaning we attach to communication efforts by others is based on what we see or feel (Fig. 3.4). A positive message can be communicated to a customer with a smile, a firm handshake, good eye contact, and a professional appearance.[24]

Nonverbal messages can reinforce or contradict the spoken word. When your verbal message and body language are consistent, they give others the impression that you can be trusted and that what you say reflects what you truly believe. When there is a discrepancy between your verbal and nonverbal messages, you are less apt to be trusted.[25]

Ruth Bell Steinhauer (see p. 41): A pleasant smile sends a positive nonverbal message.

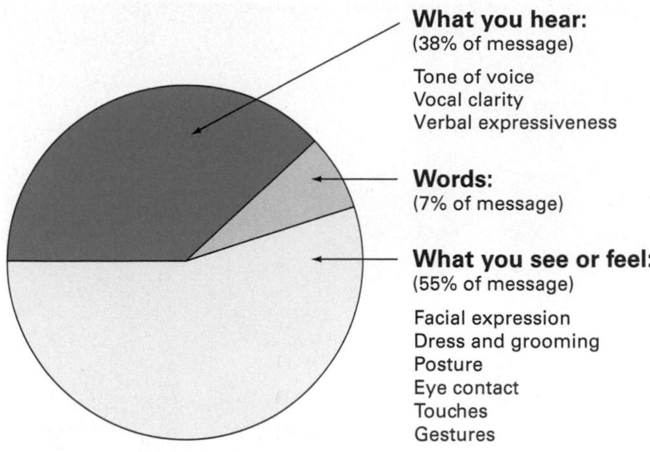

Figure 3.4 When someone else is speaking, your understanding of what is said depends heavily on what you see or feel. (Moravian Study of Nonverbal Communication)

ENTRANCE AND CARRIAGE

www.theprofessionalimage.net

As noted earlier, the first impression you make is very important. The moment a salesperson walks into a client's office, the client begins making judgments. Susan Bixler, author of *The Professional Image* and *Professional Presence*, makes this comment:

> "All of us make entrances throughout our business day as we enter offices, conference rooms, or meeting halls. And every time we do, someone is watching us, appraising us, sizing us up, and gauging our appearance, even our intelligence, often within the space of a few seconds."[26]

Bixler says that the key to making a successful entrance is simply believing—and projecting—that you have a reason to be there and have something important to offer the client. You can communicate confidence with a strong stride, good posture, and a friendly smile. A confident manner communicates to the client the message, "This meeting will be beneficial to you."

SHAKING HANDS

An inadequate handshake is like dandruff: no one will mention it, but everyone will notice it. The handshake is an important symbol of respect and, in most business settings, it is the proper greeting.[27] In the field of selling, the handshake is usually the first—and frequently the only—physical contact you make during a sales call. The handshake can communicate warmth, genuine concern for the prospect, and an image of strength. It can also communicate aloofness, indifference, and weakness to the customer. The message you communicate with a handshake will be determined by a combination of five factors:

1. *Eye contact during handshake.* Eyes transmit more information than any other part of the body, so maintaining eye contact throughout the handshaking process is important when two people greet each other.
2. *Degree of firmness.* Generally speaking, a firm handshake will communicate a caring attitude, while a weak grip (the dead-fish handshake) communicates indifference.

3. *Depth of interlock.* A full, deep grip will communicate friendship to the other person.
4. *Duration of grip.* There are no specific guidelines to tell us what the ideal duration of a grip should be. However, by extending the duration of the handshake we can often communicate a greater degree of interest and concern for the other person. Do not pump up and down more than once or twice.
5. *Degree of dryness of hands.* A moist palm not only is uncomfortable to handle but also can communicate the impression that you are quite nervous. Some people have a physiological problem that causes clammy hands, and they should keep a handkerchief within reach to remove excess moisture. A clammy hand is likely to repel most customers.[28]

In a relaxed and friendly atmosphere, the customer is more apt to open up and share information. Creating this atmosphere is part of the relationship strategy.

The best time to present your name is when you extend your hand. When you introduce yourself, state your name clearly and then listen carefully to be certain you hear the customer's name. To ensure that you will remember the customer's name, repeat it. In some cases you will need to check to be sure you are pronouncing it properly.[29]

FACIAL EXPRESSIONS

If you want to identify the inner feelings of another person, watch facial expressions closely. The face is a remarkable communicator, capable of accurately signalling emotion in a split second and capable of concealing emotion equally well. You can tell in a blink of an eye if your customer's face is registering surprise, pleasure, or skepticism (see Fig. 3.5). Facial expressions are largely universal, so people around the world tend to "read" faces in a similar way. It is worth noting that the smile is the most recognized facial signal in the world and it can have a great deal of influence on others. George Rotter, professor of psychology at Montclair University, says, "Smiles are an enormous controller of how people perceive you." People tend to trust a smiling face.[30] Get in the habit of offering a sincere smile each time you meet with a prospect.

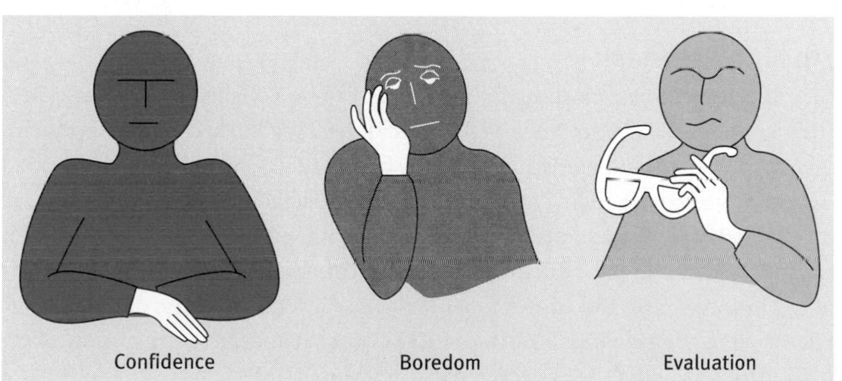

Figure 3.5 Our subtle facial gestures are continuously sending messages to others.

EYE CONTACT

When the customer is talking, eye contact is one of the best ways to say, "I'm listening." If you are looking across the room or at papers in your briefcase, the customer will assume you are not listening. However, prolonged eye contact can send the wrong message. A prolonged direct stare can be threatening. To avoid the prolonged stare, take fleeting glances at your notes. As the customer speaks, nod occasionally to indicate agreement or interest.[31]

THE EFFECT OF APPEARANCE ON RELATIONSHIPS

We form opinions about people based on a pattern of immediate impressions conveyed by appearance. The clothing we wear, the length and style of our hair, the fragrances we use, and the jewellery we display all combine to make a statement about us to others—a statement of primary importance to anyone involved in selling.

unconscious expectations Certain views concerning appropriate dress.

business casual clothing Clothing that allows you to feel comfortable but looks neat and professional.

We all have certain views, or **unconscious expectations**, concerning appropriate dress. In sales work we should try to anticipate the expectations of our clientele. The clothing worn by salespeople does make a difference in terms of customer acceptance because it communicates powerful messages. The clothing we wear can influence our credibility and likeability. Martin Siewert, a member of the business development team for Axiom Management Consulting, has adopted a flexible approach to dress. His company's policy favours an informal dress code, so he usually wears casual clothing at work unless he is meeting with a client. When he calls on customers, most of whom are *Fortune* 500 companies, he wears a suit and tie. "I want to show that I respect their culture," he says.[32]

Jay Mechling, senior vice-president of Morgan Stanley Dean Witter, believes that carefully selected casual dress is appropriate for certain customer contacts.

Most image consultants agree that there is no single "dress for success" look. The appropriate wardrobe will vary from one city or region to another and from one company to another. However, there are some general guidelines that you should follow in selecting clothing for sales work. Four factors should govern your decisions: simplicity, appropriateness, quality, and visual integrity.

Simplicity

The colour of your clothing, as well as design, will communicate a message to the customer. Some colours are showy and convey an air of casualness. In a business setting we want to be taken seriously, so flashy colours should usually be avoided.

Appropriateness

Selecting appropriate clothing for sales work can be a challenge. We must carefully consider the clients we serve and decide what will be acceptable to them. Many salespeople are guided by the type of products they sell and the desired image projected by their employers. Deciding what constitutes appropriate attire in today's business-casual world begins with an understanding of what it means to "dress down." **Business casual clothing** allows you to feel comfortable but looks neat and professional. Pay close attention to the clothing your clients wear.[33] If a client is wearing a nice sport coat and dress slacks, don't wear khaki trousers and a short-sleeve polo shirt.

Quality

The quality of your wardrobe will also influence the image you project to customers. A salesperson's wardrobe should be regarded as an investment, with each item carefully selected to look good and fit well. Susan Bixler says, "If you want respect, you have to dress as well as or better than your industry standards."[34]

Visual Integrity

Visual presence must have a certain amount of integrity and consistency. The images you project are made up of many factors, and lack of attention to important details can negate your effort to create a good impression. Too much jewellery, a shirt that does not fit well, or unshined shoes can detract from the professional look you want to project. People often are extra alert when meeting someone new, and this heightened consciousness makes every detail count.[35] Keep in mind that customer contact often takes place in several settings. The first meeting with a customer may take place in his or her office, but the second meeting may be on the golf course. And the third meeting may take place at a nice restaurant. The clothing you wear in each of these settings is important.

Effect of Voice Quality on Relationships

As noted previously, voice quality contributes about 38 percent of the meaning attached to spoken messages. On the telephone, voice quality is even more important because the other person cannot see your facial expressions, hand gestures, and other body movements. You cannot trade in your current voice for a new one; however, you can make your voice more pleasing to others. How? Consider these suggestions.

1. *Do not talk too fast or too slowly.* Rapid speech often causes customers to become defensive. They raise psychological barriers because a "rapid-fire monologue" is associated with high-pressure sales methods. Peter Urs Bender (**www.peterursbender.com**), a noted Canadian business speaker and author of *Secrets of Power Presentations*, says that 85 percent of presenters begin too fast. He says, "Remember, it's better to go slower than faster as this will make you look more confident. Also, be sure you incorporate some appropriately long pauses between sentences, particularly at the beginning."[36] The slower presentation allows others to follow, and it allows you, the speaker, time to think ahead—to consider the situation and make judgments. Another good tip is to vary the speed of your speech.

2. *Avoid a speech pattern that is dull and colourless.* The worst kind of voice has no colour and no feeling. Enthusiasm is a critical element of an effective sales presentation. It is also contagious. Your enthusiasm for the product will be transmitted to the customer. Your tone of voice

mirrors your emotional state and physical well-being. When you are feeling good and positive, your voice will naturally sound upbeat, energetic, and enthusiastic. Sometimes, however, the normal stresses and strains of life can be reflected in your voice. Then, you may have to manipulate your tone of voice to communicate greater warmth and enthusiasm. Before you make that important phone call or meet with a prospect, reflect on your state of mind. To drain tension from your voice, inhale and tense every muscle. Hold for a count of 5, and then exhale for a count of 10. If you want to sound warm and friendly, smile while speaking.[37]

Effect of Manners On Relationships

The study of manners (sometimes called etiquette) reveals a number of ways to enhance your relationship strategy. Salespeople who possess knowledge of the rules of etiquette can perform their daily work with greater poise and confidence. Think of manners as a universal passport to positive relationships and respect.

With practice, anyone can have good manners without appearing to be rigid and can, at the same time, win the respect and admiration of others. Space does not permit a complete review of this topic, but here are some of the rules of etiquette that are especially important to salespeople.

1. *Avoid the temptation to address a new prospect by first name.* In a business setting, too much familiarity too quickly can cause irritation.
2. *Avoid offensive comments or stories.* Never assume that the customer's value system is the same as your own. Rough language and off-colour stories can do irreparable damage to your image.
3. *Do not express personal views on political or religious issues.* There is seldom a "safe" position to take in these areas, so it is better to avoid these topics altogether.
4. *When you invite a customer to lunch, do not discuss business before the meal is ordered unless the client initiates the subject.* Also, order food that is easily controlled, and avoid such items as ribs, chicken, and lobster.
5. *When you use voice mail, leave a clear, concise message.* Do not speak too fast or mumble your name and number.
6. *Avoid cellular phone contempt.* Turn off the cell phone ringer any time you are with a client. Never put your telephone on the table during a meal.

It has been said that good manners make other people feel better. This is true because good manners require that we place the other person's comfort ahead of our own. One of the best ways to develop rapport with a customer is to avoid behaviour that might be offensive to that person.

Conversational Strategies That Enhance Relationships

The foundation for a long-term relationship with the customer is frequently a "get acquainted" type of conversation that takes place before any discussion of business matters. Within a few minutes it is possible to reduce the relationship tension that is so common when two people meet for the first time. This informal visit with the customer provides the salesperson with an opportunity to apply three guidelines for building strong relationships featured in *How to Win Friends and Influence People,* the classic book written by Dale Carnegie.

- *Become genuinely interested in other people.* Tim Sanders, chief solutions officer at Yahoo!, says, "How we are perceived as human beings is becoming increasingly important in the new economy."[38] When you become genuinely interested in the customer, you create an experience that is long remembered.
- *Be a good listener; encourage others to talk about themselves.* Stephen Covey, the noted author and consultant, recommends empathetic listening. This requires listening with your ears, your eyes, and your heart.[39]
- *Talk in terms of the other person's interests.*[40] When you are initiating a conversation with a customer, don't hesitate to use small talk to get the conversation started. This may involve current events, business, or sports. Be sure to focus on topics that the customer is interested in.

The length of this conversation depends on your sense of the prospect's reaction to your greeting, how busy the prospect appears to be, and your awareness of topics of mutual interest. In developing conversation the following three areas should be considered.

Comments on Here and Now Observations. Observant salespeople are aware of the things going on around them. These observations can be as general as unusual developments in the weather or as specific as noticing unique artefacts in the prospect's office.

Compliments. When you offer a *sincere* compliment to your prospect, you are saying, "Something about you is special." Most people react positively to compliments because they appeal to the need for self-esteem. Your admiration should not be expressed, however, in phony superlatives that will seem transparent. The prospect may suspect ulterior motives, which are unwelcome.

Search for Mutual Acquaintances or Interests. A frequent mode for establishing rapport with a new prospect is to find friends or interests you have in common. If you know someone with the same last name as your prospect, it may be appropriate to ask whether your friend is any relation. Anything you observe in the prospect's office or home might suggest an interest that you and your prospect share. Such topics of conversation appeal to your prospect's social needs.

SELLING MENTOR

You Can Build Relationships with Frequent Deposits

Building relationships in sales can be compared to making deposits in the bank. Regular bank deposits have a compounding effect, so that, over time, you see steady growth in your account. Each of the following contacts with a customer or prospect is a deposit that can build the relationship:

- Send articles or reports of interest to your contacts. Be sure a personal note accompanies them.
- Send cards to celebrate an event, such as a birthday or anniversary.
- Contact customers after the sale to check on their level of satisfaction with the product.
- Express appreciation for purchases with a card, letter, or phone call.
- Don't forget to make contact with secondary decision makers, support staff, and appropriate management personnel.[c]

Strategies for Self-Improvement

Orson Welles, a well-known and highly respected actor, once said, "Every actor is very busy getting better or getting worse." To a large extent, salespeople are also "very busy getting better or getting worse." To improve, salespeople must develop an ongoing program for self-improvement. It is important to keep in mind that all improvement is self-initiated. Each of us controls the switch that stimulates personal growth and development.

At the beginning of this chapter, when we introduced the concept of emotional intelligence, we noted that it can be increased with the aid of self-development activities. Would you like to develop a more positive self-image? Improve your ability to develop double-win relationships? Develop effective nonverbal communication skills? Improve your speaking voice? These relationship-building strategies can be achieved if you are willing to follow these four steps:

Step one: Set goals. The goal-setting process begins with a clear, written statement that describes what you want to accomplish. If your goal is too general or vague, progress toward achieving that goal will be difficult to observe. Next, you must identify the ways in which you plan to achieve your goal.

Step two: Use visualization. To make your goals a reality, engage in visualization. Forming a mental picture of yourself succeeding in goal attainment will actually affect your behaviour. Many Olympic athletes, such as Mary Lou Retton, have used visualization. Mary Lou described her preparation for the gymnastics event this way:

This salesperson has set a fitness goal. Physical fitness can be an important part of a self-improvement program.

"When I visualized myself going through a beam routine, I didn't imagine myself falling. I visualized myself on the beam—perfect. Always picture it perfect."[41]

You can work the same "mental magic" in goal setting by visualizing yourself as the person you want to be. For example, spend time developing mental pictures of successful experiences with prospective or established customers.

Step three: Use positive self-talk. People with a strong inner critic will receive frequent negative messages that can erode their self-esteem. It helps to refute and reject those negative messages with positive self-talk. **Self-talk** takes place silently in the privacy of your mind—a series of personal conversations you have with yourself continually throughout the day. Just like statements from other people, your self-talk can dramatically affect your behaviour and self-esteem.[42]

self-talk An effort to override past negative mental programming by erasing or replacing it with conscious, positive new directions.

Step four: Recognize your progress. When you see yourself making progress toward a goal, or achieving a goal, reward yourself. This type of reinforcement is vital when you are trying to change a behaviour. There is nothing wrong with taking pride in your accomplishments.

Self-improvement efforts can result in new abilities or powers, and they give us the motivation to draw more fully on the talents we already have. As a result, our potential for success is greater.

SUMMARY

The manner in which salespeople establish, build, and maintain relationships is a major key to success in personal selling. The key relationships in selling include management personnel, company support staff, secondary decision makers, and customers.

The concept of partnering was defined and discussed in detail. Partnering emphasizes building a strong relationship during every aspect of the sale and working hard to maintain a quality relationship with the customer after the sale.

An understanding of the psychology of human behaviour provides a foundation for developing relationship strategies. In this chapter we discussed the link between self-image and success in selling. Self-imposed fears can prevent salespeople from achieving success.

We describe several factors that influence the image you project to customers. The image others have of us is shaped to a great extent by nonverbal communication. We may choose the right words to persuade a customer to place an order, but aversive factors communicated by our clothing, handshake, facial expression, tone of voice, or general manner may prejudice the customer against us and our product or service.

The various conversational strategies that enhance relationships are reviewed. Dale Carnegie's guidelines for building strong relationships are discussed.

We also discuss the importance of self-improvement. A four-step self-improvement plan was described.

Key Terms

Business Casual Clothing **68**

Character **64**

Emotional Intelligence **55**

Integrity **64**

Nonverbal Message **65**

Partnering **58**

Self-Image **61**

Self-Talk **73**

Unconscious Expectations **68**

Review Questions

1. List the three prescriptions that serve as the foundation for development of a relationship strategy in sales.
2. How important are establishing, building, and maintaining relationships in the selling process? List the four groups of people with whom sales personnel must be able to work effectively.
3. Define the term *partnering*. Why has the building of partnerships become more important today?
4. Defend the statement, "Successful sales relationships depend on a positive self-image."
5. Describe the win-win approach to selling.
6. How is our self-image formed? Why is a positive self-image so important in personal selling?
7. Describe the meaning of the term *emotional intelligence*.
8. Identify three conversational methods that can be used to establish relationships.
9. Describe the meaning of *nonverbal messages*. Why should salespeople be concerned about these messages?
10. List and describe each step in the four-step self-improvement plan.

Application Exercises

1. Select four salespeople you know and ask them if they have a relationship strategy for working with customers, management personnel, secondary decision makers, and company support staff.
2. Emotional intelligence is a fairly new concept that has been introduced in this chapter. Go to **www.google.ca** (or another search engine if you prefer) and hit "advanced search." Type "emotional intelligence" under "Find results with exact phrase." Limit your search by typing ".ca" under "domain." Be prepared to discuss what you find in class.
3. Complete the following etiquette quiz. Your instructor will provide you with answers so you can check your responses.
   a. On what side should you wear your name tag?
   b. Is it appropriate to drink beer from a bottle at a reception?
   c. When introducing a female salesperson to a male prospect, whose name should be spoken first?
   d. At the table, when should you place your napkin in your lap?
   e. Is it ever proper to comb, smooth, or touch your hair while seated at a restaurant table?
4. It is pointed out in this chapter that clothing communicates strong messages. In this exercise you will become more aware of whether your clothes communicate the messages you want them to communicate.
   a. Make a chart like the one that follows:

Item of clothing being analyzed	What I want my clothes to say about me to others	What others think my clothing says

   b. In the first column, list the clothing you are now wearing (e.g., dress slacks, dress shoes, and sweater; athletic shoes, jeans, and T-shirt; or suit, dress shirt, and dress shoes).
   c. In the middle column, describe the message you would like the clothes you have chosen to say (e.g., "I want to be comfortable," "I want people to notice me," or "I want people to understand how proper and organized I am.").
   d. Have somebody else fill in the third column by describing what they think your clothes say about you.
   e. Compare the last two columns. Do your clothes communicate what you want them to?
5. Do the same exercise for social dress, casual dress, business attire, and hairstyle.

ROLE-PLAY EXERCISE

This is a two-part role-play exercise. Part one involves preparation for a sales call on a new prospect you have not met previously. The primary objective of this meeting is to get acquainted with the prospect and begin the process of building a long-term relationship. You anticipate that this prospect will become a very good customer. Review the text material on thought processes that will enhance your relationship strategy, nonverbal strategies that add value to your relationships, and conversational strategies that enhance relationships. Prepare a written outline of the things you plan to say and do during the first five to ten minutes of the meeting. Think of this outline as your "strategic plan." Part two involves a role play with a class member who will play the role of the prospect. Throughout the role play, try to say and do everything that was part of your plan. At the end of the role play, give your strategic plan outline to the class member playing the role of the prospect and request feedback on your performance.

CRM Application Exercise PREPARING LETTERS WITH CRM

Load the ACT! software and look up My Record. This screen identifies the person using the database—which in this case was Pat Silva and now will be you. Replace Pat Silva's name with your own.

The ACT! software demonstrates how customer relationship management programs are designed to be used by people who are in a hurry or who don't have extensive typing skills. Make menu choices by using the mouse, by typing simple key combinations, or by selecting an icon. This means that a procedure, such as preparing and printing correspondence, can be started by

a. selecting with a mouse the word Write, then the word Letter, from the menus
b. pressing the Alt key and the W (Write) key at the same time (Alt+W), and then pressing the L (Letter) key, or
c. selecting the Letter icon with the mouse.

On your screen will appear a blank letter with the date, inside address, salutation, closing line, your name, and your title. All you need to do is begin typing your letter. If you have a printer connected to your computer, you can print your letter by selecting Print from the File menu. With the File menu open, note that the right column displays key combinations, such as Ctrl+P to print.

Find the record for Brad Able by choosing Lookup, Last Name, type in "Able," and press Enter. With Brad Able's record on the screen, choose the letter icon or, from the menus, Write and Letter. Prepare, then print, a brief letter to Brad Able confirming an appointment to meet at his office next Thursday at 9:00 a.m. to discuss his training needs. Your letter should feature the win-win approach discussed in this chapter.

Case Problem

When people buy or sell a home, they hold their realtor to high standards. After all, for most people, the home purchase represents the largest single investment they will make throughout their lifetime. Most realtors understand the magnitude of the home purchase or home sale experience. They know that the customers are anxious to partner with someone who can be trusted to look after their best interests.

Sandra Khadra, vice-president of marketing with a prestigious real estate company, helps salespeople form a professional image that appeals to the type of clientele served by her company. She knows that there is a direct link between the image projected by the salespeople and the success of the company. When working with salespeople, she stresses the following points:

- Customers notice even the little details such as the quality of stationery, note paper, and business cards. If the business card features a photo of the salesperson, the person should be looking straight ahead, not away from the camera. This pose permits the salesperson to make eye contact with the customer.
- Salespeople must be able to build rapport with a variety of personality types. Some customers are quiet, reserved, and somewhat guarded when expressing their views. Others are more impulsive and express their views openly. Salespeople are encouraged to alter their communication style to increase the comfort level of the customer. Sandra Khadra encourages salespeople to mirror the behaviour of the prospect to the greatest extent possible. She says that it is always important to gauge how your communication style impacts on the prospect. A positive attitude is another important aspect of the relationship-building process.
- In some cases, salespeople must communicate across language and cultural barriers. Multicultural real estate clients are becoming more common, and effective salespeople want to gain a greater understanding and respect for cultural diversity. To impose our own way of doing business on every prospect is short-sighted.

Sandra Khadra suggests that salespeople should find out what customers value. What is the most important aspect of the home purchase or home sale? Most customers do not open up and share important information until they trust the salesperson.

Questions

1. Why should real estate salespeople spend time developing a relationship strategy? What might be some long-term benefits of this strategy?
2. Is it ever appropriate to touch your client other than a handshake? Explain your answer.
3. What are some benefits to the salesperson who can mirror the behaviour of the prospect?
4. What are some precautions to take when preparing a meeting with a client whose cultural background differs from yours?

CHAPTER 4

Communication Styles

MANAGING THE RELATIONSHIP PROCESS

LEARNING OBJECTIVES

After studying this chapter, you should be able to

1. Discuss communication-style bias and how it influences the relationship process
2. Explain the benefits derived from an understanding of communication styles
3. Identify the two major dimensions of the communication-style model
4. List and describe the four major communication styles in the communication-style model
5. Describe how to identify your preferred communication style and that of your customer
6. Summarize how to overcome communication-style bias and build strong selling relationships with style flexing

Bill Gates, chairman, and Steven Ballmer, CEO, of Microsoft Corporation **www.microsoft.com** met as undergraduates at Harvard University. Both were math whizzes. Bill dropped out of Harvard to form Microsoft and Steve started teaching at the Stanford Graduate School of Business. When Bill Gates needed a tough-minded manager at his fledgling company, he gave Steve Ballmer the assignment. Steve built a sales organization to compete with IBM in large corporate accounts. During the early years at Microsoft, Steve was known as a very aggressive executive with little patience. His explosive temper was legendary and he once needed throat surgery because he yelled so much. Despite his domineering management style and his unwillingness to delegate decision making, he accomplished a great deal. Steve Ballmer was promoted to president in 1998 and to chief executive officer in January 2000. As CEO, he has managed to fortify Microsoft's position as an industry leader. Today his leadership style is more diplomatic and he's more likely to delegate decision-making authority. Many people at Microsoft say Steven Ballmer has mellowed. In 2002 he was named one of the top 25 managers by *Business Week*.[1]

Steven Ballmer displays the characteristics of the Director communication style, one of four styles we will discuss in this chapter. In recent years, Steve Ballmer seems to be displaying communication-style flexibility in a deliberate attempt to adjust his communication style to meet the needs of others.

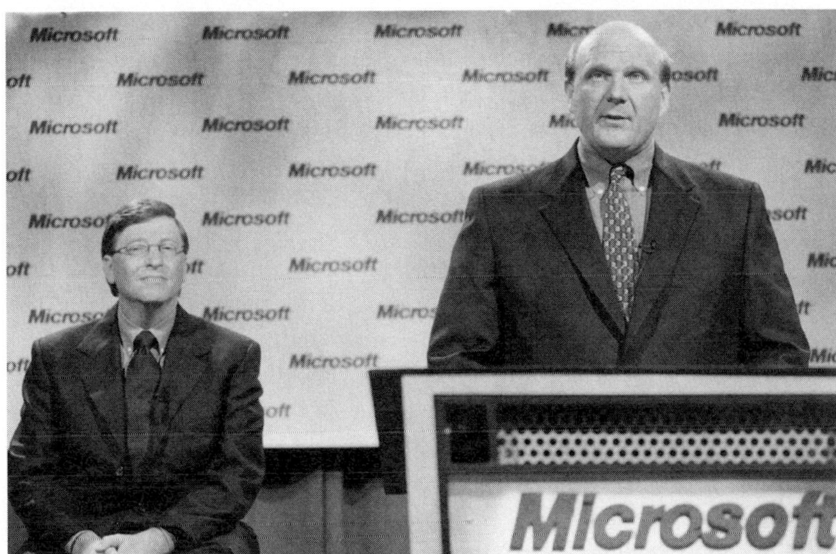

Steve Ballmer, CEO of Microsoft, provides an example of the Director communication style. In recent years he has displayed greater communication-style flexibility.

Communication Styles—An Introduction to Managing Selling Relationships

Almost everyone has had the pleasant experience of meeting someone for the first time and developing instant mutual rapport. There seems to be something about some people that makes you like them instantly—a basis for understanding that is difficult to explain. On the other hand, we can all recall meeting people who immediately "turn us off." Why do these things happen during the initial contact? The impressions that others form about us are based on what they observe us saying and doing. They have no way of knowing our innermost thoughts and feelings, so they make decisions about us based on what they see and hear.[2] The patterns of behaviour that others observe can be called **communication style**. Voice patterns, eye movement, facial expression, and posture are some of the components of our communication style.

communication style Patterns of behaviour that others observe. Voice patterns, eye movement, facial expression, and posture are some of the components of our communication style.

COMMUNICATION-STYLE BIAS

Bias in various forms is quite common in our society. In fact, governments at all levels have passed many laws to curb blatant forms of age, ethnic, religious, and gender discrimination. We also observe some degree of regional bias when people from various parts of Canada meet.

The most frequently occurring form of bias is not commonly understood in our society. What has been labelled **communication-style bias** is a state of mind that almost every one of us experiences from time to time, but the symptoms of which we usually find difficult to explain. Biases against communication style develop when we have contact with another person whose communication style is different from our own. For example, a purchasing

communication-style bias A state of mind we often experience when we have contact with another person whose communication style is different from our own.

agent was overheard saying, "I do not know what it is, but I just do not like that sales representative." The agent was no doubt experiencing communication-style bias but could not easily describe the feeling.

Your communication style is the "you" that is on display every day—the outer pattern of behaviour that others see. If your style is very different from another person's, it may be difficult for the two of you to develop rapport. All of us have had the experience of saying or doing something that was perfectly acceptable to a friend or co-worker and being surprised when the same behaviour irritated someone else. However, aside from admitting that this happens, most of us are unable to draw meaningful conclusions from these experiences to help us perform more effectively with people in the future.[3]

In recent years, thousands of sales professionals have learned to manage their selling relationships more effectively through the study of communication styles. Books such as *People Styles at Work* by Robert Bolton and Dorothy Grover Bolton, and *The Versatile Salesperson* by Roger Wenschlag serve as good references. Many training companies offer seminars that provide enrollees with a practical understanding of communication-style theory and practice. This practical theory of human behaviour, based on research by Swiss psychoanalyst Carl Jung and others, helps them achieve improved sales productivity.

COMMUNICATION STYLE PRINCIPLES

The theory of behavioural- or communication-style bias is based on a number of underlying principles. A review of these principles will be beneficial before we examine specific styles.

EVERYONE SELLS

This Dentist Communicates

Most people feel some apprehension before going to a new dentist for the first time. But patients of Dr. Steve Bajura in London, Ontario grow increasingly comfortable after each visit. That's because he talks to his patients—and not just about recommended dental procedures. He asks about their work, their children, their hobbies, and anything they wish to discuss. When they return for a second visit, they are pleasantly surprised to find that he remembers everything from their previous conversation. If they tell him that another patient referred them, he makes sure to thank that patient during their next visit.

Steve Bajura carefully manages his patient information, and this enables him to build better relationships with them, resulting in greater customer satisfaction, increased loyalty, and frequent referrals. He claims his business format just evolved naturally, but adds, "It seems to me that the way I manage patients is or should be the way all business is handled. I feel that, when the patient is in the chair, he or she deserves my full attention. That may or may not include 'small talk' which I feel is comfortable for me and probably for the patient. As time has gone on, the practice has continued to grow—far exceeding any expectations that I may have had."[a]

1. *Individual differences exist and are important.* It is quite obvious that we all differ in terms of such physical characteristics as height, shoe size, facial features, and body build, but the most interesting differences are those patterns of behaviour that are unique to each of us. As noted earlier, voice patterns, eye movement, facial expression, and posture are some of the components of our communication style. Additional characteristics are discussed later in this chapter.
2. *A communication style is a way of thinking and behaving.* It is not an ability; it is a preferred way of using abilities that you have. This distinction is very important. *Ability* refers to how well someone can do something. *Style* refers to how someone likes to do something.[4]
3. *Individual style differences tend to be stable.* Our communication style is based on a combination of hereditary and environmental factors. Our style is somewhat original at the time of birth; it takes on additional individuality during the first three to five years of life. By the time we enter elementary school, the teacher should be able to identify our communication style. This style remains fairly constant throughout life.
4. *There is a finite number of styles.* Most people display one of several clusters of similar behaviours, and this allows us to identify a small number of behavioural categories. By combining a series of descriptors, we can develop a single "label" that will describe a person's most preferred communication style.
5. To create the most productive relationships, it is necessary to get in sync with the communication style of the people you work with.[5] Differences between people can be a source of friction unless you develop the ability to recognize and respond to another person's style.

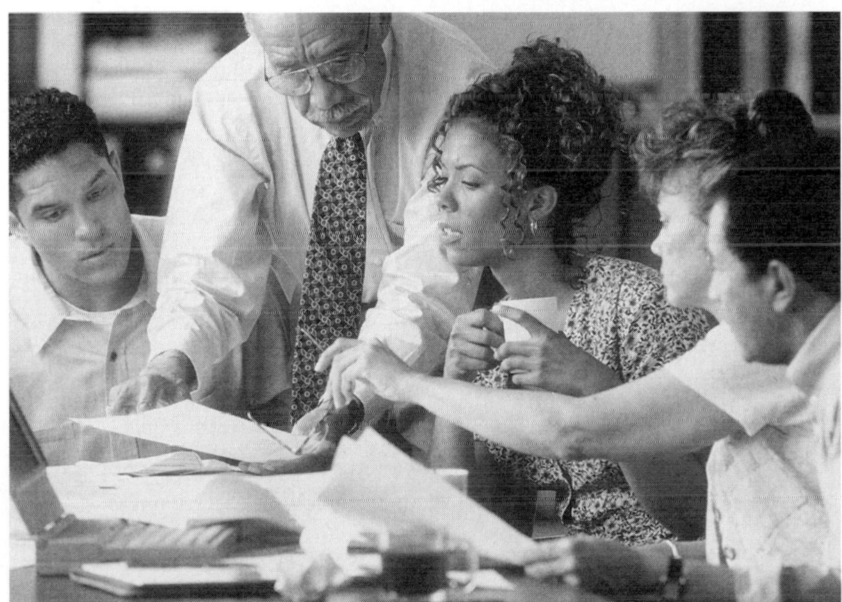

Group sales presentations can be very challenging because, in most cases, you are attempting to relate to several different communication styles.

The ability to identify another person's communication style, and to know how and when to adapt your own preferred style to it, can afford you a crucial advantage in dealing with people. The ability to "speak the other person's language" is an important skill for managing sales relationships.[6]

IMPROVING YOUR ABILITY TO MANAGE SALES RELATIONSHIPS

Anyone who is considering a career in selling will benefit greatly from the study of communication styles. These concepts provide a practical method of classifying people according to communication style and give the salesperson a distinct advantage in the marketplace. A salesperson who understands methods for classifying communication style and learns how to apply them can avoid common mistakes that threaten interpersonal relations with customers. Awareness of these methods greatly reduces the possibility of tension arising during the sales call.

The first major goal of this chapter is to help you better understand your own most preferred communication style. The second goal is to help you develop greater understanding and appreciation for styles that are different from your own. The third goal is to help you manage your selling relationships more effectively by learning to adapt your style to fit the communication style of the customer. This practice is called **style flexing**.

style flexing The deliberate adjustment of one's communication style to accommodate the needs of the other person.

Communication-Style Model

This section introduces you to the four basic communication styles. One of these will surface as your most preferred style. The communication-style model that defines these styles is based on two important dimensions of human behaviour: dominance and sociability. We look at the dominance continuum first.

DOMINANCE CONTINUUM

dominance Reflects the tendency to influence or exert one's will over others in a relationship. Each of us falls somewhere on this continuum.

Dominance can be defined as the tendency to control or prevail over others.[7] Dominant people tend to be quite competitive. They also tend to offer opinions readily and to be decisive and determined. Each of us falls somewhere on the dominance continuum illustrated by Figure 4.1.

A person classified as high in dominance is generally a "take charge" type of person who makes a position clear to others. A person classified as low in dominance is usually more reserved, unassertive, and easygoing. Dominance has been recognized as a universal behavioural characteristic. David W. Johnson developed the Interpersonal Pattern Exercise to help people achieve greater interpersonal effectiveness. He believes that people fall into two dominance categories:

1. *Low dominance:* These people have a tendency to be quite cooperative and eager to assist others. They tend to be low in assertiveness.
2. *High dominance:* These people tend to give advice freely and frequently initiate demands. They are more aggressive in dealing with others.[8]

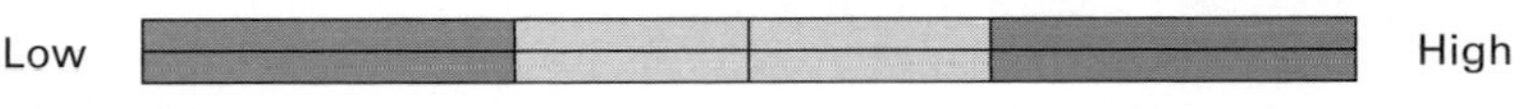

Figure 4.1 The first step in determining your most preferred communication style is to identify where you are on the dominance continuum.

The first step in determining your most preferred communication style is to identify where you fall on the dominance continuum. Do you tend to rank low or high on this scale? To answer this question, complete the Dominance Indicator form in Table 4.1. Rate yourself on each scale by placing a check mark on the continuum at the point that represents how you perceive yourself. If most of your check marks fall to the right of centre, you are someone who is high in dominance. If most of your check marks fall to the left of centre, you are someone who is low in dominance. Is there any best place to be on the dominance continuum? The answer is no. Successful salespeople can be found at all points along the continuum.

Table 4.1

Dominance Indicator

Rate yourself on each scale by placing a check mark on the continuum at the point that represents how you perceive yourself.

I Perceive Myself as Somewhat

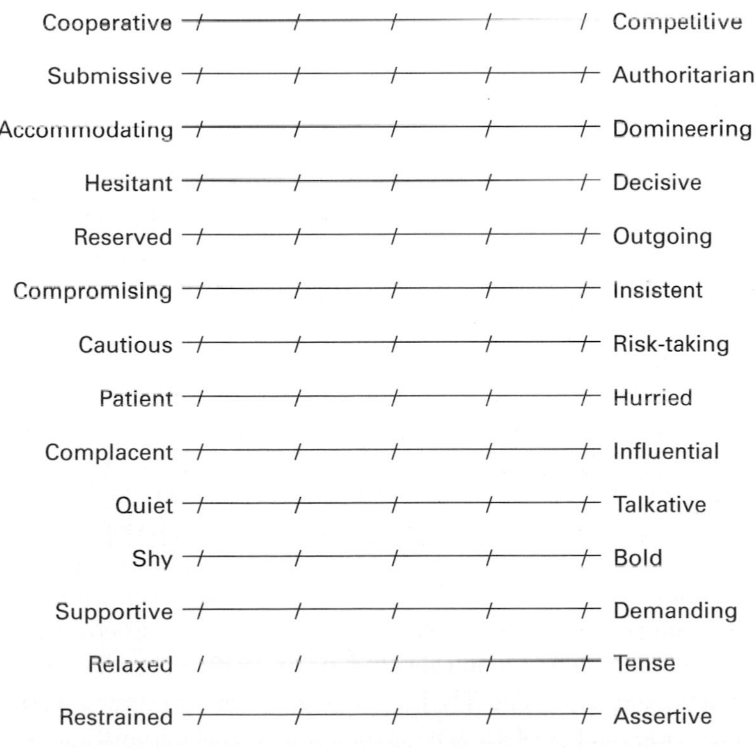

Cooperative	Competitive
Submissive	Authoritarian
Accommodating	Domineering
Hesitant	Decisive
Reserved	Outgoing
Compromising	Insistent
Cautious	Risk-taking
Patient	Hurried
Complacent	Influential
Quiet	Talkative
Shy	Bold
Supportive	Demanding
Relaxed	Tense
Restrained	Assertive

SOCIABILITY CONTINUUM

sociability Reflects the amount of control one exerts over emotional expressiveness. People who are high in sociability tend to express their feelings freely, while people who are low on this continuum tend to control their feelings.

Sociability reflects the amount of control we exert over our emotional expressiveness.[9] People who are high in sociability tend to express their feelings freely, while people who are low in this dimension tend to control their feelings. Each of us falls somewhere on the sociability continuum illustrated in Figure 4.2.

Sociability is also a universal behavioural characteristic. It can be defined as the tendency to seek and enjoy interaction with others. Charles Margerison, author of *How to Assess Your Managerial Style*, says that high sociability is an indication of a person's preference to interact with other people. He says that low sociability is an indicator of a person's desire to work in an environment where the person has more time alone instead of having to make conversation with others.[10] The person who is classified as low in the area of sociability is more reserved and formal in social relationships.

Figure 4.2 The second step in determining your most preferred communication style is to identify where you are on the sociability continuum.

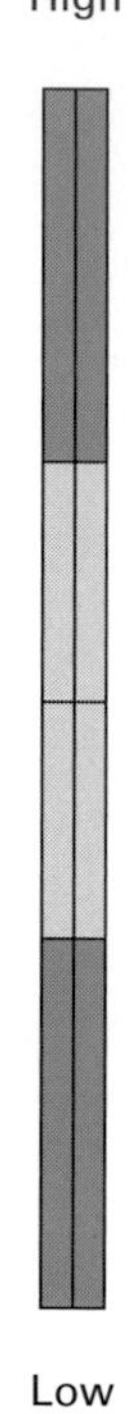

The second step in determining your most preferred communication style is to identify where you fall on the sociability continuum. To answer this question, complete the Sociability Indicator form shown in Table 4.2. Rate yourself on each scale by placing a check mark on the continuum at the point that represents how you perceive yourself. If most of your check marks fall to the right of centre (or, above centre, on Table 4.2), you are someone who is high in sociability. If most of your check marks fall to the left of centre, you are someone who is low in sociability. Keep in mind that there is no best place to be. Successful salespeople can be found at all points along this continuum.

With the aid of the dominance and sociability continuums we can now discuss a relatively simple communication-style classification plan that has practical application in the field of selling. We will describe the four basic styles: Emotive, Director, Reflective, and Supportive.

FOUR STYLES OF COMMUNICATION

By combining the two dimensions of human behaviour—dominance and sociability—we can form a partial outline of the communication-style model (see Fig. 4.3 on page 86). Dominance is represented by the horizontal axis and sociability is represented by the vertical axis. Once the two dimensions of human behaviour are combined, the framework for classifying communication styles is established.

The Emotive Style

Emotive style A communication style that displays the following characteristics: appears to be quite active, takes the social initiative in most cases, likes to encourage informality, and expresses emotional opinions.

The upper right-hand quadrant of Figure 4.4 (page 86) defines a style that combines high sociability and high dominance. We call this the **Emotive style** (see Fig. 4.5 on page 86). Emotive people usually stand out in a crowd. They are expressive and willing to spend time maintaining and enjoying a large number of relationships.[11] Oprah Winfrey, the well-known television personality, and talk show hosts David Letterman and Larry King provide excellent models of the Emotive communication style. Sports personality Don Cherry and actors Jim Carrey and Mike Myers provide additional examples. They are outspoken, enthusiastic, and stimulating. The Emotive person wants to create a social relationship quickly and usually feels more comfortable in an informal atmosphere. Some of the verbal and nonverbal clues that identify the Emotive person follow:

Table 4.2

Sociability Indicator

Rate yourself on each scale by placing a check mark on the continuum at the point that represents how you perceive yourself.

I Perceive Myself as Somewhat

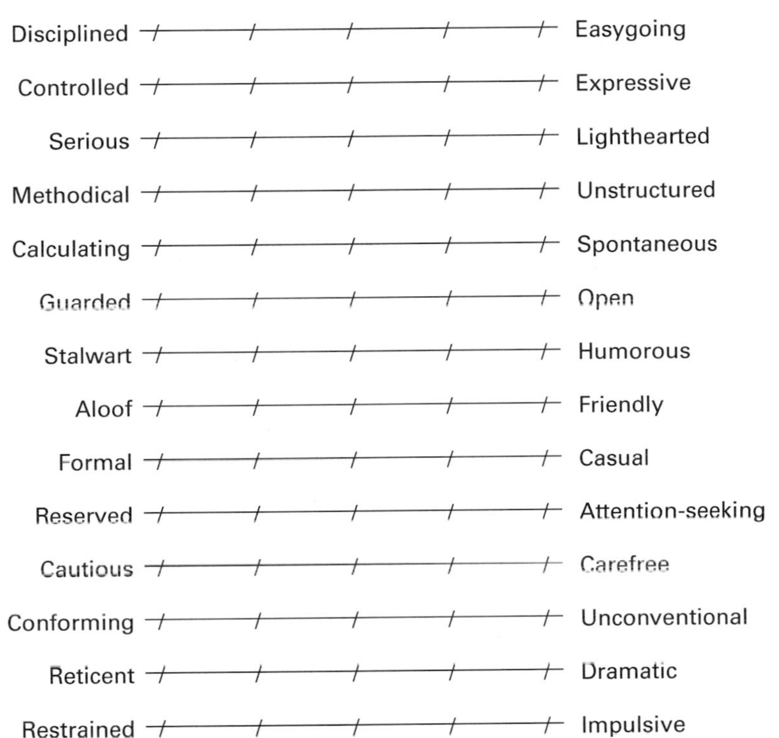

Disciplined	Easygoing
Controlled	Expressive
Serious	Lighthearted
Methodical	Unstructured
Calculating	Spontaneous
Guarded	Open
Stalwart	Humorous
Aloof	Friendly
Formal	Casual
Reserved	Attention-seeking
Cautious	Carefree
Conforming	Unconventional
Reticent	Dramatic
Restrained	Impulsive

1. *Appears quite active.* This person gives the appearance of being busy. A person who combines high dominance and high sociability is often restless. The Emotive person is likely to express feelings with vigorous movements of the hands and a rapid speech pattern.
2. *Takes the social initiative in most cases.* Emotives are the classic extroverts. When two people meet for the first time, the Emotive person will be more apt to initiate and maintain the conversation as well as to initiate the handshake. Emotives rate high in both directness and openness.
3. *Likes to encourage informality.* The Emotive person will move to a first-name basis as soon as possible (too soon in some cases). Even the way this person sits in a chair will communicate a preference for a relaxed, informal social setting.
4. *Expresses emotional opinions.* Emotive people generally do not hide their feelings. They often express opinions dramatically and impulsively.

Figure 4.3 Combining the dominance and sociability dimensions of human behaviour provides the framework for classifying communication style.

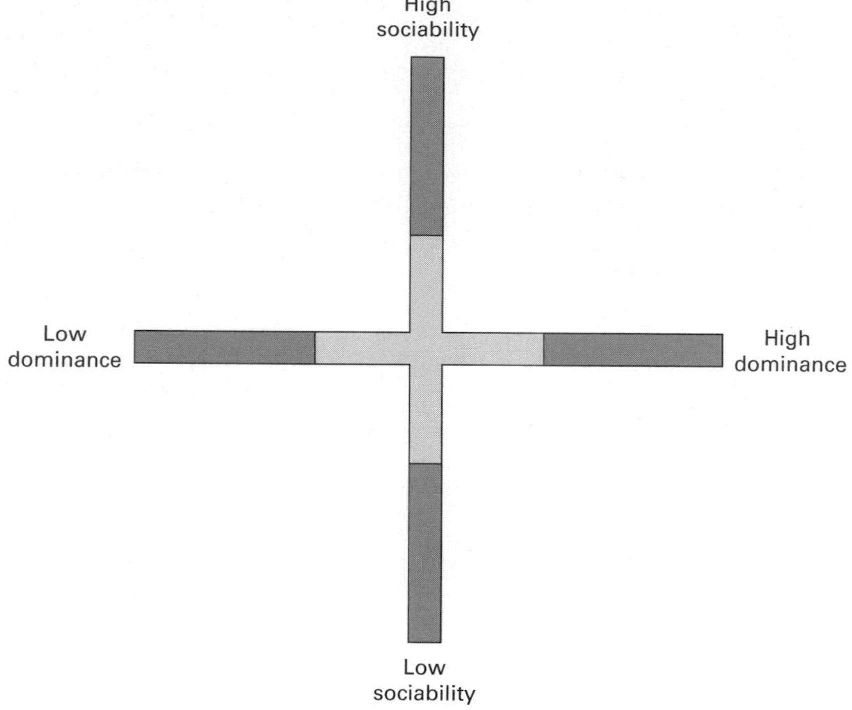

Figure 4.4 The Emotive style combines high sociability and high dominance.

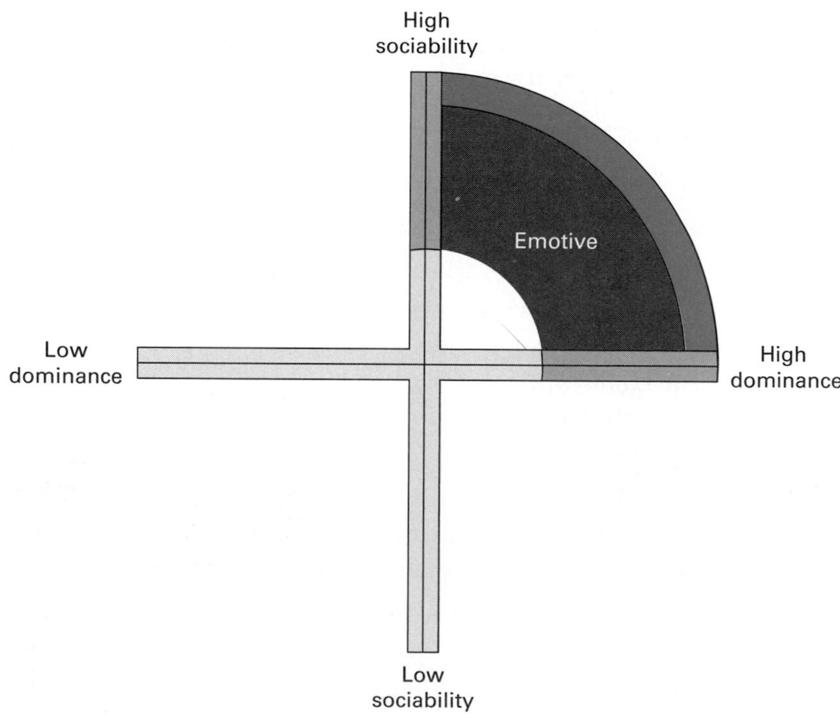

Figure 4.5 Key words for the Emotive style

Sociable	Unstructured
Spontaneous	Excitable
Zestful	Personable
Stimulating	Persuasive
Emotional	Dynamic

Emotive people like Oprah Winfrey are enthusiastic, outspoken, and stimulating.

The Director Style

The lower right-hand quadrant of Figure 4.6 defines a style that combines high dominance and low sociability. We will call this the **Director style** (see Fig. 4.7).

Director style A communication style that displays the following characteristics: appears to be businesslike, displays a serious attitude, and voices strong opinions.

To understand the nature of people who display the Director communication style, picture in your mind's eye the director of a Hollywood film. The person you see is giving orders in a loud voice and is generally in charge of every facet of the operation. Everyone on the set knows this person is in charge. While this common image of the Hollywood film director is probably exaggerated, this example will be helpful as you attempt to become familiar with the Director style.

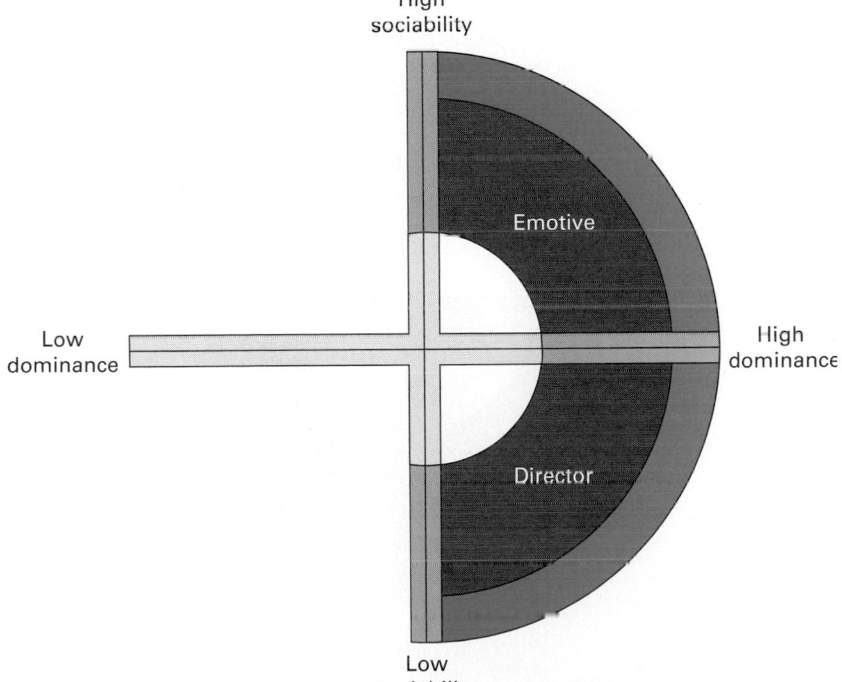

Figure 4.6 The Director style combines high dominance and low sociability.

Figure 4.7 Key words for the Director style

Aggressive	Determined
Intense	Frank
Requiring	Opinionated
Pushy	Impatient
Serious	Bold

Judith Sheindlin, better known as Judge Judy, uses a brash "take no prisoners" approach to handling disputes on the *Judge Judy* television show. She is frank, assertive, and very focused.

Many senior executives of large corporations project the Director style. Television commentator Barbara Walters and interviewer Pamela Wallin provide additional examples. They may be described as frank, demanding, aggressive, and determined.

In the field of selling you will encounter a number of customers who are Directors. How can you identify these people? What verbal and nonverbal clues can you observe? A few of the behaviours displayed by Directors follow:

1. *Appears to be quite busy.* The Director generally does not like to waste time and wants to get right to the point. Judy Sheindlin of the *Judge Judy* television show displays this behaviour.
2. *May give the impression of not listening.* In most cases the Director feels more comfortable talking than listening.
3. *Displays a serious attitude.* A person who is low in sociability usually communicates a lack of warmth and is apt to be quite businesslike and impersonal. Mike Wallace, one of the stars on the popular *60 Minutes* television show, seldom smiles or displays warmth.
4. *Likes to maintain control.* The person who is high on the dominance continuum likes to maintain control. During meetings the Director will seek to control the agenda.[12]

Reflective style A communication style that displays the following characteristics: controls emotional expression, displays a preference for orderliness, tends to express measured opinions, and seems difficult to get to know.

The Reflective Style

The lower left-hand quadrant of Figure 4.8 features a combination of low dominance and low sociability. We call this the **Reflective style** (see Fig. 4.9).

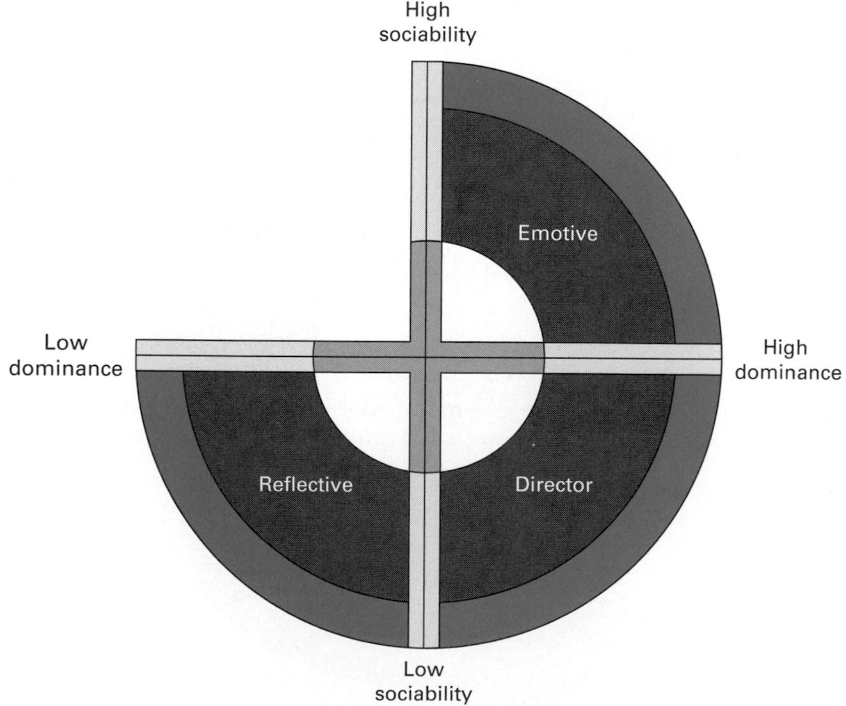

Figure 4.8 The Reflective style combines low dominance and low sociability.

The Reflective person tends to examine all the facts carefully before arriving at a decision. Like a cautious scientist, this individual wants to gather all available information and weigh it carefully before taking a position. The Reflective type is usually a stickler for detail.[13] Rex Murphy, the journalist who hosts CBC's *Cross Country Checkup*, and David Suzuki, the scientist who hosts CBC's *The Nature of Things*, are two well-known Canadians who display the characteristics of the Reflective type. The late physicist Albert Einstein is another example.

Figure 4.9 Key words for the Reflective style

Precise	Scientific
Deliberate	Preoccupied
Questioning	Serious
Disciplined	Industrious
Aloof	Stuffy

The Reflective communication style combines low dominance and low sociability; therefore people with this classification tend to be reserved and cautious. Some additional behaviours that characterize this style follow:

1. *Controls emotional expression.* Reflective people tend to curb emotional expression and are less likely to display warmth openly.
2. *Displays a preference for orderliness.* The Reflective person enjoys a highly structured environment and generally feels frustration when confronted with unexpected events.
3. *Tends to express measured opinions.* The Reflective individual usually does not express dramatic opinions. This communication style is characterized by disciplined, businesslike actions.
4. *Seems difficult to get to know.* The Reflective person tends to be somewhat formal in social relationships and therefore is viewed as aloof by many people.

Persons with the Reflective style, such as David Suzuki, tend to control their emotions and examine all the facts when making a decision.

In a selling situation the Reflective customer does not want to move too fast. This person wants the facts presented in an orderly and unemotional manner and does not want to waste a lot of time socializing.

The Supportive Style

The upper left-hand quadrant of Figure 4.10 (p. 90) defines a style that combines low dominance and high sociability. We call this the **Supportive style** (see Fig. 4.11, p. 90). These people find it easy to listen and usually do not express their views in a forceful manner. Entertainers Kevin Costner, Rita MacNeil, Anne Murray, and Meryl Streep display the characteristics of the Supportive style.

Supportive style A communication style that displays the following characteristics: appears quiet and reserved, listens attentively to other people, tends to avoid the use of power, and makes decisions in a thoughtful and deliberate manner.

Low visibility generally characterizes the lifestyle of Supportive people. They complete their tasks in a quiet, unassuming manner and seldom draw attention to what they have accomplished. In terms of assertiveness, persons with the Supportive style rank quite low. Someone who ranks high on the dominance continuum is likely to view the Supportive individual as being too easygoing. Other behaviours that commonly characterize the Supportive person follow:

1. *Gives the appearance of being quiet and reserved.* People with the Supportive behavioural style can easily display their feelings, but not in the assertive manner common to the Emotive individual.

People with the Supportive communication style are usually quiet and unassuming.

2. *Listens attentively to other people.* In selling, good listening skills can be a real asset. This talent comes naturally to the Supportive person.
3. *Tends to avoid the use of power.* Whereas the Director may rely on power to accomplish tasks, the Supportive person is more likely to rely on friendly persuasion.
4. *Makes decisions in a thoughtful and deliberate manner.* The Supportive person usually takes longer to make a decision.

POPULARITY OF THE FOUR-STYLE MODEL

We are endlessly fascinated by ourselves, and this helps explain the growing popularity of the four-style model presented in this chapter. To satisfy this insatiable appetite for information, many training and development companies offer training programs that present the four social or communication styles. Figure 4.12 features the approximate equivalents of the four styles presented in this chapter.

DETERMINING YOUR COMMUNICATION STYLE

You now have enough information to identify your own communication style. If your location on the dominance continuum is right of centre and your position on the sociability continuum is below the centre mark, you fall into the Director quadrant. If your location on the dominance continuum is left of centre and your position on the sociability continuum is above the

Figure 4.10 The Supportive style combines low dominance and high sociability.

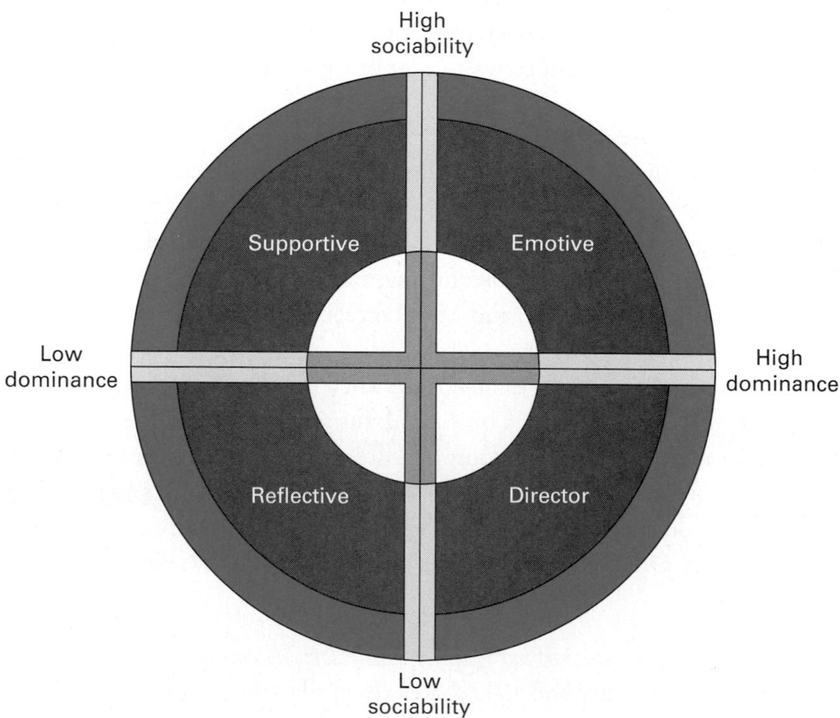

Figure 4.11 Key words for the Supportive style

Lighthearted	Patient
Reserved	Sensitive
Passive	Relaxed
Warm	Compliant
Docile	Softhearted

Supportive (Manning/Reece/MacKenzie) Amiable (Wilson Learning) Supportive-Giving (Stuart Atkins Inc.) Relater (People Smarts) Steadiness (Personal Profile System)	Emotive (Manning/Reece/MacKenzie) Expressive (Wilson Learning) Adapting-Dealing (Stuart Atkins Inc.) Socializer (People Smarts) Influencing (Personal Profile System)
Reflective (Manning/Reece/MacKenzie) Analytical (Wilson Learning) Conserving-Holding (Stuart Atkins Inc.) Thinker (People Smarts) Cautiousness/Compliance (Personal Profile System)	Director (Manning/Reece/MacKenzie) Driver (Wilson Learning) Controlling-Taking (Stuart Atkins Inc.) Director (People Smarts) Dominance (Personal Profile System)

Figure 4.12 The four basic communication styles have been used in a wide range of training programs. For comparison purposes the approximate equivalents to the four communication styles discussed in this chapter are listed.

centre mark, then your most preferred style is Supportive. Likewise, low dominance matched with low sociability forms the Reflective communication style, and high dominance matched with high sociability forms the Emotive style.

Of course, all of us display some characteristics of the Emotive, Director, Reflective, and Supportive communication styles. However, one of the four styles is usually predominant and readily detectable.[14]

Some people who study the communication-style model for the first time may initially experience feelings of frustration. They find it hard to believe that one's behavioural style tends to remain quite uniform throughout life. People often say, "I am a different person each day!" It is certainly true that we sometimes feel different from day to day, but our most preferred style remains stable. The Supportive person might say, "I sometimes get very upset and tell people what I am thinking. I can be a Director when I want to

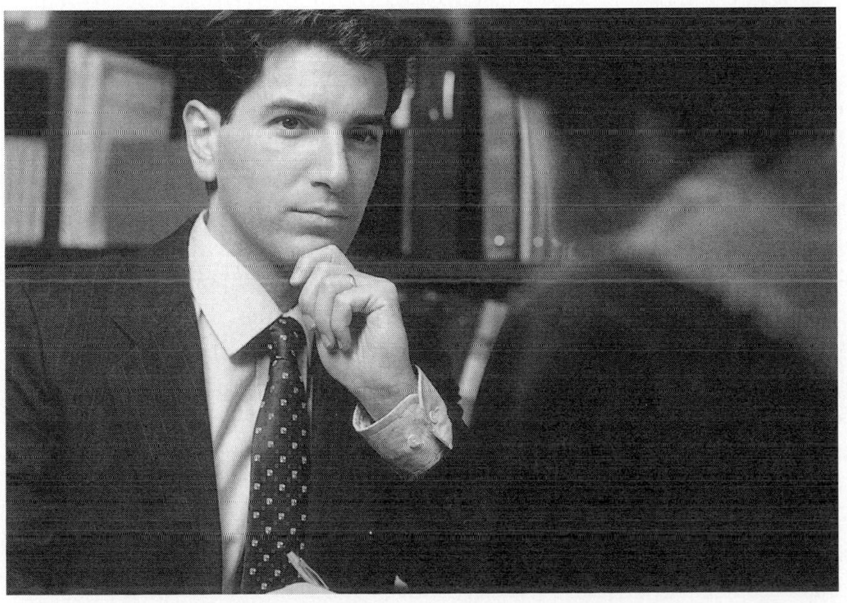

The nonverbal gestures displayed by this customer indicate a preference for the Reflective communication style.

be!" There is no argument here. Just because you have a preferred communication style does not mean you will never display the behavioural characteristics of another style. Some people use different styles in different contexts and in different relationships.[15] Reflective people sometimes display Emotive behaviour, and Emotive people sometimes display Reflective behaviour. The research shows that each person has one most preferred and habitually used communication style.

Managing Communication-Style Bias

Salespeople often make the mistake of focusing too much on the content of their sales presentation and not enough on how they deliver their message.[16] When information is presented ineffectively, salespeople miss the opportunity to add value. Biases about communication styles are a barrier to success in selling. This form of bias is a common problem in sales work simply because salespeople deal with people from all four quadrants. You cannot select potential customers on the basis of their communication style. You must be able to develop rapport with people from each of the four quadrants. When people of different styles work together but don't adjust to one another, serious problems can develop.[17]

SELLING IN THE GLOBAL ECONOMY

Bow, Hug, Kiss, or Shake?

When you do business across cultures, a lot can be communicated nonverbally. The key to relationship building is demonstrating respect for the other person's culture. A good place to start is with the greeting ritual. "How do you do? It is a pleasure to meet you" will work well in Canada, and you will likely find that foreign visitors will greet you this way. However, when you visit another country, the onus is on you to be sensitive to local customs.

In India, it is common to place your palms together at heart level in the classic prayer position and make a slight bow of the head, accompanied by saying "*Namaste*" (pronounced nah-mas-tay). This is a very respectful greeting that wishes you harmony with the universe. It is particularly appropriate when a Western businesswoman meets an Indian businessman. In Thailand, a visiting businessman should smile rather than shake a businesswoman's hand, but he may shake hands with another businessman. In Taiwan, it is not necessary to shake hands during initial greetings. A simple nod of the head is sufficient. In the Philippines, a foreign businesswoman can initiate a handshake with either men or women, but a foreign businessman should wait for a Filipino woman to extend her hand first.

In some cultures, it is common for men to greet one another with an embrace—but only after a friendship has developed. Kisses and "air kisses," where the lips don't actually touch the skin, are common in some European and Latin American countries. If you want to demonstrate your sensitivity to other cultures and your willingness to accept their customs, you should seek advice before you travel abroad. An excellent resource for travelling businesspeople is **www.executiveplanet.com**, where you can get information on etiquette in 35 countries.[b]

HOW COMMUNICATION-STYLE BIAS DEVELOPS

To illustrate how communication-style bias develops in a sales situation, let us observe a sales call involving two people with different communication styles. Mary Wheeler entered the office of Dick Harrington, a new prospect, with a feeling of optimism; she was sure that her product would save Dick Harrington's company several hundred dollars a year. She had done her homework and was 99 percent certain that the sale would be closed.

Mary is an "all business" type who is a Director in terms of communication style. Her sales calls are typically fast-paced and focused. On entering the office of Dick Harrington she immediately began to talk business. He interrupted to ask if she wanted coffee. She declined the offer and continued her sales presentation. He asked Mary if she enjoyed selling. After a glance at her watch, she responded by saying that selling was a rewarding career and then quickly returned to her sales presentation. Thirty minutes after meeting Dick Harrington, Mary walked out of his office without the order. What went wrong?

Dick Harrington's communication style is Supportive. He feels uncomfortable doing business with strangers and likes slow-paced interactions with people. He felt tension when Mary Wheeler failed to establish a social relationship. He also felt she was moving at a pace that was too fast. If Mary had spent a few minutes socializing with Dick, she would have recognized his preferred approach to communication—and she might have secured the sale. The "all business" approach she used might be appropriate for the Director or Reflective communication style.

A salesperson who is highly adaptable can usually build rapport with customers regardless of their communication style. Style flexibility is a sales strategy that can be learned.

When people are introduced to communication styles for the first time, they often label certain styles as more or less favourable for selling careers. The truth is, there is no one best place to be on the communication-style model because there are no best types of personality.[18] As noted previously, a style refers to how someone likes to do something, not how well someone can do something. Successful salespeople come from all four quadrants. What these high achievers have in common is style flexibility.

MATURE AND IMMATURE BEHAVIOUR

There is a mature and an immature side to each behavioural style. Let us examine the Emotive style to illustrate this point. People with this style are open, personable individuals who seem genuinely friendly. The natural enthusiasm displayed by the mature Emotive is refreshing. On the other hand, an Emotive person who is too talkative and too emotional, and who lacks the ability to listen to others, reflects the immature side of the Emotive communication style. You will recall that we used the words "industrious" and "precise" to describe the Reflective style. These are words that apply to the mature side of the Reflective person. We also used the words "aloof" and "stuffy." These words describe the immature side of the Reflective.

The good news is that we all have the potential for developing the mature side of our communication style. Our most preferred communication style does not change, but it matures as we mature.

STRENGTH/WEAKNESS PARADOX

It is a fact of life that your greatest strength can become your greatest weakness. If your most preferred style is Reflective, people will likely respect your well-disciplined approach to life as one of your strengths. However, this strength can become a weakness if it is exaggerated. The Reflective person can be too serious, too questioning, and too inflexible. Robert Haas, chairman of Levi Strauss & Company, is known for extraordinary—some say obsessive—attention to detail. Those who work with him say an offhand conversation can sound like a lecture. This Reflective leader, however, has the ability to flex his style. Levi's employees are fiercely loyal to Haas and describe him as compassionate to a fault.[19]

www.levistrauss.com

People with the Director style are open and frank, and express their true feelings in a direct manner. When J. P. Bryan, president and CEO of Gulf Canada Resources Ltd., was asked why he stayed away from Calgary's Petroleum Club, he stated: "I stayed away because I didn't want to get friendly with people in the oil patch. I'm not bound by these traditional relationships, so we can go after people as we see fit, and I'm not worried about ruining a friendship."[20] In most cases we appreciate candour, but we do not like to be around people who are too straightforward or too blunt in expressing their views. When people come across as opinionated, they tend to antagonize others. We should avoid pushing our strengths to the point of unproductive excess.[21]

To illustrate how strengths become weaknesses in excess, let us add more detail to our communication-style model. Note that it now features three zones that radiate out from the centre (see Fig. 4.13). These dimensions might be thought of as intensity zones.

CUSTOMER RELATIONSHIP MANAGEMENT WITH TECHNOLOGY

Being Prepared

Customer relationship management (CRM) software empowers a salesperson with information essential to continue a relationship. The software can be used to record, retain, and produce personal information including such factors as marital status, names and ages of children, and individual preferences. Before placing a call, the salesperson might review the database information, to refresh his or her memory about the prospect. This can be especially helpful when preparing to talk with someone with a specific communication style. (See the exercise, Identifying Communication Styles, p. 102, for more information.)

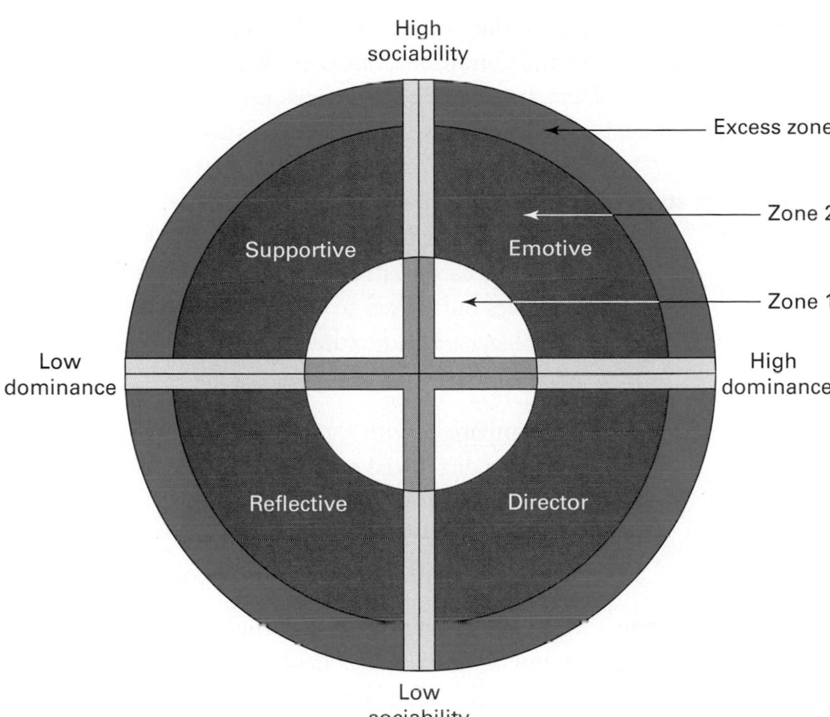

Figure 4.13 The completed communication-style model provides important insights needed to manage the relationship process in selling.

Zone one. People who fall within this zone display their unique behavioural characteristics with less intensity than those in zone two. The Emotive person, for example, is moderately high on the dominance continuum and moderately high on the sociability continuum. As you might expect, zone one communication styles are more difficult to identify because there is less intensity in both dimensions (dominance and sociability).

Zone two. Persons who fall within this zone display their unique behavioural characteristics with greater intensity than persons in zone one. The zone two Reflective, for example, falls within the lowest quartile of the dominance continuum and the lowest quartile of the sociability continuum.

The boundary line that separates zone one and zone two should not be seen as a permanent barrier restricting change in intensity. Under certain circumstances we should abandon our most preferred style temporarily. Style flexing, introduced earlier in this chapter, is a deliberate move from zone one to zone two, or vice versa in order to raise the comfort level in a discussion with someone who has a different communication style.

Excess zone. The excess zone is characterized by a high degree of intensity and rigidity. When people allow themselves to drift into this zone, they become very inflexible, which is often interpreted by others as a form of bias toward their style. In addition, the strengths of the inflexible person become weaknesses. Extreme intensity in any quadrant is bound to threaten interpersonal relations.

We are apt to move into the excess zone and exaggerate our style characteristics under stressful conditions. Stress tends to bring out the worst in many people. Here are some of the behaviours that salespeople and customers may display when they are in the excess zone:

Emotive style	Expresses highly emotional opinions Stops listening to the other person Tries too hard to promote own point of view Becomes outspoken to the point of being offensive Uses exaggerated gestures and facial expressions to make a point
Director style	Gets impatient with the other person Becomes dictatorial and bossy Will not admit being wrong Becomes extremely competitive Is cold and unfeeling when dealing with people
Reflective style	Becomes stiff and formal during social interactions Is unwilling to make a decision Avoids displaying any type of emotion Displays a strong dislike for change Is overly interested in detail
Supportive style	Agrees with everyone Is unable to take a strong stand Becomes overly anxious to win approval of others Tries to comfort everyone Constantly seeks reassurance

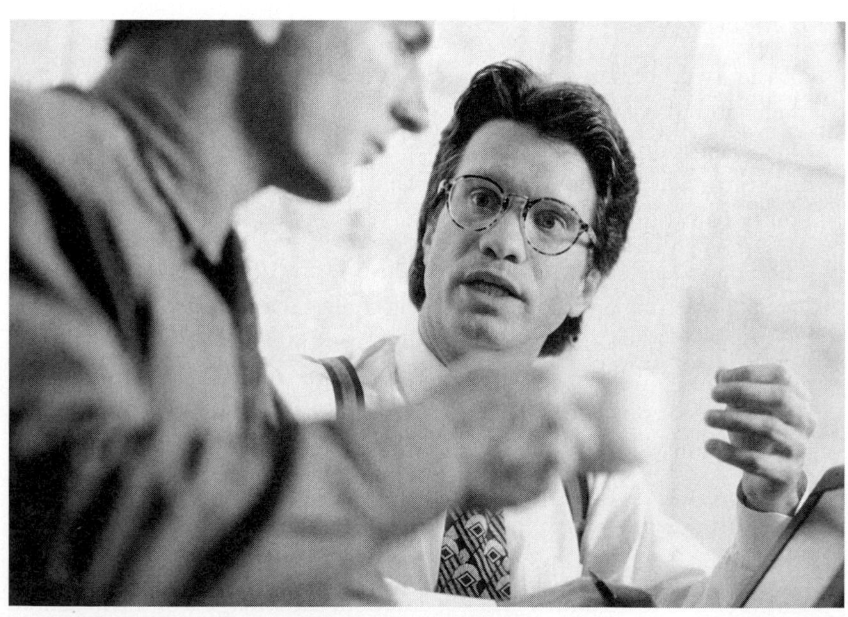

The excess zone is characterized by a high degree of intensity and rigidity. We are more apt to move into the excess zone under very stressful conditions.

Developing Communication-Style Flexibility

As noted earlier, style flexing is the deliberate adjustment of your communication style to accommodate the needs of another person. You are attempting to communicate with the other person on his or her own "channel." Ron Willingham, in his book *Integrity Selling*, reminds us that "people are more apt to buy from you when they perceive you view the world as they view the world."[22] In a selling situation you should try to determine the customer's most preferred style and flex your own accordingly. If your preferred communication style is Director, and your customer's is Supportive, try to be more personal and warm in your presentation. Once you know the customer's style, flexing your style can make the difference between a presentation that falters and one that exceeds your expectations.[23] Style sensitivity and flexing add value to the sales process.

Throughout the preapproach you should learn as much as possible about the customer and try to determine his or her style. Once you are in the customer's presence, watch and listen for clues that reveal his or her predominant style.

When you are meeting with a customer, do not become preoccupied with analyzing the person's style. If you are trying hard to analyze the person's style, you may not listen closely enough to what he or she is trying to tell you. If you are truly tuned in to the customer, you will absorb many clues that will help you determine his or her style. After the sales call, analyze the communication and record your findings. Use this information to plan your next contact with the customer.[24]

Listen closely to the customer's tone of voice. A Supportive person will sound warm and friendly. The Reflective customer's voice is more likely to be cautious and deliberate. Pay particular attention to gestures. The Emotive individual will use his or her hands to communicate thoughts and ideas. The Director also uses gestures to communicate but is more controlled and less spontaneous. The Reflective person will appear more relaxed, less intense.

The Emotive individual is an open, impulsive communicator, while the Reflective person is quite cautious. The Supportive type will be personal and friendly, while the Reflective person may seem difficult to get to know. To avoid relationship tension, consider the following suggestions for each of the four styles.

SELLING TO EMOTIVE PEOPLE

If you are attempting to sell products to an Emotive person, keep in mind the need to move at a pace that will hold the attention of the prospect. Be enthusiastic and avoid an approach that is too stiff and formal. Take time to establish goodwill and build relationships. Do not place too much emphasis on the facts and details. To deal effectively with Emotive people, plan actions that will provide support for their opinions, ideas, and dreams.[25] Plan to ask questions concerning their opinions and ideas, but be prepared to help them get back on track if they move too far away from the topic. Maintain good eye contact and, above all, be a good listener.

SELLING TO DIRECTOR PEOPLE

The key to relating to Directors is to keep the relationship as businesslike as possible. Developing a strong personal relationship is not a high priority for Directors. In other words, friendship is not usually a condition for a good working relationship. Your goal is to be as efficient, time disciplined, and well organized as possible, and to provide appropriate facts, figures, and success probabilities. Most Directors are goal-oriented people, so try to identify their primary objectives and then determine ways to support and help with these objectives. Early in the sales presentation, ask specific questions and carefully note responses. Look for specific points you can respond to when it is time to present your proposal.

SELLING TO REFLECTIVE PEOPLE

The Reflective person will respond in a positive way to a thoughtful, well-organized approach. Arrive at meetings on time and be well prepared. In most cases it will not be necessary to spend a great deal of time building a social relationship. Reflective people appreciate a no-nonsense, businesslike approach to personal selling. Use specific questions that show clear direction. Once you have information concerning the prospect's needs, present your proposal in a slow, deliberate way. Provide as much documentation as possible. Do not be in too big a hurry to close the sale. Never pressure the Reflective person to make quick decisions.

SELLING TO SUPPORTIVE PEOPLE

Take time to build a social relationship with the Supportive person. Spend time learning about the things that are important in this individual's life—family, hobbies, and major interests. Listen carefully to personal opinions and feelings. Supportive individuals like to conduct business with sales personnel who are professional but friendly. Therefore, study their feelings and emotional needs as well as their technical and business needs. Throughout the presentation, provide personal assurances and support for their views. If you disagree with a Supportive person, curb the desire to disagree too assertively; Supportive people dislike interpersonal conflict. Give them the time to contemplate your proposal. Patience is important.

As you develop your ability to identify communication styles and become more adept at style flexing, you will be better able to manage sales relationships. With these skills, you should be able to open more accounts, sell more to established customers, and more effectively meet the pressures of competition. Most important, your customers will view you as a person better able to understand and meet their needs.

A WORD OF CAUTION

It is tempting to put a label on someone and then assume the label tells you everything you need to know about that person. If you want to build an effective sales partnership with a prospect, you must acquire additional information about that person. Stuart Atkins, a respected authority on communication styles and author of *The Name of Your Game*, says that it requires real effort to look beyond the label and to experience the whole person as a dynamic process.[26] You must also be careful not to let the label you place on yourself become the justification for your own inflexible behaviour. Try not to let the label justify or reinforce why you are unable or unwilling to communicate effectively with others.[27]

www.bcon-lifo.com

SELLING IN ACTION

Versatility Is Key

One way to increase sales and enjoy selling more is to reduce the tension between you and the prospect. Personal selling is almost never a tension-free activity, but there are effective ways to control the tension that is likely to surface during the selling process. Dr. David Merrill, one of the early pioneers in development of communication-style instruments and training programs, uses the term "versatility" to describe our ability to control the tension we create in others. He believes it is important for you to understand your preferred communication style but also to control personal behaviour patterns and adapt to the people with whom you have contact. In jobs such as selling, which require a high degree of interpersonal effectiveness, versatility can be the key to success.

Roger Wenschlag, author of *The Versatile Salesperson*, defines "versatility" as "the degree to which a salesperson is perceived as developing and maintaining buyer comfort throughout the sales process." This does not mean you must become "another person" and display behaviours that make you uncomfortable. However, you should be able to adjust your behaviour temporarily to fit the buyer's style. Versatility displayed by the salesperson sends the message "I care about the relationship."

Versatility has another benefit, according to Tony Alessandra, author of *People Smarts*. He notes that this quality enables you to interact more productively with difficult people.

The wonderful thing about versatility is that it can be learned. We can learn to control what we say and do to make others more comfortable.[c]

SUMMARY

The primary objective of this chapter is to introduce communication-style bias and examine the implications of this concept for salespeople. Many sales are lost because salespeople fail to communicate effectively with the prospect. Communication-style bias contributes to this problem. Every salesperson who is willing to develop style sensitivity and engage in appropriate style flexing can minimize one of the most common barriers to success in selling.

The communication-style model is based on two continuums that assess two major aspects of human behaviour: dominance and sociability. By combining them as horizontal and vertical continuums, we create quadrants that define four styles of communication. We have called these the Emotive, Director, Reflective, and Supportive styles. With practice in observation, you should be able to increase your sensitivity to other people's styles. Practice in self-awareness and self-control will give you the ability to flex your own style and to help others feel at ease.

Key Terms

Communication Style **79**
Communication-Style Bias **79**
Director Style **87**
Dominance **82**
Emotive Style **84**
Reflective Style **88**
Sociability **84**
Style Flexing **82**
Supportive Style **89**

Review Questions

1. What is the most prominent form of bias in our society? Explain.
2. Describe the five major principles that support communication-style theory.
3. What are the benefits to the salesperson who understands communication style?
4. What two dimensions of human behaviour are used to identify communication style?
5. Describe the person who tends to be high in sociability.
6. What are the four communication styles? Develop a brief description of each of the styles.
7. What is the reaction of most people who study communication styles for the first time? Why does this reaction surface?
8. What is the major reason for introducing communication styles in a textbook on selling?
9. Explain the statement, "Your greatest strength can become your greatest weakness."
10. The Selling in Action boxed feature on page 99 suggests that we should try to control what we say and do to make others more comfortable. Is it realistic to expect salespeople to follow this advice? Explain your answer.

Application Exercises

1. Oprah Winfrey is a very popular television personality.
   a. On the dominance continuum below, mark where you think she belongs.
   b. On the sociability continuum below, mark where you think she belongs.
   c. Using the two continuums to form the communication-style model, what is Oprah Winfrey's communication style? Does she possess style flexibility? Explain this in terms of (i) the different styles of guests on her program and (ii) her apparent popularity with millions of people.

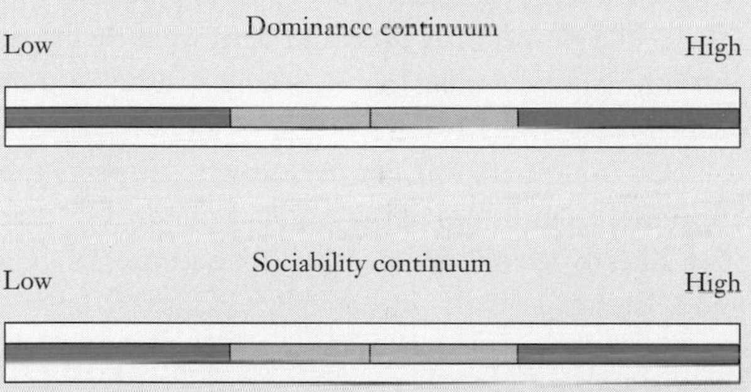

   d. Describe Oprah Winfrey's personality using statements and terms from this chapter.
   e. Have you ever observed Oprah Winfrey slipping into her excess zone? Explain.

2. Many salespeople, after being introduced to communication-style psychology, attempt to categorize each of their customers. They report that their relationships become mutually more enjoyable and productive. Select five people whom you know quite well (e.g., supervisor, subordinate, customer, teacher, friend, or member of your family). Using the two behavioural continuums in this chapter, determine these people's communication styles. Using your own descriptive terminology in conjunction with terminology in this chapter, develop a descriptive behavioural profile of each of these people. Explain how this information will improve your relationship with each of these people.

3. Self-awareness is important in personal selling. As we get to know ourselves, we can identify barriers to acceptance by others. Once you have identified your most preferred communication style, you have taken a big step in the direction of self-awareness. If you have not yet determined your most preferred communication style, take a few minutes to complete the Dominance Indicator form (Table 4.1) and the Sociability Indicator form (Table 4.2). Follow the instructions provided in the text about the tables.

4. Myers-Briggs Personality Types and Jungian Personality Types are two very popular descriptions of the material in this chapter. Visit **www.google.ca** (or another search engine if you prefer) and hit "advanced search." Type "Jungian + personality profiles" under "Find results with exact phrase" to access the Jungian personality types. Limit your search by typing ".ca" under "domain." To access the Myers-Briggs types, type in "Myers-Briggs + personality profiles." Does the number of hits indicate anything about the validity and popularity of these theories? Examine Web sites that discuss both of these theories. Be prepared to discuss what you have found in class.

ROLE-PLAY EXERCISE

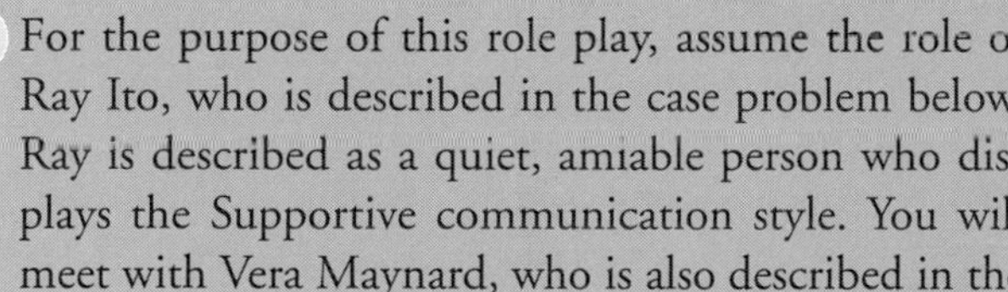

For the purpose of this role play, assume the role of Ray Ito, who is described in the case problem below. Ray is described as a quiet, amiable person who displays the Supportive communication style. You will meet with Vera Maynard, who is also described in the case problem. For the purpose of this role play, assume that Vera displays the characteristics of the Director communication style. Prior to the role play, study the chapter material on style flexing and on how to sell to persons with the Director communication style.

CRM Application Exercise IDENTIFYING COMMUNICATION STYLES

Pat Silva carefully recorded the communications styles of most of the people in the database and identified the prospects as Emotive, Director, Reflective, or Supportive. To talk to an Emotive, select Lookup, Keyword, type "Emotive," check Notes, and press Enter. After searching, Act! displays four records of people whom Pat identified as Emotives. Print these notes by selecting Report, Contact Report, Active Lookup, Printer, and Enter.

Case Problem

Ray Ito has been employed at CanTrust Real Estate for almost two years. Prior to receiving his real estate licence, he was a property manager with a large real estate agency in another community. During his first year with CanTrust, he was assigned to the residential property division and sold properties totalling $825 000. He then requested and received a transfer to the commercial division.

Three months ago, Ray obtained a commercial listing that consisted of 10.5 hectares (26 acres) of land near a growing residential neighbourhood. The land is zoned commercial and appears to be ideally suited for a medium-sized shopping centre. Ray prepared a detailed prospectus and sent it to Vera Maynard, president of Consumer Growth Corporation, a firm specializing in development of shopping centres. One week later he received a letter from Vera Maynard requesting more information. Shortly after receiving Ray's response, Vera called to set up an appointment to inspect the property. A time and date were finalized, and Ray agreed to meet her plane and conduct a tour of the property.

Ray is a quiet, amiable person who displays the Supportive communication style. Friends say that they like to spend time with him because he is a good listener.

Questions

1. If Vera Maynard displays the characteristics of the Director communication style, how should Ray Ito conduct himself during the meeting? Be specific as you describe those behaviours that would be admired by Vera Maynard.
2. If Vera Maynard wants to build rapport with Ray Ito, what behaviour should she display?
3. It is not a good idea to put a label on someone and then assume the label tells us everything about the person. As Ray Ito attempts to build rapport with Vera Maynard, what other personal characteristics should he try to identify?

CHAPTER 5

Ethics

THE FOUNDATION FOR RELATIONSHIPS IN SELLING

Herbert Schulte, a veteran sales representative for Prudential Insurance (**www.prudential.com**), was forced to make a difficult ethical decision. His sales manager gave him a list of his middle-aged customers and sales literature that described a Prudential life insurance policy as nursing home coverage. He contends that his manager was implicitly recommending an insurance-industry practice called "churning," a practice by which agents pressure customers to use built-up cash value in an existing policy to buy a new, more expensive one. In some cases information is withheld so that customers fail to understand the negative aspects of the buying decision. Herbert realized that the sales approach recommended by his sales manager would require that he mislead his established customers and he refused to go along with the plan.[1]

Herbert Schulte was one of hundreds of Prudential sales representatives encouraged to use misleading sales practices. Soon after the Prudential problems made headlines, the company began to reform its sales practices and meet its legal obligations. More than a thousand agents and managers were fired and a fine of $35 million was paid. The company purchased full-page newspaper ads to apologize for "intolerable" deceptive sales practices. Later, Prudential agreed to a class-action settlement of $2 billion that involved 650 000 policyholders. A few years later the company was embarrassed again when the Prudential Securities unit produced a poor track record in the area of investor abuses. A study prepared by Weiss Ratings Inc.

LEARNING OBJECTIVES

After studying this chapter, you should be able to

1. Discuss the influence of ethical decisions on relationships in selling
2. Describe the factors that influence the ethical conduct of sales personnel
3. Explain how role models influence the ethical conduct of sales personnel
4. Discuss the influence of company policies and practices on the ethical conduct of salespeople
5. Explain how values influence behaviour
6. Compare legal versus ethical standards
7. Discuss guidelines for developing a personal code of ethics

ranked Prudential Securities number one (i.e., the worst) in this area. The Weiss study examined arbitration awards, and regulatory and legal actions for the 18 top retail brokerage firms between 1997 and 2001.[2]

Most business decisions can be judged as right or wrong, so why did some Prudential employees make the wrong choice? Why would any company violate the moral contract it has with customers and risk the loss of goodwill built up over many years? The authors of *When Good Companies Do Bad Things* note that there is a simple and a complex answer to these questions. The simple answer is that every business enterprise must recognize the need to establish a strategic relationship between know-how and integrity. A company cannot be successful in the long term without both. The complex answer requires a careful study of the forces that influence ethical decision making in today's turbulent economy.[3] Studying the material in this chapter will help you identify ethical issues in personal selling and recognize ways to resolve them.

Making Ethical Decisions

Making ethical decisions is a daily reality in the field of personal selling. In every selling situation salespeople must judge the rightness or wrongness of their actions. As in any other professional field, personal selling offers countless temptations to compromise personal standards of conduct, or ethics, to achieve economic goals.

ethics Rules of conduct used to determine what is good or bad. They are moral principles or values concerned with what ought to be done—a person's adherence to, for example, honesty and fairness.

Ethics are the rules that direct your conduct and moral judgments.[4] They help translate your values into appropriate and effective behaviours in your day-to-day life as well as your work. Ethics reflect the moral principles and standards of a company, a culture, or society at large. Bribes and kickbacks may be acceptable practices in some places, yet may be viewed as unethical practices elsewhere. Exaggerated or inaccurate sales claims may be acceptable at one company but forbidden at another company.

There is no one uniform code of ethics for all salespeople. However, numerous business organizations, professional associations, and certification agencies have established written codes. The Canadian Professional Sales Association (CPSA), introduced in Chapter 2, requires all persons seeking to become a Certified Sales Professional to agree to abide to the CPSA Sales Institute's code of ethics (see Fig. 5.1).

Today, we recognize that character and integrity strongly influence relationships in personal selling. As noted in Chapter 3, character is composed of your personal standards of behaviour, including your honesty and integrity. Your character is based on your internal values and the resulting judgments you make about what is right and what is wrong. The ethical decisions you make reflect your character strength.

www.stephencovey.com

We are indebted to Stephen Covey, author of *The 7 Habits of Highly Effective People*, for helping us to better understand the relationship between character strength and success in personal selling. In his best-selling book Stephen Covey says there are basic principles that must be integrated into our character.[5] One example is to always do what you say you are going to do. Fulfilling your commitments builds trust, and trust is the most important precondition of sales partnering.

Figure 5.1 The CPSA Sales Institute Code of Ethics.

www.cpsa.com

The CPSA Sales Institute Code of Ethics is the set of principles and standards that a certified sales professional will strive to adhere to with customers, organizations, competitors, communities and colleagues.

The Certified Sales Professional pledges and commits to uphold these standards in all activities.

I will:

1. Maintain honesty and integrity in all relationships with customers, prospective customers, and colleagues and continually work to earn their trust and respect.
2. Accurately represent my products or services to the best of my ability in a manner that places my customer or prospective customer and my company in a position that benefits both.
3. Respect and protect the proprietary and confidential information entrusted to me by my company and my customers and not engage in activities that may conflict with the best interests of my customers or my company.
4. Continually upgrade my knowledge of my products/services, skills and my industry.
5. Use the time and resources available to me only for legitimate business purposes. I will only participate in activities that are ethical and legal, and when in doubt, I will seek counsel.
6. Respect my competitors and their products and services by representing them in a manner which is honest, truthful and based on accurate information that has been substantiated.
7. Endeavor to engage in business and selling practices which contribute to a positive relationship with the community.
8. Assist and counsel my fellow sales professionals where possible in the performance of their duties.
9. Abide by and encourage others to adhere to this Code of Ethics.

As a certified sales professional, I understand that the reputation and professionalism of all salespeople depends on me as well as others engaged in the sales profession, and I will adhere to these standards to strengthen the reputation and integrity for which we all strive. I understand that failure to consistently act according to this Code of Ethics may result in the loss of the privilege of using my professional sales designation.

Source: www.cpsa.com/institute.html. Reprinted with permission.

Colleges and universities are beginning to play a more active role in character development, now commonly offering courses that focus on ethics. When a new ethics course was developed at the University of Virginia, the faculty indicated that the purpose of the course is not to point out what is right and what is wrong. The course is designed to help students understand the consequences of their actions when they face an ethical dilemma.[6]

THE EROSION OF CHARACTER

Despite growing interest in business ethics, unethical behaviour has become all too common. One survey indicates that nearly half of the workers surveyed had engaged in unethical or illegal acts during the year preceding the study. Many of the workers who had transgressed reported that they were under pressure to act unethically or illegally on the job.[7] A survey conducted by *Newsweek* suggests that the current generation of workers may be more tolerant of deception. Many of those involved in the survey did not view lying and cheating as unacceptable.[8]

As the 1990s unfolded, many large inflexible corporations were transformed into nimble competitors. New economy thinking prevailed as business firms, large and small, worked hard to become lean, innovative, and profitable. We witnessed an almost unrelenting emphasis on earnings that was driven, in many cases, by executive greed. During this period, some of the most respected companies began to cross the ethical divide.[9]

A company cannot enjoy long-term success unless its employees are honest, ethical, and uncompromising about values and principles. Yet many employees engage in dishonest practices that erode their character. The collapse of Enron, the largest U.S. corporation ever to file for bankruptcy, can be traced to a culture that emphasized risk taking, personal ambition over teamwork, and earnings growth at any cost. While the information economy depends on innovation and aggressive development of markets, actions that weaken the moral contract with employees, customers, and shareholders can have serious consequences for business success. Let's examine some half-truths that have eroded moral character in business settings.

- *We are only in it for ourselves.* Some critics of today's moral climate feel that the current moral decline began when society's focus shifted from "what is right" to "what is right for me." In personal selling this point of view can quickly subtract rather than add value to a customer relationship. Fortunately, there are many salespeople for whom integrity and self-respect are basic values. Take Darryl Ashley, for example. A pharmaceutical representative for Eli Lilly Company, Darryl suspected that one of his customers, a pharmacist, was diluting chemotherapy drugs in order to increase profit margins. Darryl shared his suspicions with one of the cancer doctors who was purchasing the drug from the pharmacist. Tests indicated that the drug had been diluted.[10]
- *Corporations exist to maximize shareholder value.* In the past, corporations were often viewed as economic and social institutions—organizations that served their customers and communities. In recent years, analysts, stock traders, CEOs, and the media have tended to focus on a single standard of performance—share price.[11] Marjorie Kelly, editor of *Business Ethics*, says, "Managing a company solely for maximum share price can destroy both share price and the entire company."[12]

  Pressure to increase "numbers" led to sales abuses at WorldCom Incorporated. Some salespeople double-booked accounts in order to make their quota and collect increased commissions. The false reporting was identified by an internal company probe and the guilty sales representatives were fired.[13] The same pressure led financial executives at Canada's Nortel Networks to report forecast revenues and earnings that were "out of touch with reality"; as a result, the company's CEO and a number of senior financial executives were fired.[14]

Each year *Fortune* publishes a list of the best hundred companies to work for in the United States. It is encouraging to note that most of these companies still say that employees represent their most important asset and that the customer is "king."

- *Companies need to be lean and mean.*[15] Downsizing has become a common practice even when the economy is strong. After the layoffs, companies must deal with serious problems of low morale and mistrust of management. Those employees who remain after a company reduces its ranks often feel demoralized, overworked, and fearful. The stress of long hours and a faster pace can result in losses in quality and bad service that alienate customers. Richard Sennett, author of *The Corrosion of Character*, says that the decline of character strength can be traced to conditions that have grown out of our fast-paced, high-stress, information-driven economy. He states that character strength builds as we display loyalty, mutual commitment, and the pursuit of long-term goals.[16] These are the qualities needed to build strong buyer–seller relationships.

Today many business firms are struggling to align their values, ethics, and principles with the expectations of their salespeople and their customers. The process of negotiating ethical standards and practices must be ongoing. *Business Week* reports that a new era of reform is dawning that will restore core values of honesty, fairness, and integrity.[17]

Factors Influencing the Ethics of Salespeople

In the field of personal selling, the temptation to maximize short-term gains by some type of unethical conduct is always present. Salespeople are especially vulnerable to moral corruption because they are subject to such temptations. Here are a few examples:

The competition is using exaggerated claims to increase the sale of its product. Should you counteract by using exaggerated claims of your own to build a stronger case for your product?

You have visited the buyer twice and, each time, the person displayed interest in your product. During the last visit the buyer hinted that the order might be signed if you provide a small gift. Your company has a policy that gifts are not to be given under any circumstances. What do you do?

Your sales manager is under great pressure to increase sales. At a recent meeting of the entire sales staff, this manager said, "We have to beat the competition no matter what it takes!" Will this emotional appeal change your way of dealing with customers?

During a recent business trip, you treated a good friend who is not a customer to lunch. You paid for the entire bill and left a generous tip. Do you put these non–business-related expenses on your expense account?

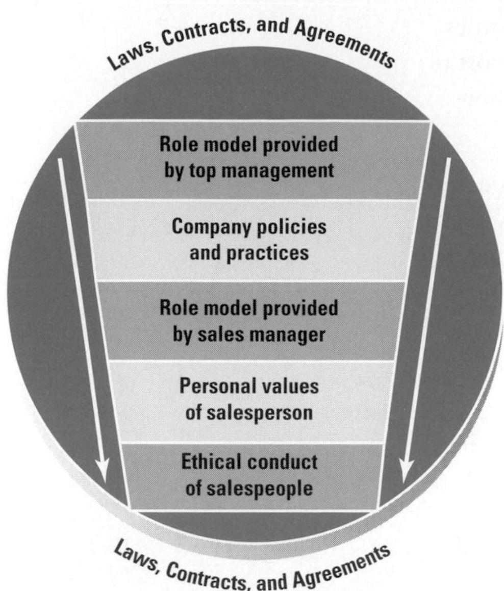

Figure 5.2 Factors determining ethical behaviour of salespeople.

You sell financial services and have developed a long list of satisfied customers. A competitor hires you. Should you attempt to take your good customers with you?

These types of ethical conflicts arise frequently in the field of selling. How do salespeople respond? Some ignore company policy, cast aside personal standards of conduct, and yield to the pressure. However, most salespeople are able to resist. They are aided by numerous factors that help them distinguish right from wrong. Figure 5.2 outlines the positive forces that help them deal honestly and openly with prospects at all times. We will discuss each of these factors.

TOP MANAGEMENT AS ROLE MODEL

Ethical standards tend to filter down from the top of an organization. According to Michael Deck, principal with Toronto-based KPMG Ethics & Integrity Services, "Corporate integrity begins with senior executives visibly and actively setting an example of respect for the rules. In this way, senior management sends a clear message that unethical and illegal behaviours are not acceptable business practices."[18] Employees look to company leaders for guidance. The organization's moral tone, as established by management personnel, is the most important single determinant of employee ethics. In addition, trust in senior leadership is a key factor in developing employee loyalty.[19]

www.kpmg.ca

COMPANY POLICIES AND PRACTICES

Company policies and practices can have a major impact on the ethical conduct of salespeople. Al Rosen, who taught accounting at York University for 30 years, says that, once you are hired, you become a product of your company and its ethics drift through you. He says, "People are telling you to forget this and that—it becomes a birds-of-a-feather atmosphere."[20] Developing policy statements forces a firm to "take a stand" on various business practices. Distinguishing right from wrong can be a healthy activity for any organization. The outcome is a clearer philosophy of how to conduct business transactions. Research has demonstrated that companies with a

THE CUSTOMER'S PERSPECTIVE

Ethics: Increasingly Becoming Front and Centre

Customers today are more likely to demand proof of integrity, particularly when choosing important vendors that must be capable of providing long-term support. Many salespeople simply try to refer customers to their company Web sites, where they can find statements of company values and ethics practices. However, many customers are now demanding more. Requests for proposals are increasingly requiring vendors to sign documents that explicitly outline their good ethical practices.

Experts in business ethics suggest four things common to vendors that follow "best practices":

1. *A top-level business executive responsible for ethics, business conduct, and compliance.* These executives are increasingly responsible to report directly and regularly to company boards of directors.
2. *The ability for all employees to be able to anonymously and confidentially report any suspected wrongdoing.* At Nortel Networks, employees are now able to call a confidential advice line, e-mail the business ethics department, or communicate directly with anyone in the organization, including individual members of the board, or the board as a whole.
3. *The ability to monitor and assess their ethics program effectiveness.* Vendors need more than simple statements of ethical conduct and values.
4. *Ethics training for all employees, including senior executives.* Sun Microsystems has provided a basic online ethics training program for all of its 35 000 employees worldwide, and requires that they take ongoing training. In addition, about 1200 top executives and some staff members are required to participate each year in a two-day workshop. Before Brian Conlon, chief information officer at Howrey, Simon, Arnold & White, a large international law firm, awarded a contract to Sun Microsystems to overhaul his company's IT infrastructure, he carefully scrutinized Sun's business conduct and compliance programs. As justification, he says, "The things we are doing with Sun are not one-offs. It will be our partner for a long time, and we need to make sure it will stay in business."[a]

defined corporate commitment to ethical practices did better financially than firms that didn't make ethics a key management component.[21]

The KPMG Ethics Survey 2000 polled the CEOs of one thousand Canadian companies. Among the respondents, 86 percent reported having written documents that outlined their values and principles. The presence of a senior-level manager responsible for the implementation, monitoring, and assurance of ethics initiatives was reported by 42 percent of the respondents, but most of these managers reported spending less than 10 percent of their time on ethical issues.

Most marketing companies provide salespeople with guidelines in such areas as sharing confidential information, reciprocity, bribery, gift giving, entertainment, and business defamation. A brief discussion of each of these areas follows.

Sharing Confidential Information

Personal selling, by its very nature, promotes close working relationships. Customers often turn to salespeople for advice. They disclose confidential information freely to someone they trust. It is important that salespeople preserve the confidentiality of information they receive.

It is not unusual for a customer to disclose information that may be of great value to a competitor. This might include development of new products, plans to expand into new markets, or anticipated changes in personnel. A salesperson may be tempted to share confidential information with a representative of a competing firm. This breach of confidence might be seen as a means of gaining favour. In most cases this action will backfire. The person who receives the confidential information will quickly lose respect for the salesperson. A gossipy salesperson will seldom develop a trusting relationship with another business associate.

Reciprocity

reciprocity A mutual exchange of benefits, as when a firm buys products from its own customers.

Reciprocity is a mutual exchange of benefits, as when a firm buys products from its own customers. Some business firms actually maintain a policy of reciprocity. For example, the manufacturer of commercial sheets and blankets may purchase hotel services from firms that use its products. Is there anything wrong with the "you scratch my back and I'll scratch yours" approach to doing business? The answer is sometimes yes. In some cases the use of reciprocity borders on commercial blackmail. Salespeople have been known to approach firms that supply their company and encourage them to buy out of obligation. The firm may be forced to buy products of questionable quality at excessive prices. A business relationship based on reciprocity often has drawbacks, such as the ever-present temptation to take reciprocal customers for granted. A customer who buys out of obligation may take a back seat to customers who were won in the open market.

Bribery

In some jurisdictions, a bribe is illegal. The book *Arrogance and Accords: The Inside Story of the Honda Scandal* describes one of the largest commercial corruption cases in North American history. Over a 15-year period Honda offi-

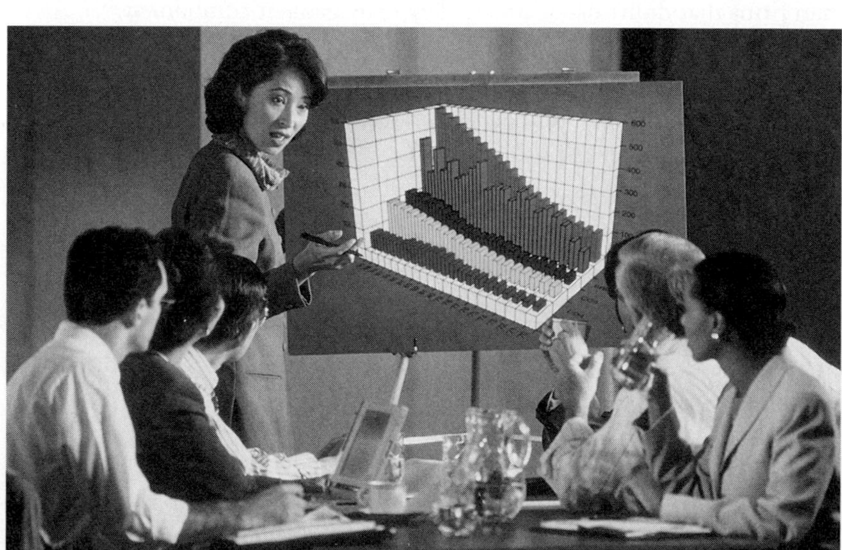

Personal selling, by its nature, promotes close working relationships. It is important that salespeople preserve the confidentiality of information they receive. Violation of this ethical responsibility will quickly erode a relationship with the customer.

cials received more than US$50 million in cash and gifts from dealers anxious to obtain fast-selling Honda cars and profitable franchises. When the bribery became public, 18 former Honda executives were convicted of obtaining kickbacks; most went to prison.[22] Unfortunately, bribery is quite common in sales. In 2002, *Sales & Marketing Management* surveyed 249 sales executives, 64 percent of whom indicated that they viewed personal gifts valued at more than $100 as bribes; however, 89 percent also indicated that they or their colleagues had offered such gifts in exchange for business.[23] While these bribes are seldom illegal, they are ethically wrong. It helps to have company policies for salespeople to use as a reference point, so they know what is not acceptable behaviour.

Gift Giving

Gift giving is a widespread business practice in Canada. However, some companies do maintain a "no gift" policy. Many companies report that their policy is either no gifts or nothing of real value. General Motors' code of ethics states: "Both as a matter of sound procurement practice and basic business integrity, we at General Motors must make our purchase decisions solely on the basis of which suppliers offer GM the best value for the goods and services we need."[24]

There are some grey areas that separate a gift from a bribe. Most people agree that a token of insignificant value, such as a pen imprinted with a company logo, is an appropriate way to foster goodwill. A bribe, on the other hand, is an attempt to influence the person who is receiving the gift.[25]

Are there right and wrong ways to handle gift giving? The answer is yes. The following guidelines will be helpful to any salesperson who is considering giving gifts to customers:

1. Do not give gifts before doing business with a customer. Do not use the gift as a substitute for effective selling methods.
2. Never convey the impression you are "buying" the customer's business with gifts. When this happens, the gift becomes nothing more than a bribe.
3. When gift giving is done correctly, the customer will clearly view it as symbolic of your appreciation—a "no strings attached" goodwill gesture.
4. Be sure the gift is not a violation of the policies of your firm or of your customer's firm. Some companies will not allow employees to accept gifts at all; others place a dollar limit on a gift's value.

In summary, if you have second thoughts about giving a gift, do not do it. When you are sure some token is appropriate, keep it simple and thoughtful.[26]

Entertainment of Customers

Entertaining customers is a widespread practice in the field of selling but may be viewed by some people as a bribe. The line dividing gifts and entertainment from bribes is often quite arbitrary. Salespeople must frequently decide how to handle entertaining. Some industries see entertaining customers as a way to build relationships with them outside the work environment.

Entertainment of customers is a highly individualized process. One customer might enjoy a professional football game while another might be impressed most by a quiet meal at a good restaurant. The key is to get to know your customer's preferences. How does the person spend leisure time? How much time can the person spare for entertainment? You will need to answer these and other questions before you invest time and money on entertainment of customers.

Business Defamation

During a sales presentation, salespeople frequently compare their product's qualities and characteristics with those of a competitor. If such comparisons are inaccurate, are misleading, or slander a company's business reputation, they are illegal.[27] Competitors have sued hundreds of companies and manufacturer's representatives for making slanderous statements while selling.

What constitutes business defamation? Steven M. Sack, co-author of *The Salesperson's Legal Guide*, provides the following examples:

1. *Business slander.* This arises when an unfair and untrue oral statement is made about a competitor. The statement becomes actionable when it is communicated to a third party and can be interpreted as damaging the competitor's business reputation or the personal reputation of an individual in that business.
2. *Business libel.* This may be incurred when an unfair and untrue statement is made about a competitor in writing. The statement becomes actionable when it is communicated to a third party and can be interpreted as damaging the company.
3. *Product disparagement.* This occurs when false or deceptive comparisons or distorted claims are made concerning a competitor's product, services, or property.[28]

The effectiveness of company policies as a deterrent to unethical behaviour will depend on two factors. The first is the firm's attitude toward employees who violate these policies. If violations are routinely ignored, the policy's effect will soon be eroded. The second factor is the support of the entire sales staff for policies that influence personal selling. Salespeople should have some voice in policy decisions; they are more apt to support policies they have helped develop.

THE SALES MANAGER AS ROLE MODEL

The salesperson's actions often mirror the sales manager's behaviour and expectations. This is not surprising when you consider the relationship between salespeople and their supervisors. They look to their supervisors for

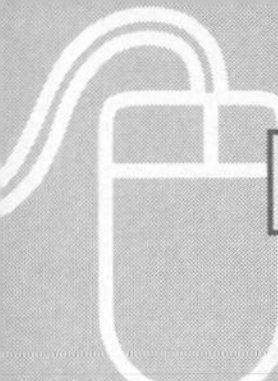

CUSTOMER RELATIONSHIP MANAGEMENT WITH TECHNOLOGY

Exercising Care with CRM Data

Customer relationship management systems enable you to collect information about people with whom you maintain relationships, including the taking of notes. It is a good practice to record more than basic transaction information, such as personal details about your customers. Reviewing your observations about their behaviour and recording their statements can help you understand them and their needs. Re-reading their comments about ethical issues can assist you to assess the value of maintaining a business relationship with them.

To be fair, it is important to record only the facts regarding your observations, not necessarily your conclusions. Information in an electronic database can last a long time and, as a result of such circumstances as litigation or company acquisitions, can be "mobile." This means that others may form an opinion about your customer based on your recorded observations, with potential detrimental consequences for your customer. Not being aware of the existence of the information in your database, your customer does not have a fair opportunity to correct any erroneous conclusions. Another reason to record only facts is the possibility that the information may be read by the customer. For example, there have been instances in which a customer has later joined the sales organization and gained access to the CRM system.

Most CRM systems contain scheduling functions, which means that you can set aside time on your calendar to attend meetings, make phone calls, and perform tasks. The scheduling tools usually include alarms, which will remind you that a deadline is approaching. The disciplined use of these features can help you get things done on time. Taking advantage of the system's reminder tools can be especially important when it involves fulfilling your commitments. The system can help you build trust by reminding you always to do what you said you would do. (See the exercise Preparing Mailing Labels with CRM on page 121 for more information.)

guidance and direction. The sales manager is generally the company's closest point of contact with the sales staff. This person is usually viewed as the chief spokesperson for top management.

Sales managers generally provide new salespeople with their first orientation to company operations. They are responsible for interpreting company policy. On a continuing basis the sales manager monitors the salesperson's work and provides important feedback regarding conduct. If a salesperson violates company policy, it is usually the sales manager who is responsible for administering reprimands. If the moral fibre of a sales force begins to break down, the sales manager must shoulder a great deal of responsibility.

Sales managers influence the ethical behaviour of salespeople by virtue of what they say and what they do. From time to time, managers must review their expectations of ethical behaviour. Salespeople are under continual pressure to abandon their personal ethical standards to achieve sales goals. Values such as integrity and honesty must receive ongoing support from the sales manager. The sales manager's behaviour must be consistent with a stated philosophy. Actions do speak louder than words; any inconsistency between words and deeds is likely to have a negative influence on the attitude of the sales staff.

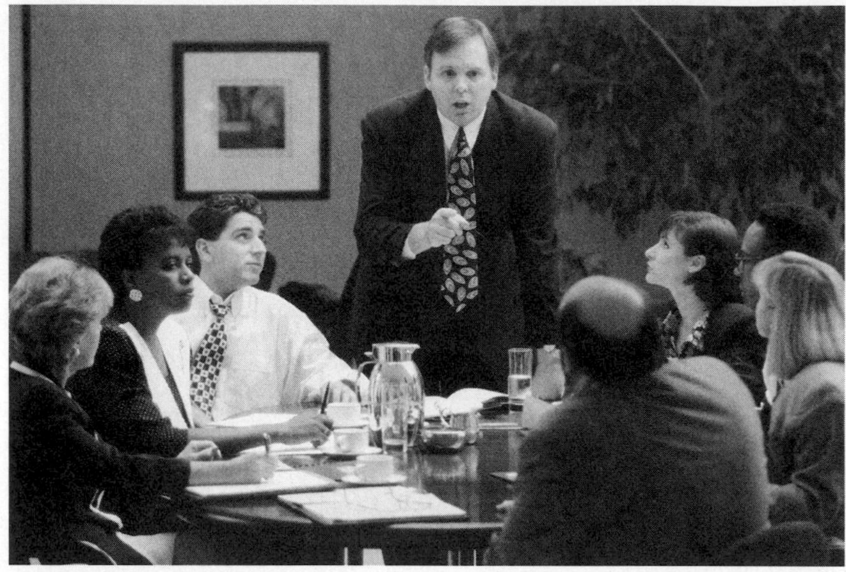

Sales managers influence the ethical behaviour of salespeople by virtue of what they say and what they do.

THE SALESPERSON'S PERSONAL VALUES

Ann Kilpatrick, a sales representative in the transportation industry, encountered something unexpected when entertaining a potential client. The client said, "Let's go to Johnny's." She was not familiar with Johnny's but, on arrival, discovered it was a raunchy bar. Kilpatrick related that she sat there for five minutes and then said, "This is not what I was expecting. This is a sleazy place. Let's go somewhere else where we can talk." She was not willing to compromise her personal values to win a new account.[29]

values Your deep personal beliefs and preferences that influence your behaviour.

Values represent the ultimate reasons people have for acting as they do. **Values** are your deep personal beliefs and preferences that influence your behaviour. To discover what really motivates you, carefully examine what it is you value.[30] Values serve as a foundation for our attitudes, and our attitudes serve as a foundation for our behaviour (see Fig. 5.3). We do not adopt or discard values quickly. In fact, the development of values is a lifelong process.

VALUES CONFLICT

Values can serve as a deterrent to unethical behaviour in a selling situation. They help to establish our own personal standards concerning what is right and what is wrong. Ron Willingham, author of *Integrity Selling*, says, "A salesperson's ethics and values contribute more to sales success than do techniques or strategies."[31] Some salespeople discover a values conflict between themselves and the employer. If you view your employer's instructions or influence as improper, you have three choices:

1. Ignore the influence of your values, and engage in unethical behaviour. The end result will likely be a loss of self-respect and a feeling of guilt. When salespeople experience conflicts between their actions and values, they also feel a loss of confidence and energy.[32] Positive energy is

Salespeople must avoid misleading sales claims. To stretch the truth is not only unethical but also illegal.

the result of creating value for the customer. Negative energy emerges when salespeople fail to honour and embrace their ethical values.

2. Voice strong opposition to the practice that is in conflict with your value system. Take a stand, and state your beliefs. A wise person once said, "Following the path of least resistance is what makes men and rivers crooked." Your objective is to influence decisions made by your superiors.

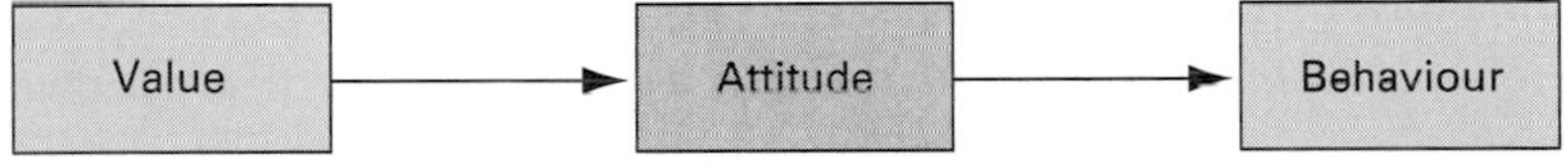

Figure 5.3 The relationship of values, attitudes, and behaviour.

SELLING IN ACTION

Honesty from a Quarterback's Perspective

Jeff Kemp, former National Football League quarterback, believes that sports can teach important moral lessons. Some of these lessons can be applied in personal selling. This is what he says about honesty: "The importance of honesty colours all the rest of life. Why is truth so important? It is because respect, relationships, and unity all depend on truth. If you cannot be honest with people, you cannot have healthy relationships." Kemp found that honesty was the foundation for harmony among team members. He says, "Without truth, I couldn't trust my teammates and they couldn't trust me."[b]

3. Refuse to compromise your values, and be prepared to deal with the consequences. This may mean leaving the job. It may also mean that you will be fired.

Salespeople face ethical problems and decisions every day. In this respect they are no different from the doctor, the lawyer, the teacher, or any other professional. Ideally, they will make decisions on the basis of the values they hold.

Laws, Contracts, and Agreements

Take another look at Figure 5.2 and you notice that all of the key elements, personnel, and policies are influenced by laws, contracts, and agreements. Everyone involved in sales and marketing is guided by legal as well as ethical standards. We live in a society in which the legal system plays a key role in preventing people from engaging in unethical behaviour.

LAWS

http://laws.justice.gc.ca/en/C-34/

The specific obligations imposed by government on the way business operates take the form of statutes. In Canada, it is necessary for salespeople not only to know federal statutes but also to recognize that there are many provincial and territorial statutes, and that important differences exist between provinces and territories. The *Competition Act* is the major federal legislation in Canada that defines illegal practices, including price fixing, bid rigging, price discrimination, predatory pricing, double ticketing, resale price maintenance, bait and switch selling, and pyramid selling.

cooling-off laws Provincial and territorial laws that give customers an opportunity to reconsider a buying decision made under a salesperson's persuasive influence.

All Canadian provinces and territories have passed legislation that establishes a cooling-off period during which the consumer may void a contract to purchase goods or services. While the provisions of **cooling-off laws** vary from jurisdiction to jurisdiction, their primary purpose is to give customers an opportunity to reconsider a buying decision made under a salesperson's persuasive influence. In most jurisdictions, this legislation is referred to as either *The Direct Sellers Act* or *The Consumer Protection Act.*

CONTRACTS AND AGREEMENTS

contract An oral or written promise enforceable by law.

The word "contract" may bring to mind the familiar multiple page, single-spaced documents that only a lawyer seems able to read. In fact, contracts can be oral or written. A **contract** is simply a promise or promises that the courts will enforce. Oral contracts are enforceable, but written contracts are preferable, as they reduce the possibility of disagreement; courts give written contracts great weight in a lawsuit. A written contract can consist of a sales slip, a notation on a cheque, or any other writing that offers evidence of the promises that the parties made.[33]

Salespeople are sometimes the legal representatives of their company and, therefore, must be careful when signing written contracts. They often oversee contracts with customers, suppliers, and resellers. A salesperson may be asked to sign an employment contract at the time he or she is hired. Most of these agreements include a noncompete clause. One of the most common clauses, a noncompete clause prohibits salespeople from joining a competing firm for a year after they leave. Most clauses are legally binding even when an employee's position is cut. Employers see employment contracts as an effective way to protect intellectual property, customer lists, and other resources an employee might take to a competing firm.[34]

ETHICS BEYOND THE LETTER OF THE LAW

Too often people confuse ethical standards with legal standards. They believe that, if they are not breaking the law then they are acting in an ethical manner.[35] A salesperson's ethical sense must extend beyond the legal definition of what is right and wrong. To view ethics only in terms of what is legally proper encourages the improper attitude, "What can I get by with?" A salesperson must develop a personal code of ethics that extends beyond the letter of the law.

A Personal Code of Ethics That Adds Value

Many people considering a career in selling are troubled by the thought that they may be pressured into compromising their personal standards of right and wrong. These fears may be justified. The authors of *The Ethical Edge*, a book that examines organizations that have faced moral crises, contend that business firms have given too little thought to the issue of helping employees to function ethically within organizations.[36] Many salespeople wonder if their own ethical philosophy can survive in the business world. These are some of their questions:

"Will I be forced to abandon my own ethical beliefs?"

"Can good business and good ethics coexist?"

"Is honesty still a valued personal trait in the business community?"

It is becoming more difficult to provide a concise yes or no answer to these questions. Times are changing, and it is getting harder and harder to tell the "good guys" from the "bad guys." We read about the unethical use of gifts and bribes by corporate officials. Investigations of provincial medicare programs turn up overbilling and other unethical behaviours by doctors, pharmacists, and operators of nursing homes. Reports from colleges and universities indicate that cheating is becoming more common. Even some of our most respected political leaders have been guilty of tax fraud, accepting illegal campaign contributions, and accepting payments for questionable favours. We are tempted to ask, "Are ethical standards changing?"

Our society is currently doing a great deal of soul-searching. Many people want to see a firming of ethical standards. Many leaders are keenly aware that unethical behaviour threatens the moral fabric of our free enterprise system. If the business community cannot police itself, more and more people will be looking to government for solutions to the problem. But one fact we have learned from history is that we cannot legislate morality.

In the field of athletic competition the participants rely heavily on a written set of rules. The referee or umpire is ever-present to detect rule violations and assess a penalty. In the field of personal selling there is no universal code of ethics. However, some general guidelines can serve as a foundation for a personal code of business ethics.

1. *Personal selling must be viewed as an exchange of value.* Salespeople who maintain a value focus are searching for ways to create value for their prospects or customers. This value may take the form of increased productivity, greater profit, enjoyment, or security. The value focus motivates the salesperson to carefully identify the prospect's wants and needs.[37] Salespeople who accept this ethical guideline view personal selling as something you do *for* customers, not something you do *to* customers. The role of the salesperson is to diagnose buyer needs and determine if value can be created. Understanding the prospect's wants and needs should always precede any attempt to sell.[38]

2. *Relationship comes first, task second.* Sharon Drew Morgan, author of *Selling with Integrity*, says you can't sell a product unless there is a level of comfort between you and the prospect. She encourages salespeople to take the time to create a level of comfort, rapport, and collaboration that encourages open communication.[39] Placing task before relationship is based on the belief that the salesperson knows more than the customer. Morgan reminds us that "the buyer has the answers; the seller has the questions."[40] These answers will surface only when the buyer–seller relationship is characterized by rapport and trust.

3. *Be honest with yourself and with others.* To achieve excellence in terms of ethical practices, you have to believe that everything you do counts. Tom Peters, in his book *Thriving on Chaos*, says, "Integrity may be about little things as much as or more than big ones."[41] It's about accuracy in completing your expense account—and resisting the temptation to inflate the expense report for personal gain. It's about avoiding the temptation to stretch the truth, to exaggerate, or to withhold information. Paul Ekman, author of *Telling Lies*, says that withholding important information is one of the primary ways of lying.[42] A complete and informative sales presentation may include information regarding the product's limitations. If you let your character and integrity be revealed in the little things, others will see you as one who acts ethically in all things. Any violation of honesty, however small, dilutes your ethical strength, leaving you weaker for the big challenges you will face sooner or later.[43]

TRUST

Everyone involved in personal selling must work hard to build relationships based on trust. When the customer and the salesperson trust each other, they will usually find ways to form a productive partnership. Although trust is an essential element of every sale, the meaning of trust changes with the type of sale.[44]

- *Transactional Sales.* The primary customer focus in this type of sale is trust in the product. Is the product reliable? Is the product priced as low as possible? Can the product be delivered in a timely fashion? The transactional buyer may purchase a product from a salesperson they do not feel totally comfortable with if it meets their purchase criteria.
- *Consultative Sales.* In a consultative sale, the customer focus shifts from the product to the person who sells the product. The consultative buyer is thinking "Can I trust this salesperson to identify my problem and offer me one or more solutions?" Customers involved in a consultative sale usually do not separate the product from the person selling it. They want to do business with a salesperson who displays such positive qualities as warmth, empathy, genuineness, competence, and integrity.
- *Relationship Selling.* The relationship buyer wants to do business with an institution that can be trusted. This buyer looks beyond the well-qualified salesperson and assesses the entire organization. Relationship customers will not feel comfortable partnering with a company whose values differ greatly from their own. Ethical accountability will greatly influence the way a partner is judged and valued.

Trust exists when we strongly believe in the integrity, ability, and character of a person or an organization. Although trust is intangible, it is at the very core of all meaningful relationships. Trust is quickly lost and slowly won.[45]

SUMMARY

At the beginning of this chapter we defined ethics as the rules that direct your conduct and moral judgments. Ethics help us establish standards of honesty, loyalty, and fairness. We have noted that ethics are not legally constituted guidelines. To consider only what is legally right and wrong limits our perception of morality. Laws alone will not bring a halt to unethical selling practices.

Company policies and practices can have a strong influence on the ethical conduct of salespeople. These policies often help salespeople cope with ethical conflicts.

Salespeople can benefit from the stabilizing influence of good role models. Although top management personnel are usually far removed from day-to-day selling activities, they can have a major impact on salespeople's conduct. Dishonesty at the top causes an erosion of ethical standards throughout an organization. Sales managers provide another important role model. They interpret company policies and help establish guidelines for acceptable and unacceptable selling practices.

Finally, salespeople must establish their own standards of personal conduct. They must decide how best to serve their company and build strong partnerships with their customers. The pressure to compromise one's ethical standards surfaces almost daily. The temptation to take the easy road to achieve short-term gains is always present. The primary deterrent is a strong sense of right and wrong. Three general guidelines that can serve as a foundation for a personal code of ethics were presented.

We strongly support the premise that "bad ethics is bad business and unethical sales practices will eventually destroy relationships with customers." Anyone who relies on unethical sales practices cannot survive in the selling field very long. These practices undermine the company's reputation and eventually reduce profits.

Key Terms

Contract **116**

Cooling-off laws **116**

Ethics **104**

Reciprocity **110**

Values **114**

Review Questions

1. What is the definition of ethics? Why are corporate ethics receiving so much attention today?
2. Carefully review Figure 5.1, the CPSA Sales Institute code of ethics. Select the three standards you feel would present the greatest challenge to salespeople. Explain your choices.
3. Select one of the half-truths that have influenced the erosion of character in the business community and indicate your agreement or disagreement with it.
4. What major factors help influence salespeople's ethical conduct?
5. A company policy on ethics will usually cover several major areas. What are they?
6. Is it ever appropriate to give gifts to customers? Explain.
7. What is business defamation? Describe three ways in which a salesperson may be guilty of business defamation.
8. Explain why the sales manager plays such an important role in influencing the ethical behaviour of salespeople.
9. What are cooling-off laws? How do they protect consumers?
10. List and describe three guidelines used as a foundation of a self-imposed code of business ethics.

Application Exercises

1. You find that you have significantly overcharged one of your clients. The error was discovered when you received his cheque. It is unlikely that the customer or your company will become aware of the overcharge. Because of this error, the company realized a high net profit on the sale. Your commissions are based on this profit. What, if anything, will you do about the overcharge? Explain why.
2. The Canadian Telecommunications Consultants Association requires all members to adhere to its code of ethics and professional conduct. Look up its code on its Web site (**www.ctca.ca**). Be prepared to discuss in class why this organization has a code of ethics and professional conduct for its members.
3. You work for a supplier of medical equipment. Your sales manager informs you that he wants you to capture a certain hospital account. He also tells you to put on your expense account anything it costs to secure the hospital as a client. When you ask him to be more specific, he tells you to use your own judgment. Up to this time you have never questioned your sales manager's personal code of ethics. Make a list of the items you feel can be legitimately charged to the company on your expense account.
4. For some time your strongest competitor has been making untrue derogatory statements about your product and about you as a salesperson. You know for a fact that her product is not as good as yours, yet hers has a higher price. Several of your best customers have confronted you with these charges. Describe how you plan to answer them.

ROLE-PLAY EXERCISE

This morning you met with a customer who has purchased office supplies from you for almost three years. You are quite surprised when she says, "I am prepared to place an order worth $10 500, but you must match an offer I received from a competitor." She then explains that the competitor is offering new customers a seven-day all-expenses-paid trip to Quebec City if they place an order for more than $10 000. What would you do?

Prepare to role-play your response with another student. Review the material in this chapter, paying special attention to ways you can add value and build long-term relationships with ethical decision making.

CRM Application Exercise PREPARING MAILING LABELS WITH CRM

Load the ACT! software and select Report, Other. From the list of mailing label formats, choose avry5160, and press OK. In the Prepare Report window, pick Active Group and Document, and press OK. The mailing information for each contact will be displayed on the screen. Select File, Print, and print this list.

A friend of yours is a salesperson with a firm that installs the cables used to connect network components, a service that your company does not offer. Your friend wants to know if you will share the customer list that you just printed. What should be your response?

Case Problem

Dave MacDonald was sitting in the outer office waiting to see Stan Hope, the purchasing agent for Strait Structural Steel, a new account that had just begun operations in a coastal location about 65 kilometres (40 miles) from the nearest city. Stan had telephoned Dave the previous week with an urgent request for four large exhaust fans that were required to remove fumes from enclosed spaces where welders were at work. The union had threatened to stop the project unless working conditions were improved. Although Dave didn't sell fans at the time, he found a line of fans and negotiated a discount from the manufacturer, along with an agreement to discuss the further possibility of representing the fan manufacturer on a national basis.

When Stan gave the order to Dave for the fans, the two men discussed other products that Dave sold. Dave sold products for a company that was both a general-line and specialty-line industrial distributor. Included in the general-line products were such items as hand and power tools, cutting tools (e.g., drills, taps, dies), safety equipment, wire rope and slings, fasteners (e.g., nuts, bolts), and fittings (e.g., stainless steel, bronze, and carbon steel flanges, elbows, tees). Included in the specialty-line products were such items as electric motors and generators, motor controls, hydraulic and pneumatic valves and cylinders, rubber dock fenders, and overhead cranes. When the men finally met, they were almost instantly friends, and it was obvious that the opportunities for them to do further business were great.

"One item that really interests me," said Stan, "is PTFE tape. We need some and we will be using a lot of it."

"We have the largest stock of PTFE tape in the country," replied Dave. "We import it directly from Italy. It's high quality and the same standard size as all others on the market: 1/2 inch wide, 0.003 inch thick, and 480 inches long. How much are you interested in?"

"Let's start with 400 rolls," Stan suggested.

PTFE tape was a white, non-adhesive tape used as a pipe thread sealant. It was wrapped around the threads of pipe or fittings before they were screwed together to make a leak-proof seal. The tape first came on the market in the late 1960s at prices as high as $3.60 per roll but, since then, prices had dropped considerably. North American manufacturers were still selling the tape for list prices near $1.80 and were offering dealer discounts between 25 and 50 percent depending on the quantities that dealers bought. Dave was importing the tape from Italy at a landed cost of $0.17 per roll.

"We have a standard price of $1.00 per roll as long as you buy 200 rolls," Dave offered.

"No question. You have an excellent price. How much would you charge M H Sales?"

"I don't know. Who is M H Sales?" asked Dave.

"A small industrial supply company located in my basement. The "H" is for Hope. I share the company with Bruce Malcolm, the "M," and he's in purchasing at Central Power Corporation. M H Sales is a small company and we are looking for additional products to sell. Between Strait Structural and Central Power, we could sell several thousand rolls of PTFE tape each year."

Questions

1. What are the ethical issues?
2. What are the relevant facts?
3. Who are the parties primarily affected?
4. What alternative actions can be considered?
5. What are the ethics of the alternatives?
6. What are the practical constraints?
7. What actions should be taken?

PART II

ROLE-PLAY EXERCISE

RELATIONSHIP STRATEGY
PRESENTATION STRATEGY
PERSONAL SELLING PHILOSOPHY
PRODUCT STRATEGY
CUSTOMER STRATEGY

Developing a Relationship Strategy

SCENARIO

You are an experienced sales representative employed by one of Canada's largest industrial distributors, a company that has been in business for nearly 70 years. Your company is a customer-focused sales organization that is known for its reputation for honesty and fairness. Your company has always been rated highly by customers and, over the past decade, customer satisfaction has been improving. Your sales force is generally respected as the best among all industrial distributors. Your customers come from a variety of industries, including pulp and paper, chemicals, steel manufacturing, shipbuilding, mining, metal working, fishing, and others. Your company also sells some products through smaller industrial distributors, called jobbers, who serve smaller accounts or accounts in geographically remote locations.

CUSTOMER PROFILE

Stan Hope is the senior purchasing agent at Strait Structural Steel, a company that has recently begun operations. He appears to be friendly and professional. Stan has recently placed a large order with you, and you are meeting him in person for the first time.

SALESPERSON PROFILE

Dave MacDonald began working in sales about seven years ago. After a probationary period, he was assigned to a territory in the Atlantic Provinces. He replaced an experienced account representative who was highly respected by his customers and by his employer. After three successful years, Dave was promoted to senior account representative.

PRODUCT

You have a wide assortment of industrial products that can be used by customers of all types.

INSTRUCTIONS

For this role play you will assume the role of Dave MacDonald. To prepare for the role play you should carefully read the case problem at the end of Chapter 5. This information will help you understand the issues that need to be addressed during this role play, in which you meet with Stan Hope. The role of Stan is to be assumed by another student.

During the early stages of the role play, you will want to obtain more information from Stan and resolve any misunderstandings. Your goal is to obtain an order for PTFE tape, but you also want to develop a good longer-term business relationship with Stan and Strait Structural Steel. Keep in mind that ethical decisions can greatly influence the relationship between a salesperson and the customer. Reflect on the important information covered in Chapter 5 as your meeting with Stan progresses.

Service is not a competitive edge, it is *the* competitive edge. People do not buy just things; they also buy expectations. One expectation is that the item they buy will produce the benefits the seller promised. Another is that, if it doesn't, the seller will make good on the promise. —Karl Albright and Ron Zemke, *Service America: Doing Business in the New Economy*

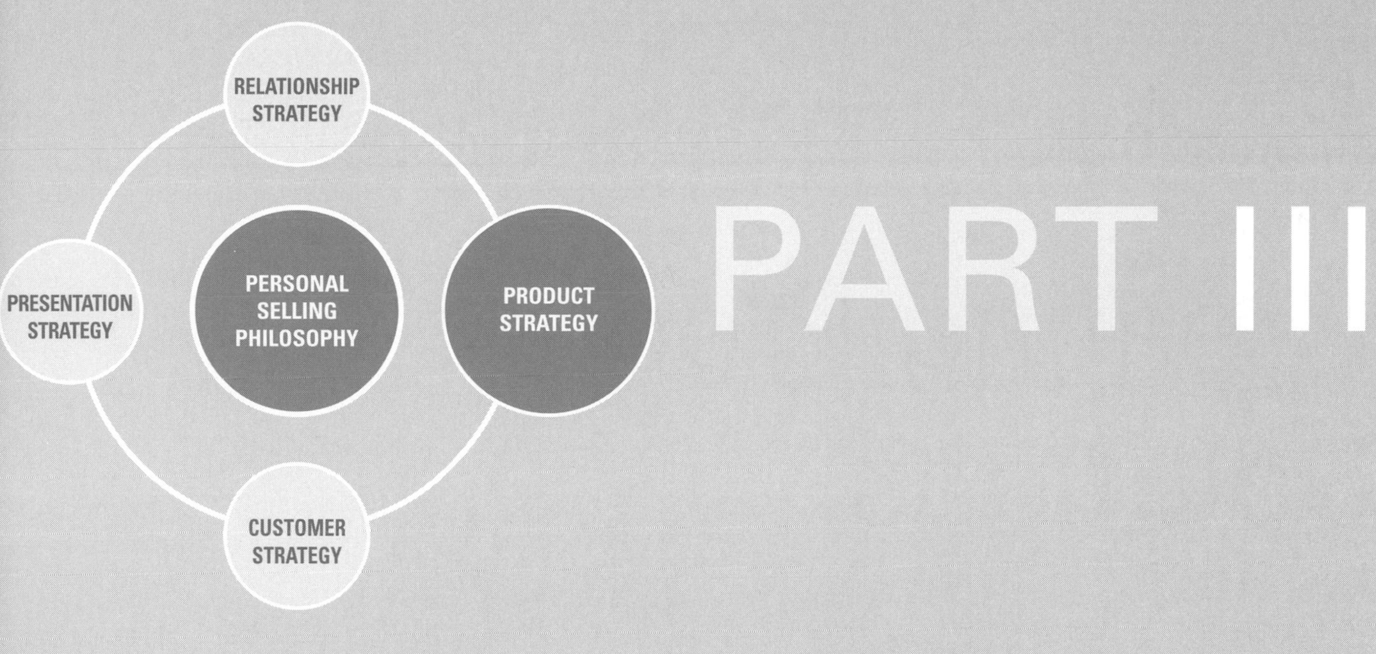

Developing a Product Strategy

Part III examines the importance of having complete and accurate product, company, and competitive knowledge in personal selling. Lack of knowledge in these areas will impair the salesperson's ability to achieve maximum customer service. Part III also describes several value-added selling strategies.

CHAPTER 6

Creating Product Solutions

LEARNING OBJECTIVES

After studying this chapter, you should be able to

1. Explain the importance of developing a product strategy
2. Describe product configuration
3. Identify reasons why salespeople and customers benefit from thorough product knowledge
4. Discuss the most important kinds of product and company information that salespeople use in creating product solutions
5. Describe how knowledge of competition improves personal selling
6. List major sources of product information
7. Explain the difference between product features and buyer benefits
8. Demonstrate how to translate product features into buyer benefits

Thousands of people decide each year to start their own business. Some want independence, some look for large profits, and others hope to have some effect on society's ills. Some of these risk takers are prospects for Cart Works, a company that manages free-standing retail booths—often called kiosks—that operate in shopping malls. Many mall managers have incorporated kiosks to create the busy and happy atmosphere of an open marketplace. Every would-be entrepreneur has choices. Some prefer to start a business on their own, make all the decisions, and reap all the rewards, while others prefer a franchise-type arrangement that includes help with major decisions. Cart Works is searching for people who do not want to go it alone. The company has conducted careful research to determine the best merchandise mix for certain types of malls. The company also provides training for persons who own and operate a kiosk. Sales representatives for Cart Works are involved in two types of personal selling. They are selling the Cart Works concept to would-be entrepreneurs and to mall managers, as the kiosks cannot operate in a mall without approval. The prospective entrepreneur and the mall manager are seeking specific kinds of product and company information.[1]

Developing a Product Solution That Adds Value

The **product strategy** is a well-conceived plan whereby a sales representative becomes a product expert, selling product benefits and creating value-added solutions (see Fig. 6.1). A product strategy helps salespeople make effective decisions concerning the selection and positioning of products or services to meet identified customer needs.

product strategy A well-conceived plan for sales that emphasizes acquiring extensive product knowledge, learning to select and communicate appropriate product benefits that will appeal to the customer, and creating value-added solutions.

Developing a product strategy has become more challenging for two reasons. First, customers are increasingly seeking a customized product solution. The industrial-age model of making things cheaper by making them the same is no longer acceptable in many markets. The customized product solution appeals to the customer's desire for choices. Noted author and speaker Regis McKenna says that choice has become a higher value than brand.[2] Second, information is the strategic resource used by today's salespeople. In this era of information overload, salespeople are expected to know which information has value and which information should be ignored. Becoming a product expert is the ultimate challenge in the information age. Most salespeople have adopted a broad definition of the term "product" to encompass information, services, ideas, tangible products, or some combination of these that satisfies the customer's needs.[3] Let's look at the sales process at two firms.

> Strategic Vista International, a Markham, Ontario–based technology leader in video security and surveillance, has begun manufacturing and distributing a new line of digital video monitoring solutions that allows customers to view multiple camera locations from anywhere in the world at any time. Salespeople can configure a range of product solutions to satisfy the needs of most consumers and small and medium-sized businesses.[4]

Strategic/Consultative Selling Model	
Strategic step	**Prescription**
Develop a Personal Selling Philosophy	✓ Value Personal Selling ✓ Adopt Marketing Concept ✓ Become a Problem Solver/Partner
Develop a Relationship Strategy	✓ Project positive, professional image ✓ Practise communication-style flexing ✓ Behave ethically
Develop a Product Strategy	• Become a product expert • Sell specific benefits • Configure value-added solutions

Figure 6.1 Developing a product strategy enables the salesperson to custom fit products or services to the customer's needs.

> Loki Management Systems, a Delta, B.C.–based software developer, has provided workforce management solutions to customers in the health-care, hospitality, and telecommunications industries. Its product solutions help companies create employee work schedules, increase employee satisfaction and retention, reduce staffing and overtime costs, save management time, and reduce payroll errors.[5]

From the customer's point of view, salespeople employed by Strategic Vista International and Loki Management Systems are selling primarily information and expertise. Customers view the problem-solving ability these salespeople provide as the product. When you sell a complex product, your knowledge and expertise create value.

TAILORING THE PRODUCT STRATEGY

A product strategy should be tailored to the customer's buying needs (see Fig. 6.2). Transactional buyers are usually well aware of their needs. Most of these customers have conducted their own research and have a good understanding of the product that will meet their needs. The office manager who frequently buys a large amount of copy paper knows that this standard item can be purchased from several vendors, and that the quality of the paper usually does not vary from one vendor to another. The consultative buyer will usually lack needs awareness and want help to evaluate possible solutions. This customer usually needs a customized product solution, as it appeals to the customer's desire for choices that are tailored to his or her needs. Developing a product strategy for the relationship customer usually offers the greatest challenge. Study of the prospective partner can be very time consuming, but the rewards of a successful partnership may be substantial. In some cases, the company that wishes to form a partnership with a new customer must be prepared to make a large investment in capital-intensive technology and additional personnel.[6]

THE EXPLOSION OF PRODUCT OPTIONS

Domestic and global markets are overflowing with a vast array of goods and services. In some industries the number of new products introduced each year is mind-boggling. Makers of consumer products, for example, churn out as

	Transactional Sale	Consultative Sale	Relationship Sale
Product characteristics	• Standard generic items • Well understood • Easily substitutable	• Hidden features • Differentiated choices • Customizable	• High cost importance • Limited substitutability

Figure 6.2 The product strategy can be tailored to meet the needs of transactional, consultative, and relationship buyers.
Source: Adapted from Neil Rackham and John R. DeVincentis, *Rethinking the Sales Force* (New York: McGraw-Hill, 1999), p. 79.

many as 30 000 new products each year. Want to buy a product in the securities and financial services field? In the fastest-growing segment—mutual funds—there are now approximately 80 fund management companies and 144 dealer firms in Canada that sell 1800 different mutual funds.[7] For the customer, this much variety creates a "good news–bad news" situation. The good news is that almost all buyers have a choice when it comes to purchasing a product or service; people like to compare various options. The bad news is that having so many choices often complicates the buying process.

One of the most important roles of the salesperson is to simplify the customer's study of the product choices. Later in this chapter we discuss how product features (information) can add value when converted into specific benefits (knowledge) that can help the buyer make an intelligent buying decision.

CREATING SOLUTIONS WITH PRODUCT CONFIGURATION

The challenge facing both customers and salespeople in this era of information overload is deciding which product applications, or combination of applications, will solve the customer's buying problem. If the customer has complex buying needs, then the salesperson may have to bring together many parts of the company's product mix to develop a custom-fitted solution. The product selection process is often referred to as **product configuration**. Salespeople representing Cisco Systems are often involved in the sale of new products to new and established customers. They use Cybrant Solutions Architect software to quickly identify solutions. The software helps salespeople ask prospects the right questions to discover their needs and then configures a solution that best meets those needs.[8] Product configuration is no less important in retail situations where the salesperson is selling a complex product. Assembling a professional wardrobe, preparing an interior design for a home or office, or putting together an automobile lease plan involves product configuration.

product configuration The solution of complex buying needs, for instance when the salesperson brings together many different parts of the company's product mix or uses specialized software to develop a custom-fitted solution.

Many companies are using product configuration software to develop customized product solutions quickly and accurately. Product configuration software incorporates product selection criteria and associates them directly with customer requirements. Members of the sales force can use the sales configurator to identify product options, prices, delivery schedules, and other parts of the product mix, while working interactively with the customer. Most of today's product configuration software can be integrated with software programs for customer relationship management (CRM) such as ACT!, Goldmine, or Maximize. In addition to improving the quality of the sales proposal, CRM software reduces the time-consuming process of manually preparing written proposals.

PREPARING WRITTEN PROPOSALS

Written proposals are frequently part of the salesperson's product strategy. It is only natural that some buyers will want the proposed solution put in

written proposal A specific plan of action based on the facts, assumptions, and supporting documentation about a buying solution that are included in the sales presentation. Written proposals vary in terms of format and content.

writing. A **written proposal** can be defined as a specific plan of action based on the facts, assumptions, and supporting documentation about a buying solution that are included in the sales presentation.[9] A well-written proposal adds value to the product solution and can set you apart from the competition. It offers the buyer reassurance that you will deliver what you have promised. Written proposals vary in terms of format and content. Many government agencies, and some large companies, issue a request for proposal (RFP) that specifies the format of the proposal. Some written proposals follow a specific format developed by the company. The length of a proposal can vary from a single page to dozens of pages for a complex product. Most effective proposals include the following parts:

Budget and overview. Tell the prospect the cost of the solution you have prescribed. Be specific as you describe the product or service features to be provided, and itemize the price.

Objective. Expressed in terms of benefits, a tangible objective might be "to reduce payroll expense by 10 percent." An intangible objective might be stated as "to increase business security offered by a company with a reputation for dependability." Focus objectives on benefits that relate directly to the customer's need.

Strategy. Briefly describe how you will meet your objective. How will you fulfill the obligations you have described in your proposal? In some cases this section of your proposal includes specific language: "Your account will be assigned to Susan Murray, our senior lease representative."

Schedule. Establish a time frame for meeting your objective. This might involve the confirmation of dates with regard to acquisition, shipping, or installation.

Rationale. With a mixture of logic and emotion, present your rationale for taking action now. Once again, the emphasis should be on benefits, not features.[10]

The proposal should be printed on quality paper and free of any errors in spelling, grammar, or punctuation. Before completing the proposal, review the content one more time to be sure you have addressed all of the customer's concerns. Bob Kantin, author of *Sales Proposals Kit for Dummies,* says the proposal is really the first "product" that the customer receives from you, so be sure it is perfect.[11]

The remainder of this chapter is divided into five major sections. The first two examine the kinds of product information and company information required by the salesperson. The third section describes the type of information about the competition that is helpful to salespeople. Sources of information are covered in the fourth section, and the fifth section describes how product features can be translated into buyer benefits.

This salesperson is making a follow-up call to determine if the customer needs any additional information regarding the written proposal, which was sent earlier.

SELLING MENTOR

Writing Effective Sales Letters

Salespeople are increasingly using sales letters to describe features and benefits, to position products, to build relationships, and to provide assurances to customers. There are several standard rules that apply to all written sales letters. These include:

1. Sales letters should follow the standard visual format of a business letter. They should contain, in the following order, either a letterhead or sender's address, date, inside address (the same as on the outside of the envelope), salutation, body, complimentary closing, typed name and handwritten signature of sender, and a notation of enclosures (if there are any).
2. Placement of the letter on the paper should provide balanced white space bordering the entire letter. Three to five blank lines should separate the date and inside address; a single blank line should separate the inside address and the salutation, the salutation and the opening paragraph of the letter, and each paragraph. A single blank line should separate the last paragraph and the complimentary closing. Single spacing should generally be used within the paragraphs.
3. Proper business punctuation includes a colon after the salutation and a comma after the complimentary closing.
4. Most sales letters include at least three paragraphs. The first paragraph should indicate why you are writing the letter, the second paragraph should be a summary of the benefits proposed, and the third paragraph should state what the next action step will be for the salesperson, the customer, or both.
5. Proper grammar and spelling must be used throughout the entire letter. Business letters provide opportunities to build a stronger relationship with the customer and to close the sale. Improper placement, punctuation, spelling errors, or weak content conveys a negative impression to the reader and may result in a lost sale.
6. The use of the personal pronoun "I" should be minimized in the sales letter. To keep the letter focused on the customer's needs, the pronouns "you" and "your" should appear throughout the body of the letter.

Product knowledge training is an ongoing activity in the life of a salesperson.

Becoming a Product Expert

One of the major challenges facing salespeople is winning the customer's trust. A survey reported in *Sales & Marketing Management* ranked product knowledge as the number one characteristic of salespeople who are able to build trust.[12] Ideally, a salesperson will possess product knowledge that meets and exceeds customer expectations.

This section reviews some of the most common product information categories: (1) product development and quality improvement processes, (2) performance data and specifications, (3) maintenance and service contracts, and (4) price and delivery. Each is important as a potential source of knowledge concerning the product or service.

PRODUCT DEVELOPMENT AND QUALITY IMPROVEMENT PROCESSES

product development The testing, modifying, and retesting of an idea for a product several times before offering it to the customer.

Companies spend large amounts of money in the development of their products. In **product development** the original idea for a product or service is tested, modified, and retested several times before it is offered to the customer. Each modifications is made to improve the product. Salespeople should be familiar with a product's development history. Often this information will set the stage for stronger sales appeals.

Wabi Iron and Steel Corp. in New Liskeard, Ontario, manufactures components for machinery that must operate under adverse conditions. The company keeps ahead of its competitors by systematically developing and testing improved alloys, in close co-operation with one of its major cus-

EVERYONE SELLS

Writing Spreads the Word

Rudolf Melik, CEO of Laval, Quebec–based Tenrox Inc. recognized he had a problem common to many smaller businesses: How do you compete with large competitors who can spend millions of dollars on marketing when you can afford only a much smaller amount? His solution: write a book. His company makes software that tracks time and expenses for project-driven businesses. With his brother, Ludwig, vice-president of sales and marketing, Rudolf wrote a book on streamlining consulting processes. Within only a few months, about a hundred companies requested a copy. Rudolf Melik says, "Some of those are new customers who are being courted by our sales reps. The book helps them understand our products and explains the benefits." Rudolph Melik has also been invited to speak at Boston's Project Management Institute where he will get to talk to 60 decision makers from major U.S. companies. "The same exposure would cost millions in advertising," says Rudolf Melik.[a]

tomers. It has been able to develop components exclusively for this customer, and its success has given Wabi the profile it needs to compete in new markets. In 2001, Wabi won an Ontario Global Traders Award.[13]

Quality improvement continues to be an important long-term business strategy for most successful companies. Salespeople need to identify processes for quality improvement that provide a competitive advantage and be prepared to discuss this information during the sales presentation. Motorola and Xerox provide examples of companies that have won awards for implementing important quality controls. **Quality control**, which involves measuring products and services against established standards, is one dimension of the typical quality improvement process. At Pfizer Inc., salespeople in the pharmaceutical group receive extensive training as an important quality control. Sales representatives must demonstrate their ability to present product information to physicians accurately and effectively.[14]

quality control The evaluation or testing of products against established standards. This has important sales appeal when used by the salesperson to convince a prospect of a product's quality.

Many companies are investing a great deal of time and money to achieve International Organization for Standardization (ISO) 9000 certification. ISO is an internationally recognized quality standard that certifies the process a company uses to develop a product or service. Independent auditors are used to verify that a company is in compliance with the standards. Purchasers recognize that ISO 9000 certification assures them a level of certainty regarding product quality.[15]

www.iso.org

PERFORMANCE DATA AND SPECIFICATIONS

Most potential buyers are interested in performance data and specifications. Here are some typical questions that might be raised by prospects:

> "What is the frequency response for this stereo loudspeaker?"
>
> "What is the anticipated rate of return on this mutual fund?"
>
> "What is the energy consumption rating for this appliance?"

A salesperson must be prepared to address these types of questions in the written sales proposal and the sales presentation. Performance data are especially critical when the customer is attempting to compare the merits of one product with another.

To become familiar with the performance of Whirlpool appliances, salespeople literally live the brand. The company rented and redesigned an eight-bedroom farmhouse near corporate headquarters and outfitted it with Whirlpool dishwashers, refrigerators, washers, dryers, and microwaves. Salespeople, in groups of eight, live at the house for two months and use all of the appliances. Whirlpool engineers visit the home and present information on design, performance data, and specifications. After completing the live-in training, salespeople report that the experience makes a difference in their performance. A recent graduate of the training program says, "I have a confidence level that's making a difference in my client contacts."[16]

BOC converts its product data and specifications into benefits. A product strategy with emphasis on selling benefits adds value because time-starved customers quickly understand how the product meets and possibly exceeds their needs. Note how BOC has quantified its benefits.

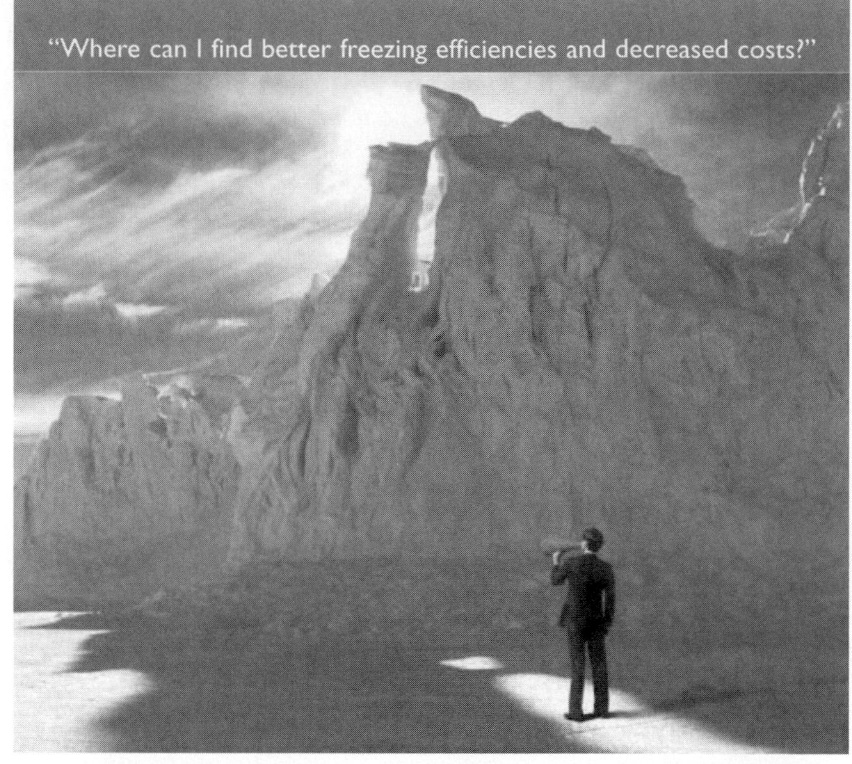

"Where can I find better freezing efficiencies and decreased costs?"

Would you benefit from efficiency improvements associated with faster freezing? Do you want to reduce your freezing costs? Is dehydration loss melting away your profits?

The world's ***only*** cryogenic Impingement Freezer might just be your coolest solution ever! Besides offering the lowest dehydration rate and a higher freezing capacity, the BOC Cryogenic Impingement Freezer provides a faster freeze than most freezing methods. It can also provide the highest efficiencies in the industry.

Your search may be over. Chill out with the BOC Cryogenic Impingement Freezer! For additional information, please call **1-800-755-9277** or email us at **boc.food@us.gases.boc.com**.

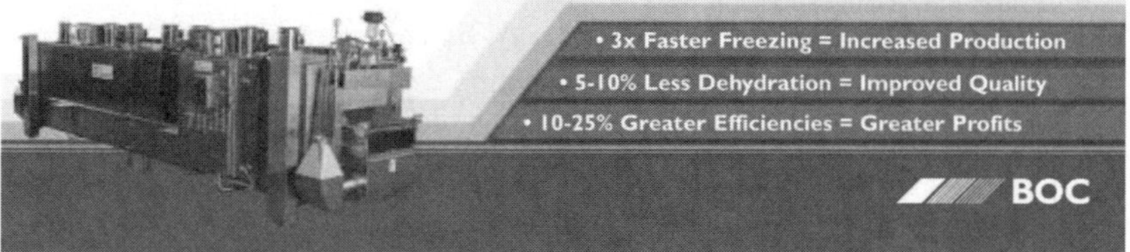

• 3x Faster Freezing = Increased Production
• 5-10% Less Dehydration = Improved Quality
• 10-25% Greater Efficiencies = Greater Profits
BOC

MAINTENANCE AND SERVICE CONTRACTS

Prospects often want information concerning maintenance and care requirements for the products they purchase. The salesperson who can quickly and accurately provide this information will have the edge. Proper maintenance will usually extend the life of the product, so this information should be provided at the time of the sale.

Today, many salespeople are developing customized service agreements that incorporate the customer's special priorities, feelings, and needs. They work hard to acquire a real understanding of the customer's specific service criteria. If call-return expectations are very important to the customer, the frequency and quantity of product-related visits per week or month can be included in the service contract. Customized service agreements add value to the sale and help protect your business from the competition.[17]

PRICE AND DELIVERY

Potential buyers expect salespeople to be well versed in price and delivery policies on their products. If a salesperson has pricing authority, buyers perceive the person as someone with whom they can really talk business. The ability to set prices puts the salesperson in a stronger position.[18] Decision-making authority in the area of pricing gives the salesperson more power and responsibility. If the salesperson negotiates a price that is too low, the company may lose money on the sale. Price objections represent one of the most common barriers to closing a sale, so salespeople need to be well prepared in this area.

In most situations the price quotation should be accompanied by information that creates value in the mind of the customer. The process of determining whether or not the proposal adds value is often called **quantifying the solution**. When the purchase represents a major buying decision, such as the purchase of a new computer system, quantifying the solution is important. One way to quantify the solution is to conduct a cost–benefit analysis to determine the actual cost of the purchase and savings the buyer can anticipate from the investment (see Table 6.1 on page 136).

quantifying the solution The process of determining if a sales proposal adds value. Quantifying the solution is especially important in situations where the purchase represents a major buying decision.

ROI SELLING APPEALS

As products and services become more complex and more expensive, customers are more likely to look at the financial reasons for buying. This is especially true in business-to-business selling. Salespeople who can develop a sales proposal that contains specific information on return on investment (ROI) are more likely to get a favourable response from key decision makers. Chief financial officers, for example, are more inclined to approve an expensive purchase if it results in a good return on investment.[19]

Performing accurate ROI calculations typically requires the collection of detailed financial information. You may need to help the prospect collect information within the company to build a case for the purchase. BAX Global, with offices throughout Canada and the United States, offers customers multi-modal shipping solutions. It has the capabilities to employ more than one mode of transportation for a customer. In order to develop a customized solution for the customer, the sales representative must collect a great deal of data from the prospect. Transportation modes (e.g., trucks, trains, ships, airplanes) vary in terms of cost, speed, dependability, frequency, and other criteria, so preparation of the sales proposal can be a complicated process.[20]

The use of ROI selling requires more work up front, but it may lead to shorter sales cycles. The salesperson who is not well schooled in financial issues or who cannot compute and supply price information accurately may be at a serious disadvantage. In Chapter 7, we discuss how to position products according to price.

Table 6.1

Quantifying the Solution with Cost–Benefit Analysis

Quantifying the solution often involves a carefully prepared cost-benefit analysis. This example compares the higher-priced Phoenix semitruck trailer with the lower-priced FB model, which is a competing product.

Cost Savings of the Phoenix Versus FB Model for a 10-Year Period (All Prices Are Approximate)

	Cost Savings
Stainless steel bulkhead (savings on sandblasting and painting)	$ 425.00
Stainless steel rear door frame (savings on painting)	425.00
Air ride suspension (better fuel mileage, longer tire life, longer brake life)	3 750.00
Hardwood or aluminum scuff (savings from freight damages and replacement of scuff)	1 000.00
LED lights (lasts longer; approximate savings: $50 per year 10 years)	500.00
Light protectors (save $50 per year on replacement 10 years)	500.00
Threshold plate (saves damage to entry of trailer)	200.00
Internal rail reinforcement (saves damage to lower rail and back panels)	500.00
Stainless steel screws for light attachment (savings on replacement cost)	200.00
Domestic oak premium floor—1 (should last 10 years under normal conditions)	1 000.00
Doors—aluminum inner and outer skin, outside white finish, inside mill finish, fastened by five aluminum hinges (savings over life of trailer)	750.00
Five-year warranty in addition to standard warranty covers bulkhead rust, LED lights, floor, scuff liner, glad hands, rear frame, mud flap assembly, and threshold plate (Phoenix provides a higher trade-in value)	1 500.00
Total approximate savings of Phoenix over 10-year period (All the preceding is standard equipment on a Phoenix; this trailer will sell for $23 500; an FB standard trailer would sell for $19 500)	$10 750.00
Less additional initial cost of Phoenix over FB standard	4 000.00
Overall cost savings of Phoenix over FB trailer	**$ 6 750.00**

Know Your Company

Many companies recognize that sales personnel are often the firm's closest point of contact with the customer, and therefore they need to be well informed. The customer's mental image of the organization from which he or she is buying is formed entirely through contact with a sales representative. In the eyes of the customer, the salesperson is the company.

Never underestimate information about the company itself as a strong appeal that can be used during the sales presentation. This is especially true in situations in which products are similar. Life insurance, for example, can be purchased from a large number of firms at nearly identical rates. Some companies, such as 3M, Procter & Gamble, IBM, and TD Waterhouse, have what might be called "brand power," because these companies and the products they sell are well known. However, if you are selling teak outdoor furniture made by Rock Wood Casual Furniture of Oakville, Ontario, or outsourced e-mail services offered by The Electric Mail Company Inc. of Burnaby, B.C., you may find it necessary to spend time providing information about your company.

Acquiring knowledge about your company is an important step toward developing complete product knowledge. In this section we examine the types of information needed in most selling situations.

COMPANY CULTURE AND ORGANIZATION

Many salespeople take special pride in the company they work for. Salespeople employed by Pfizer Canada feel good that their company has been consistently chosen among the best companies to work for in Canada.[21] Pride can also develop in smaller companies. Vancouver-based Intrinsyc Software Inc. attributes its success, at least in part, to giving employees challenging work and the opportunity to be creative. President Derek Spratt says, "We're a young high-tech firm with an environment that challenges employees to learn more. You don't stagnate at Intrinsyc. People roll out of bed and get excited about going to work every day."[22]

Every organization has its own unique culture. **Organizational culture** is a collection of beliefs, behaviours, and work patterns held in common by people employed by a specific firm. Most organizations over a period of time tend to take on distinct norms and practices. At British Columbia Buildings Corporation, a statement of core values that communicates what the company holds important guides employees. Research indicates that the customer orientation of a firm's salespeople will be influenced by the organization's culture. A supportive culture that encourages salespeople to offer tailor-made solutions to buyer problems will set the stage for long-term partnerships.[23]

organizational culture A collection of beliefs, behaviours, and work patterns held in common by people employed by a specific firm.

Many prospects will use the past performance of a company to evaluate the quality of the current product offering. If the company has enjoyed success in the past, there is good reason to believe that the future will be bright. At least this is the way most prospects are likely to view such an organization.

Companies such as British Columbia Buildings Corporation communicate their core values to customers, suppliers, employees, and other stakeholders.

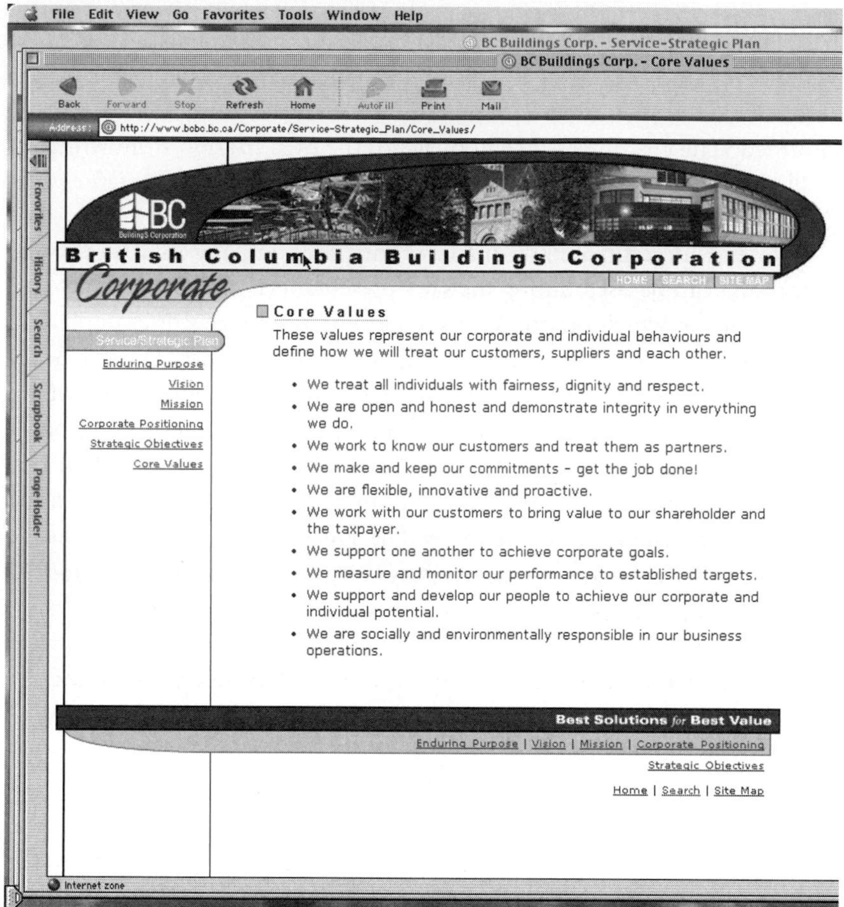

COMPANY SUPPORT FOR PRODUCT

Progressive marketers support the products they sell. When customers buy promotional products from Toronto-based distributor Aware Marketing Group Ltd., they receive an after-sale phone call to gauge their level of satisfaction. Founder Craig Morantz says customers are asked four questions: "Did we meet expectations on this order? Are you satisfied with the product quality? Are you satisfied with communications during the order? And did we keep you updated on the status of the order?" This focus on customer satisfaction has been an important factor in the company's rapid growth.[24] Husky Injection Molding Systems Ltd. of Bolton, Ontario, is a world-class manufacturer of injection moulding machinery. The company frequently sends teams of sales and technical specialists to call on major accounts. Mike Urquhart, vice-president of sales, says: "Our spare parts manager is one of the key people we often include in our sales presentations. It's his role to say, 'Here's how we back you up. Here's how we can help you when you have problems.' This is one way we convince customers that we are committed to helping them before, during, and after the sale."[25]

Know Your Competition

Acquiring knowledge of your competition is another important step toward developing complete product knowledge. Salespeople who have knowledge of their competitors' strengths and weaknesses are better able to understand their own position, and adjust their selling strategy accordingly.[26] Prospects often raise specific questions concerning competing firms. If you cannot provide answers or if your answers are vague, the sale may be lost.

YOUR ATTITUDE TOWARD YOUR COMPETITION

Regardless of how impressive your product is, the customer will naturally seek information about similar products sold by other companies. Therefore, you must acquire facts about competing products before the sales presentation. Once armed with this information, you are more confident in your ability to handle questions about the competition.

The attitude you display toward your competition is of the utmost importance. Every salesperson should develop a set of basic beliefs about the best way of dealing with competing products. Here are a few helpful guidelines:

1. In most cases, do not refer to the competition during the sales presentation. This shifts the focus of attention to competing products, which is usually not desirable.
2. Never discuss the competition unless you have all your facts straight. Your credibility will suffer if you make inaccurate statements. If you do not know the answer to a specific question, simply say, "I do not know."
3. Avoid criticizing the competition. You may be called on to make direct comparisons between your product and competing products. In these situations, stick to the facts and avoid emotional comments about apparent or real weaknesses.
4. Be prepared to add value. The competition may come to your prospect with a comparative advantage in price, delivery, or some other area. Be prepared to neutralize the competitor's proposal with a value-added approach.

Customers appreciate an accurate, fair, and honest presentation of the facts. They generally resent highly critical remarks about the competition. Avoid mudslinging at all costs. Fairness is a virtue that people greatly admire.

BECOME AN INDUSTRY EXPERT

Salespeople need to become experts in the industry they represent. In many cases this means moving beyond the role of product specialist and becoming a business analyst. Staying current and developing an understanding of business processes takes time and may require additional education.[27] If, for

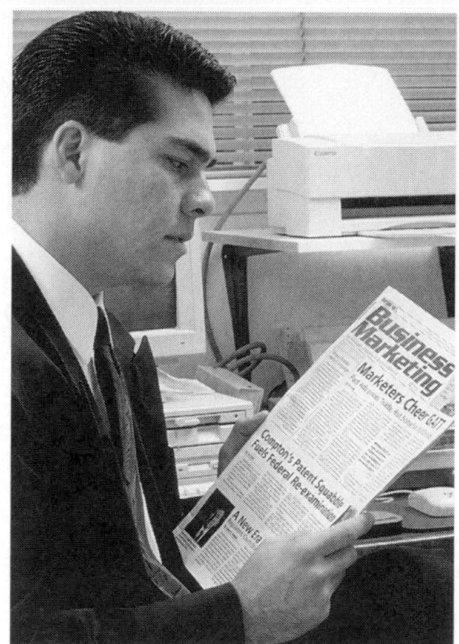

Salespeople should closely examine the sources of information about their products and the industries where these products are used.

example, your clients work in the banking industry, read the appropriate trade journals and become active in professional associations that serve bankers' needs.

Sources of Product Information

There are several sources of product information available to salespeople. Some of the most common include: (1) product literature developed by the company, (2) sales training programs, (3) plant tours, (4) internal sales and sales support team members, (5) customers, (6) the product, (7) the Internet, and (8) publications.

PRODUCT LITERATURE

Most companies prepare materials that provide a detailed description of their product. This information is usually quite informative, and salespeople should review it carefully. If the company markets a number of products, a sales catalogue is usually developed. To save salespeople time, many companies give them computer software that provides a constantly updated, online product catalogue. Advertisements, promotional brochures, and audio cassettes or compact discs can also be a valuable source of product information. Some salespeople develop their own product literature with the aid of electronic marketing encyclopedias. These libraries put a wide range of sales and marketing information at your fingertips. EnCyc Inc., for example, has developed an encyclopedia that allows salespeople to create PowerPoint presentations automatically by pulling slides from an organized database.[28]

SALES TRAINING PROGRAMS

As noted previously, company-sponsored sales training programs frequently focus on product knowledge. These programs are delivered in a variety of formats. In addition to traditional classroom presentations, companies can use online learning, interactive distance learning networks delivered via satellite, and other forms of technology.

E-learning has become popular because it is inexpensive and fast, and it can be geared to the flexible schedules of salespeople who can review the latest product information by turning on their laptop. The Internet is also an excellent source of technical reports on various products. Many salespeople turn to the Internet to access information concerning competing products.

PLANT TOURS

Many companies believe that salespeople should visit the manufacturing plant and see the production process first-hand. Such tours not only provide valuable product information but also increase the salesperson's enthusiasm for the product. A new salesperson may spend several days at the plant getting acquainted with the production process. Experienced personnel within the organization can also benefit from plant tours.

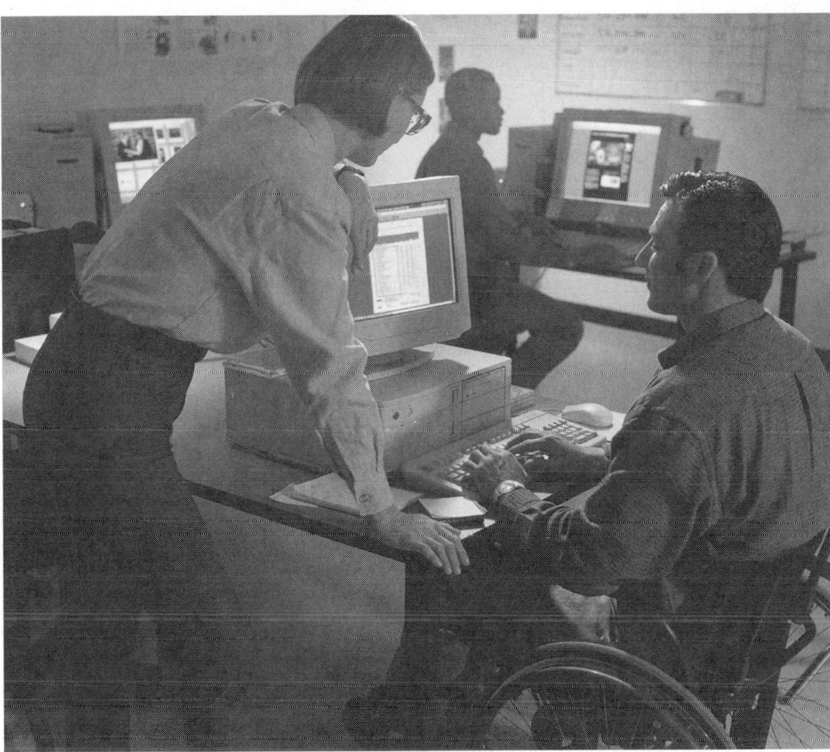

Surveys indicate that product knowledge training should be a basic element of any sales training program.

CUSTOMER RELATIONSHIP MANAGEMENT WITH TECHNOLOGY

Starting Fast with CRM

New salespeople can be overwhelmed by the amount of information they need to master. This includes information about the company and its processes, products, and customers. Companies can now make learning easier with information technology. Information about the company and its processes can be stored on the company's network, on its virtual private network, or on CD-ROM. Computer-based training permits new employees to learn at their own pace about a product's specifications, features, benefits, uses, and selling points.

Companies can now provide salespeople with software that they can use to accurately and effectively create product solutions. Product configuration software allows salespeople to select the components necessary to assemble a custom-tailored solution to meet their prospects' needs. This software guides users through the product selection process while ensuring that the components will be compatible with one another.

Companies can deliver to new salespeople a rich body of customer information through a strong commitment to the use of customer relationship management (CRM) software. The salesperson who carefully records his or her business and relationship contacts with customers and prospects will, over time, accumulate a valuable store of information. A new salesperson taking over these accounts can quickly come up to speed with these people and their needs. (See the exercise Finding Product Information in CRM on page 150 for more information.)

INTERNAL SALES AND SALES SUPPORT TEAM MEMBERS

Team selling has become popular, in part, because many complex sales require the expertise of several sales and sales support personnel. Expertise in the areas of product design, finance, or transportation may be needed to develop an effective sales proposal. Pooled commissions are sometimes used to encourage team members to share information and work as a team.

CUSTOMERS

Persons who actually use the product can be an important source of information. They have observed its performance under actual working conditions and can provide an objective assessment of the product's strengths and weaknesses. Some companies collect testimonials from satisfied customers and make this persuasive information available to the sales staff.

THE PRODUCT

The product itself should not be overlooked as a source of valuable information. Salespeople should closely examine and, if possible, use each item they sell to become familiar with its features. Investigation, use, and careful evaluation of the product will provide a salesperson with additional confidence.

PUBLICATIONS

www.bizlink.com/cangrocer.htm

www.adage.com AdAge.com

www.consumerreports.com

Trade and technical publications such as *Canadian Grocer* and *Advertising Age* provide valuable product and industry information. Popular magazines and the business section of the newspaper also offer salespeople considerable information about their products and their competition. Publications such as *Consumer Reports* test products extensively and report the findings in non-technical language for the benefit of consumers. These reports are a valuable source of information.

A WORD OF CAUTION

Is it possible to be overly prepared? Can salespeople know too much about the products and services they sell? The answer to both questions is generally no. Communication problems can arise, however, if the salesperson does not accurately gauge the prospect's level of understanding. There is always the danger that a knowledgeable salesperson will overwhelm the potential buyer with facts and figures. This problem can be avoided when salespeople adopt the feature–benefit strategy.

Adding Value with a Feature–Benefit Strategy

Frederick W. Smith, founder of Federal Express, first proposed the concept of overnight delivery in a paper that he wrote as an undergraduate at Yale University. The now-famous paper was given a C by his professor. Many

DOONESBURY **by Garry Trudeau**

years later Smith said, "I don't think that we understood our real goal when we first started Federal Express. We thought that we were selling the transportation of goods; in fact, we were selling peace of mind."[29]

Throughout this chapter we emphasize the importance of acquiring information on the features of your product, company, and competition. Now it is important to point out that successful sales presentations translate product features into buyer benefits. The "peace of mind" that Frederick W. Smith mentioned is a good example of a buyer benefit. Only when a product feature is converted to a buyer benefit does it make an impact on the customer. People do not buy features; they buy benefits.

DISTINGUISH BETWEEN FEATURES AND BENEFITS

To be sure we understand the difference between a product feature and a buyer benefit, let us define these two terms.

> A **product feature** is information or a characteristic of your product or service. Features often relate to craftsmanship, design, durability, and economy of operation. They may reveal how the product was developed and manufactured. Product features are often described in the technical section of the written sales proposal and in the literature provided by the manufacturer.

product feature Anything that a customer can feel, see, hear, taste, smell, or measure to answer the question, "What is it?" Features include craftsmanship, durability, design, and economy of operation.

> A **buyer benefit** is whatever provides the consumer with personal advantage or gain. It answers the question, "How will I benefit from owning or using the product?"

buyer benefit Something that provides the customer with personal advantage or gain to answer the question, "How will the customer benefit from owning or using the product?"

If you mention to a prospect that a certain tire has a four-ply rating, you are talking about a product feature. If you go on to point out that this tire will provide greater safety, last longer, and reduce your gas consumption, you are pointing out benefits.

GENERAL VERSUS SPECIFIC BENEFITS

Neil Rackham, author of *The SPIN Selling Fieldbook*, says that a statement can only be a benefit if it meets a specific need expressed by the buyer. When you

www.huthwaite.com

link a benefit to a buyer's expressed need, you demonstrate that you can help solve a problem that has been described by the customer. A general benefit shows how a feature can be helpful to a buyer, but it does not relate to a specific need expressed by the buyer. Here are two examples of specific benefits:

> "Our water purification system meets the exact specifications you have given us for environmental compliance."
>
> "Our XP400 model meets the safety criteria you've spelled out."

Neil Rackham says that benefit statements linked to the customer's expressed need are especially effective in large and complex sales.[30]

Some sales training programs suggest that salespeople need to include advantages in the sales presentation. Advantages are characteristics of the product (i.e., features) that can be used or will help the buyer. Consider the advantage in the following statement: "Prior to shipping, all of our containers are double wrapped. This means that our product is completely free from contamination when it arrives at your hospital."

Some salespeople develop an advantage statement for each important product feature. Unfortunately, these advantages are often included in the sales presentation even when the buyer has not expressed a need for this information. When this happens, the advantage can be described as a general benefit.

Successful salespeople focus on specific benefits that relate to a need explicitly expressed by the customer. Less successful salespeople take the position that the best way to create value is to present as many benefits as possible. High-performance salespeople work hard to discover which benefits the customer really cares about. Today's customer measures value by how well your product benefits fit their needs.[31] Jerry Vass, consultant and sales trainer, says the buyer has three questions about the product you sell: So what? What's in it for me? and Can you prove it? He cautions salespeople to avoid burying the prospect with features that, by themselves, would not answer any of these questions. Vass also believes that very few salespeople have the ability to sell benefits rather than features.[32]

USE BRIDGE STATEMENTS

bridge statement A transitional phrase that connects one or more product features with potential customer benefits.

We know that people buy benefits, not features. One of the best ways to present benefits is to use a bridge statement. A **bridge statement** is a transitional phrase that connects a statement of features with a statement of benefits. This method permits customers to connect the features of your product to the benefits they will receive. A sales representative for a food wholesaler, for example, might use a bridge statement to introduce a new snack food: "This product is nationally advertised, which means you will benefit from more presold customers." Some companies prefer to state the benefit first and the feature second. When this occurs, the bridge statement may be a word such as "because." For example: "You will experience faster turnover and increased profits because the first order includes an attractive display rack."

Noggin 250
Features & Benefits

The Noggin 250 combines the latest subsurface imaging technology with ease-of-use and affordability. Some features and benefits of the Noggin 250 include:

Features	Benefits
• Noggin unit contains transmitter, receiver, and console electronics in one "box"	→ minimal setup necessary → easy to transport and use → no external cables to trip over
• weighs 16 lbs	→ easily portable → low shipping costs → cuts down on user fatigue in the field
• 12V battery operated	→ enables portability → no external power source needed
• can locate metallic and non-metallic objects	→ can be used for virtually all of your subsurface investigations
• easily operated by one person	→ no need for a large survey crew
• no experience necessary to operate	→ can be used right "out of the box"
• includes SpiView software	→ no need to buy operating software → provides the user with real-time data display
• weatherproof and will run reliably at -40°C to +40°C	→ can be used dependably in virtually any harsh environment
• rugged exterior shell	→ greatly reduces the likelihood of damage to electronics

For more information on Noggin or SpiView, please contact Sensors & Software Inc. at the address below.

209

subsurface imaging solutions

Sensors & Software Inc.
1040 Stacey Court
Mississauga, ON L4W 2X8 Canada
Tel: (905) 624-8909
Fax: (905) 624-9365
E-mail: sales@sensoft.ca
Website: www.sensoft.ca

Sensors & Software knows that customers buy benefits, not features. Salespeople who can link product features to customer benefits are more successful.

IDENTIFY FEATURES AND BENEFITS

A careful analysis of the product will help identify both product features and customer benefits. Once all the important features are identified, arrange them in logical order. Then write beside each feature the most important benefit the customer will derive from that feature. Finally, prepare a series of bridge statements to connect the appropriate features and benefits. Using this three-step approach, a hotel selling conference and convention services, and a manufacturer selling electric motors used to power mining equipment, developed feature–benefit worksheets (see Tables 6.2 and 6.3 on page 147). Notice how each feature is translated into a benefit that would be important to someone purchasing these products and services. Table 6.3 reminds us that company features can be converted to benefits.

THE CUSTOMER'S PERSPECTIVE

Customer Needs Determine New Product Sales Success

When Xerox introduced the 9200 mega-copier, sales were far below expectations. Buyers initially interested in the copiers became more resistant as sales presentations proceeded—a finding that surprised company officials. A questionnaire administered to the sales force found a negative correlation between enthusiasm and sales. That is, salespeople who were less enthusiastic sold more copiers than those who had higher enthusiasm—another surprising finding. When researchers made sales calls with Xerox salespeople, they discovered two differences between how salespeople tried to sell the new copiers and how they sold more established products.

First, they asked 40 percent fewer questions. Second, they provided three times as many product details. Instead of being customer-centred and asking questions to discover customer needs, the salespeople were product-centred, performing "feature dumps." One theory was that salespeople would introduce new products to customers the same way the products were introduced to them. That is, if management described all the "bells and whistles" to the salespeople, the sales representatives would do the same to customers.

To test this theory, researchers intervened in a new product launch for a Kodak blood analyzer. Researchers described to 12 randomly chosen salespeople how the product solved customer problems, without describing any of the product's "bells and whistles." The salespeople were further coached to avoid describing product features and to ask questions that uncovered needs. After one year, the salespeople in the experimental group achieved sales 54 percent higher than a matched group who had experienced the company's standard product launch—one with all the "bells and whistles." This finding supports David Milliken's views. The national director of business development at Deloitte & Touche says, "Any minute you spend talking about a product or feature that doesn't connect to an explicit need is a minute wasted."[b]

AVOIDING INFORMATION OVERLOAD

Knowing your product has always been essential to good selling, but concentrating on product alone can be a serious mistake. Salespeople who love their products and possess vast product knowledge about them may overload their customers with product data they neither need nor want. This practice is sometimes described as a "data dump."[33] With the aid of specific types of questions (see Chapter 11), the customer's needs can be identified. Once the customer's needs are known, the salesperson can develop a customized sales presentation that includes selected features that can be converted to specific benefits.

Table 6.2

Convert Product Features to Benefits

Salespeople employed by a hotel can enhance the sales presentation by converting product features to benefits.

Feature	Benefit
Facilities	
Our hotel conference rooms were recently redecorated.	Which means all your meetings will be held in rooms that are attractive and comfortable.
Our rooms were completely redecorated this year and many are now designated non-smoking.	Which means your people will find the rooms clean and attractive. In addition, those who wish can select a non-smoking room.
Food Services	
We offer four different banquet entrées prepared by our executive chef, who was recently selected Chef of the Year by the Canadian Federation of Chefs and Cooks.	Which means your conference will be enhanced by delicious meals served by a well-trained staff.
Our hotel offers 24-hour room service.	Which means your people can order food or beverages at their convenience.

Table 6.3

Convert Company Features to Benefits

Here we see company features translated into customer benefits.

Feature	Benefit
Our company has the largest selection of motors in the area.	Which means you will have an excellent choice of models to interface with your equipment.
We hire only certified service technicians.	Which means your equipment will be kept running in peak condition by well-qualified service personnel.
Our company has an inventory of all major spare parts.	Which means you will have less equipment downtime and will make higher profits.

SUMMARY

A salesperson whose product knowledge is complete and accurate is better able to satisfy customers. This is without doubt the most important justification for becoming totally familiar with the products you sell. It is simply not possible to provide maximum assistance to potential customers without this information. Additional advantages to be gained from knowing your product include greater self-confidence, increased enthusiasm, improved ability to handle buyer resistance, development of stronger selling appeals, and the preparation of more effective written sales proposals.

A complete understanding of your company will also yield many personal and professional benefits. The most important benefit, of course, is your ability to serve your customer most effectively. In many selling situations, customers inquire about the company's business practices. They want to know things about support personnel, product development, credit procedures, warranty plans, and product service after the sale. When salespeople are able to provide the necessary company information, they gain respect. They also close more sales.

This chapter also stresses knowing your competition. It pays to study other companies that sell similar products to determine whether they have competitive advantages or disadvantages. The Internet is a good source of information about competing products.

Salespeople gather information from many sources. Company literature and sales training meetings are among the most important. Other sources include factory tours, customers, competition, sales support personnel, publications, and actual experience with the product itself.

In the sales presentation and the written sales proposal, your knowledge of the product's features and your company's strengths must be presented in terms of the resulting benefits to the buyer. The information and benefits you emphasize will depend on your assessment of the prospect's needs and motivation.

Key Terms

Review Questions

1. What is a *product strategy*? Why is it important for salespeople to have a clearly defined product strategy?
2. Some sales managers state, "Training given to sales personnel should stress product knowledge over any other area." List three reasons that support this view.
3. What is *product configuration*? Provide an example of how this practice is used in the sale of commercial stereo equipment.
4. List and briefly describe the five parts included in most written sales proposals.
5. Review the Everyone Sells boxed feature on page 132. Explain how the book written by Rudolph and Ludwig Melik will be a benefit to Tenrox Inc.
6. Review the British Columbia Buildings Corporation statement of corporate values on page 138 and explain how its core values can contribute to its salespeople's career success.

7. What is *organizational culture*? How might knowledge of a company's organizational culture benefit a salesperson?
8. Basic beliefs underlie the salesperson's method of handling competition. What are three guidelines a salesperson should follow in developing basic beliefs in this area?
9. Discuss six common sources of product information.
10. Distinguish between *product features* and *buyer benefits.* Select a product of your choice, identify three features of that product, and connect those product features to buyer benefits.

Application Exercises

1. Obtain, if possible, a copy of a customer-oriented product sales brochure or news release that has been prepared by a marketer. (Many salespeople receive such selling tools.) Study this information carefully, then develop a feature–benefit analysis sheet.
2. Today many companies are automating their product configuration and proposal-writing activities. Go to the Internet and find these providers of software: **www.qwikquote.com** (for simple sales configuration) and **www.results-online.com** (for moderately complex sales configuration). Click on each company's demonstration software and study the design of each product.
3. Select a product you are familiar with and know a great deal about. (This may be an item you have shopped for and purchased, such as a compact disc player or an automobile.) Under each of the categories listed, fill in the required information about the product.
   a. Where did you buy the product? Why did you choose this seller?
   b. Did product design influence your decision?
   c. How and where was the product manufactured?
   d. What different applications or uses are there for the product?
   e. How does the product perform? Are there any data on the product's performance? What are they?
   f. What kinds of maintenance and care does the product require? How often?
   g. Could you, as a sales representative, sell the product you have written about in categories (a) through (f)? Why or why not?

ROLE-PLAY EXERCISE

Study the convention centre information included in "Partnership Selling: A Role Play/Simulation" on your Companion CD-ROM and also posted online in the Student Resources at **www.pearsoned.ca/manning.** Pay particular attention to pricing on the meals and meeting rooms. Configure a sales proposal (see p. 27) for your instructor who is responsible for setting up a student awards meeting. Use your school name and address. The meeting includes a banquet-style meal of chicken Wellington for 26 attendees from 5:30 to 8:00 p.m. on the last Wednesday of next month. The meal will be served at 5:45 p.m., and the awards session is scheduled from 6:45 to 8:00 p.m. in the same room. The seating should be banquet style. Present the completed proposal to another student (acting as your customer) and communicate the features and benefits of your proposal.

CRM Application Exercise FINDING PRODUCT INFORMATION IN CRM

Providing immediate access to product information can increase a salesperson's efficiency and responsiveness to customer requests. Computers excel at the task of quickly providing information. An example can be found in the ACT! CRM case study software. Basic information about networks is available in the Reference Library, a feature of this version of ACT!: select View, Reference Library, to view the networking information. Print this information by selecting File, Print. While in the Reference Library, you can open other library documents by selecting File, Open, and by double-clicking on one of the files that ends with "wpd." When finished, these ACT! word processing files can be closed by selecting File, Close (Alt+F C).

Case Problem

Cart Works manages several free-standing retail booths called kiosks that operate in shopping malls. Many of the newer malls have incorporated kiosks to create the busy and happy atmosphere of an open marketplace. The design of the kiosk varies from a stationary booth to a movable cart. A typical kiosk offers a specialized product line such as greeting cards, inexpensive jewellery, T-shirts, sunglasses, candy, or snacks. A small number of kiosks can add a new dimension to the shopping atmosphere.

Cart Works offers training and help in selecting a high-traffic location in the mall. Once a location is selected, members of the Cart Works staff decide what products are most likely to be popular at that location. Cart Works wants to expand its business and is looking for many new entrepreneurs who are interested in operating a kiosk in a shopping mall as their own business. A decision has been made to promote the Cart Works concept by placing in selected newspapers throughout the country ads that briefly explain the business opportunity and invite prospects to attend an information meeting at a local hotel. A representative of Cart Works will conduct the meeting. Persons who attend the meeting will be given an overview of the company that includes the following features:

- Cart Works has conducted research to determine what type of merchandise sells best from a booth or movable cart. The company knows what type of mall shopper is most likely to buy a product from a booth or cart.
- Cart Works can provide merchandise that sells well from a booth or cart. Entrepreneurs also have the option of providing their own merchandise, which can be purchased from another vendor.
- Cart Works will provide the training needed to successfully establish and operate the business.
- Cart Works will meet with the mall manager and obtain permission to operate the business within the mall. Most malls will require a contract that outlines the business relationship. All malls charge a fee for operation of the booth or cart.

Persons who attend the meeting will be given a package of materials that explains the business opportunity. Serious prospects will be contacted after the meeting. They will be invited to meet with a Cart Works representative. (See chapter opening material on page 126.)

Questions

1. Explain how a Cart Works representative can use the three prescriptions for a product-selling strategy in preparing and presenting product solutions.
2. What are the major benefits that could be incorporated into the group and individual presentations?
3. In addition to the actual product strategy, how important will company information (e.g., history, mission, past performance, product support) be in closing the sale during individual meetings with prospects?

Partnership Selling:

A ROLE PLAY/SIMULATION

Included with your CD-ROM. A Contents page lists appropriate page references for the activities.

Read *Employment Memorandum 1* (p. 5), which introduces you to your new training position with the Hotel Convention Centre. You should also study the product strategy materials that follow the memo to become familiar with the company, product, and competitive knowledge you will need in your new position.

Read *Customer Service/Sales Memorandum 1* (p. 26) and complete the three-part customer/service assignment provided by your sales manager. In item 1 you are to complete a feature–benefit worksheet; in item 2 you are to configure a price–product sales proposal; and in item 3 you are to write a sales cover letter for the sales proposal. Note that the information presented in the price–product sales proposal will consist of product facts or features, and the information presented in your sales cover letter should present specific buyer benefit statements. These three forms should all be custom fitted to meet your customer's—B. H. Rivera's—specific needs. All the product information you will need is in the product strategy materials provided as enclosures and attachments to *Employment Memorandum 1.*

CHAPTER 7

Product-Selling Strategies That Add Value

LEARNING OBJECTIVES

After studying this chapter, you should be able to

1. Describe positioning as a product-selling strategy
2. Discuss product differentiation in personal selling
3. Explain how today's customer is redefining the product
4. Describe how to sell products at various stages of the product life cycle
5. Explain how to sell your product with a price strategy
6. Explain how to sell your product with a value-added strategy
7. List and describe the four dimensions of the total product

You just finished paying off your college loans and it's time to replace that old rust bucket with a new car. You have looked at the sport-compact cars available, but they all seem so small. Now you are eagerly looking at cars in the sports-sedan category. The cars in this niche offer a good blend of comfort, design, and performance. However, there are almost too many choices. *Road & Track* says there are 11 different automobiles in this group. The list price is $70 700 for the Cadillac CTS-V and $53 000 for the Saab 9-5 Aero. The Audi A4 and Jaguar X-Type offer all-wheel drive; all the rest offer front- or rear-wheel drive. As you learn more about the choices available, it becomes clear that each manufacturer has taken steps to differentiate its product.

Several years ago automobile manufacturers from around the world began to develop and position cars for the sports-sedan segment. Research indicated that demand for these cars would increase. The result was the introduction of 11 different marques, each with its own unique characteristics. At the dealer level, the process of product differentiation continues. If you want something more than standard equipment, the salesperson can describe a variety of options that can add $10 000 or more to the price. Accessories can be added to each car to meet your personal needs. The dealer can also help position this product with modern facilities, customer-friendly service policies, and a reputation for honesty and integrity.

Salespeople at the dealer level can play an important role in positioning the automobile for competitive advantage. They can describe the quality control process that ensures the build quality of the BMW 330i or demonstrate the sports car driving characteristics of the Lexus IS 330. Adding value depends on the salesperson's ability to provide a competitive analysis using knowledge of the manufacturer, the automobile, and the dealership.[1]

Product Positioning—A Personal Selling Strategy

Long-term success in today's dynamic global economy requires the continual positioning and repositioning of products. **Product positioning** involves those decisions and activities intended to create and maintain a certain conception of the firm's product in the customer's mind. A product's "position" is the customer's concept of the product's attributes relative to his or her concept of competing products.[2] In a market that has been flooded with a variety of sport-utility vehicles (SUVs), Land Rover has been positioned as a dependable vehicle that can climb a steep, rock-covered hillside with ease. Every effort has been made to create the perception that a Land Rover is safe, durable, and secure. To give sales representatives increased confidence in the Land Rover, the company has arranged plant tours and the opportunity to observe actual testing of the Land Rover under extremely demanding conditions. Good positioning means that the product's name, reputation, and niche are well recognized. However, a good positioning strategy does not last forever. The positioning process must be continually modified to match the customer's changing wants and needs.[3]

product positioning Decisions, activities, and communication strategies for creating and maintaining a firm's intended conception of its product in the customer's mind.

THE ESSENTIALS OF PRODUCT POSITIONING

Most companies use a combination of marketing and sales strategies to give their products a unique position in the marketplace. Every salesperson needs a good understanding of the fundamental practices that contribute to product positioning. This chapter begins with a brief introduction to the concept of product differentiation. This introduction is followed by an explanation of how products have been redefined in the age of information. The remainder of the chapter is devoted to three selling strategies that can be used to position a product. We emphasize positioning your product with a value-added strategy. In the age of information, salespeople who cannot add value to the products they sell will diminish in number and influence.

Achieving Product Differentiation in Personal Selling

One of the basic tenets of sales and marketing is the principle of product differentiation. The competitors in virtually all industries are moving toward differentiating themselves on the basis of quality, price, convenience, economy, or some other factor. Salespeople, who are on the front line of many marketing efforts, assume an important role in the product differentiation process. Differentiating your product helps you stand out from the crowd. It often allows you to distance yourself from the competition. In many cases, the process of differentiation creates barriers that make it difficult for the buyer to choose a competing product simply on the basis of price.[4]

A well-informed customer will usually choose the product that offers the most value. Therefore, salespeople need to position their product with a value proposition. A **value proposition** summarizes the mix of key buyer benefits on which the product is positioned.[5]

value proposition The key buyer benefit on which the product is positioned.

Edmonton-based ZCL Composites Ltd. is a manufacturer of fibreglass-reinforced underground fuel storage tanks. To compete against approximately 150 other tank manufacturers, the company had to reposition itself. President and CEO Ven Côté says, "We began to offer entire systems that included not just the tank but all the accessories that go with it. Through vertical integration we positioned ourselves not as a tank manufacturer, but as a whole-solution provider." This positioning strategy has allowed the company to grow regionally, nationally, and internationally.[6] ZCL Composites works hard to achieve product and service differentiation, and offer customers a well-defined value proposition.

www.zcl.com

Redefining Products in the Age of Information

satisfactions The positive benefits that customers seek when making a purchase. Satisfactions arise from the product itself, from the company that makes or distributes the product, and from the salesperson who sells and services the product.

Theodore Levitt, former editor of the *Harvard Business Review*, says that products are problem-solving tools. People buy products if they fulfill a problem-solving need. Today's better-educated and more demanding customers are seeking *a cluster of satisfactions*. **Satisfactions** arise from the product itself, from the company that makes or distributes the product, and from the salesperson who sells and services the product.[7] Figure 7.1 provides a description of a three-dimensional Product-Selling Model. As noted in a previous chapter, many companies are attempting to transform themselves from selling products to selling solutions. To develop and sell solutions, salespeople must be familiar with the satisfactions that meet the needs of each customer.

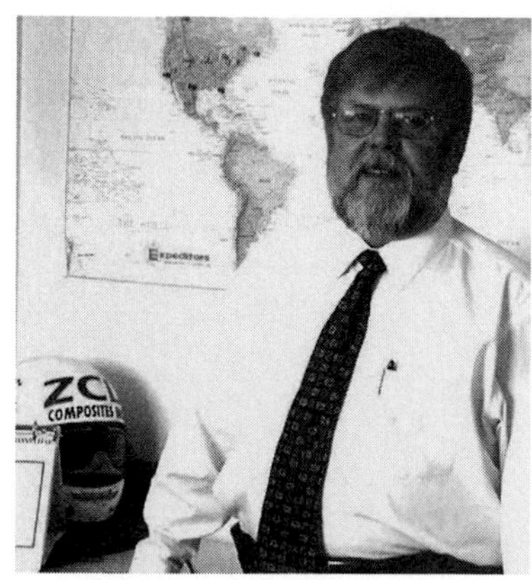

Positioning ZCL Composites as a whole-solution provider has allowed Ven Côté, president and CEO, to grow the company both within Canada and internationally.

To illustrate how the concept of a cluster of satisfactions works in a business setting, let us examine an important buying decision. Elaine Parker, a sales representative for Elmore Industries Incorporated, sells metals for manufacturing operations. Over a period of six months, she frequently called on a prospect that had the potential to become a valued customer. During every call, the buyer's receptionist told her the company was happy with its present supplier. Elaine refused to give up and finally the buyer agreed to see her. At first, she was greeted with cool silence, so she decided to ask him some questions about his business, such as: "How's the slow economy affecting your sales?" The buyer's answers focused on materials costs. He said his company could not raise prices nor cut quality. He wanted to lower costs but was unsure how it could be done. Elaine suggested his company consider trying some new alloys that are less expensive than the standard metals he had been purchasing. As she described the new alloys, the buyer's interest began to build. She offered to make a full presentation to the buyer and his engineers at a follow-up meeting. The second meeting was a success. Soon after that meeting, Elaine received her first order from the customer. Within a year, she had become the customer's most trusted adviser on technological developments in the industry and his exclusive supplier.[8]

Elaine Parker used questions to engage the customer and identify his problem. She also provided answers to questions raised by the customer, such as:

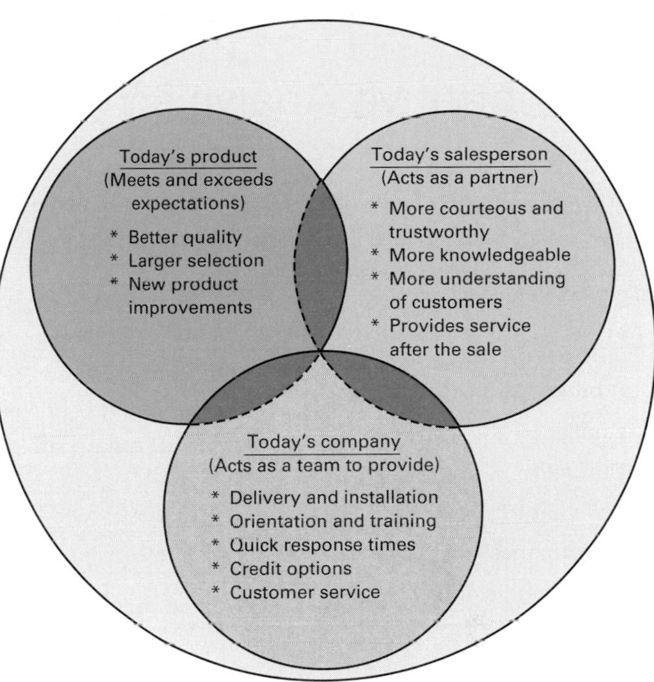

Figure 7.1 Product-Selling Model. The product strategy should include a cluster of satisfactions that meet the needs of today's better-educated and more-demanding customers. Drawing from this cluster, the salesperson can custom fit presentations to meet a wide range of customer needs.

Questions Related to the Product
What product is best for our type of operation?
Does the product meet our quality standards?
Given the cost of this product, will we maintain our competitive position in the market place?

Questions Related to the Company
Does this company provide the most advanced technology?
What is the company's reputation for quality products?
What is the company's reputation for standing behind the products it sells?

Questions Related to the Salesperson
Does the salesperson possess the knowledge and experience needed to recommend the right product?
Can the salesperson clearly communicate specific buyer benefits?
Can the salesperson serve as a trusted adviser?
Will this salesperson provide support services after the sale?

The purchase of a service may be no less complicated. Let us assume that you are planning a retirement banquet for the president of your company. The location of the banquet would likely depend on the type of food and beverage service available at hotels and restaurants in your community. This would be the *product* decision. The qualifications of the food and beverage salesperson or sales manager would also influence your buying decision, because this is the person who describes the food, beverage, and meeting room options and works with you after the buying decision. You must be convinced that this person has the experience and skills necessary to do the job. In the final analysis, you would make a buying decision based on your perception of the "whole" product.

Salespeople who have a strong knowledge base are in the best position to redefine a product. Knowledge helps you achieve product differentiation, understand the competition, and prepare an effective value proposition. The competitive analysis worksheet can help you discover ways to position your product as the superior choice over your competition (see Table 7.1, p. 156).

Table 7.1

Competitive Analysis Worksheet

A value-added product-selling strategy is enhanced when salespeople analyze product, company, and salesperson attributes of the competition in relation to benefits they offer. This information helps the salesperson create value within the sales process.

	My Company	Competitor A	Competitor B
Product Attributes			
Quality			
Durability			
Reliability			
Performance			
Packaging flexibility			
Warranty			
Brand			
Company Attributes			
Reputation			
Industry leadership			
Facilities			
Ease of doing business			
Distribution channels			
Ordering convenience			
Returns, credits, etc.			
Salesperson Attributes			
Knowledge/Expertise			
Responsiveness			
Pricing authority			
Customer orientation			
Honesty/Integrity			
Follow-through			
Presentation skills			

A WORD OF CAUTION

Because many of today's products are very complex, product differentiation must be handled with care. Salespeople are sometimes tempted to use technical lingo—real and invented—to impress the buyer. This problem often

EVERYONE SELLS

Technical Staff Assume Sales Role

Reggie Daniel, CEO of Scientific & Engineering Solutions, says, "The company culture is to have every employee bringing in business." His three full-time salespeople and a selected 15 non-salespeople get paid commissions or bonuses based on the profitability of sales they help close. Steve Newcomb, a technical staff member, helped close a sale that resulted in a $700 000 contract. He not only collected the commission on the sale, he received a trip to the Super Bowl. Reggie wants his technical staff to have access to the business world because sales opportunities often surface when they are involved in technical problem solving.[a]

surfaces in a situation in which the salesperson is not sure how to describe the value-added features of the product. Robert Notte, technology chief for travel outfitter Backroads, says that, during the telecom boom, salespeople representing WorldCom and other firms babbled endlessly, using industry jargon that was often unintelligible. "They wanted you to be impressed," Robert Notte says. Some customers were so intimidated they were afraid to ask questions—or make a buying decision.[9]

Product-Positioning Options

Product positioning is a concept that applies to both new and existing products. Given the dynamics of most markets, it may be necessary to reposition products several times in their life, because even a solid popular product can lose market position quickly. Salespeople have assumed an important and expanding role in positioning products. To succeed in our information-drenched society, marketers must use a more direct and personalized form of communication with customers. Advertising directed toward a mass market will often fail to position a complex product.

Throughout the remainder of this chapter we discuss specific ways to use various product-positioning strategies. We explain how salespeople can (1) position new and emerging products versus mature and well-established products, (2) position products with price strategies, and (3) position products with value-added strategies.

POSITIONING NEW AND EMERGING PRODUCTS VERSUS MATURE AND WELL-ESTABLISHED PRODUCTS

Products, like human beings, are born, grow up, mature, and grow old. In marketing, this process is known as the **product life cycle**; it includes the stages a product goes through from the time it is first introduced until it is discontinued. As the product moves through its cycle, the strategies relating to competition, promotion, pricing, and other factors must be evaluated and

product life cycle Stages of a product from the time it is first introduced to the market until it is taken off the market, including the stages of introduction, growth, maturity, and decline.

possibly changed. The nature and extent of each stage in the product life cycle are determined by several factors, including:

1. The product's perceived advantage over available substitutes;
2. The product's benefits and the importance of the needs it fulfills;
3. Competitive activity, including pricing, substitute product development and improvement, and effectiveness of competing advertising and promotion; and
4. Changes in technology, fashion, or demographics.[10]

As you develop a product-selling strategy, you must consider where the product is positioned within its life cycle. The sales strategy used to sell a new and emerging product will be much different from the strategy used to sell a mature, well-established product (see Fig. 7.2).

SELLING NEW AND EMERGING PRODUCTS

Selling strategies used during the new and emerging stage are designed to develop a new level of expectation, change habits, and in some cases establish a new standard of quality (see Fig. 7.2). The goal is to build desire for the product.

When Brother International Corporation introduced its line of Multi-Function Centre (MFC) machines, the goal was to convince buyers that one machine could replace five separate machines. However, before buyers would give up their copy machine, fax machine, laser printer, and other machines, they asked some hard questions. Is a multifunction machine reliable? Does the quality match that of the current machines? Finding the best machine for each customer is challenging because Brother offers more than 10 different MFC models to choose from.

In some cases the new product is not a tangible item. A few years ago Kinko's began making a big push into the business-to-business market.

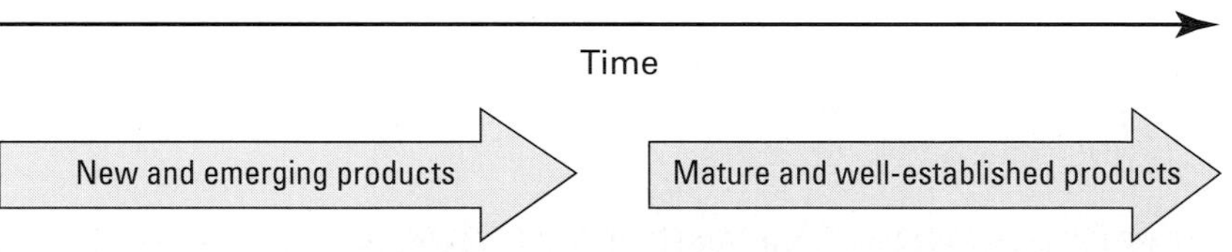

Product-selling strategy	Product-selling strategy
• Develop new levels of expectations • Change habits • Establish new standards • Build desire for product • Focus on creating new markets	• Emphasize brand superiority • Emphasize company superiority • Point out unique features • Provide outstanding customer service • Focus on sustaining existing market share

Figure 7.2 Product-selling strategies for positioning new and emerging products versus mature and well-established products.

Today, the company is no longer viewed as a simple corner copy shop. Kinko's is partnering with large business firms that need digital solutions to large jobs. Gary Kusin, CEO of Kinko's Incorporated, says, "Right now, the biggest service we can sell is competence: the ability to listen to our customers, to understand their problems, and to apply our knowledge to come up with creative solutions."[11] When Kinko's decided to create a field sales force, the company did not clearly establish its mission. Salespeople were happy to sign any deal, large or small. In the late 1990s Kinko's reorganized the sales force around a single mission: "Create long-term profitable relationships with big companies that want to outsource their printing and copy needs." In 2004, the company was bought by FedEx. Today FedEx Kinko's sales force of more than 700 salespeople—called commercial account managers—contact large accounts. The value proposition they present emphasizes customized plans for each customer, quality documents, and on-time completion. These benefits have helped the sales team sign up large customers such as IBM and Hewlett-Packard.[12]

www.kinkos.ca

SELLING MATURE AND WELL-ESTABLISHED PRODUCTS

Mature and well-established products are usually characterized by intense competition as new brands enter the market. At this point, customers accept

CUSTOMER RELATIONSHIP MANAGEMENT WITH TECHNOLOGY

Managing New Product Information with CRM

Today, salespeople are challenged to manage a steady stream of information about customers' needs and products or solutions. From this stream of information, the sales professional must select product information that will be relevant to a specific customer and deliver the information in a manner that the customer can understand. CRM assists the busy salesperson by providing tools that can collect information and link it to those who need it. Most CRM systems can receive and organize information from e-mail, from Web sites, and from the files of reference material that are kept within a company's information system. Sales professionals can add value to this information by summarizing, combining, and tailoring the information to meet a customer's needs.

When new product information is received, databases of customer data can be quickly searched to find those customers who might have an interest. The new product information can be merged into an e-mail, fax, or letter to that customer, along with other information (e.g., benefits) that help the customer assess its value. Later, the CRM system can display a follow-up alert, while reminding the sales professional of the information that was shared with the customer. (See the exercise Informing Customers with CRM on page 168 for more information.)

the well-established products and are aware of competing products. With new and emerging products, salespeople may initially have little or no competition and their products may dominate the market. However, this condition may not last long.

www.sunlife.ca

Sun Life Assurance Company of Canada regularly provides its 1500 independent sales agents with new products. Yet the company finds that competing insurance companies quickly copy its new products. When competing products enter the market, Sun Life sales agents must adopt new strategies. One positioning strategy Sun Life uses is to emphasize the company's 125 years of superior service to policyholders and its undeniable financial strength. Agents often describe Sun Life as a supportive company that gives high priority to service after the sale, and a stable company that will be around to service future needs.[13] The objective is to create an awareness in the customer's mind that Sun Life is a solid company with a long history of good service to policyholders.

The relationship strategy is often critical in selling mature and well-established products. To preserve market share and ward off competitors, many salespeople work hard to maintain a strong relationship with the customer. At Sun Life, salespeople have found that good service after the sale is one of the best selling strategies because it builds customer loyalty.

POSITIONING PRODUCTS WITH A PRICE STRATEGY

Pricing decisions must be made at each stage of the product life cycle. Therefore, setting the price can be a complex process. The first step in establishing price is to determine the firm's pricing objectives. Some firms set their prices to maximize their profits; they aim for a price as high as possible without causing a disproportionate reduction in unit sales. Other firms set a market share objective; management may decide that the strategic advantage of an increased market share outweighs a temporary reduction in profits. Many of the new companies doing business on the Internet have adopted this approach.

Pricing strategies often reflect the product's position in the product life cycle. When DVD players were introduced to consumers, customers who wanted this innovative equipment were willing to pay $1000 or more for a unit. Now, DVD players can be purchased for less than $100.

TRANSACTIONAL SELLING TACTICS THAT EMPHASIZE LOW PRICE

Some marketers have established a positioning plan that emphasizes low price and the use of transactional selling tactics. These companies maintain a basic strategy that focuses on meeting competition. If the firm has meeting competition as its pricing goal, it makes every effort to charge prices that are identical or close to those of the competition. Once this positioning strategy has been adopted, the sales force is given several price tactics to use. Salespeople can alter (i.e., lower) the base price through the use of discounts and allowances. Discounts and allowances can take a variety of forms. A few of the more common ones follow:

SELLING IN ACTION

Setting Your Professional Fees

The age of information has created many career opportunities for people who want to sell professional services. Strong demand for professional services has surfaced in such diverse fields as telecommunications, banking, computer technology, training, and health care. Gary Svoboda recently resigned his position as vice-president at the Canadian Innovation Centre, where he worked for 18 years, to start his own consulting business, Adventus Research. It specializes in new product application identification and research, primarily in technology and industrial markets. Like thousands of other professional service providers, Gary had to decide how much to charge for his service. Should he price his service on an hourly basis or on a project basis? Here are some things to consider when determining fees:

- *Experience:* In the case of Gary Svoboda, new clients benefit from what he has learned during his many years at the Canadian Innovation Centre.
- *Exclusivity:* If you are one of only a small number of people with a particular capability, you may be able to charge more. Specialists often charge higher fees than generalists.
- *Target Market:* Some markets are very price sensitive. If you are selling your services to large corporations that are accustomed to paying high fees, you may be able to set your fees higher. If you are providing your services to small business clients, expect resistance to high fees.
- *Value:* How important is your service to the client? Some service providers charge higher fees because they create greater value for their customers.[b]

The **quantity discount** allows the buyer a lower price for purchasing in multiple units or above a specified dollar amount.

With **seasonal pricing**, the salesperson adjusts the price up or down during specific times to spur or acknowledge changes in demand. Lower off-season travel and lodging pricing is an example.

A **promotional allowance** is a price reduction given to a customer who participates in an advertising or a sales support program. Many salespeople give supermarkets promotional allowances for advertising or displaying a manufacturer's products.

Channel intermediaries, such as wholesalers, often perform credit, storage, or transportation services. A **trade** or **functional discount** covers the cost of these services.[14]

quantity discount A price reduction made to encourage a larger volume purchase than would otherwise be expected.

seasonal discount Adjusting prices up or down during specific times to spur or acknowledge changes in demand.

promotional allowance A price reduction given to a customer who participates in an advertising or sales support program.

trade or **functional discount** A discount given to channel intermediaries to cover the cost of the services they provide.

Another option available to salespeople facing a buyer with a low-price buying strategy is to "unbundle" product features. Let's assume that a price-conscious customer wants to schedule a conference that will be accompanied by a buffet-style meal, thereby eliminating the need for servers. This product configuration involves less cost to the seller, and the cost savings can be passed on to the buyer. A salesperson representing a line of computer products might reduce the selling price by altering or eliminating certain assurances and/or warranties.

These examples represent only a small sample of the many discounts and allowances salespeople use to compete on the basis of price. Price discounting

EDGAR-ARGO
"WE HAVE QUALITY AND WE HAVE LOW PRICES... WHICH DO YOU WANT?"

Agency Sales Magazine from the Manufacturing Agent National Association (MANA)

is a competitive tool available to large numbers of salespeople. Excessive focus on low prices and generous discounts, however, can have a negative impact on profits and sales commissions.

CONSEQUENCES OF USING LOW-PRICE TACTICS

Pricing is a critical factor in the sale of many products and services. In markets where competition is extremely strong, setting a product's price may be a firm's most complicated and important decision. The authors of *The Discipline of Market Leaders* encourage business firms to pick one of three disciplines—best price, best product, or best service—and then do whatever is necessary to outdistance the competition. However, the authors caution us not to ignore the other two disciplines: "You design your business to excel in one direction, but you also have to strive to hit the minimum in the others."[15] Prior to using low-price tactics, everyone involved in sales and marketing should answer these questions:

- *Are you selling to high- or low-involvement buyers?* Some people are emotionally involved with respected brands, such as BMW, Sony, and American Express. A part of their identity depends on buying the product they consider the best. Low-involvement buyers care mostly about price.[16]
- *How important is quality in the minds of buyers?* If buyers do not fully understand the price–quality relationship, they may judge the product by its price. For a growing number of customers, long-term value is more important than short-term savings that result from low prices. A broad-based desire for high quality and "value" as opposed to the lowest possible price suggests that price alone is an inadequate competitive tool.
- *How important is service?* For many buyers, service after the sale is a critical factor. Even online customers, thought to be very interested in price, rate quality of service very highly. This is especially true in business-to-business sales. A survey conducted by Accenture reported that 80 percent of nearly a thousand corporate buyers rate a strong brand and reliable customer service ahead of low prices when deciding which companies to do business with online.[17]

THE INFLUENCE OF ELECTRONIC BUSINESS ON PRICING

Companies large and small are racing to discover new sales and marketing opportunities on the Internet. Products ranging from personal computers, to airline tickets, to equity stocks and mutual funds can now be purchased online. Salespeople who are involved primarily in transactional selling and add little or no value to the sales transaction will often not be able to compete with online vendors. To illustrate, consider the purchase of stocks online from one of Canada's many discount brokers. At the present time it's possible to make an online purchase for a fraction of the cost of using a full-service broker. A well-informed buyer, willing to visit several Web sites, can make decisions based on online information and investing tools that were considered to be beyond the understanding of the average investor only a few years ago. Persons who need little or no assistance buying stocks can visit Canada's largest discount broker, TD Waterhouse Discount Brokerage, or one of the many others, including E*Trade Canada, RBC Action Direct, CIBC Investor's Edge, to name only a few of the many choices available to informed consumers. The person who wants help selecting a stock can turn to a full-service broker such as Merrill Lynch, BMO Nesbitt Burns, or Scotia McLeod. Full-service broker revenues are still about five times that of discount brokers, but their share is decreasing.[18] Full-service brokers can survive and may prosper as long as they can add value to the sales transaction. The new economy is reshaping the world of commerce, and every buyer continues to have more choices.

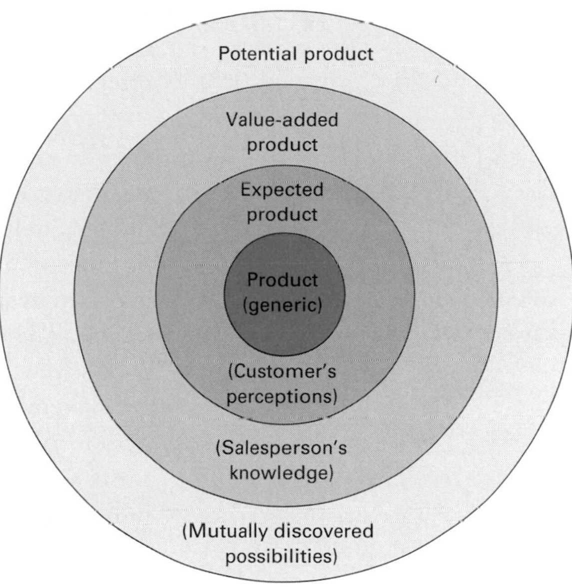

Figure 7.3 The Total Product Concept. An understanding of the four possible products is helpful when the salesperson develops a presentation for different customers.

POSITIONING YOUR PRODUCT WITH A VALUE-ADDED STRATEGY

Many progressive marketers have adopted a market plan that emphasizes **value-added strategies**. Companies add value to their product with one or more intangibles such as better-trained salespeople, increased levels of courtesy, more dependable product deliveries, better service after the sale, and innovations that truly improve the product's value in the eyes of the customer. In today's highly competitive marketplace these value-added benefits give the company a unique niche and a competitive edge.

value-added strategies Relationship, product, or service strategies that a company uses to add value for the customer.

To understand fully the importance of the value-added concept in selling, and how to apply it in a variety of selling situations, it helps to visualize every product as having four dimensions. The total product is made up of four possible products: the generic product, the expected product, the value-added product, and the potential product (see Figure 7.3).[19]

GENERIC PRODUCT

The **generic product** is the basic substantive product you are selling. Generic product describes only the product category, for example, life insurance, rental cars, clothing, hotels, or personal computers. Every Ritz-Carlton hotel offers guest rooms, food and beverage service (i.e., restaurants, bars, and banquet space), meeting rooms, guest parking, and other basic services. For customers who visit Toronto-based Tilley Endurables, the generic product is the men's and women's travel and adventure clothing and accessories they find there. The generic products at a bank are money that can be loaned to customers and basic chequing account services. The capability of delivering

generic product The basic substantive product being sold.

a generic product gives the marketer the right to play in the game, to compete in the marketplace.[20] Generic products, even the lowest-priced ones, often cannot compete with products that are expected by the customer.

EXPECTED PRODUCT

Every customer has minimal purchase expectations that exceed the generic product itself.[21] Ritz-Carlton must offer not only a comfortable guest room, but also a clean one. Some customers expect an exceptionally clean room. The **expected product** is everything that represents the customer's minimal expectations. The customer at Tilley Endurables will expect quality products, a good selection, fashionable accessories, and well-informed salespeople.

expected product Everything that represents the customer's minimal expectations.

The minimal purchase conditions vary among customers, so the salesperson must acquire information concerning the expected product that exists in the customer's mind. Every customer will perceive the product in individualized terms, which a salesperson cannot anticipate. When the customer expects more than the generic product, the product can be sold only if those expectations are met. Top salespeople encourage customers to think more deeply about the problems they face and discover for themselves the value of the solution. They avoid offering solutions until the needs are clearly spelled out. If the buyer says, "The average gas consumption for our fleet of delivery trucks is only 5.5 kilometres per litre," the salesperson might respond: "How does this low gas consumption rate affect your profitability?" To move the customer's attention from the expected product to the value-added product, you need to keep the customer focused on solutions.[22]

To determine each customer's expectations requires the salesperson to make observations, conduct background checks, ask questions, and listen to what the customer is saying. You are attempting to discover both feelings and facts.

Research reported in the *Harvard Business Review* indicates that it is very difficult to build customer loyalty if you are selling only the expected product. Customer satisfaction and loyalty do not always move in tandem. The customer who purchases the services of a consulting firm may feel satisfied after the project is completed but may choose a different consulting firm the next time. Customer loyalty is more likely to increase when the purchase involves a value-added product.[23]

VALUE-ADDED PRODUCT

The **value-added product** exists when salespeople offer customers more than they expect. When you make a reservation at one of the Ritz-Carlton hotels and request a special amenity such as a tennis lesson, a record of this request is maintained in the computer system. If you make a reservation at another Ritz-Carlton at some future date, the agent will inform you of the availability of a tennis court. The guest who buys chocolate chip cookies in the gift shop at one location may find some waiting in the room for his or her next stay weeks later. The hotel company uses modern technology to surprise and delight guests, and provide a value-added product.[24] Tilley Endurables pro-

value-added product Product that exists when salespeople offer the customer more than they expect.

vides many things to enhance customers' shopping experiences. At their retail store locations, customers get free cookies, shop in an engaging environment, and can get alterations to clothing in minutes. Even at its online location, the company adds value for its customers. It provides information on its products, service, and guarantees, and even travel information on almost anywhere in the world customers might be travelling. One of the most powerful value-added strategies is personalized service. Larry Wilson, noted author and sales consultant, says that adding value means *always* working outside your job description to exceed customer expectations.[25] Salespeople who have adopted the value-added philosophy routinely meet clients' expectations and then exceed those expectations.

www.tilley.com

POTENTIAL PRODUCT

After the value-added product has been developed, the salesperson should begin to conceptualize the **potential product**—what may remain to be done; that is, what is possible.[26] As the level of competition increases, especially in the case of mature products, salespeople must look into the future and explore new possibilities.

potential product What may remain to be done to a product—that is, what is possible.

In the highly competitive food services industry, restaurant owners like to do business with a distribution sales representative (DSR) who wants to help make the business profitable. The DSR who assumes this role becomes a true partner and looks beyond the customer's immediate and basic needs. The potential product might consist of a careful study of the restaurant's current menu and appropriate recommendations to the owner. To deliver the potential product, a salesperson must discover and satisfy new customer needs, which requires imagination and creativity.

Steelcase Incorporated, a leading manufacturer of office furniture, recently developed the Personal Harbor Workspaces. The product is designed to be clustered around common work areas that invite teamwork and collaboration. These circular workstations offer buyers a twenty-first–century version of the traditional office cubicle. The podlike workstation is such a departure from conventional office design that customers were initially unable to comprehend its potential. Salespeople quickly learned that a traditional product-oriented presentation would not work. Meetings between Steelcase salespeople and customers involved discussions of concepts such as team building, organizational communication, and employee interaction. Steelcase developed "advanced solution" teams that adopted a truly consultative role. These teams meet with people in the organization who are more interested in the potential of the Personal Harbor Workspaces than in their price.[27]

The potential product is more likely to be developed by salespeople who are close to their customers. Many high-performing salespeople explore product possibilities with their

Lexus, a company that emphasizes engineering sophistication, agrees to treat and refer to its customers as "guests."

WHAT IS LEXUS?

Lexus is... Engineering sophistication and manufacturing quality.
Lexus is... Luxury and performance.
Lexus is... An image and an expectation of excellence.
Lexus is... Valuing the customer as an important individual.
Lexus is... Treating customers the way THEY want to be treated.
Lexus is... A total experience that reflects professionalism and a sincere commitment to satisfaction.
Lexus is... "Doing it right the first time".
Lexus is... Caring on a personal level.
Lexus is... Exceeding customer expectations.

And... In the eyes of the customer
I AM LEXUS !!!

customers on a regular basis. Potential products are often mutually discovered during these exchanges.

Investments in Value Creation for Transactional, Consultative, and Relationship Buyers

In most cases, investments in value creation during the transactional sale are minimal. With such sales, salespeople usually place emphasis on finding ways to eliminate any unnecessary costs and on avoiding delays in processing the order. Technology investments can sometimes play a big role in improving efficiencies.[28] For example, customers may be encouraged to order other products.

By contrast, sales representatives frequently invest in value creation in consultative sales. Higher investments in value creation are permitted because companies need to invest in developing a good understanding of the customer's needs and problems. This is especially true in large complex sales where creating custom-tailored solutions and delivering more real benefits to the customer provides the opportunity for higher margins. If, for example, your company is selling mobile autonomous robots, the sales cycle will be quite long, and investments will be quite high. Sales representatives may take several weeks to study the applications of this product in a hospital, a manufacturing plant, or a large warehouse facility. The use of these robots may eventually result in significant cost savings for the customer.[29]

Investments in value creation are made most often in relationship sales. As noted in Chapter 3, partnering represents the highest form of selling relationship. Building a partnership is always preceded by careful study of the proposed partner. Creating value often requires leveraging the full assets of the company, so that investments go well beyond the sales force. Partnerships may be developed by a team of specialists from such areas as finance, engineering, and marketing. A proposed alliance may require investments in new technology, manufacturing facilities, and warehouses.[30]

SUMMARY

Success in today's dynamic global economy requires the continual positioning and repositioning of products. Product positioning involves those decisions and activities intended to create and maintain a certain concept of the firm's product in the customer's mind. Salespeople can make an important contribution to the process of product positioning. In many cases they assume an important role in product differentiation.

We noted that today's better-educated customers are often seeking a cluster of satisfactions that arise from the product itself, from the company that makes or distributes the product, and from the salesperson who sells and services the product.

We introduced the major product-positioning strategies available to salespeople: positioning new and emerging products versus mature and well-established products, positioning with a price strategy, and positioning with a value-added strategy.

Part of this chapter was devoted to the total product concept. The total product is made up of four possible products. This range of possibilities includes the generic product, the expected product, the value-added product, and the potential product.

Key Terms

Review Questions

1. Why has product differentiation become so important in sales and marketing?
2. According to Theodore Levitt, what is the definition of a product? What satisfactions do customers want?
3. Explain what is meant by *positioning* as a product-selling strategy. What is a *value proposition*?
4. Why have salespeople assumed an important role in positioning products?
5. Briefly describe the influence of electronic business on pricing. What types of products are sold on the Internet?
6. What are the possible consequences a salesperson might experience when using low-price tactics?
7. What are some of the common ways salespeople add value to the products they sell?
8. What are the four possible products that make up the *total product* concept?
9. Describe the differences between a generic product and a value-added product.
10. Refer to the Selling in Action boxed feature on page 161. Explain four things which any professional must consider when setting fees for the services they offer.

Application Exercises

1. Obtain catalogues from two competing industrial-supply firms or two competing direct-mail catalogue companies. Assume one of the represented businesses is your employer. After studying the catalogues, make a comparative analysis of your company's competitive advantages.
2. Padinox Inc. has been making stainless steel cookware in Prince Edward Island for more than 20 years. Visit its Web site (**www.padinox.ca**) and view information on its products. Describe how Padinox positions its products in the market. How does Padinox add value for its customers?
3. Interview the manager of a local supermarket that sells a large assortment of national brands such as Nabisco, Kellogg's, and McCain. Ask this manager what kinds of appeals sales representatives of national brand products use when they request more shelf space. Determine how frequently they offer trade or advertising allowances.
4. Call a local financial services representative who specializes in stock, bond, or equity fund transactions. Ask what percentage of clients relies on the information given to make complex decisions on their investments. Also ask this manager if customers feel that advice in custom-fit investment programs adds value to their decision making. Find out whether financial products are getting more or less complex, and what effect this will have on providing value-added service in the future.

ROLE-PLAY EXERCISE

Study the convention centre information included in "Partnership Selling: A Role/Play Simulation" on your Companion CD-ROM and also online in the Student Resources at **www.pearsoned.ca/manning**. Analyze this information and determine the value-added product that would appeal to a meeting planner, the customer. Prepare a value proposition that summarizes the mix of key benefits on which your product is positioned. The proposition might include the free limousine service to and from the airport. Present your value proposition to another class member who will assume the role of the customer. Consider using information sheets, pictures, and other materials that will enhance your presentation.

CRM Application Exercise **INFORMING CUSTOMERS WITH CRM**

The notes in the ACT! database software contain two references to extranets, another system offered by SimNet Systems. One account is a prospective buyer of an extranet who needs more information. The other account has an extranet and is willing to show it to others. The Reference Library also contains information about virtual private networks (VPN), including extranets. Find the two accounts by selecting Lookup, Keyword, type "Extranet," check Notes, uncheck Contact, and press Enter.

After searching, ACT! will display two records. An examination of the notes will show the account with an extranet and the one with an interest. Make a note of the name of the organization now using an extranet. Close the notes screen (File, Close) and use the Page Up or Page Down key to display the account that needs information. Select View, Reference Library to display the information about networks. Page Down to the last paragraph of that document, entitled VPN. Highlight the paragraph with your mouse and select Edit, Copy. Select File,Close to close the library.

Select Write, Letter, and enter the following: "You might find this of interest." Press Enter twice to begin a new paragraph. Select Edit, Paste to add the information from the Reference Library. Press Enter twice again for a new paragraph and type "If you wish, I can arrange for you to look at the extranet in use at" then enter the name of the person and organization using the extranet. Select File, Print (Ctrl+P) to print the letter and File, Close to close the letter window.

Case Problem

Many of the most profitable companies have discovered that there are "riches in market niches." They have developed products and services that meet the needs of a well-defined or a newly created market. Steelcase Incorporated, a leading source of information and expertise on work effectiveness, has been working hard to develop products that meet the needs of people who do most of their work in an office environment. The company motto is "The Office Environment Company." One of its newest products is the Personal Harbor Workspaces, a self-contained, fully equipped, and totally private podlike workstation. Steelcase sales literature describes the product as ideal for companies that are tired of waiting for the future: "They were developed to support the individual within a highly collaborative team environment, and they work best when clustered around common work areas equipped with mobile tables, carts, benches, screens, and other Steelcase Activity Products. These "commons" are meant to be flexible spaces that enhance communication and facilitate interaction."

Steelcase realized that selling this advanced product would not be easy, so a decision was made to develop an advanced sales team to presell the Personal Harbor before its major introduction. Once the team started making sales calls, it became evident that a traditional product-oriented sales presentation would not work. The Personal Harbor was such a departure from conventional office design that many customers were perplexed. Sue Sacks, a sales team member, said, "People acted as if we had fallen from Mars." Team members soon realized that, to explain the features and benefits of the product, they had to begin studying new organizational developments such as team-oriented workforces and corporate re-engineering. The advanced sales team was renamed the "advanced solutions" team. Sales calls put more emphasis on learning about the customers' problems and identification of possible solutions. Members of the team viewed themselves as consultants who were in a position to discuss solutions to complex business problems.

The consultative approach soon began to pay off in sales. One customer, a hospital, was preparing to build a new office building and needed workstations for 400 employees. The hospital had formed a committee to make decisions concerning the purchase of office equipment. After an initial meeting between the Steelcase sales team and the hospital committee, a visit to the Steelcase headquarters was arranged. The hospital committee members were able to tour the plant and meet with selected Steelcase experts. With knowledge of the hospital's goals and directions, Sue Sacks was able to arrange meetings with Steelcase technical personnel who could answer specific questions. As a result, the hospital placed an order worth more than a million dollars.

Questions

1. To fulfill a customer's needs, salespeople must be prepared to communicate effectively with customers who are seeking a cluster of satisfactions. Is it likely that a customer who is considering the Personal Harbor Workspaces will seek information concerning all three dimensions of the Product-Selling Model (see Fig. 7.1)? Explain your answer.
2. What product-selling strategies are most effective when selling a new and emerging product such as the Personal Harbor Workspaces?
3. Sue Sacks and other members of her sales team discovered that a traditional product-oriented presentation would not work when selling the workspaces. Success came only after the team adopted the consultative style of selling. Why was the product-oriented presentation ineffective?
4. Sue Sacks and other members of the advanced solutions team found that the consultative approach resulted in meetings with people higher in the customer's organization. "We get to call on a higher level of buyer," she said. Also, the team was more likely to position the product with a value-added strategy instead of a price strategy. In what ways did the advanced solutions team members add value to their product? Why was less emphasis placed on price during meetings with the customer?

PART III

ROLE-PLAY EXERCISE

Developing a Product Strategy

SCENARIO

TD Canada Trust is a full-service bank with a reputation for excellent customer service. Personal selling efforts by customer service representatives, financial advisers, and financial planners are considered an integral part of the bank's customer service program.

CUSTOMER PROFILE

At age 45, Angela Cormier is looking forward to early retirement. To supplement her company-sponsored retirement program, she has purchased a guaranteed insurance certificate (i.e., a term deposit) in the amount of $4000 each year. The annual percentage yield earned on these term deposits is currently in the range of 1.2 to 2.4 percent. Angela is not interested in stocks and bonds because she sees these products as high-risk investments.

SALESPERSON PROFILE

Susan Ray is a financial planner with TD Canada Trust. She can provide a wide range of financial products, such as stock and bond mutual funds, blue chip stocks, diversified mutual funds, fixed annuities, money market funds, and guaranteed insurance certificates. Susan feels that Angela Cormier may be a good candidate for investment in fixed annuities. She plans to call Ms. Cormier to request an appointment.

PRODUCT

Susan plans to suggest that, instead of purchasing term deposits each year, Angela Cormier purchase a five-year term fixed annuity at an annual yield of 3.0 percent. The minimum single premium purchase is $5000. This product, offered by General Electric Capital Assurance Company, gives the customer a guaranteed principal and a fixed rate of return. At the contract maturity date, the customer can select several payout options. This is a tax-deferred annuity, which means that the customer won't pay income taxes on earnings until she chooses to withdraw the funds. Angela could add funds to her fixed annuity account throughout the contract period. Also, she need not close the account at the end of the contract period but could allow her money to continue to grow at the same interest rate. If Angela withdraws funds prior to the end of the contract, she would be assessed a withdrawal charge.

INSTRUCTIONS

For this role-play activity you will assume the role of Susan Ray. You will meet with Angela Cormier, role-played by another student, and determine her current and future financial plans. You will determine if she might benefit by investing in this fixed annuity.

Prior to meeting with Angela, review the following material in Chapter 6:

- Adding value with a feature–benefit strategy
- Use of bridge statements
- General versus specific benefits

Also, think about the implications of the Product-Selling Model (Fig. 7.1).

At the beginning of the role play, use appropriate questions to acquire information regarding Angela's needs. Be prepared to recommend this product and close the sale if you feel that Angela will benefit from this purchase.

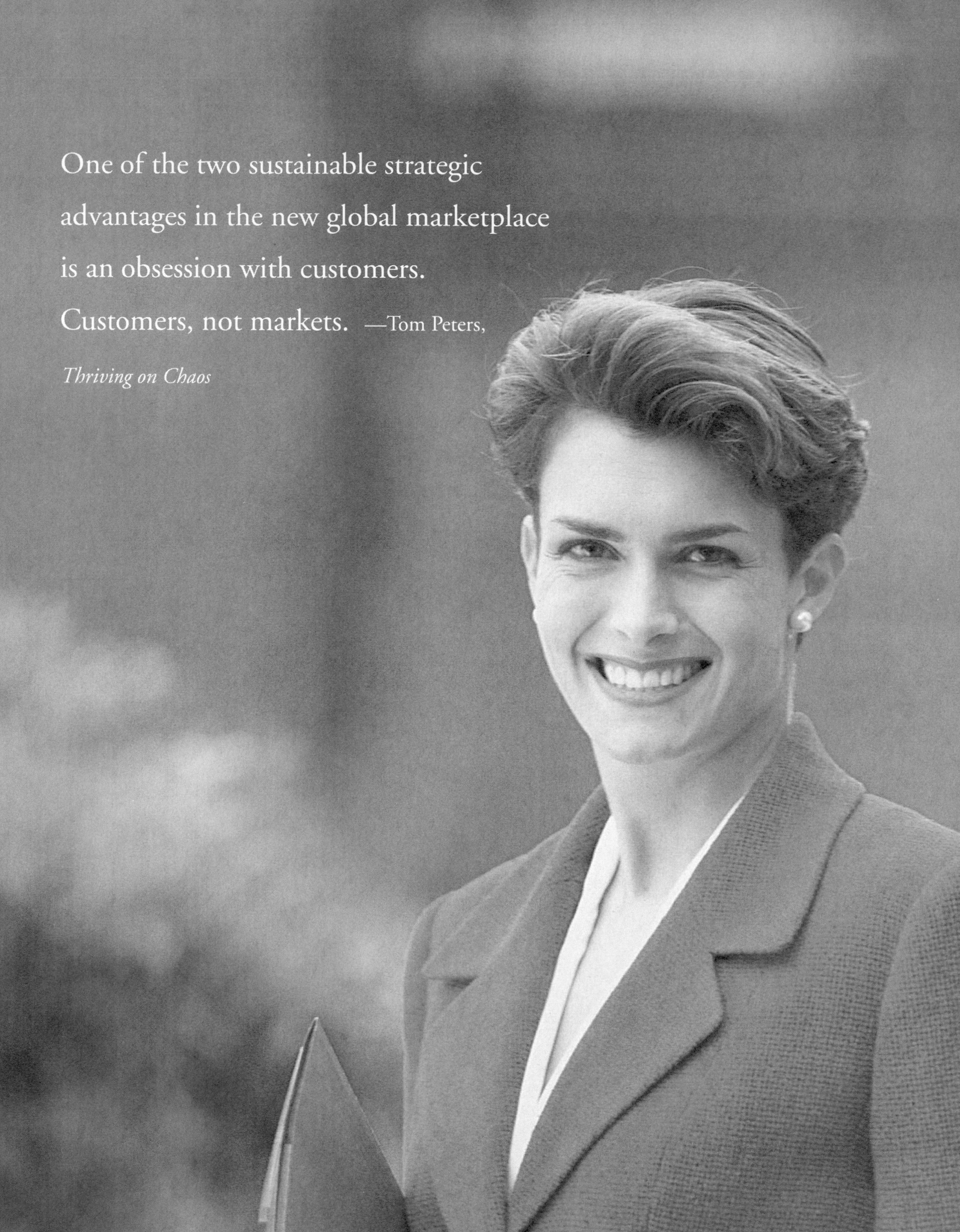

One of the two sustainable strategic advantages in the new global marketplace is an obsession with customers. Customers, not markets. —Tom Peters, *Thriving on Chaos*

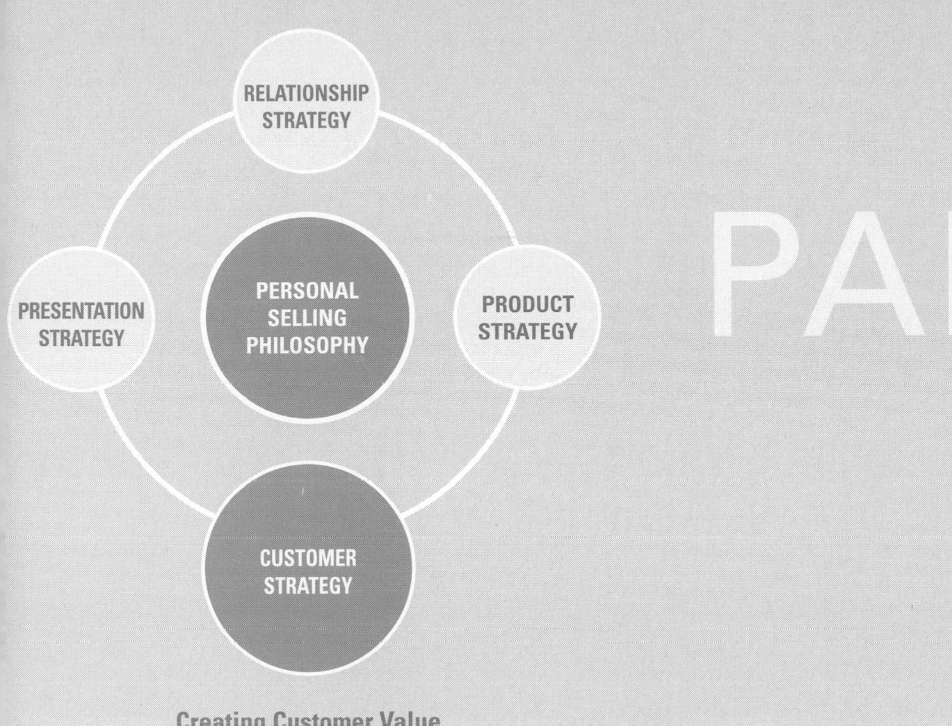

PART IV

Developing a Customer Strategy

With increased knowledge of the customer, the salesperson is in a better position to achieve sales goals. This part presents information on understanding buyer behaviour, discovering customer needs, and developing a prospect base.

CHAPTER 8

The Buying Process and Buyer Behaviour

LEARNING OBJECTIVES

After studying this chapter, you should be able to

1. Discuss the meaning of a customer strategy
2. Explain the difference between consumer and organizational buyers
3. List and describe the steps in the typical buying process
4. Discuss the buying process of the transactional, consultative, and relationship buyer
5. Understand the importance of alignment between the selling process and the customer's buying process
6. Discuss the social and psychological influences that shape customer buying decisions

Throughout the past few years, we have seen a major power shift in selling in the direction of the customer. Today's customers have greater access to information that lets them make more informed decisions. They are more demanding, and salespeople must work harder to meet their needs. Every sales call must begin with the customer as the central focus of attention. Tom Peters, noted author and consultant, says we must "Become one with the customer."[1] The customer focus must encompass the buying process—how people buy—and buyer behaviour—why people buy.

We know that new products must satisfy the customer's needs, but identifying these needs can be very challenging. Pembina Dodge Chrysler, one of five Chrysler dealerships in Winnipeg, understands this challenge. Several times Pembina has won the President's Challenge Award that requires superior performance in three areas: parts, service, and sales. Ron Trudel, a senior salesperson at the dealership, has been recognized many times as one of the best Chrysler Canada dealer salespeople. In an environment that has been growing increasingly competitive with both new product introductions and strong global competitors, Ron Trudel continues to be successful because he understands the customer buying process and buyer behaviour. He has a clear strategy focused on the customer.[2]

Developing a Customer Strategy

The greatest challenge to salespeople in the age of information is to improve responsiveness to customers. In fact, many sales professionals believe that the customer has supplanted the product as the driving force in sales today. This is especially true where the products of one company in an industry are becoming more and more similar to those of the competition. The salesperson can distinguish between similar products and services, and help customers perceive important differences. The development of valuable, customer-specific services and information is the hallmark of value-added selling.

ADDING VALUE WITH A CUSTOMER STRATEGY

A **customer strategy** is a carefully conceived plan that will result in maximum customer responsiveness. One major dimension of this strategy is to achieve a better understanding of the customer's buying needs and motives. As noted in Chapter 1, information has become a strategic resource (see Fig. 1.1). When salespeople take time to discover needs and motives, they are in a better position to offer customers a value added solution to their buying problem.

customer strategy A carefully conceived plan that will result in maximum customer responsiveness.

Every salesperson who wants to develop repeat business should figure out a way to collect and systematize customer information. The authors of *Reengineering the Corporation* discuss the importance of collecting information about the unique and particular needs of each customer:

> "Customers—consumers and corporations alike—demand products and services designed for their unique and particular needs. There is no longer any such notion as the customer; there is only this customer, the one with whom a seller is dealing at the moment and who now has the capacity to indulge his or her own personal tastes."[3]

The first prescription for developing a customer strategy focuses on the customer's buying process (see Fig. 8.1 on page 176). Buying procedures and policies can vary greatly from one buyer to another. This is especially true in business-to-business selling. If a salesperson fails to learn how the buyer plans to make the purchase, then he or she may find the selling process out of alignment with the customer's buying process. Keith Eades, author of *The New Solution Selling*, says: "If we haven't defined how our buyers buy, then we make assumptions that throw us out of alignment with our buyers. Misalignment with buyers is one of selling's most critical mistakes."[4]

The second prescription focuses on why buyers buy. This topic will be discussed in detail later in this chapter. The third prescription for developing a customer strategy emphasizes building a strong prospect base, which is discussed in Chapter 9.

The Complex Nature of Customer Behaviour

The forces that motivate customers can be complex. Arch McGill, a former vice-president of IBM, reminds us that individual customers perceive the product in their own terms, and that these terms may be "unique, idiosyncratic, human, emotional, end-of-the-day, irrational, erratic terms."[5] Different people doing the same thing—such as purchasing a personal computer—may have different needs that motivate them, and each person may have several motives for a single action. With the proliferation of market research studies, public opinion polls, surveys, and reports of "averages," salespeople might easily fall into the trap of thinking of the customer as a number. The customer is a person, not a statistic. Companies that fully accept this basic truth are likely to adopt a one-to-one marketing strategy based on a bedrock concept: *Treat different customers differently.*[6]

consumer buyer behaviour Buying behaviour of individuals and households who buy goods and services for personal consumption.

business buyer behaviour Buying behaviour of organizations that buy goods and services for use in the production of other products and services or for the purpose of reselling or renting them to others at a profit.

Consumer versus Business Buyers

Consumer buyer behaviour refers to the buying behaviour of individuals and households who buy goods and services for personal consumption. The Canadian consumer market consists of more than 31 million people who purchase many billions of dollars' worth of goods and services each year. **Business buyer behaviour** refers to the buying behaviour of organizations that buy goods and services for use in the production of other products and services or for the purpose of reselling or renting them to others at a profit.[7]

It is not uncommon for salespeople to sell products and services to both consumer and business buyers. A well-established interior decorating firm will likely work with homeowners as well as commercial clients who own hotels, restaurants, and art galleries. A salesperson employed by an automobile dealership will often sell to corporate customers who maintain a fleet of cars or trucks as well as to consumers who buy vehicles for personal use.

There are some similarities between consumer markets and business markets. Both involve people who assume the role of buyer and make purchase decisions to satisfy needs. These two markets differ, however, in some important areas. Figure 8.2 provides a brief review of some of these differences. A business purchase is likely to involve more participants in the decision making who may be well trained. Most purchasing agents spend time learning how to buy more effectively.[8]

Figure 8.1 The greatest challenge to salespeople today is to improve responsiveness to customers. Understanding how and why customers buy and knowing who prospects are form the foundation blocks for the salesperson to develop a highly responsive customer strategy.

Strategic/Consultative Selling Model	
Strategic step	Prescription
Develop a Personal Selling Philosophy	✓ Value Personal Selling ✓ Adopt Marketing Concept ✓ Become a Problem Solver/Partner
Develop a Relationship Strategy	✓ Project positive, professional image ✓ Practise communication-style flexing ✓ Behave ethically
Develop a Product Strategy	✓ Become a product expert ✓ Sell specific benefits ✓ Configure value-added solutions
Develop a Customer Strategy	• Understand the buying process • Understand customer behaviour • Develop prospect base

TYPES OF BUSINESS BUYING

There are three major types of business buying. The amount of time and effort organizational buyers spend on a purchase usually depends on the complexity of the product and how often the decision must be made.[9] At one extreme is the new-task buy which may require extensive research. At the other extreme is the straight rebuy which is a fairly routine decision. In the middle is the modified rebuy which will require some research.[10]

Consumer Buyers	Business Buyers
Purchases made for individual or household consumption	Purchases made for some purpose other than personal consumption
Decisions usually made by individuals	Decisions frequently made by several people
Purchases often made based on brand reputation or personal recommendations with little or no product expertise	Purchases often made according to precise technical specification based on product expertise
Purchases based primarily on emotional responses to product or promotions	Purchases based primarily on rational criteria
Individual purchasers may make quick decisions	Purchasers may engage in lengthy decision process
Products are consumer goods and services for individual use	Products are often complex; classified by how organizational customers use them

Figure 8.2 Differences between Consumer and Business Buyers
Source: Adapted from Michael R. Solomon and Elnora W. Stuart, *Marketing: Real People, Real Choices*, Third Edition (Upper Saddle River, NJ: Prentice Hall 2003), p. 193.

NEW-TASK BUY

A first-time purchase of a product or service is a **new-task buy**. Depending on the cost and complexity of this purchase, the buying decision may require several weeks for information gathering and the involvement of numerous participants in the decision making. In some cases, a buying committee is formed to consider the new product's quality, price, and service provided by suppliers. Salespeople who are involved in new-task buying must rely heavily on consultative selling skills.

new-task buy A first-time purchase of a product or service.

STRAIGHT REBUY

A **straight rebuy** is a routine purchase of items needed by a business-to-business customer. Let's assume you have decided to open a new restaurant and need a steady supply of high-quality cooking oil. After talking to several restaurant suppliers and testing several oils, you select one that meets your needs. Your goal now is to simplify the buying process with the use of a straight rebuy plan. As long as the supplier meets your criteria for price, quality, service, and delivery, future purchases will be routine. Organizations use the straight rebuy approach for such items as cleaning supplies, copy paper, and cartridges for computer printers. Salespeople must constantly monitor every straight rebuy to be sure the customer is completely satisfied. A competing supplier will be quick to exploit any sign of dissatisfaction by the customer.

straight rebuy A routine purchase of previously purchased goods or services.

MODIFIED REBUY

The tide of change is a powerful force in the world of business. From time to time, your customers may wish to modify product specifications, change delivery schedules, or renegotiate prices. Several years ago, the North American automobile manufacturers—faced with greater competitive pressures from China, Germany, Japan, Korea, and other nations—turned to their suppliers and demanded price reductions. Suppliers were required to become involved in a **modified rebuy** or risk loss of the account. A modified rebuy often requires the involvement of several participants. Well-trained professional salespeople work hard to provide outstanding service

modified rebuy Purchasing when the buyer wants to reconsider product specifications, prices, or suppliers.

after the sale and anticipate changes in customer needs. Some salespeople regularly ask their customers what they value most about the existing buying situation and how improvements can be made in this area.

BUILDING CLOSER, LONGER-TERM BUYER–SELLER RELATIONSHIPS

systems selling A type of selling that appeals to buyers who prefer a packaged solution from a single seller, thereby avoiding the series of separate decisions sometimes involved in a complex buying situation.

Buyers and sellers are increasingly forming closer, longer-term relationships. These are formed when companies have similar business interests and believe that a closer, longer-term relationship will help them gain a mutual competitive advantage. We introduced partnering in Chapter 3 as a high-quality relationship focused on solving a customer's buying problem. In fact, many partnering relationships are initiated by buyers. Another form of closer, longer-term buyer–seller relationship involves **systems selling**, the selling of a packaged solution to a buyer's problem. Systems selling appeals to buyers who prefer a packaged solution from a single seller, thereby avoiding the series of separate decisions sometimes involved in a complex buying situation.[11]

Several years ago, Kinko's reinvented itself from a photocopying service to a provider of document solutions for business firms. Full-service Kinko's stores began offering the buyer networks of computers equipped with popular software, ultra-fast colour printers, high-speed Internet connections, and a variety of document preparation services. More recently, Kinko's was purchased by FedEx. There are now 1200 digitally connected FedEx Kinko's locations offering customized, needs-based document solutions. One large financial institution consolidated the services of 13 vendors by forming a partnering relationship with FedEx Kinko's.[12] Systems selling efforts at FedEx Kinko's has become an important strategy for winning and holding accounts.

TYPES OF CONSUMER BUYING SITUATIONS

As noted previously, consumer buying behaviour refers to purchases of products for personal or household use. The amount of time consumers devote to a purchasing decision can vary greatly depending on the cost of the product, familiarity with the product, and the importance of the item to the consumer. Few buyers invest much effort in selecting a tube of toothpaste, but most will devote extensive time to decision making over the purchase of a new automobile or a home. Consumer buying can fall into one of three categories depending on the degree of consumer involvement: habitual, variety-seeking, or complex buying.

HABITUAL BUYING DECISIONS

habitual buying decision A consumer buying decision that requires very little involvement and where brand differences are usually insignificant.

A **habitual buying decision** usually requires very little consumer involvement and brand differences are usually insignificant.[13] For frequently purchased, low-cost items such as shampoo or paper towels, consumer involvement in the decision-making process may be very low. Supermarket shoppers often display habitual buying behaviour as they select items.

VARIETY-SEEKING BUYING DECISIONS

A **variety-seeking buying decision** is also characterized by low customer involvement, but important perceived brand differences.[14] Brand switching is not uncommon for such decisions because buyers can be influenced by advertising appeals, coupons, or lower prices to try a new brand. Brand switching is usually motivated by the desire for variety rather than product dissatisfaction.

variety-seeking buying decision A consumer buying decision motivated by the desire for variety rather than product dissatisfaction.

COMPLEX BUYING DECISIONS

A **complex buying decision** is characterized by a high degree of involvement by the customer. Consumers are likely to be highly involved when the product is expensive, purchased infrequently, and highly self-expressive.[15] Examples of complex buying decisions might include the purchase of a vacation home, a long-term care insurance policy, an expensive boat, or a costly piece of art. The learning process for some purchases can be very lengthy.

complex buying decision An often lengthy consumer buying decision characterized by a high degree of involvement.

Achieving Alignment with the Customer's Buying Process

The foundation of a successful sales effort is knowing how buyers buy. As noted previously, if salespeople have not defined how buyers buy, then they make assumptions that throw their sales process out of alignment with the buyer's buying process.[16] Too often salespeople rely on generalizations about the buyer's decision-making process rather than acquire specific information.

The buying process is a series of systematic actions or defined and repeatable steps intended to achieve a result.[17] Organizational purchasing structures and buying procedures can vary greatly from company to company, so we need to be clear on how decisions are being made within each account. In some cases, the steps in the buying process have been clearly defined by the organization and this information is available to any potential supplier. However, this information may not tell us the whole story. Salespeople need to obtain answers to these types of questions:

How urgent is the buyer's need? When will the buying decision be made?

Will "political" factors within the organization influence how the decision is made?

Has the money needed to purchase my product been allocated?

Who within the organization will actually use the product I am selling?[18]

Customers make buying decision in many ways, so understanding each individual buyer's decision-making process is central to success in personal selling. Some buyers will have multiple buying processes. Buying decisions involving a straight rebuy, for example, will likely differ from buying decisions involving a new-task buy.

STEPS IN THE TYPICAL BUYING PROCESS

buying-decision process The stages a buyer goes through when making a buying decision.

The term "process" brings to mind a set formula that applies to every situation. But buying decisions are made in different ways, so it would be inappropriate to view the buying process as a uniform pattern of decision making. However, there is a model, a form of decision making that buyers usually apply to their unique circumstances. Figure 8.3 shows the typical stages in the **buying-decision process**: need awareness, evaluation of solutions, resolution of problems, purchase, and implementation. This model is especially helpful in understanding business-buying decisions and large consumer acquisitions. Consumers who make routine purchases often skip or reverse some of these stages.[19]

NEED AWARENESS

Need awareness is the first stage in the buying process. The buyer recognizes that something is imperfect or incomplete. The need for energy conservation technology may surface when oil prices rise to higher levels. The need for a customer service training program may become evident when surveys show a decline in customer satisfaction. Salespeople can create value at this stage of the buying process if they can help determine the magnitude of the customer's problem and identify a solution. For example, a sales representative may be able to help the buyer estimate the cost of poor customer service and recommend a way to improve service. Customers need help in determining whether they have a problem large enough to justify the cost of a proposed solution.[20]

EVALUATION OF SOLUTIONS

Buyers who become aware of a need usually begin searching for information that will help them evaluate possible problem solutions. They realize that some solutions may work better than others and require comparative study. Salespeople can add value at this stage by providing useful information that helps the customer make an informed choice. In some cases, the justification for proposed added value can be presented in terms of cost reduction or increased revenue. In other cases, the value added may be intangible, such as customer satisfaction, improved security, or reduced stress. In business-to-business selling, value justification that can be measured is usually the most powerful.

To establish a true partnership with the customer, you need to be sure that you are offering them information that will help them achieve their objectives.

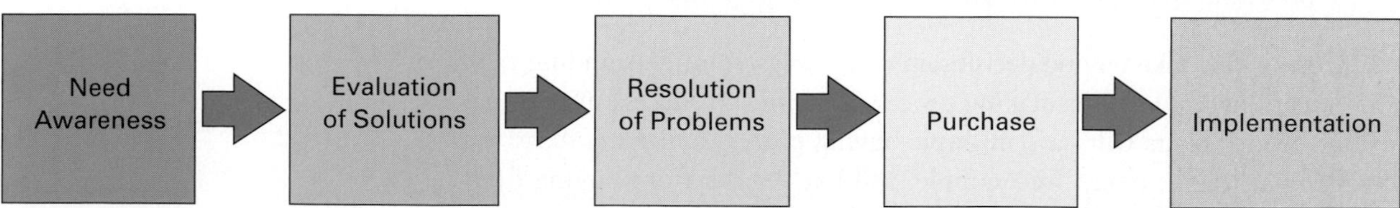

Figure 8.3 Steps in Typical Buying-Decision Process

If you possess a good understanding of the customer's buying process, you will know what they are trying to accomplish to solve their buying needs.[21]

RESOLUTION OF PROBLEMS

At this stage of the buying process, the customer is aware of a need and has evaluated one or more solutions. While the customer has decided to do something, he or she is likely to have issues that must be resolved before moving ahead. This is especially true in the case of complex sales.[22]

Some customers will want the proposed solution in writing. Competitors may be invited to submit written proposals. A well-written proposal is one way to add value, as described in Chapter 6. Customers may request specific information that can only be provided by your company's engineers or accountants. Customers may insist on visiting your company's manufacturing plant so that they can see the production process at first hand. Buyers often need help to overcome obstacles that prevent them from moving to the purchase stage of the buying-decision process.

PURCHASE

Once the customer has, with the help of the salesperson, overcome obstacles and resolved concerns, he or she can make the decision to purchase. Professional salespeople create value in many ways at this stage of the buying process. First, they can make sure the purchase is "hassle free." This may mean working with the customer to arrange the best financing, or supervising delivery and installation of the product. Salespeople can add value by becoming an advocate for the customer within their own organization. This may mean, for example, negotiating with various departments to expedite the order. Buyers want to work with salespeople who are able to quickly solve problems that might prevent the order from being fulfilled.[23]

IMPLEMENTATION

The first sale is only the beginning of the salesperson's relationship with the buyer. Repeat sales occur when your company as supplier has demonstrated the ability to add value in various ways after the sale. Value creation can take the form of timely delivery, superior installation, accurate invoicing, follow-up contacts by the salesperson, or servicing or anything else that is important to the customer.

Understanding the Buying-Decision Process for Transactional, Consultative, and Relationship Selling

The next step in understanding the customer's buying process is to discuss three approaches to creating value in sales that appeal to certain customers. In Chapter 1, we briefly introduced transactional, consultative, and relationship selling. We will now discuss when to use each approach.[24]

TRANSACTIONAL SELLING

In transactional selling, buyers are well aware of their needs and usually know a great deal about the products or services they intend to purchase. In a truly transactional sale, buyers will become frustrated if the salesperson attempts to use need assessment, problem solving, or relationship building. They are not looking for new information or advice from the salesperson. Most transactional buyers have conducted their own research and, in most cases, have decided which product best meets their needs. They don't want hand holding and they don't want the salesperson to waste their time.[25]

How can a salesperson add value to a transactional sale? If the buyer is already aware of his or her needs, has evaluated solutions, and has no issues or concerns that need to be resolved, then the salesperson needs to focus on the purchase stage of the buying process model (see Fig. 8.3). Do whatever is necessary to facilitate a convenient and "hassle-free" purchase. Eliminate any unnecessary costs or delays in having your company process the order. The transactional buyer may quickly turn to a competitor if he or she experiences unnecessary costs or delays.

CONSULTATIVE SELLING

Consultative selling, a major theme of this text, was described in Chapter 1. This sales approach appeals to buyers who need help assessing needs or evaluating possible solutions. Some buying decisions require assistance from a consultative salesperson because the product is very complex and/or the cost of the product is very high, for example, in the purchase of a new home; home buyers usually seek the assistance of an experienced realtor. For business buyers, the purchase of Internet phone-calling equipment provides a good example where consultative selling is beneficial. Organizations that are considering such a purchase might seek answers to such questions as: Can we keep a portion of our traditional phone network? Will the new system provide the same voice quality as our traditional system? Internet phone-calling equipment is available from several suppliers, including Avaya Incorporated and Cisco Systems Incorporated. Some customers will need help comparing the technology available from these and other suppliers.[26]

www.avaya.com

www.cisco.com

Successful consultative salespeople focus a great deal of attention on the needs awareness step in the buying process model (see Fig. 8.3). This is where salespeople can create the most value by helping customers to gain an understanding of their problems and by suggesting solutions that correct these problems.[27] Many customers seek help with defining needs and solutions but avoid dealing with sales representatives who simply want to sell a product.

For consultative selling, salespeople should conduct a systematic assessment of the prospect's situation. This usually involves collecting as much information as possible prior to the sales call and, during the sales call, using a series of carefully worded questions to obtain the customer's point of view. Two-way communication can provide a mutual exchange of ideas, feelings, and perceptions.

The consultative salesperson will help the customer evaluate solutions and help resolve any problems that surface prior to the purchase stage. Consultative salespeople also work hard to add value at the implementation stage of the buying process, perhaps by supervising product delivery and installation, servicing warranties, and providing other services after the sale.

RELATIONSHIP SELLING

As noted previously, closer, longer-term buyer–seller relationships are often formed by companies that have similar business interests and seek to gain a mutual competitive advantage. Nortel implemented a series of partnerships for several groups of products that it was buying when it found that its purchasing people were spending as much as 80 percent of their time to purchase items that accounted for only 20 percent of their purchases. These partnering relationships resulted in the creation of a number of one-stop–shopping sources for Nortel, and considerable cost savings for the company.[28]

www.nortelnetworks.com

Before these types of relationships are formed, both the buyer and the seller must carefully study each other. Depending on the particular relationship, people from various departments within the two organizations may be involved, including purchasing, sales, marketing, finance, engineering, and distribution. Both parties must be prepared to explain how they will add value once the relationship is formed. Both must be prepared to commit considerable resources to establish and maintain the relationship.

THE BUYER RESOLUTION THEORY

Several theories explain how customers arrive at a buying decision. One traditional point of view is based on the assumption that a final buying decision is possible only after the prospect has answered five logical questions (see Fig. 8.4 on page 184). This is called the **buyer resolution theory**. One strength of this buying theory is that it focuses the salesperson's attention on five important factors that the customer is likely to consider before making a purchase: need, product, source, price, and time. Answers to these five questions—the five Ws—provide valuable insights about the customer's buying strategy. One important limitation of this theory is that a salesperson cannot always anticipate which of the five buying decisions might be most difficult for the prospect to make. There is no established sequence in which prospects make these five decisions, so a highly inflexible sales presentation would not be effective. If the selling process does not mesh with the buying process, a sale is less likely.

buyer resolution theory A selling theory that a purchase will be made only after the prospect has made five buying decisions about need, product, source, price, and time.

Understanding Buyer Behaviour

While every customer is unique, salespeople need to understand the important social and psychological influences that tend to shape customer buying decisions. To present the many forces that influence customers, we will review concepts that come from the fields of psychology, sociology, and anthropology. Figure 8.5 illustrates forces that influence buying decisions.

www.customerexpressions.com

Figure 8.4 Buyer Resolution Theory. This view of the buying-decision process recognizes that a purchase is made only after the prospect has made five buying decisions that result from specific, affirmative responses to the five key questions.

Buyer Resolution Theory recognizes that a purchase is made only after the prospect has made five buying decisions that result from specific, affirmative responses to the five key questions.	
Why Should I Buy?	Realistically, it is difficult to provide prospects with an answer to this question. In many cases salespeople fail to help customers become aware of a need. Therefore, large numbers of potential customers are not sufficiently persuaded to purchase products that will provide them with genuine buyer benefits.
What Should I Buy?	If a prospect agrees that a need does exist, then a sales representative is ready to address this buying decision. He or she must convince the prospect that the product being offered will satisfy the need. In most cases the buyer can choose from among several competing products.
Where Should I Buy?	As products become more complex. customers are giving more attention to "source" decisions. In a major metropolitan area someone who wants to buy a LaserJet 3160 or a competing product will be able to choose from several sources.
What Is a Fair Price?	Today's better-educated and -informed consumers are searching for the right balance between price and value (i.e., buyer benefits). They are better able to detect prices that are not competitive or that do not correspond in their minds with the product's value.
When Should I Buy?	A sale cannot be closed until a customer has decided when to buy. In some selling situations, the customer will want to postpone the purchase because of reluctance to part with the money.

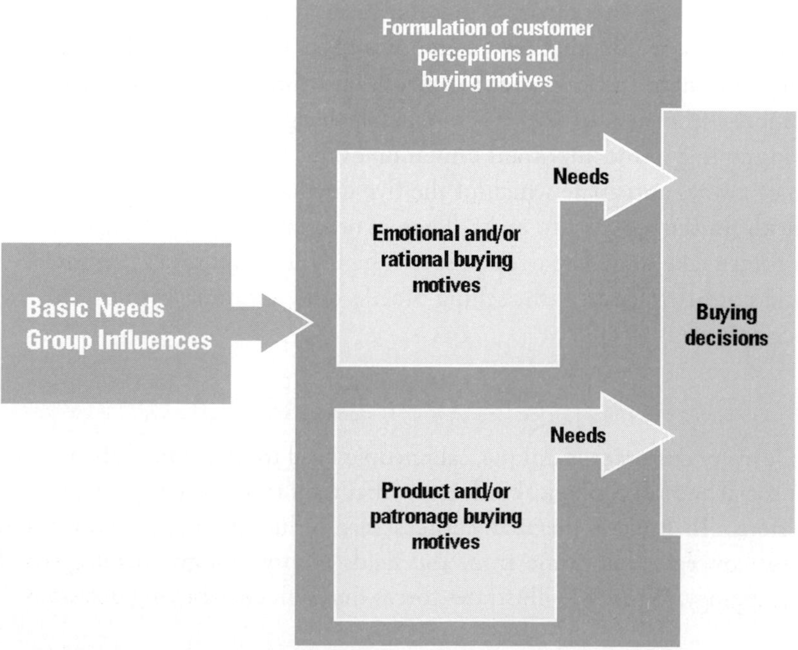

Figure 8.5 Developing a Customer Strategy Model. This model illustrates the many factors that influence buying decisions. It can serve as a guide for developing a highly responsive customer strategy.

THE CUSTOMER'S PERSPECTIVE

Butterfly Behaviour

In *The Butterfly Customer*, Susan O'Dell and Joan Pajunen, two Toronto-based management consultants, describe a customer who would rather switch than fight. This "butterfly customer" is one who flits from business to business, from relationship to relationship, always looking for the latest, the closest, the cheapest. There is, however, a special butterfly that businesses should value. That is the monarch, the one butterfly that returns to the same place, year after year, with total loyalty. Susan O'Dell and Joan Pajunen describe five characteristics of monarch butterflies to help you identify them so that you can encourage their loyalty.

1 *Monarch butterflies always return—sooner or later!* You need to keep regular staff who will recognize them, who will make them feel welcome and important, and who can communicate with them to find out where they have been if they have not patronized you recently, and what has brought them back.
2. *Monarch butterflies often send others in their place.* Even if they do not continue to patronize your business, monarch butterflies refer others to you. You need to train your staff to find out why new customers come to your business, where they have heard about you.
3. *Monarch butterflies have opinions.* They not only have opinions, they express them freely. These customers are highly involved with your business and are motivated to help you improve it. What appears to be a "nuisance" complaint may be a monarch butterfly who is committed to your business. To reward these customers, you need to ensure that your staff and systems can provide feedback on every complaint.
4. *Monarch butterflies share their homework.* They are curious and informed, and love to provide you with details on what your competitors are doing. You must ensure that your staff members have appropriate listening skills, and that they know what to do with this information when they receive it.
5. *Monarch butterflies are forgiving and giving.* They will allow you to mess up occasionally, and will pitch in and help you with your service delivery when the going gets rough. They don't mind helping themselves and may even help you serve other clients.

According to Susan O'Dell and Joan Pajunen, trust is what leads Monarch butterflies to return. They trust when you consistently deliver what you promise, how you promised it. High-profit, low-maintenance customers are your reward for being trustworthy.[a]

BASIC NEEDS THAT INFLUENCE BUYER BEHAVIOUR

Basic human needs have changed little throughout our economic history. However, the ways in which needs are fulfilled has changed greatly in the age of information.[29] The starting point for developing an understanding of the forces influencing buyers is a review of the individual needs that shape the customer's behaviour. To gain insights into customer behaviour motivated by both physiological and psychological needs, it is helpful to study the popular hierarchy of needs developed by Abraham Maslow.

MASLOW'S HIERARCHY OF NEEDS

According to Abraham Maslow, basic human needs are arranged in a hierarchy according to their strength (see Fig. 8.6 on page 186). His theory rests on the assumption that, as each lower-level need is satisfied, the need at the next level demands attention.

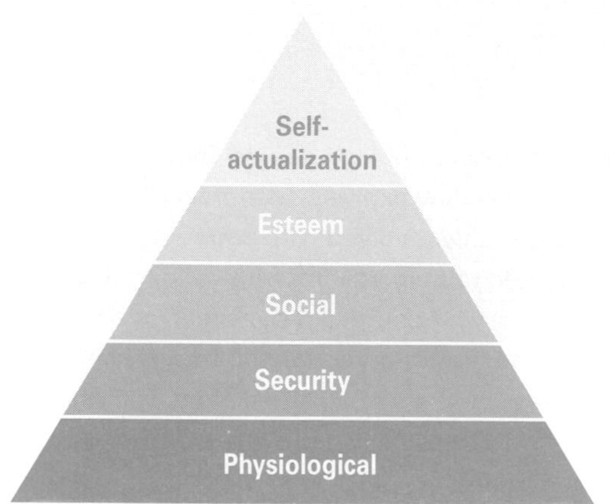

Figure 8.6 The forces that motivate customers to make specific buying decisions are complex. This model illustrates Maslow's hierarchy of needs.

Physiological Needs. Sometimes called primary needs, **physiological needs** include food, water, air, shelter, warmth, and sleep. Maslow placed our physiological needs at the bottom of the pyramid. He believed that these basic needs tend to be strong in the minds of most people.

Security Needs. Maslow theorized that, after physiological needs have been satisfied, people next tend to need safety and security. **Security needs** represent our desire for protection from the elements, and to be free from danger and uncertainty. The desire to satisfy the need for safety and security might motivate people to purchase such items as medical and life insurance or a security alarm for their home or business.

Social Needs. The need to belong, or **social needs**, reflects our desire for affection, identification with a group, and social approval from others. These needs help explain our continuing search for friendship, companionship, and long-term business relationships.

Esteem Needs. At the fourth level of Maslow's needs hierarchy are **esteem needs**, which reflect our desire to feel worthy in the eyes of others. We seek a sense of personal worth and adequacy, a feeling of competence.

Self-Actualization. Maslow defined the term **self-actualization** as a need for self-fulfillment, a tapping of one's full potential. It is the need to "be all that you can be," to have mastery over things you are doing. In selling, you must be sensitive to the needs of buyers who are searching for a way to achieve self-actualization.

The needs hierarchy developed by Maslow is theoretical and, therefore, somewhat artificial. At times, several of our needs interact simultaneously. Consider the business lunch where you are not only conducting business with a client but are also satisfying your need to consume food and beverages, to engage in social activities, and perhaps to seem important in your own eyes and, you hope, the eyes of your customer.[30] However, the model does provide salespeople with a practical way of understanding which need is most likely to dominate customer behaviour in certain buying circumstances.

physiological needs Primary or physical needs, including food, water, air, shelter, warmth, and sleep.

security needs These represent our desire for protection from the elements, and to be free from danger and uncertainty; buying decisions to support these needs could include clothing, shelter, and insurance.

social needs Needs that reflect a person's desire for affection, identification with a group, and approval from others.

esteem needs The desire to feel worthy in the eyes of others, to develop a sense of personal worth and adequacy or a feeling of competence and importance.

self-actualization The need for self-fulfillment; a tapping of one's full potential to meet a goal; the need to be everything one is capable of being.

group influences Forces that other people exert on customers' buying behaviour.

role A set of characteristics and expected social behaviours based on the expectations of others. All the roles we assume may influence our buying behaviour.

GROUP INFLUENCES THAT INFLUENCE BUYING DECISIONS

As noted earlier, the people around customers also influence their buying decisions. These **group influences** can be classified in four major areas: (1) role, (2) reference groups, (3) social class, and (4) culture and microcultures[31] (see Fig. 8.7). Salespeople who understand these influences can develop valuable insights into customers' buying decisions.

ROLE INFLUENCES

Throughout our lives we belong to families, groups, organizations, and institutions. In each relationship, we have a **role**—a set of characteristics and expected social behaviours based on the expectations of others. All the roles we assume (e.g., student, member of the school board, our position at work) influence not only our general behaviour but also our buying behaviour. A woman, for example, may assume the roles of mother at home, volunteer in the community, and purchasing manager at work. As a mother and volunteer, she regularly buys many items as a consumer. In the manager's role, she may feel the need to purchase a conservative wardrobe, enroll in a leadership training course, or join a professional association.

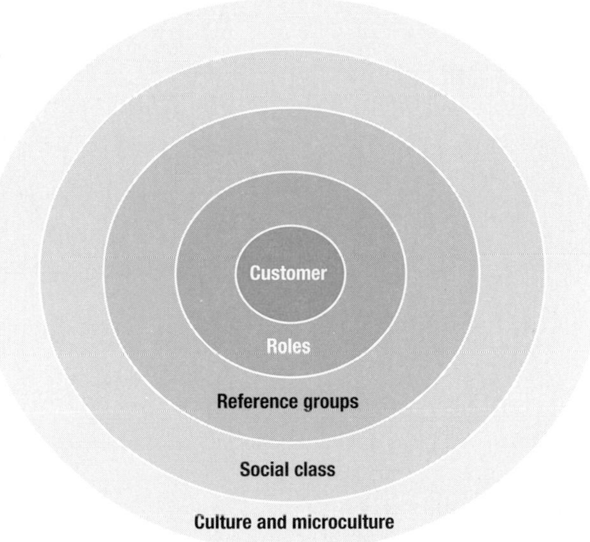

Figure 8.7 To gain additional insights into customers' motivations, salespeople can study group influences that affect buying decisions.

REFERENCE GROUP INFLUENCE

A **reference group** consists of a group to which you belong and habitually compare yourself. Members of a reference group tend to influence the values, attitudes, and behaviours of one another.[32] The reference group may act as a point of comparison and a source of information for the individual member. In the business community, the Canadian Professional Sales Association may be a reference group for its members. As a member of a reference group, each of us may observe other people in the group to establish our own norms; these norms may become a guide for our purchasing activities.

reference group Two or more people who have well-established interpersonal communications and tend to influence the values, attitudes, and buying behaviours of one another. They act as a point of comparison and a source of information for a prospective buyer.

SOCIAL CLASS INFLUENCE

A **social class** is one of society's relatively permanent and ordered divisions whose members share similar values, interests, and behaviours.[33] The criteria used to rank people according to social class vary from one society to another. In some societies, land ownership differentiates members of one social class from another; in other societies, education is a major key to achieving upper-class status. Social class, in most cases, is not determined by a single factor. It is determined by a combination of such factors as income, education, occupation, and accumulated wealth.

social class A group of people who share similar values, interests, and behaviours.

CULTURAL INFLUENCE

Culture can be defined as the accumulation of values, rules of behaviour, forms of expression, religious beliefs, and transmitted behaviour patterns for a people or society that shares a common language and environment. Culture tends to encourage or discourage particular behaviours and mental processes.[34] Culture has considerable influence on buying behaviour. Today, culture in Canada is getting more attention because of rapid increases in immigration. As cultural diversity increases, companies must re-examine their sales and marketing strategies. Within most societies, there are communities whose members share value systems based on common life experiences and situations that differ from those of the dominant culture. We call such value system a **microculture**. Some microcultures, such as elderly consumers, Blacks, Southeast Asians, and Aboriginal Canadians, are important market segments.

culture The values, beliefs, institutions, transmitted behaviour patterns, and thoughts of a people or society.

microculture Value systems shared by communities based on common life experiences and situations that differ from those of the dominant society's culture.

"It would never work out between us, Tom—we're from two totally different tiers of the upper middle class."

Perception—How Customer Needs Are Formed

perception A process through which sensations are interpreted, using our knowledge and experience.

Perception is the process through which sensations received through sight, hearing, touch, taste, and smell are interpreted, using our knowledge and experience. Buyer behaviour is often influenced by perception.[35] When Volkswagen announced that it would build an ultra-luxury car selling for more than $100 000, many people questioned the merits of this decision. Could the maker of the Beetle and the Golf compete in the market segment dominated by Lexus, Mercedes Benz, Jaguar, and BMW? So far, sales of the Volkswagen Phaeton have been slow even though most automobile journalists view it as a truly luxurious car. [36] Is perception the barrier to the Phaeton's sales growth?

CUSTOMER RELATIONSHIP MANAGEMENT WITH TECHNOLOGY

Managing Multiple Contacts with CRM

Salespeople often find that groups of their contacts have common interests and buying motives. Customers and prospects may be segmented into groups by buying influences, by the products they purchase, by the industries in which they are involved, or by their size. Customer relationship management software can enable the salesperson to easily link contacts as groups and to produce accumulated information that is custom-fitted to the needs of people in a specific group. For example, each owner of a specific product may receive a telephone call, personalized letter, or report that describes the benefits of a new accessory available from the salesperson. (See the exercise Managing Multiple Contacts with CRM on page 195 for more information.)

We tend to screen out or modify stimuli, a process known as selective perception, for two reasons. First, we cannot possibly be conscious of all sensations we're receiving at one time; just the commercial messages we see and hear each day are enough to cause sensory overload. Second, we are conditioned by our social and cultural background, and by our physical and psychological needs, to use selectivity. Similarly, buyers may screen out or modify information presented by a salesperson if it conflicts with their previously learned attitudes or beliefs. The prospect who is convinced that "I will never be able to master the personal computer" is apt to use selective perception when the salesperson begins discussing user-friendly features. Salespeople who can anticipate this problem of selective perception should acquire as much background information as possible before meeting with the prospect. During the first meeting with the customer, the salesperson should make every effort to build a strong relationship so that the person opens up and freely discusses personal perceptions. Salespeople who do this have accepted one of the great truisms in sales and marketing: "Facts are negotiable. Perception is rock solid."

BUYING MOTIVES

Every buying decision has a motive behind it. A **buying motive** can be thought of as an aroused need, drive, or desire that stimulates purchasing behaviour intended to satisfy that need, drive, or desire. Our perceptions influence or shape this behaviour. An understanding of buying motives provides the salesperson with the reasons why customers buy.

buying motive An aroused need, drive, or desire that initiates the buying-decision process.

As you might expect, some buying decisions are influenced by more than one buying motive. The buyer of catering services may want food of exceptional quality served quickly so that all the guests can eat together. This customer may also be quite price conscious. In this situation, the caterer should attempt to discover the **dominant buying motive (DBM)**. The DBM will have the greatest influence on the buying decision.[37] If the customer is anxious to make a good impression on guests who have discriminating food tastes, then food quality may be the dominant buying motive. Successful salespeople are those who adopt product strategies that uncover the dominant buying motives that will influence the purchase decision. In Chapter 11 we describe a process that identifies buyer needs that you can use to discover customers' buying motives.

dominant buying motive The motive that has the greatest influence on a customer's buying decision.

EMOTIONAL VERSUS RATIONAL BUYING MOTIVES

A careful study of buyer perceptions and behaviour reveals that people make buying decisions based on both emotional and rational buying motives. An **emotional buying motive** is one that prompts the prospect to act because of an appeal to some sentiment or passion. When customers buy expensive Harley-Davidson motorcycles, they are paying for much more than a high-flying "hog"; they are purchasing entry into a community of like-minded enthusiasts who share a passion for all things Harley.[38] Emotions can be powerful and often serve as the foundation of the dominant buying motive. A **rational buying motive** usually appeals to the prospect's reason or judgment

emotional buying motive A motive that prompts the prospect to act as a result of an appeal to some sentiment or passion.

rational buying motive A motive that prompts the prospect to act because of an appeal to the prospect's reason or better judgment such as price, quality, and availability of technical assistance. Generally these result from an objective review of available information.

THE CUSTOMER'S PERSPECTIVE

How Do Customers Judge Service Quality?

In the growing service industry there is intense price competition. One gets the impression that every buyer decision hinges on price alone. However, a closer examination of service purchases indicates that service quality is an important factor when it comes to developing a long-term relationship with customers.

How do customers judge service quality? Researchers have discovered valuable insights about customer perceptions of service quality. From their survey of hundreds of customers in a variety of service industries, they discovered that five service-quality dimensions emerged:

1. *Tangibles* are things the customers can see, such as personnel and equipment.
2. *Reliability* is the ability to perform the desired service dependably, accurately, and consistently.
3. *Responsiveness* is the willingness of sales and customer service personnel to provide prompt service and help customers.
4. *Assurance* includes the employees' knowledge, courtesy, and ability to convey trust and confidence.
5. *Empathy* means the provision of caring, individualized attention to customers.

Customers apparently judge the quality of each service transaction in terms of these five quality dimensions. Companies need to review these service-quality dimensions and make sure that what they offer measures up to the customer's expectations. Salespeople should recognize that these dimensions have the potential to add value to the services they sell.[b]

based on objective thought processes. Some common rational buying motives include quality, price, and availability of technical assistance.

Emotional Buying Motives

Many purchases are guided by emotional buying motives, which is why many firms use emotional selling appeals. An ad for Trimark Investments says, "Introducing four investment solutions that will put you to sleep." Even technology firms sometimes rely on appeals to emotions. GTE, the giant telecommunications firm, says, "We're working to help make your life easier." Doing business in Canada is never purely rational or logical. To inspire people and move them in the right direction, salespeople often have to engage them emotionally.[39] In a world filled with look-alike products, emotional factors can have considerable influence. If two vendors have nearly identical products, then the influence of each vendor's salespeople becomes more important. The salesperson who is able to connect with buyers at a personal level will have the advantage.

Rational Buying Motives

A purchase based on rational buying motives is generally the result of an objective review of available information. The buyer closely examines product or service information with an attitude that is relatively free from emotion. Professional buyers or purchasing agents are most likely to be motivated by such rational buying motives as on-time delivery, financial gain, competent installation, saving of time, increased profits, reduced costs, or durability. Business buyers representing large firms, such as Nortel, Air Canada, and Canadian National Railways, rely on a buying

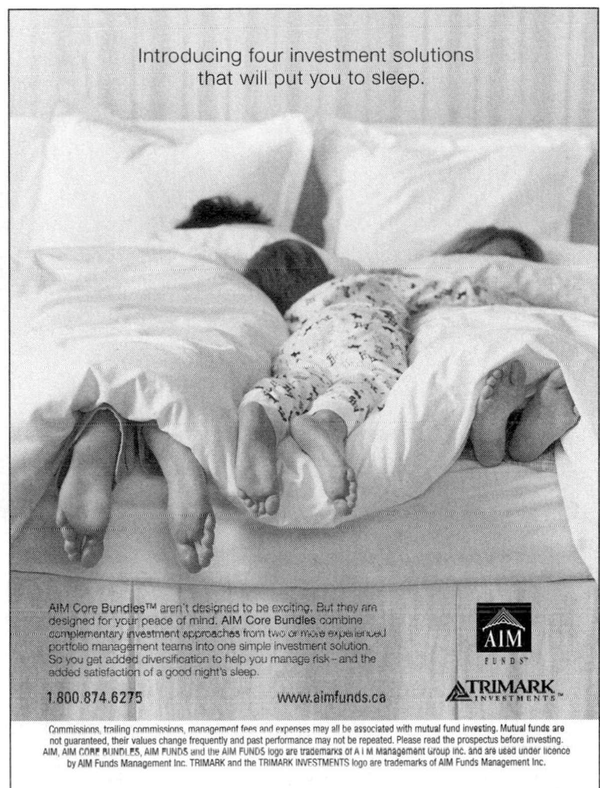

This Trimark Investments ad appeals to a customer's emotional buying motives.

This Samsung Electronics Canada ad appeals to a customer's rational buying motives.

Rational buying motives usually influence the purchase decisions of the professional buyer.

process that is more formalized than the consumer buying process. Purchases made by these companies usually call for detailed product specifications, written purchase orders, and formal approval. The business buyer and the salesperson work closely during all stages of the buying process that begins with a precise definition of the customer's problem. Salespeople who sell to business buyers spend a great deal of time gathering, interpreting, and disseminating customer-specific information.[40]

PATRONAGE VERSUS PRODUCT BUYING MOTIVES

Another way to help explain buyer perceptions and behaviour is to distinguish between patronage and product buying motives. Patronage buying motives and product buying motives are learned reasons for buying. These buying motives are important because they can stimulate repeat business and referrals.

Patronage Buying Motives

patronage buying motive A motive that causes the prospect to buy a product from one particular company rather than another. Typical patronage buying motives include superior service, attractive decor, product selection, and competence of the salesperson.

A **patronage buying motive** is one that causes the prospect to buy products from one particular business. The prospect has usually had prior direct or indirect contact with the business and has judged this contact to be beneficial. In those situations where there is little or no appreciable difference between two products, patronage motives can be highly important. At a time when look-alike products are very common, these motives take on extra importance. Some typical patronage buying motives are superior service, complete selection of products, competence of sales representatives, and ability to buy online.

PRODUCT BUYING MOTIVES

product buying motive A motive that causes the prospect to buy one particular product brand or label over another. Typical product buying motives include brand, quality, price, and design or engineering preference.

A **product buying motive** is one that leads a prospect to purchase one product in preference to another. Interestingly enough, this decision is sometimes made without direct comparison between competing products; the buyer simply feels that one product is superior to another. Numerous buying motives trigger prospects to select one product over another, including brand, quality, price, and design or engineering preference.

SUMMARY

The importance of developing a customer strategy is introduced in this chapter. This type of planning is necessary to ensure maximum customer responsiveness. Buying procedures and policies can vary greatly from one buyer to another. If a salesperson does not learn how each buyer plans to make a purchase, then his or her selling process will likely be out of alignment with the customer's buying process.

Business buyer behaviour was compared to consumer buyer behaviour. Three types of business buying situations were described: new-task buy, straight rebuy, and modified rebuy. Systems selling, a common business buying strategy, was also described. Three types of consumer buying situations were described: habitual, variety-seeking, and complex. Customers make buying decisions in many ways, so it is inappropriate to view the buying process as a uniform pattern of decision making. However, there is a common decision-making model that most buyers apply to their unique circumstances. The typical stages in the buying-decision process are needs awareness, evaluation of solutions, resolution of problems, purchase, and implementation. This model is especially helpful in understanding organizational buying decisions and large consumer acquisitions. Three selling approaches for creating value appeal to certain types of transactional, consultative, and relationship customers.

We note that buyer behaviour is influenced in part by individual physiological and psychological needs. Maslow's hierarchy ranks these needs. Numerous group influences—the roles we assume, reference groups, social class, and culture—shape our psychological needs and influence buyer behaviour.

"Perception" is defined as the process of selecting, organizing, and interpreting sensations received by our five senses to produce meaning. We discuss emotional and rational buying motives. Emotional buying motives prompt the prospect to act because of an appeal to some sentiment or passion. Rational buying motives tend to appeal to the prospect's reasoning power or judgment. We also compare patronage and product motives. Patronage buying motives grow out of a strong relationship that has developed between the customer and the supplier. When competing products are quite similar, patronage motives can be very important. Product buying motives are usually in evidence when a prospect purchases one product in preference to another.

Key Terms

Business Buyer Behaviour **176**
Buyer Resolution Theory **183**
Buying-Decision Process **180**
Buying Motive **189**
Complex Buying Decision **179**
Consumer Buyer Behaviour **176**
Culture **187**
Customer Strategy **175**
Dominant Buying Motive **189**
Emotional Buying Motive **189**
Esteem Needs **186**
Group Influences **186**
Habitual Buying Decision **178**
Microculture **187**
Modified Rebuy **177**
New-Task Buy **177**
Patronage Buying Motive **192**
Perception **188**
Physiological Needs **186**
Product Buying Motive **192**
Rational Buying Motive **192**
Reference Group **187**
Role **186**
Security Needs **186**
Self-Actualization **186**
Social Class **187**
Social Needs **186**
Straight Rebuy **177**
Systems Selling **178**
Variety-Seeking Buying Decision **179**

Review Questions

1. According to the Strategic/Consultative Selling Model, what are the three prescriptions for the development of a successful customer strategy?
2. List and describe the three most common types of business buying situations.
3. Describe the five major steps in the typical buying process.
4. List and describe three selling approaches for creating value that appeal to various types of customers.
5. According to the buyer resolution theory, a purchase is made only after the prospect has made decisions about five buying factors. What are they?
6. Explain how Maslow's hierarchy of needs relates to buyer behaviour.
7. Describe four group influences that affect buyer behaviour.
8. What is meant by the term "perception"?
9. Distinguish between emotional and rational buying motives, and between product and patronage buying motives.
10. J. D. Power, founder of J. D. Power and Associates, says, "We define quality as what the customer wants."[40] Do you agree or disagree with his observations? Explain your answer.

Application Exercises

1. Select several advertisements from a trade magazine. Analyze each one, and determine which rational buying motives the advertiser is appealing to. Explain whether these advertisements also appeal to emotional buying motives.
2. The $100 000 Volkswagen Phaeton is a far cry from the Volkswagen Beetle. VW's new flagship model is designed to challenge Lexus, Mercedes Benz, and BMW. The Phaeton, like the original Lexus LS400, is positioned as another choice in the luxury-car market. Do you think potential customers accept the Phaeton as a truly luxurious car? Will customer perceptions play a role in the acceptance of this new model? Explain your reasoning.
3. J. D. Power and Associates is a global marketing information services firm that helps businesses and consumers make better decisions through credible customer-based information. The company provides an unbiased source of marketing information based on opinions of consumers. Visit **www.jdpower.com** and become familiar with the type of information services offered. View some of the studies done on Canadian consumer satisfaction and be prepared to discuss interesting findings in class.

ROLE-PLAY EXERCISE

In this role play, you will assume the role of a salesperson working at a clothing store. The inventory includes a wide range of business professional clothing such as suits, sports coats, dress shirts, and accessories; the store also offers a full range of business casual clothing. A member of your class will assume the role of a customer who visits your store for the purpose of buying clothing for work. He or she is about to graduate and will start work at a new job in approximately two weeks. In addition to clothing, your store offers complete alteration services and credit plans. During the role play, you should develop a relationship with the customer using strategies discussed in previous chapters and determine the customer's needs. At the conclusion of the role play, ask the customer to evaluate your sales methods.

CRM Application Exercise MANAGING MULTIPLE CONTACTS WITH CRM

The ACT! database software identifies four firms involved with architecture. You can look up these firms and arrange to contact them. Start by selecting Lookup, Other and, on the blank record, enter "architectural" in the Account Code field and click OK. ACT! will display four records with architectural in that field.

Scheduling Multiple Telephone Calls. Starting with the first record, Bryan Enterprises, select the schedule call icon or select the following menu choices: Schedule, Calls. Use your mouse to select the following Monday, pick OK, select 9:00 a.m., pick OK, and on the menu, choose Follow up, and pick OK. On the next window, called Schedule an Activity, select the box labelled "Contact . . . ," which displays another window called Select a Contact. On the Select a Contact window, pick the box labelled Lookup. This will return you to the Schedule an Activity window, where you can pick OK. To confirm that a phone call was scheduled with each person in these architectural firms, select View, Task List. When the Task List window appears, choose the Time Period, Future, and pick OK when finished.

Creating Form Letters. You can create a form letter to send to each of the people in the four architectural firms by selecting Write, Edit Template, typing the word "letter," and pressing Enter. A template with codes will be displayed. Type the words, "I'll call Monday," then select File, Save As, and type "Form" then press Enter. Select File, Close. To prepare the four letters, select Write, Form Letter, type "Form," and press Enter. On the next window, labelled Prepare Form Letter, choose Active Lookup and Document, then pick OK. The first form letter will be displayed on your screen. By pressing the Page Down key, you can review all four letters. Select Print (Ctrl+P) to print the four letters and File, Close to close the letter window.

Case Problem

Ron Trudel has been selling cars for Pembina Dodge Chrysler in Winnipeg since 1985. Before that, he sold farm machinery, worked in retail, owned an import company, and operated as a manufacturer's agent. Ron Trudel has been recognized four times by Chrysler Canada with a Senate Membership, an award that recognizes the top 50 salespeople in Canada each year. When asked why he has done so well, Ron Trudel says,

> Selling is easy. The first thing you have to remember is the golden rule: Treat every customer as you would want to be treated. The next most important thing is enthusiasm. Customers know immediately if you don't have enthusiasm, and I think I have as much today as when I started selling. I greet customers as soon as they come into our dealership, and I try to develop some rapport within the first 35 seconds. That's important too. I ask questions and I listen. It's very important to understand customer needs before you start making recommendations. When families are involved, I always encourage the husband and wife to visit our showroom together. I also like to see the children come along. Each family member has different buying motives and, if you listen to them interact while they visit your showroom, you can easily see what buying motives each person has, and you can try to appeal to all of them. It's also nice when the whole family is involved because this is a major decision, one which everyone should enjoy, and one which everyone will remember for years to come. The first responsibility of the salesperson is to ensure that everyone has good memories of the occasion. That's why I also take such good care of my customers after the sale.

What does Ron Trudel do for his customers? He regularly calls them to see if they are happy with their purchase and the service they are getting. In fact, he even gets his customers to call him when they want service so that he arranges it with the service department for them; he says, "Even if they just want an oil change, I ask them to call me. If they're tied up at the office and can't get away, I'll even pick up their vehicle for them, have it serviced, and deliver it back to them when it's done."

Ron Trudel has been selling cars long enough now that he gets a lot of business from repeat customers and from referrals. Customers will come to the dealership to see him and, if he's not there, they will go away and come back again. Some have even called him at home to see if he was going to be in the next day. His effort and customer dedication have been paying off to the point where he is currently selling about twice as many vehicles as the average salesperson.

And he does put in a lot of effort. Ron Trudel looks after a lot of little things. He makes sure customers leave with all the relevant information, as many customers want to think about their vehicle purchase for some time and to compare dealerships. For many customers this is a very major decision, probably the biggest after buying a home. Ron Trudel calls all prospects a few days after they visit the showroom to see if he can help them further. This has resulted in many sales for him that might otherwise have gone elsewhere. When it comes to effort, Ron Trudel is always selling. He estimates that about 30 percent of his time is spent prospecting. One of his favourite methods is to look through old company sales slips to see which customers have bought cars from salespeople who are no longer at the dealership. Then he calls them to see if they are thinking about another purchase, or if there is anything he can do to help them. Ron Trudel is also an active member in his church group, golfs regularly, and belongs to several fraternal and service organizations, where he also networks. In fact, Ron Trudel says, "I'm always prospecting. Nothing gets mailed from our house without my business card in it. I even send one with my telephone and electricity payments each month. I've left them in restaurants, posted them on bulletin boards, and generally leave them anywhere they might get noticed."

Recently, a prospect walked into the showroom holding one of Ron's business cards. When Ron Trudel began to ask him some questions toward the need-discovery process, it was quickly apparent that the customer knew exactly what he wanted. Ron quoted him a price, to which the customer responded that he had a slightly better offer from one of the other Chrysler dealerships in Winnipeg. Further questioning revealed that the customer had bought his last car from that other dealership, but the salesperson he had bought the car from no longer worked there. The new salesperson that he had been talking to didn't seem to be particularly interested in his business. While Ron Trudel was trying to decide whether to meet the price, he asked the prospective customer, "Where did you get my card?"[41]

Questions

1. Does it appear that Ron Trudel has built his customer strategy on the three prescriptions featured in the Strategic/Consultative Selling Model? Explain.
2. If this prospective customer had already been offered a low price on a new car, why did he come to see Ron Trudel?
3. Should Ron Trudel focus on patronage or product buying motives while making his presentation to this customer? Explain.
4. What does it appear that Ron Trudel has learned about customer behaviour from his years as a car salesperson?

CHAPTER 9

Developing a Prospect Base

The Stevens Company Limited **www.stevens.com** is the largest distributor of supplies to physicians, hospitals, and nursing homes in Canada. Its sales representatives sell more than 500 000 medical supplies and equipment products from Ontario to British Columbia. It also employs inside telesales people to service inactive accounts, smaller accounts, and new accounts that are not sufficiently large to justify the time of a field sales representative. Inside telesales staff use ACT! contact software, with which, Jeff Stevens says, the company maintains a detailed profile of customers, prospects, and all support personnel. With a single computer keystroke, staff can bring up detailed information on any of more than 8000 contacts in the database. Customer service has been improved because the ACT! software reminds the sales representatives when it's time to make a follow-up call and shows them important account information at a glance.[1]

The makers of ACT! and other software vendors such as Epicor, EDSI, and ActiveSales are helping companies develop effective customer relationship management systems. These systems are at the heart of every successful one-to-one marketing initiative. Success in selling depends on one's ability to identify prospects, gain insight into the prospect's needs, and develop an accurate picture of a prospect's importance to your business.[2]

LEARNING OBJECTIVES

After studying this chapter, you should be able to

1. Discuss the importance of developing a prospect base
2. Identify and assess important sources of prospects
3. Describe criteria for qualifying prospects
4. Explain common methods of organizing prospect information
5. Name some characteristics that are important to learn about customers as individuals and as business representatives
6. Describe the steps in developing a prospecting and sales forecasting plan

Prospecting—An Introduction

Gerhard Gschwandtner, editor of *Selling Power*, says, "The main purpose of a salesperson is not to make sales, but to create customers."[3] Identifying potential customers is an important aspect of the customer strategy. In the terminology of personal selling, this process is called **prospecting**, as a potential customer—someone who meets the qualification criteria established by you or your company—is referred to as a prospect.

prospecting A systematic process of identifying potential customers.

Finding prospects who can make the decision to purchase is not an easy process. This is especially true in business-to-business sales. In many situations, the salesperson must make the sales presentation to many people involved in the purchase decision. This group of people is referred to as the **buying centre**. One member of the buying centre might be the *technical influencer* who can influence the purchase by getting a positive answer to the question "Does the product meet the company's specifications?" Another member might be the *user influencer*, or the person who will actually use the product. This person is usually in the best position to assess the product or service features that are important, so that the purchase can do the job that needs to be done. Of course, there is generally a *financial influencer*. This is the person who controls the "purse strings" and may want answers to the questions "What is our initial cost?" and "What will be our longer-term operating costs?"

buying centre The group of people involved in making a purchase decision.

Any or all of these people may be involved in a purchase decision, and a salesperson must be able to identify all of them and ensure that their needs are satisfied. During periods of economic uncertainty, or when the importance of the purchase decision increases for the company, the decision-making process typically moves upward in the organization. It is sometimes difficult for salespeople to make connections with upper-level executives. One solution is to plan a joint sales call involving a higher-level executive from your own company.[4]

The goal of prospecting is to build a **prospect base** made up of current customers and potential customers. Many successful companies find that current customers account for a large percentage of their sales. Every effort is made to keep these clients satisfied because they provide the repeat business that is necessary to maintain profitability.

prospect base A list of current and potential customers.

THE IMPORTANCE OF PROSPECTING

Every salesperson must cope with customer attrition—that is, the inevitable loss of customers over a period of time, which can be attributed to a variety of causes. Unless new prospects are found to replace lost customers, a salesperson will eventually face a reduction in income and possible loss of employment. To better understand the significance of prospecting, let us examine a few common causes of customer attrition.

1. *The customer may move to a new location outside the salesperson's territory.* The Canadian population is very mobile. This cause of attrition is especially common in the retail and service areas.

2. *A firm may go out of business or merge with another company.* In some areas of business the failure rate is quite high. In recent years we have witnessed a record number of mergers, which have caused massive changes in purchasing plans.

3. *A loyal buyer or purchasing agent may leave the position because of promotion, retirement, resignation, or serious illness.* The replacement may prefer to buy from someone else.

4. *Sales are lost to the competition.* In some cases, the competition offers more value. The added value may take the form of better quality, a better price, a stronger relationship, better service, or some combination of these factors.

Some studies reveal that the average company loses 15 to 20 percent of its customers every year. Depending on the type of selling, this figure might be higher or lower. Clearly, many customers are lost for reasons beyond the salesperson's control. If salespeople want to keep their earnings at a stable level, they will need to develop new customers.

Joe Girard, a popular sales trainer, uses the analogy of the Ferris wheel to illustrate the relationship between prospecting and customer attrition. As people (i.e., customers) get off the Ferris wheel, the operator (i.e., salesperson) fills their seats one at a time, moves the wheel a little, and continues this process until all the original riders have left the wheel and new ones come aboard (see Fig. 9.1 on page 200). In selling, of course, established customers do not come and go this fast. With the passing of time, however, many customers will be replaced.

PROSPECTING REQUIRES PLANNING

Prospecting should be viewed as a systematic process of locating potential customers. Some prospecting efforts can be easily integrated into a regular sales call. Progressive marketers are doing three things to improve the quality of the prospecting effort:

1. *Increase the number of prospects.* You want to see a continuous flow of potential prospects who, in the analogy of Figure 9.1, board the Ferris wheel, because they are the source of sales opportunities. If the number of potential prospects declines sharply, the number of sales closed will also decline.

2. *Improve the quality of the prospects.* Companies that have adopted quality improvement view this phase of prospecting as critical. They have established quality standards that ensure a steady supply of prospects with high profit potential.[5] In the absence of such quality standards, it may be necessary to drop unproductive customers, for example, when they demand more sales and service resources than their purchase volume justifies.[6]

3. *Shorten the sales cycle by qualifying prospects.* Quickly determine which of the new prospects are *qualified* in terms of need, ability to pay, and authority to purchase the product. Gerhard Gschwandtner says, "Time is the ultimate scorekeeper in the game of selling." He points out that

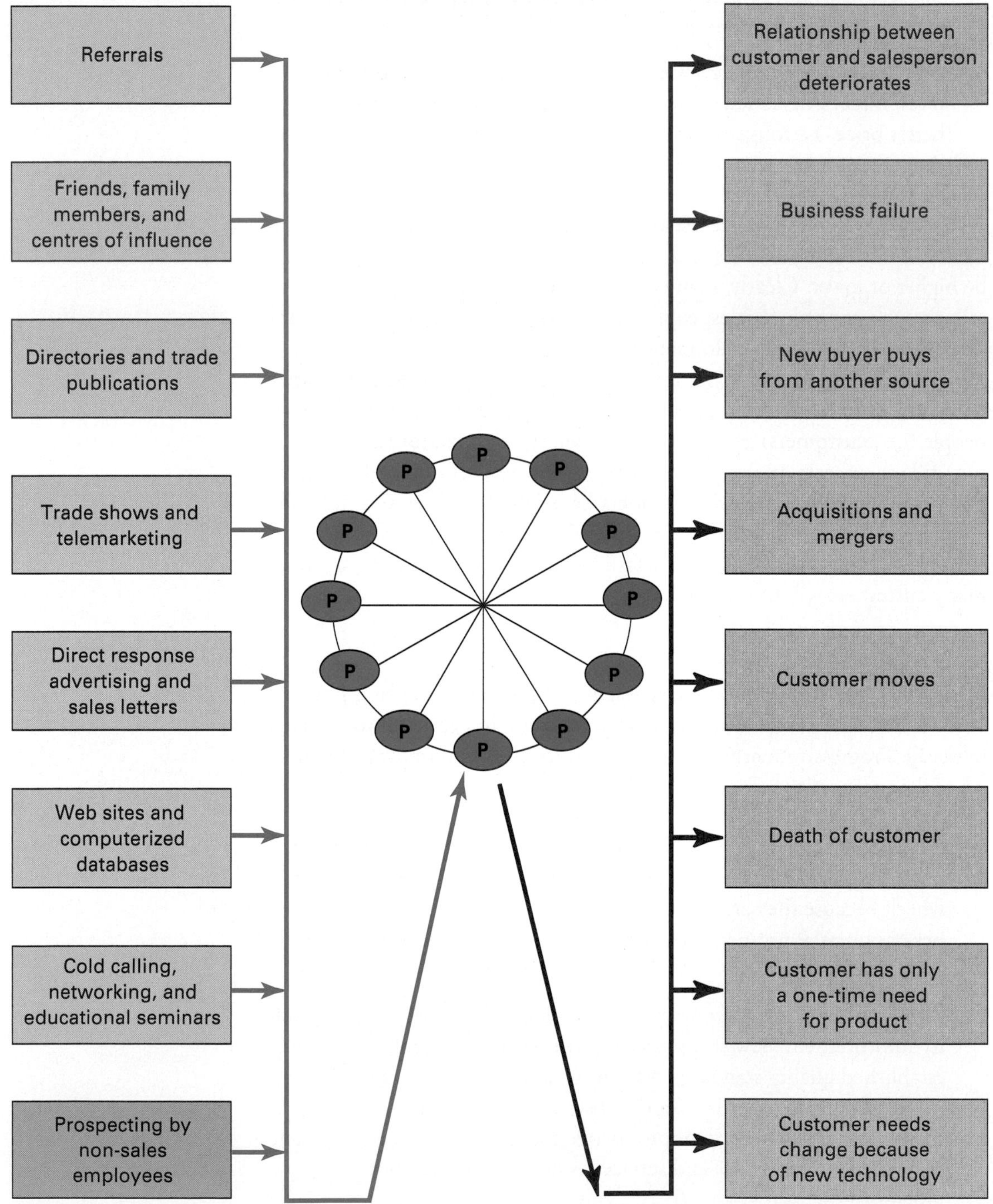

Figure 9.1 The Ferris wheel concept, illustrates the resupply of an ongoing list of prospects to combat customer attrition. It is part of the customer strategy of Joe Girard, world sales record holder.

many salespeople do not meet their sales goals because they do not quickly qualify new prospects.[7] Later in this chapter we examine qualifying practices and discuss how to shorten the sales cycle with sales force automation methods.

In most selling situations, prospecting begins with a study of the market for your product or service. When Pitney Bowes first developed the desktop postage meter, the company conducted a careful study of the market. At first glance, equipment of this nature seemed well suited only to large business firms. With additional market analysis the company identified many additional customers who could benefit from purchasing the product.

Colonel Harland Sanders, founder of Kentucky Fried Chicken, visited 1008 restaurants before he received his first sale.

PROSPECTING ATTITUDE

As noted in Chapter 4, attitudes serve as a foundation for our behaviour. Salespeople who view prospecting as an important key to success spend time every day on this activity. Prospecting is not thought of as a chore, but an opportunity to identify persons who can benefit from your product or service. Prospecting is viewed as a process that can take place in virtually any environment—social situations, on an airplane, while attending a professional meeting, or wherever people are present.[8]

Prospecting requires self-discipline. Ian Selbie, president of Vancouver-based Power Marketing, argues that salespeople should give prospecting

CUSTOMER RELATIONSHIP MANAGEMENT WITH TECHNOLOGY

Using the Same CRM Software As AT&T

AT&T implemented a customer relationship management program that resulted in major increases in productivity and improved customer service. The first stage of the automation project involved 11 000 desktop computers and the popular ACT! software. This combination of hardware and software resulted in a reported 15 to 20 percent improvement in productivity. AT&T salespeople gained easier and quicker access to such account information as the prospect's name, title, company, assistant's name, and notes concerning the account. Placing the database on a server gives all network users access to this important information.

Information in a CRM database can be reviewed before a salesperson calls or visits a prospect, thereby ensuring a more personalized contact. By using CRM, salespeople gain a competitive edge in relating to their prospects' needs and interests.

You have the opportunity to use a demonstration version of the same software that AT&T uses. Just as an AT&T salesperson would be, you are assigned 20 prospect accounts and given individual and company information about each account's contact person in the database. Your participation in the CRM case studies and exercises will give you hands-on experience with the strategic development of a prospect base using modern sales technology. Not only will you be using the same software that is being used by thousands of salespeople, you will also be working with data that are derived from authentic selling challenges. (See the CRM case study Reviewing the Prospect Database on page 219 for more information.)

greater priority: "Every sales person should not only have a revenue quota, but also a quota for meetings with new prospective clients monthly. Nobody can manage results, only the activity that leads to results."[9] Colonel Harland Sanders, founder of Kentucky Fried Chicken, relied on prospecting to succeed as an entrepreneur. In his initial attempts to sell his secret fried chicken recipe, he visited more than a thousand restaurants. The first 1008 sales calls ended in rejection, but number 1009 gave him his first Yes. With the passing of years, the number of restaurants serving his special recipe grew to 600 and Harland Sanders became a multimillionaire.[10]

Sources of Prospects

Every salesperson must develop a prospecting system suited to a particular selling situation. There are several sources of prospects, and each should be carefully examined.

- Referrals
- Friends, family members, and centres of influence
- Directories
- Trade publications
- Trade shows and special events
- Telemarketing
- Direct response advertising and sales letters
- Web sites
- Computerized databases
- Cold calling
- Networking
- Educational seminars
- Prospecting by non-sales employees

REFERRALS

referral A prospect who has been recommended by a current customer or by someone who is familiar with the product or service.

The use of referrals as a prospecting approach has been successful in a wide range of selling situations. In most cases referrals result in higher rates in closing sales, larger sales, and a shorter sales cycle. A **referral** is a prospect who has been recommended by a current customer or by someone who is familiar with the product. Satisfied customers, business acquaintances, and even prospects who do not buy can often recommend the names of persons who might benefit from owning the product or using your service. Customers are more likely to give a referral if they perceive value in the product you sell. When you build value into your sales process, you increase the odds that the customer will give you a referral.

Endless Chain Referrals

One approach to obtaining referrals, called the endless chain referral, is easy to use because it fits naturally into most sales presentations. A salesperson selling long-term health care insurance might ask "Miss Chen, who do you know who might be interested in our insurance plan?" This open-ended question gives the person the freedom to recommend several prospects and is less likely to be answered with a no response. Be sure to use your reference's name when you contact the new prospect, as in this example: "Mary Chen suggested that I call you."

Trade shows are very effective for prospecting. Barry Siskind has helped many North American companies benefit from trade show participation.

Referral Letters and Cards

Another approach, a variation of the endless chain technique, is the referral letter. In addition to requesting the names of prospects, the salesperson asks the customer to prepare a note or letter of introduction that can be delivered to the potential customer. The correspondence is an actual testimonial prepared by a satisfied customer. Some companies give their salespeople a preprinted referral card to use to introduce the salesperson. The preprinted card has a place for your customer to sign the new prospect's name and his or her own name.

FRIENDS, FAMILY MEMBERS, AND CENTRES OF INFLUENCE

A person who is new in the field of selling often uses friends and family members as sources of information about potential customers. It is only natural to contact people we know. In many cases these people have contacts with a wide range of potential buyers. The centre-of-influence method involves establishing a relationship with a well-connected influential person who is willing to provide information about potential prospects. This person may not make buying decisions but has influence on other people who do. To illustrate, consider the challenge facing Gary Schneider, creator of a powerful software product that would help small farmers optimize their crop selection. After spending several years developing the product, Gary and his wife began selling the product one copy at a time. During one cold call on a major crop insurer, Gary met a senior researcher who immediately saw the benefits of his product. This respected researcher was in a position to influence buying decisions at his company and to provide prospect information for other crop insurers.[11]

PRECISION TARGET MARKETING

Use Scott's Directories and Selectories

• for personal contact to arrange a face-to-face sales call

• to save valuable time by pinpointing hot prospects that need your product or service

• to prepare telemarketing call sheets

• to produce mailing labels and personalized letters for sales literature and promotions

• to build a personalized prospect database

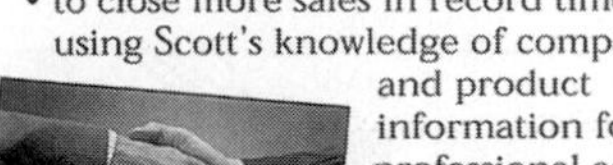

• to close more sales in record time... using Scott's knowledge of company and product information for a professional and well prepared presentation!

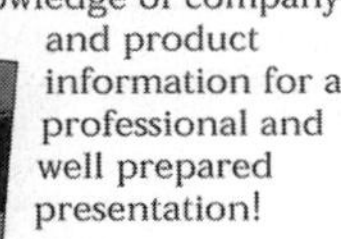

SCOTT'S
DIRECTORIES

1450 Don Mills Road
Don Mills, Ontario M3B 2X7
(416) 442-2122, 1-800-668-2374
Fax (416) 510-6875

3300 Côte Vertu, Suite 410
Ville St-Laurent, QC H4R 2B7
(514) 339-1397, 1-800-363-1327
Fax (514) 339-1396

Scott's directories are good sources of prospects for salespeople.

DIRECTORIES

Directories can help salespeople search out new prospects and determine their buying potential. A list of some of the more popular national directories is provided here.

The Blue Book of Canadian Business, published by Canadian Newspaper Services International Limited, lists 2500 medium- to large-size Canadian firms with sales of more than $10 million or having more than 500 employees.

The Canadian Key Business Directory, available from Dun & Bradstreet, lists and profiles the top 20 000 businesses in Canada.

Canadian Directory of Industrial Distributors lists industrial distributors by product specialty and geographic location. Also contains information on age of company, types of accounts serviced, main contacts within firms.

Canadian Trade Index, published by Canadian Manufacturers & Exporters, is available in print, on CD-ROM, and online; it lists more than 30 000 manufacturers, distributors, and industrial service companies.

Fraser's Canadian Trade Directory containing 350 000 listings in four volumes is designed to help you find suppliers of specific products or services, including many non-Canadian companies that have distributors or agents in Canada.

Scott's Directories publishes separate regional volumes—Atlantic, Quebec, Ontario, and Western—which are also available on CD-ROM. They are designed to help locate businesses by company name, province or city, or type of business. (There is also a *Greater Toronto Directory* available from Southam Inc.)

Polk city directories provide detailed information on the citizens of a specific community. Polk, in business for more than 125 years, publishes about 1100 directories covering 6500 communities in Canada and the United States. Each directory can usually be obtained from the local government or chamber of commerce.

These are just a few of the better-known directories. There are hundreds of additional directories covering national, regional, and local business and industrial firms. Some directories are free, while others must be purchased at a nominal fee. One of the most useful sources of free information is the telephone directory, most of which have a classified section that groups businesses and professions by category (i.e., Yellow Pages).

If you are involved in the sale of products in international markets, International Trade Canada offers several services to assist you, such as the Canadian Trade Commissioner Service. Canada has trade commissions in more than 125 cities throughout the world, which can provide such essential services as market intelligence and identification of potential customers, suppliers, or distributors and agents. Another valuable resource is the Export Development Corporation, a Crown corporation that helps Canadian exporters compete throughout the world. The corporation provides a wide range of financial and risk management services, and country and market information on most countries where Canadians sell. On its Web site (**www.edc.ca**), you can also view Canadian export performance data by country, and view country economic and credit summaries.

www.dfait-maeci.gc.ca

TRADE PUBLICATIONS

Trade publications provide a status report on every major industry. If you are a sales representative employed by one of the huge food wholesalers that supply supermarkets, then you will benefit from a monthly review of *Canadian Grocer* magazine. Each month this trade publication reports on trends in the retail food industry, new products, problems, innovations, and related information. Trade journals such as *Women's Wear Daily*, *Home Furnishings*, *Canada IT*, *Pulp & Paper Canada*, and *Canadian Underwriter* are examples of publications that might help salespeople identify prospects.

TRADE SHOWS AND SPECIAL EVENTS

A trade show is a large exhibit of products that are, in most cases, common to one industry, such as electronics or office equipment. The prospects walk into the booth or exhibit and talk with those who represent the exhibitor. Trade shows, according to Darrell Komick, president of Calgary-based Prairie Stage Productions Ltd., are "a fundamental way of collecting sales

Bentley Motor Cars invited a number of potential clients to the famous Le Mans 24-hour endurance race. This special event helped the company develop its prospect base.

leads." He also points out that, in some instances, trade shows can reduce the cost of making a sales call by one-third, and salespeople can make contacts in a shorter period of time.[12] In some cases sales personnel invite existing customers and prospects to attend trade shows where they will have an opportunity to demonstrate their newest products.

A special event can be a hockey game, a golf tournament, a reception for a dignitary, or a charity event. Bentley Motor Cars invited a number of potential clients to the famous Le Mans 24-hour endurance race where prospects watched the Bentley race car compete while sipping champagne. In Canada, charity events serve as a venue for cultivating wealthy clientele who can afford a Bentley automobile.[13]

TELEMARKETING

telemarketing The practice of using telephone contact to prospect for, qualify, sell to, and service customers.

www.deerhurst.com

Telemarketing is the practice of using telephone contact to prospect for, qualify, sell to, and service customers. It is becoming increasingly important as companies look for ways to increase their sales productivity; telemarketing is much less expensive than field sales calls. When Mass Mutual Life Insurance was considering buying Deerhurst Resort, about two hours north of Toronto, it hired Outlook Marketing to research market potential. Outlook began by compiling corporate profiles from such sources as Web sites, business journals, and chambers of commerce. Then Outlook's team of telemarketers went to work to gain additional information: how many people travel for a company, where they go, how long they stay, which types of hotels they use, who selects the travel locations and who influences the decisions, and much more. The information was then given to the sales staff in Toronto to use in developing and implementing its sales strategy. Sales the next year increased by 35 percent, and the following year by another 22 percent. Sean Mullen, director of sales at Deerhurst, admits that keeping account information accurate is a challenge for his six field salespeople. Each quarter, he uses an inside salesperson to update the entire database originally developed by the telemarketers.[14]

DIRECT RESPONSE ADVERTISING AND SALES LETTERS

Many advertisements invite the reader to send for a free booklet or brochure that provides detailed information about the product or service. In the category of business-to-business marketing, advertising has the greatest power to generate inquiries. Some firms distribute postage-free response cards (also known as *bingo cards*) to potential buyers. Recipients are encouraged to complete and mail the cards if they desire additional information. In some cases the name of the person making the inquiry is given to a local sales representative for further action.

Sales letters can easily be incorporated into a prospecting plan. The prospecting sales letter is sent to persons who are in a position to make a buying decision. Shortly after the letter has been mailed (i.e., three or four days), the prospect is called and asked for an appointment. The call begins with a reference to the sales letter. To make the letter stand out, some salespeople include a promotional item. As noted in Chapter 6, all sales letters must be written with care. To get results, sales letters must quickly get the reader's attention.

WEB SITES

Thousands of companies and business people have established Web sites, one purpose of which is to prospect for potential customers. Mary Kay Canada has more than 26 000 beauty consultants. When customers contact the company though its Web site, they are asked for the name of their beauty consultant. If they do not have one, they are asked for the first three characters of their postal code, and an independent beauty consultant is recommended to them. Mary Haurilak, co-ordinator of communications and public relations, sees the Internet as a great way to attract new customers but, she says, "Consultants are always meant to have the personal contact first and any online ordering would be afterwards. . . . The Internet is completely being used as a complement and not as a replacement."[15]

New technologies can be used to enhance your online sales message. LifeFX is working with Kodak to develop personalized e-mail messages that will include a photo of the salesperson and a verbal message in the salesperson's own voice. With this technology, a salesperson could send an e-mail to an advance list of trade-show attendees to invite them to attend his or her booth.[16]

COMPUTERIZED DATABASES

With the aid of electronic data processing salespeople can match product features with the needs of potential customers quickly and accurately. In many situations a firm will develop its own computerized database. In other cases it is more economical to purchase the database from a company that

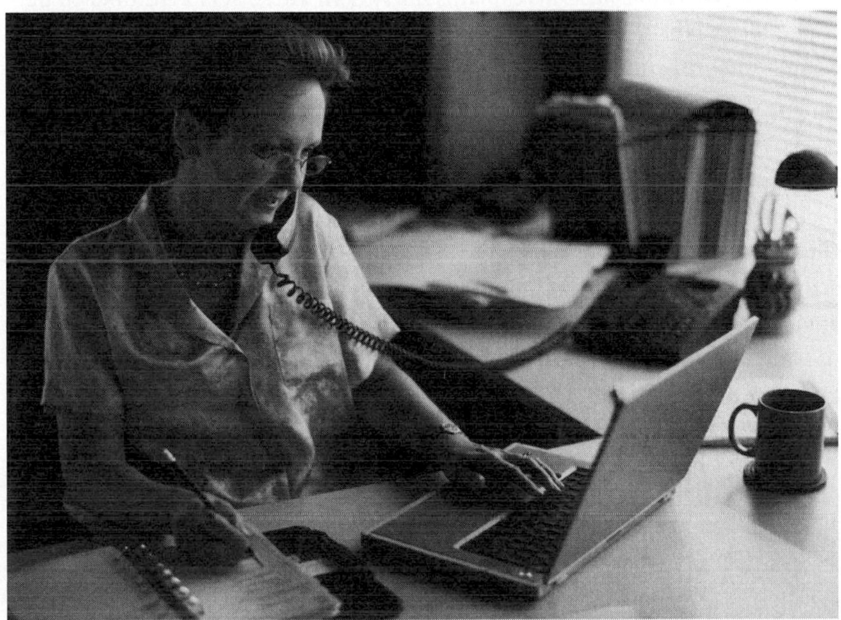

An up-to-date customer database can enhance prospecting.

specializes in collection of such information. For example, lists are available for boat enthusiasts, computer industry professionals, and subscribers to many magazines.

With the aid of a personal computer (PC), salespeople can develop their own detailed customer files. As newer PCs provide expanded storage capacity at a lower price than in the past, salespeople can accumulate a great deal of information about individual customers and use this information to personalize the selling process.[17] For example, a PC can help an independent insurance agent maintain a comprehensive record for each policyholder. As the status of each client changes (e.g., through marriage, the birth of children), the record can easily be updated. With the aid of an up-to-date database the agent can quickly identify prospects for various existing and new policy options.

COLD CALLING

cold calling A method of prospecting in which the salesperson selects a group of people who may or may not be actual prospects, and then calls on each one.

With some products, cold call prospecting is an effective approach to prospect identification. In **cold calling** the salesperson selects a group of people who may or may not be actual prospects and then contacts each one. For example, the sales representative for a wholesale medical supply firm might call on every hospital in a given community, assuming that each one is a potential customer. Many new salespeople must rely on cold calling because they are less likely to get appointments through referrals.[18] It takes time to develop a group of established customers who are willing to give referrals.

Successful cold calls do not happen spontaneously. Some strategic thinking and planning must precede telephone calls and personal visits. Canadian sales trainer and coach Steven J. Schwartz suggests that cold calls can be turned into hot calls through a telephone contact system that uses good call planning, strategic scripting, and effective script delivery. His book *How to Make Hot Cold Calls* explains his system and offers a number of personal diagnostic tools for salespeople.[19] We will answer many questions related to contacting customers in Chapter 10.

www.hotcoldcalls.com

NETWORKING

networking The practice of making and using contacts. It involves people meeting people and profiting from the connections.

In simple terms, **networking** is the art of making and using contacts: people meeting people and profiting from the connections.[20] Barry Siskind, an Ontario-based consultant and author of *Making Contact*, sees networking as a three-act process. In act one, you must be able to approach someone and engage them in conversation. Act two is when you "net-chat," a term Siskind uses to describe the technique of collecting and giving information, finding out as much as you can about the other person in the shortest time possible. Act three is where you disengage.

Many networkers spend too much time networking with too few people. Successful networkers must develop a number of skills. They must be able to engage people in conversation, make a good impression, gather information, disengage from conversation, and follow up on their contacts.[21] The following are some tips for networking.

1. *Be focused.* You should consider whom you need to network with, and where you are likely to meet these people.
2. *Be a listener.* Listening is important to any successful interpersonal activity. Besides, you learn more when you listen.
3. *Be sincere.* If you are superficial or only wish to use people, you will quickly be shunned.
4. *Be mobile.* Move around the room and mingle. Don't get trapped in one place.
5. *Be a joiner.* Many valuable contacts are made in charity organizations, on boards of trade, and in athletic clubs.
6. *Be sensitive to cultural and physical differences.* With the trend of increasing diversity in the workplace, salespeople who meet an individual from a different culture or with a physical difference need to focus on the person and not on the difference. You need to have empathy, show respect, and demonstrate sensitivity to differences.

There are three types of networks salespeople should nurture. Every salesperson will be well served by networking within his or her own organization. You never know when someone in finance or shipping will be needed to help solve a problem or provide you with important information. A second form of networking involves establishing contacts inside your industry. Make contact with experts in your field, top performers, leaders, successful company representatives, and even competitors. The third form of networking involves business contacts with people outside your industry, such as bankers, government officials, developers, and other people in your community. The local golf course may be a good place to make these contacts.[22]

EDUCATIONAL SEMINARS

Many salespeople are using educational seminars as a method of identifying prospects. Seminars provide an opportunity to showcase your product without pressuring prospects to buy. Polaroid Canada Inc. has been conducting seminars throughout Canada to display and demonstrate imaging products. Approximately 150 prospects have been attending each of these seminars, where Polaroid imaging specialists ensure that prospects' toughest questions are answered and prospects are able to explore imaging solutions in a hands-on environment.[23] The purpose of these seminars is not to sell products, but to demonstrate them and to educate prospects on Polaroid solutions. Microsoft, IBM, and Xerox have all used seminar selling at many locations throughout Canada. Many banks, investment firms, accounting firms, wine

*info*CANADA is just one of several companies that maintain databases of consumers and businesses, and that provide salespeople with an excellent way to prospect for customers.

www.polaroid.com

merchants, and consulting companies use seminars to generate new prospects. When inviting prospects, be clear about the seminar's content, and always deliver what you promise.[24]

PROSPECTING BY NON-SALES EMPLOYEES

Should service technicians, receptionists, bank tellers, and other non-sales personnel be involved in prospecting? For many organizations the answer is Yes. Prospecting need not be the exclusive responsibility of the sales force. At Computer Specialists Incorporated, employees have been given an incentive to pass along names of prospective customers. If the prospect becomes an account, the employee receives a bonus of up to $1000, depending on the value of the job. Over a one-year period this program generated 75 leads, resulting in nine new accounts.[25]

Employees do not have to work in sales to identify potential customers. However, they may not be alert to opportunities unless they are given an orientation to this role. Non-sales personnel need special training to function effectively in this role. An incentive program will keep them focused on new business opportunities for the organization.

SELLING IN ACTION

Seminar Selling

The use of educational seminars has become an important prospecting method. You can educate prospective customers with brochures, news releases, catalogues, or your Web site, but educational seminars offer the advantage of face-to-face contact. Barbara Siskind, in her book *Seminars to Build Your Business*, identifies 15 objectives for hosting seminars. Here are a few of the most important.

- *Obtain sales leads.* This is one of the most common objectives for seminars. You can obtain the names of attendees and arrange appointments for future sales calls. Seminars may also help identify actual product users, technical support people, or engineers who, while they may not be the decision makers, may influence the purchase decision.
- *.Promote your place of business.* Your place of business can become a destination for people who might otherwise not consider visiting it. You have an opportunity to create awareness of your company and develop a positive image for your entire operation and its capabilities.
- *Showcase and demonstrate your expertise.* Seminars allow you to show a carefully targeted group of people that you really know your stuff. Technical experts and others in the organization who can address clients' specific concerns can support salespeople.

Toronto-based Charon Systems, Inc., a systems integrator that deploys networks for organizations, regularly organizes seminars for 80 to 100 technology people from mid-sized firms. President David Fung estimates that 25 percent of prospects become clients.[a]

COMBINATION APPROACHES

In recent years we have seen an increase in the number of prospecting approaches used by salespeople. In many cases, success in selling depends on your ability to use a combination of the methods described in this chapter. For example, the large number of prospects identified at a trade show might be used to develop an effective telemarketing program. Prospects are called and an effort is made to set up a personal call. Prospects identified at a trade show or educational seminar might also be sent a sales-oriented newsletter, a sales letter, or an e-mail message.

Qualifying the Prospect

One of the most important keys to success in personal selling is the ability to qualify prospects. **Qualifying** is the process of identifying prospects who should be contacted. The qualification process is important for two reasons. First, a salesperson cannot afford to spend time calling on persons who are not legitimate prospects. Time conservation should always be a primary concern. Calling on potential customers is much more time consuming than calling on established customers. In terms of sales closings, a new customer can require several contacts. Second, a salesperson should identify prospects who can place an order large enough to cover sales expenses. Salespeople often rank prospects according to anticipated sales volume. The average sales call costs more than $200, so salespeople should restrict calls for customers who have limited buying potential.

qualifying The process of identifying prospects who are likely to become customers.

Every salesperson needs to establish qualifying criteria. The process involves finding answers to several basic questions.

1. *Does the prospect have a need for my product?* If you sell copy machines, it might appear that every business firm is a prospect. However, a firm that is outsourcing its copy work to FedEx Kinko's may not be a legitimate prospect. Qualifying involves probing for real needs. Let's assume you sell real estate for a large agency. You receive a call from someone who believes that owning a home is a good investment. At this point, it's important to find out what else makes owning a home important for that person. Get permission to ask questions and then determine the person's real needs. In the final analysis, you may decide it would be a waste of your time and the prospect's time to visit several homes that are on the market.[26]

2. *Can the prospect make the buying decision?* Ideally, you should talk to a person who has authority to buy or who can influence the buying decision. Talking to the right person within a large organization may involve collecting information from several sources. Some buying decisions are made by individuals and others are made by a committee. Expensive products often require the approval of a decision maker higher up in the organization.

3. *Can the prospect pay for the purchase?* It is usually not difficult to obtain credit information for consumers and business buyers. If you are selling products to a business, the *Dun & Bradstreet Reference Book* is an excellent source of credit information. A local credit bureau can provide credit information for a consumer. While the collection of credit information is not difficult, detecting financial instability can be much more complicated. In recent years, we have seen a steady stream of corporate scandals involving accounting irregularities, inflated balance sheets, and outright fraud.[27] Salespeople must be aware of the possibility that a customer may provide incorrect or misleading information.
4. *Will anyone close the sale?* Rick Page, author of *Hope Is Not a Strategy*, reminds us that many prospects evaluate products but do not buy. When an evaluation stalls, the prospect may have determined that the need is not of great enough magnitude or urgency to make the purchase. Also, in some cases there is not enough support within the company to reach closure. Rather than walk away from this situation, some salespeople move higher in the organization to determine the level of support for the purchase.[28] Numerous senior executives say they get involved in the sale early in the decision-making process, yet salespeople have difficulty meeting with high-level decision makers. Most senior executives will not meet with salespeople who are making cold calls. When appointments are granted, the time allocated may be very short; 5 to 10 minutes is not uncommon. How do you establish credibility for yourself and your company in a short time period? Be sure you know a great deal about the company before the appointment and be prepared to demonstrate your knowledge of the company and the industry it serves. Do not propose solutions until you fully understand the buyer's needs. Be sure to communicate value.[29]

This list can be revised to meet the needs of many different types of salespeople. A sales representative for an industrial equipment dealer will see the qualifying process differently from the person who sells commercial real estate. The main consideration is providing accurate answers to each question.

Organizing Your Prospect Information

When it comes to organizing prospect information, the salesperson has two choices. Some salespeople record prospect information on blank file cards (the 4 × 6-inch size is the most popular) or on preprinted file cards that have space for specific kinds of information; others record information in looseleaf notebooks.

At some retail stores, for example, salespeople record information about each customer in a "personal" book. Successful salespeople often have three or four bulging books that help them provide more personalized service to each customer. In addition to the customer's name, address, and account number they record the person's sizes, style preferences, hobbies and interests, birthday,

EVERYONE SELLS

Debi Rosati Helps Sell Business Ideas to Investors

Debi Rosati graduated in 1984 from Brock University with an Honours Bachelor of Business Administration and, in 1985, became a chartered accountant. During her career, Debi has held senior finance positions with Tundra, Cognos, and BDO Dunwoody. She was co-founder and chief financial officer for TimeStep Corporation, where she gained financing and operational experience at first hand in a technology start-up company. In 1999, TimeStep was acquired by Newbridge Networks Corporation. Shortly after, Debi joined the venture capital firm Celtic House as a general partner. She was involved in all aspects of venture investing, including evaluating investment opportunities, negotiating deal structure, and guiding operations.

Debi Rosati founded RosatiNet in 2001 as a venture catalyst firm that brings together technology start-up companies and investors. As a venture catalyst, she helps entrepreneurs get the right amount of money, at the right time, with the right investors and the right terms. To recognize both her business success and her long-standing involvement in and commitment to various community events and associations, Debi was awarded the *Ottawa Business Journal* Top 40 under 40 Award in 2001 and the Brock University Faculty of Business Distinguished Graduate Award in 2003. Debi also teaches in the professional programs at Sprott School of Business at Carleton University.

Reflecting on her career, Debi says, "Accounting is an important technical skill that I have used to bring value as a chief financial officer, venture capitalist, business advisor, and board member and community builder. However, my selling skills are equally important to my success as a venture catalyst. I am constantly networking for RosatiNet and its many clients."[b]

previous items purchased, and any other appropriate information. With this information available, each customer becomes a "prospect" for future purchases. Sales personnel often call their customers when new products arrive.

Author Harvey Mackay instructs his salespeople to develop a 66-question customer profile. The form is divided into categories such as education, family, business background, special interests, and lifestyle. In the process of collecting and analyzing this information, the salesperson gets to know the customer better than competing salespeople do. Harvey Mackay describes the benefits of developing a customer profile:

> "If selling were just a matter of determining who's got the low bid, then the world wouldn't need salespeople. It could all be done on computers. The 'Mackay 66' is designed to convert you from an adversary to a colleague of the people you're dealing with and to help you make sales."[30]

Mackay says that the 66-item customer profile helps the salesperson systematize information in a way that will make it more useful and accessible.

The use of file cards and notebooks is adequate for salespeople who deal with a small number of prospects and do not get involved in complex sales. The use of some type of computerized system is more appropriate for salespeople who deal with large numbers of prospects, frequently get involved in complex sales, and must continually network with management and members of the sales support team. A recent study conducted by *Sales & Marketing Management* magazine found that more than one-third of the companies surveyed use an automated lead-management system.[31] With the aid of modern technology salespeople can retrieve data from various sources no matter where they are. Regardless of the system used, most salespeople need to collect and organize two kinds of data: information about the prospect as an individual and information about the prospect as a business representative.

THE PROSPECT AS AN INDIVIDUAL

The foundation for a sales philosophy that emphasizes the building of partnerships is the belief that we should always treat the other person as an individual. Each prospect is a one-of-a-kind person with unique characteristics. The only possible way we can treat the prospect as an individual is to learn as much as possible about the person. The starting point is to learn the correct spelling and pronunciation of the prospect's name. Then acquire information about the person's educational background, work experience, special interests, hobbies, and family status. Interview industry people or employees at the company to acquire personal information.[32]

In Chapter 4 you were introduced to the concept of communication-style bias and the benefits derived from an understanding of communication styles. You also learned how to overcome communication-style bias and build strong selling relationships with style flexing. If at all possible, acquire information concerning the prospect's communication style before the sales call.

A lasting business partnership is based in large part on a strong personal relationship. Dale Carnegie, a pioneer in the field of human relations training and author of *How to Win Friends and Influence People*, recognized the importance of taking a personal interest in others. He said, "You can make more friends in two months by becoming interested in other people than you can in two years by trying to get other people interested in you."

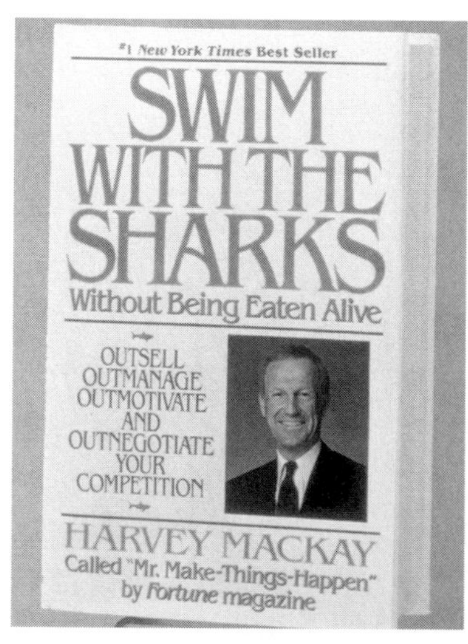

Well-known author Harvey Mackay instructs his salespeople to develop a 66-question customer profile. This information helps them to know the prospect both as an individual and as a business representative.

THE PROSPECT AS A BUSINESS REPRESENTATIVE

In addition to personal information about the prospect, it is important to collect certain business-related facts. This is especially important in business-to-business selling. Before calling on the prospect it pays to review various aspects of the company operation. Research starts with a document search for information about the company and industry.[33] What does the company manufacture or sell? How long has the firm been in business? Is the firm a leader in the field? Does the firm have expansion plans? Each company has a unique culture.

Most established firms have been doing business with one or more other suppliers. When possible, find out whom the company buys from and why. It always helps to know in advance who the competition is. Salespeople who take time to study personal and business facts will be in a stronger position to meet the prospect's needs.

SELLING MENTOR

Designing and Using Your Business Card

The business card continues to be a powerful tool for salespeople and sales support personnel. It provides a personal touch in our high-tech world. The business card communicates important information to prospects and customers. Donald Cooper, Canadian marketing consultant and judge in *Profit*'s first Canadian Business Card Competition, wants a card to explain what the company does as his first test of effectiveness. A card that simply says "Your source for innovative solutions" fails. To create effective business cards, here are some other tips to keep in mind.

- Use graphics, words, shape, colour, and texture to convey what you do, but use them tastefully.
- Make your cards pleasing to view and easy to read. Remember that some people will have difficulty reading small type.
- The card should feature all current contact information such as your e-mail address, telephone and fax numbers, and mailing address.
- Consider using both sides of the card. You might print your customer service philosophy or list the products you sell on the back of your card, or use other languages for international contacts.

Give your cards generously to people who might need to contact you later. Always offer your business card when networking. The card is useful when the contact tells others about your products or services.[c]

Developing a Prospecting and Sales Forecasting Plan

A major barrier to prospecting is time. There never seems to be enough time for a salesperson to do everything that needs to be done. In many situations, less than half of the workweek is devoted to actual sales calls. The remainder of the time is spent identifying and screening prospects, travel, paperwork, planning, sales meetings, and servicing accounts. Time devoted to prospecting often means that less time is available for actual selling. Given a choice, salespeople would rather spend their time with established customers. Attrition, of course, will gradually reduce the number of persons in this category, and prospecting will be necessary for survival.

Prospecting activities can be approached in a more orderly fashion with the aid of a plan. It is difficult to prescribe one plan that will fit all selling situations; however, most situations require the following similar types of decisions:

1. *Prepare a list of prospects.* You will recall that the prospect base includes current and potential customers. The process of enlarging the prospect base to include potential customers will vary from one industry to another. In the food service distribution industry, salespeople often start with a territorial audit.[34] This involves the collection and analysis of information about every food service operator (e.g., restaurants, hotels, colleges) in a given territory. Important information—such as the name of the operation, name of the owner or manager, type of menu—is

recorded on a card or entered into a computer. Some salespeople in this industry pinpoint each operator on a map of the territory. When the audit is complete, the salesperson analyzes the information on each food service operator and selects those that should be contacted. A salesperson who sells hotel and convention services could use a variation of the territorial audit. The list of prospects might include local businesses, educational institutions, civic groups, and other organizations that need banquet or conference services.

sales forecast Outlines expected sales for a specific product or service to a specific target group over a specific period of time.

2. *Forecast the potential sales volume that might be generated by each new account for each product.* A **sales forecast** outlines expected sales for a specific product or service to a specific target group over a specific period of time. With a sales forecast the salesperson is able to set goals, establish a sales budget, and allocate resources with greater accuracy. Preparing an accurate sales forecast can be a real challenge. Jack Stack, author of *The Great Game of Business,* says sales forecasts are too often based on gut feelings and wishful thinking. Salespeople need to begin the forecasting process with a careful estimate of sales volume to current customers. This is followed by an assessment of new sales to prospects that will be identified during the sales forecast period.[35]

routing The procedure used to determine which customers and prospects will be visited during a certain period of time.

3. *Anticipate prospect calls when planning the sales route; a systematic routing plan saves time and reduces travel expenses.* The procedure used to determine which customers and prospects will be visited during a certain period of time is called **routing**. Consider calls on prospective customers in developing your route plan. This approach helps minimize the cost of developing new accounts.

A plan helps give prospect identification greater purpose and direction. It also helps reduce the cost of developing new customers. Without a plan, salespeople tend to give prospecting too little attention. Paul Tindall of Toronto-based Coaching Works says, "Top performers prospect consistently. Low performers don't.[36] Planning for prospecting, and then prospecting, is important to selling success.

SUMMARY

Prospect identification has been called the lifeblood of selling. A continuous supply of new customers must be found to replace those lost for various reasons. *Prospecting* is the systematic process of locating potential customers.

Analysis of both your product or service and your existing customers can help to identify, locate, and even profile your prospects. Important sources of new customers include referrals (endless chain referrals, and referral letters and cards); friends, family members, and centres of influence; directories; trade publications; trade shows; telemarketing; direct response advertising and sales letters; Web sites; computer databases; cold calling; educational seminars; networking; and prospecting by non-sales employees. These prospecting techniques produce a list of names that must be evaluated using criteria developed by each salesperson. The process of prospect evaluation is called "qualifying."

Basic questions that can be used to qualify a prospect include: Is the person already buying from you? Is the person a former customer? Is the person a user of your product? and Is the person currently buying from a competitor? An estimate of the amount of sales that could be generated from this prospect and the prospect's credit rating should also be determined.

Information about both customers and prospects should be recorded systematically, whether on a special form, in a notebook, on cards, or in a computerized database. Information that is important to record about customers as individuals includes their correct name; their age and experience; and their education, family status, special interests and hobbies; and their communication style. Information that is important to record about customers as representatives of their business includes their authority to buy, the business's ability to pay, the company operations, and the company buying practices.

Development of a prospecting and sales forecasting plan requires preparation of a list of prospects, creating a forecast of potential sales volume from each new account, and anticipating prospect calls when planning a sales route.

Key Terms

Buying Centre **198**

Cold Calling **208**

Networking **208**

Prospect Base **198**

Prospecting **198**

Qualifying **211**

Referral **202**

Routing **216**

Sales Forecast **216**

Telemarketing **206**

Review Questions

1. List and briefly explain the common causes of customer attrition.
2. During periods of economic uncertainty, the decision-making process often moves upward. What basic tips would you give a salesperson who is calling on senior executives?
3. Describe three steps progressive marketers are taking to improve the quality of the prospecting effort.
4. List the major sources of prospects.
5. Explain how the endless chain referral method works for prospecting.
6. Discuss how direct-response advertising and sales letters can be used to identify prospects.
7. What are the most common methods of organizing prospect information?
8. What is *networking*? How might a real estate salesperson use networking to identify prospects?
9. What does the term "qualifying" mean? What are the four basic questions that should be answered during the qualifying process?
10. What is routing? How does this relate to the prospecting plan?

Application Exercises

1. You are a sales representative for Xerox Canada, which has just designed a new, less expensive, and better quality copying machine. Make a list of 15 prospects you would plan to call about this machine. From the material in this chapter, identify the sources you would use in developing your prospect list.
2. You are in the process of interviewing for a sales position with Sun Life Assurance of Canada. In addition to filling out an application form and taking an aptitude test, one of the items the agency manager requests of you is to develop a list of prospects with whom you are acquainted. He informs you that this list will represent the

prospects you will be working with during the first few weeks of employment. The agency manager recommends that you list at least 50 names. Prepare a list of 10 acquaintances you have who would qualify as prospects.

3. Visit **www.hotcoldcalls.com** and hit "Toolbox." Here you will find a "hot calls" self-assessment tool that asks you to complete 24 questions to help you identify mistakes you might make when making an initial telephone contact with prospective customers. Complete the survey and assess how well you did. Continue until you get all answers correct.

4. Locating companies to work for is a form of prospecting. Assuming you are interested in changing careers, develop a list of 10 companies for which you would like to work. Assign each company a priority according to your interest, from the most desirable (1) to the least (10). Organize your list in six columns showing the company name, telephone number, address, person in charge of hiring, prospect information, and priority. What sources did you use to get this information?

ROLE-PLAY EXERCISE

For this role play, you will assume a sales position at a Lexus dealership. You will just have completed a successful sale by signing the papers for the second new Lexus this customer has purchased in the past four years. Because you know your customer has had a very successful experience with his first Lexus, you have decided to use the referral methods described in this chapter. Review the material on referrals and plan what you will say to your customer to build your prospect base. Pair off with another student who will assume the role of your customer. Explain that satisfied customers often know other people who would consider purchasing a Lexus. You might say, "Considering the positive experience you have had as a Lexus owner, you probably know others who appreciate fine automobiles. Is there anyone who comes to mind?" If, after probing, your customer doesn't recall someone immediately, ask permission to call him later to see if anyone has come to mind. Ask this person for actual names, addresses, and other qualifying information about prospective customers whom he knows. Also, ask the customer if he would write a referral note or letter that you could use.

Case Problem

Many sales people are finding that once you have a customer, maintaining the relationship is a lot cheaper than finding a new customer. Salespeople are increasingly using contact software to improve service to existing customers. Marisa Trichilo is Ontario Accounts Coordinator for Western Inventory Service Ltd. (visit **www.inventoryservice.com.**), a national company that counts inventories and fixed assets for all types of businesses across Canada. She is giving her customers added value with ACT! contact software. Like most salespeople, she is trying to cope with expanded duties, faster work pace, and customers with high expectations. ACT! software helps her in the following ways:

- **Customer profile.** Complete information on each customer is available onscreen at the touch of a key. In addition to name, phone number, and address, she has a complete record of all past contacts. The profile also includes important personal and business information about the customer.
- **Organization and planning.** It is no longer necessary for Marisa to prepare a written "to do" list or a

planning calendar. All of this information can easily be entered into her portable computer. In the morning she simply clicks her Day At A Glance command and she is reminded of scheduled appointments, phone calls to be followed up, and other activities. If she needs to make a call at 2:00 P.M., she can press the Set Alarm button, which works like an alarm clock.

- **Correspondence.** ACT! software features a built-in word processor that makes it easy to prepare memos, letters, and reports. To send a standard follow-up letter to a customer, she simply brings up the letter from storage, enters the customer's name, and presses the appropriate key. The word processor automatically prints the inside address and mailing label. With ACT! software you can even send and receive e-mail. Most salespeople are responsible for numerous reports. The ACT! software can be used to generate a wide range of reports with a minimum of effort. It features 30 predefined reports for use in a wide range of sales and sales support areas.

David Florence, a sales representative with Motorola–EMBARC, makes more than a hundred phone calls each day. He appreciates the ACT! feature that permits automatic dialling. He simply identifies the customer's name and presses a key.

Questions

1. If your goal is to maintain long-term partnerships with each of your customers, what features of the ACT! contact software will be most helpful?
2. Let us assume you are selling copy machines in a city with a population of 100 000 people. Your territory includes the entire city. What features of the ACT! software would you use most frequently?
3. Some salespeople who could benefit from use of ACT! software continue to use a Rolodex or note cards to keep a record of their customers. What are some barriers to adoption of this type of technology?
4. Examine the first ACT! contact screen presented in Appendix A.
   - **a.** What is Bradley Able's position within the company?
   - **b.** What is the "date expected" for the sale to close?
   - **c.** What is the dollar amount forecast for this potential sale?

CRM Case Study REVIEWING THE PROSPECT DATABASE

Becky Kemley is the sales manager in the Dallas, Texas, office of SimNet Systems, which sells network products and services. Selecting and using the correct system—LAN (local area network), WAN (wide area network), or VPN (virtual private network)—can considerably enhance the productivity and the critical mission of Becky's customers. Becky's company is called a value-added reseller because its people help customers to maximize the value of the products bought through SimNet.

Becky's sales and technical support people may spend several months in the sales process or cycle. Salespeople telephone and call on prospects to determine whether they qualify for SimNet's attention. Time is taken to study the customer's needs (i.e., needs identification). The expert opinion of SimNet's technical people is incorporated into a sales proposal that is presented to the prospective customer. The presentation may be made to a number of decision makers in the prospect's firm. The final decision to purchase may follow weeks of negotiations with SimNet and consideration within the firm. Once a decision is made by a customer to buy from SimNet, Becky's people begin the process of acquiring, assembling, and installing the network system; they then follow through with appropriate training, integration, and support services.

Becky's company must carefully prospect for customers. SimNet may invest a significant amount of time helping a potential customer configure the right combination of products and services. This means that only the most serious prospects should be cultivated. Further,

Becky's people must ascertain that, if the investment of time is made in a prospective customer, the prospect will follow through with purchases from SimNet.

Becky is responsible for ensuring that prospect information is collected and used effectively. The network salespeople use the ACT! CRM software to manage their prospect information. The system, which is the same as the software available for use with this textbook, allows salespeople to document and manage their sales efforts with each prospect.

Becky has just hired you to sell for SimNet beginning December 1. Becky has given you the files of Pat Silva, a salesperson who has just been promoted to SimNet's corporate headquarters. Becky has asked you to review the status of Pat's 20 prospect accounts. Pat's customers have been notified that Pat is leaving and that a new salesperson, you, will be contacting them. Becky wants you to review each prospect's record. You are to meet with Becky next Monday. Be prepared to answer the following questions.

Questions

1. Which contact can you ignore immediately as a prospect for making a potential purchase?
2. Referring only to the "date close" category, which four prospects would you call immediately?
3. Referring only to the dollar amount of "sales forecast" category, which four accounts would you call first? Does the likelihood of "closing percentage" category have any influence on decisions concerning which prospects to call first? Why?
4. According to information on the Records and Notes (View, Notes) windows, which prospecting method did Pat Silva appear to use the most? Give examples.

ROLE-PLAY EXERCISE

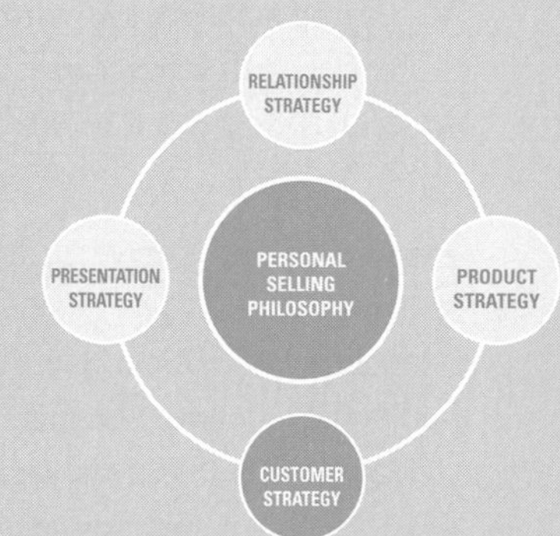

Developing a Customer Strategy

SCENARIO

You are a sales representative employed by the Park Inn International Hotel and Convention Centre. One of your primary responsibilities is to identify prospects and make sales calls that result in the development of new accounts. During each of these calls, you plan to build a relationship with the customer and describe selected value-added guest services and amenities offered by the Park Inn. You also try to learn as much as possible about the customer's buying process.

CUSTOMER PROFILE

Gabriela Ansari is the founder and chief executive officer of Cantrol Security Inc., a growing high-tech firm with more than a hundred employees. The company manufactures and sells security systems for use in residential homes, retail stores, and other commercial buildings. According to a recent article in *The Globe and Mail*, Cantrol Security is poised to grow very rapidly in the next year. The article described Gabriela Ansari as a workaholic who usually works 80 hours each week. Delegation does not come easily to this personable, hard-charging entrepreneur.

SALESPERSON PROFILE

Simon Julian has just completed the Park Inn sales training program and now wants to develop some new accounts. In addition to taking care of established customers, he plans to call on at least four new prospects every week.

PRODUCT

Park Inn International is a full-service hotel and convention centre located in Toronto, Ontario. The hotel recently completed a $2.8 million renovation of its meeting and banquet rooms.

INSTRUCTIONS

For this role play activity you will assume the role of Simon Julian. You will meet with Gabriela Ansari, role-played by another student, who appears to be a good prospect. During the first sales call, plan to learn more about Gabriela as an individual and acquire more information about Cantrol Security. This meeting will provide you with the opportunity to begin building a long-term partnership.

During the first meeting with a prospect, you like to present a limited amount of important product information. In this case the length of the appointment is 15 minutes, so you should not try to cover too much information. To prepare for the first sales call, read *Employment Memorandum Number 1* (pp. 5–7 of Partnership Selling on the CD-ROM). This memo describes the value-added guest services and amenities offered by the Park Inn.

For the purpose of this role play, Gabriela Ansari should be considered a consultative process buyer. You can assume that she will need help identifying and evaluating possible solutions. As you prepare for the first call, think about what may take place during future calls. Review the steps in the typical buying process (see Fig. 8.3). Keep in mind that today's more demanding customers are seeking a cluster of satisfactions. Study the Product Selling Model (Fig. 7.1) prior to meeting with Gabriela Ansari.

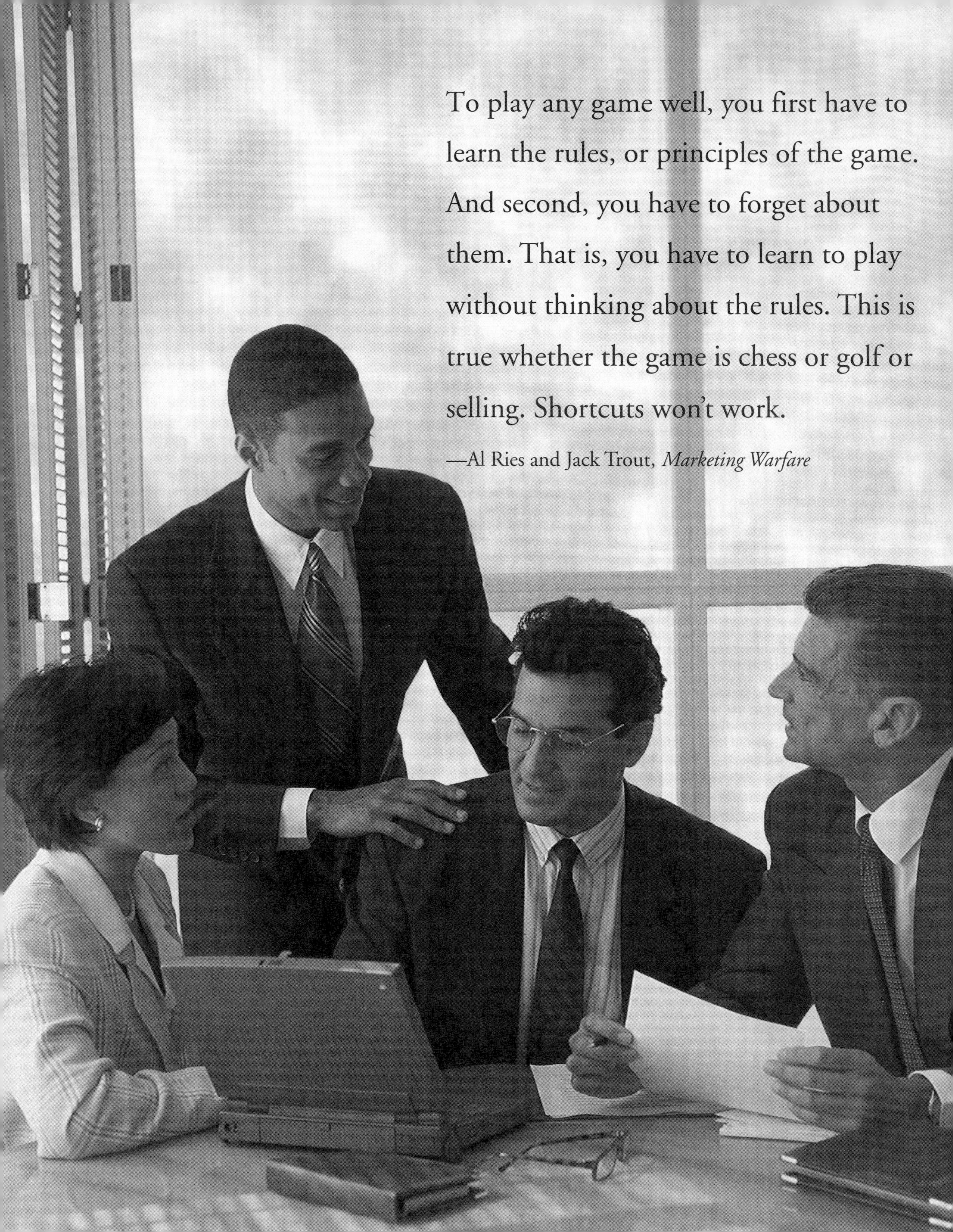

To play any game well, you first have to learn the rules, or principles of the game. And second, you have to forget about them. That is, you have to learn to play without thinking about the rules. This is true whether the game is chess or golf or selling. Shortcuts won't work.

—Al Ries and Jack Trout, *Marketing Warfare*

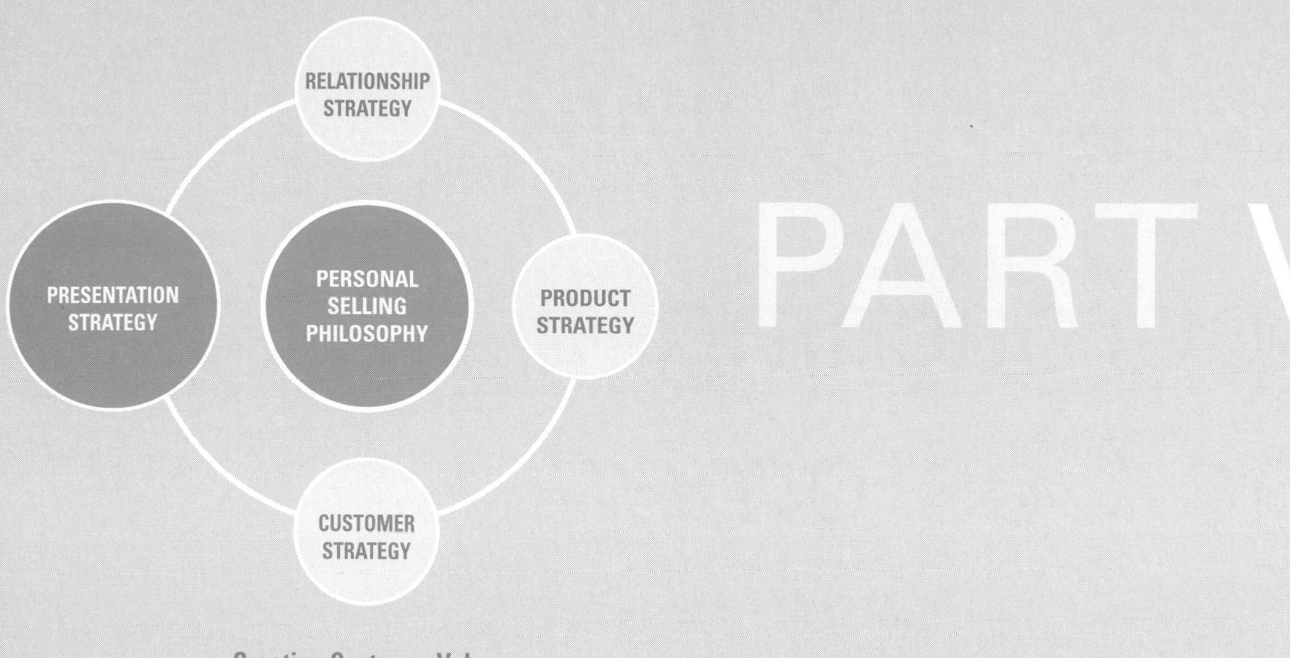

Creating Customer Value

PART V

Developing a Presentation Strategy

The chapters included in Part V review the basic principles used in the Strategic/Consultative Sales Presentation. You will use this information as you prepare presentation objectives, develop a presentation plan, and identify ways to provide outstanding service after the sale.

CHAPTER 10

Approaching the Customer

LEARNING OBJECTIVES

After studying this chapter, you should be able to

1. Describe the three prescriptions that are included in the presentation strategy
2. Describe the role of objectives in developing the presale presentation plan
3. Discuss the basic steps of the preapproach
4. Explain the merits of a planned presentation strategy
5. Describe the nature of team versus one-person presentation strategies
6. Describe the six main parts of the presentation plan
7. Explain how to effectively approach the customer
8. Describe seven ways to capture the prospect's attention and arouse interest

You might think that a sales force is unimportant for a pharmaceutical company that has a number of drugs needed by patients with serious health problems. Not true. Once Health Canada approves a drug, the sales force has to inform everyone who can be influential in the purchase decision for it, and they must ensure that it is available where and when needed.

Brenda Fisher (see page 37, Chapter 2) is one of about 150 Canadian salespeople at Janssen-Ortho Inc. Selling is not what she expected to be doing when she completed her B.Ed.: "I applied for teaching positions everywhere, but I didn't even get a thank you because there were so many applicants. When I applied for this sales job, the manager was skeptical as to why I wanted to sell. I tried to convince him that selling a product is the same as teaching a concept. You have to understand what the customer needs to know, and you have to communicate knowledge about your product and company and how you can meet their needs."

On any particular day, Brenda Fisher may have to approach general practitioners, specialists, nurses, residents, interns, wholesalers, pharmacists, or any combination of these. She may have to educate them about her company, her products, or herself. She may have to persuade them to buy her products, or she may simply need to remind them about Janssen-Ortho and the products that it manufactures.[1]

Everything you have studied in Chapters 1 through 9 is important to your success, but it is all part of preparing you for the actual face-to-face interaction with prospects and customers—the place where "the rubber meets the road." Chapters 10 though 15 will help you develop an effective presentation strategy to build credibility and trust. In particular, Chapter 10 provides you with the information needed to assume the role of consultant when approaching the customer.

Developing the Presentation Strategy

The presentation strategy combines elements of the relationship, product, and customer strategies. Each of the other three strategies must be developed before a salesperson can develop an effective presentation strategy.

The **presentation strategy** is a well-conceived plan that includes three prescriptions: (1) establishing objectives for the sales presentation, (2) developing the presale presentation plan needed to meet these objectives, and (3) renewing one's commitment to providing outstanding customer service (see Fig. 10.1).

presentation strategy A well-conceived plan that includes three prescriptions: establishing objectives for the sales presentation, preparing the presale presentation plan needed to meet these objectives, and renewing one's commitment to providing outstanding customer service.

The first prescription reminds us that we need to establish one or more objectives for each sales call. High-performance salespeople like Brenda Fisher understand that it is often possible to accomplish several things during a single call. A common objective of sales calls is to collect information

Figure 10.1 The Strategic/Consultative Selling Model provides the foundation for a successful consultative-style presentation strategy.

Strategic/Consultative Selling Model*

Strategic step	Prescription
Develop a Personal Selling Philosophy	✓ Value Personal Selling ✓ Adopt Marketing Concept ✓ Become a Problem Solver/Partner
Develop a Relationship Strategy	✓ Project positive, professional image ✓ Practise communication-style flexing ✓ Behave ethically
Develop a Product Strategy	✓ Become a product expert ✓ Sell specific benefits ✓ Configure value-added solutions
Develop a Customer Strategy	✓ Understand customer behaviour ✓ Discover customer needs ✓ Develop prospect base
Develop a Presentation Strategy	• Understand buying process • Prepare objectives • Provide outstanding service

* Strategic/consulative selling evolved in response to increased competition, more complex products, increased emphasis on customer needs, and growing importance of long-term relationships.

about the prospect's needs. Another common objective is to build relationships with those who will make the buying decision.

A carefully prepared presentation plan ensures that salespeople will be well organized during the sales presentation and prepared to achieve their objectives. A six-step presentation plan is introduced later in this chapter. Establishment of objectives for the sales presentation and preparation of the presale presentation plan must be guided by a strong desire to offer outstanding customer service. Achieving excellence is the result of careful needs analysis, correct product selection, clear presentations, informative demonstrations, win-win negotiations, and flawless service after the sale. Salespeople who are committed to doing their best in each of these areas will be richly rewarded.

PRESENTATION STRATEGY ADDS VALUE

How does precall planning add value? Value is added when you position yourself as a resource—not just a vendor. You must prove that you have important ideas and advice to offer.[2] A well-planned presentation adds value when it is based on carefully developed objectives for the sales call and on a presentation plan created to meet those objectives. Good planning ensures that the presentation is customized to meet the needs and time constraints of the prospect.

Salespeople need to be aware of the changing needs of their customers or risk losing out to their competition. Some salespeople do not pay enough attention to how they conduct business with their established customers. Without a precall plan, it's easy to miss opportunities to increase your knowledge of the customer's business, sell new products, or discover ways to improve service.[3]

Planning the Preapproach

preapproach Activities that precede the actual sales call and set the stage for a personalized sales approach, tailored to the specific needs of the prospect. This involves the planning necessary for the actual meeting with a prospect.

approach The first contact with the prospect, either face-to-face or by telephone. The approach has three objectives: to build rapport with the prospect, to capture the person's full attention, and to generate interest in the product you are selling.

Preparation for the actual sales presentation is a two-part process. Part one is referred to as the preapproach. The **preapproach** involves preparing presale objectives and developing a presale presentation plan. Part two is called the **approach** and involves making a favourable first impression, securing the prospect's attention, and transitioning to need identification (see Fig. 10.2). The preapproach and approach, when handled correctly, establish a foundation for an effective sales presentation.

The preapproach should be viewed as a key step in preparing for each sales presentation. Professional salespeople complete the preapproach for every presentation whether it involves a new account or an established customer. The preapproach includes the first two prescriptions for developing a presentation strategy: establishing objectives and creating a presale presentation plan.

ESTABLISHING PRESENTATION OBJECTIVES

Sales representatives employed by Nalco Chemical Company prepare for each sales call by filling out a 13-point precall planner. One section of this

Figure 10.2 Preparing for the presentation involves planning for the activities that will occur before meeting the prospect and for the first few minutes of actual contact with the prospect.

form requires the salesperson to identify the objectives of the call. Nalco is a company that emphasizes professionalism, long term partnerships, and staying focused on customer needs.[4]

www.nalco.com

In Chapter 8, we introduced the five stages of the typical buying process (see Fig. 8.3). When you are calling on a consultative or relationship buyer, you will usually not cover all of these stages during a single sales call. **Multi-call sales presentations** are especially common in complex sales. Therefore, it's best to develop presentation objectives suitable for each stage of the buying process. During the first stage—need awareness—prospects may or may not be aware of their needs or problems. The need awareness stage is the "investigation" stage. To uncover and clarify needs will require the use of appropriate questions (covered in detail in Chapter 11). The following presentation objectives would be appropriate during the first call on a new prospect:

multi-call sales presentations A standard practice in some industries where products are complex and buying decisions are made by more than one person. The purpose of the first call is to collect and analyze certain basic information that is used to develop a specific proposal.

- Establish rapport and begin building a relationship with the prospect.
- Obtain permission to ask about a prospect's needs.
- Obtain personal and business information to establish the prospect's profile.

During stage two of the buying process—evaluation of solutions—the customer is ready to consider possible solutions to solve his or her problems

SELLING IN THE GLOBAL ECONOMY

Approaching Prospects in Relationship-Focused Countries

In most countries of the world, business is conducted through established relationships and social networks. People in relationship-focused countries—including most of Africa, Central and South America, Arab countries, and the Asia/Pacific region—prefer to do business after personal relationships and trust have been established. It is often difficult to approach prospects directly in these countries so, if you are trying to make new contacts, you may need a third-party introduction to help bridge the relationship gap. You may use trade associations, chambers of commerce, banks, or even consultants who specialize in arranging introductions in some countries. International trade shows are popular and one of the best methods to make foreign contacts. People attend these shows expressly to make business contacts. An increasingly popular method is to participate in a trade mission. International Trade Canada organizes trade missions to many important foreign markets (**www.dfait-maeci.gc.ca**). Team Canada, led by the prime minister, has conducted seven trade missions since 1994 and has helped more than 2800 Canadian business representatives gain access to important international business leaders and decision makers. The Team Canada missions have contributed more than $30.6 billion to Canadian companies. Export sales account for more than 43 percent of all goods and services sold in Canada and provide excellent opportunities for Canadian salespeople.[a]

or fulfill his or her needs. In some cases, several solutions must be evaluated. Presentation objectives for stage two might include the following:

- Involve the customer in a product demonstration.
- Provide value justification in terms of cost reduction and increased revenue.
- Compare and contrast the features of a lease option with an outright purchase option.

Selecting presentation objectives with care can pay big dividends. When the sales presentation is guided by carefully established objectives, the sales cycle is usually shorter. In the business world, where everyone subscribes to the belief that "time is money," efficient planning and execution of the sales process is greatly valued by customers.

Once you have an appointment with the prospect and the presentation objectives have been established, consider sending a fax that outlines the agenda for the meeting. The fax will confirm the appointment and clarify the topics to be discussed.[5]

www.richardsonline.com

Multi-call sales presentations are common in many areas, including the retail field. The sale of recreational vehicles, leased automobiles, boats, and quality sound systems for the home or business typically require more than one sales call. Some clothing stores and independent tailors make office calls to sell tailored clothing. One example is Mitchells/Richards, a progressive retailer with a reputation for superior customer service. Its salespeople will

Extensive strategic planning is required for salespeople who use computer graphics tied into a desktop projection system such as this one from Proxima.

make office calls on request. Working with a customer at his office usually requires more than one sales call.[6]

TEAM SELLING PRESENTATION OBJECTIVES

In today's ever-changing business environment, team selling has surfaced as a major development. Team selling is ideally suited to organizations that sell complex or customized products and services that require direct communication between customers and technical experts. Sales teams can often uncover problems, solutions, and sales opportunities that an individual salesperson working alone might not discover.[7] In some situations, the involvement of technical experts can shorten the selling cycle. The team approach often results in more precise need identification, improved selection of the solution, and more informative sales presentation.

www.waterhousegroup.com/services/teamselling.html

Team sales presentations require a more detailed precall plan than individual sales calls. Each team member must have a clear understanding of the role he or she will play during the sales call. Sales presentation objectives should be clearly stated. Team members should share detailed information about the customer, understand the basics of a consultative sales presentation, and be prepared to add value.[8]

Often, teams are involved in developing the customer relationship and making purchase decisions after a partnership is established. As noted in Chapter 1, relationship selling is growing more popular. The long-term partnerships that develop are especially common in business-to-business sales. When a customer's decision-making process is guided by a team, the seller is likely to use a team-selling approach.[9]

Salespeople are trained to seek the assistance of another salesperson or to actually turn the customer over to another salesperson when problems surface. The other salesperson may bring to the selling situation a greater ability to identify the customer's needs or to select the appropriate product. Salespeople who have well-prepared presale objectives know when to seek assistance from another professional.

SELLING TO A BUYING TEAM

In some cases salespeople must address and satisfy both the individual and collective concerns of each participant in a multi-buyer situation. The decision makers may be members of a well-trained buying team, a buying committee assembled for a one-time purchase, or a board of directors.

As in any type of selling situation, the salesperson should attempt to determine the various buying influences. When possible, the role of each decision maker, the amount of influence he or she exerts, and each decision maker's needs should be determined before or during the presentation.

Some presentation strategies involve a team approach. The sales team might include a technical specialist or a senior company executive.

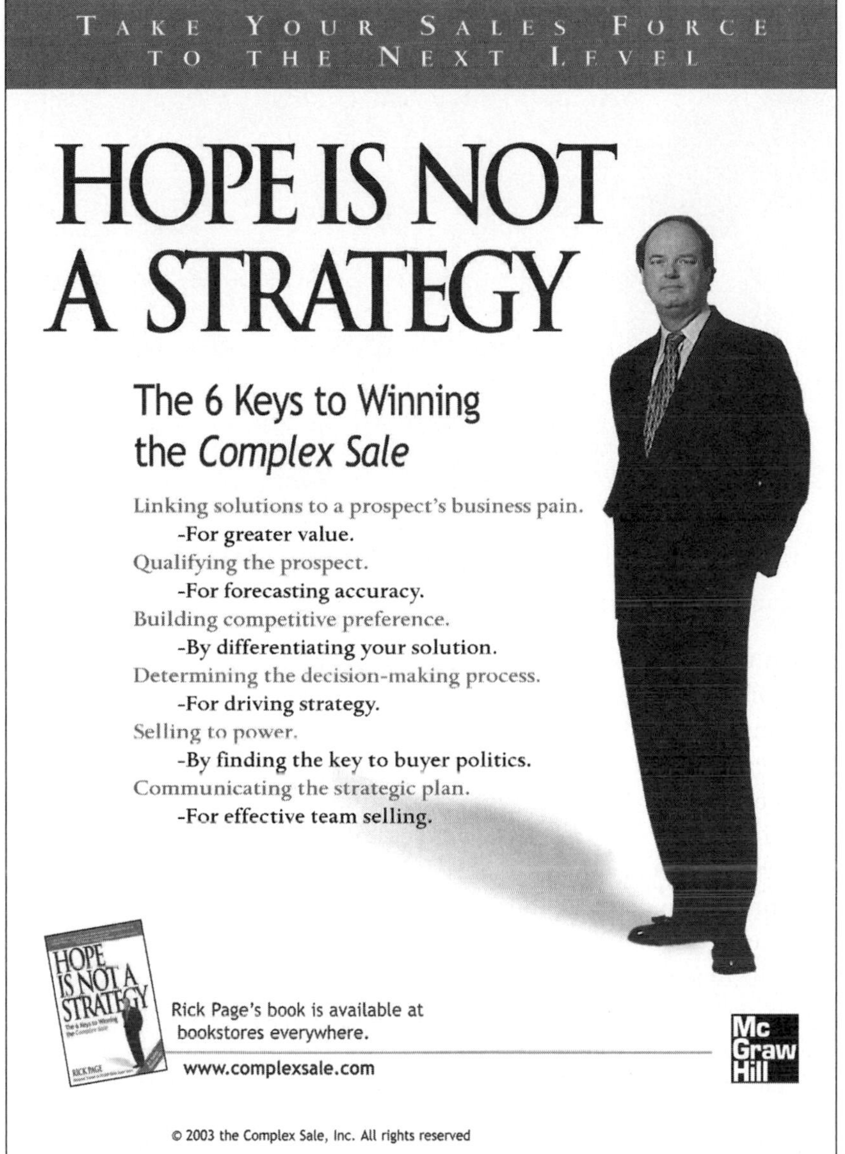

Rick Page's best-selling trade book *Hope Is Not a Strategy* emphasizes the need for strategic planning during the preapproach. His six keys to winning the complex sale in the age of information help salespeople move to the next level of selling.

Careful observation during the presentation can reveal who will use the product, who controls the finances, and who will provide the expertise necessary to make the correct buying decision.

When you make a group selling presentation, make sure all parties feel involved. Any member of the group who feels ignored could prevent you from closing the sale. Be sure to direct questions and comments to all potential influencers who might affect the buying decision. Find out if there are any silent team or committee members. A silent member is one who will influence the buying decision but does not attend the presentation. Silent members are usually senior managers who have a major influence on the buying decision. If a silent member does exist, you must find a way to communicate, directly or indirectly, with this person.[10]

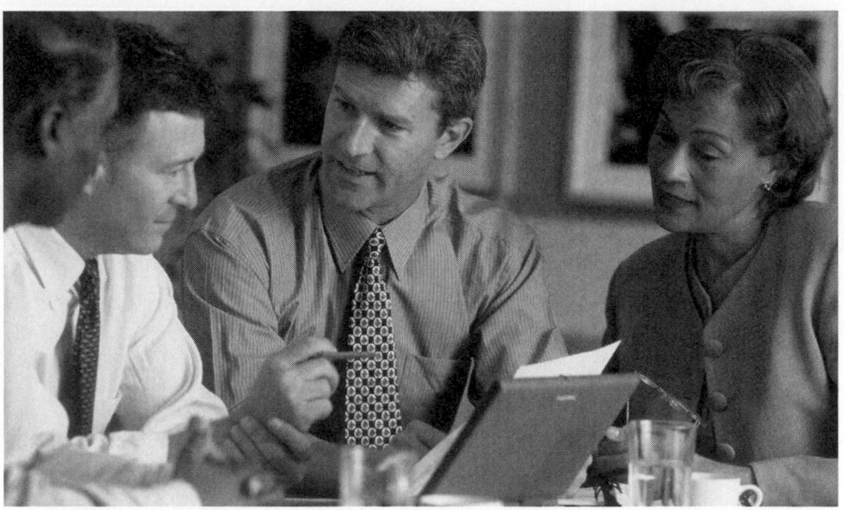

Well-prepared presale objectives will help salespeople address the needs of each person in a group selling situation.

INFORMATIVE, PERSUASIVE, AND REMINDER PRESENTATION OBJECTIVES

When preparing presale presentation objectives, it is important to make a decision concerning the overall purpose of the presentation. The major purpose may be to inform, persuade, or remind. The sale of highly technical products and services may begin with an informative sales presentation; the customer needs to be familiar with the product before making a buying decision. In another situation, where the customer's needs have been carefully identified and your product is obviously suited to these needs, a persuasive presentation would be appropriate. In the case of repeat customers, it is often necessary to remind them of the products and services you offer.

The time available to prepare presale objectives and create presale presentations varies depending on the complexity of the product, the customer's knowledge of the product, and other factors. The successful outcome of the complex sale is usually dependent on the time and effort invested in preparation. In some selling situations, the salesperson is given little time to prepare for the sales presentation. This is the case in some retail and service situations in which customers arrive unannounced.

Informative Presentation

The objective of a presentation that involves a new or unique product is generally to inform customers of its features and explain how these features will benefit the customer. Typically, people will not purchase a product or service until they become familiar with its application. Informative presentations are usually more prevalent when the product is first introduced to the market. A detail salesperson (introduced in Chapter 2) usually spends a great deal of time informing customers of new products and changes in existing products.

Persuasion The act of presenting product appeals so as to influence the prospect's beliefs, attitudes, or behaviour.

Persuasive Presentation

Some degree of persuasion is common to nearly all sales presentations. **Persuasion**—the act of presenting product appeals so as to influence the prospect's beliefs, attitudes, or behaviour—is a strategy designed to encourage the buyer to make a buying decision. Persuasion can be integrated into every phase of the sales presentation. A friendly greeting and a firm handshake at the time of initial customer contact represent a relationship-oriented form of persuasion. An enthusiastic sales demonstration is another type of persuasion common in sales. Additional forms of persuasion include converting features to buyer benefits, repeating feature–benefit statements, and asking for the sale. Persuasive strategies are designed to elicit a positive response from the prospect. It is never a good idea, however, to apply too much persuasion in an attempt to sell a product or service. These actions can perpetuate the stereotype of the pushy, unprofessional salesperson.

Reminder Presentation

In some selling situations, the primary objective of the sales call will be to remind the prospect of products and services offered by the company. Without this occasional reminder the prospect may forget information that is beneficial. Computer salespeople might periodically remind customers about special services (e.g., training classes, service contracts, and customized programming) available from the company they represent. An occasional reminder can prevent the competition from capturing the business.

Consideration of whether the overall presentation objective should be to inform, persuade, or remind will have a significant influence on your presale presentation plan and your efforts to provide outstanding service.

Developing the Six-Step Presentation Plan

Once you have established objectives for the sales presentation, you are ready for the next prescription: developing the presentation plan. This plan helps you achieve your objectives. Today, with increased time constraints, fierce competition, and rising travel costs, the opportunity for a face-to-face meeting with customers may occur less frequently. The few minutes you have with your customers may be your only opportunity to win their business, so careful planning is more critical than ever. Steve Schiffman, president of DEI Management Group, recalls meeting with a Yellow Pages sales representative who had failed to do even the most basic research prior to the sales call. The salesperson began the meeting with a question: "Are you happy with your advertising in the Yellow Pages?" DEI was not, at that time, listed in the Yellow Pages. A quick search of the Yellow Pages would have prevented this embarrassing experience.[11]

In preparation for development of the presentation strategy, it is helpful to review the three broad strategic areas that have been described in previous chapters: relationship strategy, product strategy, and customer strategy. Why is this review so critical? It is because today's dynamic sales presentations require consideration of the simultaneous influences of the relationship, product, and customer strategies. A careful review of these three areas sets the stage for flexible presentations that meet the needs of the customer.

PLANNING THE PRESENTATION

six-step presentation plan
Preparation involving consideration of those activities that will take place during the sales presentation.

Once you have sufficient background information, you are ready to develop a customized presale presentation plan. The plan is developed after a careful review of the **six-step presentation plan** (see Fig. 10.3). This planning aid is a tentative list of activities that will take place during the sales presentation. This presale activity will further strengthen your self-confidence and help avoid confusion in the presence of the prospect. Each step in this plan will be explained in chapters 10 to 15.

CUSTOMIZING THE PRESENTATION

Preparing a customized sales presentation can take a great deal of time and energy. Nevertheless, this attention to detail will give you added confidence and help you avoid delivering unconvincing hit-or-miss sales talks.

A well-planned sales presentation is a logical and orderly outline that features the salesperson's own thoughts from one step to the next. The presentation is usually divided into six main parts (see Fig. 10.3):

1. *Approach.* Preparation for the approach involves making decisions concerning effective ways to make a favourable first impression during the initial contact, to secure the prospect's attention, and to develop the prospect's interest in the product. The approach should set the stage for an effective sales presentation.

2. *Presentation.* The presentation is one of the most critical parts of the selling process. If the salesperson is unable to discover the prospect's buying needs, select a product solution, and present the product in a convincing manner, the sale may be lost. Chapter 11 covers all aspects of the sales presentation.

3. *Demonstration.* An effective sales demonstration helps verify parts of the sales presentation. Demonstrations are important because they provide the customer with a better understanding of product benefits. The demonstration, like all other phases of the presentation, must be carefully planned. Chapter 12 is devoted exclusively to this topic.

4. *Negotiation.* Buyer resistance is a natural part of the selling–buying process. An objection, however, does present a barrier to closing the sale. For this reason, all salespeople should become skillful at negotiating buyer concerns. Chapter 13 covers this topic.

5. *Close.* As the sales presentation progresses, there may be several opportunities to close the sale. Salespeople must learn to spot closing clues. Chapter 14 provides suggestions on how to close sales.

6. *Servicing the sale.* The importance of developing a long-term relationship with the prospect was noted earlier in this chapter. This rapport is often the outgrowth of postsale service. Learning to service the sale is an important aspect of selling. Chapter 15 deals with this topic.

The Six-Step Presentation Plan	
Step One: APPROACH	○ Review Strategic/Consultative Selling Model ○ Initiate customer contact
Step Two: PRESENTATION	● Determine prospect needs ● Select solution ● Initiate sales presentation
Step Three: DEMONSTRATION	● Decide what to demonstrate ● Select selling tools ● Initiate demonstration
Step Four: NEGOTIATION	● Anticipate buyer concerns ● Plan negotiating methods ● Initiate win-win negotiations
Step Five: CLOSE	● Plan appropriate closing methods ● Recognize closing clues ● Initiate closing methods
Step Six: SERVICING THE SALE	● Follow-through ● Follow-up calls ● Expansion selling
Service, retail, wholesale, and manufacturer selling.	

Figure 10.3 The Six-Step Presentation Plan. A presale plan is a logical and orderly outline that features a salesperson's thoughts from one step to the next in the presentation.

A truly valuable idea or concept is timeless. The six parts of the presale presentation plan checklist have been discussed in the sales training literature for several decades; therefore, they might be described as fundamentals of personal selling. These steps are basic elements of almost every sale and frequently occur in the same sequence. Of course some sales are made without an objective, and some customers buy before the salesperson attempts to close.

While these six basic selling steps are part of nearly every seminar, workshop, and course devoted to sales training, the emphasis given to each will vary depending on the nature of the selling situation. Keep in mind the understanding that each step in the plan provides an opportunity to add value.

The Approach

After a great deal of preparation, it is time to communicate with the prospect, either by face-to-face contact or by telephone. We refer to the initial contact with the customer as the *approach.* All the effort you have put into developing relationship, product, and customer strategies can now be

The sales presentation should be a model of good two-way communication.

applied to the presentation strategy. If the approach is effective, you will be given the opportunity to make the sales presentation. If, however, the approach is not effective, the chance to present your sales story may be lost. You can be the best-prepared salesperson in the business but, without a good approach, there may be little chance for a sale.

The approach has three important objectives:

- First, you want to build rapport with the prospect.
- Second, you want to capture the person's full attention. Never begin your sales story if the prospect seems preoccupied and is not paying attention.
- Third, you want to make a transition to the need discovery stage of the sales presentation.

In some selling situations the first contact with the customer is a telephone call. The call is made to schedule a meeting or, in some cases, to conduct the sales presentation. The face-to-face sales call starts with the social contact and continues with the business contact. The telephone contact, social contact, and business contact are discussed in this section.

ESTABLISH YOUR CREDIBILITY

Thomas A. Freese, author of *Secrets of Question Based Selling*, says credibility is critical to your success in sales. Credibility is an impression that people form about you very early in the sales process.[12] Sometimes little things can erode your credibility before you have a chance to prove yourself. Arriving late for appointment, spending 45 minutes with the prospect when you said you would need only 15 minutes, or failure to send the prospect information that was promised can quickly weaken a relationship. Failure to be well prepared for the sales call will also undermine your credibility. Credibility grows when the customer realizes you are a competent sales representative who can add value throughout the sales process.

THE TELEPHONE CONTACT

A telephone call provides a quick and inexpensive method of scheduling an appointment. Appointments are important because many busy prospects will not meet with a salesperson who drops in unannounced. When you schedule an appointment the prospect knows about the sales call in advance and can therefore make the necessary advance preparation.

Some salespeople use the telephone exclusively to establish and maintain contact with the customer. As noted in Chapter 2, inside salespeople rely almost totally on the telephone for sales. **Telesales**—not to be confused with *telemarketing*—includes many of the same elements as traditional sales: gathering customer information, determining needs, prescribing solutions, negotiating buyer concerns, and closing sales. Telesales is usually not scripted, a practice widely used in telemarketing. In some situations, telesales is as free-wheeling and unpredictable as a face-to-face sales call.

telesales Using the telephone to acquire information about the customer, determine needs, suggest solutions, negotiate buyer concerns, close the sale, and service the sale.

In Chapter 3 we examined some of the factors that influence the meaning we attach to an oral message from another person. With the aid of this information we can see that communication via telephone is challenging. As the person who receives the call cannot see our facial expression, gestures, or posture, he or she must rely wholly on the sound of our voice and the words used. The telephone has some additional limitations. A salesperson accustomed to meeting prospects in person may find telephone contact impersonal. Some salespeople try to avoid using the telephone because they believe it is too easy for the prospect to say no.

These drawbacks are more imagined than real. With proper training a salesperson can use the telephone effectively to schedule appointments. When you make an appointment by telephone, use the following practices:

1. *Plan in advance what you will say.* It helps to prepare written notes to use as a guide during the first few seconds of the conversation. What you say will be determined by the objectives of the sales call. Have a calendar available to suggest and confirm a date, time, and place for the appointment. Be sure to write it down.
2. *Politely identify yourself and the company you represent.* Set yourself apart from other callers by using a friendly tone and impeccable phone manners. This approach will help you avoid being shut out by a wary gatekeeper (secretary or receptionist).
3. *State the purpose of your call and explain how the prospect can benefit from a meeting.* In some cases, it is helpful to use a powerful benefits statement that will get the prospect's attention and whet the person's appetite for more information. Present only enough information to stimulate interest.
4. *Show respect for the prospect's time.* Tell the person how much time the appointment will take. Emphasize that you know his or her time is valuable.

The telephone contact can set the stage for the social and business contact. The first few seconds of the call are crucial to the image you project.

5. *Confirm the appointment.* Send a brief note or letter with the date, time, and place of your appointment. Enclose your business card and any printed information that may be of interest to the prospect.[13]

You should anticipate resistance from some prospects. After all, most decision makers are very busy. Be persistent and persuasive if you genuinely believe a meeting with the prospect will be mutually beneficial.

THE EFFECTIVE USE OF VOICE MAIL

The growing popularity of voice mail presents a challenge to salespeople. What type of message sets the stage for a second call or stimulates a return call? It's important to anticipate voice mail and know exactly what to say if you reach a recording. The prospect's perception of you is based on what you say and voice quality. The following message almost guarantees that it will be ignored: "Ms. Simpson, I am Paul Watson and I am with Elliott Property Management Services. I would like to visit with you about our services. Please call me at 862-1500."[14] Note that this message provides no compelling reason for the prospect to call back. It offers no valid item that would stimulate interest. The voice mail message should be similar to the opening statement you would make if you had a face-to-face contact with the prospect:

> Ms. Simpson, I am Paul Watson and I am with Elliott Property Management Services. We specialize in working with property managers. We can help you reduce the paperwork associated with maintenance jobs and provide an easy way to track the progress of each job. I would like the opportunity to visit with you and will call back in the morning.[15]

Note that this message is brief and describes benefits that customers can receive. If Paul Watson wants a call back, then he needs to give the best time to reach him. He should give his phone number slowly and completely. It's usually best to repeat the number. If you are acting on a referral, be sure to say who referred you and why.

In some cases a secretary, assistant, or receptionist will screen incoming telephone calls. Be prepared to convince this person that your call is important. Always treat the gatekeeper with respect and courtesy.

"I don't think of myself as the Jenkins Doolittle & Bloom gatekeeper. I rather prefer lead blocker."

EFFECTIVE USE OF E-MAIL

Many prospects and established customers like the convenience of e-mail correspondence and prefer it to telephone contact. Your challenge is to make it easy for your correspondents to read and handle your e-mail. Always use a meaningful, specific subject line. People who receive large amounts of e-mail may selectively choose which ones to read by scanning the subject lines and deleting those of no interest.

The e-mail message should tell the reader what you want and then encourage a response. Always use the grammar and spell check tools. Messages that contain errors may misrepresent your competence. Finally, use a signature file—a small block of text that automatically follows each e-mail you send. A typical signature file includes full name, title, affiliation, phone number, and in some cases a slogan.

THE SOCIAL CONTACT

According to many image consultants, "First impressions are lasting impressions." This statement is essentially true, and some profitable business relationships never crystallize because some trait or characteristic of the salesperson repels the prospective customer. Sales personnel have only a few minutes to create a positive first impression. Dr. Leonard Zunin, co-author of *Contact: The First Four Minutes*, describes what he calls the "four-minute barrier." In this short period of time a relationship can be established or denied. Susan Bixler, author of *The New Professional Image*, describes the importance of the first impression this way:

> Books are judged by their covers, houses are appraised by their curb appeal, and people are initially evaluated on how they choose to dress and behave. In a perfect world this is not fair, moral, or just. What's inside should count a great deal more. And eventually it usually does, but not right away. In the meantime, a lot of opportunities can be lost.[16]

CUSTOMER RELATIONSHIP MANAGEMENT WITH TECHNOLOGY

Planning Personal Visits

Personally visiting prospects and customers helps build strong relationships, yet travelling is expensive and time consuming. A salesperson is challenged to plan visits that will optimize the investment represented by each trip. Access to CRM prospect records helps salespeople quickly identify all the accounts in a given geographic area.

CRM empowers salespeople to rapidly review and compare an area's prospects on the basis of position in sales cycle, potential size of account or purchase, likelihood of sale, and the contribution that the visit could make to information gathering and relationship building. A well-managed CRM database will provide salespeople with appropriate business and social topics to discuss when calling selected prospects for an appointment. (See the exercise Planning Personal Visits on page 248 for more information.)

Building rapport leads to credibility, which leads to trust. Once trust is established, the prospect is likely to open up and share information. This information will provide clues regarding ways to create value. To be certain that your first impression is appropriate, review the material in Chapter 3. The information in this chapter is timeless and will serve you well today and in the future.

DEVELOPING CONVERSATION

The brief general conversation during the social contact should hold the prospect's attention and establish a relaxed and friendly atmosphere for the business contact that is to follow. As mentioned in Chapter 3, there are three areas of conversation that should be considered in developing a social contact:

1. *Comments on "here and now" observations.* These comments may include general observations about the victory of a local athletic team, an article in *The Globe and Mail,* or specific comments about awards on display in the prospect's office.
2. *Compliments.* Most customers will react positively to sincere compliments. Personal items in the prospect's office, achievements, or efficient operation of the prospect's business provide examples of things that can be praised.
3. *Search for mutual acquaintances or interests.* Discovering that you have mutual friends or interests can serve as the foundation for a strong social contact.

Communication on a personal basis is often the first step in establishing a common language that will improve communication between the salesperson and the prospect. How much time should be devoted to the social contact? There is no easy answer to this question. The length of the conversation will depend on the type of product or service sold, how busy the prospect appears to be, and your awareness of topics of mutual interest. In many cases, the conversation will take place over lunch or dinner. Many successful sales have been closed during or after a meal. This explains why some companies enroll their sales staff and other customer contact personnel in dining etiquette classes.

THE BUSINESS CONTACT

Moving the prospect's attention from the social contact to the business proposal is an important part of the approach. When you convert and hold your prospect's attention, you have fulfilled an important step in the selling process. Furthermore, without success in the beginning, you may find the door has been closed before you can complete the remaining steps of the sale.

Some salespeople use a carefully planned opening statement or a question to attract the customer's attention to the sales presentation. A statement or question that focuses on the prospect's dominant buying motive is, of course, more likely to achieve the desired results. Buyers must like what they see and hear, and must be made to feel that it will be worthwhile to hear more.

Throughout the years, salespeople have identified and used a number of effective ways to capture the prospect's attention and arouse interest in the presentation. Seven of the most common will be explained in the following material. We also discuss combining two or more of these approaches.

- Agenda approach
- Product demonstration approach
- Referral approach
- Customer benefit approach
- Question approach
- Survey approach
- Premium approach

Agenda Approach

One of the most effective ways to move from the social contact to the business contact is to thank the customer for taking time to meet with you and then review your goals for the meeting. You might say, "Thank you for meeting with me this morning. I would like to accomplish three things during the time you have given me." This statement shows you value the person's time and you have preplanned a specific agenda. Always be open to changing the agenda based on suggestions from the prospect.[17]

Product Demonstration Approach

Sales representatives who sell copy machines, photographic equipment, automobiles, construction equipment, office furniture, and many other products use this straightforward method of getting the prospect's attention. If the actual product cannot be demonstrated, salespeople can use appropriate audiovisual technology such as computer-generated graphics, slides, and videotapes. Trish Ormsby, a sales representative who sells security systems, uses her portable computer to create a visual image of systems that meet the customer's security needs.[18]

Referral Approach

Research indicates that another person will be far more impressed with your good points if these points are presented by a third party rather than by you. The referral approach is quite effective because a third party—a satisfied customer—believes the prospect will benefit from your product. This type of opening statement has universal appeal among salespeople from nearly every field. When you use the referral approach, your opening statement should include a direct reference to the third party. Here is an example: "Mrs. Follett, my name is Kurt Wheeler, and I represent the Cross Printing Company. We specialize in printing all types of business forms. Mr. Ameno—buyer for Raybale Products, Incorporated—is a regular customer of ours, and he suggested I mention his name to you."

Customer Benefit Approach

One of the most effective ways to gain a prospect's attention is immediately to point out one benefit of purchasing your product. Start with the most

SELLING MENTOR

The Social Contact

The social contact should be viewed as effective communication on a personal basis. This brief conversation establishes the foundation for the business contact, so it should never be viewed as an insignificant part of the presentation strategy. The following guidelines can help you develop the skills needed to make good social contact.

1. *Prepare for the social contact.* Conduct a background check on topics of interest to the person you are contacting. This includes reviewing information in the prospect database, reading industry reports, and searching the Internet. Once you arrive at the customer's office, you will discover additional information about the person's interests. Most people communicate what is important to them in the way they personalize their work environment.
2. *Initiate social contact.* The most effective opening comments should be expressed in the form of an open-ended question, such as "I understand you have just been elected president of the United Way?" You can improve the possibility of a good response to your verbal question by applying nonverbal communication skills. Appropriate eye contact, voice inflections that communicate enthusiasm, and a warm smile will increase the customer's receptivity to your opening comments.
3. *Respond to the customer's conversations.* When the customer responds, it is imperative that you acknowledge the message both verbally and nonverbally. The verbal response might be "That is really interesting" or any other appropriate comment. Let the customer know you are listening and you want him or her to keep talking.
4. *Keep the social contact focused on the customer.* Because you cannot control where a conversation might go, you may be tempted to focus the conversation on topics with which you are familiar. A response such as "Several years ago I was in charge of our company's United Way campaign and we had a difficult time meeting our goal" shifts the focus of the conversation back to you. Instead, continue to focus the conversation on topics that are of interest to the customer. Dale Carnegie said that one of the best ways to build a relationship is to encourage others to talk about themselves.

important issue (or problem) facing the client.[19] When using this approach, the most important buyer benefit is included in the initial statement. For example, the salesperson selling a Sony projector might open with this statement:

> "The Sony VPL-CS4 lightweight projector strikes a balance between cost, size, brightness, and convenience. It's a good choice for a quick business trip or for a work-at-home presentation."

Another example taken from the financial services field follows:

> "When you meet with a Charles Schwab investment specialist, you can obtain advice on more than 1200 mutual funds with no load and no transaction fee."

The key to achieving success with the customer benefit approach is advance preparation. Prospects are annoyed when a salesperson cannot quickly communicate the benefits of meeting with them. Bruce Klassen, sales manager for Do All Industrial Supply, says, "Our salespeople begin the sales process by researching the prospect and the company. We need to be sure that our product line is going to benefit that prospect before we make even an initial sales approach."[20]

Question Approach

The question approach has two positive features. First, a question will almost always trigger prospect involvement. Very few people will avoid answering a direct question. Second, a question gets the prospect thinking about a problem that the salesperson is prepared to solve.

Molly Hoover, a sales training consultant, conducts training classes for sales managers and car dealers who want to better understand the subtleties of selling to the first-time woman car buyer. She suggests an approach that includes a few basic questions such as:

> "Is the vehicle for business or pleasure?"
>
> "Will you be buying within the next week or so?"[21]

These opening questions are not difficult to answer, yet they get the customer mentally involved. Some of the best opening questions are carefully phrased to arouse attention. The authors of *The Sales Question Book* offer some good examples:

> "Are you aware that we just added three new services to our payroll and accounting package? Could I tell you about them?"
>
> "We are now offering all our customers a special service that used to be reserved for our largest accounts. Would you be interested in hearing about it?"[22]

Once you ask the question, listen carefully to the response. If the answer is yes, proceed with an enthusiastic presentation of your product. If the answer is no, then you may have to gracefully try another approach or thank the prospect for his or her time and depart.

Survey Approach

Larry Short, a financial advisor with RBC Dominion Securities and a former winner of the Atlantic Canada Award of Distinction by the Investment Dealers Association of Canada, frequently uses the survey approach as part of his

The survey approach can be used to capture the prospect's attention.

customer strategy. He has new clients fill out a detailed questionnaire before he sees them for a first appointment.[23] He studies the completed questionnaire and other documents before making any effort to find a solution to any of the customer's financial planning needs. Data collection through the survey is an important part of the problem-solving philosophy of selling. It is often used in selling office machines, business security systems, insurance, and other products where the need cannot be established without careful study.

The survey approach offers many advantages. It is generally a nonthreatening way to open a sales call. You are simply asking permission to acquire information that can be used to determine the buyer's need for your product. Because the survey is tailor-made for a specific business, the buyer is given individual treatment. Finally, the survey approach helps avoid an early discussion of price. Price cannot be discussed until the survey is completed.

Premium Approach

The premium approach involves giving the customer a free sample or an inexpensive item. A financial services representative might give the customer a booklet that can be used to record expenses. Sales representatives for one textbook publisher give faculty members a monthly planner. Product samples are frequently used by persons who sell cosmetics. Creative use of premiums is an effective way to get the customer's attention.

The agenda, product demonstration, referral, customer benefit, question, survey, and premium approaches offer the salesperson a variety of ways to set the stage for the presentation strategy. With experience, salespeople learn to select the most effective approach for each selling situation. Table 10.1 provides examples of how these approaches can be applied in real-world situations.

COMBINATION APPROACHES

A hallmark of consultative selling is flexibility. Therefore, a combination of approaches sometimes provides the best avenue to need identification. Sales personnel who have adopted the consultative style will, of course, use the question and survey approaches most frequently. Some selling situations, however, require that one of the other approaches be used, either alone or in combination with the question and survey approaches (see Fig. 10.4). An example of how a salesperson might combine referral and question approaches follows:

Salesperson: Carl Hamilton at Simmons Modern Furniture suggested that I visit with you about our new line of compact furniture designed for today's smaller homes. He believes this line might complement the furniture you currently feature.

Customer: Yes, Carl called me yesterday and mentioned your name and company.

Salesperson: Before showing you our product lines, I would like to ask you some questions about your current product mix. First, what do you currently carry in the area of bedroom furniture?

Table 10.1
Business Contact Worksheet

This worksheet illustrates how to prepare effective real-world approaches that capture the customer's attention.

Method of Approach	What will you say?
1. Agenda	1. (Office supply) "Thank you for meeting with me, Ms. Ramotse. During the next 45 minutes, I plan to accomplish three things
2. Product demonstration	2a. (Retail clothing) "We have just received a shipment of new fall sweaters from Braemar International."
	2b. (Business forms manufacturer) "Our plant has just purchased a $300 000 Harris Graphics composer, Mr. Reichart; I would like to show you a copy of your sales invoice with your logo printed on it."
3. Referral	3. (Food wholesaler) "Paula Doeman, procurement manager for St. Joseph's Hospital, suggested that I provide you with information about our computerized 'Order It' system."
4. Customer benefit	4. (Real estate) "Mr. and Mrs. Stuart, my company lists and sells more homes than any other company in the area where your home is located. Our past performance would lead me to believe we can sell your home within two weeks."
5. Question	5. (Hotel convention services) "Mrs. McClaughin, will your 2002 Annual Franchisee Meeting be held in April?"
6. Survey	6a. (Custom-designed computer software) "Mr. Pham, I would like the opportunity to learn about your accounts receivable and accounts payable procedures. We may be able to develop a customized program that will significantly improve your cash flow."
	6b. (Retail menswear) "May I ask you a few questions about your wardrobe? The information will help me better understand your clothing needs."
7. Premium	7. (Financial services) "I would like to give you a publication entitled *Guaranteed Growth Annuity*."

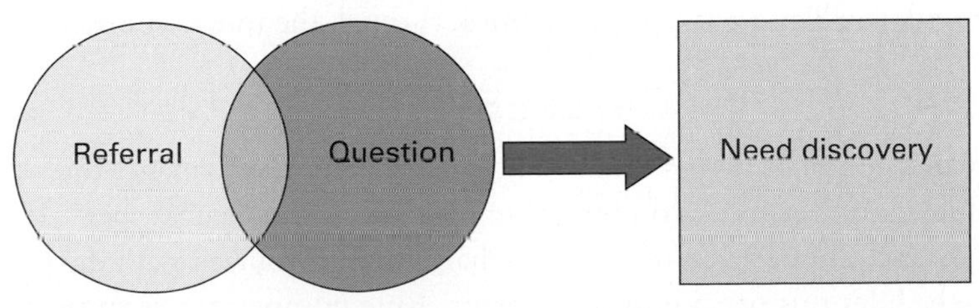

Figure 10.4 Combination approaches provide a smooth transition to the need discovery part of the consultative-style presentation.

DEALING WITH THE "BAD-TIMING" RESPONSE

If your approach is effective, you will usually be given an opportunity to make the sales presentation. However, the prospect may attempt to delay the presentation with a statement such as "The time just isn't right, call me back later." Before you agree to a follow-up call, try to determine whether the prospect is really interested in your product and willing to take action in the future. Your response might sound like this: "I certainly do not mind scheduling another call. But first, do you agree that my product is one you see yourself using?" You do not want to waste time on a follow-up call if the person is not a prospect.

COPING WITH SALES CALL RELUCTANCE

sales call reluctance Fear of making the initial contact with the prospect.

The transition from the preapproach to the approach is sometimes blocked by **sales call reluctance**. Fear of making the initial contact with the prospect is a problem for rookies and veterans in every selling field. For new salespeople the problem can be career-threatening. Sales call reluctance may stem from concern about interrupting or intruding on the prospect, or from fear of saying the wrong thing, or from concern about not being able to respond effectively to the person who quickly begins asking questions. Sales call reluctance may surface because the salesperson fears rejection.

Regardless of the reasons for sales call reluctance, you can learn to deal with it. Here are some suggestions:

- *Be optimistic about the outcome of the initial contact.* It is better to anticipate success than to anticipate failure. Martin Seligman, professor of psychology at the University of Pennsylvania and author of the best-selling book *Learned Optimism*, says that success in selling requires a healthy dose of optimism.[24] The anticipation of failure is a major barrier to making the initial contact.
- *Practise your approach before making the initial contact.* A well-rehearsed effort to make the initial contact will increase your self-confidence and reduce the possibility that you may handle the situation badly.
- *Recognize that it is normal to feel anxious about the initial contact.* Even the most experienced salespeople experience some degree of sales call reluctance.
- *Develop a deeper commitment to your goals.* Abraham Zaleznik, professor emeritus at the Harvard Graduate School of Business, says, "If your commitment is only in your mind, then you'll lose it when you encounter a big obstacle. If your commitment is in your heart and your mind, you'll create the power to break through the toughest obstacles."[25]

MANAGING THE "GATEKEEPER"

Many decision makers have an assistant or secretary who manages their daily schedule. This person is commonly referred to as the "gatekeeper." If you want to reach the decision maker, work hard to align yourself with the person who schedules this person's appointments. Rule number one is to treat this person with respect. Learn his or her name and what he or she does. Keep in mind that this person can be an important source of information. For example, he or she can tell you how the buying process works and provide information regarding new developments in the company. This person may be able to help you make a preliminary qualification before you reach the decision maker. When you treat this person as an expert by soliciting his or her views, you establish a relationship that can pay big dividends today and in the future.[26] When possible, use personal referrals from someone the prospect knows. If you have met the prospect previously, describe the meeting and tell the "gatekeeper" why you feel a second meeting would be beneficial.

SUMMARY

One sales consultant has noted that: "Organization multiplies the value of anything to which it is applied." This is especially true of precall planning. The well-prepared salesperson approaches the sales call with an attitude of confidence and expectancy.

Developing a presentation strategy involves preparing presale objectives, developing a presale presentation plan, and providing outstanding customer service. The presentation strategy combines elements of the relationship, product, and customer strategies.

Preparation for the sales presentation is a two-part process. Part one, the *preapproach,* involves preparing presale objectives and developing a presale presentation plan. It's best to develop presentation objectives for each stage of the buying process. Part two, the *approach,* involves making a good first impression, securing the prospect's attention, and developing the prospect's interest in the product.

Over the years, salespeople have identified several ways to convert the prospect's attention and arouse interest in the presentation. Some of the most common ways include the agenda approach, product demonstration approach, referral approach, customer benefit approach, question approach, survey approach, and premium approach. This chapter also includes information on dealing with "bad timing" response, how to cope with sales call reluctance, and managing the "gatekeeper."

Key Terms

Approach **226**

Multi-call Sales Presentations **227**

Persuasion **232**

Preapproach **226**

Presentation Strategy **225**

Sales Call Reluctance **246**

Six-Step Presentation Plan **234**

Telesales **237**

Review Questions

1. What is the purpose of the preapproach? What are the two prescriptions included in the preapproach?
2. Explain the role of objectives in developing the presale presentation plan.
3. Why should salespeople establish multiple-objective sales presentations? List four possible objectives that could be achieved during a sales presentation.
4. Describe some common applications for telesales.
5. Describe the major purpose of the informative, persuasive, and reminder sales presentations.
6. What are the major objectives of the approach?
7. Review the Selling Mentor boxed feature on page 242. Briefly describe the four guidelines that can help you make a good social contact.

8. What are some rules to follow when leaving a message on voice mail? on e-mail?
9. What methods can the salesperson use to convert the prospect's attention to the sales presentation?
10. Discuss why combination approaches are considered an important consultative-selling practice. Provide one example of a combination approach.

Application Exercises

1. Assume that you are a salesperson who calls on retailers. For some time, you have been attempting to get an appointment with the head buyer of one of the best retailers in the city to persuade her to carry your line. You have an appointment to see her in 90 minutes. You are sitting in your office now and it will take you about 30 minutes to drive to your appointment. Outline what you should be doing between now and the time you leave to meet your prospect.
2. Tom Nelson has just graduated from Algonquin College with a major in marketing. He has three years of experience in the retail grocery business and has decided he would like to go to work as a salesperson for the district office of Procter & Gamble. Tom has decided to telephone and set up an appointment for an interview. Write out exactly what Tom should plan to say during his telephone call.
3. Concepts from Dale Carnegie's *How to Win Friends and Influence People* are noted in this chapter. Access the Dale Carnegie Web site (**www.dale-carnegie.com**) and click on "Find it Now." Then click on "Find a course or seminar," then click on "USA and Canada." Finally, find "Sales Advantage." You may need to select a province to see information on this course. Read the description and look at the price. What does this Carnegie course offer that your course does not? How is this course offered in Canada? Why do you think this Carnegie course is priced at its current price?

ROLE-PLAY EXERCISE

Research the new computer that you would like to purchase in the future or that you have just purchased. Strategically, prepare to meet a prospect who has been referred to you by a friend and who would like to purchase a similar computer. Using Table 10.1, prepare four different business contact statements or questions you could use to approach your prospect. Review the material in this chapter and then work with another student who will assume the role of your prospect. First, role-play the telephone contact and set up an appointment to get your prospect into your store to meet with you and look at the computer. Second, role-play the approach you will use when the prospect actually comes into the store. Review how well you made the approach.

CRM Application Exercise PLANNING PERSONAL VISITS

CRM software allows trip planners to examine the status of prospects in the geographic area to be visited. Assume that a salesperson using the ACT! software wishes to visit the city of Bedford, Texas. The software permits a fast field search capability to select and sort the records of prospects in that city: Lookup, City, type "Bedford," and press Enter. After arranging by phone to visit these people, you can print the information contained in these records and take it along: Report, Contact Report, Active Lookup, Printer, and Enter. You should now have printed information about all customers in Bedford. Salespeople today use the Internet to schedule trip transportation and lodging, and to check the weather forecast.

Case Problem

In April 2006, Hal Maybee was discussing the five salespeople at Astro Distribution with Don Rodgers, the company owner. Don wanted Hal to make some sales calls with his two newest salespeople, and provide an assessment of their training needs.

"Don," said Hal, "can you tell why you're not concerned about the rest of them?"

"Well, Stan has been with me for 15 years. His sales have been consistently growing 4 to 5 percent per year. Bruce has the highest sales revenue in the company. Ronnie took over a poor territory when he joined us last year, and he has nearly doubled sales there since then."

"Can you estimate your annual price increase across all the product lines you sell?"

"It's been quite low for the past few years. Maybe 2 percent, maybe a bit more," Don replied.

"What about new product lines? Do you regularly add new products to the list of things you sell? Do you ever drop old product lines?"

"Sure. We add one or two manufacturers each year. In fact, our accountant just calculated some interesting figures for me the other day. She told me that product lines that we have added within the last five years now account for more than 30 percent of our sales. But we seldom drop lines. I think we dropped one manufacturer in the past five years. It didn't want to work with us and kept selling direct to some of our customers behind our back."

"Don, I think it's wise to spend a half-day with each salesperson. If we focus on only a few, that may send the wrong message. Also, I may have some interesting advice for you when I'm done," said Hal. "Would you object to that?"

After reflecting for a few moments, Don replied, "How do we convince Stan to take you along?"

They were both somewhat surprised when Stan seemed to agree almost immediately. Don had said that it was important to have them all participate, and Hal said he would appreciate making the first calls with Stan because, as the most experienced salesperson, he could help Hal understand the company and the products more quickly.

Stan was less receptive a week later when Hal phoned him. "Stan," said Hal, "I'd like to make two sales calls with you next Wednesday morning. Can we arrange that?'

"Sure," Stan replied, "I have two accounts in mind already.

"Well, actually, I was hoping we could call on Alberta Chemco and Trusty Tanks. Would that be possible?"

"Why those two?" Stan queried with a hint of concern.

Hal had expected the concern. "Well, I know you have been calling on Alberta Chemco for years and have been doing very well with the account. I thought it would be good to see one of your better customers. I have to admit, I hadn't heard of Trusty Tanks until last week but, if we take the main highway back to the office, they're only about five minutes out of our way." Hal didn't directly state that it was because Trusty Tanks was not a current customer, but Stan would certainly guess that. Stan was skeptical, but he did agree.

On Wednesday morning, Stan and Hal stopped at Alberta Chemco to meet Bob Jordan, the supplies buyer.

"Hi, Bob." Stan said, extending his hand. "This is Hal Maybee. Hal is a consultant who is working with our company and, after our sales call, he wants to stay behind for about five minutes to ask you a few confidential questions about our products and service."

"Good to see you, Stan. Pleasure to meet you as well, Hal." Bob shook their hands. "Please be seated."

"Bob, I came by today on my regular visit to see if there is anything you need. Can I help you with anything? Are you having any problems?"

"No, Stan. As far as I know everything is fine," Bob smiled.

"No complaints from receiving, or accounts payable?"

"No. Everything's fine."

"Any orders for us in the works? Anything I can write up today?"

"No, I don't have anything immediately. You know that, when we need more fasteners or fittings, we'll simply send the order along to you."

"Yes, and I appreciate it. That's why I come by regularly to make sure you're not having any problems with us or any of our products."

"Oh, if we have problems, you'll hear." Bob smiled again.

Following that, Stan exited, and Hal stayed behind to ask some questions concerning Astro Industrial Supply and Stan Andrews. It was apparent that Bob liked doing business with both the company and Stan, the salesperson.

On the way back to the office, they stopped at Trusty Tanks. Stan had called the previous week and made an appointment. He and Hal were greeted by Angela Ahuja, the company's purchasing agent. "Good morning, Mr. Andrews. How may I help you?" she asked without any apparent emotion.

"Well, as I said when I called you last week, I wanted to come by and introduce myself and my company to you, and to let you know what we have that may interest you. Astro Distribution has been doing business here for over 20 years and I have been with them all that time. We have quite a complete line of consumable supplies—everything from abrasives, cutting tools, electric and pneumatic hand tools, to safety equipment, fasteners and fittings, valves, even hose."

"That's quite a list. Do you have a catalogue, or a product listing?"

"Absolutely. I wasn't sure which catalogues to bring, but I do have a complete product listing on this attractive sheet for you. Do you have any immediate needs I might help you with?"

"Nothing I can think of, but leave your product listing. If anything comes up, I'll call your office and check your prices and your service." She glanced at Hal.

"I'm sorry," said Stan. "This is Hal Maybee. He is a consultant who is visiting some of our important customers to ask questions about our service. Since you're not a customer yet, he can't very well ask much of you."

Hal reached forward to shake hands. "Pleasure to meet you, Ms. Ahuja."

"Thank you. I hope you will provide them good value. I like to see companies that are concerned with improving their service for their customers," Angela smiled.

"Thank you. If I can make a small difference, then customers like you will win, Astro Industrial will win, and, ultimately, I will win. It's hard to beat that." Hal smiled and waited for Stan to continue but was surprised when he simply asked Ms. Ahuja to give Astro Industrial a try. As they left the building, Stan turned to Hal and said, "When they do call, I'll make sure we impress them with our prices and service. I think they'll be a good account."

Questions

1. Has Stan adopted the three prescriptions for a presentation strategy? Explain.
2. Consider Stan's two presentations. Explain if each is an informative, a persuasive, or a reminder presentation.
3. How effectively has Stan been at establishing the social contact? Describe how you would improve the social contact for each presentation.
4. How effectively has Stan been at establishing the business contact? Describe how you would improve the business contact for each presentation.
5. If you were Hal Maybee, what advice would you give to Stan?

CRM Case Study ESTABLISHING YOUR APPROACH

Becky Kemley, your sales manager at SimNet Systems, has notified Pat Silva's former prospects by letter that you will be calling on them soon. She wants to meet with you tomorrow to discuss your preapproach to your new prospects. Review the records in the ACT! database.

Questions

1. Becky wants you to call on Robert Kelly. Describe what your call objectives will be with Mr. Kelly.
2. Describe a possible topic of your social contact with Mr. Kelly and how you would convert that to a buying contact.
3. Becky has given you a reprint of a new article about using networks for warehouse applications. Which of your prospects might have a strong interest in this kind of article? How would you use this article to make an approach to that prospect?

Partnership Selling

A ROLE PLAY/SIMULATION (see Partnership Selling on CD-ROM, pp. 29–33)

DEVELOPING A RELATIONSHIP STRATEGY

Read *Employment Memorandum 2*, which announces your promotion to account executive. In your new position you will be assigned by your instructor to one of the two major account categories in the convention centre market. You will be assigned to either the association accounts market or the corporate accounts market. Association accounts includes customers who are responsible for planning meetings for the association or group they are a member of or are employed by. Corporate accounts include customers who are responsible for planning meetings for the company they represent. You will remain in the account category for the rest of the role plays.

Note the challenges you will have in your new position. Each of these challenges will be represented in the future sales memoranda you will be receiving from your sales manager.

Read *Sales Memorandum 1* for the account category you are assigned. (Note that "A" means association and your customer is Erin Adkins, and "B" means corporate and your customer is Leigh Combs.) Follow the instructions in the sales memorandum and strategically prepare to approach your new customer. Your call objectives will be to establish a relationship (social contact), share an appealing benefit, and find out if your customer is planning any future conventions (business contact).

You will be asked to assume the role of a customer in the account category that you are not assigned as a salesperson. Your instructor will provide you with detailed instructions for correctly assuming this role.

CHAPTER 11

Creating the Consultative Sales Presentation

LEARNING OBJECTIVES

After studying this chapter, you should be able to

1. Describe the characteristics of the consultative sales presentation
2. Explain how to determine the prospect's needs
3. Discuss the use of questions to determine needs
4. Select product that matches the prospect's needs
5. List and describe three types of need-satisfaction presentation strategies
6. Present general guidelines for creating value-added presentations

While dot.com companies have been failing faster than you can say Maserati, Google.com has been growing at 20 percent per month and now has offices in major cities around the world. It describes itself as "the closest thing the Web has to an ultimate answer machine."

Why has Google been so successful? In part, it's the sales strategy of its 90-person sales team. Google has sales specialists with expertise in particular market segments such as automotive and health care. These specialists make sales calls but also help Google salespeople sell advertising. Regional sales manager Andrea Zurek tells how she sold advertising to Sun Microsystems. First, they did a search on keywords important to Sun: server, JAVA tool, and Java tech, for example. Then, they approached Sun with the results and a forecast of likely traffic patterns, demonstrating Google's advantage over its competitors.

Google salespeople promise customers that, by advertising on the Google Web site, they will get a click-through rate of 2.5 percent, five times the industry standard. To ensure they meet their promise, Google salespeople work carefully with customers to place their ads on appropriate pages on Google's site. Then, they follow up after the sale to ensure they have satisfied customers, that is, whether customers have received what they were promised. As part of its consultative sales approach, Google salespeople refuse to sell to accounts that fail to fit their model, and who would then become dissatisfied customers.[1]

Most salespeople have adopted the consultative sales presentation, the second step in the Six-Step Sales Presentation Plan (see Fig. 11.1). They support the selling philosophy expressed by Suzanne Vilardi, area sales manager for Swift Transportation: "Be a consultant, a partner, an extension of your client's business. Be a friend, a problem solver. Balance your client's best interests with those of your own and your company."[2] Key concepts related to creating the consultative sales presentation are featured in Figure 11.2 on page 254. This approach can be used effectively in all types of selling: service, retail, wholesale, and manufacturing. It results in increased customer satisfaction, more sales, fewer cancellations and returns, more repeat business, and more referrals.

The Consultative Sales Presentation

As we noted in Chapter 10, an effective approach sets the stage for the sales presentation. Once you have established rapport with the prospect, captured the prospect's full attention, and generated interest in your product, you can begin the sales presentation with confidence. To be most effective, the salesperson

The Six-Step Presentation Plan	
Step One: APPROACH	✓ Review Strategic/Consultative Selling Model ✓ Initiate customer contact
Step Two: PRESENTATION	Determine prospect needs Select solution Initiate sales presentation
Step Three: DEMONSTRATION	Decide what to demonstrate Select selling tools Initiate demonstration
Step Four: NEGOTIATION	Anticipate buyer concerns Plan negotiating methods Initiate win-win negotiations
Step Five: CLOSE	Plan appropriate closing methods Recognize closing clues Initiate closing methods
Step Six: SERVICING THE SALE	Follow-through Follow-up calls Expansion selling
Service, retail, wholesale, and manufacturer selling.	

Figure 11.1 Creating the sales presentation.

Figure 11.2 Salespeople who truly represent value to their customers plan ahead strategically for the actions taken during the presentation.

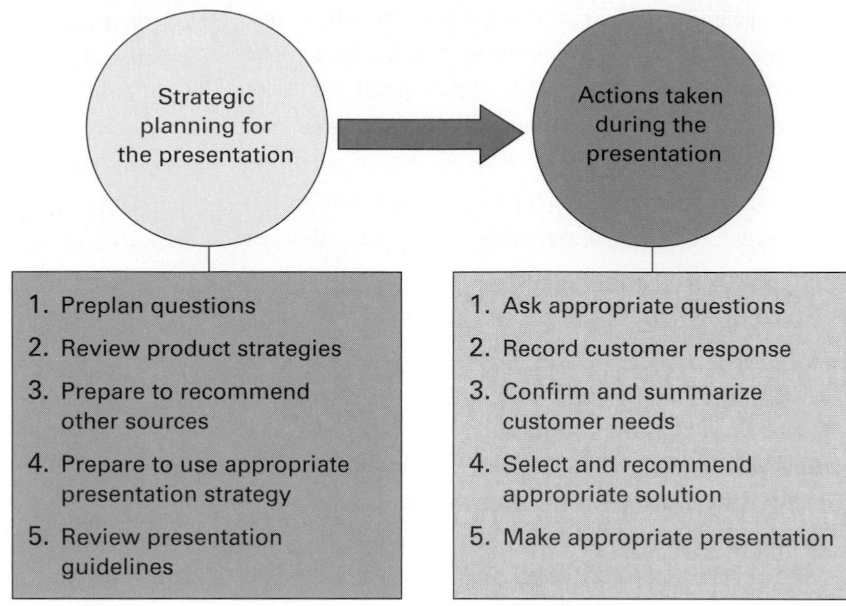

should think of the presentation as a four-part process. The Consultative Sales Presentation Guide (see Fig. 11.3) features these four parts.

1. **Need Discovery.** A review of the behaviours displayed by high-performance salespeople helps to understand the importance of discovering a customer's needs precisely. Top salespeople have learned how to skillfully diagnose and solve the prospect's problems better than their competitors can. This problem-solving capability translates into more repeat business and referrals, and fewer order cancellations and returns.

   Unless the selling situation requires mere order taking (i.e., from customers who know exactly what they want), need discovery is a standard part of the sales presentation. It may begin during the approach, if the salesperson uses questions or a survey during the initial contact with the customer. If neither is used during the approach, need discovery begins immediately after the approach.

   The pace, scope, depth of inquiry, and time allocated depend on a variety of factors, including the sophistication of the product, the selling price, the buyer's knowledge of the product, the product applications, and, of course, the time available for dialogue between the salesperson and the prospect. Each selling situation is different, so a

Figure 11.3 The Consultative Sales Presentation Guide. To be most successful, the salesperson should think of the sales presentation as a four-part process.

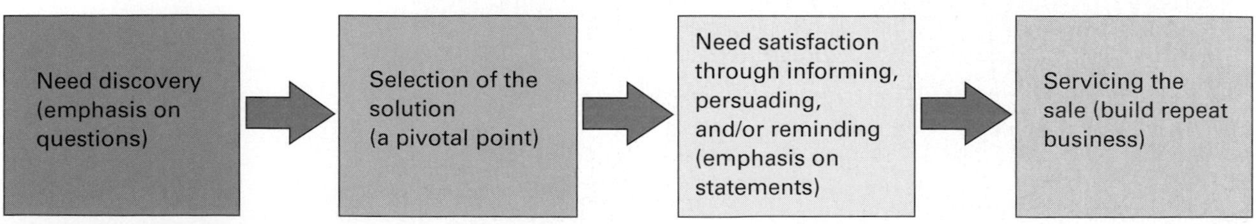

standard set of guidelines for need discovery is not practical. Additional information on need discovery is presented later in the chapter.

2. **Selection of the Solution.** The emphasis in sales and marketing today is on determining buyer needs and then selecting or configuring custom-fitted solutions to satisfy these needs. Therefore an important function of the salesperson is product selection and recommendation. The salesperson must choose the product or service that will provide maximum satisfaction. When making this decision, the salesperson must be aware of all product options, including those offered by the competition. Salespeople who have the ability to conduct an effective value-added needs analysis can achieve the status of trusted adviser.

   Mary Langston is a personal salesperson who works in a large department store and helps customers update their wardrobes. When asked what her days are like, she says, "It starts and ends with being a good listener." She promises her customers that she will never let them walk out of the store with clothing that does not look right.[3]

3. **Need Satisfaction through Informing, Persuading, or Reminding.** The third part of the consultative sales presentation consists of communicating to the prospect, both verbally and nonverbally, the satisfaction that the product or service will provide. The salesperson places less emphasis on the use of questions and begins making statements. These statements are organized into a presentation that informs, persuades, or reminds the prospect of the most suitable product or service. Later in this chapter, and in several of the remaining chapters, we discuss specific strategies used in conjunction with the demonstration, negotiating buyer concerns, and closing the sale.

4. **Servicing the sale.** The final part of the consultative sales presentation is a major dimension of the selling process. These activities, which

The sales presentation can inform, persuade, or remind.

occur after closing the sale, ensure maximum customer satisfaction and set the stage for a long-term relationship with the customer. Service activities include suggestion selling, making credit arrangements, following through on assurances and promises, and dealing effectively with complaints. Servicing the sale is covered in detail in Chapter 15.

In those cases where a sale is normally closed during a single sales call, the salesperson should be prepared to go through all four parts of the Consultative Sales Presentation Guide. However, when a salesperson uses a multi-call approach, preparation for all the parts is usually not practical. The person selling computer systems or investments, for example, will almost always use a multi-call sales presentation. Need discovery (part one) is the focus of the first call.

Need Discovery Activities That Create Value

A lawyer does not give the client advice until the legal problem has been carefully studied and confirmed. A doctor does not prescribe medication until the patient's symptoms have been identified. In like manner, the salesperson should not recommend purchase of a product without thoroughly identifying the prospect's need.

You start with the assumption that the prospect's need or problem is not known. The only way to determine and confirm the need or problem is to get the other person talking. You must obtain information to properly clarify the need. Many prospects do not realize that they actually have a problem. Even when they are aware of their need, they may not realize that your company has a solution to their problem.

Need discovery The salesperson establishing two-way communication by asking appropriate questions and listening carefully to the customer's responses.

Need discovery (sometimes called *need analysis*) begins with precall preparation, when the salesperson is acquiring background information on the prospect. It continues once the salesperson and the prospect are engaged in a significant dialogue. Through the process of need discovery the salesperson establishes two-way communication by asking appropriate questions and listening carefully to the prospect's responses. These responses will usually provide clues concerning the prospect's dominant buying motive (see Fig. 11.4).

ASKING QUESTIONS

The effective use of questions to achieve need identification and need satisfaction is the single greatest challenge facing most professional salespeople. The types of questions you ask, the timing of those questions, and how you pose them will greatly affect your ability to create customer value. Questions span the entire sales process, and today they are the tools salespeople use to gather information, probe, confirm, and persuade.

In every selling situation we want the prospect to be actively thinking, sharing thoughts, and asking questions. Until the person begins to talk

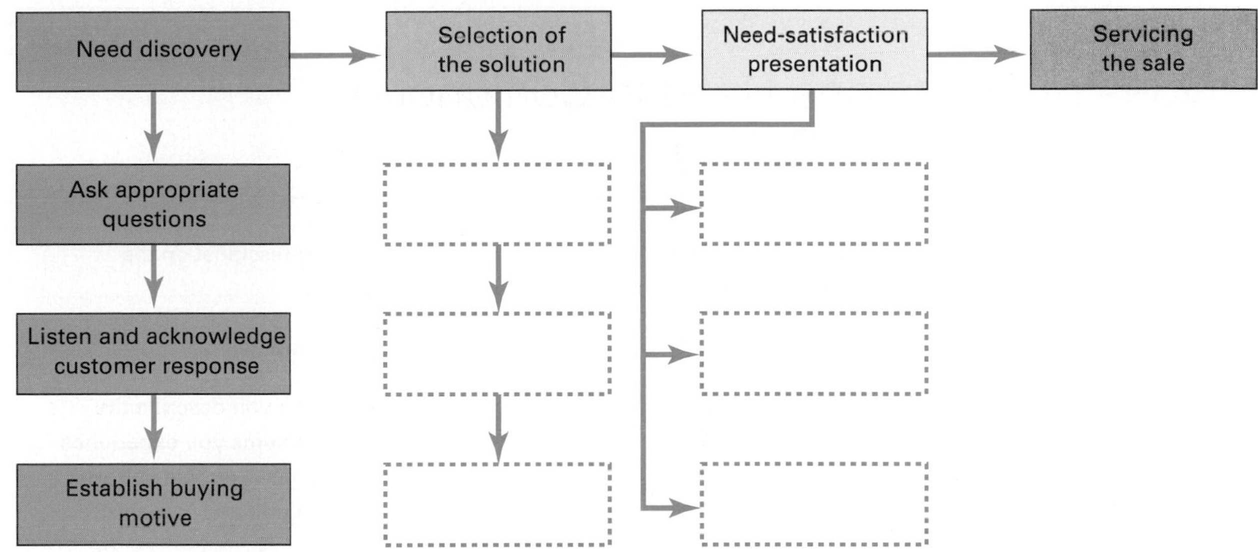

Figure 11.4 Three dimensions of need discovery.

freely, the salesperson will have difficulty diagnosing and solving the customer's problems. A well-planned sales presentation includes a variety of preplanned questions (see Table 11.1 on page 258). We describe the four most common types of question used in the field of personal selling.

SURVEY QUESTIONS

At the beginning of most sales presentations, there is a need to collect information about the buyer's existing situation and problem. A **survey question**—or *information-gathering question* as survey questions are sometimes called—is designed to obtain this knowledge. To accomplish this, there are two types of survey questions: general and specific.

survey question A question used to help the salesperson collect information about the buyer's existing situation and problem.

A **general survey question** can help the salesperson discover facts about the buyer's existing situation and are often the first step in the partnership-building process. Here is a sampling of general information-gathering questions that can be used in selected selling fields:

general survey question A question used early in the sales presentation to help the salesperson discover facts about the buyer's existing situation.

> "Tell me about the challenges you are facing in the area of data storage." *(File Server)*
>
> "What is your current rate of employee turnover?" *(Customer Service Training)*
>
> "Can you provide me with information on the kinds of meetings and conventions you plan for your clients and employees?" *(Hotel Convention Services)*
>
> "Can you describe the style of home furnishings you prefer?" *(Retail Home Furnishings)*

General survey questions can help you identify potential problems and dissatisfactions. The focus of these questions is on the buyer's existing situation.

Table 11.1

Types of Questions Used in Conjunction with Consultative Selling

(*Note:* Salesperson selling fractional ownership of a jet aircraft to a well-known golf professional on the Professional Golf Association (PGA) Tour, who is currently using commercial air travel)

Type of Question	Definition	When Used	Example
Survey	Discovers basic facts and information about buyer's current situation	Usually at the beginning of a sale	"Can you describe the problems you experience travelling to the various pro golf tournaments?"
Probing	Designed to focus on the consequences of the problem, or links the problem to other unforeseen problems	When you feel the need to obtain more specific information to fully understand the problem	"Are the travel problems affecting your concentration when you are preparing for the event?"
Confirmation	Used throughout the sales process to verify the accuracy and assure a mutual understanding of information exchanged by the salesperson and buyer	After important information has been exchanged	"So, you think the uncertainty associated with commercial air travel is having some effect on your game?"
Need-Satisfaction	Designed to move the sales process toward commitment and action	When you change the focus from the problem to a discussion of the solution	"With fractional ownership of your own jet, what personal benefits would this bring to your performance in the 30 tournaments you play each year?"

specific survey question A question designed to give prospects a chance to describe in more detail a problem, issue, or dissatisfaction from their point of view.

In most selling situations, general survey questions are followed by specific survey questions. A **specific survey question** is designed to give prospects a chance to describe in more detail a problem, issue, or dissatisfaction from their point of view. These questions give you an opportunity to delve more deeply into the customer's buying situation. Four examples of specific survey questions follow:

"How do you feel about adding another server to your system?" *(File Server)*

"To what extent is employee turnover affecting your customer service?" *(Customer Service Training)*

"What meal function features are most important to your guests?" *(Hotel Convention Services)*

"Are you looking for an entertainment centre that blends in with the existing furniture you have?" *(Retail Home Furnishings)*

Survey questions, general or specific, should not be used to collect factual information that can be acquired from other sources prior to the sales call. The preapproach information gathering effort is especially important when the salesperson is involved in a large or complex sale. These buyers expect the salesperson to do his or her homework and to not waste the buyer's time discussing basic factual information that is available from other sources.

Although survey questions are most often used at the beginning of the sales presentation, they can be used at other times. Information gathering may be necessary at any time during the sales presentation. We present the four types of questions in a sequence that has proven to be effective in most selling situations. However, it would be a mistake to view this sequence as a rigid plan for every sales presentation.

High-performing salespeople spend time strategically preparing questions that might prove useful before they make the sales call. The worksheet in Table 11.2 provides some examples of preplanned questions. Note that both open and closed questions are listed. An **open question** requires the prospect to go beyond a simple Yes or No response. A **closed question** can be answered with a Yes or No, or with a brief response.

open question A question that requires the prospect to respond with more than just a Yes or No response.

closed question A question that can be answered with a Yes or No, or a brief response.

Table 11.2

Need Discovery Worksheet

Preplanned questions—sometimes used in conjunction with preprinted forms—are often used in service, retail, wholesale, and manufacturer selling. Salespeople who use the consultative approach frequently record answers to their questions and use this information to correctly select and recommend solutions that build repeat business and referrals.

1. "Tell me a little bit about your investment portfolio." *(Survey/General—Open)*
2. "What are your major concerns when managing your financial affairs?" *(Survey/Specific—Open)*
3. "Is providing for your children's college education a major concern at this time?" *(Probing/Closed)*
4. "So, tax savings and providing for your children's college education are of primary importance. Is that correct?" *(Confirmation/Closed)*
5. "Are there any other benefits you see to converting some of your non-registered guaranteed investment certificates to a Registered Education Savings Plan?" *(Need-Satisfaction/Open)*

A good salesperson and a good doctor have one thing in common: they encourage questions.

Open questions are very effective in certain selling situations because they provoke thoughtful and insightful answers. The question "What are the biggest challenges you face in the area of plant security?" focuses the prospect's attention on problems that need solutions. Closed questions, however, can be equally effective when the sales conversation needs to be narrowed or focused on a specific issue. The question "Is your security concern primarily in the area of inventory control?" narrows the focus to a more specific problem.

PROBING QUESTIONS

Early in the sales process, the salesperson should make every effort to fully understand the buying problem and the consequences surrounding the problem. This clarification process will assure that the solution ultimately recommended and agreed upon will perform as intended.

probing question A question that helps the salesperson to uncover and clarify the prospect's buying problem and the circumstances surrounding the problem.

A **probing question** helps you to uncover and clarify the prospect's buying problem and the circumstances surrounding the problem. Probing questions are used more frequently in large, complex sales. They often uncover the current level of customer concern, fear, or frustration related to the problem. The following probing questions are more focused than the survey questions presented earlier:

> "What would be the consequences if you choose to do nothing about your current server situation?" *(File Server)*

> "How does your senior management feel about employee turnover and the related customer service problem?" *(Customer Service Training)*

> "Is poor service at the meal function negatively affecting the number of people returning to your seminar?" *(Hotel Convention Services)*

> "Is it important that you have easy access for connecting your DVD, TIVO, and wireless LAN network? *(Retail Home Furnishings)*

Probing questions help the salesperson and the prospect reach a mutual understanding of why a problem is important. Asking appropriate specific probing questions requires extensive knowledge of your company's capabilities, detailed insight into your customer's buying problem, and a great deal of practice.

The best sales presentations are characterized by active dialogue. As the sales process progresses, the customer becomes more open and shares perceptions, ideas, and feelings freely. A series of appropriate probing questions stimulates the prospect to discover things that he or she had not considered before.

CONFIRMATION QUESTIONS

A **confirmation question** can be used throughout the sales process to verify the accuracy and assure a mutual understanding of information exchanged by the salesperson and the buyer (see Table 11.1). These questions help determine if there is mutual understanding of the problems and circumstances the prospect is experiencing. Throughout the sales process there is always the potential for a breakdown in communication. Perhaps the language used by the salesperson is too technical. Maybe the prospect is preoccupied and has not listened closely to what has been said. Many confirmation questions are simple and to the point.

confirmation question A question used throughout the sales process to verify the accuracy and assure a mutual understanding of information exchanged by the salesperson and the buyer.

> "If I understand you correctly, the monitoring system must be set up at both your corporate headquarters and the manufacturing operation. Is that correct?" *(File Server)*
>
> "I want to be sure I am clear that you feel there is a direct relationship between employee turnover and the problem that exists in customer service." *(Customer Service Training)*
>
> "Did you say your seminar attendance dropped 12 percent last year?" *(Hotel Convention Services)*
>
> "So you want a new entertainment centre that blends with your current light-coloured oak furniture?" *(Retail Home Furnishings)*

The length of the sales process can vary from a few minutes during a single-call presentation to several weeks in a complex multi-call sales presentation. As the sales process progresses, the amount of information available to the salesperson and the customer increases. As the need discovery progresses, the customer's buying criteria or conditions surface. A **buying condition** is a qualification that must be available or fulfilled before the sale can be closed. The prospect may buy only if the product is available in a certain colour or can be delivered by a certain date. In some selling situations, product installation and service after the sale are considered important buying conditions by the customer. In a large, complex sale, several buying conditions may surface. The salesperson has the responsibility of clarifying and confirming each condition.

buying condition A qualification that must be available or fulfilled before the sale can be closed.

One of the best ways to clarify and confirm buying conditions is with a **summary confirmation question**. To illustrate, let us consider a situation in which Laura Feng, sales manager at a major hotel, has interviewed a prospect who wants to schedule a large awards banquet. After a series of survey, probing, and confirmation questions, Laura feels confident she has

summary confirmation question A question used to clarify and confirm buying conditions.

collected enough information to prepare a proposal. However, to be sure that she has all the facts and has clarified all of the important buying conditions, she asks the following summary confirmation question:

> "Let me summarize the major items you have mentioned. You want all of the banquet attendees served within an eight-minute time frame after the opening speaker has finished his speech?"

If the customer responds in the affirmative, Laura continues with another summary confirmation question:

> "And, you need a room that will comfortably seat 60 persons banquet-style, and 10 of these persons will be seated at the head table. Is this correct?"

Once all the buying conditions are confirmed, Laura can prepare a proposal that reflects the specific needs of her customer. The result is a win-win situation for the customer and the salesperson. The chances of closing the sale greatly improve. In multi-call sales processes, it is wise to begin subsequent calls with summary confirmation questions that re-establish what was discussed during the previous call(s). This enables the salesperson to verify that the previously discovered buying conditions have remained the same and not changed since the last meeting.

NEED-SATISFACTION QUESTIONS

need-satisfaction question
A question designed to move the sales process toward commitment and action by helping to clarify the problem in the prospect's mind, and by building a desire for your solution.

The fourth type of question used in the sales process in fundamentally different from the other three. A **need-satisfaction question** is designed to move the sales process toward commitment and action. These are helpful questions that focus on the solution. The chances of closing the sale greatly improve because these questions help clarify the problem in the customer's mind and build desire for a solution.

Survey, probing, and confirmation questions focus on understanding and clarifying the customer's problem. Need-satisfaction questions help the prospect see how your product or service provides a solution to the problem you have uncovered.

In most cases need-satisfaction questions are used after the salesperson has created awareness of the seriousness of the buyer's problem. The questions you ask will offer relief from his or her current levels of concern, fear, or frustration. The following examples provide insight into the use of need-satisfaction questions: "Tests on similar applications show a new file server can increase data storage by 30 to 40 percent. How much do you feel you would achieve?" *(File Server).*

In some selling situations a product demonstration is an essential stage in the sales process. In this case, the salesperson might use the following need-satisfaction question: "Would it be helpful if we provided a demonstration of one of our training modules to senior management so they can understand what you and I have discovered about reducing employee turnover? *(Customer Service Training).*

Once the prospect's needs are clearly identified, need-satisfaction questions can be valuable closing tools. Consider these examples:

"Considering the benefits we have summarized and agreed on, and noting the fact that our staff will deliver an outstanding meal function, would you like to sign this confirmation so we can reserve the rooms and schedule the meals that you need? *(Hotel Convention Services)*

"The wood grain in this oak entertainment unit adds a feeling of warmth. Do you see this unit fitting nicely with your current furniture?" *(Retail Home Furnishings)*

Need-satisfaction questions, such as those above, are very powerful because they build desire for the solution and give ownership of the solution to the prospect. When the prospect understands which parts of the problem(s) your solution can solve, you are less likely to invite objections. In some cases, you may identify problems that still need to be clarified. When this happens, you can use survey, probing, or confirmation questions to obtain more information.

At this point you have received only a basic introduction to the four most common types of questions used during the selling process. Many major books on personal selling emphasize the importance of using questions as part of the consultative selling process, as shown in Table 11.3. We will revisit these important sales tools later in this chapter and in Chapters 12, 13, 14, and 15.

Table 11.3

Comparison of Strategic Approaches to Questioning in Complex Sales

The use of questions to discover needs and present solutions is discussed in several popular books on personal selling. For comparison purposes, the approximate equivalents to the four types of questions described in this chapter are listed. These questions are listed in the sequence presented by the authors. To determine the exact definition of each question, you need to check the source.

***Selling Today*: Manning, Reece, MacKenzie**	***The SPIN Selling Fieldbook*: Rachman**	***The New Solution Selling*: Eades**	***The New Conceptual Selling*: Heiman, Sanchez, Tuleja**	***Secrets of Question-Based Selling*: Freese**
Survey	Situation	Diagnose Reasons	Confirmation	Status
Probing	Problem	Explore Impact	New Information	Issue
Confirmation	Implication	Visualize Capability	Attitude	Implication
Need-Satisfaction	Need-Payoff		Commitment	Solution
			Basic Issue	

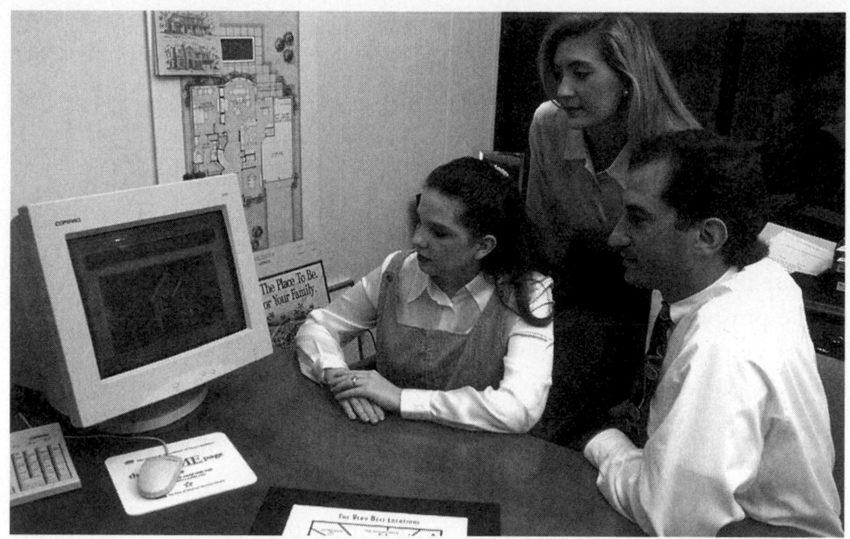

This real estate salesperson, with the help of a computerized database of homes, is using probing and confirmation questions to clarify the needs of the customer.

ELIMINATING UNNECESSARY QUESTIONS

It is important to avoid the use of unnecessary questions during a sales call. As noted previously, salespeople need to acquire as much information as possible about the prospect before the first meeting. This preliminary information gathering is especially important when the prospect is a corporate buyer. These buyers expect the salesperson to be well informed about their operation and not waste time asking basic survey questions to gather information. Increasingly, corporate buyers want to establish a long-term partnership with suppliers. They assume that potential partners will conduct a careful study of their company before the first sales call.

LISTENING AND ACKNOWLEDGING THE CUSTOMER'S RESPONSE

To fully understand the prospect, a salesperson must listen closely and acknowledge every response. The authors of *First Impressions* offer these words of advice to salespeople who use questions as part of need discovery: "What you do after you ask a question can reveal even more about you than the questions you ask. You reveal your true level of interest in the way you listen."[4] We are born with the ability to hear, but we have to learn how to listen. The starting point is developing a listening attitude. Always regard the prospect as worthy of your respect and full attention. Once you have made a commitment to becoming a good listener, develop active listening skills.

active listening The process of sending back to the prospect what you as a listener think the person meant, both in terms of content and in terms of feelings. It involves taking into consideration and exhibiting both verbal and nonverbal messages.

DEVELOPING ACTIVE LISTENING SKILLS

Active listening is the process of sending back to the prospect what you as a listener think the person meant, both in terms of content and in terms of feelings. Active listening requires intense involvement as you concentrate on what you are hearing, exhibit your listening attitude through your nonverbal messages (see Chapter 3), and feed back to the prospect what you think he or she meant.[5] Developing active listening skills involves three practices that can be learned by any salesperson willing to make the commitment:

- *Focus your full attention.* This is not easy because the delivery of the messages we hear is often much slower than our capacity to listen. Thus, we have plenty of time to let our minds roam, to think ahead, and to plan what we are going to say next. Our senses are constantly feeding us new information while someone is trying to tell us something. Staying focused is often difficult and involves use of both verbal and nonverbal messages.[6] To show that you are paying attention, lean toward the prospect while murmuring "uh-huh," "Okay," or "I understand," and nod in agreement when appropriate. Avoid nodding rapidly or saying "uh-huh" loudly or frequently because this will communicate impatience or a desire to turn the conversation back to yourself.[7]
- *Paraphrase the prospect's meaning.* After the prospect stops talking, pause for two or three seconds and then state in your own words what you think the person meant. This technique not only helps ensure understanding but also is an effective relationship-building strategy. The prospect feels good knowing that not only are you listening to what has been said but you are making an effort to ensure accuracy. In addition to paraphrasing the content, do not hesitate to use paraphrasing for perception checks.[8] The use of survey or probing questions is appropriate any time you need to clarify what is being said by the prospect.
- *Take notes.* Although note taking is not necessary in every sales presentation, it is important in complex sales where the information obtained from the prospect is critical to the development of a buying solution. Taking notes is a good way to demonstrate to the prospect that you are actively listening. When you take notes, you increase your memory of what was heard. Your notes should be brief and to the point.[9]

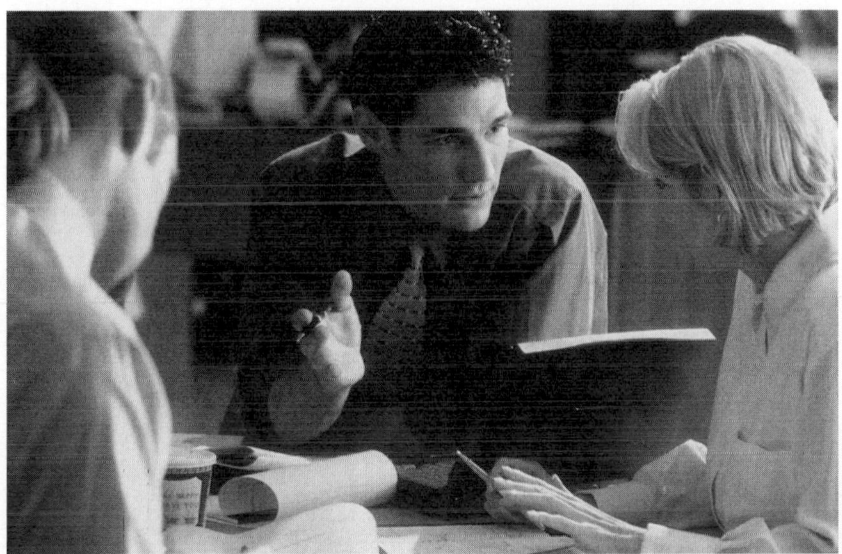

In many selling situations, note taking will demonstrate a high level of professionalism.

CUSTOMER RELATIONSHIP MANAGEMENT WITH TECHNOLOGY

Reviewing Account Status

Salespeople regularly review the status of their prospects' records in their CRM databases. In some cases, this is done on the computer screen. In other situations, a printed copy of the records can enhance the process.

Salespeople review their files to ascertain at what phase in the Consultative Sales Presentation Guide each prospect is in the sales cycle. Then they will decide which action to take to help move the prospect to the next phase. Sales managers can be helpful with this process, especially for new salespeople. Managers can help salespeople evaluate the available information and suggest strategies designed to move to the next phase.

Even experienced salespeople count on their sales managers to help plan presentations. Managers can help salespeople evaluate their prospects' needs, select the best solution, and plan a presentation most likely to succeed. (See the exercise Printing the Customer Database on page 279 for more information.)

ESTABLISHING BUYING MOTIVES

The primary goal of questioning, listening, and acknowledging is to uncover prospect needs and establish buying motives. Our efforts to discover prospect needs will be more effective if a salesperson focuses his or her questioning on determining the prospect's primary reasons for buying. When a prospect has a definite need, it is usually supported by specific buying motives.

Selecting Solutions That Add Value

The second part of the consultative sales presentation consists of selecting or creating a solution that satisfies the prospect's buying motives. After identifying the buying motives, the salesperson carefully reviews the available product options. At this point, the salesperson is searching for a specific solution to satisfy the prospect's buying motives. Once the solution has been selected, the salesperson makes a recommendation to the prospect (see Fig. 11.5).

If the sale involves several needs and the satisfaction of multiple buying motives, selection of the solution may take several days or even weeks and involve the preparation of a detailed sales proposal. A company considering the purchase of automated office equipment would likely present this type of challenge to the salesperson. The problem needs careful analysis before a solution can be identified.

MATCH SPECIFIC BENEFITS WITH BUYING MOTIVES

As we noted in Chapter 7, products and services represent problem-solving tools. People buy products when they perceive that they fulfill a need. We also noted that today's more demanding customers seek a cluster of satisfactions that arise from the product itself, from the company that makes or distributes the product, and from the salesperson who sells and services the product (see Fig. 7.1). Tom Riley, author of *Value-Added Selling*, says "Value-

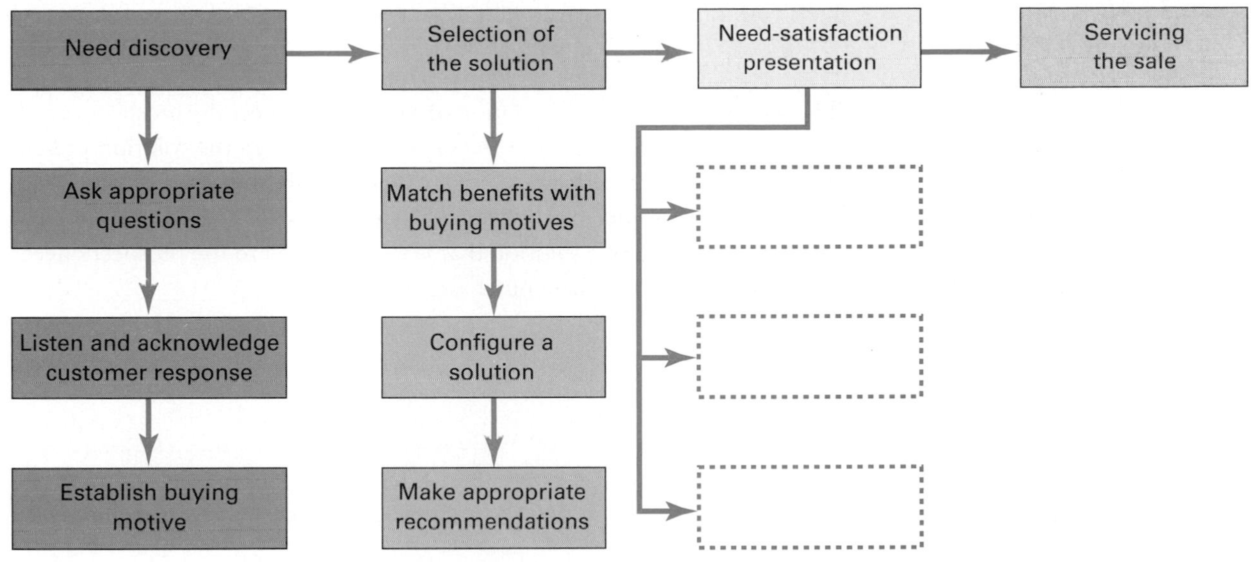

Figure 11.5 Three dimensions of product selection.

added salespeople sell three things: the product, the company, and themselves. This is the three-dimensional bundle of value."[10] When possible the salesperson should focus on benefits related to each dimension of value. Of course, it is a mistake to make benefit statements that do not relate to the specific needs of the customer.

CONFIGURE A SOLUTION

Most salespeople bring to the sale a variety of products or services. Salespeople who represent food distributors can offer customers a mix of several hundred items. Most pharmaceutical sales representatives can offer the medical community a wide range of products. Best Buy, a large retailer of electronics, offers customers a wide range of audio and visual entertainment options. The customer who wants to purchase a sound system, for example, can choose from many combinations of receivers, speakers, and other equipment.

www.bestbuy.ca

MAKE APPROPRIATE RECOMMENDATIONS

The recommendation strategies available to salespeople are similar to those used by a doctor who must recommend a solution to a patient's medical problem. In the medical field, three possibilities for providing patient satisfaction exist. In situations in which the patient easily understands the medical problem and the appropriate treatment, the doctor can make a recommendation and the patient can proceed immediately toward well-being. If the patient does not easily understand the medical problem or solution, the doctor may need to discuss thoroughly with the patient the benefits of the recommended treatment. If the medical problem is not within his or her medical specialty area, the doctor may recommend a specialist to provide the treatment. In consultative selling the salesperson has these same three counselling alternatives.

RECOMMEND SOLUTION—PROSPECT BUYS IMMEDIATELY

The selection and recommendation of a product to meet the prospect's needs may occur at the beginning of the sales call, such as in the solution presentation; during the interview, just after the need discovery; or near the end, when minor resistance has been negotiated. At any of these three opportunities, presentation of a solution that is well matched to the prospect's needs may result in an immediate purchase.

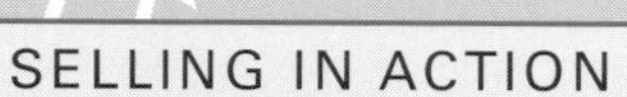

Selling to Couples

There are many situations where salespeople sell to a couple, rather than to an individual: real estate, mutual funds, cars, wedding rings, insurance. These situations can pose additional challenges for salespeople. Each person in a couple may, for example, bring hidden agenda to the purchase. An unseasoned salesperson risks alienating or offending one partner and, perhaps as a result, losing the sale.

According to Marilyn Powers, a practising therapist, couples exhibit one of three communications stages: a fusion stage, a power struggle stage, or an independent stage. Couples in the fusion stage think and feel alike, and try to avoid conflict. As a result, they make hasty decisions, often without providing adequate information to the salesperson. This may result in the sale being cancelled, or in after-sale customer dissatisfaction. To prevent this, the salesperson needs to ask sufficient questions during the need discovery stage of the sales process, to be sure he or she fully understands the couple's needs.

Couples in the power struggle stage actively seek a win-lose solution, where one partner's "win" over the other partner is more important than the actual purchase decision. Here, the salesperson needs to slow the sales process and craft a "win-win" solution for the couple. The best way to do this is to focus on each person, being sure to establish and understand each individual's needs. Through active listening—paraphrasing and restating each participant's comments—the salesperson may be able to defuse the emotional situation, keeping the communication lines open and establishing some common ground. Unfortunately, there will be instances where it is apparent that one key decision maker will win the power struggle. Here, some salespeople argue that it is best to align with that person as it will be impossible to keep both participants happy; other salespeople argue that it is best to remain impartial and to avoid getting involved in the power struggle.

Couples in the independent stage often have different opinions about what they should buy, but they are willing to continue their search for a third solution that may be better than either of their independent solutions. A salesperson who encounters this situation may need to give the couple additional time to communicate with each other, and should not try to close the sale too quickly.

Judith C. Tingley and Lee E. Robert, authors of *GenderSell: How to Sell to the Opposite Sex*, suggest some tips to use, depending on whether the salesperson is a man or a woman. They suggest that male salespeople must be careful to avoid being patronizing or condescending toward women when trying to sell to a mixed-gender couple. A male salesperson should greet the woman first, keep her involved throughout the sales process, and be careful to use gender-neutral language. Female salespeople need to build credibility quickly, be more rational and less emotional in their selling style, and treat both partners with equal respect.[a]

RECOMMEND SOLUTION—SALESPERSON MAKES NEED-SATISFACTION PRESENTATION

This alternative requires a presentation of product benefits, including demonstrations and negotiating resistance, before the sale is closed. In this situation, the prospect may not be totally aware of a buying problem, and the solution may not be easily understood or apparent. The salesperson will need to make a detailed presentation to define the problem and communicate a solution to the prospect.

Earlier in this book, we indicated that professional salespeople may recommend that a prospect buy a product or service from another source, maybe even a competitor. If, after a careful needs assessment, the salesperson concludes that the products represented will not satisfy the customer's needs, the consultative salesperson should recommend another source.

Need Satisfaction—Selecting a Presentation Strategy

Decisions concerning which presentation strategy to emphasize have become more complex because of several factors discussed in previous chapters: longer sales cycles, multiple buying influences, emphasis on repeat sales and referrals, greater emphasis on custom fitting solutions, and building of long-term partnerships. Conducting business today, based on the assets of knowledge and information, requires that we think about ways to improve the sales presentation. Here is how one author described this challenge:

> "As we move from the rutted byways of the Industrial Age to the electronic thoroughfares of the Information Age, business presentations become a measure of our ability to adapt to new surroundings. The most successful and forward-thinking companies already have assigned presentations a new, fundamental and strategic importance."[11]

Today we need a broader range of presentation strategies. Today, the need-satisfaction strategy involves assessing the prospect's needs; selecting the solution; and deciding whether to use an informative, persuasive, or reminder presentation (see Fig. 11.6, page 270).

cathy® **by Cathy Guisewite**

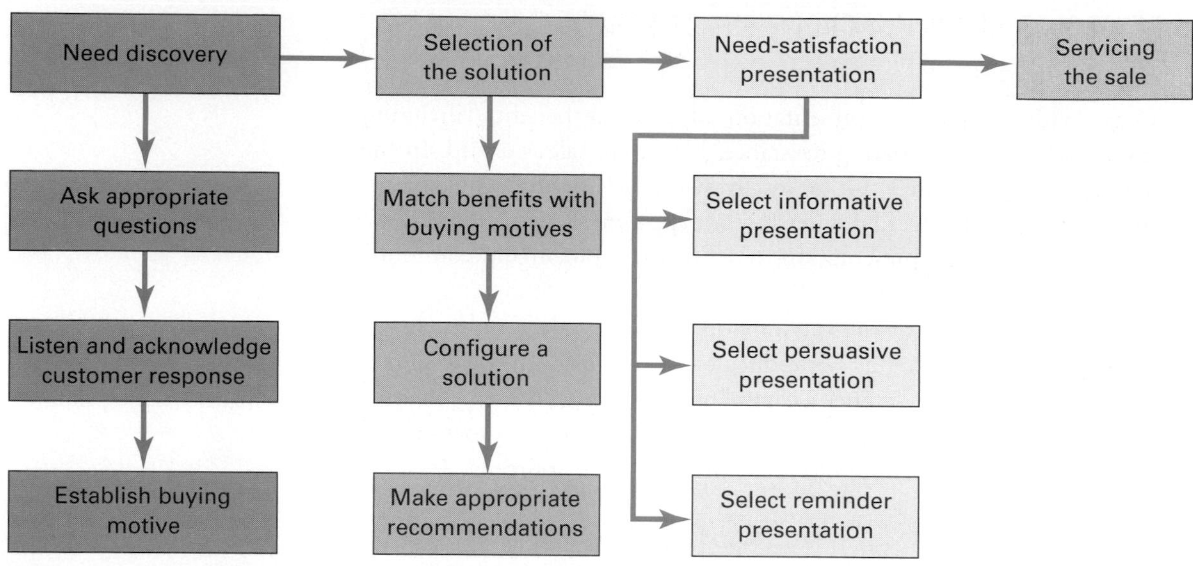

Figure 11.6 The three strategies to use in developing an effective need-satisfaction presentation.

INFORMATIVE PRESENTATION

informative presentation Emphasizes factual information, which is often taken from technical reports, company-prepared sales literature, or written testimonials from people who have used the product.

To be informative, a message must be clearly understood by the prospect. Of course, clarity is important in any presentation, but it needs special attention in a presentation in which the primary purpose is to inform. The **informative presentation** emphasizes factual information typically taken from technical reports, company-prepared sales literature, or written testimonials from persons who have used the product. This type of presentation is commonly used to introduce new products and services. Within most major industries, new products are appearing at a rapid rate and many of them are introduced through informative sales presentations. This strategy emphasizes clarity, simplicity, and directness.

A variety of factors motivate sales personnel to adopt the informative presentation. Some have discovered that this strategy works best when they sell highly complex products that have to be custom fitted to unique needs. In addition, if the price of the solution is quite high, a factual presentation, devoid of emotion, may be the best approach. Some salespeople simply think that it is not appropriate to use persuasion during the sales presentation. They believe that a product should stand on its own merits and that persuasion should not be necessary to sell it.

PERSUASIVE PRESENTATION

persuasive presentation A sales strategy that influences the prospect's beliefs, attitudes, or behaviour and encourages buyer action.

Many salespeople believe that, when a real need for their product exists, the stage is set for a persuasive presentation. The major goals of the **persuasive presentation** are to influence the prospect's beliefs, attitudes, or behaviour, and to encourage buyer action. Persuasive sales presentations include a subtle transition stage where the dialogue shifts from an intellectual emphasis to an emotional appeal. Every business decision is influenced by both reason and emotion, but the amount of weight given to each of these elements during the decision-making process can vary greatly depending on the prospect.[12]

In the field of personal selling, persuasion is an acceptable strategy once a need has been identified and a suitable product has been selected. When it is clear that the buyer will benefit from ownership of the product or service, an enthusiastic and persuasive sales presentation is usually appropriate. As a strategy, the persuasive presentation requires a high level of training and experience to be effective, because a poorly planned and delivered persuasive presentation may raise the prospect's anxiety level. The persuasive presentation, when handled properly, does not trigger fear or distrust.

REMINDER PRESENTATION

Studies show that awareness of a company's products and services declines as promotion is stopped. This problem represents one of the reasons many companies employ "missionary" salespeople to maintain an ongoing awareness of and familiarity with their product lines. Other types of salespeople also use this strategy by delivering a **reminder presentation** (sometimes called a *reinforcement presentation*). Route salespeople rely heavily on reminder presentations to maintain their market share. They know that, if they do not make frequent calls and remind customers of their products, the competition will likely capture some customers. The 12 800 Frito-Lay salespeople are in a strong position to use the reminder presentation as a strategy because they use handheld computers to manage orders. It takes only a minute or two to review a programmed product list in the presence of a customer.[13]

reminder presentation Sometimes called the *reinforcement presentation*, this strategy assumes that the prospect has already been involved in an informative or persuasive presentation and understands at least the basic product features and buyer benefits.

The reminder presentation also has many applications at the retail level. Sales personnel working with repeat customers are in a good position to remind them of products or services offered in their own department or another department located in some other area of the business.

Salespeople using the reminder presentation understand the value of repetition. They know that many of their recommendations will not be accepted until the second, third, or fourth time.

Guidelines for Developing a Persuasive Presentation

There are many ways to incorporate persuasion into a sales presentation. In this section we review a series of guidelines that should be followed during preparation of a persuasive presentation.

PLACE SPECIAL EMPHASIS ON THE RELATIONSHIP

Throughout this book we have emphasized the importance of the relationship strategy in selling. Good rapport between the salesperson and the prospect establishes a foundation for an open exchange of information. Robert Cialdini, writing in the *Harvard Business Review*, says the science of persuasion is built on the principle of liking: *People like those who like them.* Establish a bond with the prospect early by uncovering areas of common interest, using praise when it's appropriate, and being completely trustworthy.[14] Always do what you say you will do.

SELL BENEFITS AND OBTAIN PROSPECT REACTIONS

People do not buy things; they buy what the things will do for them. They do not buy an auto battery; they buy a sure start on a cold morning. Office managers do not buy laser printers; they buy better-looking letters and reports. Every product or service offers the prospect certain benefits. The benefit might be greater comfort, security, a feeling of confidence, or economy.

www.allstate.ca

If you are selling Allstate insurance, for example, you should become familiar with the service features. One feature is well-trained employees, and another is the convenient location of Allstate offices throughout Canada. The benefit to prospects is greater peace of mind in knowing that they will receive good service at a nearby location.

After you state the feature and convert it to a buyer benefit, obtain a reaction from the prospect. You should always check to see if you are on the right track and if your prospect is following the logic of your presentation. The reactions can be triggered by a simple confirmation question. Here are some examples:

Feature	Benefit	Confirmation question
Commercial-size package	Money saved	"You are interested in saving money, are you not?"
Automatic climate control system for automobile	Temperature in car not varying after initial setting	"Would you like the luxury of setting the temperature and then not worrying about it?"

The feature–benefit–reaction (FBR) approach is used by many high-performance salespeople. Involving the prospect with a confirmation question helps you maintain two-way communication.

MINIMIZE THE NEGATIVE IMPACT OF CHANGE

As we noted earlier, salespeople are constantly threatening the status quo. They sell people the new, the different, and the untried. In nearly all selling situations the prospect is being asked to consider change of some sort and, in some cases, it is only natural for the person to resist change. Whenever possible, salespeople should try to help the prospect view change in a positive and realistic way. Change is more acceptable to people who understand the benefits of it and do not see it as a threat.

PLACE THE STRONGEST APPEAL AT THE BEGINNING OR END

Research indicates that appeals made at the beginning or end of a presentation are more effective than those given in the middle. A strong appeal at the beginning of a presentation, of course, will get the prospect's attention and possibly develop interest. Made near the end of the presentation, the appeal sets the stage for closing the sale.

TARGET EMOTIONAL LINKS

An **emotional link** is a connector between your messages and the prospect's emotions.[15] Some common emotional links in the business community are quality improvement, on-time delivery, increased market share, innovation, customer service, and reduction of operating expenses. Targeting just a few emotional links can increase your chances of closing the sale. When you target emotional links use persuasive words such as "proven," "efficient," "save," "convenient," "world-class," "new," and "improved." Also, use the terminology to which your prospect is attuned.

emotional link A connector that links a salesperson's message to the customer's internal emotions and increases the chances of closing a sale—for example, quality improvement, on-time delivery, service, innovation.

USE METAPHORS, STORIES, AND TESTIMONIALS

Metaphors, sometimes referred to as *figurative language*, are highly persuasive sales tools. Metaphors are imaginative words or phrases that suggest pictorial relationships between objects or ideas. With the aid of metaphors you can paint vivid visual pictures for prospects that will command their attention and keep their interest. The success of the metaphor rests on finding common ground (i.e., shared or well-known experiences) so that your message gets a free boost from a fact already known or believed to be true. A salesperson presenting a new computer system that has a very fast data analysis capability might say, "The speed of our system, compared to what you are used to, would be like comparing an Olympic sprinter to a toddler just learning to walk."[16]

Donald J. Moine, noted speaker and sales trainer, says that stories will not only help you sell more products, but they will also help you enrich relationships with your customers. A good story not only focuses the customer's attention, it can effectively communicate the value of a product or service. Xerox and IBM represent just two examples of companies that use stories to inspire the selling effort.[17]

www-306.ibm.com/software/solutions/webservices/testimonials.html

Many salespeople find it beneficial to quote a specific third party. Third-party testimonials from satisfied customers can help a prospect feel confident about using your product.

Guidelines for Creating Effective Presentations

There are many ways to make all three need-satisfaction presentation strategies more interesting and valuable. A more effective presentation can be developed using the following general guidelines. Each of these guidelines will be discussed in more detail in chapters 12 to 15.

STRENGTHEN THE PRESENTATION STRATEGY WITH AN EFFECTIVE DEMONSTRATION

The need-satisfaction presentation can be strengthened if the salesperson preplans effective demonstrations that clarify the product features and benefits. Many salespeople encounter doubt or skepticism during the sales presentation. The prospect often wants some kind of assurance or proof. The salesperson must be prepared to substantiate claims made with factual information. This information can be provided in several ways. The following list of proof strategies is explained in detail in Chapter 12.

- Product itself
- Models
- Photos and illustrations
- Portfolios
- Testimonials and case histories
- Reprints
- Graphs, charts, and test results
- Laptop computers and demonstration software
- Audiovisual technology
- Bound paper presentations

PREPLAN METHODS FOR NEGOTIATING AND CLOSING THE SALE

Salespeople who make the most efficient use of time are adding value. To make your presentation as concise and to the point as possible, you should preplan methods for negotiating misunderstandings or resistance that might surface during the presentation. You need to bring some degree of urgency to the selling environment by presenting focused solutions.[18] In most cases, the focus of the negotiation is on one of the following areas:

- Need awareness is vague or nonexistent.
- Price does not equal perceived value.
- The buyer is satisfied with present source or product.
- Product does not meet the buyer's perceived requirement.
- Buyer does not see that this is the right time.

Methods used to negotiate buyer resistance in each of these areas are introduced in Chapter 13. It also is important to preplan closing and confirming

Sales Force Automation. Salespeople can enhance their presentation strategy with proof devices produced using computer software packages such as the popular Microsoft PowerPoint.

EVERYONE SELLS

Low-Tech Pitchman

When *Canadian Business* selected its "dream team" of Canadian executives, it chose Randy Van Der Starren as "The Pitchman." Van Der Starren, who worked for several advertising agencies, eventually came to Young & Rubicam in Toronto. While there, he made a presentation to Blake Golding, CEO of AGF Management Ltd. "I'll never forget his presentation," says Blake Golding. "He was a breath of fresh air." It was a straight pitch—without any of the usual PowerPoint, charts, or graphs. He was sufficiently impressed with Randy Van Der Starren that he convinced him to join the AGF team.

As senior vice-president of marketing for AGF, Randy Van Der Starren takes his business seriously but he maintains, "You don't have to take yourself so seriously." His challenge today is to sell the number crunchers at AGF that superheroes and mutual funds go well together. After all, the AGF "What are you doing after work?" campaign featuring the Incredible Hulk, Spider-Man, and Gumby won a CASSIES award for raising brand awareness and market share.[b]

of the sale. This planning should include a review of closing clues that may surface during the sales presentation and methods of closing the sale. These and other topics are discussed in Chapter 14.

PREPLAN CUSTOMER SERVICE METHODS THAT ADD VALUE

Customer service, in its many forms, provides an opportunity to add value. Very often prospects want a preview of the customer service options during the sales presentation. And, in some cases, customer service is the key to closing the sale. Consider the purchase that must be financed and the customer expects you to be familiar with various credit options. You can also add value with timely delivery of the product, proper installation, and follow-up to ensure customer satisfaction. Customer service will be discussed in detail in Chapter 15.

KEEP YOUR PRESENTATION SIMPLE AND CONCISE

The best way to achieve conciseness is to preplan your sales call. Think ahead of time about what you are going to say and do. Anticipate questions and resistance the prospect may voice, and be prepared with accurate information and concise answers.

Preplanning also involves time allocation. Figure 11.7 on page 276 illustrates an ideal breakdown of time allocation between the salesperson and the prospect during all three parts of the sales presentation. In terms of involvement, the prospect assumes a greater role during the need discovery stage. As the salesperson begins the product selection process, the prospect's involvement decreases. During the need-satisfaction stage, the salesperson is doing most of the talking; but note that the prospect is never excluded totally.

In addition to preplanning the sales presentation, consider rehearsing in front of your colleagues. A less-threatening approach might be to practise

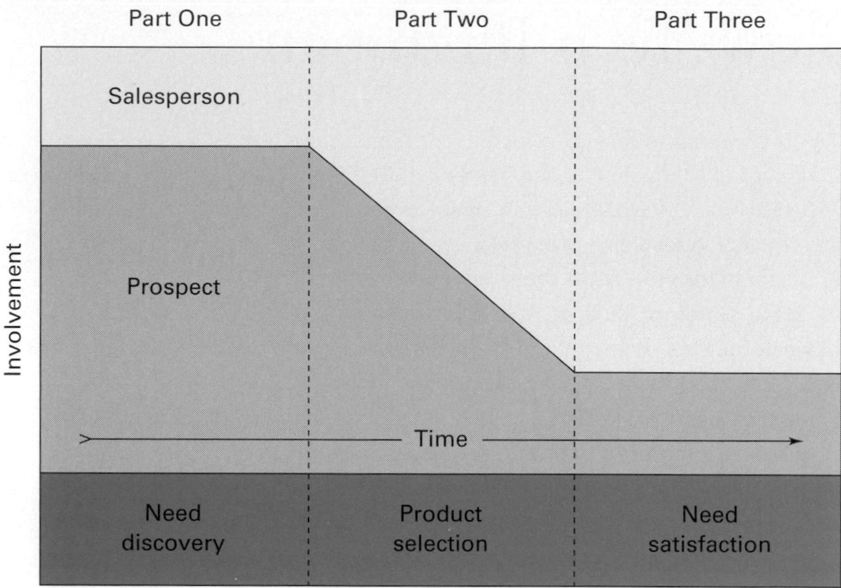

Figure 11.7 Time used by salesperson and prospect during each part of the consultative sales presentation.

your presentation for your spouse or a close friend. Videotaping the rehearsal can help you see how you really look. Do you appear too stiff and motionless? Do you talk too fast or too slow? It's a good idea to practise presentations with specific customers in mind.[19]

THE CONSULTATIVE SALES PRESENTATION AND THE TRANSACTIONAL BUYER

Throughout this chapter you have been given a comprehensive introduction to the consultative sales presentation. It is important to keep in mind that the fundamentals of consultative selling must be customized to meet the individual needs of the prospect. For example, some of the guidelines for developing an effective presentation must be abandoned or greatly altered when you are working with a transactional buyer. In Chapter 1 we described transactional selling as a process that most effectively satisfies the needs of the buyer who is primarily interested in price and convenience. In most cases transactional buyers understand what product they need and when they need it. In many situations they are interested only in the product itself and not what the company or salesperson can do to create additional value. The buyer may even resent time spent with the salesperson, especially time spent on need discovery. The Internet has armed many transactional buyers with a great deal of information, so the salesperson who spends time asking information-gathering questions or making a detailed informative presentation may be wasting the prospect's time. Most of these buyers want the salesperson to configure a product solution that focuses on pricing and delivery issues.[20]

SUMMARY

A well-planned and well-executed presentation strategy is an important key to success in personal selling. To be most effective, the consultative sales presentation should be viewed as a four-part process: need discovery; selection of the solution; need satisfaction through informing, persuading, or reminding; and servicing the sale.

The most effective sales presentation is characterized by two-way communication. It should be a dialogue between the salesperson and the prospect, whose involvement should be encouraged with survey, probing, confirmation, and need-satisfaction questions. Beware of assuming things about the prospect, and be sure the language of your presentation is clearly understood. Listen attentively as the prospect responds to your questions or volunteers information.

After making a good first impression during the approach and getting the prospect's full attention, the salesperson begins the presentation. The salesperson's ability is tested during this part of the sale, because this is where the prospect's buying motives are established. The salesperson's ability to verbalize solution benefits will also be tested during this part of the sale.

Once you have selected a solution that matches the prospect's needs, you must decide which presentation strategy to emphasize. Need satisfaction can be achieved through informing, persuading, or reminding. The salesperson will, of course, use a combination of these presentation strategies in some cases. An effective presentation is an important part of the sales call and will often determine the ease or difficulty of proceeding through the rest of the steps to a successful sale.

Key Terms

Review Questions

1. List and describe the four parts of the Consultative Sales Presentation Guide.
2. List and describe the four types of question commonly used in the selling field.
3. Define the term "buying conditions." What are some common buying conditions?
4. What is the listening efficiency rate of most people? Describe the process of active listening and explain how it will improve the listening efficiency rate.
5. Discuss the major factors that should be considered during the product selection phase of the consultative-style sales presentation.

6. Distinguish among the three types of need-satisfaction presentations: informative, persuasive, and reminder.
7. What are the guidelines to follow when developing a persuasive sales presentation?
8. What are some advantages of using the feature-benefit–reaction approach?
9. What role does *figurative language* play in personal selling? Distinguish among three types of figurative language commonly used by salespeople.
10. The opening vignette on page 252 describes how Google.com salespeople refuse to sell to accounts that fail to fit their model. Explain why this is a good practice for salespeople who use a consultative selling approach.

Application Exercises

1. Assume that you are a salesperson working in each of the following kinds of selling careers, and assume further that the prospect has given you no indication of what he or she is looking for. Identify the types of question you would use to discover your prospect's specific needs.
   a. Personal computer
   b. Carpet
   c. Financial planning
2. You are a department manager and have called a meeting with the five staff members in your department. The purpose of your meeting is to inform your staff of a new procedure your company has adopted. It is important that you develop understanding and support. What steps can you take to enhance communication with the group?
3. Pick a job that you would really like to have and for which you are qualified. Assume you are going to be interviewed for this job tomorrow afternoon. You really want this position and therefore want to be persuasive in presenting your qualifications. List facts about your qualifications, including where you have worked previously, how much education you have, and what hobbies and activities you have been involved in. Use a feature-benefits worksheet like the one in Table 6.2 as a guide to convert these employee facts to employer benefits in the form of selling statements.
4. Go to **www.google.ca** (or another search engine if you prefer) and hit "advanced search." Type "active listening" under "Find results with exact phrase." Limit your search by typing ".ca" under "domain." Do the same for "listening skills." To what other groups besides salespeople do these terms appear to be most relevant? Why? Be prepared to discuss some of what you find in class.

ROLE-PLAY EXERCISE

Research the type of new computer that you would like to purchase in the future or that you have just purchased. Strategically, prepare to meet a potential customer who has been referred to you by a friend and who would like to purchase a similar computer. Using Table 11.1, prepare survey (i.e., information-gathering) questions you could use to discover the potential customer's specific computer needs. Also prepare a transition statement and permission question to move you directly into the need discovery part of the consultative sales presentation. Using the materials you have created, role-play the questioning process with another person. Review how well you conducted the need discovery.

CRM Application Exercise PRINTING THE CUSTOMER DATABASE

Sales managers regularly help salespeople review the status of their accounts. These strategic account review meetings may involve examining all of the information available on the salespeople's most promising prospects. The sales manager and salesperson will each have a copy of all information currently available for the accounts either on their computer screens or on paper. To produce a paper record of the information contained in the ACT! database, select Lookup, Everyone, Report, Contact Report, Active Group, Printer, and Enter. Approximately 40 pages of information will be printed.

Case Problem

Annette Peterson is a real estate salesperson for Canwest Homes, Inc. The sales manager referred a young couple, John and Beth Reems, to Annette. John and Beth are being transferred to the city for John's job as a manager of a local men's clothing store. Beth had been a computer systems analyst in a department store and will be looking for a similar position after the move.

Annette had no opportunity to visit with John and Beth until they arrived in the city today. The sales manager set up an appointment for them to meet at the office at 1:00 p.m. On their arrival, Annette made the following sales presentation:

Annette: Good afternoon, Mr. and Mrs. Reems. My name is Annette Peterson.

John: Good afternoon. I'm John Reems and this is my wife, Beth.

Beth: Good afternoon, Mrs. Peterson, we've been looking forward to meeting you.

Annette: Please call me Annette. And how was your flight?

Beth: Oh, we had a lovely flight and got a wonderful view of the city as we circled for landing.

John: I enjoyed the flight also and am looking forward to seeing the city and driving around to see the homes for sale. Our flight back leaves at 8:30 p.m. so we are not going to have a lot of time. Our looking is going to have to move rather quickly.

Annette: My sales manager told me you would have limited time, so I've prepared an agenda for us to follow this afternoon. I have four homes that I have selected from our computerized database. I picked up the keys for all four of them so we can drive out and take a look. Before we get going, though, I would like to show you a picture of each home and tell you a little about it. I am sure you will find all four of them very appealing.

John and Beth: Oh!

Annette: Here is the first one. It is priced at $246 000, has 2000 square feet in two storeys. This house has two bathrooms and is located on a 65- by 135-foot lot. It was built in 1975 and has Acan windows.

John and Beth: Uh-huh! [Beth looks for a pencil in her purse.]

Annette: Now here is a picture of the second house. I do not like this one as well as the first, but I thought you might like to see it. This home was built in 1987 and is priced at $240 000. The taxes are $3000 a year. It has 1600 square feet and has vinyl siding on it. It also has an attached 22- by 24-foot garage. The lot is 80 by 140 feet. It is a ranch-style home.

John and Beth: We do like ranch-style homes.

Annette: This picture is of the third home that I chose. I really like this one. It is a split-level, priced at $238 900. The taxes are—oh, I'm sorry, the taxes do not seem to be listed for this one. I am sure we can find out what they are, however, if you are interested.

John: Well, we really are not interested in split-level homes. There are too many stairs to climb. By the way, how far are these homes from the store?

Annette: Well, most customers I have worked with do not concern themselves with how far, but rather how long it will take them to get to work. You will find that the city has an excellent system of streets with rapid uncongested travelling. The homes I am going to show you are all located in a suburb called Majestic Oaks. It will take you about 20 minutes to drive from there to your store.

John: I see. [John looks at his watch.]

Annette: Here is a picture of the fourth home I picked out. This one is also a two-storey and has a 24- by 24-foot garage. The price is $239 000 and it has an assumable mortgage of $130 500 with two years remaining at 4.5 percent interest. The home is located on a cul-de-sac, with a 90- by 160-foot lot. I went through this house last week and remember that it has oak wainscotting in the family room and also vinyl siding. It has a high-efficiency furnace, air conditioner, and Maytag appliances.

Questions

1. Describe what you think John and Beth's impressions are of Annette.
2. Evaluate the strength of Annette Peterson's presentation strategy.
3. Evaluate the weaknesses of this presentation strategy.
4. Assume you are Annette Peterson. Prepare an outline that you would follow in giving your sales presentation.
5. Assume that Annette Peterson follows the same pattern in the demonstration and close that she has already established in the presentation thus far. Is she likely to close the sale? Why or why not?
6. Select five features brought out by Annette and convert them to buyer benefits. Use the forms presented in tables 6.2 and 6.3.

CRM Case Study PLANNING PRESENTATIONS

Becky Kemley, your sales manager at SimNet Systems, wants to meet with you this afternoon to discuss the status of your accounts. It is common for prospects to have several contacts with SimNet before ordering a network system. These multiple call contacts, or *sales cycle phases*, usually include getting acquainted and prequalifying, need discovery, proposal presentation, closing, and account maintenance. Becky wants to know what phase each account is in and, particularly, which accounts may be ready for a presentation.

Questions

1. Which five accounts have already had a need discovery? Which two accounts are scheduled for a need discovery? Which six accounts are likely to buy but have not yet had a need discovery?
2. Which two accounts have had a need discovery and now need a product solution to be configured?
3. Which three accounts do not now have a network and appear to be ready for your sales presentation?
4. For those accounts listed next that are ready for your sales presentation, which strategy would you use for each: informative, persuasive, or reminder?

   Able Profit Machines — International Studios

   Big Tex Auto Sales — Lakeside Clinic
5. Which accounts appear to be planning to buy without a need discovery or product configuration/proposal? What risks does this pose?

Partnership Selling

A ROLE PLAY/SIMULATION **(see Partnership Selling on CD-ROM, p. 36)**

UNDERSTANDING YOUR CUSTOMER'S BUYING STRATEGY

Read *Sales Memorandum 2* ("A" or "B" depending on the account category you were assigned in Chapter 10). Your customer has called you back because you made such a good approach in call 1, and he or she wants to visit with you about a convention recently assigned. In this call you are to use the information gathered in sales call 1 to re-establish a good relationship, discover your customer's convention needs, and set an appointment to return and make a presentation.

Follow the instructions carefully and prepare information-gathering questions prior to your appointment. Keep your information-gathering questions general and attempt to get your customer to share information openly. Use probing questions later during the appointment to gain more insight. Be careful about doing too much of the talking. In the need discovery your customer should do most of the talking, with you taking notes and using them to ask confirmation, and summary confirmation questions in order to check the accuracy of your perceptions concerning what the customer wants. After this meeting you will be asked to prepare a sales proposal from the information you have gathered.

Your instructor may again ask you to assume the role of a customer in the account category that you are not assigned as a salesperson. If so, you will receive detailed customer instructions, which you should follow closely. This will provide you with an opportunity to experience the strategic/consultative/partnering style of selling from a customer's perspective.

CHAPTER 12

Creating Value with the Sales Demonstration

LEARNING OBJECTIVES

After studying this chapter, you should be able to

1. Discuss how sales demonstrations add value
2. Explain the guidelines to be followed when planning a sales demonstration
3. Complete a demonstration worksheet
4. Develop selling tools that can strengthen your sales presentation
5. Discuss how to use audiovisual presentations effectively

SimGraphics Engineering Corporation **www.simg.com** specializes in the development of visual simulation systems based on virtual reality. These systems have application in such diverse areas as television programming, the training of medical doctors, and product design. For example, students are using one virtual reality system to learn and practise eye surgery skills before working on real patients. The SimGraphics system animates virtual characters from the motion-captured performance of a human actor in real time—as the performance is taking place. Performance animation enjoys advantages in immediacy and cost-effectiveness that cannot be matched by a traditional animation system. Needless to say, it's not easy to explain this without a well-planned demonstration.[1]

Importance of the Sales Demonstration

In today's fuzzy, complex, out-of-focus world, customers greatly appreciate help with making decisions. The salesperson who can simplify things and who can communicate with clarity will be welcomed with open arms. Every effort that is made to uncomplicate the situation adds value.[2] Throughout this text, we have defined value-added selling as a series of creative improvements that enhance the customer experience. The perception of value is enhanced with a well-developed demonstration.

One of the scarcest resources today is people's attention. If the customer isn't paying attention, there is little chance of closing the sale. The increase in look-alike products and greater competition present additional challenges. The sales demonstration has become a more important communication tool. A well-planned **demonstration** adds sensory appeal to the product (see Fig. 12.1 on page 284). It attracts the customer's attention, stimulates interest, and creates desire. It is usually not possible to make this type of impression with words alone. The salesperson finds it easier to show what the product can do and how it can fit the customer's needs. Strategic planning, of course, sets the stage for an effective demonstration that adds value to the sale (see Fig. 12.2 on page 285). Some of the most important ways to create value with the demonstration are discussed next.

demonstration A sales and marketing technique that adds sensory appeal to the product. It attracts the customer's attention, stimulates interest, and creates desire.

IMPROVED COMMUNICATION AND RETENTION

In Chapter 3 we noted the limitation of the verbal presentation: words provide only part of the meaning attached to messages that flow between the salesperson and the prospect. When we try to explain something with words alone, we may fail to reach people as we intend. People frequently do not

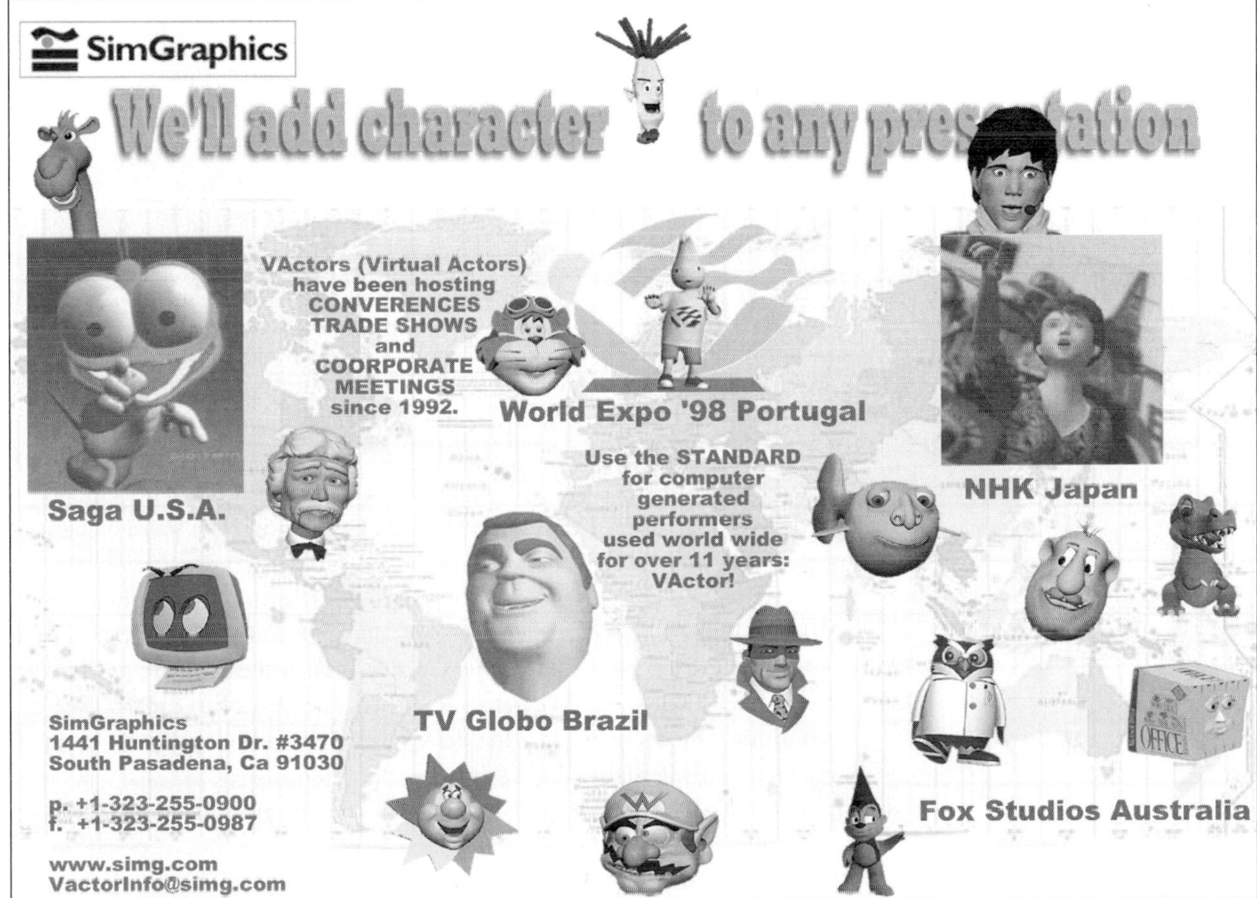

The sales force at SimGraphics must develop a well-planned, value-added demonstration to explain their virtual-reality–based visual simulation systems. Customers with complex simulation training needs, such as a medical school, need custom-fitted demonstrations.

Figure 12.1 Conducting the sales demonstration.

The Six-Step Presentation Plan	
Step One: APPROACH	✓ Review Strategic/Consultative Selling Model ✓ Initiate customer contact
Step Two: PRESENTATION	✓ Determine prospect needs ✓ Select solution ✓ Initiate sales presentation
Step Three: DEMONSTRATION	○ Decide what to demonstrate ○ Select selling tools ○ Initiate demonstration
Step Four: NEGOTIATION	○ Anticipate buyer concerns ○ Plan negotiating methods ○ Initiate win-win negotiations
Step Five: CLOSE	○ Plan appropriate closing methods ○ Recognize closing clues ○ Initiate closing methods
Step Six: SERVICING THE SALE	○ Follow-through ○ Follow-up calls ○ Expansion selling
Service, retail, wholesale, and manufacturer selling.	

understand our verbal-only messages. Why is communication via the spoken word alone so difficult? One major reason is that people are visually oriented from birth. We grow up surrounded by the influence of movies, television, commercial advertising, road signs, and all kinds of visual stimulation. People are accustomed to learning new things through the sense of sight or through a combination of seeing and hearing.

Many sales representatives recognize the limitations of the spoken word. When talking to prospects about the economic benefits of delivering training programs with a satellite system, a salesperson used a table to illustrate savings (see Table 12.1). With the aid of this table, prospects can visualize the economic benefits of the satellite delivery system compared with a competing system using high-bandwidth terrestrial lines.

When we rely on verbal messages alone to communicate, we must recognize that retention of information by listeners will be minimal. Several studies provide evidence to support this important point. Research has also found that retention increases from 14 to 38 percent when the spoken word is accompanied by effective visuals. In addition, the time needed to present a concept can be reduced by up to 40 percent with the use of appropriate visuals.[3]

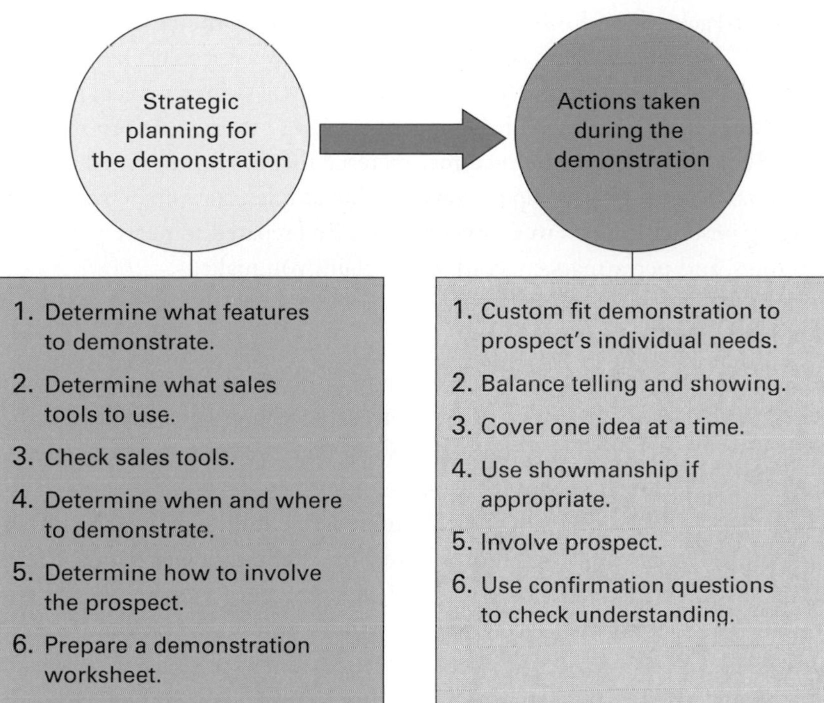

Figure 12.2 Poorly conducted demonstrations usually result from a lack of strategic planning and preparation.

PROOF OF BUYER BENEFITS

A well-planned and well-executed sales demonstration is one of the most convincing forms of proof. This is especially true if your product has dramatic points of superiority. Salespeople representing Epson, Canon,

Table 12.1

Sample table to illustrate potential savings to a prospect

How Much Can a Satellite System Save You?

Type of System	Per-Person Cost—20 Sites	Per-Person Cost—30 Sites	Per-Person Cost—40 Sites	Per-Person Cost—50 Sites
Satellite delivery system	*$10.70*	*$9.90*	*$9.00*	*$8.20*
High-bandwidth terrestrial lines	*$9.70*	*$10.10*	*$10.50*	*$11.00*

These cost estimates are based on current satellite broadcast rates and rates for use of terrestrial lines. The per person cost is based on an audience size of 25 trainees at each site.

Hewlett-Packard, and other manufacturers can offer the customer a wide range of printers. What is the real difference between a $200 basic printer and a $1000 laser printer? The laser equipment will print a neater and more attractive letter or report. The most effective way to provide proof of this buyer benefit is to show the customer material that has been printed on both printers. By letting the prospect compare the samples, the salesperson is converting product features to a buyer benefit. Be prepared to prove with tests, findings, and performance records every claim you make.

PROOF DEVICES

proof device A device such as a statement, report, testimonial, customer data, or photograph that is used to enhance the salesperson's credibility during a sales presentation.

We have noted that, when trust is present, customers are more open to the sales presentation. One way to build trust is to use a **proof device** that enhances your credibility. Proof devices can take the form of a statement, a report, a testimonial, customer data, or a photograph. A salesperson selling conference services for a large hotel/conference centre might use the following proof statement: "We were selected by *Training* magazine as one of Canada's top ten conference centres." Later the salesperson shows the customer photographs of the conference facilities and guest rooms. Then the customer is given a copy of a testimonial letter from a satisfied customer. The statement, photos, and letter help build the customer's confidence in the product. Later in this chapter we will examine proof devices in more detail.

FEELING OF OWNERSHIP

Many effective sales demonstrations give the prospect a temporary feeling of ownership. This pleasant feeling builds desire to own the product. Let us consider the person who enters a men's clothing store and tries on a Hart Shaffner and Marx suit. During the few moments the customer is wearing the suit, a feeling of pride is apt to develop. If the suit fits well and looks good, desire to own it probably builds.

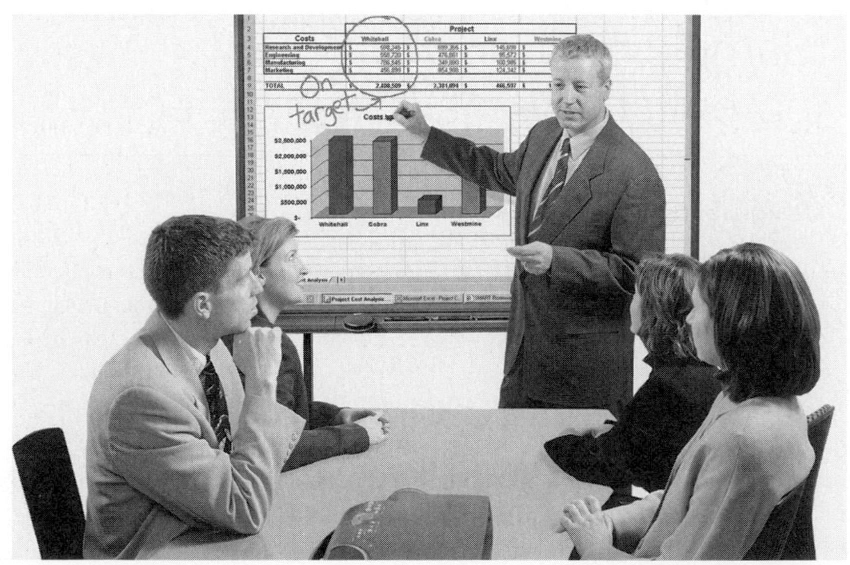

When salespeople use effective visual proof devices in their presentations, research indicates that retention increases from 14 to 38 percent and the time needed to present a concept is reduced by up to 40 percent.

Many firms offer prospects an opportunity to enjoy products on a trial basis. This is done to give people a chance to assess the merits of the product in their own home or business. Some firms that sell office equipment and office furniture use this sales strategy.

QUANTIFYING THE SOLUTION

In Chapter 6, we explained the process of determining whether a sales proposal adds value is called *quantifying the solution.* If the cost of the proposal is offset by added value, closing the sale will be much easier. In business-to-business selling, quantifying the solution is very common. Let's assume you represent a manufacturing company that sells robots—a reprogrammable machine capable of performing a variety of tasks. The two primary benefits are (1) payroll cost savings and (2) vastly improved quality. One way to quantify the solution in this case is to use simple **cost–benefit analysis.** This involves listing the costs to the buyer and the savings to be achieved from the purchase of the robots.

cost–benefit analysis An analysis of the costs versus the benefits to the customer as a result of making a particular purchase.

Another way to quantify the solution is to calculate the net profits or savings, or **return on investment (ROI)**, expressed as a percentage of the original investment. Using the following formula, you can determine the return on a given investment:

return on investment (ROI) The net profits or savings that the customer will see from investing in a particular purchase.

$$\text{ROI} = \text{Net Profits (or Savings)} \div \text{Investment} \times 100$$

If the robotic system costs \$16 000 but saves the firm \$4000, the ROI is 25 percent (\$4000 ÷ \$16 000 · 100 = 25%). Some companies set a minimum ROI for new products or cost-saving programs. Salespeople typically acquire this information at the need assessment stage, then include it in the written proposal.

Space does not permit a review of the many methods of quantifying the solution. Some of the additional ways include payback period, opportunity cost, net present value, after-tax cash flow, turnover, and contribution margin.

THE VALUE PROPOSITION REVISITED

Most customers are searching for the product that offers the best value. Salespeople are in a strong position to close a sale if they position their product with a value proposition (introduced in Chapter 7). The value proposition includes the mix of key benefits on which the product is positioned. Very often the sales demonstration is the vehicle used to present several, if not all, of the major benefits. Harry Rosen has been positioned as Canada's clothing expert and his namesake store as a retailer of the finest quality men's clothing. He sells more than 50 famous brands. Customers who wish can make an appointment with a Harry Rosen sales associate who is trained to assist with wardrobe selection. Harry Rosen associates work hard to provide excellent customer service. All of the major benefits offered to Harry Rosen customers can be highlighted during in-store demonstrations made by sales associates.

www.harryrosen.com

The value proposition includes a mix of key benefits to meet the needs of the customer. This ad illustrates the three parts of Durkee's value proposition: support, flavour, and performance.

Planning Demonstrations That Add Value

A sales demonstration that adds value is the result of both planning and practice. Planning gives the salesperson a chance to review all the important details that should be considered in advance of the actual demonstration. Practice (or rehearsal) provides an opportunity for a trial run to uncover areas that need additional polish. Experts agree that salespeople should spend as much as one hour of preparation time for every minute of presentation time.[4] During the planning stage it helps to review a series of guidelines that have helped salespeople over the years to develop effective demonstrations.

DEVELOP CREATIVE DEMONSTRATIONS

Presenting product features and buyer benefits in an interesting and appealing way requires some amount of creativity. One study indicated that 90 percent of the salespeople who were surveyed agreed that creativity is critical in selling.[5] Creativity is needed to develop a sales demonstration that can gain attention, increase desire, and add value. The ability to come up with problem-solving answers or different ways of looking at situations is greatly valued in today's fast-changing business environment. Some of the creative skills we need to cultivate include capacity for divergent thinking, ability to break problem-solving habits (i.e., mental sets), persistence in problem solving, and willingness to take risks.[6] One way to develop a more creative approach to sales demonstrations is to ask "What if...?" questions, and then to record your answers. This exercise is best done when you feel relaxed and rested. Relaxation enhances the creative process.[7]

USE CUSTOM-FITTED DEMONSTRATIONS

In nonmanipulative selling, each presentation is custom tailored because each client problem and priority is unique. In other words, every aspect of the sales presentation, including the demonstration, should relate to the needs or problems mutually identified by the prospect and the salesperson.

It is possible to develop a sales demonstration so structured and so mechanical that the prospect feels like a number. We must try to avoid what some veteran marketing people refer to as the depersonalization of the selling–buying process. If the demonstration is overly structured, it cannot be personalized to meet specific customer wants and needs.

Bell Helicopter manufactures helicopters in Canada and the United States. It sells a product with countless custom options, and each option changes its price and performance. One customer may want a helicopter for emergency medical care and another may want one for electronic news gathering. Bell's 18-member sales force, all of whom are licensed helicopter pilots, can introduce the Bell product line with a video presentation and then follow up with a demonstration flight if requested. Sales representatives also have access to a sales configuration system that supports the customization process. Price and performance data can be quickly determined for each accessory needed by the customer. The software automatically provides answers to the numerous questions that can surface during the sales presentation.[8]

Bell's 18-member sales force, all of whom are licensed helicopter pilots, can introduce the Bell product line with a video presentation and then follow up with a demonstration flight if requested.

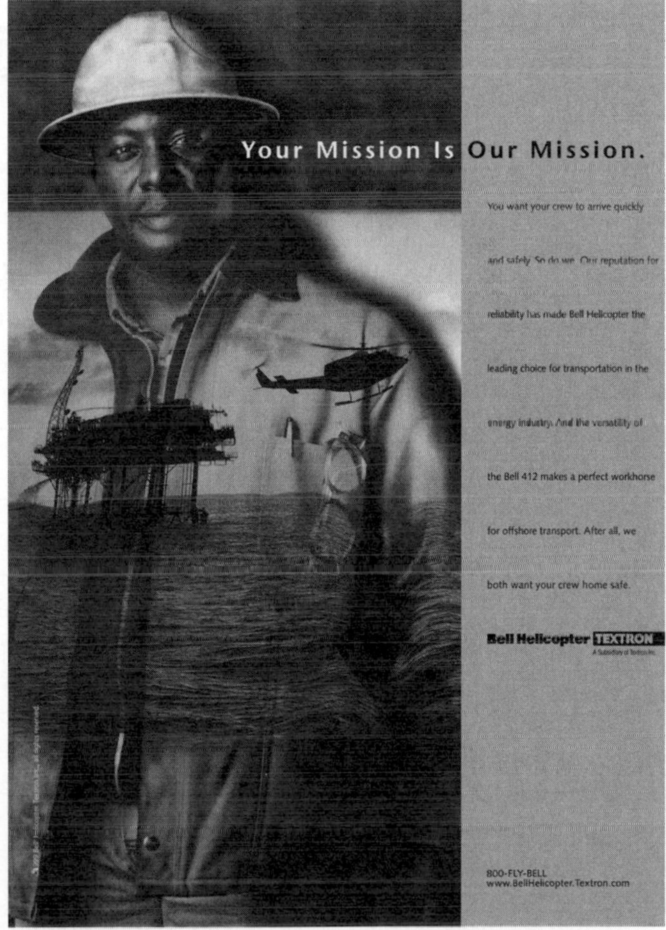

Your Mission Is Our Mission.
You want your crew to arrive quickly and safely. So do we. Our reputation for reliability has made Bell Helicopter the leading choice for transportation in the energy industry. And the versatility of the Bell 412 makes a perfect workhorse for offshore transport. After all, we both want your crew home safe.
Bell Helicopter TEXTRON
800-FLY-BELL
www.BellHelicopter.Textron.com

EVERYONE SELLS

Two Great Gals

Susan Abramson and Rachel McGarry are two great gals. They first met while improving their interior decorating skills at Seneca College, and soon became friends. Susan and Rachel were quick to recognize they had other complementary skills and, in 2002, they decided to offer decorating and organizing advice for homeowners.

Customers who contract with 2 Great Gals (**www.2greatgals.com**) can expect a visit from both gals. Susan, the gal with the business skills, says, "We spend the first half of the consultation doing a 'walk through' of the house and asking lots of questions. We need to know who lives there, what they value, and how they use their home. Do they have children? pets? Do they entertain a lot? How is the home situated for natural sunlight? It's a very consultative process."

Rachel, the gal with the artistic skills, says, "Once we have enough information, we can begin to explore ideas with the homeowners. Before we leave, I prepare a customized attractive binder with drawings and visuals to help them implement the decorating and organizing ideas we discussed."[a]

CHOOSE THE RIGHT SETTING

The location of the sales demonstration can make a difference. Some companies routinely rent space at a hotel, motel, or conference centre so that the demonstration can be conducted in a controlled environment free of noise and other interruptions.

CHECK SALES TOOLS

Be sure to check every item to be used in conjunction with the sales demonstration. If you are using audiovisual equipment, be certain that it is in good working condition. Always carry an extension cord and a spare bulb. If you are making a laptop presentation, be sure you can go online in front of the customer. If you plan to demonstrate a Web site, save it on a hard disk instead of going online. Be prepared for technological snags by having multiple backups. Always carry extra batteries for your laptop.[9]

COVER ONE IDEA AT A TIME

Pace the demonstration so that the customer does not become confused. Offer one idea at a time, and be sure the customer understands each point before moving on. This practice is especially important if the primary purpose of your sales presentation is to inform. If you neglect this practice, there is the danger that the customer's concentration will remain fixed on a previous point. Some demonstrations are ruined by a salesperson who moves too rapidly from one point to another. Consider using a confirmation question to get agreement on each key point before moving on to the next.

One objective of the sales demonstration is to increase the customer's desire for a solution to their problem. Therefore, a need-satisfaction question can help move the sale forward (see Chapter 11). During the demonstration of an animation publishing platform, the salesperson might say, "This program can help you produce a complex animation in a very short period of time. Do you often work on projects with tight deadlines?"

APPEAL TO ALL SENSES

In conducting a sales demonstration, it is a good idea to appeal to all appropriate senses. Each of the five senses—sight, hearing, smell, touch, and taste—represents an avenue by which the salesperson can attract the prospect's attention and build desire. Although sight is considered the most powerful attention-attracting sense, it may not be the most important motivating force in every selling situation. When presenting a food product, the taste and aroma may be critical. Designers and decorators tell us that most furniture buyers still want to touch and feel the product before they buy.

Christa-Lee McWatters understands the importance of reaching the prospect through as many senses as possible. She sells 28 different wines bottled by Sumac Ridge Estate Winery Ltd. in Summerland, British Columbia, to beer and wine stores, restaurants, and even to individuals and companies.[10] The sales presentation for a quality wine usually highlights four areas:

www.sumacridge.com

- *Consumer demand.* The wine's sales potential is described in realistic terms.
- *Marketing strategies.* Suggested ways to merchandise the wine are discussed.
- *Bouquet.* The distinctive fragrance of the wine is introduced.
- *Taste.* A sample of the wine is given to the prospect in a good-quality wineglass.

Note that a sales presentation featuring these appeals will reach the prospect through four of the five senses. Collectively, these appeals develop a strong motivating force. When you involve more than one sense, the sales presentation is more informative and persuasive.

Comprehension and retention can be enhanced with visual images.

BALANCE TELLING, SHOWING, AND INVOLVEMENT

Some of the most effective sales demonstrations combine telling, showing, and involvement of the prospect. To plan an effective demonstration, consider developing a demonstration worksheet like the sample in Figure 12.3, page 293. In the first column, list the major features you plan to demonstrate in proper sequence. In the second column, describe the proof devices you will use. In the third column, describe what you will say about the feature, converting the feature to a customer benefit. In the fourth column, describe what you (or the customer) will do at the time this benefit is discussed.

Prospects can be involved in many demonstrations. Two retail examples follow:

Furniture: To prove comfort or quality, have the buyer sit in a chair, lie on a mattress, or feel the highly polished finish of a coffee table.

Clothing: Have the customer try on garments to highlight style, fit, and comfort. This involvement is especially important in the sale of high-quality garments.

SELLING IN ACTION

Tracking Down a Sale

CareTrak is a product designed to locate patients suffering from the effects of brain injuries or Alzheimer's disease who have wandered away from a care centre and become lost. During a sales call at one nursing home, a sales representative was explaining the benefits of Care Trak when a doubting staff member picked up the transmitter and asked the salesperson to wait 20 minutes, then try to find him. After a 20-minute wait, the salesperson began the search under the watchful eyes of the nursing home administrator and members of the nursing staff. After tracking the transmitter on the staff member to a specific location, the locator signal became very strong in spite of the fact that everyone was standing in the middle of an otherwise empty hallway. At that point, other staff members began having doubts about the value of the equipment. Then the salesperson pointed the directional antenna straight up to the ceiling. He pushed aside a ceiling tile to reveal the nursing home employee in his hiding place. The nursing home placed an order for the product that day.[b]

If it is not possible for the prospect to participate in the demonstration or handle the product, then place sales literature, pictures, or brochures in the person's hands. After the sales call these items will remind the prospect of not only who called, but why.

REHEARSE THE DEMONSTRATION

While you are actually putting on the demonstration, you will need to be concentrating on a variety of things. The movements you make and the multitude of things you do should be so familiar to you that each response is nearly automatic. To achieve this level of skill, you will need to rehearse the demonstration.

"GET READY, I THINK THEY'RE STARTING TO DRIFT."

Rehearse both what you are going to say and what you are going to do. Merrie Spaeth, consultant and author of *Marketplace Communication*, says, "If you don't rehearse, the best-conceived idea can go wrong."[11] Say the words aloud exactly as if the prospect were present. It is surprising how often a concept that seems quite clear as you think it over becomes hopelessly mixed up when you try to discuss it with a customer. Rehearsal is the best way to avoid this embarrassing situation. Whenever possible, have your presentation and demonstration videotaped before you give it; this is perhaps the best way to catch trouble spots, so that you can perfect what you will say and do.

PLAN FOR THE DYNAMIC NATURE OF SELLING

The sales presentation is a dynamic activity. From the moment the salesperson and the customer meet, the sales presentation is being altered and fine-tuned to reflect the new information available. The salesperson must be able to execute strategy instantaneously. In the movie *Top Gun*, Kelly McGillis asks Tom Cruise, "What were you thinking up there?" His reply was, "You

Demonstration Worksheet			
Feature to Be Demonstrated	**Proof Device to Be Used**	**What I Will Say (Include Benefit)**	**What I or the Customer Will Do**
Special computer circuit board to accelerate drawing graphics on a colour monitor screen.	Monitor and software	"This monitor is large enough to display multiple windows. You can easily compare several graphics."	Have the customer bring up several windows using the computer keyboard.
Meeting room setup at a hotel and conference centre.	Floor plan	"This setup will provide a metre of elbow space for each participant. For long meetings, the added space provides more comfort."	Give the customer a tour of the room and invite her to sit in a chair at one of the conference tables.

Figure 12.3 The demonstration worksheet enables the salesperson to plan strategically and then rehearse demonstrations that strengthen the presentation.

don't have time to think. You take time to think up there, you're dead." By that he meant that the response must be habitual and reflexive.[12]

During a typical presentation, the salesperson asks numerous questions, discusses several product features, and demonstrates the appropriate product benefits. The customer also is asking questions and, in many cases, voicing concerns. The successful sales presentation is a good model of two-way communication. Because of the dynamic nature of the sales presentation, the salesperson must be prepared to apply several different selling skills to meet the variety of buyer responses. Figure 12.4 on page 294 illustrates how the various selling skills can be applied during all parts of the sales presentation. In creating effective presentations, the salesperson should be prepared to meet a wide range of buyer responses with effective questions, benefit statements, demonstrations, negotiating methods, and closing methods.

Proof Devices for Effective Demonstrations

Nearly every sales organization provides its staff with sales tools or proof devices of one kind or another. Many of these, when used correctly, augment the sales effort. If the company does not provide these items, the creative salesperson secures or develops sales tools independently. In addition to technology-based presentations, sales personnel can use a wide range of other selling aids. Creative salespeople are continually developing new types of sales tools. The following section summarizes some of the most common tools used today.

Product and Plant Tours

Without a doubt the best selling aid is usually the product itself. As noted previously, Bell Helicopter uses an effective video to describe various prod-

Consultative Selling Skills	Parts of the Sales Presentation			
	Need Discovery	**Selecting Solution**	**Need-Satisfaction Presentation**	**Servicing the Sale**
Questioning Skills	As a question approach To find needs and buying motives To probe for buying motives To confirm needs and buying motives	To confirm selection	To confirm benefits To confirm mutual understanding To increase desire for a solution	To make suggestions To confirm delivery and installation To resolve complaints To build goodwill To secure credit arrangements
Presenting Benefits	As a benefit approach To discover specific benefits	To match buying motives	To build support for the solution	To make suggestions To use credit as a close
Demonstrating Skills	As a product approach To clarify need	To clarify selection	To strengthen product claims	When making effective suggestions
Negotiating Skills	To overcome initial resistance to sales interviews To overcome buyer's need concerns	To overcome buyer's product concerns	To overcome buyer's source, price, and time concerns	In handling complaints To overcome buyer's financing concerns
Closing Skills	When customer has made buying decision	When buyer immediately recognizes solutions	Whenever buyer presents closing signals	After suggestion To secure repeats and referrals

Figure 12.4 The Selling Dynamics Matrix. A sales demonstration that creates value increases the dynamic nature of personal selling

ucts. However, some customers want to see the real thing. When Airbus executives were trying to get business from British Airways, they flew an A320 into London's Heathrow Airport and parked it directly in front of a Boeing 737. They then asked British Airways executives to make a direct comparison. Airbus president Henri Courpron says, "It was a gimmick. But it built a positive image and momentum. And we did end up getting the order, our first from British Airways."[13]

Doug Adams was the first salesperson hired by a major manufacturer of high-quality optical equipment. Although he was not a technician or an engineer, he quickly realized that the equipment had product superiority that physicians would recognize if they saw it demonstrated. During the first year, he sold 28 machines, far surpassing the expectations of his employer.[14]

As noted in a previous chapter, plant tours provide an excellent source of product information. EMP (Engineered Machine Products) makes high-efficiency thermal management systems for cooling engines. Products are made at its state-of-the art manufacturing facility, and the company has learned that the key to closing many large, complex sales is a tour of this innovative facility.

Models

Sometimes it is not practical to demonstrate the product itself because it is too big or immobile. In such cases it is easier to demonstrate a small-scale model or cross-section of the original equipment. A working model, like the actual product, can give the prospect a clear picture of how a piece of equipment operates.

With the aid of modern technology it is possible to create a model in picture form. ClosetMaid, a manufacturer of ventilated wire for commercial closets and other storage products, uses desktop visualization software to create a three-dimensional presentation that allows customers to see exactly what the finished facility will look like. Sales representatives can print out a hard copy so the customer has a picture of the custom-designed model for future reference. With the aid of this visualization technology, ClosetMaid salespeople can modify closet layouts on screen and produce a detailed bill of materials for each project.[15]

Photos, Illustrations, and Brochures

The old proverb "One picture is worth a thousand words" can be put into practical application by a creative salesperson. A great deal of information can be given to the prospect with the aid of photos and illustrations. Amir Hooda of Anar Jewellers Inc. in Toronto takes Polaroid pictures and gives them to clients who have tried on jewellery but who are not ready to make a

The most effective demonstrations balance telling, showing, and customer involvement. The use of sales tools can help with the process.

purchase. Amir Hooda says, "I don't pressure them. I just take a photo and attach my card. People don't throw away photos and it almost always results in business."[16]

Many companies develop brochures that visually reinforce specific need or benefit areas. Brochures can be effective during the initial discussion of needs when the salesperson wants to provide a brief overview of possible solutions. Someone planning to remodel a living room might, for example, collect a number of brochures that show colour photos of several examples of designs, materials, and colours that they could consider.

Portfolio

portfolio A portable case or loose-leaf binder containing a wide variety of sales-supporting materials. It is used to add visual life to the sales message and to prove claims.

A **portfolio** is a portable case or loose-leaf binder containing a wide variety of sales-supporting materials. The portfolio is used to add visual life to the sales message and to prove claims. A person who sells advertising might develop a portfolio including the following items:

- Successful advertisements used in conjunction with previous campaigns
- Selected illustrations that can be incorporated into advertisements
- A selection of testimonial letters
- One or more case histories of specific clients who have used the media with success

The portfolio has been used as a sales aid by people who sell, for example, interior design services, insurance, real estate, securities, and convention services. It is a flexible sales aid that can be revised at any time to meet the needs of each customer.

Reprints

Leading magazines and journals sometimes feature articles that directly or indirectly support the salesperson's product. A reprint of the article can be a forceful selling aid. It is also an inexpensive selling tool. Pharmaceutical and medical sales representatives often use reprints from journals that report on research in the field of medicine. A few years ago, Closure Medical Corporation received approval to sell Dermabond, a surgical glue used to close cuts. This innovative product received national attention when the prestigious *Journal of the American Medical Association* concluded that gluing a wound could be just as effective as sewing it shut. Salespeople representing Dermabond used the article to help educate doctors on the product's merits and applications.[17] In many cases the prospect will be far more impressed with the good points of your product if a third party presents them than if you do. A reprint from a respected journal can be very persuasive.

Catalogues

A well-designed catalogue shows the range and comprehensiveness of your product line. It may include specifications needed for installation and current price information. If you plan to give customers a copy of your catalogue, review the important features, such as a comprehensive index or important appendix material.[18]

Graphs, Charts, and Test Results

Graphs and charts can be used to illustrate change of some variable such as payroll expense, fuel consumption, or return on investment. For example, a bar graph might be used to illustrate the increase in fuel costs over a 10-year period. While graphs are usually quite descriptive, the layperson may misunderstand them. It is best to interpret the graph for the prospect. Do not move too fast, because the full impact of the message may be lost.

Test results from a reliable agency can be convincing. This is especially true when the test results are published by a respected independent agency, such as J. D. Power and Associates.

Laptop Computers and Demonstration Software

A survey conducted by *Selling Power* magazine found that 87 percent of salespeople use laptops during their sales presentations.[19] Many salespeople will tell you that the laptop computer is the single most powerful sales tool they use. Many of the things needed during the demonstration can be stored in the computer. If the customer is interested in a specific product, pull up the appropriate brochure on your laptop screen. If the client wants a copy of printed material or video tape, you can either print the pages or send them via e-mail. If the customer raises a question regarding product availability, use your laptop to access the information. You can place an order and in some cases print an invoice with a laptop computer and portable printer.[20]

Thanks to modern computer technology, it's possible to conduct impressive multiple, simultaneous product demonstrations without leaving your office. Let's assume you are presenting a new employee disability insurance plan to members of the 3M Canada human resources staff. One key decision maker is based in London, Ontario, and the other is in the United States. With the aid of Pixion PictureTalk software or a similar product, you can use the Internet to conduct the demonstration for both persons in real time. Sales managers might use this same approach to train members of their sales team in remote offices.

www.pixion.com

Personal computers (PCs), with the support of online presentation technologies and presentation software, have played an important role in increasing sales force productivity. Salespeople have instant access to customer data, so they can easily customize the sales presentation. Many salespeople report that PC-based presentations, using graphics software, are very effective. Today's PC can produce striking visuals and attractive printed material that can be given to the customer for future reference.

Enhancing Demonstrations with PowerPoint

The PowerPoint software program from Microsoft has been available to salespeople for almost 20 years. PowerPoint is so common that many prospects will find the standard presentation graphics very familiar, even dull. When developing a PowerPoint presentation, use bold, simple and large fonts (such as Arial and Veranda) and put graphics on several slides. Limit the number of words to 15 or fewer per slide.[21] Salespeople who want their demonstration to look unique can create their own corporate template, animate their logo, or put video clips of their own company information into a PowerPoint presentation.[22]

Creating Electronic Spreadsheets

For many years, salespeople have been using electronic spreadsheets to prepare sales proposals. The electronic spreadsheet is an excellent tool to organize the numbers involved in preparing quotes, such as quantities, costs, and prices. The electronic spreadsheet allows the user to answer "What if..." questions about the effects of lowering costs or raising prices. Once the preparation work is finished, the electronic spreadsheet itself can be printed and used as the proposal or to accompany the proposal.[23] The spreadsheet data can also be converted to a chart or graph that can enhance the proposal. Figure 12.5 shows a graph that might be used to demonstrate a comparison of group rates to a customer who might be considering holding a conference.

Many computers sold today include an electronic spreadsheet program. The leading electronic spreadsheet, Excel, is part of Microsoft's Office suite of products. If you have access to Excel, or any other electronic spreadsheet software, you can explore the power of this tool for preparing proposals.

Web-Based Demonstrations

www.webex.com

Some salespeople create computerized demonstrations that are stored in a central library and accessed on demand. With a few clicks of a mouse, presenters can call up the information they wish to showcase using a Web browser. Salespeople can also use WebEx's Meeting Center to deliver interactive presentations to customers in various locations. Meeting Center presentations integrate data, voice and video with a standard Web browser. The salesperson can show PowerPoint presentations, present product features and conduct question-and-answer sessions in real time.[24] The WebEx Presentation Studio solution is available for added client convenience. Salespeople create the demonstration, record it, and then make it available to prospects. The prospect decides when and where to view the presentation.[25]

Figure 12.5 Comparing Hotel Rates. Graphs produced with Excel software can add value and be very persuasive in demonstrating key benefits of a sales presentation. This Excel graph also uses a PowerPoint background design to add more value.

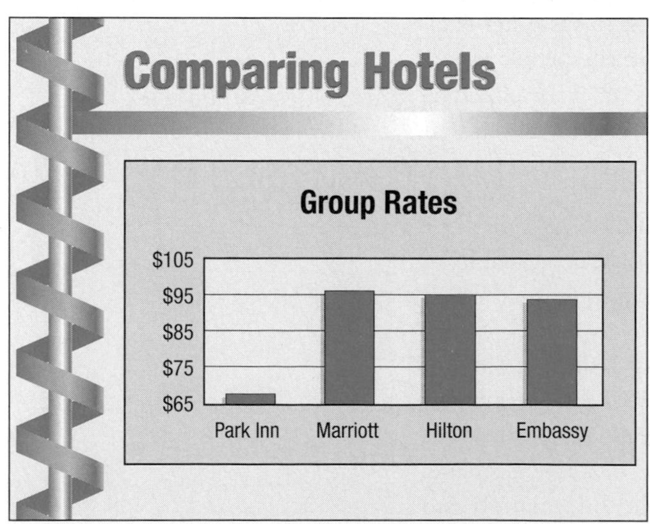

Bound Paper Presentations

While many salespeople are using some type of presentation technology in conjunction with the sales demonstration, paper is still widely used. For many sales and marketing organizations, bound paper presentations continue to be the most popular medium.[26] With the aid of computer-generated graphics, salespeople find it is easy to print attractive graphs, charts, and other proof information. Product guarantees and warranties are sometimes included in a bound paper presentation. Some marketers use guarantees and warranties to differentiate their products from competing products. Customer testimonials represent another common element of bound paper presentations. A testimonial letter from a prominent satisfied customer provides persuasive evidence that the product has support in the industry. Here, proof letters describing tangible benefits of the product can also enhance credibility. Prospects

SELLING MENTOR

Make Better Presentations

Presentations are important to your success in sales. Here are some tips for you:

1. *Tell them, tell them, tell them.* That is, tell them what you are going to tell them (the agenda), then tell them (the presentation), and then tell them what you told them (the summary). Back up whatever you tell them with evidence or proof.
2. *Be creative—use visual aids.* Most people remember what they see better than what they hear. But be careful: don't let the visual aids take the attention away from the message you wish to get across.
3. *Don't read.* Use notes, but do so sparingly. You need to be comfortable with your material. If you use visual aids, do not load them with too much information as this will encourage both you and the audience to read.
4. *Invite questions.* Don't ask if there are any questions. Ask, "Who has the first question?" If the question is hostile, paraphrase it for the group in a more neutral way. When responding, always respond to the entire audience, not directly to the questioner.

Group presentations require some special considerations:

1. *Prepare as a group.* Everyone needs to be familiar and comfortable with where they fit in the overall presentation. Meeting an hour before the presentation, or worse, having someone "parachute in" at the last minute without practising with the group, invites poor performance.
2. *Decide who's driving.* The work may be shared, but someone has to be clearly in charge to avoid confusion. One way to designate that person to the audience is to have that person introduce the agenda, the participants, and the roles they will play.
3. *Be aware of body language.* The positions, movements, and gestures of group members can be distracting and take attention from your message. All group members should be focused on the person who is presenting; that will encourage the audience to do so too.[c]

like bound paper presentations because the document is readily available for future reference.

AUDIOVISUAL PRESENTATION FUNDAMENTALS

Many companies provide their salespeople with such audiovisual aids as video tapes or computer-based presentations. Unfortunately, they sometimes fail to explain how to use these tools in the most effective way. Here are some suggestions on how to use audiovisual presentations to achieve maximum impact.

- Never rely too heavily on "bells and whistles" to sell your products. Audiovisual technology provides support for the major points in your presentation, but it does not replace an interactive sales demonstration.
- Be sure the prospect knows the purpose of the presentation. Preview the material and describe a few highlights. Always try to build interest in advance of the audiovisual presentation.
- Be prepared to stop the presentation to clarify a point or to allow the prospect to ask questions. Do not permit the audiovisual presentation to become a barrier to good two-way communication.
- At the conclusion of the audiovisual presentation, review key points and allow the prospect an opportunity to ask questions.

SUMMARY

In selling, the prospect is moving from a known quantity (i.e., the money in hand or an obligation for future payment) to something of an unknown quantity (i.e., amount of satisfaction to be gained from the potential purchase). With most people this process produces anxiety and insecurity. The professional salesperson reduces prospect anxiety and insecurity by supplying proof of product performance. The objective of the demonstration is to supply this proof. The demonstration can also help the customer better understand the solution to his or her problem.

People receive impressions through the five senses. In the presentation, the salesperson communicates verbally to the prospect primarily through the sense of sound. In the demonstration, the salesperson broadens the communication strategy to include as many of the other senses as possible. Generally, the more senses we appeal to, the more believable our sales appeal becomes.

This chapter includes a series of guidelines to be followed when planning a sales demonstration. Completion of a demonstration worksheet is an important first step in preparing an effective sales demonstration.

Nearly every marketing-driven organization provides its salespeople with a variety of sales tools to use in the demonstration. A partial list of these tools includes the product itself and plant tours, models, photos, illustrations, brochures, reprints, portfolios, graphs, charts, test results, testimonials, audiovisual presentations via laptop computers, demonstration software, catalogues, and bound paper presentations.

Key Terms

Cost–Benefit Analysis **287**

Demonstration **283**

Portfolio **296**

Proof Device **286**

Return on Investment (ROI) **287**

Review Questions

1. List the benefits of using a sales demonstration during the presentation of a product or service.
2. What effect does showing (i.e., appealing to the sense of sight) have on retention when combined with an oral presentation?
3. Discuss the advantages of using the demonstration worksheet.
4. Explain why a salesperson should organize the sales presentation so that it appeals to as many of the five senses as possible.
5. List the guidelines to follow in planning an effective demonstration.
6. Develop a list of the sales tools that the salesperson should consider when planning a sales demonstration.
7. Describe the merits of a bound paper presentation. What can be done to strengthen the persuasive power of a bound paper presentation?
8. Explain how magazines and trade journals can be used to assist the salesperson in a persuasive sales presentation.
9. Explain why audiovisual presentations are becoming more popular as a means of support for sales demonstrations.
10. What are some of the common sales functions performed by laptop computers and demonstration software?

Application Exercises

1. In many selling situations, it is difficult, if not impossible, to demonstrate the product itself. List means other than the product itself that can be used to demonstrate the product features and benefits.
2. Develop a list of sales tools you could use in a job interview. What tools could you use to demonstrate your skills and capabilities?
3. As noted in this chapter, demonstration software is becoming increasingly popular. Real estate products are customarily showcased on the Internet. Assume you have just taken a job in Calgary, Alberta. Access Homestore Canada at **www.realestate.ca** and select "Alberta." Then choose the type of house you would like and examine the properties that match your request. Select the home you personally like best from among the ones that were found by the search. Click on it and examine the information available.

ROLE-PLAY EXERCISE

Study the product selling strategy memo and proof devices found on pages 40–44 in Partnership Selling on the CD-ROM. In this role play, you will be selling to another student role-playing a human resource manager who is interested in controlling costs for a regional meeting of company employees. All 75 of the attendees will be staying at the hotel—50 of them will be driving to the hotel, whereas the other 25 will be flying. Prepare a comparative cost–benefit graph to show the total amount this meeting planner can expect to save by selecting your hotel. Use the proof devices you have prepared to demonstrate the cost savings to the meeting planner. Plan also to use the map on page 12 to demonstrate the ease of finding the hotel.

Case Problem

Simulation has proven to be a very cost effective training method. Commercial airline pilots can practise takeoff and landing procedures over and over again without endangering the lives of passengers. The Marine Institute in St. John's, Newfoundland and Labrador, boasts a state-of-the-art ship's bridge simulator where ship's officers can practise their skills under a variety of weather and ocean conditions. Medical students can practise basic surgery skills with the aid of a virtual reality system before working on real patients.

SimGraphics specializes in the development of virtual simulation systems. Steve Tice, president, and Steve Glenn, vice-president of new business development, are frequently involved in sales presentations. Prior to a sales call, they try to answer several questions:

- *What is the customer's area of expertise?* Someone with an engineering background will usually want to know how the system was developed and may ask specific technical questions. In contrast, the customer who works primarily in entertainment or the design of training programs will be more focused on the creative applications of a particular system.
- *What type of demonstration is best for this client?* SimGraphics has developed a system that animates virtual characters from the motion-captured performance of a human actor in real time—as the performance is taking place. One option is to videotape the human actor who is preparing the performance animation. The video can be shown in the client's office or conference room. The other option is to let the customer see the actual performance animation process. Moving the equipment from the SimGraphics laboratory to the client's office is possible. The sales staff must also decide which finished

products—developed for other clients—should be integrated into the demonstration.

- *What is the most effective way to quantify the solution?* Performance animation enjoys advantages in cost-effectiveness that traditional animation systems cannot match. The sales staff must determine the best way to illustrate cost-effectiveness. This will usually require obtaining certain information from the customer.
- *Will it be necessary to develop a prototype visual simulation prior to the sales demonstration?* In some cases, the needs of the customer are unique and no existing product is suitable for the demonstration. In this case, a prototype is required.

Questions

1. You have decided to prepare a value proposition for a customer who has indicated an interest in your product. What are some of the key benefits you would include in the proposition?
2. Assume that you are preparing a sales presentation for a customer who has spent several years as a movie director. Today, he is developing training programs for a *Fortune* 500 company. Describe how you would organize the sales demonstration for this client.
3. How might you quantify the solution if the customer is a small manufacturing company with a need for a safety training program?

CRM Case Study CUSTOM FITTING THE DEMONSTRATION

Your SimNet Systems sales manager, Becky Kemley, has asked you to meet with her to discuss demonstrations. She wants you to tell her if any of your accounts needs a demonstration and, if so, what type of demonstration.

Questions

1. Which two accounts need a demonstration of the speed and power capabilities of the recommended network?
2. Which account needs to be shown that the recommended network product configuration will meet the account's specifications?
3. Which account with many sites will need a demonstration of SimNet's ability to put together a complex solution?
4. Which account seeking a low price needs a testimonial of SimNet's value-added ability to help customers maximize the power of their network?
5. Which account needs a demonstration of SimNet's financial stability?

Partnership Selling

A ROLE PLAY/SIMULATION **(see Partnership Selling on the CD-ROM, p. 40)**

DEVELOPING A SALES PRESENTATION STRATEGY—THE DEMONSTRATION

Read *Sales Memorandum 3* ("A" or "B" depending on the category you were assigned in sales call 1). In this role play, your call objectives are to make a persuasive presentation, negotiate any customer concerns, and close and service the sale.

At this time you should complete item 1 of the presentation plan, and prepare and price a product solution. This will include completing the sales proposal form. Also, you should obtain a three-ring binder with pockets in the front and back for the development of a portfolio presentation. In this binder you should prepare your presentation and demonstration, following the instructions in items 2a, 2b, 2c, and 2d under the presentation plan. The presentation and demonstration materials should be placed in the three-ring binder as a part of your portfolio presentation. (Use the product strategy materials—i.e., photos, price lists, menus, awards—provided to you with *Employment Memorandum 1.*) You may want to select a person as your customer and rehearse the use of these materials.

CHAPTER 13

Negotiating Buyer Concerns

LEARNING OBJECTIVES

After studying this chapter, you should be able to

1. Describe negotiations as part of a win-win strategy
2. Describe common types of buyer concerns
3. Outline general strategies for negotiating buyer concerns
4. Discuss specific methods of negotiating buyer concerns
5. Describe ways to deal effectively with buyers who are trained in negotiating

The Banff Centre for Management (BCM) **www.banffcentre.ca/departments/leadership/** is a not-for-profit organization dedicated to training and developing executives, managers, and professionals. It is acclaimed as the best organization of its type in Canada, and one of the five best in North America. Operating for nearly 50 years, it has delivered programs to more than 250 000 participants from Canada and around the world.

Doug Macnamara, the general manager, has a ready response when prospective clients raise concerns about external training programs such as the ones offered by the BCM. He describes their ability to provide innovative, experiential, and unforgettable learning in exceptional facilities situated in one of the most attractive locations in the world. The BCM has developed a network of faculty who are experienced at the mid- to senior-executive level and who are superior learning facilitators. Of course, prospective clients do not communicate some forms of sales resistance to Doug. He must often work hard to identify the resistance, clarify it, then overcome it.[1]

Negotiating Buyer Concerns and Problems

Many sales professionals are very proficient in need discovery and selecting the right solution, but are weak in the area of negotiating an agreement that is favourable to the customer and the salesperson's firm. Some salespeople fail to anticipate buyer concerns and to plan negotiating methods (see Fig. 13.1). A

Figure 13.1 Negotiating customer concerns and problems.

The Six-Step Presentation Plan	
Step One: APPROACH	✓ Review Strategic/Consultative Selling Model ✓ Initiate customer contact
Step Two: PRESENTATION	✓ Determine prospect needs ✓ Select solution ✓ Initiate sales presentation
Step Three: DEMONSTRATION	✓ Decide what to demonstrate ✓ Select selling tools ✓ Initiate demonstration
Step Four: NEGOTIATION	● Anticipate buyer concerns ● Plan negotiating methods ● Initiate win-win negotiations
Step Five: CLOSE	● Plan appropriate closing methods ● Recognize closing clues ● Initiate closing methods
Step Six: SERVICING THE SALE	● Follow-through ● Follow-up calls ● Expansion selling
Service, retail, wholesale, and manufacturer selling.	

common mistake is making last-minute concessions in order to close the sale.[2] In this chapter, we describe effective strategies for anticipating and negotiating buyer concerns.

We have noted previously that the heaviest time investment in value-added selling is at the outset of the sale. This is especially true for large, complex sales that require a long sales cycle. Identifying the customer's needs and developing the best solution can be very time consuming. However, when you do these things effectively, you are creating value in the eyes of the customer. When you build value on the front end of the sale, price becomes less of an issue later in the sales process. [3]

NEGOTIATION—PART OF THE WIN-WIN RELATIONSHIP STRATEGY

Frank Acuff, negotiations trainer and author of *How to Negotiate Anything with Anyone, Anywhere Around the Globe*, says, "Life is a negotiation."[4] Negotiating skills have application almost daily in our personal and professional lives. Some of the traditional personal selling books discussed how salespeople should "handle" buyer objections. The message communicated to the reader was that personal selling is an "us versus them" process: somebody wins and somebody loses. The win-win solution, where both sides win, was not offered as an option.

The foundation for win-win negotiations is a relationship with the customer built on trust and rapport. Ron Willingham, author of two books on selling with integrity, says: "When trust and rapport are strong, negotiation becomes a partnership to work through customer concerns. But when trust and rapport are weak, almost any negotiation becomes too combative."[5] Trust and rapport must be established on the front end of the sale and maintained throughout the sales process. High-performance salespeople take time to discover the customer's needs and try to recommend the best possible solution. And always keep in mind that any agreement that leaves one party dissatisfied will come back to hurt you later, sometimes in ways that you cannot predict.[6]

negotiation Working to reach an agreement that is mutually satisfactory to buyer and seller.

What is **negotiation**? One definition is "working to reach an agreement that is mutually satisfactory to both buyer and seller." It involves resolving the problems or concerns that prevent people from buying.[7] As we noted in Chapter 1, the salesperson increasingly serves as a consultant or resource, and provides solutions to buyers' problems. The consultant seeks to establish and maintain long-term relationships with customers. The ability to negotiate problems or concerns is one of the most effective ways to create value for the customer. Figure 13.2 outlines the steps a salesperson can take to anticipate and negotiate problems.

NEGOTIATION IS A PROCESS

Negotiations can take place before the sales call or at any time during the sales presentation. Early negotiations may involve the meeting location, who will attend the sales presentation, or the amount of time available for the first

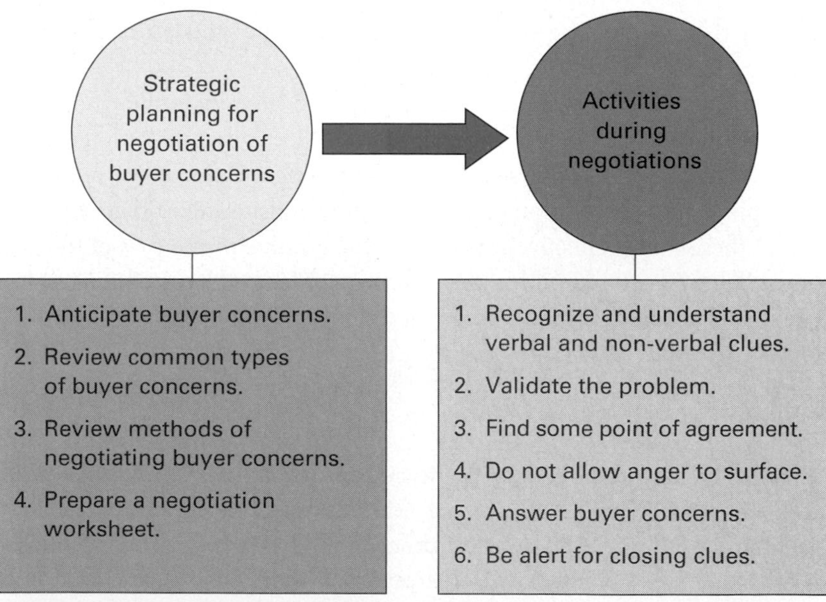

Figure 13.2 Salespeople today must be prepared to anticipate and negotiate buyer concerns and problems.

meeting. Salespeople sometimes make early concessions to improve the relationship. This approach, however, may set a costly precedent for later in the sale.[8] Some concessions can have a negative influence on the sales presentation. If, for example, you need 40 minutes for an effective product demonstration, do not agree to a 20-minute meeting.

In most cases you can anticipate that the most important negotiations will take place during stage three of the buying process (see Fig. 8.3). Resolution of problems can sometimes be time consuming. Establishing strong partnering relationships requires lengthy negotiations that may extend over weeks, months, or even years. As these relationships continue to develop and strengthen, negotiations will continue when concerns voiced by one party or the other surface.

Common Types of Buyer Concerns

Salespeople learn that patterns of buyer resistance exist, and they can therefore anticipate that certain concerns will arise during the sales call. With this information, it is possible to be better prepared for each meeting with a customer. The majority of buyer concerns fall into five categories: need, product, source, price, and time.

CONCERNS RELATED TO NEED FOR THE PRODUCT

If you have done your homework satisfactorily, then the prospect you call on probably has a need for your product or service. You can still expect, however, that the initial response may be, "I do not need your product." This might be a conditioned response that arises nearly every time the prospect meets with a sales representative. It may also mask the real reason for not buying, which might be lack of funds, lack of time to examine your proposal carefully, or some other reason. Sincere need resistance is one of the greatest challenges that face a salesperson. Think about it for a moment. Why would any customer want to purchase a product that does not seem to provide any real benefits? Unless we can create need awareness in the prospect's mind, there is no possible way to close the sale.

If you are calling on business prospects, the best way to overcome need resistance is to prove that your product is a good investment. Every privately owned business hopes to make a profit. Therefore you must demonstrate how your product or service will contribute to that goal. Will your product increase sales volume? Will it reduce operating expenses? If the owner of a hardware store says, "I already carry a line of high-quality tools," point out how a second line of less expensive tools will appeal to another large segment of the buying public. With the addition of the new line, the store will be in a better position

Negotiation is defined as "working to reach an agreement that is mutually satisfactory to both buyer and seller." It involves building relationships instead of making one-time deals.

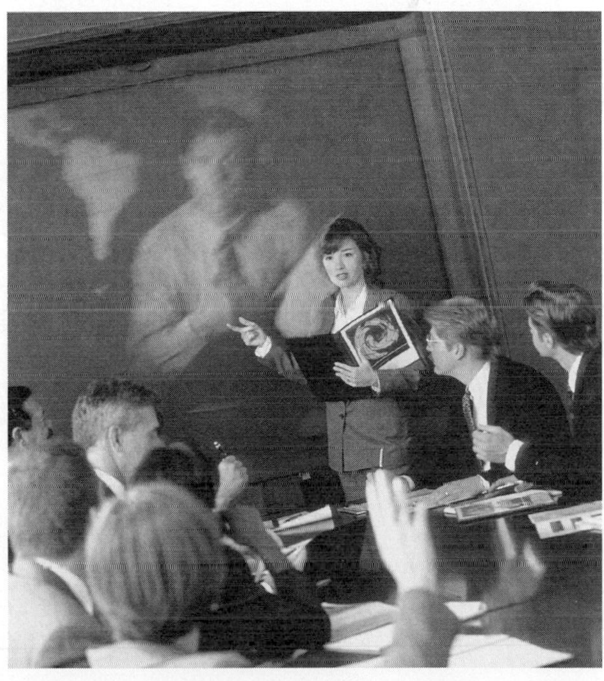

to compete with other stores (e.g., discount merchandise stores and supermarkets) that sell inexpensive tools.

In some selling situations you must help the prospect solve a problem before you have any chance of closing the sale. Suppose the prospect says, "I am already overstocked." If you call on wholesalers or retailers, expect to hear this concern quite frequently. Often the prospect is unwilling to buy additional merchandise until older stock is sold. If there is no demand for the older merchandise, then a real problem exists. In this situation your best bet is to offer the buyer one or more solutions to the problem. Some value-added tactics are:

1. *Suggest that the prospect hold a special sale to dispose of the unsold merchandise.* It may even be necessary to sell the stock at a loss to recover at least part of the original investment. Close-outs can be painful but may be the best option.
2. *Ask the prospect to accept a trial offer on a guaranteed sale or consignment basis.* This option will allow the customer to acquire new merchandise without an initial cash investment and will open the door for your product.
3. *If company policy permits, consider negotiating the purchase of the prospect's inventory.* Give the customer a credit against a minimum opening order.

In many cases, the key to negotiating need resistance is creative problem solving. Work closely with the prospect to overcome the barrier that prevents closing the sale.

The desire to buy low is quite common. However, faced with information overload, buying decisions become more difficult. When concerns surface, salespeople need to explain the benefits that add value and use skillful negotiations to gain acceptance of the selling price. If the selling price is too low, profit margins will suffer.

CONCERNS ABOUT THE PRODUCT

You will recall from Chapter 8 that consultative process buyers often lack needs awareness or need help evaluating possible solutions. Therefore, the product that offers a solution can become the focal point of buyer resistance. When this happens, try to discover specific reasons why the prospect has doubts about your product. Often you will find that one of the following factors has influenced the buyer's attitude:

1. *The product is not well established.* This is a common form of buyer resistance if you are selling a new or relatively new product. People do not like to take risks. They need plenty of assurance that the product is dependable. Use laboratory test results, third-party testimonials from satisfied users, or an effective demonstration to create value.
2. *The product will not be popular.* If the product is for resale, discuss sales results at other firms. Discuss the success other firms have had with your product. Also, discuss any efforts your company has taken to increase demand. For example, show the prospect sample advertisements that have appeared in the newspaper, or commercials that have appeared on television.
3. *Friends or acquaintances did not like the product.* It is not easy to handle this form of buyer resistance. After all, you cannot say, "Your friend is all wet—our product is the best on the market!" Move cautiously to acquire more information. Use questions to pinpoint the problem, and clarify any misinformation that the person may have concerning your product.
4. *The present product is satisfactory.* Change does not come easily to many people. Purchasing a new product may mean adopting new procedures or retraining employees. In the prospect's mind the advantages do not outweigh the disadvantages, so buyer resistance surfaces. To overcome this resistance, a salesperson must build a greater amount of desire in the prospect's mind. Concentrate on superior benefits that give your product a major advantage over the existing product or reconfigure the product to better meet the customer's needs.

CONCERNS RELATED TO SOURCE

Concerns related to source can be especially challenging when the prospect is a relationship buyer. The buyer may already have well-established partnerships with other companies. If the prospect feels genuine loyalty to his or her present supplier, you will have to work harder to establish a relationship and begin the need discovery process.

When dealing with the loyalty problem, it is usually best to avoid direct criticism of the competing firm. Negative comments are apt to backfire because they damage your professional image. It is best to keep the sales presentation focused on the customer's problems and your solutions.

There are positive ways to cope with buyer loyalty. Here are some suggestions:

1. *Work harder to identify problems your company can solve with its products or services.* With the help of good questions you may be able to understand the prospect's problems better than your competitors.
2. *Point out the superior benefits of your product or company.* By doing this, you hope the logic of your presentation will overcome the emotional ties that may exist between the prospect and the present supplier.
3. *Point out that the business may profit from the addition of a second line.* You do not expect the person to drop the present supplier, but you do want the person to try your product.
4. *Encourage the prospect to place a trial order and then evaluate the merits of your product.* Again, you are not asking the person to quit the present supplier.
5. *Work on recruiting internal champions to build more support for your message.* Use referrals whenever possible.[9]

Try to stay visible and connected. Every contact with the prospect is one more step in building a relationship. David Haslam, president of Toronto-based Presidential Plumbing Ltd., devotes time to a number of community projects. He says, "I believe in community involvement, but I'm also gaining invaluable experience, getting contacts."[10] One subtle way to regularly keep in touch with a large number of contacts is with a newsletter.

CONCERNS RELATED TO PRICE

There are two important points to keep in mind concerning price concerns. First, it is one of the most common forms of buyer resistance in the field of selling. Therefore you must learn to negotiate skillfully in this area. If you are selling a product or service to a transactional buyer, price may be the primary barrier to closing the sale. Second, it is one of the most common excuses. When people say, "Your price is too high," they probably mean, "You have not sold me yet." In the eyes of most customers value is more important than price. Always try to position your product with a convincing value proposition. Customers who perceive added value are less likely to choose a competing product simply on the basis of price.

WORKING WITH BUYERS WHO ARE TRAINED IN NEGOTIATION

www.pmac.ca

In recent years we have seen an increase in the number of training programs developed for professional buyers. For example, the Purchasing Management Association of Canada (PMAC) offers a two-day seminar designed to enhance

SELLING MENTOR

Apply Negotiation Skills in the Job Market

Chester L. Karrass, creator of the Effective Negotiating seminar, says, "In business, you don't get what you deserve; you get what you negotiate." This is good advice for the job seeker. Most employers will not propose the highest wage possible at the beginning of the offer. If you want a higher starting wage, you must ask for it. Employers often have a predetermined range for each position and the highest salary is reserved for the applicant who brings something extra to the job. To prepare for a productive negotiation, you must know your own needs and you must know something about the worth of the position. Many employers will tell you the salary range prior to the interview. The Internet can be a good source of salary information for certain types of job. In terms of your needs, try to determine what you care about the most: interesting work? future promotion? flexible work schedule? If you are willing to negotiate, you can increase your pay by hundreds or even thousands of dollars. Be prepared to sell yourself, negotiate the salary you feel is appropriate, and achieve a win-win solution in the process.[a]

the negotiating skills of purchasing people. Enrollees learn how to negotiate with salespeople. Some salespeople are also returning to the classroom to learn negotiation skills. SalesForce Training & Consulting Inc., of Carp, Ontario, offers a one-day seminar called "Win-Win Negotiating for Salespeople," which covers many of the negotiating techniques that salespeople need to know. The Canadian Professional Sales Association offers a popular seminar, "The Persuasive Communicator: Motivating People to Buy," which is designed to help salespeople negotiate buyer concerns.

www.salesforcetraining.com

www.cpsa.com

Professional buyers often learn to use specific tactics in dealing with salespeople. Homer Smith, author of *Selling through Negotiation*, provides these examples:

Budget Limitation Tactic.[11] The buyer may say, "We like your proposal, but our budget for the convention is only $8500." Is the buyer telling the truth, or is the person testing your price? The best approach in this instance is to take the budget limitation seriously and use appropriate negotiation strategies. One strategy is to reduce the price by eliminating some items. In the case of a truck fleet sale, the salesperson might say, "We can deliver the trucks without radios and, thus, meet your budget figure. Would you be willing to purchase trucks without radios?"

Take-It-or-Leave-It Tactic.[12] How do you respond to a buyer who says, "My final offer is $3300, take it or leave it"? A price concession is, of course, one option. However, this is likely to reduce profits for the company and lower your commission. An alternative strategy is to confidently review the superior benefits of your product and make another closing attempt. Appealing to the other person's sense of fairness also may move the discussion forward. If the final offer is totally without merit, consider calling a halt to the negotiation to allow the other party to back down from his or her position without losing face.[13]

Let-Us-Split-the-Difference Tactic.[14] In some cases, the salesperson may find this price concession acceptable. If the buyer's suggestion is not acceptable, then the salesperson might make a counteroffer.

These tactics represent only a sample of those used by professional buyers. To prepare for these and other tactics, salespeople need to plan their negotiating strategies in advance and have clear goals. Decide in advance on the terms you can and cannot accept. It is important that you have the authority to set prices. Buyers want to do business with someone who has decision-making authority. Daniel Skarlicki, a specialist in organizational behaviour at the University of British Columbia, says, "Simply put, negotiations are won or lost in the planning and preparation, not at the negotiating table. Don't wing it."[15]

NEGOTIATING PRICE WITH A LOW-PRICE STRATEGY

As noted in Chapter 7, some marketers have positioned their products with a price strategy. The goal is to earn a small profit margin on a large sales volume. Many of these companies have empowered their salespeople to use various low-price strategies such as quantity discounts, trade discounts, seasonal discounts, and promotional discounts. Some salespeople are given permission to match the price of any competitor. Transactional buyers will always give price a high priority during negotiations.

HOW TO DEAL WITH PRICE CONCERNS

As we have noted, price concerns are common, so salespeople must prepare for them. There are some important "dos and don'ts" to keep in mind when the price concern surfaces.

Do Clarify Price Concerns with Questions

When you are confronted with a price objection, determine what the customer is really saying. You will recall from Chapter 11 that probing questions encourage the customer to give you more details. The following probing questions might be used when price concerns surface: "When you say we are higher, could you be more specific, please?" or "What did you anticipate the price to be?" When the customer says budget is the primary reason for delaying the purchase, you might ask, "If you had the budget, would you buy?" Questions can help you determine what the customer is really thinking.[16]

Do Add Value with a Cluster of Satisfactions

As noted in Chapter 7, customers are increasingly seeking a cluster of satisfactions that includes a good product, a company that stands behind its products and a salesperson who is truly a partner (see Fig. 7.1). Many business firms are at a competitive disadvantage when price alone is considered. When you look beyond price, however, it may become obvious that your company offers more value for the dollar.

Stephen Smith, senior account manager for Bell Atlantic, says that price is like the tip of the iceberg—it is often the only feature the customer sees.

Salespeople need to direct the customer's attention to the value-added features that make up the bulk of the iceberg that is below the surface (see Fig. 13.3).[17] Do not forget to sell yourself as a high-value element of the sales proposal. Emphasize your commitment to customer service after the sale.

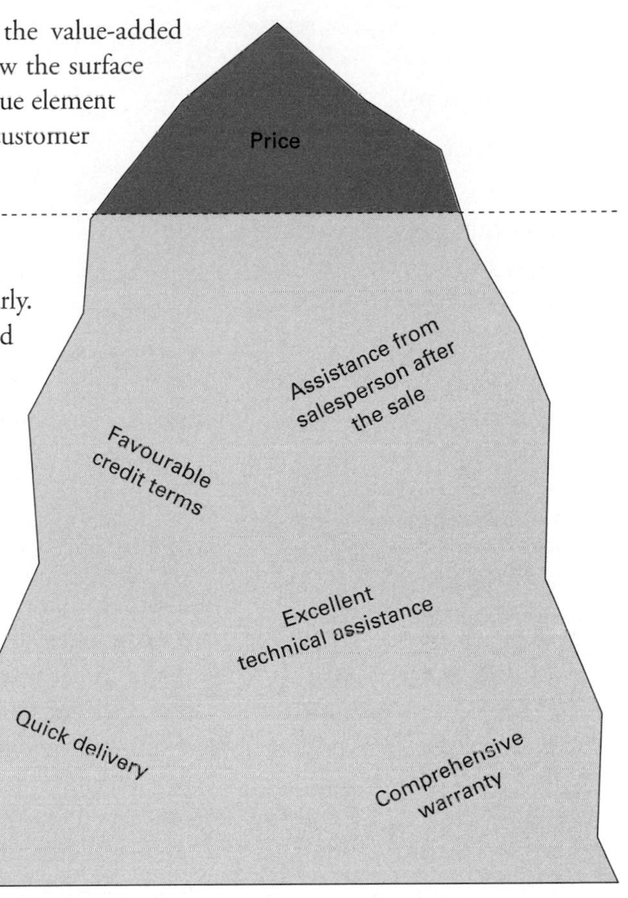

Figure 13.3 A sales proposal is sometimes like an iceberg. The customer sees the tip of the iceberg the price—but does not see the value-added features below the surface.

Do Not Make Price the Focal Point of Your Sales Presentation

You may need to discuss price, but do not bring it up too early. The best time to deal with price is after you have reviewed product features and discussed buyer benefits. You increase the chances for a win-win outcome by increasing the number of issues you can resolve. If you negotiate price along with delivery date, support services, or volume purchases, you increase the opportunities for a trade-off so you and the customer both win something of value.[18]

Do Not Apologize for the Price

When you do mention price, do so in a confident and straightforward manner. Do not have even a hint of apology in your voice. Convey to the prospect that you believe your price is fair and make every effort to relate price to value. Many people fear paying too much for a product or service. If your company has adopted a value-added strategy, point this fact out to the prospect. Then discuss how you and your company add value.

Do Point Out the Relationship between Price and Quality

In our highly competitive, free-enterprise economy, there are forces at work that tend to promote fair pricing. The highest quality can never be obtained at the lowest price. Quality comes from the Latin word *qualitas*, meaning "what is the worth." When you sell quality, price will more likely be secondary in the prospect's mind. Always point out the value-added features that create the difference in price. Keep in mind that cheap products are built down to a price rather than up to a standard.[19]

Do Explain the Difference between Price and Cost

Price represents the initial amount the buyer pays for the product; *cost* represents the amount the buyer pays for a product as it is used over a period of time. The price–cost comparison is particularly relevant if your product or service lasts longer, is more reliable, or provides greater operating efficiencies when compared to competitors' products or services. Today, airlines are comparing the price and cost of small regional jets manufactured by Canada's Bombardier and Brazil's Embraer with large jets sold by Boeing and Airbus. Figure 13.4 on page 314 compares Bombardier's CRJ200 with the A320 offered by Airbus. Sales representatives at Bombardier point out the fast speed (859 kilometres per hour) and low fuel consumption of the CRJ200.[20]

	CRJ200	A320
Passengers (seats)	50	150
Cost of aircraft	$21.0 million	$48.2 million
SHORT TRIP (925 km)		
Cost per seat per km	3.34¢	2.85¢
Total cost of trip	$961	$2460
LONG TRIP (1850 km)		
Cost per seat per km	2.79¢	2.16¢
Total cost of trip	$1604	$3722

Figure 13.4 The Winner in the Short Run. Airlines are comparing the price and cost of small regional jets with large jets sold by Boeing and Airbus. The cavernous Airbus leads on seat cost per kilometre, but the much lower price per trip of the CRJ200 makes it a winner in the minds of some buyers. Adapted from *Fortune*, 9/4/00 © 2000 Time Inc. All rights reserved.

Do Not Make Concessions Too Quickly

Give away concessions methodically and reluctantly, and always try to get something in return. A concession given too freely can diminish the value of your product. Also, giving a concession too easily may send the signal you are negotiating from a position of weakness. Neil Rackham, author of several books on SPIN selling, says, "Negotiate late, negotiate little, and never let negotiation become a substitute for good selling."[21]

Many transactional buyers are primarily interested in price and convenience, so consider eliminating, or unbundling, features that contribute to a higher selling price. If the buyer is only interested in the lowest possible price, and you represent a marketer committed to a value-added sales strategy, consider withdrawing from negotiations.

CONCERNS RELATED TO TIME

stall Resistance related to time.

If a prospect says, "I want time to think it over," you may be encountering resistance related to time—often referred to as the **stall**. A stall usually means the customer does not yet perceive the benefits of buying now. In most cases the stall indicates that the prospect has both positive and negative feelings about your product. Consider using probing questions to determine the negative feelings: "Is it my company that concerns you?" "Do you have any concerns about our warranty program?"

It is all right to be persuasive if the prospect can truly benefit from buying now. If the price will soon rise, or if the item will not be available in the future, then you should provide this information. You must, however, present this information sincerely and accurately. It is never proper to distort the truth in the hope of getting the order.

EVERYONE SELLS

Renting Pandas

Ron Barbaro, currently chairman and CEO of the Ontario Lottery and Gaming Corporation, says that, when he first started in sales, he was not a good salesperson but he had determination and he was a good worker. It was this determination and hard work that enabled him to sell more than $1 million–worth of insurance in his first year. He went on to become president of Prudential Insurance Company of America's Canadian and worldwide operations. His determination—and undoubtedly the negotiating and problem-solving skills he learned while selling—helped him close what he refers to as his toughest, but most rewarding, sale.

When Ron Barbaro was chairman of the board for the Metro Toronto Zoo, he was instrumental in bringing the first Giant Panda exhibit to Canada from Asia. "They wouldn't give the pandas to us, nor would they sell them to us," says Ron. He eventually succeeded in negotiating a panda exhibit rental.[b]

General Strategies for Negotiating Buyer Concerns

The successful negotiation of buyer concerns is based in large part on understanding human behaviour (see Table 13.1). This knowledge, coupled with a good measure of common sense, will help salespeople overcome most forms of buyer concerns. It is also helpful to be aware of general methods for negotiating buyer resistance.

ANTICIPATE AND FORESTALL BUYER CONCERNS

Many people who sell, such as Doug Macnamara for the Banff Centre for Management (p. 304), have learned to anticipate certain problems and forestall them with a well-planned and well-executed presentation. While buyer concerns are by no means insurmountable, it is a good idea to take preventive measures whenever possible. By anticipating problems, a salesperson can approach the prospect with greater confidence and save valuable time.

KNOW THE VALUE OF WHAT YOU ARE OFFERING

It is important that a salesperson know what is of real value to the customer and not consider value only in terms of purchase price. The real value of what you are offering may be a value added intangible such as superior product knowledge, good credit terms, prompt delivery, or a reputation for honest dealings. An important aspect of the negotiation process is discovering what is of utmost importance to the buyer. The focus of personal selling today should be the mutual search for value. Some salespeople make the

Table 13.1

Negotiating Buyer Concerns

Objections are often requests for more information to justify the buying decision. Objections can tell us a lot about the real source of hesitation and what type of information the customer is seeking

Buyer's Concern	Source of Hesitation	Request For
"Price too high."	Perceived cost vs. benefit	Value articulation
"Think about it."	Afraid to make a bad decision	Create comfort, provide proof
"Talk to boss."	Unable to justify decision	Risk reduction, benefit review
"Need more quotes."	Unsure you're the best option	Targeted solutions, value
"Set with current supplier."	Doesn't see benefit of change	Differentiation
"Bad history."	Past experience is affecting current review	Offer proof of change

SELLING IN THE GLOBAL ECONOMY

Negotiating Across Cultures

Negotiations in the global economy vary from one country to another because of cultural differences. German buyers are more apt to look you in the eye and tell you what they do not like about your product. Japanese buyers, on the other hand, do not want to embarrass you and, therefore, bury their concerns beneath several layers of courtesy. In China, now one of the most important markets for Canadian businesses, negotiations are more straightforward. People who have been doing business in China for many years suggest a very direct approach to negotiations. However, do not become antagonistic or discourteous. Do get involved in Chinese business rituals that are intended to create a friendly atmosphere.

When you enter into negotiations in foreign countries, it is important to understand and accommodate the customer's culture. You may not get every detail exactly right, but you win respect by trying. Selling in certain cultures often requires more time in bonding and building rapport. Several meetings may be needed to lay the groundwork for the actual sale.[c]

mistake of offering a lower price the moment buyer concerns surface. In the customer's mind, price may be of secondary importance compared with the quality of service after the sale. As noted previously, do not be in a hurry to make price concessions.

Many salespeople have learned to anticipate certain problems and forestall them with a well-planned and well-executed presentation.

PREPARE FOR NEGOTIATIONS

It helps to classify possible resistance with the aid of a negotiations worksheet. To illustrate how this form works, let us review an example from the food industry. Mary Turner is a salesperson for Durkee Famous Foods. She represents more than 350 products. Mary calls on supermarkets daily and offers assistance in the areas of ordering and merchandising. Recently her company decided to offer retail food stores an allowance of $1 per case of olives if the store purchased 15 or more cases. Prior to talking with her customers about this offer, Mary sat down and developed a negotiations worksheet, shown in Figure 13.5. We cannot anticipate every possible problem, but it is possible to identify the most common problems that are likely to arise. The negotiations worksheet can be a useful tool.

UNDERSTAND THE PROBLEM

David Stiebel, author of *When Talking Makes Things Worse!*, says we need to understand the difference between a misunderstanding and a true disagreement. A *misunderstanding* is a failure to accurately understand the other person's point. For example, the salesperson believes the customer is primarily interested in price, but the customer's primary need is on-time delivery. A *disagreement*, in contrast, is a

Negotiations Worksheet

Customer's concern	Type of concern	Possible response
"Fifteen cases of olives will take up valuable space in my receiving room. It is already crowded."	Need	Combination Direct denial/Superior benefit "You will not have to face that problem. With the aid of our merchandising plan you can display 10 cases immediately on the sales floor. Only 5 cases will become reserve stock. You should move all 15 cases in about two weeks."
"This is a poor time of the year to buy a large order of olives. People are not buying olives at this time."	Time	Combination Indirect denial/Third-party testimony "I agree that it has been a problem in the past, but consumer attitudes seem to be changing. We have found that olives sell well all year long if displayed properly. More people are using olives in the preparation of omelets, pizza, and other dishes. Of course, most relish trays feature olives. We will supply you with point-of-purchase material that provides kitchen-tested ways to use this high-profit item."
"I have to stay within my budget."	Price	Superior benefit "As you know, olives represent a high-profit item. The average margin is 26 percent. With the addition of our $1.00 per case allowance the margin will rise to about 30 percent. This order will give you a good return on your investment."
"I am very satisfied with my present supplier."	Source	Combination question/Trial order "What can I do to get you to take just a trial order?"

Figure 13.5 Before the presentation it is important to prepare a negotiations worksheet.

failure to agree that would persist despite the more accurate understanding.[22] Be certain that both you and the prospect are clear on the true nature of what needs to be negotiated. When the prospect begins talking, listen carefully and then listen some more. With probing questions, you can fine-tune your understanding of the problem.

CREATE ALTERNATIVE SOLUTIONS

When the prospect finishes talking, it is a good practice to validate the problem, using a confirmation question. This helps to isolate the true problem and reduce the chance of misunderstanding. The confirmation question might sound like this: "I think I understand your concern. You feel the warranty does not provide you with sufficient protection. Is this correct?" By taking time to ask this question, you accomplish two important things. First, you are giving personal attention to the problem, which will please the customer. Second, you gain time to think about the best possible response.

The best possible response is very often an alternative solution. Many of today's customers do not want to hear that there is only one way or a single solution. In the age of information, people have less time to manage their work and their lives, so they expect new levels of flexibility.

FIND SOME POINT OF AGREEMENT

Negotiating buying problems is a little like the art of diplomacy. It helps to know what points of agreement exist. This saves time and helps establish a closer bond between you and the prospect. At some point during the presentation you might summarize by using a summary confirmation question: "Let us see if I fully understand your position. You think our product is well constructed and will provide the reliability you are looking for. Also, you believe our price is fair. Am I correct on these two points?" Once all the areas of agreement have been identified, there may be surprisingly few points of disagreement. The prospect suddenly sees that the advantages of ownership far outweigh the disadvantages. Now that the air is cleared, both the salesperson and the customer can give their full attention to any remaining points of disagreement.

KNOW WHEN TO WALK AWAY

For many reasons salespeople must sometimes walk away from a potential sale. If the customer's budget doesn't allow the purchase of your product, don't press the issue. If the customer's best offer is not favourable for your company, don't continue to waste your time. If you discover that the prospect is dishonest or fails to keep his or her word, discontinue negotiations. Be aware of how much flexibility you have in terms of such factors as price, specifications, or delivery schedules and know when you have reached your "walk-away" point.[23]

Specific Methods of Negotiating Buyer Concerns

There are seven specific methods of negotiating buyer concerns. In analyzing each problem, a salesperson should try to determine which method will be most effective. In most cases you will use a combination of the following methods to negotiate buyer concerns.

DIRECT DENIAL

direct denial Involves refuting the prospect's opinion or belief. The direct denial of a problem is considered a high-risk method of negotiating buyer concerns.

Direct denial involves refuting the opinion or belief of a prospect. The direct denial of a problem is considered a high-risk method of negotiating buyer concerns. Therefore you should use it with care. People do not like to be told they are wrong. Even when the facts prove the prospect is wrong, resentment can build if a salesperson fails to handle the situation properly.

When a prospect offers buyer resistance that is not valid, a salesperson sometimes has no option other than to disagree openly. If the person is misinformed, you must provide accurate information. For example, if the customer questions the product's quality, meet the concern head-on with whatever proof seems appropriate. It is almost never proper to ignore misinformation. High-performance salespeople counter inaccurate responses from the prospect promptly and directly.

The manner in which you state the denial is of major importance. Use a win-win approach. Be firm and sincere in stating your beliefs but do not be offensive. Above all, do not patronize the prospect. A know-it-all attitude can be irritating.

INDIRECT DENIAL

Sometimes the prospect's concern is completely valid, or at least accurate to a large degree. This method is referred to as the **indirect denial**. The best approach is to bend a little and acknowledge that the prospect is at least partly correct. After all, if you offered a product that is concern-proof, you would likely have no competitors. Every product has a shortcoming or limitation.[24] The success of this method is based in part on the need most people have to feel that their views are worthwhile. For this reason the indirect denial method is the most widely used.

indirect denial Often used when the prospect's concern is completely valid, or at least accurate to a large degree. The salesperson bends a little and acknowledges that the prospect is at least partly correct.

An exchange that features the use of this approach follows. The salesperson is a key account representative for Tele-Direct Atlantic.[25]

> **Salesperson:** The total cost of placing your one-quarter–column ad in the Yellow Pages of the five different directories you have chosen is approximately $10 000.
>
> **Prospect:** As a builder I want to reach people who are planning to build a home. I am afraid my ad will be lost among the hundreds of ads featured in your directories.
>
> **Salesperson:** Yes, I agree the Yellow Pages in our directories do feature hundreds of ads, but the section for general contractors features fewer than 30 ads. Our design staff can prepare an ad that will be highly visible and will set your company apart from ads placed by other contractors.

Note that the salesperson used the words "Yes, I agree" to reduce the impact of denial. The prospect is less likely to feel his or her point of view has been totally disproved.

FEEL—FELT—FOUND

Successful salespeople are sensitive to clues that indicate the client feels something is wrong. One way to empathize with the client's concerns is to use the "feel—felt—found" strategy. George Hutchison, chairman and CEO of North Bay, Ontario–based Equisure Financial Network Inc., is an ace negotiator who regularly uses this method. When someone raises a major concern, he will often say to the person, "I know how you *feel.* Others have

www.equisure.ca

felt the same way. However, we've *found* that...." Hutchison says that, besides offering empathy, this method reassures the person that others have successfully overcome the same concerns.[26]

QUESTIONS

Throughout this chapter, we have described several situations where probing or confirmation questions can enhance the negotiation process. We must also keep in mind the important role of need-satisfaction questions. In Chapter 11 we noted that need-satisfaction questions are designed to move the sales process toward commitment and action. These questions focus on the solution.[27] Consider the following exchange that involves a price concern:

> **Buyer:** It would be difficult for our Human Resources Department to absorb the cost of your psychological tests.
>
> **Seller:** What would a 10-percent reduction in employee turnover save your company?

In this example the question is designed to get the customer's attention focused on the solution. This question also gives ownership of the solution to the prospect. (See Chapter 11 for more examples of the need-satisfaction question.)

SUPERIOR BENEFIT

Sometimes the customer raises a problem that cannot be answered with a denial. For example: "Your copy machine does not feature an automatic document feed mechanism. This means that our employees will have to spend more time at the machine." You should acknowledge the valid concern and then discuss one or more superior benefits: "We have not included the automatic feature because it is less reliable than the manual approach. As you know, downtime is not only costly but also inconvenient." A **superior benefit** is a benefit that will, in most cases, outweigh the customer's specific concern.

superior benefit A benefit that will, in most cases, outweigh the customer's specific concern.

DEMONSTRATION

If you are familiar with your product as well as that of your competition, this method of negotiating buyer concerns is easy to use. You know the competitive advantages of your product and can discuss these features with confidence. The product demonstration is one of the most convincing ways to overcome buyer skepticism. With the aid of an effective demonstration you can overcome specific concerns.

Sometimes a second demonstration is needed to overcome buyer skepticism. This demonstration will provide additional proof. High-achieving sales personnel know when and how to use proof to overcome buyer concerns.

TRIAL OFFER

trial offer Involves giving the prospect an opportunity to try the product without making a purchase commitment.

A **trial offer** involves giving the prospect an opportunity to try the product without making a purchase commitment. The trial offer—especially with new products—is popular with customers because they can get fully acquainted with your product without making a major commitment. Assume that a buyer for a large restaurant chain says, "I am sure you have a good cooking oil, but we are happy with our present brand. We have had no complaints from our managers." In response to this comment you might say, "I can understand your reluctance to try our product. However, I do believe our oil is the finest on the market. With your permission, I would like to ship you 125 litres of our oil at no cost. You can use our product at selected restaurants and evaluate the results. If our oil does not provide you with superior results, you are under no obligation to place an order."

In the case of office equipment the customer may be given the opportunity to use the product on a trial basis. An office manager might respond to the salesperson who sells dictation equipment in this manner: "I would not feel comfortable talking to a machine." In response to this issue a salesperson might say, "I can understand how you feel. How about using one of our demonstration models for a few days?"

THIRD-PARTY TESTIMONY

Studies indicate that the favourable testimony of a neutral third party can be an effective method of responding to buyer resistance. Let us assume that the owner of a small business states that he or she can get along without a personal computer. The salesperson might respond in this manner: "Many small business owners think the way you do. However, once they use a personal computer, they find it to be an invaluable aid. Mark Williams, owner of Williams Hardware, says that his PC saves him several hours a week. Plus, he has improved the accuracy of his record keeping." Third-party testimony provides a positive way to solve certain types of buying problems. The positive experiences of a neutral third party will almost never trigger an argument with the prospect.

POSTPONE METHOD

At the beginning of this chapter, we noted that many of today's customers are well informed and may want to engage in negotiations early in the sales

CUSTOMER RELATIONSHIP MANAGEMENT WITH TECHNOLOGY

Automated Sorting and Productivity

The notes of a busy salesperson can quickly become extensive. Paper notes make it difficult, if not impossible, to cross-reference important information within those notes. The notes in a CRM system give salespeople immediate access to records containing needed words or phrases. This feature offers users many advantages, including a method of quickly finding information about buyers with similar interests or concerns. (See the exercise Finding Keywords in a CRM Database on page 325 for more information.)

Aramark lists several of its larger customers in this ad, a form of third-party testimony.

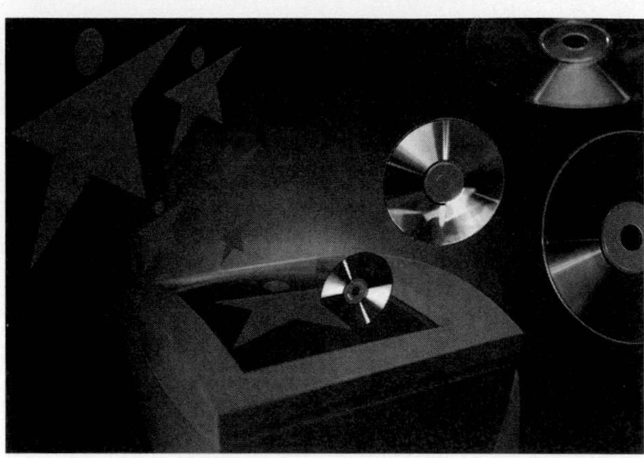

WHO'S GOT THE SOLUTIONS FOR MORE EFFICIENT OFFICE SYSTEMS?

We're ARAMARK Office Services and while our name is new, we bring our clients years of experience in providing total office management solutions. Our point of difference lies in our approach to your business, which is solutions based supported by technology and equipment, not the other way around.

Our range of services includes on-site print on demand, copy centre, mail centre management, Electronic Document Management Systems, distribution, fulfilment and stationery and forms control. ARAMARK provides you with the most advanced equipment available with dedicated specialists in each area.

In addition, ARAMARK's unique "Unlimited Partnership" culture offers a wide range of managed services from food service to cleaning to office coffee. All designed for cost effectiveness and to save you time, time that can be focused on your core business.

Now isn't that the best solution of all.

ARAMARK
Managed Services, Managed Better.
FORMERLY VERSA SERVICES

ARAMARK Managed Services for Business, Education, Healthcare, Sports & Entertainment, Offshore and Remote, and Government: Food, Refreshment, Office Management, and Facility Services. Visit us at www.aramark.ca

process. The customer may raise concerns that you would prefer to respond to later in the presentation. Let's assume you are calling on an office manager who is interested in well-equipped cubicles for eight employees. Soon after you present some product information, the customer says, "How much will eight well-equipped cubicles cost us?" Using the **postpone method**, your response might be, "I would prefer to answer that question in a few minutes. Once I learn what features you prefer, I can calculate a cost estimate." Every customer concern should be taken seriously. Always try to explain why you want to postpone the response.

postpone method A method salespeople use to delay a response when a customer raises a concern that would be better handled later in a sales presentation.

COMBINATION METHODS

As noted previously, consultative selling is characterized by flexibility. A combination of methods sometimes proves to be the best way to deal with buyer resistance. For example, an indirect denial might be followed by a question: "The cost of our business security system is a little higher than the competition's. The price I have quoted reflects the high-quality materials used to develop our system. Wouldn't you feel better entrusting your security needs to a firm with more than 25 years of experience in the business security field?" In this situation, the salesperson might also consider combining the indirect denial with an offer to arrange a demonstration of the security system.

SUMMARY

Sales resistance is natural and should be welcomed as an opportunity to learn more about how to satisfy the prospect's needs. Buyers' concerns often provide salespeople with precisely the information they need to close a sale.

Concerns may arise from a variety of reasons, some related to the content or manner of the presentation strategy and others related to the prospect's own concerns. Whatever the reasons, the salesperson should negotiate sales resistance with the proper attitude, never making too much or too little of the prospect's concerns.

General strategies for negotiating buyer concerns include anticipating them, knowing the value of what you are offering, preparing for negotiations, understanding the problem, creating alternative solutions, finding some point of agreement, and avoiding anger.

The best strategy for negotiating sales resistance is to anticipate it and preplan methods to answer the prospect's concerns. If a salesperson uses a negotiations worksheet, then it will be much easier to deal with buyer resistance.

We discuss the various types of problems likely to surface during the sales presentation: need, product, source, price, and time.

Specific methods and combinations of methods for negotiating resistance will vary depending on the particular salesperson, product, and prospect. We have described several common methods, but you should remember that practice in applying them is essential and that there is room for a great deal of creative imagination in developing variations or additional methods. With careful preparation and practice, negotiating the most common types of buyer concerns should become a stimulating challenge to each salesperson's professional growth.

Key Terms

Direct Denial **318**

Indirect Denial **319**

Negotiation **306**

Postpone Method **322**

Stall **314**

Superior Benefit **320**

Trial Offer **320**

Review Questions

1. Explain why a salesperson should welcome buyer concerns.
2. List the common types of buyer concerns that might surface in a presentation.
3. How does the negotiations worksheet help the salesperson prepare to negotiate buyer concerns?
4. Explain the value of using a confirmation question as a general strategy for negotiating buyer concerns.
5. List seven general strategies for negotiating buyer concerns.

6. While it might be unwise for a buyer to pay too much when making a purchase, some salespeople argue that it is worse to pay too little. Do you agree or disagree with this statement? Explain.
7. What is the most common reason prospects give for not buying? How can salespeople deal effectively with this type of concern?
8. Professional buyers may have learned to use specific negotiation tactics in dealing with salespeople. List and describe two tactics that are commonly used today.
9. When a customer says, "I want time to think it over," what type of resistance is the salesperson encountering? Suggest ways to overcome this type of buyer concern.
10. What are some positive ways to cope with the buyer's source concern?

Application Exercises

1. During an interview with a prospective employer, the interviewer raises a concern that you are not qualified for the job for which you are applying. On the basis of your observation, you do not believe the interviewer fully understands the amount of experience you have or that you really have the ability to perform the job requirements. Write how you would overcome the concern the interviewer has raised.
2. Assume you have decided to sell your own home. During an open house, a prospect whom you are showing through the house begins to criticize every major selling point about your home.
   a. You have taken excellent care of your home, believe it to be a good home, and have done a lot of special projects to make it more enjoyable. What will be your emotional reaction to this prospect's criticisms? Should you express this emotional reaction?
   b. You think this prospect is really interested in buying your home, despite this surface criticism. How would you negotiate the buyer's concerns that he or she is showing?
3. Much valuable information on negotiating can be found on the Internet. Two important sources are the Web sites of BayGroup International, the makers of DealMaker software (**www.baygroup.com**), and Roger Dawson, author of *Secrets of Power Negotiating for Salespeople* and founder of the Power Negotiating Institute (**www.rdawson.com**). Visit these Web sites and view some of the free articles on negotiating. Be prepared to discuss your findings in class.

ROLE-PLAY EXERCISE

You have had two previous interviews for a career position that really interests you. You understand that, with the hiring process in this company, most interviewers want to "buy low." However, you want to "sell high." The vice-president of sales indicated that she really wants you to be a part of the department and has offered you a position. However, the first year's salary and benefits are $10 000 below what you feel you are worth. This salary is also several thousand dollars below what you will need to cover the kind of lifestyle you want. The only thing between you and the position is the difference in compensation. Using a negotiations worksheet, plan your response to the following statements made by the vice-president: (1) "Our salary budget limits us." (2) "Can we split the difference?" (3) "Either take it or leave it." Decide at what point in the salary negotiations you will decide to turn down the offer or accept the offer. Role-play your response to each of these statements with another student role-playing the vice-president. Afterward, discuss how effective your negotiating was.

CRM Application Exercise FINDING KEYWORDS IN A CRM DATABASE

During sales training this week, your sales manager Becky Kemley led a discussion about negotiating buyer resistance and managing their concerns. The discussion included methods of identifying and responding to price concerns. You wish to find those contacts who might have a price concern so that you can better prepare for working with them. Using the ACT! software, access all records containing the word "price" by selecting Lookup, Keyword, type "price," check Notes, and press Enter. After searching, ACT! will display three records in which price is an issue. Print contact reports for these three records by selecting Report, Contact Report, Active Lookup, Printer, and OK.

Case Problem

Each year, private and public organizations throughout Canada, including not-for-profit agencies, send thousands of employees to management training seminars. Training has become a multi-million–dollar business, and the number of programs has been growing rapidly. Some of the largest providers of management training and related services are catering to clients in new and exciting ways.

The Banff Centre for Management (BCM) (see p. 304) provides a good example of this type of service provider. The goal of the BCM is to advance the state of leadership excellence in both individuals and organizations throughout Canada. In total, the BCM offers about 150 programs yearly, in areas such as executive development, general leadership and management, not-for-profit and community leadership, Aboriginal leadership, and environmental leadership. The program-design staff members each work with approximately 10 to 15 partnered client organizations annually to develop customized programs. They promise an unforgettable experience, with guaranteed results. Part of the process includes individual competency measurement and, if improvement cannot be demonstrated six to twelve months after the program, the BCM will refund that person's portion of the learning costs or will re-engage with that individual free of charge.

The BCM has a wide range of accommodations for participants, including 433 guest rooms in five facilities. There is a resource room with a printer and computers with Internet connections, and a full range of current management books and periodicals. Classrooms are equipped with the latest in multimedia technology. The BCM has a 500-seat dining room, six private function rooms that can be configured for various-sized groups for banquets or receptions, and numerous lounges that are licensed for private functions. There are outstanding indoor recreational facilities for swimming, squash, racquetball, weight training, track, and aerobic training. Outdoor sports are also available, including fishing, hiking, climbing, kayaking, river rafting, skiing, trail riding, golfing, mountain biking, and more. Participants can also attend a number of cultural events provided by the Banff Centre for the Arts.

In an ideal situation, Doug Macnamara, general manager of the BCM, likes to guide prospects through the facilities. This tour in some ways fulfills the function of a sales demonstration. He describes special amenities and services that the BCM can offer, and uses this time to become better acquainted with the prospect's needs. Then he escorts the prospect back to his office and completes a needs assessment, before preparing a detailed sales proposal. In most cases the proposal will be presented to the prospect at a second meeting. The proposal needs to contain accurate and complete information because, when signed, it becomes a legally enforceable sales contract.

Rarely will the sales proposal for a program be accepted without negotiating some modifications. Some clients Doug Macnamara deals with are experienced negotiators, who are likely to press for concessions that might include a lower daily participant rate, lower rates for accommodations or meals, complimentary barbecues or receptions, or passes for cultural or sporting events.

Of course some buyer concerns are not easily identified. Doug Macnamara says he follows three steps in dealing with buyer concerns:

1. *He locates the concerns.* Some prospects are reluctant to accept a sales proposal, but the reason may be unclear. Doug has discovered that some clients are concerned whether instructors can relate "theoretical" material to the real world of business, and whether they can relate to adult learners who respond better to a more active style of learning rather than simple lecture-based learning. Once these perceptions are uncovered, Doug knows how to deal with them.
2. *He clarifies the concerns.* If a prospect says, "I like your facilities and your program, but your price is too high," Doug must clarify what the prospect means. Is the prospect seeking a major price concession or a very small price concession?
3. *He overcomes the buyer concerns.* Doug says, "You must know the value of what you are offering. The BCM must be able to cover its costs, so concessions can only be made after careful consideration. Sometimes there are things included in the proposal that the prospect does not value or need, and removing them allows both parties to win: the client gets a program configured to meet his or her specific needs, and the BCM controls its costs."

Doug Macnamara's ability to configure value-added solutions for clients and to negotiate buyer concerns have helped the BCM achieve its goals.

Questions

1. If you were selling management training programs to businesses, what types of buyer concerns would you expect from a new prospect?
2. Let's assume that you are representing the Banff Centre for Management and you are meeting with a new prospect in her office. She is located some distance from Banff and cannot visit your facilities. What are some tools that you might use during the sales presentation? What proof devices might you use to support your claims?
3. If you meet with a professional buyer who is trained in negotiations, what tactics can you expect the person to use? How would you respond to each of these tactics?

CRM Case Study NEGOTIATING RESISTANCE

Becky Kemley has asked you to review Pat Silva's former prospect accounts. She wants you to look for accounts with which you might anticipate buyer concerns during a presentation.

Questions

1. Which account might voice a time concern and say, "We want to put off our decision for now." How would you propose dealing with this buyer concern?
2. Which account is most likely to try to get you to agree to a lower price and how would you respond?
3. Which account might you anticipate would use the phrase "we want to shop around for a good solid supplier"? What would be your response?

Partnership Selling

A ROLE PLAY/SIMULATION **(see Partnership Selling on the CD-ROM, pp. 40–41)**

DEVELOPING A SALES PRESENTATION STRATEGY—NEGOTIATING

Refer to *Sales Memorandum 3* and strategically plan to anticipate and negotiate any buyer concerns and/or concerns your customer may have to your presentation. You should prepare a negotiations worksheet to organize this part of your presentation.

The instructions for item 2e direct you to prepare negotiations for the time, price, source, and product concerns. You will note that your price is approximately $200 more than your customer budgeted for this meeting. You will have to be very effective in negotiating a value-added strategy because your convention centre is not a low-price supplier. (See Chapter 6 on value-added product strategies.)

During the presentation you should use proof devices from the product strategy materials provided in *Employment Memorandum 1* to negotiate concerns you anticipate. You may also want to use a calculator to negotiate any financial arrangements, such as savings on parking or airport transportation. Place these materials in the front pocket of your three-ring binder (portfolio) for easy access during your presentation. You may want to ask another person to be your customer, instructing him or her to voice the concerns you have anticipated and then responding with your negotiation strategies. This experience will provide you with the opportunity to rehearse your negotiation strategies.

CHAPTER 14

Closing the Sale

AND CONFIRMING THE PARTNERSHIP

LEARNING OBJECTIVES

After studying this chapter, you should be able to

1. Describe the proper attitude to have about closing the sale
2. List and discuss selected guidelines for closing the sale
3. Explain how to recognize closing clues
4. Discuss selected methods of closing the sale
5. Explain what to do when the buyer says Yes and what to do when the buyer says No

Dana Bengtson, sales representative for Ryder Commercial Leasing & Services **www.ryder.com**, understands the importance of patience in selling. It took him two years to convince a major food distributor to replace its in-house truck fleet with leased trucks from Ryder. Soon after his first contact he arranged for efficiency studies of the prospect's existing transportation system. With this information he was able to demonstrate the cost advantages of leasing. Although he seemed to be moving toward a close, he heard from the prospect's officials that they did not want to continue talks about leasing, at least for the time being. Dana realized that he had to slow down negotiations and be patient. In his words, it was time to "do nothing." Later Dana resumed his closing efforts. He sent the prospect's officials articles on long-term vehicle leasing and information on the food distribution business. He restructured his proposal to make it more appealing. After six more months of hard work he was rewarded with a seven-year lease agreement worth more than $4 million annually to Ryder. Dana Bengtson closed this sale because he knew when to speed up and when to slow down negotiations.[1]

Closing the Sale—Yesterday and Today

Throughout the evolution of personal selling, we have seen major changes in the way closing is perceived. Prior to the introduction of consultative selling and the partnering era, closing was typically presented as the most important aspect of the sales process. The early sales training literature also presented closing methods that encouraged manipulation of the customer; for example, some sales training programs included the standing-room-only close in which the sales trainee was encouraged to emphasize the negative consequences of waiting: "If you don't place the order today, I can't guarantee delivery by June 1." If the salesperson's statement is true, this information should be given to the customer. However, this important deadline should be discussed much earlier in the sales process. Use of any closing method that is perceived by the customer as pushy or manipulative will damage your chances of building a long-term partnership.

Some companies have taken steps to avoid the use of closing methods that might damage trust. Bill Goodwin, manager of training, sales, and marketing at 3M, says that closing methods are no longer included in 3M's sales training program. 3M wants salespeople to become more diagnostic and more responsive to feedback from the customer. Goodwin believes that thorough diagnostic efforts at the outset of the sales presentation will result in less buyer resistance as the salesperson moves toward closing the sale.[2]

www.3m.com

We take the position that, in many selling situations, the salesperson needs to assume responsibility for obtaining commitment from the customer. Some closing methods can move the customer from indecision to commitment. When these methods are used effectively, the prospect will not feel pressured. In some cases, we need to simply replace defence-arousing language—such as "This is the lowest price available anywhere"—with a positive need-satisfaction question, such as "Wouldn't this new software help you achieve more efficient inventory control?" Commitment is more readily obtained when the salesperson is strategically prepared for the close. Preparation for the close involves planning appropriate closing methods. Throughout the sales presentation, the salesperson should recognize closing clues and be prepared to use effective closing methods (see Fig. 14.1, p. 330).

Review the Value Proposition from the Prospect's Point of View

Closing the sale is usually easier if you look at the value proposition from the prospect's point of view. Have you effectively summarized the mix of key benefits? Will your proposal fulfill the customer's needs? Is your proposal strong enough to win over a customer who is experiencing buying anxieties?

Gene Bedell, author of *3 Steps to Yes*, reminds us that buying often causes emotional stress. The following buying anxieties help explain why some customers are reluctant to make a commitment to your proposal.[3]

> *Loss of options.* If the customer agrees to purchase a $5000 design proposal, then that money will not be available for other purchases or investments. Agreeing to purchase a product or service often means that some other purchase must be postponed. Anxiety and stress build as the customer thinks about allocating limited resources.

Figure 14.1 Effective closing methods require careful planning.

The Six-Step Presentation Plan	
Step One: APPROACH	✓ Review Strategic/Consultative Selling Model ✓ Initiate customer contact
Step Two: PRESENTATION	✓ Determine prospect needs ✓ Select solution ✓ Initiate sales presentation
Step Three: DEMONSTRATION	✓ Decide what to demonstrate ✓ Select selling tools ✓ Initiate demonstration
Step Four: NEGOTIATION	✓ Anticipate buyer concerns ✓ Plan negotiating methods ✓ Initiate win-win negotiations
Step Five: CLOSE	● Plan appropriate closing methods ● Recognize closing clues ● Initiate closing methods
Step Six: SERVICING THE SALE	● Follow-through ● Follow-up calls ● Expansion selling
Service, retail, wholesale, and manufacturer selling.	

Fear of making a mistake. If the customer believes that agreeing with a closing request may be the wrong thing to do, he or she may back away just when the decision seems imminent. Fear of making a mistake can be caused by lack of trust in the salesperson.

Social or peer pressures. Some customers make buying decisions with an eye on the opinions and reactions of others. A business buyer may have to justify a purchase to her boss or employees who will actually use the product. Be prepared to deal with these anxieties as you get closer to closing the sale. Sometimes, just a little gentle persuasion will help the anxious customer to make a decision.

CLOSING THE SALE—THE BEGINNING OF THE PARTNERSHIP

Closing should be thought of as the beginning of a long-term partnership. Tom Riley, in his book *Value-Added Selling*, says, "You don't close sales... you build commitment to a course of action that brings value to the customer and profit to the seller."[4] There is a building process that begins with an

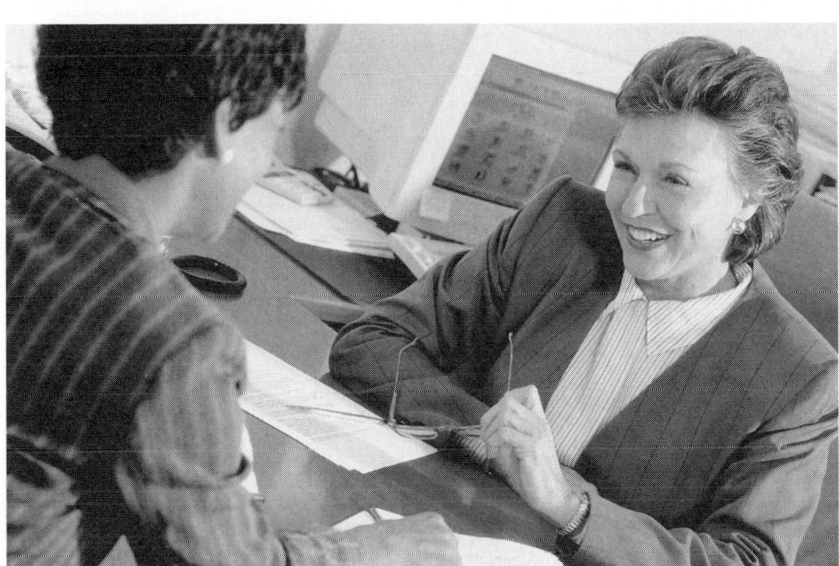

Closing should be viewed as part of the selling process—the logical outcome of a well-planned presentation strategy.

interesting approach and need discovery. It continues with effective product selection and presentation of benefits, which build desire for the product. After a well-planned demonstration and after negotiating sales resistance, it is time to obtain commitment. Dan Kennedy, author of *No B.S. Sales Success*, says, "If closing is difficult, something is wrong with earlier parts of the selling process."[5] Closing ought to be a natural conclusion to the selling process.

Guidelines for Closing the Sale

Several factors increase the odds that you will close the sale (see Fig. 14.2). These guidelines for closing the sale have universal application in the field of selling.

FOCUS ON DOMINANT BUYING MOTIVES

Most salespeople incorporate the outstanding benefits of their product into the sales presentation. This is only natural. They are, however, alert to the one benefit that generates the most excitement. The buying motive that is of greatest interest deserves special attention. Vince Peters, director of sales training and development for Wyeth-Ayerst International, tells his 8000 pharmaceutical salespeople that the key to closing "is to find out exactly what a prospect is looking for."[6] Throughout the need discovery stage, pay close attention to the buyer's interests. Focus your closing efforts on the point of greatest interest and give the prospect a reason for buying.

LONGER SELLING CYCLES REQUIRE MULTIPLE COMMITMENTS

Longer, more complex selling cycles have become a fact of life. One reason for this change is that more decision makers are involved in purchasing

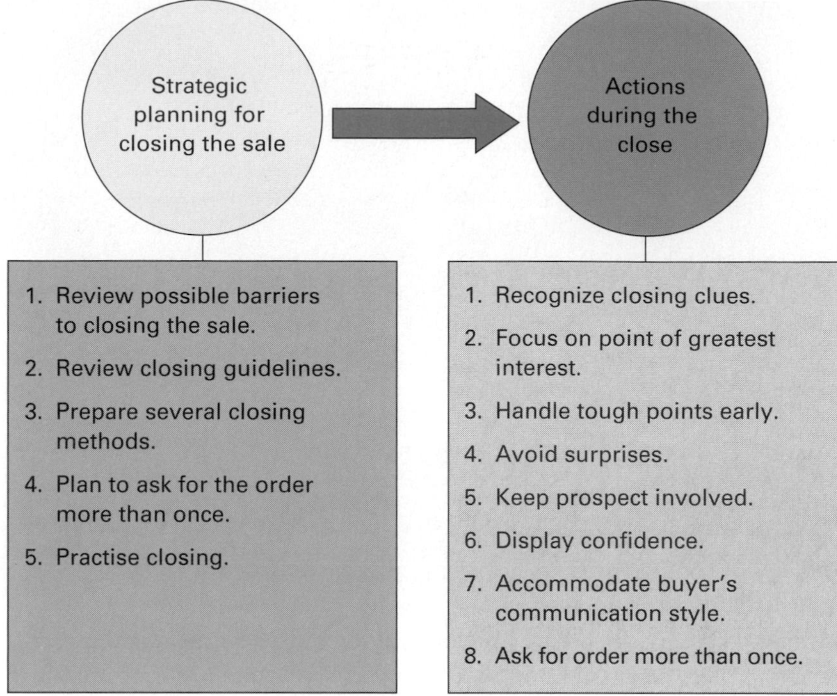

Strategic planning for closing the sale
Actions during the close
1. Review possible barriers to closing the sale.
2. Review closing guidelines.
3. Prepare several closing methods.
4. Plan to ask for the order more than once.
5. Practise closing.
1. Recognize closing clues.
2. Focus on point of greatest interest.
3. Handle tough points early.
4. Avoid surprises.
5. Keep prospect involved.
6. Display confidence.
7. Accommodate buyer's communication style.
8. Ask for order more than once.

Figure 14.2 The presentation strategy should include reviewing these guidelines for closing and confirming the sale.

some products. The purchase of highly technical products—such as computer systems that serve the entire company, security equipment, and robotics—may involve persons from many areas of the organization. In some cases the buyer has more options than in the past and will take more time to make a buying decision.

incremental commitment Gradually moving the customer to total commitment (i.e., closing on a purchase) by gaining cumulative commitment with each sales call.

When you are working on a large, complex sale you should try to achieve **incremental commitment** throughout the sales process. Assume you are a sales representative for Canada Security, a company that develops and implements high-quality security systems. You have presented your security plan to the vice-president of operations at a Winnipeg transportation company and she is committed to your proposal. However, this person cannot give final approval to the sale. In this case, you should request her help in arranging a meeting with the person who can approve your proposal. Some form of incremental commitment should be obtained during each step in a multi-call sales presentation. Otherwise, you are not moving the sale forward toward obtaining a signed order.[7]

It is helpful to view each customer commitment as a "close." At the conclusion of the first sales call, you may need to obtain commitment to an agenda for a second call. Getting this commitment aids closing.

NEGOTIATE THE TOUGH POINTS BEFORE ATTEMPTING THE CLOSE

Many products have what might be thought of as an Achilles heel. In other words, the product is vulnerable or appears to be vulnerable in one or more

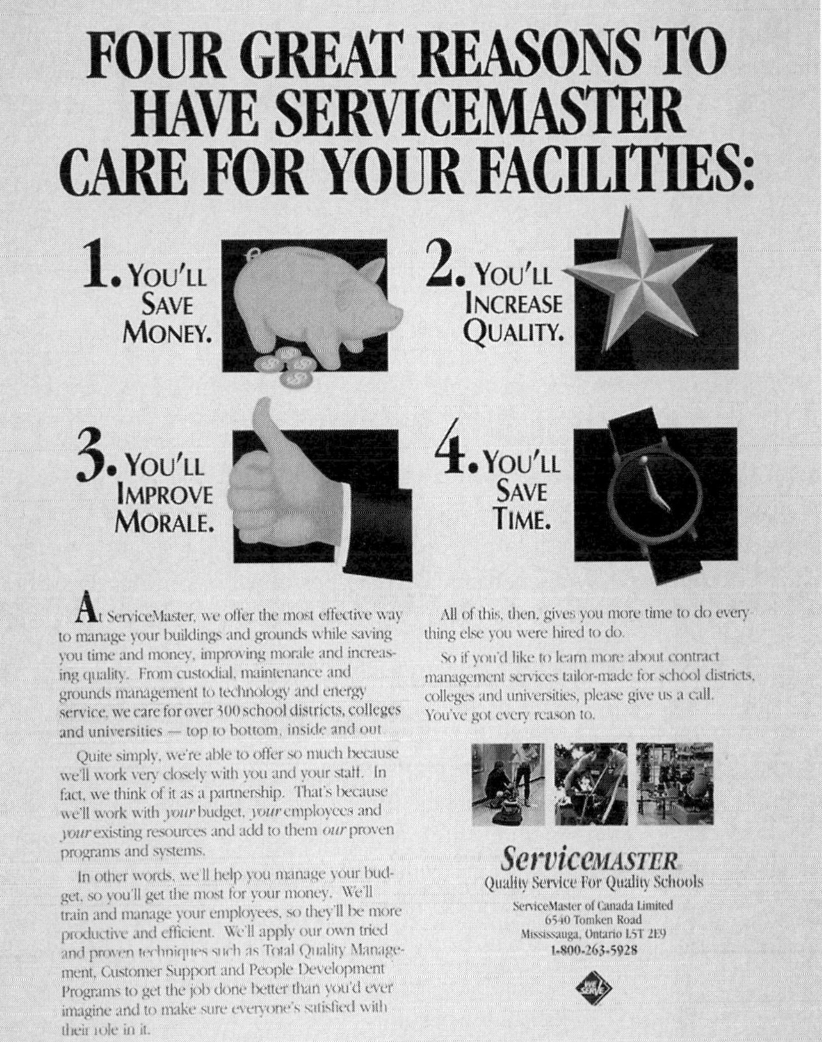

ServiceMaster of Canada recognizes that different customers can have different dominant buying motives. Focusing on dominant buying motives helps close sales.

areas. Negotiate a win-win solution to the tough points before you attempt to close the sale. Such factors can lose the sale if you ignore them. The close should be a positive phase of the sales presentation. This is not the time to deal with a controversial issue or problem.

In the case of Rolex watches, Lexus automobiles, or Banff Springs Hotel conference facilities, the Achilles heel may be price. Each of these products may seem expensive by comparison with competing ones. People who sell them find ways to establish the value of their product before attempting the close.

AVOID SURPRISES AT THE CLOSE

Some salespeople make the mistake of waiting until the close to reveal information that may come as a surprise to the prospect. For example, the salesperson quotes a price but is not specific concerning what the price includes. Let us assume that the price of a central air-conditioning unit is $1800. The prospect believes that the price is competitive in relation to similar units on the market and is ready to sign the order form. Then the salesperson mentions casually that the installation charge is an extra $225. The prospect had assumed that the $1800 fee included installation. Suddenly the extra fee looms as a major obstacle to closing the sale.

Other surprises might come in the form of an accessory that costs extra, terms of the warranty, customer service limitations, or some other issue. Do not let a last-minute surprise damage the relationship with the buyer and threaten the completion of a sale.

DISPLAY A HIGH DEGREE OF SELF-CONFIDENCE AT THE CLOSE

Do you believe in your product? Do you believe in your company? Have you identified a solution to the customer's problem? If you can answer Yes to each of these questions, then there is no need to display timidity. Look the prospect in the eye and ask for the order. Do not be apologetic at this important point in the sales presentation. The salesperson who confidently asks for the sale is displaying the boldness that is so effective in personal selling.

ASK FOR THE ORDER MORE THAN ONCE

Too often, salespeople make the mistake of not asking for the order or asking just once. If the prospect says No, they give up. Michael LeBoeuf, author of *How to Win Customers and Keep Them for Life*, reports that almost two-thirds of all sales calls conclude without the salesperson asking for the order. He also says that a majority of customers say No several times before saying Yes.[8] Some of the most productive salespeople ask for the order three, four, or even five times. They are not surprised by the number of Yes responses that come on the fourth or fifth attempt. Of course, they do not make all of these closing attempts during one call.

SELLING IN ACTION

Ask for the Order

Even though salespeople have the ultimate responsibility for bringing all of their selling activities to a close, many do not ask for the order. This problem motivated Arthur R. Bauer and Gerald L. Manning, sales trainers, authors, and consultants, to produce a video-based sales training course entitled *Ask for the Order.* They point out that most customers expect the salesperson to ask for the order and will be puzzled when the salesperson fails to ask for their business. Fear of rejection is a major reason salespeople don't ask for the sale. Lack of discipline and determination can also serve as barriers to the use of closing attempts.[a]

RECOGNIZE CLOSING CLUES

As the sales presentation progresses, you need to be alert to closing clues (sometimes called *buying signals*). A **closing clue** is an indication, either verbal or nonverbal, that the prospect is preparing to make a buying decision. It is a form of feedback, which is so important in selling. When you detect a closing clue, it may be time to attempt a close.

closing clue An indication, either verbal or nonverbal, that the prospect is preparing to make a buying decision.

Many closing clues are quite subtle and may be missed if you are not alert. This is especially true in the case of nonverbal buying signals. If you pay careful attention—with your eyes and your ears—many prospects will tell you how to close the sale. As we have noted earlier in this text, one of the most important personality traits salespeople need is empathy, the ability to sense what the other person is feeling. In this section we will review some of the most common verbal and nonverbal clues.

Verbal Clues

Closing clues come in many forms. Spoken words, or verbal clues, are usually the easiest to perceive. These clues can be divided into three categories: (1) questions, (2) recognitions, and (3) requirements.

Questions. One of the least subtle buying signals is the question. You might attempt a trial close after responding to one of the following questions:

Do you have a credit plan to cover this purchase?

What type of warranty do you provide?

How soon can our company get delivery?

Recognitions. A recognition is any positive statement concerning your product or some factor related to the sale, such as credit terms or delivery date. Some examples follow:

We like the quality control system you have recommended.

I have always wanted to own a boat like this.

Your delivery schedule fits our plans.

Requirements. Sometimes customers outline a condition that must be met before they will buy. If you are able to meet this requirement, it may be a good time to try a trial close. Here are some requirements that the prospect might voice:

We will need shipment within two weeks.

Our staff will need to be trained in how to use this equipment.

All our equipment must be certified by the plant safety officer.

In some cases, verbal buying clues will not jump out at you. Important buying signals may be interwoven into normal conversation. Listen closely whenever the prospect is talking.

Nonverbal Clues

Nonverbal buying clues will be even more difficult to detect. Once detected, this type of signal is not easy to interpret. Nevertheless, you should be alert to body movement, facial expression, and tone of voice. Here are some actions that suggest that the prospect may be prepared to purchase the product.[9]

- The prospect's facial expression changes. Suddenly the person's eyes widen and genuine interest is clear in the facial expression.
- The prospect begins showing agreement by nodding.
- The prospect leans forward and appears to be intent on hearing your message.
- The prospect begins intently to examine the product or study the sales literature.

When you observe or sense one of these nonverbal buying clues, do not hesitate to ask for the order. Keep in mind that the modern approach to selling holds that there may be several opportunities to close throughout the sales presentation. Important buying signals may surface at any time. Do not miss them.

Specific Methods for Closing the Sale

The sales presentation is a process, not a single action. Each step during the process should create another layer of trust and move the customer closer to making a commitment. Throughout the sales process, you are positioning yourself as a valued resource.[10]

There is no best closing method. Your best bet is to preplan several closing methods and use the ones that seem appropriate (see Fig. 14.3). Given the complex nature of many sales, it is often a good idea to be prepared to use a combination of closing methods. Do keep in mind that your goal is not only to close the sale but also to develop a long-term partnership. A win-win closing strategy results in repeat business and the opportunity to obtain referrals.

TRIAL CLOSE

trial close A closing attempt made at an opportune time during the sales presentation to encourage the customer to reveal readiness or unwillingness to buy.

A **trial close**, also known as a *minor point close*, is a closing attempt made at an opportune time during the sales presentation to encourage the customer to reveal readiness or unwillingness to buy. When you are reasonably sure that the prospect is about to make a decision but is being held back by natural caution, the trial close may be appropriate. It is a good way to test the buyer's attitude toward the actual purchase. A trial close is often presented in the form of a probing or confirmation question. Here are some examples:

We can arrange an August 1 shipment. Would this date be satisfactory?

Would you rather begin this plan on July 1 or July 15?

Do you want one of our staff members to supervise the installation?

Will a $250 down payment be possible at this time?

Closing Worksheet		
Closing clue (prospect)	Closing method	Closing statement (salesperson)
"That sounds fine."	Direct appeal close	"Good. May I get your signature on this order?"
"What kind of financing do you offer?"	Multiple options close	"We have two financing methods available: 90-day open credit or two-year long-term financing. Which of these do you prefer?"
"Well, we don't have large amounts of cash available at this time."	Assumptive close	"Based on your cash position, I would recommend you consider our lease–purchase plan. This plan allows you to pay a very small initial amount at this time and keep the cash you now have for your everyday business expenses. I will be happy to write up your order on the lease–purchase plan."
The prospect completes a careful reading of the proposal, then looks satisfied (a nonverbal clue).	Combination Summary-of-benefits/Direct appeal close	"That solution surpasses your quality requirements, meets your time deadlines, and provides your accounting department with the details it requested. Can you get your chief financial officer's signature on the order?"

Figure 14.3 Preparing for the close requires the preplanning of several closing methods. Research indicates that in many selling situations several closing attempts will be necessary.

Some salespeople use the trial close more than once during the sales presentation. After the salesperson presents a feature, converts that feature to a buyer benefit, and confirms the prospect's agreement that the benefit is important, it would be appropriate to use a trial close.

In broader terms, it would be appropriate to attempt a trial close after steps two, three, or four of the six-step presentation plan (see Fig. 14.4, p. 338).

SUMMARY-OF-BENEFITS CLOSE

Let us assume that you have discussed and demonstrated the major benefits of your product and you detect considerable buyer interest. However, you have covered a great deal of material. There is a chance that the prospect will not be able to put the entire picture together without your help. At this point you should provide a concise summary of the most important buyer benefits. Your goal in the **summary-of-benefits close** is to re-emphasize the benefits that will help bring about a favourable decision. This closing statement gives you the opportunity to restate how the benefits will outweigh the costs.[11]

summary-of-benefits close Involves summarizing the most important buyer benefits, re-emphasizing the benefits that will help bring about a favourable decision.

Let us see how this closing method works in the management education industry. Bill Morrissey, manager of Memorial University's Centre for Management Development, recently called on Ray Busch, director of mar-

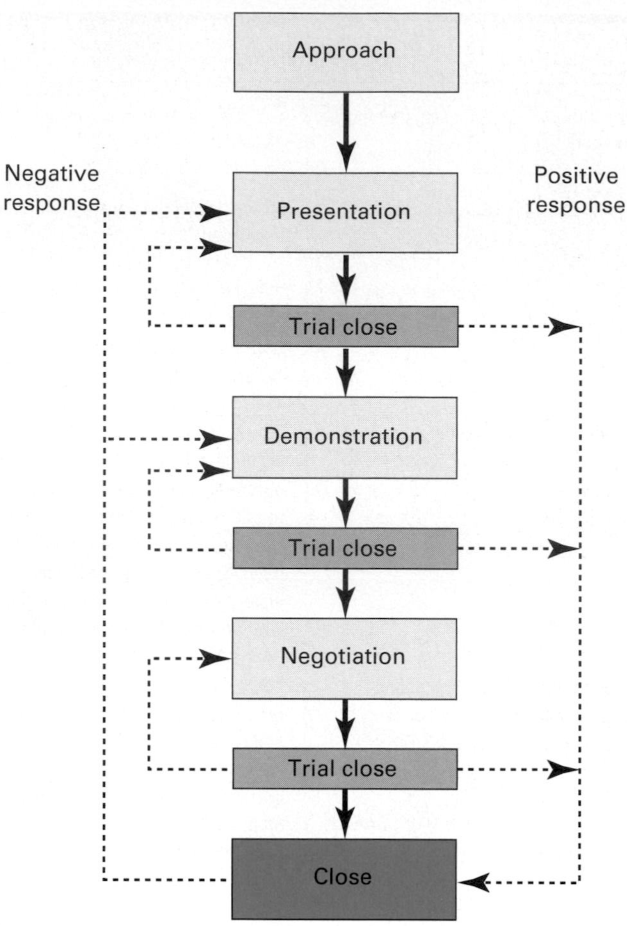

Figure 14.4 The trial close should be attempted at an opportune time during the sales presentation. It is appropriate to initiate a trial close after steps two, three, or four of the six-step presentation plan.

keting for a large corporation. Near the end of the sales presentation, Bill summarized the major benefits in this manner:

> Mr. Busch, we can provide you with a state-of-the-art seminar room that will seat 30 people comfortably and four smaller rooms for the workshops you have planned. Our staff will serve a noon lunch. The cost will be $195 per person, including the instructor's fees. Finally, we will see that each of your employees receives a pad of paper, a pen, and a copy of the conference program. Today I can reserve these facilities for November 24, which is your first preference for a meeting date. Can I go ahead and enter your reservation into our computer?

Notice that the salesperson has reviewed all the important elements of the value proposition and then asked a need-satisfaction question. This question is designed to move the sales process toward commitment and action.

assumptive close After the salesperson identifies a genuine need, presents solutions in terms of buyer benefits, conducts an effective sales demonstration, and negotiates buyer concerns satisfactorily, the salesperson assumes that the prospect has already made a buying decision.

ASSUMPTIVE CLOSE

When you use the **assumptive close**, you simply assume that the customer is going to buy. Kelley Robertson, author of *Stop, Ask, and Listen*, says, "This is one of the simplest and most effective closes since it places no emotional stress on the customer."[12]

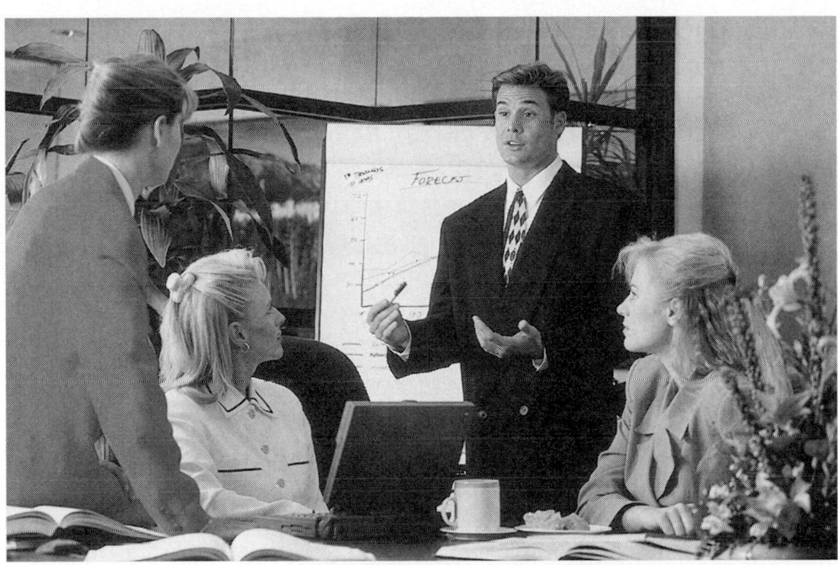

The assumptive close asks for a minor decision, assuming that the customer has decided to buy.

This closing approach comes near the end of the planned presentation. If you have identified a genuine need, presented your solutions in terms of buyer benefits, presented an effective sales demonstration, and negotiated buyer concerns satisfactorily, it may be natural to assume the person is ready to buy. The assumptive close usually takes the form of a question that focuses on a minor point. Here are some examples:

> If you feel the Model 211 gives you the major benefits you are looking for, let's schedule delivery for next Tuesday.

> Since our production systems provide you with the order fulfillment flexibility you require, let's go ahead and place your order.

Most customers will view either of these statements as the natural conclusion of the events that preceded it. Assumptive closes often include a benefit with your request for action.[13] This is a subtle way to ask for a decision when you are quite certain the customer has already decided to buy. You are only bringing the selling–buying process to a close.

SPECIAL CONCESSION CLOSE

The **special concession close** offers the buyer something extra for acting immediately. A special inducement is offered if the prospect will agree to sign the order. The concession may be part of a low-price strategy such as a sale price, a quantity discount, a more liberal credit plan, or an added feature that the prospect did not anticipate.

special concession close Offers the buyer something extra for acting immediately.

You should use this closing approach with care, because some customers are skeptical of concessions. This is especially true when the concession comes after the salesperson has made what appears to be the final offer.

Nicholas Graham, founder and chairman of Joe Boxer Corporation, spends considerable time presenting his novelty underwear line to retailers.

www.joeboxer.com

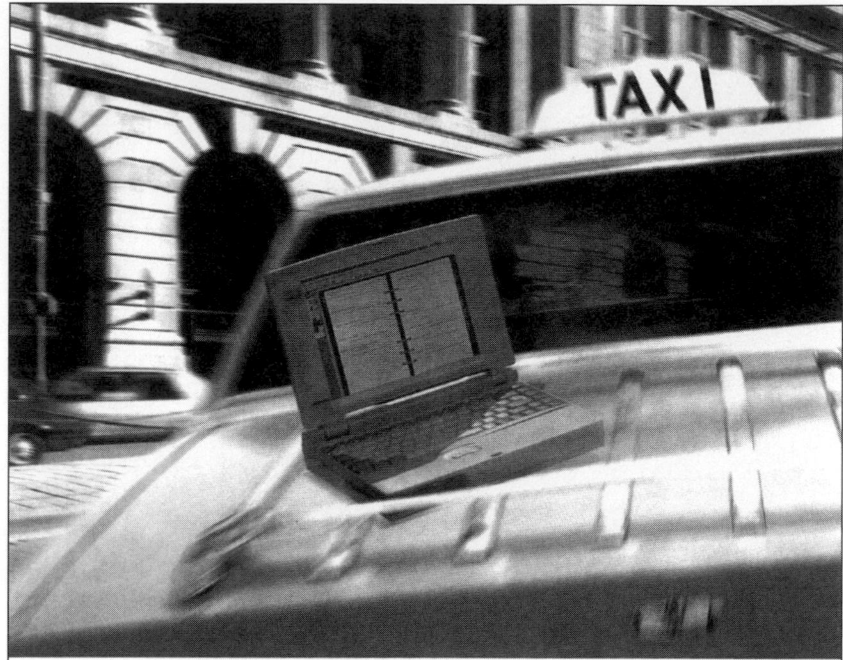

Take one of our notebooks for a test drive.

When you take a Toshiba for a spin, you'll see why more Canadians use our notebook computers than any other. We have a model to suit every need, budget and luggage rack. But, more importantly, Toshiba notebooks are packed with state-of-the-art technology and built to withstand business travel (even cab rides).
Toshiba notebooks. Tough enough for today's world.

TOSHIBA

1·800·387·5645
www.toshiba.ca

Instantaneous information can be very helpful in closing the sale. Toshiba's notebook computers offer salespeople easy access to information.

Graham recalls that one of his most difficult sales involved Saks Fifth Avenue, the prestigious department store company. He wanted the company to carry Joe Boxer underwear and suggested a Daniel Boone–inspired boxer with a detachable raccoon tail. Graham says, "They had never seen anything so absurd in their life." To close the sale, he let the store take 24 pairs on consignment. "They sold out in one hour," Graham says. Saks has been a committed customer ever since.[14]

MULTIPLE OPTIONS CLOSE

In many selling situations, it is a good idea to provide the prospect with options regarding product configuration, delivery options, and price. This is especially true when you are dealing with the price-conscious transactional buyer. As noted in the previous chapter, today's customer expects new levels of flexibility. In the **multiple options close**, allow the person to examine several different options and try to assess the degree of interest in each one. As you near the point where a close seems appropriate, remove some of the options. This will reduce confusion and indecision.

multiple options close When the salesperson gives the prospect several options to consider and tries to assess the prospect's degree of interest in each.

The multiple options technique is often used in office equipment sales. If a small business owner wants to purchase a copy machine, most vendors will offer several models for consideration. Let us assume that the prospect has examined four models and seems to be uncertain about which one would be the best choice. The salesperson might determine which copier is least appealing and eliminate it as an option. Now the prospect can choose among three copiers. If the prospect seems to favour one copier, it would be appropriate to ask for the order.

When using the multiple options close, follow these simple steps:

1. Configure more than one product solution.
2. Cease showing product options when it appears that the prospect has been given ample selection. Too many choices can result in confusion and indecision.
3. Remove products (or features) that the prospect does not seem genuinely interested in and concentrate on the options the prospect seems to be interested in.

BALANCE SHEET CLOSE

The **balance sheet close** appeals to customers who are having difficulty making a decision even though they have been given plenty of information. Let's assume that the customer feels he or she has a choice: buy now or buy later. The salesperson draws a T on a sheet of paper and writes the captions below on each side of the crossbar.

balance sheet close Is a visual way of showing the customer the reasons for making a decision now versus not making a decision now.

Reasons for buying now	Reasons for not buying now
1.	1.
2.	2.
3.	3.
4.	4.

To get the process rolling, the salesperson might say, "Let's see how many reasons we can list for buying now." On the left side of the T, the salesperson lists some reasons for buying now. These should be benefits in which the customer has already expressed an interest. On the right side, reasons for not buying now are listed. Throughout the listing process, the salesperson should engage the customer in a dialogue. This closing method will not be effective if the salesperson is doing all the talking.

MANAGEMENT CLOSE

management close A close that involves bringing the sales manager or senior management to the sales presentation as a way to help close a sale.

In previous chapters, we have discussed the merits of involving the sales manager or senior executives in sales calls. To close a major account, salespeople sometimes call on top management for help. This is the **management close**. Ryan Hegman, who works for Hegman Machine Tool Inc., recalls a sale that involved a $1.5 million automated manufacturing system. During the sales process, he brought in the president of the company, the vice-president of sales, and the lead engineer. "Each added value in a separate way," Ryan Hegman explains. One important reason to involve management is to make prospects feel your whole company's resources will be available to support the customer.[15]

DIRECT APPEAL CLOSE

direct appeal close Involves simply asking for the order in a straightforward manner.

The **direct appeal close** has the advantages of clarity and simplicity. This close involves simply asking for the order in a straightforward manner. It is the most direct closing approach, and many buyers find it attractive. Realistically, most customers expect salespeople to ask for the sale.

The direct appeal should not, of course, come too early. It should not be used until the prospect has displayed a definite interest in the product or service. The salesperson also must gain the prospect's respect before initiating this appeal. Once you make the direct appeal, stop talking. Raymond Slesinski, Digital Equipment sales trainer, tells his trainees, "After asking a closing question, do not speak, even if the prospect doesn't answer quickly." His advice is to give the prospect time to think about your offer.[16]

A variation of the direct appeal close involves using a question to determine how close the customer is to making a buying decision. The

EVERYONE SELLS

Once a Salesman...

Many of Canada's most successful salespeople have demonstrated their aptitude for selling at an early age. Greg Brophy, president and CEO of Oakville, Ontario–based Shred-it, started a lawn-watering business when he was in elementary school. In high school, he started a driveway-sealing business with his brother and went door-to-door in the evenings selling the service. In university, he bought and sold real estate. Following graduation from McMaster University, Greg Brophy started Shred-it, a company that now employs more than 2200 people at 130 branches in 13 countries on 5 continents. Shred-it has more than 150 000 customers, including *Fortune* 500 companies, hospitals, banks, and government departments and agencies.

In the early days of the company, Greg was both president and salesperson. As the company grew, he was able to coach new salespeople how to sell Shred-it service. Today, Greg Brophy still sees himself fulfilling an important sales role. Greg Brophy says, "I still consider myself very much a salesperson and really enjoy the interaction with potential clients."[b]

question might be "How close are we to closing the sale?" This direct question calls for a direct answer. The customer is encouraged to reflect on the progress of the sale.[17]

COMBINATION CLOSE

In some cases the most effective close is a **combination close** that combines two or more of the closing methods we have discussed. To illustrate, let us observe Colleen White as she attempts to close a sale in the office of a buyer for a large department store. Colleen represents a firm that manufactures a wide range of leather clothing and accessories. Near the end of her planned presentation she senses that the prospect is quite interested in her products but seems reluctant to make a decision. This is how she handles the close:

combination close When the salesperson tries to use two or more closing methods at the same time.

> Ms. Taylor, I have described two benefits that seem especially important to you. First, you agree that this line will be popular with the fashion-conscious shoppers your store caters to. Second, you indicated that the prices I quoted will allow you excellent profit margins. If we process your order now, you will have the merchandise in time for the pre–Christmas buying period. We can guarantee the delivery at this point.

Notice that this close starts with a summary of benefits and ends with a special concession.

Practise Closing

Your success in selling will depend in large part on learning how to make these eight closing methods work for you. You will not master these approaches in a few days or a few weeks, but you can speed up the learning process with preparation and practice. Role-playing is the best-known way to experience the feelings that accompany closing, and to practise the skills needed to close sales. To prepare the role play, anticipate various closing scenarios and then prepare a written script.[18] Find someone (e.g., your sales manager, friend, or spouse) to play the role of the customer and give that person a script to act out. Practise the role play in front of a video recorder, and then assess your performance for ways to improve your closing technique. The video monitor provides excellent feedback. Use the closing worksheet (see Fig. 14.3) to prepare for practice sessions.

Confirming the Partnership When the Buyer Says Yes

Congratulations! You have closed the sale and have established the beginning of what you hope will be a long and satisfying partnership with the customer. Before preparing to leave, be sure that all details related to the purchase agreement are completed. Check everything with the buyer, and then ask for a signature if necessary.

Once the sale has been closed, it is important to take time to reassure the customer. This is the **confirmation step** in closing the sale. Before you leave, reassure the customer by pointing out that he or she has made the correct

confirmation step Reassuring the customer after the sale has been closed, pointing out that he or she has made the correct decision. This may involve describing the satisfaction of owning the product.

decision, and describe the satisfaction that will come with ownership of the product. The reason for doing this is to resell the buyer and to prevent buyer's remorse. **Buyer's remorse** (sometimes called *cognitive dissonance*) is an emotional response that can take various forms such as feelings of regret, fear, or anxiety.[19] It's common to wonder whether we have made the right decision. Compliment the customer for making a wise decision. Once the sale is closed, the customer may be required to justify the purchase to others. Your words of reassurance will be helpful.

buyer's remorse Feelings of regret, fear, or anxiety that a buyer may feel after placing an order.

Before leaving, thank the customer for the order. This is very important. Everyone likes to think that a purchase is appreciated. No one should believe that a purchase is taken for granted. Even a small order deserves words of appreciation. In many cases a follow-up thank you letter is appropriate.

In several previous chapters we said that a satisfied customer is one of the best sources of new prospects. Never hesitate to ask, "Do you know anyone else who might benefit from owning this product?" or a similar question. Some customers may even agree to write an introductory letter on your behalf.

What to Do When the Buyer Says No

High-performance salespeople learn to manage disappointment. A strong display of disappointment or resentment is likely to close the door to future sales. Losing a sale may be painful, but it can also be a valuable learning opportunity. Doing some analysis of what went wrong can help you change the outcome of future sales. Here are some things you should do after a lost sale.[20]

1. *Make sure the deal is really dead.* There is always a chance that the prospect's decision can be changed. You might want to mount a last-ditch effort and reopen the presentation.

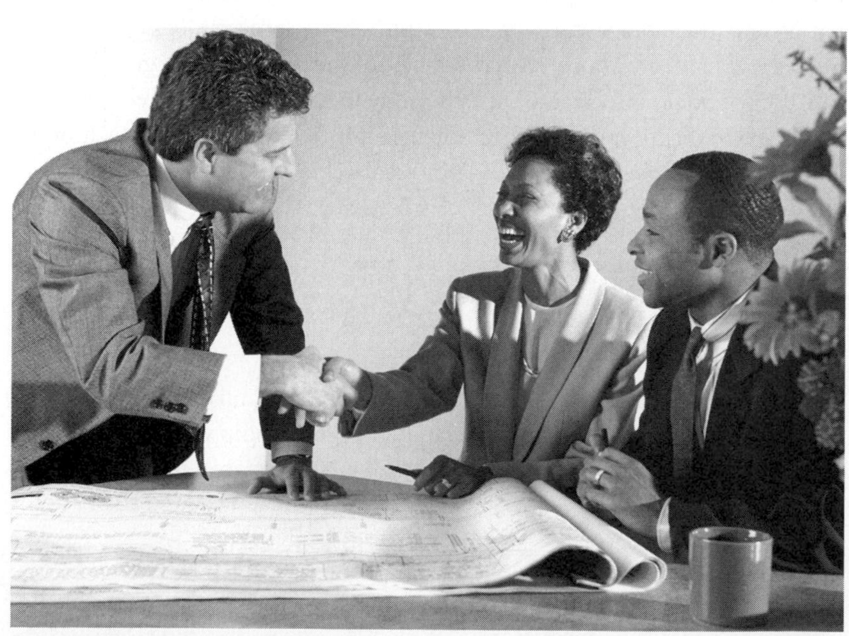

When the customer says Yes, take a few moments to express appreciation and to congratulate the person for making a wise decision.

2. *Review the chain of events.* When you experience a no-sale call, try to benefit from the experience. If you were part of a sales team, get each member's reaction. Soon after the prospect says No, schedule a debriefing session. If you worked alone, engage in honest self-analysis. If you carefully look at your performance during every aspect of the sales process, you may be able to identify weaknesses that can be corrected.
3. *Interview the customer.* Obtaining feedback requires a delicate approach. If you probe too aggressively, you may appear argumentative. If your approach is too passive, and the client's comments are general, you will not know how to improve. The key is to couch your questions in neutral terms. Rather than asking "Why didn't we get the order?" try this approach: "Thank you for considering our company. We hope to do business with you at some time in the future. Would you mind helping me understand any shortcomings in our sales proposal?"

Always keep the door open for future sales. Tell the prospect you would love to work with him or her at some time in the future. Then, put this person back on your prospect list, record any new information you have learned about the prospect, and continue to keep in touch.

PREPARE THE PROSPECT FOR CONTACT WITH THE COMPETITION

Some prospects refuse to buy because they want to take a close look at the competing products. This response is not unusual in the field of selling. You should do everything possible to help the customer make an intelligent comparison. It is always a good practice to review your product's strong points one more time. Give special emphasis to areas in which your product has a superior advantage over the competition. Make it easy for the person to buy your product at some future date.

CUSTOMER RELATIONSHIP MANAGEMENT WITH TECHNOLOGY

Adding and Deleting Prospects

Prospect and customer databases are continually changing. Promotions, transfers, mergers, and many other events require additions and deletions to a salesperson's automated data. Most CRM software makes this an easy process and warns users against the inadvertent removal of an account. (See the exercise Adding and Deleting Prospects on page 348 for more information.)

SUMMARY

Prior to the introduction of consultative selling and the partnering era, closing was often presented as the most important aspect of the sales process. Some of the early closing methods encouraged manipulation of the customer. Use of any closing method that is perceived by the customer as pushy or manipulative will damage your chances of building a long-term partnership. For consultative selling, closing should be perceived as part of the sales process and part of building a long-term relationship with the buyer.

The salesperson must be alert to closing clues from the prospect. These clues fall into two categories: verbal and nonverbal. Verbal clues are the easiest to recognize, but some may be subtle. Here again it is important to be an attentive listener. The recognition of nonverbal clues is more difficult, but practice in careful observation will help in detecting them.

Several closing methods may be necessary to get the prospect to make a buying decision; therefore, it is wise for the salesperson to preplan several closes. Eight were described in this chapter: trial, summary-of-benefits, assumptive, special concession, multiple options, balance sheet, management, and direct appeal. The salesperson customizes the appropriate closing method to fit the product and type of buyer for each sale. In some selling situations the use of a combination of closes is very effective.

The professional salesperson is not discouraged or offended if the sale is not closed. Every effort should be made to be of further assistance to the prospect; the sale might be closed on another call. Even if the salesperson loses the sale, he or she can gain valuable experience by analyzing the loss to learn from it.

Key Terms

Assumptive Close **338**

Balance Sheet Close **341**

Buyer's Remorse **344**

Closing Clue **335**

Combination Close **343**

Confirmation Step **343**

Direct Appeal Close **342**

Incremental Commitment **332**

Management Close **342**

Multiple Options Close **341**

Special Concession Close **339**

Summary-of-Benefits Close **337**

Trial Close **336**

Review Questions

1. List some aspects of the sales presentation that can make closing and confirming the sale difficult to achieve.
2. Describe three buying anxieties that sometimes serve as barriers to closing the sale.
3. What guidelines should a salesperson follow for closing the sale?
4. Why is it important to review the value proposition from the prospect's point of view?
5. What three verbal clues can the prospect use to indicate that it is time to close the sale? For what nonverbal clues should the salesperson be alert?
6. Explain how the multiple options close might be used in the sale of men's and women's suits.

7. Is there a best method to use in closing the sale? Explain.
8. What is meant by a trial close? When should a salesperson attempt a trial close?
9. Explain the summary-of-benefits close.
10. What confirming steps should a salesperson follow when the customer says Yes? What should be done when the customer says No?

Application Exercises

1. Which of the following statements, often made by prospects, would you interpret as buying signals?
    a. "How much would the payments be?"
    b. "Tell me about your service department."
    c. "The company already has an older model that seems good enough."
    d. "We do not have enough cash flow right now."
    e. "How much would you allow me for my old model?"
    f. "I do not need one."
    g. "How does that switch work?"
    h. "When would I have to pay for it?"
2. You are an accountant who owns and operates an accounting service. You have been contacted by the president of an advertising agency about the possibility of you auditing her business on a regular basis. The president has indicated that she investigated other accounting firms and thinks that they price their services too high. With the knowledge you have about the other firms, you know you are in a strong competitive position. Also, you realize her account would be profitable for your firm. You really would like to capture this account. How will you close the deal? List and describe two closing methods you might use in this situation.
3. Zig Ziglar, Brian Tracy, and Tom Hopkins are well-known authors and speakers on the subject of closing the sale, Access each of their Web sites by using **www.[their name].com** and research the books, courses, and videos they have available for companies and individuals to purchase and learn more about closing the sale. Prepare a summary of what you find available. Does the material in this chapter parallel the kind of information these individuals present?

ROLE-PLAY EXERCISE

Examine the superior benefits of the convention centre identified in Partnership Selling on the CD-ROM. Specifically research the qualities of the five-star executive chef, the award-winning renovation of the facility, the cost of parking and transportation to and from the airport, and the easy access on and off the location relative to the highway. You should assume the role of director of sales and, with this information, prepare a closing worksheet on the combination of summary-of-benefits and direct appeal closes for a prospective customer. Also, using this information from the audiovisual presentation guide, prepare a special concession close, allowing free use of the laser pointer and wireless microphone with a value of $107.50 for a group presentation to the 23 people who will be staying in single rooms at the hotel. Role-play the close of a sale using these closing methods to another student role-playing a prospect who is also seriously considering using one of your competitors.

CRM Application Exercise ADDING AND DELETING PROSPECTS

Adding and deleting contacts is easy with the ACT! software, as it is with most CRM software. Create a contact record for B. H. Rivera by selecting Edit, New Contact or by pressing the Insert key. (This key is Ins on some keyboards.) This will display a blank record that can be completed by selecting fields with the mouse or by using the Tab key to move from field to field. In the Company field, type "Graphic Forms" and type 3195556194 (no hyphens) into the Phone field. "2134 Martin Luther King" is the address, and the city, state, and zip code are Atlanta, GA, and 61740.

Most CRM software permits you to save time and avoid errors by selecting field data from menus. For example, point at the ID/Status field label and double-click with your mouse on the label, not the field. A menu of choices should appear. Another way to obtain this menu is to place the cursor in the field and press the F2 function key. From this menu, select Prospect as the ID/Status for the B. H. Rivera record.

You have just added a new record to the ACT! database. The demonstration version of the ACT! software limits the number of contacts to 25. The full version of ACT! has no such limit. Do not enter more than 25 contacts into this demonstration version. Print this new record by selecting Report, Contact Report, Active Contact, Printer, and OK.

To remove a contact, select Edit, Delete Contact. The window is displayed with a box for Contact, Lookup, and Cancel. Picking Contact will cause the individual record to be deleted, Lookup will delete all records currently being looked up, and Cancel will terminate the procedure without making changes. Choosing to delete a record will cause a warning window to be displayed. This window asks if you are sure that you wish to delete the contact. Caution is advised when deleting records or using the delete function. Press the F1 function key to display the appropriate help screen.

Case Problem

Ruan and Clark Distributing is a respected wholesale-broker of building products, including a quality line of carpeting. Three years ago, Bob Thompson graduated from college and accepted a sales position with Ruan and Clark as the representative for the carpet line.

During the past six months Bob has been calling on Woodside Building and Supply Company, one of the firms in his territory. Woodside already carries carpet lines from several of Bob's competitors. Woodside dominates its trading area in several product lines, including carpet. Bob has called on the buyer, Jim Cooney, four times. However, he has not been able to close the sale. Recently, Ruan and Clark took on a new line of carpet that Bob felt offered his dealers an excellent buy.

In calling on Woodside for the fifth time, Bob decided to use the new product line to try to close the sale. The following sales presentation took place:

Bob: Hello, Jim. It's good to see you.

Jim: [In a warm, friendly tone of voice] Good to see you again, Bob, but I'll tell you right up front, I don't have a budget to buy additional goods! I would like to find out what you have but, even if you gave me a roll of carpet, I wouldn't be able to find a place here to store it.

Bob: I'm sorry to hear that, because we have just added another product line that we think is going to revolutionize the carpet industry. [Bob shows Jim a sample of the new line—a toast colour with alternating rows of cut and uncut yarn.] Our carpet mill took the popular traditional candy stripe, built it up to a higher quality, and changed its styling to appeal to more of your customers. In short, with this new toast-coloured, 10-year-guaranteed carpet you will no longer have to compete with your competitors on the same product. This will give your salespeople a strong competitive advantage in their sales presentation. Our sales forecasting indicates that, within 12 months, this new product will take over 25 percent of the traditional market.

Jim: Bob, this is an appealing line.

Bob: [Handing the sample to Jim] Because of our mill's innovation in construction you get a much better feel in the surface yarns, don't you?
Jim: Yes, it does feel good.
Bob: This construction feature, along with the improved rubber backing, will give your customers a better-quality piece of goods. In addition, Jim, the mill has been able to hold the price on these goods to a competitive level. What do you think of it?
Jim: [Inspecting the goods a second time] I like it, Bob, but as I said before —
Bob: [Breaking in and focusing on the space problem] Jim, I can appreciate your space problem, but I am in a position to ship you as little as one roll now, so you can get into the market immediately and find out how well this product is suited for your situation.
Jim: [Showing more interest] Well, I would like to try it, but I just cannot see how I can do it today.
Bob: That is too bad, Jim, because we are running this new line at a special introductory price. The regular price on these goods is $8.99 a metre, but we are introducing it at $6.99. [Bob feels he now has Jim wanting the goods. However, he thinks Jim may want to put the sale off until later.]
Jim: That is a good price, Bob, but I am just—
Bob: [Interrupting Jim] Also, we will pay the freight at $6.99, which will save you an additional 15 percent. [Bob really wants to open the Woodside account because of the high sales Woodside will experience and the future profitability his company will achieve. Under any other circumstances he would not have offered to pay the freight at this price.]
Jim: [In a quiet voice] That sure sounds like something I should take advantage of.

Questions

1. Based on the information given, do you think this sale can be closed?
2. Assume you are Bob. After Jim's last comment, which close would you use next? Why?
3. What appeared to be the major obstacle to closing this sale?
4. Did Jim give any closing clues? Identify them.
5. Did Bob use any trial closes? Identify them.
6. What did you like and what did you dislike about the way Bob attempted to close this sale?

CRM Case Study FORECASTING THE CLOSE

You are interested in discovering what your commissions may be for the next few months from Pat Silva's former accounts. To do this, you will review the information on each contact record. There are four fields on the first page of the Contact screen from which you can forecast your expected sales: Network Need, Likelihood, Dollar Amount, and Date Close. When working with these accounts, Pat entered the information found in each of these fields: in the Network Need field, Pat entered the type of network that the prospect might order; in the Likelihood field, Pat estimated the percentage of possibility that the account might place an order (0.80 means 80 percent); the Dollar Amount field refers to how much Pat thought the account would spend; the month Pat felt they would order is in the Date Close field (01/31 means January 31).

You can estimate each month's likely sales by multiplying the number in the Dollar Amount field times the percentage in the Likelihood field. An 80 percent chance of an estimated sale worth $100 000 is a forecast of $80 000 in sales. If the Date Close field for several accounts is the same, for example 12/31, you can calculate the sales for that month (December) by totalling the forecasts for each account. For an estimate of your commission income, multiply each month's forecast by 10 percent.

Pat did not show that any forecast sales were 100 percent. Pat recognized that the sales might not close, the amount anticipated in the Dollar Amount field might not be achieved, and the close might not take place during the month projected. Pat knew that these transactions would not close themselves; certain steps would have to be taken to increase the possibility that the prospect would place an order. To collect your commissions, you have to discover the steps most likely to close these sales.

Questions

1. What would your commission income be for all Pat's accounts if you closed them as Pat forecast?
2. What kind of special concession might be necessary to close the sale with Quality Builders?
3. What kind of close may be necessary to get an order from Computerized Labs?
4. What kind of close would be appropriate for the Lakeside Clinic?

Partnership Selling

A ROLE PLAY/SIMULATION **(see Partnership Selling on the CD-ROM, pp. 40–41)**

DEVELOPING A SALES PRESENTATION STRATEGY—CLOSING THE SALE

Refer to *Sales Memorandum 3* and strategically plan to close the sale with your customer. To consider the sale closed you will need to secure the signature of your customer on the sales proposal form. This will guarantee your customer the accommodations listed on the form. These accommodations may change depending on the final number of people attending your customer's convention. This is an important point to keep in mind when closing the sale; however, you still must get the signature to guarantee the accommodations.

Follow the instructions carefully, and prepare a closing worksheet listing at least four closes using the methods outlined in this chapter. Two of these methods should be the summary of benefits and the direct appeal. Remember that it is not the policy of your convention centre to cut prices, so your methods should include value-added strategies.

Use proof devices to make your closes more convincing, and place them in the front pocket of your three-ring binder/portfolio for easy access during your presentation. You may want to ask another person to be your customer and practise the closing strategies you have developed.

CHAPTER 15

Servicing the Sale

AND BUILDING THE PARTNERSHIP

Toronto-based Aware Marketing Group is "wowing" its customers. Every 90 days, it introduces a new "wow" service. An example of a "wow" is a promise to return every voice-mail message within 90 minutes or the customer gets the next order setup free, a $40 value. Chief visionary officer Craig Morantz says, "That $40 is the best $40 I've spent because they then tell everybody in their office and it gets promoted within their own company." Another "wow" is confirming to customers when their orders are shipped. Customers get a fax that tells them when the shipment left and how much the shipment will cost, and that provides a courier tracking number. This service is not only popular with customers, it saves time and money for Aware Marketing Group. Morantz says that the average order involves approximately 10 phone calls from customers, many asking if their order has been shipped. This service reduces those calls, and is an example of how outstanding service after a sale can benefit both buyers and sellers.[1]

LEARNING OBJECTIVES

After studying this chapter, you should be able to

1. Explain how to build long-term partnerships with customer service
2. Describe current developments in customer service
3. List and describe the major customer service methods that add value to the partnership
4. Explain how to work effectively with customer support personnel
5. Explain how to deal effectively with complaints

Building Long-Term Partnerships with Customer Service

In a world of increased global competition and narrowing profit margins, customer retention through value-based initiatives can mean the difference between increasing or eroding market share. Progressive marketers are searching for ways to differentiate their service from competitors and build emotional loyalty through value.[2]

customer service All those activities that enhance or facilitate the sale and use of a product or service, including expansion selling, delivery and installation, assistance with the warranty or service contract, securing credit arrangements, and making postsale courtesy calls.

Customer service can be defined as those activities that enhance or facilitate the purchase and use of the product (see Fig. 15.1). A sales organization that can develop a reputation for servicing each sale is sought out by customers who want a long-term partner to help them with their buying needs. Satisfied customers represent an auxiliary sales force—a group of people who will recommend customer-driven organizations to others. If customers are pleased with the service they receive after the sale, be assured that they will tell other people. Recent research shows that, when someone experiences good customer service, he or she tells an average of six people; when someone experiences outstanding customer service, he or she tells twice as many.[3]

ACHIEVING SUCCESSIVE SALES

We previously defined *partnering* as a strategically developed, long-term relationship that solves the customer's problem. A successful partnering effort results in successive sales and referrals (see Fig. 1.4).

Many of today's large companies want to partner with suppliers who sell and deliver quality products and services that continually improve their processes and profits. The first sale is only the beginning of the relation-

Figure 15.1 Servicing the sale involves three steps: follow-through, follow-up calls, and expansion selling.

The Six-Step Presentation Plan	
Step One: APPROACH	✓ Review Strategic/Consultative Selling Model ✓ Initiate customer contact
Step Two: PRESENTATION	✓ Determine prospect needs ✓ Select solution ✓ Initiate sales presentation
Step Three: DEMONSTRATION	✓ Decide what to demonstrate ✓ Select selling tools ✓ Initiate demonstration
Step Four: NEGOTIATION	✓ Anticipate buyer concerns ✓ Plan negotiating methods ✓ Initiate win-win negotiations
Step Five: CLOSE	✓ Plan appropriate closing methods ✓ Recognize closing clues ✓ Initiate closing methods
Step Six: SERVICING THE SALE	Follow-through Follow-up calls Expansion selling
Service, retail, wholesale, and manufacturer selling.	

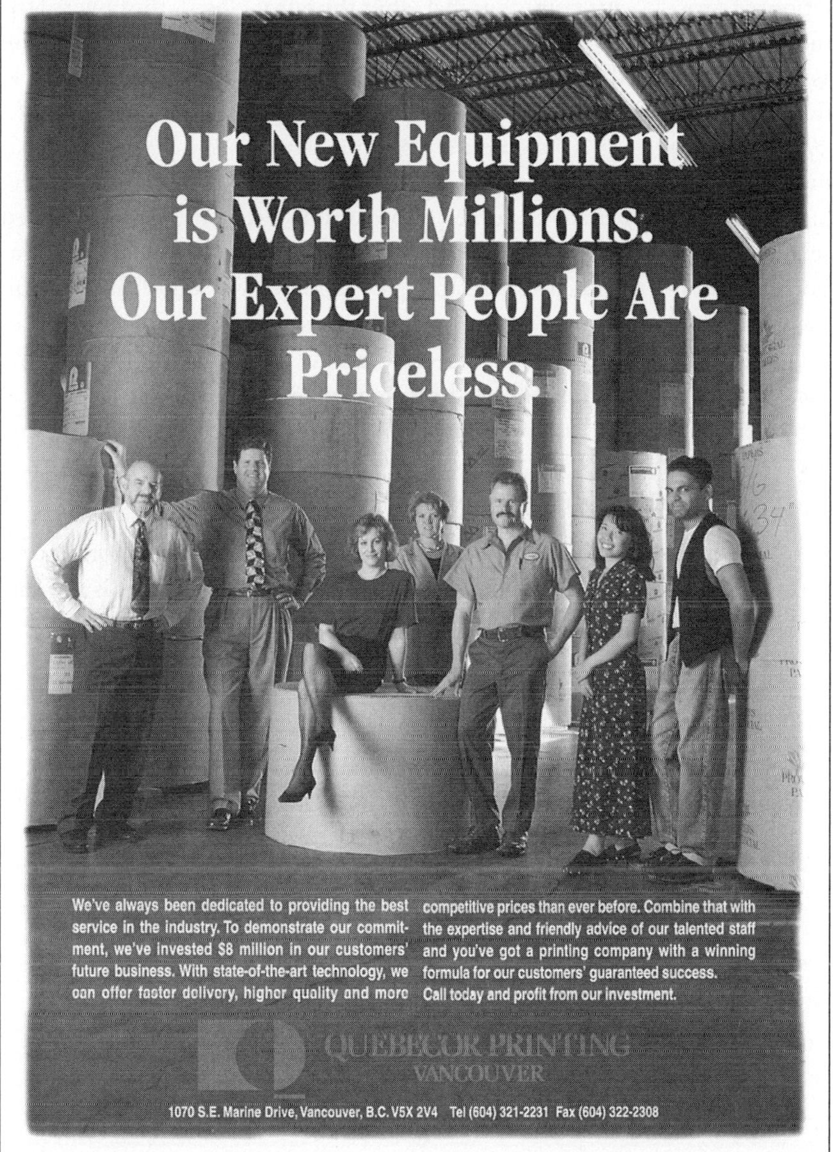

Our New Equipment is Worth Millions. Our Expert People Are Priceless.
We've always been dedicated to providing the best service in the industry. To demonstrate our commitment, we've invested $8 million in our customers' future business. With state-of-the-art technology, we can offer faster delivery, higher quality and more competitive prices than ever before. Combine that with the expertise and friendly advice of our talented staff and you've got a printing company with a winning formula for our customers' guaranteed success. Call today and profit from our investment.
QUEBECOR PRINTING
VANCOUVER
1070 S.E. Marine Drive, Vancouver, B.C. V5X 2V4 Tel (604) 321-2231 Fax (604) 322-2308

Some companies, such as Quebecor Printing, recognize that customer service is an excellent way to achieve a competitive advantage in a highly competitive market, and that people are important in maintaining service quality.

www.quebecorworldinc.com

ship—an opportunity to earn a repeat sale. Repeat sales come after the supplier demonstrates the ability to add value in various ways.[4] This value may take the form of timely delivery, superior installation, accurate invoicing, technical know-how, social contacts, or something else that is important to the customer. In business-to-business sales, the relationship should intensify as the supplier delivers extensive postsale support.

RESPONDING TO INCREASED POSTSALE CUSTOMER EXPECTATIONS

According to Ted Levitt, author of *The Marketing Imagination*, people buy expectations, not things. They buy the expectations of benefits that salespeople like you promised. Once the customer buys your product, expectations increase. Levitt points out that, after the sale is closed, the buyer's attitude changes. The buyer expects the salesperson to remember the purchase as a favour bestowed on him or her by the buyer. Nitin Nohria, business professor and co-author of *What Really Works: The 4-2 Formula for Sustained Business Success*, says, "Customers are enormously punishing when companies don't meet their expectations."[5]

Fulfilling increased customer expectations after the sale is closed requires a strategic plan for servicing the sale. Certain aspects of the relationship, product, and customer strategies can have a positive influence on the customer's heightened expectations. In most business-to-business sales the salesperson cannot service the sale alone. To properly manage the account, the salesperson will need assistance from the shipping, technical support, engineering, and other departments. Customer service is increasingly a team effort.

How do you respond to a customer who has increased expectations?

- *First, you should be certain your customer strategy is on target.* You must fully understand the needs and wants of the customer. What is the customer trying to accomplish, and how can you help the person do it better?
- *Second, you should focus like a laser beam on follow-through and follow-up activities.* Throughout every sales presentation, the salesperson will offer assurances and make some promises. The salesperson's credibility will be tarnished if any of these commitments are ignored.
- *Third, you should re-examine your product strategy.* In some cases you can enhance customer satisfaction by suggesting related products or services. If the product is expensive, you can follow through and offer assistance in making credit arrangements. If the product is complex, you can make suggestions concerning use and maintenance. Each of these forms of assistance may add value to the sale.

SELLING MENTOR

Job Searches Require Widening the Net

You have a good education but you don't have a job. This scenario is being played out in the lives of thousands of people throughout Canada. Before you send out another thousand résumés via the Internet or spend more time searching the net for employment opportunities, consider the results of a study conducted by Drake Beam Morin (DBM), a workplace-consulting firm. Networking is the top tactic for landing a job, outpacing other strategies such as the Internet and newspaper ads. The report indicates that 66 percent of DBM clients found new jobs via networking, whereas just 6 percent found employment through the Internet. Don't overlook the value of personal contact that gives you the opportunity to sell yourself.[a]

THE HIGH COST OF CUSTOMER ATTRITION

Financial institutions, public utilities, airlines, retail stores, restaurants, manufacturers, and wholesalers face the problem of gaining and retaining the patronage of clients and customers. These companies realize that keeping a customer happy is a good strategy. To regain a lost customer can be four to five times more expensive than keeping a current customer satisfied.[6]

There is no longer any doubt that poor service is the primary cause of customer attrition. Surprisingly few customers (12 to 15 percent) are lost because of product dissatisfaction. No more than 10 to 15 percent of lost customers leave because of price considerations. Some studies have found that from 50 to 70 percent of customer attrition is because of poor service.[7] A carefully developed strategic plan to reduce customer defection will pay big dividends.

Harry Rosen, president of Harry Rosen Gentlemen's Apparel, fully embraces the customer-for-life philosophy of doing business. Rosen's obsession with customer service has enabled the store to expand to several Canadian cities, and Harry Rosen now has a licensing agreement with Hugo Boss to open 20 boutiques in the United States over the next few years. Rosen says, "We don't look at a person that walks into our store as an immediate sale. We look at him with a potential lifetime value."[8]

www.harryrosen.com

Current Developments in Customer Service

In his book *Business @ the Speed of Thought*, Bill Gates predicts that, in this millennium, customer service will become the primary value-added function.[9] He recognizes that customer service is the primary method of building and extending the partnership. Customer service, in its many forms,

Bill Gates, author of *Business @ the Speed of Thought*, predicts that, in the new economy, customer service may become the primary value-added function.

nourishes the partnership and keeps it alive. The age of information has ushered in a series of customer service initiatives that affect the daily work of salespeople. We will discuss three of these current developments.

www.eastman.com

- *Salespeople must spend more time monitoring customer satisfaction.* There is a growing trend in which companies rely on their salespeople to continually monitor their customers' needs, concerns, and future plans. In the past many salespeople would live or die by the number of sales closed, and too little attention was given to service after the sale. Eastman Chemical Company provides a good example of a company that involves its salespeople in the customer service process. Eastman developed the "customer advocacy" program, which is designed to objectively measure customer satisfaction levels and give salespeople the responsibility for improving and maintaining that performance. Members of the sales force conduct ongoing surveys to assess levels of customer satisfaction. The survey form is delivered by a salesperson who emphasizes the importance of helping Eastman improve sales and service performance.[10]

  Salespeople who have frequent contact with the customer are in an excellent position to assess the health of the relationship. Mack Hanan, author of *Consultative Selling*, encourages salespeople to seek answers to several questions:[11] Is the customer still growing because of your products and your expertise? How much more growth can take place in the future? How much is the partner growing you? In other words, is your company benefiting enough from the partnership? The more important the partnership is to both the seller and the buyer, the more important will be the answers to these questions.

- *Customer knowledge is viewed by sales and support personnel as an important key to improving customer service.* Bob Johnson, vice-president of Information Technology Services Marketing Association, says the ability to manage your customer knowledge is the number one lesson for anyone who wants to build customer loyalty: "If you can't capture, manage and leverage customer history (as well as information regarding current and future needs), you can forget about loyalty. Limited knowledge management capability fosters the sense that the company has no real interest in the customer—or his repeat patronage."[12]

  www.cphotels.ca

  Once you acquire knowledge about your customer, you can tailor your customer service initiatives for them. Canadian Pacific (CP) Hotels found that business travellers valued recognition of their individual quirks and preferences, and it began a frequent-guest club to customize service. For example, customers could state their preference for bed size, or even a specific drink in their mini-bar, and CP Hotels would ensure they got it. Following implementation of this program, CP Hotels saw its share of business travel grow by 16 percent in a year that the market as a whole grew by only 3 percent. Much of the growth was because of increased customer loyalty, as many club members stopped spreading their business among competing hotels.[13]

- *Customer-friendly, computer-based systems will frequently be used to enhance customer service.* Computers give both the salesperson and the customer ready access to information and problem-solving alternatives. In the future, human involvement in service will shift from routine, low-value tasks to a high-value, personal consultancy on important customer problems or desires.[14] We will see greater use of technology to gather information on unhappy customers, and technology will quickly deliver this information to people who can deal with the problem.

Customer Service Methods That Strengthen the Partnership

Customer service encompasses all activities that enhance or facilitate the sale and use of one's product or service. The skills required to service a sale are different from those required prior to the sale (see Fig. 15.2). High-performance sales personnel do not abdicate responsibility for delivery, installation, and warranty interpretation, or other customer service responsibilities. They continue to strengthen the partnership with follow-through, follow-up, and expansion selling.

ADDING VALUE WITH FOLLOW-THROUGH

A major key to an effective customer service strategy is follow-through on assurances and promises that were part of the sales presentation. Did your sales presentation include claims for superior performance; promises of speedy delivery; assistance with credit arrangements; guaranteed factory assistance with installation, training, and service?

Most sales presentations are made up of claims and promises that the company can fulfill. However, fulfillment of these claims will depend to a

Figure 15.2 The completed Consultative Sales Presentation Guide illustrates the ways in which high-performance salespeople use value-added strategies to service the sale and build repeat business and referrals. Customer service provides many opportunities to strengthen the partnership.

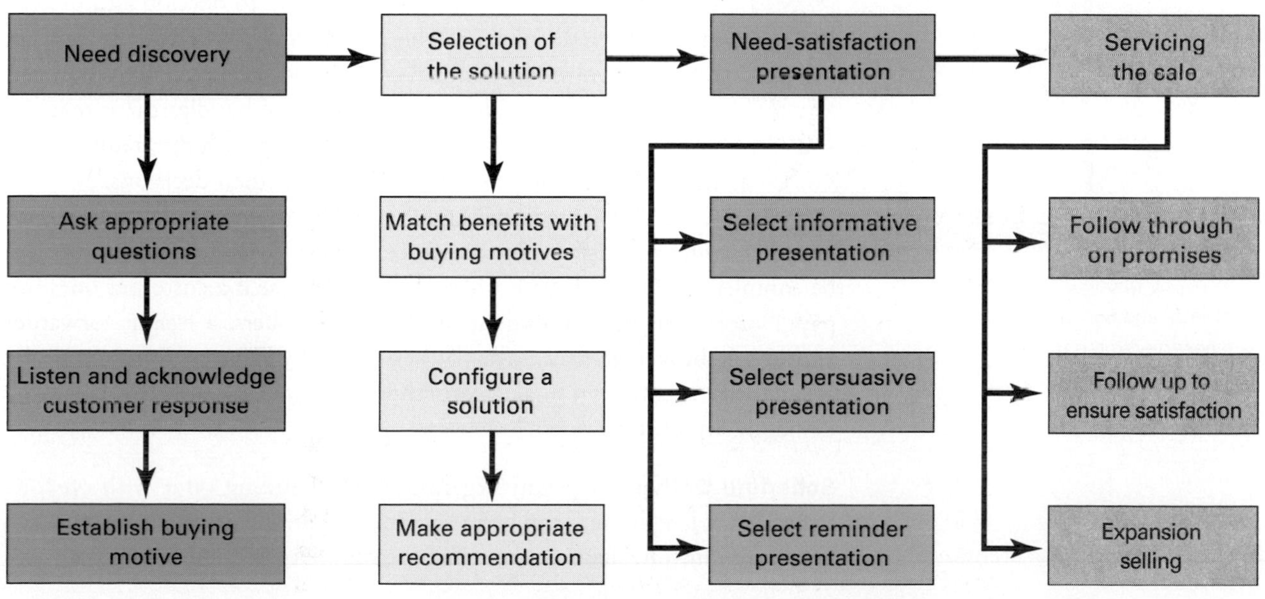

THE CUSTOMER'S PERSPECTIVE

The Moment of Magic

Tony Alessandra is a well-known sales trainer and consultant (**www.alessandra.com**). He says that there are three possible outcomes when a customer does business with an organization:

The moment of truth. In these selling situations, the customer's expectations were met. Nothing happened to disappoint the customer, nor did the salesperson do anything to surpass the customer's expectations. The customer is apt to have somewhat neutral feelings about his or her relationship with the salesperson. The moment of truth will usually not build customer loyalty.

The moment of misery. This is the outcome of a selling situation where the customer's expectations were not met. The customer may feel a sense of disappointment or even anger. Many customers who experience the moment of misery will share their feelings with others and often make a decision to "fire" the salesperson.

The moment of magic. This is the outcome of a sale where the customer received more than he or she expected. The salesperson surpassed the customer's expectations by going the extra mile and providing a level of service that added value to the customer–salesperson relationship. This extra effort is likely to establish a foundation for increased customer loyalty.[b]

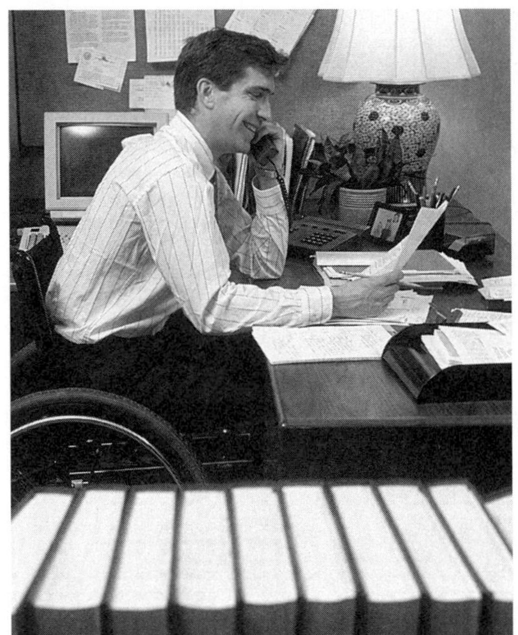

A follow-up phone call to thank the customer and find out if he or she is pleased with the product will strengthen the relationship after the sale.

large degree on after-sale action. Postsale follow-through is the key to holding that customer you worked so hard to develop.

Common Postsale Services

The first sale can be the beginning of a long-term partnership or it can be the last sale. The following services can help ensure a second sale and successive sales.

Make Credit Arrangements. Credit has become a common way to finance purchases. This is true of industrial products, real estate, automobiles, home appliances, and many other products. Closing the sale will often depend on your ability to develop and present attractive credit plans to the customer. Even if you do not get directly involved in the firm's credit and collection activities, you must be familiar with how the company handles these matters. Salespeople need to establish a relationship with the credit department and learn how credit analysts make their decisions.[15]

Making credit decisions gets a lot tougher when you are conducting business in foreign countries. Overseas transactions can be complex, and in some cases there is little recourse if a customer does not pay. Doron Weissman, president of Overseas Brokers, a freight forwarder and export brokerage firm, says, "When I sell my services, I automatically qualify the account to make sure they're financially able to meet my demands. If not, I move on."[16]

Schedule Deliveries. Many organizations are adding value with on-time deliveries. A late delivery can be a problem for both the supplier and the customer. To illustrate, let us assume that the supplier is a manufacturer of small appliances and the customer is a department store chain. A late delivery may mean lost sales because of out-of-stock conditions, cancellation of the order by the department store, or loss of future sales.

The causes of late delivery may be beyond your control. It is your responsibility, however, to keep the customer informed of any delays. You can also take steps to prevent a delay. Check to be sure your order was processed correctly. Follow up to see if the order was shipped on time. Always remember: "Every time an order is handled, the customer is handled. Every time an order sits unattended, the customer sits unattended."[17]

Be present during delivery. When the first delivery is made, be there to be sure the customer is comfortable with the purchase. Check to determine if the order is complete and be available to offer assistance.[18]

Monitor Installation. Buyer satisfaction is often related to proper installation of the product. This is true of consumer products such as security systems, central air-conditioning, solar heating systems, and carpeting. It is also true of industrial products such as electronic data processing equipment and air quality control systems. Some salespeople believe it is to their advantage to supervise product installation; they are then able to spot installation problems. Others make it a practice to follow up on the installation to be sure no problems exist.

Offer Training in the Use or Care of the Product. For certain industries it is essential that users be trained in how to use the new product. This is true of factory equipment, electronic cash registers, farm implements, and a host of other products. Technology has become so complex that many suppliers must provide training as part of the follow-up to ensure customer satisfaction. Most organizations that sell computers and other types of electronic equipment for office use now schedule training classes to ensure that customers can properly use and care for the products. These companies believe that users must be skilled in handling their equipment.

Provide Price Change Information. Price changes need not be a serious problem if they are handled correctly. The salesperson is responsible for maintain-

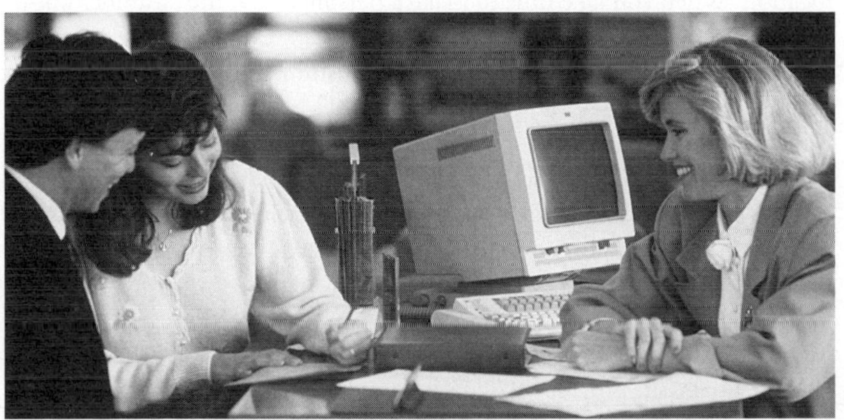

Salespeople often assist with credit arrangements and provide counsel to prospective customers.

ing an up-to-date price list. As your company issues price changes, record them accurately. Customers expect you to quote the correct price the first time.

Prevent Postsale Problems

There are ways to prevent postsale problems. The key is conscientious follow-up to be sure everything has been handled properly. Get to know the people who operate your shipping department. They are responsible for getting the right products shipped on time, and it is important that they understand your customers' needs.

Become acquainted with people in the credit department. Be sure that they maintain a good, businesslike relationship with your customers. This is a delicate area; even small mistakes—a "pay now" notice sent too early, for example—can cause hurt feelings. If your company uses a customer support staff to resolve postsale problems, be sure to get acquainted with the people who provide this service.

ADDING VALUE WITH CUSTOMER FOLLOW-UP

Customer follow-up methods usually have two major objectives. One is to express appreciation for the purchase and, thus, to enhance the relationship established during the sales presentation. You no doubt thanked the customer at the time the sale was closed, but appreciation should be expressed again a few days later. The second purpose of the follow-up is to determine whether the customer is satisfied with the purchase. Both of these methods will strengthen the buyer–seller relationship and build a partnership that results in additional sales.

In survey after survey, poor service and lack of follow-up after the sale are given as primary reasons people stop buying from a particular supplier. Most customers are sensitive to indifferent treatment by the sales representative. With this fact in mind, you should approach follow-up in a systematic and businesslike way. There are five follow-up methods.

Personal Visit

This is usually the most costly follow-up method, but it may produce the best results. It is the only strategy that allows face-to-face, two-way communication. When you take time to make a personal visit, the customer knows that you really care.

Use the personal follow-up to keep the customer informed of new developments, new products, or new applications. This information may pave the way for additional sales. Use the personal visit to reassess where you stand with the account. The reassessment process should involve something more than a "How's it going?" question. If you want the customer to see you as a partner, ask the tough questions: "Are there any problems that I need to address?" "Can you suggest any ways we can better serve your business?" Tom Reilly, author and sales trainer, says, "Your perceptions of your performance are meaningless. It's the customer's perceptions that count."[19]

value reinforcement Reinforcing to the customer the value they are getting from their purchase.

Personal visits provide a wonderful opportunity to engage in **value reinforcement**. Value reinforcement means getting credit for the value you cre-

"Due to unusually high call volume, let us remind you of the satisfaction of solving your own problem."

ate for the customer. You might review all of your follow-through activities so the customer realizes the many ways you have added value. Whenever possible, document your value-added services and point out any benefits that the customer has received. In some cases, positive bragging is an effective value reinforcement technique.[20]

Telephone Call

The telephone provides a quick and efficient way to follow up a sale. A salesperson can easily make 10 or 12 phone calls in a single hour, and the cost will be minimal. If you plan to send a thank-you card or letter, follow it up with a thank-you call. The personal appeal of the phone call will increase the effectiveness of the written correspondence. The telephone call has one major advantage over written correspondence: it allows for a two-way exchange of information. Once an account is well established, you may be able to obtain repeat sales by telephone.

E-mail Message

In many cases it is a lot quicker to send an e-mail message than to make a phone call. Salespeople report that they waste a lot of time playing "phone tag." Some customers prefer e-mail messages and may become irritated if you do not adhere to their wishes. If you know that a customer is not in the habit of checking their e-mail all that often, use the telephone as a back-up method. When in doubt, use parallel channels of communication.

Letter or Card

Written correspondence is an inexpensive and convenient way to thank the customer for the order and to promise continued service. Some companies encourage their salespeople to use a formal letter typed on company stationery. Other companies have designed special thank-you cards, which are signed and sent routinely after a sale is closed. The salesperson may enclose a business card. These thank-you cards do have one major limitation: they are mass produced and, therefore, lack the personal touch of handwritten cards and envelopes. Personalized notes, birthday cards, and anniversary cards can make a positive impression.

Call Report

call report A written summary that provides information on a sales call to people in the sales organization so that follow-up action can be taken as necessary.

The **call report** is a form that serves as a communications link with persons who can assist with customer service. The format varies, but generally it is a simple form with only four or five spaces. The sample call report form that appears in Figure 15.3 is used by a company that installs security systems at banks and other financial institutions.

A form such as this is one solution to the problem of communication between the company personnel and the customer. It is a method of follow-through that triggers the desired action. It is simple, yet businesslike.

Follow-up programs can be as creative or ingenious as you wish. Every sales organization competes on value, so you must continually think of new ways to add value. Creative use of your interpersonal communication skills can keep your messages fresh and personalized. Keep in mind that people buy both from the head and from the heart. Let customers know how much you care about their business.[21] You can use these five methods independently or in combination. Your main consideration should be some type of appropriate follow-up that (1) tells customers you appreciate their business, and (2) determines whether they are satisfied with the purchase.

ADDING VALUE WITH EXPANSION SELLING

Personal selling is the process of identifying and filling the customer's needs. As the salesperson learns more about the customer, and establishes a relationship based on trust and mutual respect, opportunities for expansion selling will arise. **Expansion selling**, used by salespeople to increase revenue or sales from a customer, can take three forms: full-line selling, cross-selling, and upselling.

expansion selling Any of three forms of selling used by salespeople to increase revenue or sales from a customer.

Full-line Selling

full-line selling The process of suggesting products or services that are related to the main item being sold to the customer.

Sometimes called *suggestion selling*, **full-line selling** is the process of recommending products or services that are related to the main item sold to the customer. The recommendation is made when, in the salesperson's judgment, the product or service can provide additional satisfaction. To illustrate, let's look at the sale of new houses. Many contractors offer customers who

Figure 15.3 The Call Report

Sales Call Report Date: October 26, 2007

To: Walt Higgins, service engineer
From: Diane Ray, sales representative

Action Promised: Visit the bank's Ottawa location within the next week to check on installation of our security system.

Assistance Needed: System B-420 was installed at the bank's main Ottawa branch on October 24. As per our agreement, you should make a follow-up call to check the installation of the system and provide bank personnel with a Form 82 certification checklist. The form should be given to Mr. Sandeep Khosla, the branch manager.

Copies to: Mr. Sandeep Khosla

CUSTOMER RELATIONSHIP MANAGEMENT WITH TECHNOLOGY

Islands of Information

Companies typically use many different software programs to manage information about customers. The firm will have customer purchase and payment history in its accounting system. Customer service problems may be recorded in the service department's software. People in customer support may use a help desk program.

The company's salespeople may be using one software program to manage its contacts with customer personnel, another program to prepare quotes, and yet another for correspondence with customers. To reduce these "islands" of customer information, more companies are finding ways to merge this information, or are acquiring software that performs more than one of these functions. Some CRM systems are combining a number of these functions into one integrated package. (See the CRM case study Servicing the Sale with CRM on page 372 for more information.)

want to differentiate their home a variety of options, including marble in the entryway, granite countertops, gourmet kitchen appliances, or Jacuzzi-like tubs for the bathroom. Customization is an important value-added service for many customers.

Full-line selling is no less important when selling services. For example, a travel agent has many opportunities to suggest related products. Let us assume that a customer purchases a two-week vacation in Ireland. The agent can offer to book hotel reservations or schedule a guided tour. Another related product would be a rental car.

Sometimes a new product is simply not "right" without related merchandise. A new business suit may not look right without a new shirt and tie. An executive training program held at a fine hotel can be enhanced with a refreshment break featuring a variety of soft drinks, fresh coffee, and freshly baked pastries.

Customers will view full-line selling as a form of value-added service when it is presented correctly. There is a right way and a wrong way to make recommendations. Here are some guidelines to follow:

1. *Plan for full-line selling during the preapproach step.* Before meeting with the customer, develop a general plan that includes your objectives for this important dimension of selling. Full-line selling is easier when you are prepared.
2. *Make recommendations after you have satisfied the customer's primary need.* While there are some exceptions to this rule, it's usually best to meet the primary need first. In the case of a new home purchase, for example, the customer should first select the model home and then make decisions regarding the upgrades.
3. *Make your suggestions thoughtful and positive.* "We just received a new order of silk ties that would go well with your new shirt. Let me show

you the collection." Avoid questions like, "Can we ship anything else?" This question invites a negative response.

4. *When appropriate, demonstrate the suggested item or use sales tools to build interest.* If you have suggested a shirt to go with a new suit, allow the customer to see it next to the suit. In industrial selling, show the customer a sample, or at least a picture if the actual product is not available.

Full-service selling is a means of providing value-added service. When you use it correctly, customers will thank you for your thoughtfulness and extra service. It is also a proven sales-building strategy.

Cross-Selling

cross-selling Selling to an established customer products that are not directly related to products the customer has already bought.

We have seen an increase in the use of cross-selling to grow sales volume. **Cross-selling** involves selling products that are not directly associated with products that you have sold to an established customer. A bank customer who has a home equity loan might be contacted and asked to consider purchase of a mutual fund. The customer who has purchased a townhouse might be a candidate for a security service. One financial services company, Quick & Reilly, has trained its 600 customer service representatives to use cross-selling when customers call regarding their current investments. By completing the cross-selling training programs, the representatives learned how to assess the caller's financial goals and develop a tailored proposal of products and services. Quick & Reilly achieved a 35 percent sales increase after developing the cross-selling program.[22]

More and more companies use cross-selling to discover additional sources of business within established accounts. Buyers generally welcome cross-selling efforts because they are searching for ways to consolidate purchases. They like the convenience of buying several items from the same source.[23]

Cross-selling is most effective in those situations in which the salesperson and the customer enjoy a true partnership. Salespeople who have a good understanding of the customer's needs and have earned the customer's respect, will face less resistance when recommending a product or service. Prior to implementing a cross-selling program, salespeople must learn about products that might meet the customer's needs. Many Canadian banks now train employees who have customer contact responsibility with how to cross-sell products and services.

Upselling

upselling Effort to sell better-quality products.

The effort to sell better-quality products is known as **upselling**. It is an important selling method that often adds customer value. Mike Weber, sales manager at Young Electric Sign Company, offers us two important tips on upselling. First, you need a well-established relationship with the customer—a relationship built on trust. Second, you need to continually qualify the prospect throughout the buying process. As you hear customers tell you more about their needs, you may see an opportunity to upsell. Weber says his salespeople usually engage in upselling at the design stage. The customer is shown

Servicing the Sale Worksheet

Method of Adding Value	What You Will Say or Do
Follow-through Set up a secure Web site or extranet so the client can track the production and delivery of custom-engineered seed research equipment.	Set up the secure Web site in a timely manner and then contact the customer when it is operational. Explain how to access the Web site and review the benefits of using this source of assistance.
Schedule training for persons who will be using the new technology.	Send training schedule to customer and confirm the dates with a follow-up call.
Follow-up Send a thank-you letter to each member of the team who made the purchase decision.	Express sincere appreciation for the purchase and explain the steps you will take to ensure a long-term partnership.
Check to be certain that the training was effective.	Visit the customer's research facility and talk with the employees who completed the training. Answer questions and provide additional assistance as needed.
Expansion Selling *Full-line selling.* Recommend Simonize System 5 paint protection program to a new car buyer.	Explain that this paint protection program—with Teflon Surface Protector—protects the vehicle's good looks and resale value for five years.
Cross-selling. A vacation home rental and real estate company contacts a customer who has rented a vacation home for more than 10 years. The customer is given information regarding vacation home ownership and construction services.	Discuss vacation home ownership as an investment opportunity. Describe lot selection, home design options, and finance plans.
Upselling. A large consulting firm wants to replace the commercial grade carpet in its office complex. Suggest the company purchase a high-grade carpet that will be more crush- and mat-resistant.	Explain and demonstrate with samples how a tight yarn twist, a short nap, and more stitches per centimetre will make the carpet more crush- and mat-resistant.

Figure 15.4 Servicing the Sale Worksheet. Follow-through on assurances and promises, customer follow-up, and expansion selling must be carefully planned. Use of this worksheet will help you preplan ways to add value.

a rough sketch of the desired sign and another rendition of something better. The added value of the more expensive option will become obvious to the customer.[24] In many selling situations, such factors as durability, comfort, or operating economy help justify the higher-priced product. A professional salesperson explains to the customer why it is in his or her best interest to spend "just a little more" and get the best value for the dollar. Most customers are more concerned with making the right purchase than they are with making the least expensive purchase.[25]

PREPLAN YOUR SERVICE STRATEGY

Servicing the sale is a very important dimension of personal selling, so a certain amount of preplanning is essential. It helps to preplan your service strategy for each of the three areas we have discussed: follow-through, follow-up, and expansion selling. You cannot anticipate every aspect of the service, but you can preplan important ways to add value once the sale is implemented. Develop a "servicing the sale" worksheet, like the one shown in Figure 15.4, prior to each sales presentation.

Partnership-Building Strategies Should Encompass All Key People

Some salespeople do a great job of communicating with the prospect but ignore other key people involved in the sale. To illustrate how serious this problem can be, let us look at the approach used by Jill Bisignano, a sales representative for a major restaurant supply firm. Jill had called on Bellino's Italian Restaurant for several years. Although she was always very friendly to Nick Bellino, she treated the other employees with nearly total indifference. One day she called on Nick and was surprised to learn that he was retiring and had decided to sell his restaurant to two long-time employees. As you might expect, it did not take the new owners long to find another supplier. Jill lost a large account because she failed to develop a good personal relationship with other key employees. It pays to be nice to everyone.

Here is a partial list of people in your company and in the prospect's company who can influence both initial and repeat sales:

1. *Receptionist.* Some salespeople simply do not use common sense when dealing with the receptionist. This person has daily contact with your customer and may schedule most or all calls. To repeatedly forget this individual's name or display indifference in other ways may cost you dearly.

2. *Technical Personnel.* Some products must be cleaned, lubricated, or adjusted on a regular basis. Take time to get acquainted with the people who perform these duties. Answer their questions, share technical information with them if necessary, and show appreciation for the work they are doing.

3. *Stock Clerks or Receiving Clerks.* People who work in the receiving room are often responsible for pricing incoming merchandise and making sure that these items are stored properly. They may also be responsible for stock rotation and processing damage claims.

4. *Management Personnel.* Although you may be working closely with someone at the departmental or division level, do not forget the person who has the final authority and responsibility for this area. Spend time with management personnel occasionally and be alert to any concerns they may have.

This is not a complete list of the people you may need to depend on for support. There may well be other key people who influence sales. Always look beyond the customer to see who else might have a vested interest in the sale.

Partnering with an Unhappy Customer

We have learned that unhappy customers generally do not initiate a verbal or written complaint. This means that postsale problems may not come to the attention of salespeople or other personnel within the organization. We also know that unhappy customers do share their negative experiences with other people. A dissatisfied customer will typically tell eight to ten people about their problem.[26] A double loss occurs when the customer stops buying your products and takes steps to discourage other people from buying your products. When complaints do surface, salespeople should view the problem as an opportunity to strengthen the business relationship. To achieve this goal, follow these suggestions:

1. *Give customers every opportunity to disclose their feelings.* Companies noted for outstanding customer service rely heavily on telephone systems, such as toll-free hotlines, to ensure easy access. At Federal Express, Cadillac Division of General Motors, and IBM—to name a few companies—specially trained advisers answer the calls and offer assistance. When a customer purchases a Ford vehicle, the salesperson introduces the customer to service staff who provide a key role in providing postsale service. The goal is to personalize the relationship with another member of the service team. Ford has discovered that after-sale contact builds a perception of value.[27] When customers do complain, by telephone or in person, encourage them to express all their anger and frustration. Do not interrupt. Do not become defensive. Do not make any judgments until you have heard all the facts as the customers see them.[28] If they stop talking, try to get them to talk some more.

2. *As the customer is talking, listen carefully and attentively.* You will need accurate information to solve the problem. One of the biggest barriers to effective listening is emotion. Do not become angry, and do not get into an argument. Once you feel the customer has fully vented, paraphrase what he or she said to prove you cared enough to listen.[29]

3. *Keep in mind that it does not really matter whether a complaint is real or perceived.* If the customer is upset, you should be polite and sympathetic. Do not yield to the temptation to say, "You do not really have a problem." Remember, problems exist when customers perceive they exist.[30]

4. *Accept responsibility.* Avoid the temptation to blame the shipping department, the installation crew, or anyone else associated with your company. Never tear down the company you work for. The problem has been placed in your hands, and you must accept responsibility for handling it. "Passing the buck" will only leave the customer with a feeling of helplessness.

5. *Politely share with the customer your point of view concerning the problem's cause.* At least explain what you think happened. The customer deserves an explanation. At this point a sincere apology is usually appropriate.

6. *Decide what action must be taken to remedy the problem.* Take action quickly and offer a value-added atonement. Don't just do what is expected; delight the customer by exceeding their expectations. Winning customer loyalty today means going beyond making it right.[31]

The value of customer complaints can emerge in two forms. First, complaints can be a source of important information that may be difficult to obtain by other means. Second, customer complaints provide unique opportunities for companies to prove their commitment to service. Loyalty builds in the customer's mind if you do a good job of solving his or her problem.[32]

A WORD OF CAUTION

When you are dealing with major or minor customer service problems and an apology is necessary, do not use e-mail. When a minor problem surfaces, call the customer personally. Do not delegate this task to someone else in your organization. If you need to apologize for a major problem that has occurred, meet with the customer in person. Schedule the meeting as soon as possible.[33]

SUMMARY

Servicing the sale is a major dimension of the selling process, with the objectives of providing maximum customer satisfaction and establishing a long-term buyer–seller partnership. Good service ensures that the product will meet the customer's current needs and builds a foundation for the future. A reputation for good service is essential in attracting new accounts and keeping old ones. The goal is to develop lifetime customers. We review several current developments in customer service. Salespeople must spend more time monitoring customer satisfaction. Customer knowledge is an important key to improving customer service, and computer-based systems are being used to enhance customer service.

The customer service strategy is made up of three activities: adding value with follow-through, adding value with follow-up, and adding value with expansion selling. These activities can create a positive impression of the salesperson and the company.

A salesperson depends on the support of many other people in servicing a sale. Maintaining good relationships with support staff members who help service your accounts is well worth the time and energy required. This chapter also includes information on ways to effectively solve the customer's problem. Regular and objective self-evaluation is also a valuable practice. Efficient performance of the functions involved in customer service is important to ensure continuing customer satisfaction and should be a matter of professional pride.

Key Terms

Call Report **362**

Cross-Selling **364**

Customer Service **352**

Expansion Selling **362**

Full-Line Selling **362**

Suggestion Selling *See* Full-Line Selling

Upselling **364**

Value Reinforcement **360**

Review Questions

1. You are currently a sales manager employed by a company that sells long-term care insurance. Tomorrow you will meet with five new sales trainees. Your major goal is to explain why it is important to service the sale. What important points will you cover?
2. Define "customer service." List the three major activities associated with this phase of personal selling.
3. Explain how full-line selling fits into the definition of customer service. How does *full-line selling* differ from *cross-selling*?
4. List and describe three current developments in customer service.
5. Adding value with follow-through can involve several postsale services. List five possible services.
6. How does credit become part of servicing the sale?
7. This chapter describes the value of the lifetime customer. Is it realistic to believe that people will become lifetime customers in our very competitive marketplace?
8. Define "upselling" and explain how it can add value.
9. What types of customer service problem might be prevented with the use of a call report?
10. What are six things you should do when trying to re-establish a partnering relationship with a dissatisfied customer?

Application Exercises

1. You are a salesperson working in the paint department at a Canadian Tire store. A customer has just purchased 75 litres of house paint. Assume that your store carries everything in the painting line, and list as many items as you can think of that could be used for expansion selling. Explain how your suggestions of these items could be a service to the customer.

2. You work as a wholesale salesperson for a plumbing supply company. One of your customers, a contractor, has an open line of credit with your company for $10 000–worth of products. He is currently at his limit; however, he is not overdue. He just received word that he has been awarded a $40 000 plumbing contract at the local airport. The contract requires that he supply $9000–worth of plumbing products. Your customer does not have the cash to pay for the additional products. He informs you that, unless you can provide him with some type of financing, he may lose the contract. He says that he can pay you when he finishes his next job in 60 days. Explain what you will do.
3. Go to **www.google.ca** (or another search engine if you prefer) and hit "advanced search." Type in "customer satisfaction" + selling, and restrict your search by typing ".ca" under "domain." Are you surprised by the number of hits on this subject? Examine some of the hits related to what customers have said about specific company customer service programs. Be prepared to discuss some of what you find in class.

ROLE-PLAY EXERCISE

An important aspect of personal selling is the need to add value with follow-through and follow-up. Both of these account management activities can be time consuming, especially if the salesperson is not skilled at setting up appointments that fit into a busy schedule. In this role play, you are to set up three follow-through meetings with a customer who has just purchased conference services from the convention centre you represent (see Partnership Selling on the CD-ROM). First, you must contact your client three days from today to confirm the availability of the Revolving Platform Room (see Partnership Selling, p. 5) for the meeting of 300 people. Second, you must contact this same client a week from today to get approval on the number of chicken Wellington banquet-style dinners needed (see Partnership Selling, p. 15, and Guarantees on p. 7). And, third, because your client isn't sure about the need for a microphone (see Partnership Selling, p. 22), you need to call your client the day before the meeting, which is scheduled four weeks from today, to verify whether you or your client will supply a microphone.

Equipped with a calendar, you should establish dates and times when your client will be available to talk or meet with you. Before you meet with your client, plan to recommend at least two times of the day that fit into your schedule for each of your meetings. If your client cannot meet at either of these times, ask your client to recommend a time. Do not start out by asking when your client is available because this could conflict with your busy schedule. Write the agreed-on times and dates in your calendar, suggesting your client does the same, so there will be no misunderstandings. Because these dates are deadlines, suggest that your client call you back if, for some reason, the schedule changes. Inform your client that you will plan to be at the hotel when the client's meeting starts and that you will be available to make sure everything is properly scheduled. Give your client your phone number and e-mail address and ask your client to contact you if there are any questions between now and the meeting date. Have another student role-play the customer and, after the role play, assess your customer service.

Case Problem

Good renovators are often distinguished by their ability and willingness to service the customer after a sale has been made. Garnet Kindervater has been a renovator for more than 25 years and has earned an excellent reputation among his clients and peers. In 1998, he won a Canadian Home Builders' Association National Sam Award in the Home Renovation Award category Over–$100 000. In 1999, he won the "Renovator of the Year Award" in St. John's, Newfoundland and Labrador, in the Under–$25 000 category. He recently served as president of the Canadian Home Builders' Association in Ottawa.

Garnet describes the renovation business as a highly personal one. His sees his role as renovator to manage the client from the time a project is started until after its completion. When he receives the first phone call from a potential client, Garnet likes to get as much information as he can during the conversation. Here's how he describes his approach to customer service.

> Just by knowing their address, often I can picture their house and even its layout. I have been in this business so long that I know what has been built throughout the city and when various neighbourhoods were constructed. I can usually tell simply from the address how much work might be involved, and what additional problems might be uncovered once work is started. It's also important to find out how much planning the client has done; that is, where are they in the purchase decision stage, and whether they are actually serious about having the work completed. If there is exterior work involved, I sometimes take a drive past the property for a quick assessment before I actually meet with the client.
>
> In the earliest stage, the clients usually have a general idea that they want something done, but it is often only at the concept stage and has not been clearly defined in their own mind. Renovators must be careful here to fill only a consultative role, making sure that the client knows what can be done and what will be involved. If the client talks to several renovators at this stage, the concept might change as the client continues to discuss it with more and more people. Sometimes, the final renovation that the client decides on may have little resemblance to what was initially discussed. When renovators quote on exactly the same job, price differences are usually not very great.
>
> I generally refuse to play a price game with clients. I think there is a real trap you can fall into as you then think about how you can manage a project to come in under cost. Quality gets sacrificed, the client becomes unhappy, and your reputation suffers. I always try to ensure the client gets superior value and that there are no surprises once work has been started. If there might be additional work necessary, it is a good idea to let the client know before work starts. For example, you might be replacing a wall in a bathroom and notice once you have started that a window has been leaking and is in very bad shape. That could add several hundreds of dollars to the project. Sometimes, clients will ask for changes to the project once a contract is signed. I accepted a job last week, and even before I started, the customer decided to make additional changes to the main entranceway, including new floor covering. In situations like this, you need to be sure the client understands and accepts any additional costs that will be involved.
>
> When there are major renovations, there are often a number of tradespeople involved in the project, such as plumbers, roofers, plasterers, or electricians. Any of them may have contact with the client. As the renovator, I must make sure the client is happy not only with the work the tradespeople do, but how they manage the process while they do it. Tradespeople need to be sensitive to the fact that they are working in someone's home and they need to be aware of things such as appearance, language, cleanliness, and courtesy. Clients can't always judge the quality of work that is done, but they can certainly tell whether they are happy with who did it and how it was done.
>
> When the project is completed, I always ask the client to develop a deficiency list, anything that may still need to be done or that they are dissatisfied with. Then, we do a walk-through together to

ensure we agree on whatever actions should be taken. If the project is handled properly throughout the renovation process, there is seldom anything that the client is unhappy with at this stage.

I did, for a period in the 1980s, begin to see more client problems. I had tried to grow my business too fast. At one point I had as many as 50 people working for me, but I found that it was impossible to properly manage all my clients. As problems continued to increase, I realized it was better to serve a smaller number of clients and do it well. Reputation is what gets you renovation business, and I guard my reputation carefully. I only work with tradespeople who have my standards of excellence, and who are good at relationship management. If all they can offer is technical competence, I let them work with someone else. Quality work is important in this business, but the ability to communicate with clients and to service the sale is even more so.[34]

Questions

1. Explain why it is so important for renovators to manage the renovation process rather than to wait for the end of the project to service the sale.
2. Should a renovator use expansion selling? What problems might arise for a renovator who uses expansion selling improperly?
3. Would you consider the following-through of assurances and promises and customer follow-up to be examples of superior customer service? Explain.

CRM Case Study SERVICING THE SALE WITH CRM

You have taken over a number of accounts of another salesperson, Pat Silva. Most of these accounts are prospects, which means that they have not yet purchased from SimNet. Two accounts did purchase networks from Pat: Karen Murray, of Murray D'Zines, and Judith Albright, owner of Piccadilly Studio. You now want to be sure that these sales are well serviced.

Questions

1. With whom should you speak, within SimNet, before following through and contacting each of the customers? What do you need to discover?
2. What will be your follow-up strategy for each customer?
3. These customers were not sold the products; they bought them. Does the fact that these customers initiated their orders influence your follow-up strategy?
4. Might other customers or prospects be affected by your service activities? How will this influence your activities? Could customer service be your competitive edge?
5. Do you see any expansion selling opportunities with these two accounts? Which expansion selling methods should you consider?

Partnership Selling

A ROLE PLAY/SIMULATION **(see Partnership Selling on the CD-ROM, p. 40)**

DEVELOPING A SALES PRESENTATION STRATEGY—SERVICING THE SALE

Refer to *Sales Memorandum 3*, and strategically plan to service the sale with your customer. After closing the sale—getting the customer's signature—there are several steps to add value and build customer confidence and satisfaction. These steps are important to providing total quality customer service, and should provide for repeat sales and a list of referred customers.

Following the instructions in item 2g of your presentation plan, you need to schedule a future appointment to telephone or personally call and confirm the number of people attending the convention, and final room and menu needs (see the convention centre policies). Also, during this conversation you might suggest beverages for breaks, audiovisual needs, and any other items that will make this an outstanding convention for your customer.

You should have your calendar available to suggest and write down dates and times for this future contact. Any special materials, such as a calendar, can be placed in the back pocket of your portfolio. You may want to ask another person to be your customer and practise the customer service strategies you have prepared.

At this point you should be strategically prepared to make the presentation to your customer outlined in *Sales Memorandum 3*. Your instructor will provide you with further instructions.

PART V

ROLE-PLAY EXERCISE

RELATIONSHIP STRATEGY
PRESENTATION STRATEGY
PERSONAL SELLING PHILOSOPHY
PRODUCT STRATEGY
CUSTOMER STRATEGY

Developing a Presentation Strategy

SCENARIO

This role play is a continuation of the Part IV role-play exercise. You recently met with Gabriela Ansari, founder and chief executive officer of Cantrol Security Inc. The purpose of the first sales call was to begin the relationship-building process and present selected value-added guest services and amenities offered by the Park Inn International Hotel and Convention Centre. You also obtained some information regarding the customer's buying process. For this role play, you will prepare a persuasive presentation for a second sales call to Gabriela Ansari, during which you must elicit information you need to prepare a formal sales proposal.

CUSTOMER PROFILE

Prior to starting Cantrol Security, Gabriela Ansari spent 12 years working in sales and sales management at General Electric Corporation (GE), described by *Fortune* magazine as America's most admired company. Working for GE was a great learning experience for Gabriela, who is trying to apply the GE success formula to Cantrol Security. She is the classic extravert, a person who combines high sociability and high dominance.

SALESPERSON PROFILE

Simon Julian is new to the field of sales but is a quick learner. The first visit with Gabriela Ansari went well, and now he is preparing for the second sales call. Gabriela is planning a large banquet to recognize her employees but has not yet selected a location for this event. While working for GE, Gabriela attended more than 25 business conferences and was disappointed by many of them. Too often, they were held at look-alike hotels that served bland food typically served by poorly trained waiters who displayed little enthusiasm. Simon took notes throughout the meeting and will address these concerns during the second sales call.

PRODUCT

The Park Inn is a full-service hotel and convention centre. After completion of a recent $2.8 million renovation, the Park Inn received the Excellence in Renovation Design Award from the Ontario Architectural Association.

INSTRUCTIONS

The first sales call was basically an informative presentation. Near the end of the visit Gabriela Ansari did disclose her plans for a large recognition banquet to be held on October 25, the company's second anniversary. No other information was provided, but Gabriela agreed to a second meeting to be held the following week.

Based on the information collected during the first call, you—as Simon Julian—are now planning a persuasive presentation that will involve the first three steps of the six-step presentation plan (see Fig. 10.3). At the office of Gabriela Ansari—to be role-played by another student—you will need to re-establish the relationship and then initiate the agenda approach (see Chapter 10). Begin the presentation with appropriate survey, probing, and confirmation questions. These questions should be preplanned using information found in Chapter 11.

As the need discovery phase of the presentation progresses, the customer's buying criteria or buying conditions should surface. Prior to the second sales call you should also select and be prepared to demonstrate appropriate selling tools (i.e., proof devices). A variety of selling tools suitable for reproduction can be found in Partnership Selling on your Companion CD-ROM. Ensure that you preplan feature–benefit selling statements that appeal to Gabriela Ansari's needs. The importance of selling specific benefits and obtaining customer reactions cannot be overemphasized (see Chapter 11).

A major objective of the second sales call is to move the sale forward by convincing Gabriela Ansari that the Park Inn offers an outstanding combination of value-added guest services and amenities and is prepared to meet her needs. The sale will not be closed during the second call, but you will try to obtain a commitment to prepare a formal sales proposal to be presented to Gabriela Ansari within 48 hours. (See Partnership Selling, p. 45, on your CD-ROM for a sample sales proposal form.)

Joyful people exude a humble self-confidence gained from mastering a succession of situations. They are enthusiastic, energetic, creative, and fun to be around. They welcome changes, ignore rivalry, enjoy life, enjoy their work, and enjoy other people. —Derek A. Newton,

Feed Your Eagles: Building and Managing a Top-Flight Sales Force

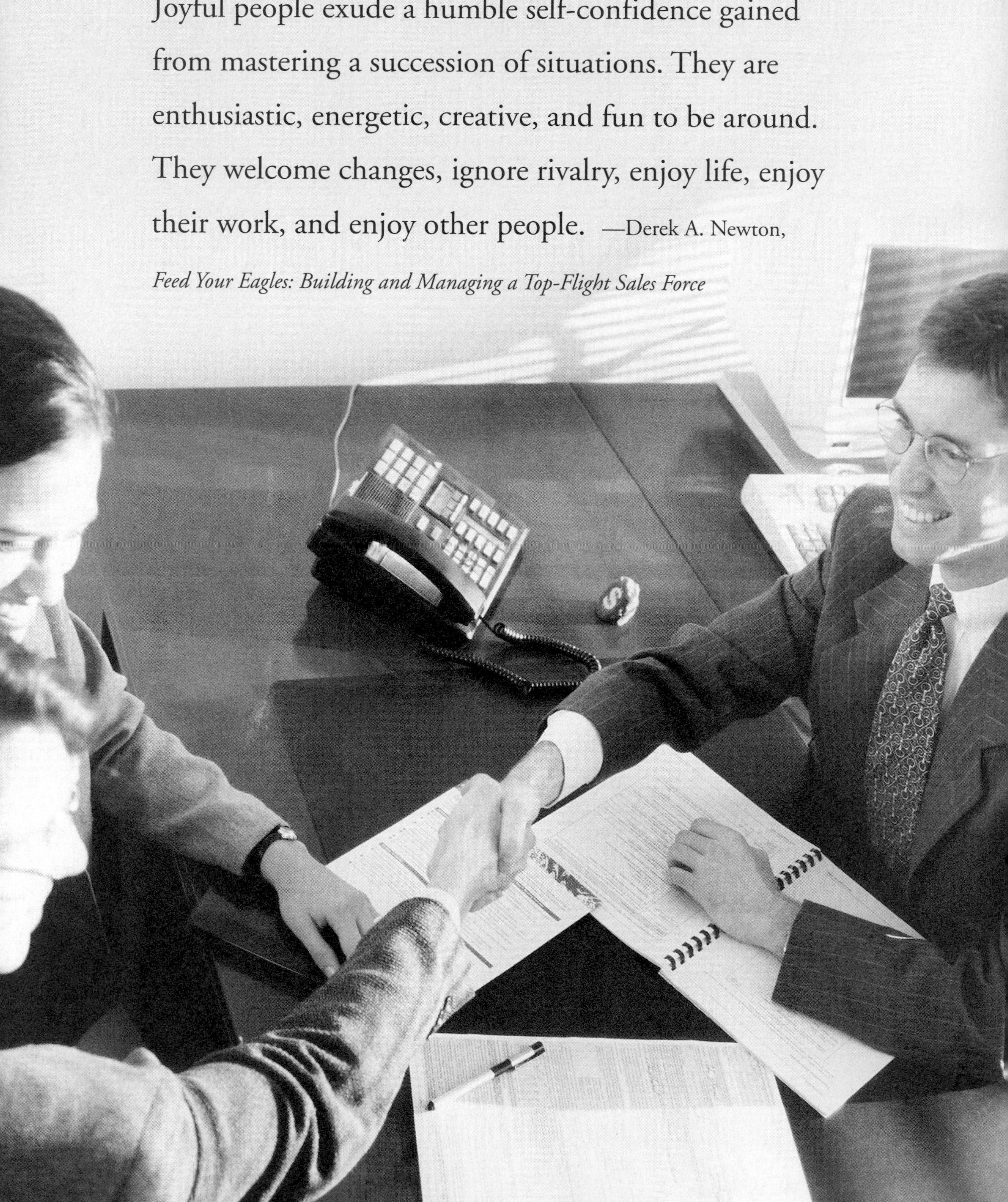

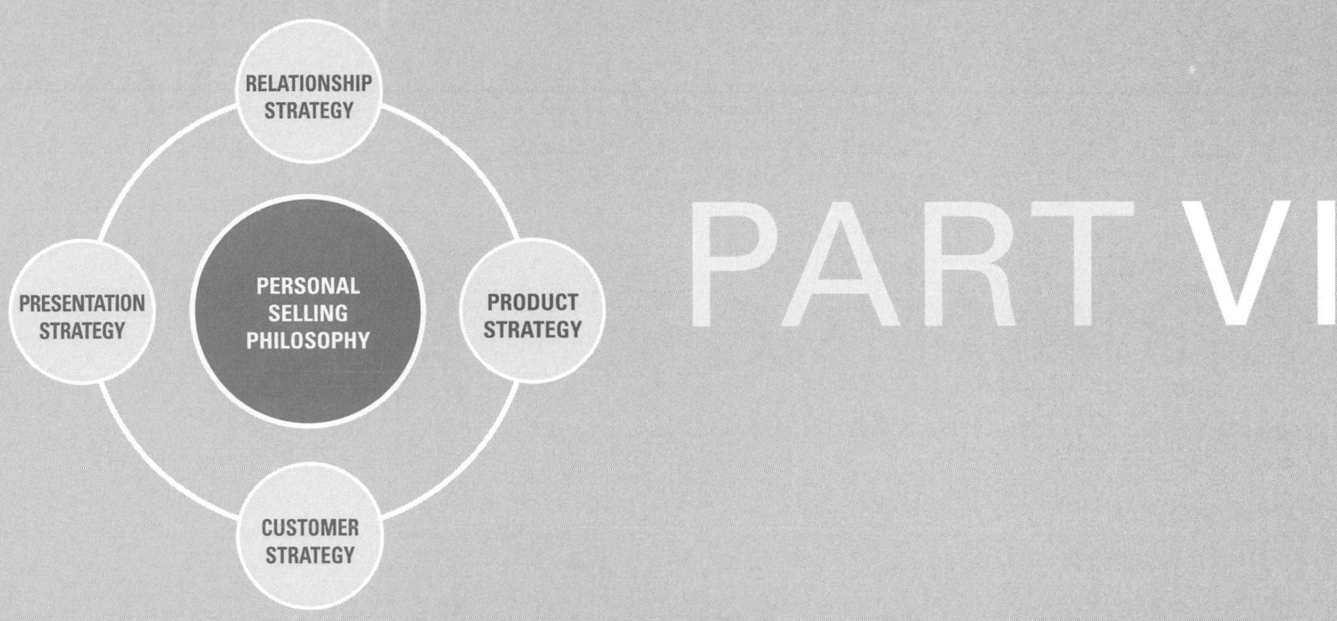

PART VI

Management of Self and Others

Personal selling requires a great deal of self-discipline and self-direction. Chapter 16 examines the four dimensions of self-management. The final chapter examines the fundamentals of sales force management.

CHAPTER 16

Management of Self

THE KEY TO GREATER SALES PRODUCTIVITY

LEARNING OBJECTIVES

After studying this chapter, you should be able to

1. Discuss the four dimensions of self-management
2. List and describe time management strategies
3. Explain factors that contribute to improved territory management
4. Identify and discuss common elements of a records management system
5. Discuss stress management practices

Many of the best salespeople we know had no intention to pursue a career in sales, but had experiences early in their lives that helped them develop personality traits and abilities that have certainly contributed to their success. During her school years, Paula Shannon acted in plays, practised public speaking, and participated in a number of competitive sports, most notably gymnastics. She spent a year studying in Belgium where she learned to adapt to another culture and social setting, and learned a third language. Paula now speaks six languages.

Paula credits managing a large paper route at a young age with helping to teach her about responsibility. Later, she worked as a waitress, did some interpretation on a tour bus, sold clothing and other items at retail, and spent a summer in customer service for a large commercial waste management firm. In Europe, Paula worked as a management trainee for Berlitz International. This program helped give her a solid grounding in general business: operations, finance, accounting, human resources, and sales. Following her management training, Paula Shannon began to handle sales for several Berlitz language centres. Paula says her belief and confidence in the product she was selling was evident. She credits her boss at the time, Anita Komlos, whom she describes as "one of the most natural and effective salespeople I have ever known," with helping her learn how to probe effectively and when to "shut up."

Paula Shannon has managed to learn something of value from everything she has done. She is clearly focused on managing herself and her career. Today, Paula Shannon is chief sales officer for Boston-based Lionbridge Technologies, Inc. She manages its global sales force of 70 from her home office in Montreal.[1]

Management of Self—A Four-Dimensional Process

What makes a salesperson successful? Some people believe the most important factor is hard work. This is only partly true. Some people work hard but do not accomplish much. They lack purpose and direction. This lack of organization results in wasted time and energy. Wasting time and energy is the slippery slope to failure in the age of information. Many salespeople are drowning in information and the flood of messages each day leaves little time to think and reflect. Sales and sales support personnel, like most other knowledge workers, are working under tighter deadlines. The response time to customer inquiries has been shortened and customers are less tolerant of delays.

In this chapter we approach management of self as a four-dimensional process consisting of the following components:

1. *Time management.* There are only about 250 business days per year. Within each day there is only so much time to devote to selling. Selling hours are extremely valuable. A group of 1300 salespeople was asked to evaluate 16 challenges they face in their work. "Not enough time" was ranked first; "achieving balance between work and family" was ranked second; "dealing with information overload" was ranked third.[2]
2. *Territory management.* A **sales territory** is a group of customers and prospective customers assigned to a single salesperson. Every territory is unique. Some territories consist of one or two cities or counties, while others encompass several provinces. The number of accounts within each territory will also vary. Today, territory management is becoming less of an art and more of a science.
3. *Records management.* A wise salesperson never relies on memory. Every salesperson must maintain a certain number of records for systematic data collection and storage. Some of the most common records include planning calendars, prospect forms, call reports, summary reports, and expense reports.
4. *Stress management.* A certain amount of stress comes with any selling position. Some salespeople have learned how to take stressful situations in stride. Others allow stress to trigger anger and frustration. Learning to cope with various stressors that surface in the daily life of a salesperson is an important part of the self-management process.

sales territory A group of customers and prospective customers assigned to a single salesperson.

Most people who achieve success in selling have a strong work ethic. They are self-starters who are committed to more than the 8-hour day or the 40-hour week.

Time Management

A salesperson can increase sales volume in two major ways. One is to improve selling effectiveness, and the other is to spend more time in face-to-face selling situations. The latter objective can best be achieved through improved time and territory management.

Improving the management of both time and territory is a high priority in the field of selling. These two closely related functions represent major challenges for salespeople.

Let us first look closely at time management. There is definitely a close relationship between sales volume and number of customer contacts made by the salesperson. You have to make calls to get results.

TIME-CONSUMING ACTIVITIES

The major time-consuming activities in personal selling are travel, time spent waiting to see a customer, completion of sales records, casual conversation, time spent on customer follow-through and follow-up, and time spent in face-to-face selling. Some salespeople who have kept careful records of how they spend their time each day are surprised to learn how little is spent in face-to-face selling situations. Salespeople need to examine carefully each of these activities and determine whether too much or too little time is spent in any area. One way to assess time use is to keep a log of your activities, recording

SELLING IN ACTION

Sales Trainer Carefully Manages His Personal Self-Development

Kip Grant, sales trainer and keynote speaker, says, "If most people drove their cars the way they lead their lives, they would be in an accident before they got out of their driveway!" By that, he simply means that most people lack a personal self-development plan. Kip Grant manages his own self-development very carefully. Each year, he conducts more than 120 seminars or workshops, and attends six or more as a participant. He enrolled in the certification program offered by the Canadian Professional Sales Association www.cpsa.com and earned his designation as a Certified Sales Professional (CSP).

Kip Grant reads one new book each week: 70 percent are business-related to keep him aware of new developments in his profession and 30 percent are fiction. He also reads the journals and other literature that his customers read. He recommends that you read in time blocks rather than by chapter. It is easier to schedule specific periods of time, even 15-minute blocks, and you will retain more. Finally, Kip Grant uses his driving time effectively. Even for short trips, he listens to cassettes. Spaced-repetition learning has been shown to be the most effective for long-term retention. Kip Grant says, "Whether you get better or worse is a function of your willingness to expand your personal comfort zone."[a]

what you do each hour for a week. Then, you can use a fluorescent marker to highlight the time you wasted.[3] Pick one or two of the most wasteful areas and then make plans to correct the problem. Set realistic goals that can be achieved. Keep in mind that wasting time is usually a habit. To manage your time more effectively, you will need to form new habits.

TIME MANAGEMENT METHODS

Sound time management methods can pave the way to greater sales productivity. The starting point is forming a new attitude toward time conservation. You must view time as a scarce resource not to be wasted. The time-saving strategies presented here are not new, nor are they unique. Time-conscious people in all walks of life are using them.

Develop a Series of Personal and Business Goals

Bob Urichuck is a master trainer (CMT) and a sales professional (CSP), and author of *Up Your Bottom Line.* He recommends that you set both personal and business goals: "Goal setting is the process you use to select, define and put into operation the expectations you have for yourself."[4] The goal-setting process focuses your efforts and requires that you be clear about what you want to accomplish. It makes you aware of your strengths and weaknesses, and points you to areas where you should focus on self-improvement. Bob Urichuck recommends that, to be effective, goals must be "S.M.A.R.T.":

S. *Specific.* "I want to sell more" is too general. "I want to close three new deals next week" is specific. If your goal is too general or vague, progress toward achieving that goal will be difficult to achieve.

M. *Measurable.* You must be able to measure your progress toward achieving your goal.

A. *Attainable.* Effective goals have psychological value. They can serve as a strong motivational force if you believe you can achieve them, and they can help build self-esteem when you do achieve them.

R. *Relevant.* Goals should reflect the values that govern your life. You need to see that achieving a specific goal is really what you want to accomplish.

T. *Trackable.* You need to be able to keep track of progress toward achieving your goals. Once you set a goal, you can set benchmark dates and either confirm that you are on the right track or make adjustments.[5]

Prepare a Daily To-Do List

Cy Charney is a leading Canadian consultant in the area of performance improvement and president of Charney & Associates Inc. (**www.askcharney.com**). He says, "Plan each day the afternoon or evening before. Doing this will give you assurance that your day will be productive and enable you to have a good night's sleep."[6] He recommends you begin by making a list of things that you have to get done, leave some time for contingencies, and do the things on your list before attempting anything not on your list. He also recommends that you prioritize your list:

1. anything relating to existing or potential customers
2. anything important to your reputation within the company
3. anything deferrable or social

Then, you should act on them in that order.[7]

Preparing a daily to-do list should become a habit. Try not to let "busy-work" crowd planning out of your schedule. A small investment in planning time can pay big dividends. Toronto-based productivity consultant Mark Elwood says that the average person spends 1.3 hours per week planning, 13.2 hours on administrative tasks, and an additional 3.7 hours on non-essential activities. However, people who spend 3.4 hours per week planning and prioritizing only spend 9.5 hours on administrative duties and 1.5 hours on miscellaneous activities. That is, 2 hours of planning provides a net gain of 4 hours.[8]

www.prioritymanagement.com

Vancouver-based Priority Management offers an online quiz to help you assess whether you are efficient or effective, and a number of online articles to help you manage time and tasks better (**www.prioritymanagement.com**).

Maintain a Planning Calendar

Ideally, a salesperson needs a single place to record daily personal and business appointments, deadlines, and tasks. Dennis Heinzlmeir, who teaches time management at Mount Royal College in Calgary, says, "Our brains are very poor organizers." The solution is to create systems "to relieve our overburdened minds."[9] Unfortunately, many salespeople write daily tasks and appointments on any slip of paper they can find: backs of envelopes, business cards, napkins, or Post-it notes. Hyrum W. Smith, author of *The 10 Natural Laws of Successful Time and Life Management,* calls these pieces of paper "floaters." Salespeople who use floaters are often unfocused, lose critical information, and miss appointments.

Salespeople increasingly prefer to use personal digital assistants. As well as keeping daily to-do lists (see Fig. 16.1), these organizers can store contact information for hundreds of people, keep track of appointments, and serve as a perpetual calendar. Other salespeople still prefer to use a paper-based planning calendar (e.g., Franklin Covey Day Planner) to bring efficiency to their planning efforts. It is easy to tell at a glance what is coming up in the days, weeks, or even months ahead (see Fig. 16.2 on page 384).

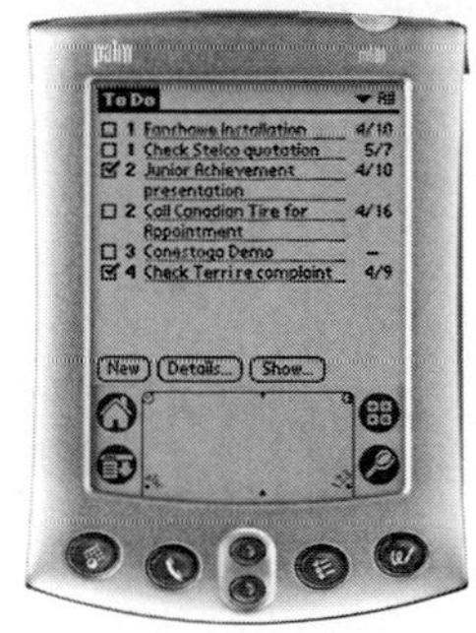

Figure 16.1 A daily list of activities can help a salesperson set priorities and save time.

Organize Your Selling Tools

You can save valuable time by finding ways to organize sales literature, business cards, order blanks, samples, and other items needed during a sales call. You may waste time on a callback because some item was not available during your first call. You may even lose a sale because you forgot or misplaced a key selling tool.

If you have a great deal of paperwork, invest in one or more file cabinets. Some salespeople purchase small, lightweight cardboard file boxes to keep their materials organized. These boxes can easily be placed in your car trunk and moved from one sales call to another. The orderly arrangement of selling tools is just one more method of time conservation.

The key to regular use of the four time-saving techniques already described is commitment. Unless you are convinced that efficient time management is important, you will probably find it difficult to adopt these new habits. A salesperson who fully accepts the "time is money" philosophy will use these techniques routinely.

SAVING TIME WITH TELEPHONES, FAX MACHINES, AND E-MAIL

As the cost of a face-to-face sales call increases, more and more salespeople are asking the question, "Is this trip necessary?" In many situations a telephone call can replace a personal visit. The telephone call may be especially useful in dealing with accounts that are marginal in terms of profitability. Some customers actually prefer telephone contact for certain types of business transaction. Here are some situations in which the phone call is appropriate.

- Call the customer in advance to make an appointment. You will save time, and the customer will know when to expect you.
- Use the telephone to keep the customer informed. A phone call provides instant communication with customers at a low cost.
- Build customer goodwill with a follow-up phone call. Make it a practice to call customers to thank them for buying your product and to determine if the customer is satisfied with the purchase.

Some customers prefer to be contacted by e-mail, and it would be a mistake to ignore their preference. Busy people often discourage telephone calls to minimize interruptions. They review e-mail messages only at specific times of the day.

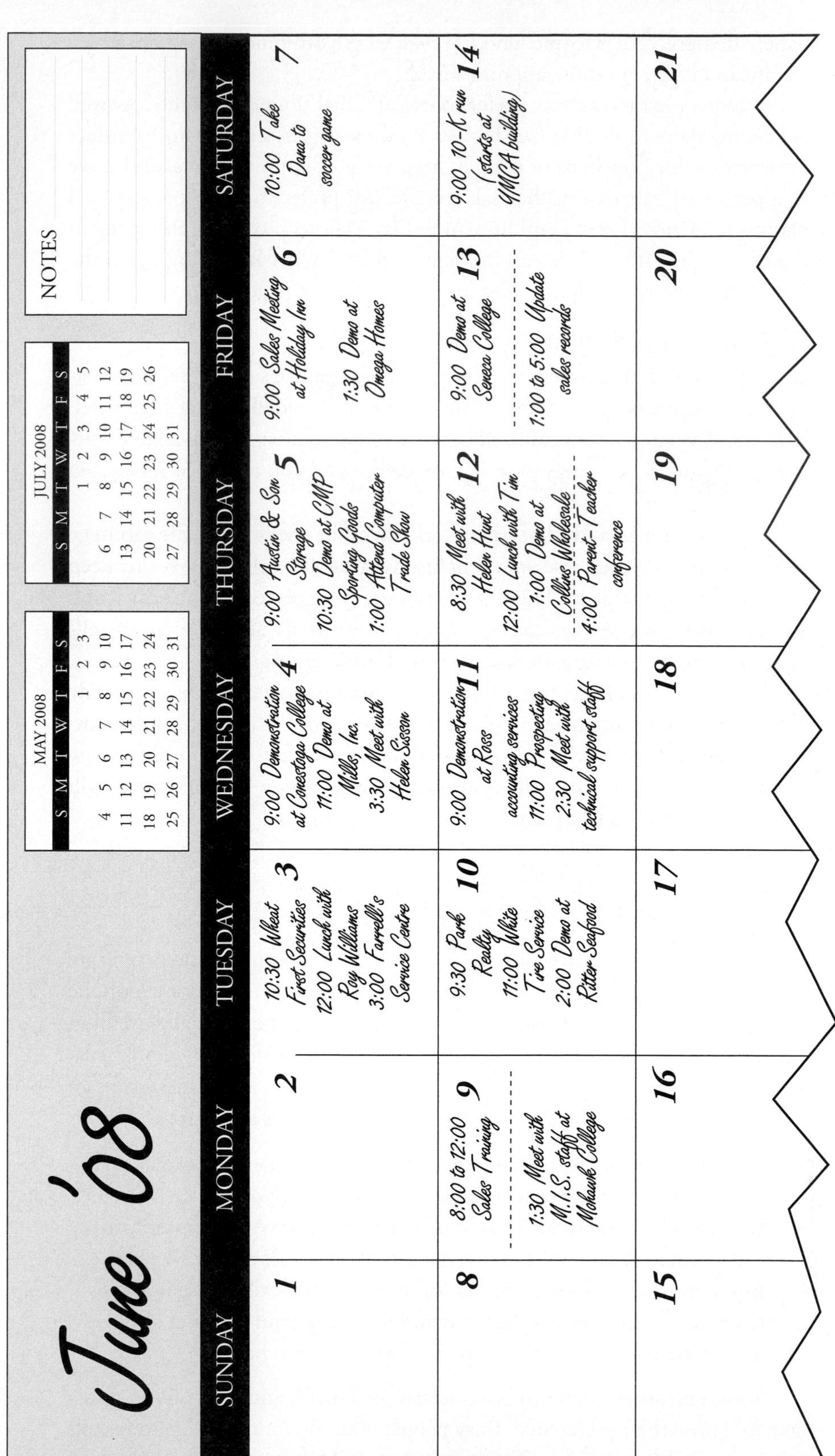

Figure 16.2 Monthly Planning Calendar. This sample shows the first 15 days of a monthly planning calendar for a computer service sales representative.

The cellular telephone has become a convenient and time-saving sales tool.

Voice mail automated telephone systems are now being used by companies of all sizes. These systems not only answer the phone and take messages but also provide information-retrieval systems that are accessible from remote locations. For many salespeople the cellular telephone and the pager have become convenient and time-saving sales tools. These technologies are especially useful for salespeople who spend a lot of time away from the office and who need to exchange information with others.

The fax machine takes telecommunication a step further. With the aid of a fax machine, salespeople can send and receive documents in seconds, using standard public or cellular telephone lines. Detailed designs, charts, and graphs can be transmitted across the country or around the world.

Territory Management

Many marketing organizations have found it helpful to break down the total market into manageable units called sales territories. As noted earlier, a sales territory is the geographic area where prospects and customers reside. While some firms have developed territories solely on the basis of geographic considerations, a more common approach is to establish a territory on the basis of classes of customers. Territories are often classified according to sales potential. Some marketers assign sales representatives to key industries. The *Ottawa Citizen* newspaper divides its customer base into major business lines, such as real estate and automotive.[10] Regardless of how the sales territory is established, it is essentially a specific number of present and potential accounts that can be called on conveniently.

With a fax machine, salespeople can send and receive documents in seconds.

WHAT DOES TERRITORY MANAGEMENT INVOLVE?

To appreciate fully the many facets of territory management, it will be helpful to examine a typical selling situation. Put yourself in the shoes of a salesperson

CUSTOMER RELATIONSHIP MANAGEMENT WITH TECHNOLOGY

Confirming Immediately

Sharing close-up and personal information creates a core on which successful relationships may be built and sustained. Friends have long supplemented their personal visits with notes, letters, and telephone calls. Contemporary technology offers new ways to save time in addition to enhancing and extending relationship-rich communications. Enlightened salespeople use the fax and computer modem as fast, and therefore effective, methods to give information to their customers.The fax function can be particularly useful to quickly convey temporary messages that confirm, affirm, or verify. (See the exercise Corresponding with CRM on page 398 for more information.)

who has just accepted a position with a firm that manufactures a line of high-quality tools. You are responsible for a territory that covers Manitoba and Saskatchewan, which includes 88 auto supply firms that carry your line of tools. It also includes 38 stores that do not carry your tools. On the basis of this limited information, how would you carry out your selling duties? To answer this question, it will be necessary to follow these steps:

Step 1: Classify All Customers. If you classify customers according to potential sales volume, then you must answer two questions: What is the dollar amount of the firm's current purchases? What amount of additional sales might be developed with greater selling effort? Store A may be purchasing \$3000–worth of tools each year, but potential sales for this firm amount to \$5000. Store B currently purchases \$2000–worth of tools a year, and potential sales amount to \$2500. In this example, store A clearly deserves more time than store B.

It is important to realize that a small number of accounts may provide a majority of the sales volume. Many companies get 75 to 80 percent of their sales volume from 20 to 25 percent of their total number of customers. The problem lies in accurately identifying which accounts and prospects fall into the top 20 to 25 percent category. Once this information is available, you can develop customer classification data that can be used to establish the frequency of calls.

Step 2: Develop a Routing and Scheduling Plan. Many salespeople have found that travel is one of their most time-consuming nonselling activities. A great deal of time can also be wasted just waiting to see a customer. The primary objective of a sales routing and scheduling plan is to increase actual selling by reducing time spent travelling between accounts and waiting to see customers.

If a salesperson called on only established accounts and spent the same amount of time with each customer, routing and scheduling would not be difficult. In most cases, however, you need to consider other variables. For example, you may be expected to develop new accounts on a regular basis. In this case, you must adjust your schedule to accommodate calls on prospects. Another variable involves customer service. Some salespeople devote considerable time to adjusting warranty claims, solving customer problems, and paying goodwill visits.

There are no precise rules to observe in establishing a sales routing and scheduling plan, but the following guiding principles apply to nearly all selling situations:

1. Obtain or create a map of your territory, and mark the location of present accounts with pins or a marking pen. Each account might be colour-coded according to sales potential. This will give you a picture of the entire territory. Mapping software is now available that can estimate travel time, create optimal calling plans, reduce average driving time, and even recommend optimal locations for field salespeople.

www.terralign.com

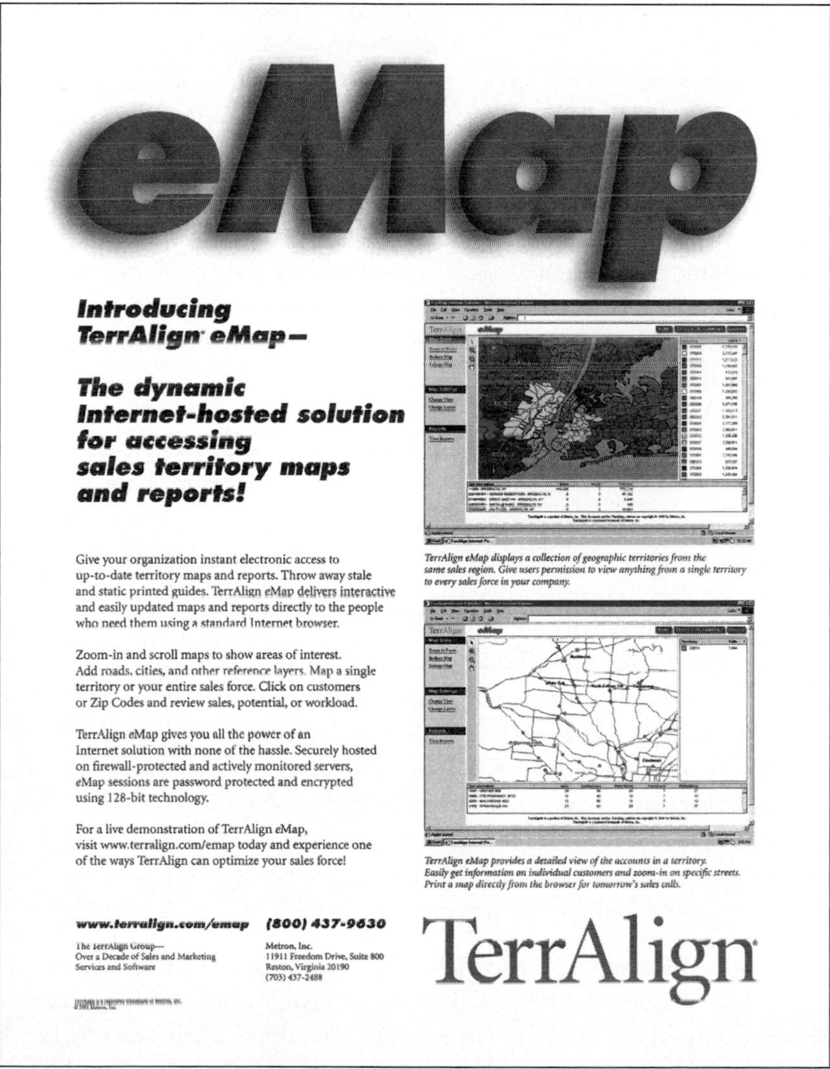

Mapping software such as eMap allows companies to instantly communicate up-to-date territory maps and reports to field salespeople.

2. If your territory is geographically quite large, consider dividing it into smaller areas. You can then plan work in terms of several trading areas that make up the entire territory.
3. Develop a routing plan for a specific period of time. This might be a one- or two-week period. Once the plan is firm, notify customers of your anticipated arrival time by telephone, letter, or e-mail.
4. Develop a schedule that accommodates your customers' needs. Some customers appreciate getting calls on a certain day of the week or at a certain hour of the day. Try to schedule your calls in accordance with their wishes.
5. Think ahead, and establish one or more tentative calls in case you have some extra time. If your sales calls take less time than expected or if there is an unexpected cancellation, you need optional calls to fill the void.
6. Decide how frequently to call on the basis of sales potential. Give the greatest attention to the most profitable customers.

SALES CALL PLANS

sales call plan A plan developed with information taken from the routing and scheduling plan. The primary purpose of the plan is to ensure efficient and effective account coverage.

You can use information from the routing and scheduling plan to develop a **sales call plan**. This proposal is a weekly action plan, usually initiated by the sales manager. Its primary purpose is to ensure efficient and effective account coverage.

The form most sales managers use is similar to the one shown in Figure 16.3. One section of the form is used to record planned calls. A parallel section is for completed calls. Additional space is provided for the names of firms called on.

The sales manager usually presents the sales call plan to individual members of the sales staff. Some salespeople may be asked to allocate calls across all categories of customers; sometimes the sales manager may ask senior or field salespeople to call on one category of account, and more junior or inside salespeople to call on another category of account. The Royal Bank of Canada, for example, segmented its customers into A, B, and C accounts on the basis of dollar activity and profitability. Account managers were asked to focus on larger accounts, offering them additional products and services. As a result, the average profit per A account increased 268 percent and the number of A accounts increased 292 percent over a two-year period.[11] The success of such a plan will depend on how realistic the goals appear to the sales staff, how persuasive the sales manager is, and what type of training accompanies the plan's introduction.

Records Management

Although some salespeople complain that paperwork is too time consuming and reduces the amount of time available for actual selling, others recognize that accurate, up-to-date records actually save time. Their work is better organized, and quick accessibility of information usually makes it possible to close more sales and improve customer service.

Sales Call Plan

Salesperson ______________ For week ending ______________

Territory ______________ Days worked ______________

Planned Calls		**Total Completed Calls**	
Number of planned calls	______	Number of calls only	______
Number of planned presentations	______	Number of presentations	______
Number of planned telephone calls	______	Number of telephone calls	______
Account Category Planning		Number of orders	______
A. Account calls	______	Total km travelled	______
B. Account calls	______	A. Account calls	______
C. Account calls	______	B. Account calls	______
		C. Account calls	______

Companies called on	Address	Date	Customer rating	Comments about call

Figure 16.3 Sales call plan.

A good record-keeping system gives salespeople useful information with which to check their own progress. For instance, an examination of the sales call plan at the end of the day provides a review of who was called on and what was accomplished. The company also benefits from complete and accurate records. Reports from the field help management make important decisions. A company with a large sales force operating throughout a wide geographic area relies heavily on information sent to the main office.

RECORDS COMMONLY KEPT BY SALESPEOPLE

A good policy is never to require a record that is not absolutely necessary. The only records worth keeping are those that provide positive benefits to the customer, the salesperson, or the personnel who work in sales-supporting areas of the company. Each record should be brief, easy to complete, and free of requests for useless detail. Where possible, the format should provide for the use of check marks as a substitute for written responses. Completing sales record forms should not be a major burden.

What records should you keep? The answer to this question will vary depending on the type of selling position. Some of the records most commonly kept by salespeople are described in this section.

Customer and Prospect Card Files Most salespeople find it helpful to keep records of customers and prospects. Each of these cards has space for name, address, telephone and fax numbers, and e-mail address. Other information recorded might be the buyer's personal characteristics, the names of people who might influence the purchase, or appropriate times to make calls. Of course, many salespeople have replaced their card files with computerized record systems.

Call Reports The call report (also called an *activity report*) is a variation of the sales call plan described earlier in this chapter. It is used to record information about the people you have called on and what took place. The call report is one of the most basic records used in the field of selling. It provides a summary of what happened during the call and an indication of what future action is required. The call reports (daily and weekly) featured in Figure 16.4 are typical of those used in the field.

We are seeing less emphasis on call reports that require only numbers (e.g., calls made each day, number of proposals written). With increased interest in customer relationship management and customer databases, companies are putting more emphasis on collecting information that will expand the customer's profile, and provide knowledge on current buying behaviour and short- and long-range buying plans.

Expense Records Both your company and the government agencies that monitor business expenses will require a record of selling expenses. These usually include such items as meals, lodging, travel, and, in some cases, entertainment expenses. Several expense-reporting software packages are now available to streamline the expense-reporting process. Automated expense reports save the salesperson a great deal of time and allow expenses to be reimbursed while the salesperson is still on the road.

Sales Records The records used to report sales vary greatly in design. Some companies require daily reports, others weekly ones. As you would expect, one primary use of the sales report is to analyze salespeople's performance.

You can take certain steps to improve a reporting system. Some records should be completed right away, while you can easily recall the information. Accuracy is always important. It can be embarrassing to have an order sent to the wrong address simply because you have transposed a figure. Take time to proofread forms for accuracy. Neatness and legibility are also important when you are preparing sales records.

WEEKLY REPORT OF SALES ACTION
3M COMPANY
Industrial Abrasives Division
Mail to your Sales Manager no later than Saturday of each week.
White Sales Mgr. Canary Sales Rep.
Sales Representative | Date Prepared | For Week Ended | No. Days Worked | Days Absent | Reason for Absence
CALLS FOR WEEK: DISTRIBUTOR | CONSUMER | O. E. M.
NEW BUSINESS AS A RESULT OF MY EFFORTS: CUSTOMER | DISTRIBUTOR | PRODUCT | VALUE | NEW/REPEAT
Manager Action
RESUME OF
Identify territ… developmen… as follows:
1)
2)
3)
4)
5)
6)

3M COMPANY TRAVEL EXPENSE VOUCHER FORM 48 A | EMPLOYEE NAME (Print) | PERIOD ENDING | T/A USE | DEPT NO | SPECIAL MAILING ADDRESS Bldg Floor Log Number | EMPLOYEE NO
HOME ADDRESS: City State Zip | EMPLOYEE SIGNATURE | APPROVED BY (Print & Sign) Date | CO CAR YR & MAKE | CO CAR NO "n" if temp.
DATE | ITINERARY FROM INTERMEDIATE TO | Miles on Pers Car | COMPANY CAR Bus Miles Cash Gas Gas Cost | PKG TOLLS. | TAXI & LIMO | ROOM | MEALS COST CD | PHONE | MISCELLANEOUS COST EXPLANATION | SUMMARY CATEGORY AMOUNT
Personal car allow | Co. Car Gas | Parking and tolls | Taxi &
TOTALS
ENTERTA…
DATE
PURPO…
DISTR…

DAILY CALL REPORT
Industrial Abrasives Division
3M COMPANY
Sales Rep | Terr Code | Branch Mgr | Date
C D | ACCOUNT NAME AND ADDRESS | SELL THRU DISTRIBUTOR | DISTRIBUTOR CLASSIFICATION | CONSUMER DEALER CLASSIFICATION | TRAVEL EXPENSE ACTUAL | BUDGET
Total Distributor | Total Consumer Dealer | Total Days Worked
3M Action 200 Paper

Figure 16.4 Call report, expense voucher, and weekly sales report. These are three of the records most commonly kept by 3M salespeople.

You should re-examine your territory management plan continually. Update it often so it reflects the current status of your various accounts. When possible, use a portable computer and appropriate software to improve your records management system. Computers can help you to achieve increased selling time and to enhance customer service.

Stress Management

Personal selling produces a certain amount of stress, in part from the non-routine nature of sales work. Each day brings a variety of new experiences, some of which may cause stress. Prospecting, for example, can be threatening to some salespeople. Long hours on the job, the loss of leisure time, and too little time for family members also can be stressful. While "variety is the spice of life," there is a limit to how much diversity one can cope with. One of the keys to success in selling is learning how to bring order to the many facets of the job. We also must be physically and mentally prepared to handle work-related stress.

stress The response of the body or mind to demands on it, in the form of either psychological or physiological strain.

Stress can be defined as the behavioural adjustments to change that affect you physically and psychologically. It is a process by which your body and mind mobilize energy for coping with change and challenge.[12] Repeated or prolonged stress can trigger a variety of warning signs. Physical signs might include headaches, loss of appetite, muscle tension, hypertension, or fatigue. Psychological symptoms might include anxiety, depression, loss of memory, or irritability. Stress interferes with your ability to concentrate, make decisions, think creatively, and engage in productive relationships.[13] This latter problem can be a serious barrier to success in sales. Lucille Peszat, executive director of the Canadian Centre for Stress and Well-Being, says, "Changes in your behaviour—you're more sarcastic, preoccupied, and inclined to procrastinate—could indicate you're overstressed."[14] Some stress is beneficial because it helps keep us motivated, but too much stress can be unhealthy if left unchecked.

Stress might be caused by trying to figure out ways to meet a sales quota or schedule travel throughout a sales territory. Missed appointments, presentations before large groups, and lack of feedback concerning your performance also can create stress. Ironically, some of the time-saving tools used by salespeople (e.g., fax machines, cellular phones, and e-mail) make it difficult for them to escape the pressures of their job. Many salespeople feel they are on call 24 hours a day.

As noted in Chapter 1, information surplus has replaced information scarcity as an important new problem in the age of information. Increasingly, knowledge workers report tension with colleagues, loss of job satisfaction, and strained personal relationships as a result of information overload. Too much information also crowds out quiet moments needed for reflection and to restore balance in our lives. It is not possible to eliminate stress from your life, but you can adopt stress management strategies that can help you cope with stress in your life. Four stress management strategies are discussed next: maintaining a stress-free home office, maintaining an optimistic outlook, practising healthy emotional expression, and maintaining a healthy lifestyle.[15]

MAINTAIN A STRESS-FREE HOME OFFICE

Many salespeople maintain a home office. With a little effort, it's possible to create a less stressful home office environment. Install a business line for phone, e-mail, and fax that rings only in the office. It's not professional to have other family members answering business calls. If your office is not an appropriate meeting space, meet with clients at their office or at a restaurant. Establish set hours. Try not to let work hours extend into evenings and weekends. Let your neighbours and friends know you keep office hours and cannot be disturbed for socializing during them.[16]

MAINTAIN AN OPTIMISTIC OUTLOOK

Passion Group Ltd., a publisher that helps companies reach the student market, is one of many newer, Canadian technology-based companies concerned with providing a work environment where employees can have fun and feel comfortable. One of its employees, Rufus, is a five-year-old Jack Russell terrier. Rufus has been "employed" for three years and shares under-the-desk space with a six-month-old Border terrier named Oliver. His official position is mascot; he is responsible for "promoting a positive attitude in the office."[17]

Researchers who evaluated the coping strategies of 101 salespeople from three companies found that those who faced job-related stress with an optimistic outlook fared better than those with a pessimistic attitude. The research team found that the optimists used problem-focused coping strategies while the pessimists used emotion-focused techniques. The optimistic salespeople most frequently focused on various ways to solve the problem. The pessimistic salespeople were more likely to try to avoid the problem and to direct their feelings toward other people.[18]

PRACTISE HEALTHY EMOTIONAL EXPRESSION

When stress occurs, you may undergo physiological and psychological changes. Your heartbeat quickens, your blood pressure rises, and tension builds. To relieve the pressure you may choose a *fight* or a *flight response.* With

THE CUSTOMER'S PERSPECTIVE

Customers Like to See Happy Salespeople

Vancouver businessman Jim Pattison related one of the most interesting examples of how a positive attitude can have an impact on sales performance. His earliest selling experiences were selling garden seeds and then pots and pans, door-to-door. He tells of having to sell one set of pots per day to earn his living. He says, "I could sell one set on average if I got three evening appointments and, to get three appointments, I needed to knock on about 30 doors. One day, I realized that, if I whistled while going door to door, more people would open their doors to me and I only needed to make 22 calls on a street to get three appointments in order to sell one set. That's when I discovered that people like dealing with happy people, so I increased my productivity by whistling and being happy." For a man with humble beginnings and who describes himself as "having no other skills except as a salesman," Jim Pattison is now the sole owner of Canada's third-largest privately held company. The Jim Pattison Group www.jimpattison.com has 25 000 employees and annual sales in excess of $5 billion.[b]

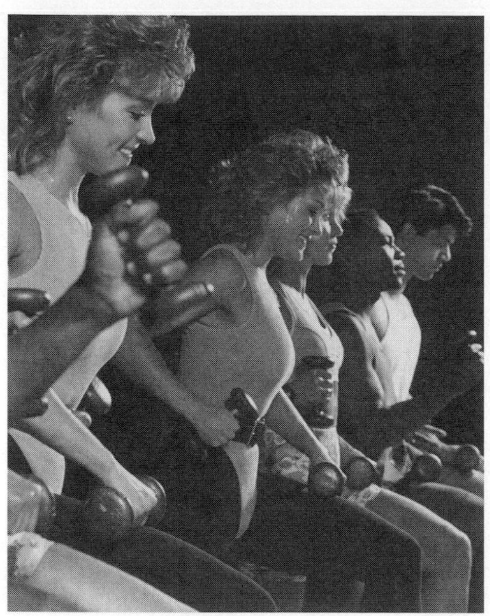

Exercise is an excellent way to moderate stress.

a fight response, you might unleash an avalanche of harsh words or ignore a person with whom you are dealing. These reactions, of course, are not recommended. At work, this behaviour may damage relationships with team members, customers, or customer support personnel. A flight response is running away from the problem: rather than face the issue squarely, you decide to turn your back on it. Flight is usually not satisfactory, as the problem will seldom go away by itself.

If you feel stress from an impractical quota, talk to your sales manager and try to get the quota reduced. Don't just give in to the feeling of being overwhelmed. If you are spending too much time away from family, take a close look at your territory management plan and try to develop a more efficient way to make sales calls. If you feel perpetually overwhelmed by job demands and you cannot negotiate a less demanding work schedule, then the only solution may be to leave this stressful environment. To achieve a more balanced life, consider a sales career in a less hectic industry.[19]

MAINTAIN A HEALTHY LIFESTYLE

www.burntsand.com

An effective exercise program—jogging, tennis, golf, racquetball, walking, or some other favourite exercise—can counter the harmful chemicals that build up in your bloodstream after a prolonged period of stress. Toronto-based IT consulting company Burntsand Inc. provides a recreation room to help employees de-stress.[20] The majority of companies currently offering employee fitness programs usually do so through athletic and fitness club memberships.

SELLING IN THE GLOBAL ECONOMY

Clean Your Filters

The selling environment today is growing increasingly diverse. According to Shirley Roberts, president of Toronto-based Market-Driven Solutions Inc., visible minorities will account for 24 percent of the Canadian population by 2016. As a salesperson, you will need to build relationships with customers and co-workers with very diverse backgrounds. Mark Williams, author of *The Ten Lenses: Your Guide to Living and Working in a Multicultural World*, says that people view others through a set of perceptual filters based on their own experiences and what they have learned. The better you understand your own perceptual filters and those of others, the better you will be able to communicate with and respond to other people. You need to consider your views on race, religion, culture, nationality, and ethnicity, because your ability to relate to people from diverse populations will increasingly determine your success in sales and management. An important part of managing yourself is to make sure your filters are clean.[c]

One in five members of fitness clubs join as a result of company-sponsored programs; 83 percent of clubs offer special corporate rates.[21]

The food you eat can also play a critical role in helping you manage stress. Health experts agree that the typical Canadian diet—high in saturated fats, refined sugars, additives, caffeine, and even too much protein—is the wrong menu for coping with stress. Employees of Husky Injection Molding Systems Ltd. in Bolton, Ontario, enjoy fresh, healthy cafeteria food, including butternut squash soup, vegetable fajitas, and abundant fruit and salad choices. In addition, there are on-site aerobics classes, a fitness centre, a naturopath, a masseuse, a doctor, and a physiotherapist. The company also sponsors a smoking-cessation program, and rewards fit employees with an extra day of vacation each year.[22]

www.husky.ca

Leisure time can also provide you with the opportunity to relax and get rid of work-related stress. Jovan Vuksanovich uses billiards to help increase relaxation skills among corporate clients, frequently combining lectures and demonstrations for an entertaining, relaxing, and informative evening. His clients have included CHUM and Nortel.[23]

In many respects, salespeople must possess the same self-discipline as a professional athlete. Sales work can be physically demanding. Lack of proper rest, poor eating habits, excessive drinking, and failure to exercise properly can reduce one's ability to deal with stress and strain.

SELLING MENTOR

Quick Tips to Help Reduce Stress

1. *Take 10 deep breaths.* It increases brain chemicals, such as serotonin, which help calm you. If your muscles feel tense, stretch them.
2. *Drink six to eight glasses of water daily.* This flushes stress-induced chemical by-products from your body. Eat lots of fruit and vegetables. In particular, such greens as broccoli increase your reserves of vitamins B and C, and zinc, all important stress fighters.
3. *Get sufficient sleep.* Drink camomile tea or warm milk before going to bed. The number of hours of sleep required for good health varies from person to person, but seven or eight hours seems to be about right for most people. Stress increases when you are tired.
4. *Take a 15-minute break.* Close your eyes; take a short nap; or simply tune in to your favourite music. Look at a cartoon or read a joke. Laughter releases endorphins that will help you deal with stress.
5. *Unplug, ignore, or simply tune out.* Learn to create technology-free zones and times at work and at home. Fewer interruptions will help you manage your time better and you will be healthier and happier with less stress.
6. *Go for a walk.* Any exercise helps, and walking is a readily available and easy exercise no matter where you are.[d]

SUMMARY

In this chapter we described management of self as a four-dimensional process. It involves time management, territory management, records management, and stress management.

All salespeople can learn more about their products and improve their selling skills. However, there is no way to expand time. Our only option is to find ways to improve time and territory management. The four time-saving techniques discussed in this chapter should be used by every salesperson. When used on a regular basis, they will set the stage for more face-to-face selling time.

The first step in territory management is classification of all customers according to sales volume or some other appropriate criterion. You normally should spend the most time with accounts that have the greatest sales potential. The second step requires developing a routing and scheduling plan. This plan should reduce time spent travelling between accounts. In some cases you can substitute telephone calls or e-mail messages for personal calls.

A good record-keeping system provides many advantages. Accurate, up-to-date records can actually save time because work is better organized. The company also benefits because sales reports provide an important communication link with members of the sales force. Today computers are used to develop more efficient record-keeping systems.

There is a certain amount of stress associated with sales work, in part from the non-routine nature of personal selling. Salespeople must learn to cope with the factors that upset their equilibrium. Four stress management strategies were discussed: maintaining a stress-free home office, maintaining an optimistic outlook, practising healthy emotional expression, and maintaining a healthy lifestyle.

Key Terms

Sales Call Plan **388**

Sales Territory **379**

Stress **392**

Review Questions

1. The Selling in Action boxed feature (on p. 380) describes Kip Grant's self-improvement plan. Why is it important for salespeople to have a self-improvement plan?
2. Management of self has been described as a four-dimensional process. Describe each dimension.
3. What are the two major ways a salesperson can increase sales volume?
4. How can a salesperson use a time log to improve time management?
5. List four techniques the salesperson should use to make better use of valuable selling time.
6. Effective territory management involves two major steps. What are they?
7. What is a *sales call plan*? Explain how it is used.
8. Describe the records most commonly kept by salespeople.
9. What is the definition of "stress"? What are some indicators of stress?
10. The Selling Mentor boxed feature (on p. 395) describes six ways to reduce stress. Which of these do you think are most important for persons employed in the sales field? Explain.

Application Exercises

1. Deciding on a goal can be the most crucial decision of your life. It is more damaging not to have a goal than it is not to reach a goal. It is generally agreed that the major cause of failure is the lack of a well-defined purpose. A successful life results not from chance, but from a succession of successful days. List three goals for yourself in these four categories: career, family, education, interpersonal relations.

2. You have just been hired as a salesperson for a major Canadian industrial distributor. Your sales manager has told you she expects you to make sales calls 210 days per year (you get four weeks of vacation, two weeks of sales training, 10 paid holidays, and are not required to call on customers during the two weeks around Christmas). She wants all salespeople to average 3.5 calls per day. She has advised you that your best customers should see you twice each month, and you should call personally on every account at least once each year. She has provided you with the following information on your accounts, based on last year's sales. She wants your suggested sales call plan (i.e., how you will allocate your sales calls across customers) for next year, based on this information. How would you allocate your calls to these customers? What other recommendations would you make to your sales manager?

Accounts	Sales
Top 10 accounts	$300 200
Next 10 accounts	$180 500
Next 10 accounts	$164 200
Next 20 accounts	$135 600
Next 20 accounts	$128 800
Next 20 accounts	$ 99 300
Next 30 accounts	$135 210
Last 30 accounts	$ 53 460

3. Interview someone you know who uses a planning calendar. What kind is it: pocket, desk, or some other type? How long has the person been using it? How important is the calendar to daily, weekly, monthly, and yearly planning? Has the person ever considered discontinuing its use? What are the person's suggestions for someone who does not use one? Write your answer.

4. Go to **www.google.ca** (or another search engine of your choice) and hit "advanced search." Type "time management" under "Find results with exact phrase." Limit your search by typing ".ca" under "domain." Do the same for "stress management." To what other groups besides salespeople do these terms appear to be most relevant? Why? Be prepared to discuss some of what you find in class.

ROLE-PLAY EXERCISE

Using the information in the Chapter 15 role-play exercise, develop a contact plan regarding the future contacts you set up. Your sales manager has scheduled a status report meeting to go over your activities with this account. With this information and with the information written into your calendar, meet with another student who will role-play your sales manager to talk over the account management meetings you have scheduled. Discuss how this schedule enhances both your time and territory management and adds value to the sale.

CRM Application Exercise CORRESPONDING WITH CRM

Waiting for a client who forgot an appointment can be very time consuming. The client who promptly receives a faxed reminder note is more likely to remember and honour a commitment to meet. Quickly confirming an agreement reached by telephone is easy for CRM systems such as ACT! Look up the Contact Ian Program, select Write, and Fax Cover to display the fax cover sheet which, by itself, may be used to convey a short confirmation message. Position the cursor at Subject and type "Lunch," then press Enter twice and type "I look forward to lunch with you Friday noon at Jimmy's." Select File, Print (Ctrl+P) to print the fax cover note. If your computer is running fax software, you could send the fax cover note directly to your client's fax machine.

Case Problem

Paula Shannon, introduced at the beginning of this chapter, spends part of most weeks away from her Montreal home-based office, managing a global team of 70 sales professionals for Boston-based Lionbridge Technologies, Inc. One indicator of her success at building a strong sales team is that Lionbridge placed second in 2003 for Best Sales Team in the American Business Awards. In 2004, Paula was recognized with the inaugural International Stevie Award as Best Sales Executive. This award recognizes leadership, innovation, perseverance, creativity, teamwork, and integrity. There are many things that must come together to create success at this level. Paula Shannon is a person who has managed herself and her career with meticulous detail; her success is not an accident. Paula Shannon notes six principles that she believes have contributed to her success:

1. *Be self-confident, but be humble and respectful.* Customers buy from salespeople who are confident and professional, not from those who are arrogant or self-centred. Paula says, "Some of the best people I have worked with have been able to combine self-confidence with a genuine interest and respect for our customers' business issues and needs."
2. *Communicate clear, simple customer solutions in a language they understand.* Some salespeople have a tendency toward bafflegab—sprinkling their discussion with technical jargon without explaining it—mistakenly believing that this will impress their customers. Yet, most customers want a clear simple solution to their buying problems. Paula says, "The art of making complex issues simple seems to be one of the most important things a salesperson can do. When done well, this results in a 'call to action' and a sense of mission or purpose to see the job through."
3. *Be a prolific reader.* Paula Shannon reads both fiction and nonfiction for pleasure. She also reads the *Wall Street Journal* daily, *Fortune*, *CIO Insight*, *Selling Power*, *The Economist*, *Harvard Business Review*, and numerous reports, industry newsletters, and specialized publications. Paula says, "I know that the ability to digest large volumes of information has always been a key to my success. Whether I am getting up to speed on a project, a new deal, or an opportunity, or staying current on business trends or technology shifts, my reading is something that has helped me at every level of my secondary education and my career."
4. *Have fun and love what you do.* Salespeople who work too hard are often subject to burnout. You need time for yourself and to relax. Paula logs more than 240 000 kilometres by air a year. There is no doubt she works hard, but she also plays hard. Paula says, "I rarely schedule work for myself over the weekends and save time for my family, sports, friends, and fun. As a result, I remain energetic, positive, and upbeat. These are all things that are important when interacting with both colleagues and customers."
5. *Develop a competence with technology.* At one point in her career, Paula purchased her own laptop. She

recognized that she could improve her own efficiency if she could work on correspondence and client proposals while away from her office. Paula says, "Sales requires extraordinary time management, immediacy, customer focus, and access to and the exchange of information. Technology is an essential tool in the equation." Speaking of the impact of technology on herself and her sales team, she adds, "Our ability to respond to customers, solve problems, and deliver information has improved five-fold. Remote access to a shared store of centralized information has helped us, as service providers, to manage global projects, report on status, improve quality, and co-ordinate worldwide teams."

6. *Develop both depth and breadth of knowledge.* Paula credits some of her success to the fact that she has taken several "career meanderings" during her career—lateral moves and an occasional step downward. Speaking of this, Paula says, "In sales—deep technical or product and service—offering expertise is crucial to your success and credibility with customers. However, those skills alone, without broader business or cultural context, result in someone whose options become increasingly limited as their career progresses."

Questions

1. Which of Paula Shannon's "six principles for success" will make the most important contribution to a career in personal selling? Explain.
2. Reflect on your own approach to accomplishing things. Then select two of Paula Shannon's principles that you would find easy to adopt. Also, select two principles you would find difficult to adopt. Explain your choices.
3. What things, among the many that Paula Shannon does, do you think help her manage stress most effectively? Explain.
4. How important do you think time management is to Paula Shannon? records management? territory management?

CRM Case Study MANAGING YOURSELF WITH CRM

A key objective in managing your time is to confirm that, at any time, you are working on your highest priorities. Contacting prospective customers is the highest priority for most salespeople. The next challenge is to decide in which order prospects should be contacted. Many salespeople prioritize their accounts on the basis of their value, the amount that they are likely to spend with the sales organization.

Questions

1. On the basis of the dollar amount that Pat Silva estimated that each account might spend, in what order would you contact the prospects in the ACT! database?
2. If you were to rank these prospects on the basis of your sales commission, would this priority list be different from the list developed in question 1? If so, why?
3. There are several ways that this list of prospects could be prioritized: by date; dollar amount; or commission. Which of these rankings is best?

CHAPTER 17

Management of the Sales Force

LEARNING OBJECTIVES

After studying this chapter, you should be able to

1. Describe the responsibilities and activities of a sales manager
2. List and discuss the qualities of an effective sales manager
3. Discuss recruitment and selection of salespeople
4. Describe effective orientation, training, and motivation practices
5. Describe selected compensation plans
6. List and discuss criteria for evaluating sales performance

When Brad Lawson joined SAS Institute as a district sales manager, he faced a number of major challenges. His sales team was at the bottom. It had sold only half of its assigned quota for the previous year. SAS Institute is a highly respected provider of sophisticated computer programs serving more than 35 000 business, government, and university sites. However, sales in his district were disappointing.

At age 30, Brad was working with a group of veteran high-tech sales representatives, most of whom were at least 10 years older than him. To gain credibility, he began going on sales calls with his salespeople and doing presale planning with them. He also told the sales team he would work hard to obtain the type of support they needed from other SAS units. Brad set high goals for the district, and some salespeople who felt he was too aggressive quit.[1]

Many salespeople aspire to become a sales manager. They generally have an expectation that, if they excel in sales, they will be promoted. Many companies do, in fact, reward superior salespeople by promoting them to sales management. Unfortunately, it is possible that, by doing this, companies may lose their best salesperson and gain their worst sales manager. Those who achieve success as sales manager may advance to more senior management positions, but the skills required to be successful as a sales manager are different from those required to be successful in sales.

Sales Management Functions

The **sales manager** has two main areas of responsibility. The first is to help plan and to implement the firm's sales strategy. To do this, the sales manager must be able to think strategically to identify high-value market opportunities that will evolve from changes within their industry, or changing customer needs. They must make strategic decisions related to account selection, penetration, and retention, and to product line development and emphasis. To implement the sales strategy, sales managers must ensure that the sales force has the resources and support necessary to succeed. They must champion the needs of the sales force at the executive level, and they must gain and maintain co-operation with many internal departments, including marketing, finance, accounting, human resources, and distribution.

sales manager The person who is responsible to help plan and to implement the firm's sales strategy, and to manage and develop the firm's sales force.

The second main area of responsibility is to manage and develop the firm's sales force. To do this, sales managers perform many management activities including recruiting, training, organizing, and supervising salespeople. The sales manager's activities may, however, vary somewhat from one marketing organization to another. Today, some of them even function in a virtual office environment. Sales force automation permits salespeople to receive data on their laptops or their home computers. The use of other technology—videoconferencing, teleconferencing, e-mail, and voice mail—reduces the need for frequent face-to-face contact with members of the sales team.[2]

Sales managers maintain a steady flow of information to salespeople and also provide a variety of selling tools and aids. Successful sales managers also help salespeople cope with the rapid change and uncertainty that permeates today's business environment.[3]

Qualities of a Good Sales Manager

Sales managers can have a dramatic influence on the attitudes and behaviours of the salespeople they supervise. Effective leadership has been discussed in hundreds of books and articles. A careful review of this material indicates that most successful supervisory management personnel have certain behaviours in common. Writers of this material agree that there are two important dimensions of effective leadership.[4] We label these dimensions *structure* and *consideration.*

STRUCTURE

Sales managers who display **structure** clearly define their own duties and those of the sales staff. They assume an active role in directing their subordinates' work. Policies and procedures are clearly defined, and subordinates know what is expected of them. Salespeople also know how well they are doing because the structured supervisor evaluates their productivity and provides feedback. Members of the sales force usually appreciate the predictable

structure A leadership characteristic displayed by sales managers who clearly define their own duties and those of the sales staff, and who assume an active role in directing their subordinates.

nature of the highly structured sales manager. The following behaviours provide evidence of structure:

1. *Planning takes place on a regular basis.* The effective sales manager thinks ahead and decides what to do in the future. Strategic planning is the process of determining the company's current position in the market, determining where you want to be and when, and making decisions on how to secure the position you want.[5] Strategic planning gives meaning and direction to the sales force.
2. *Expectations are clearly communicated.* Expectations of sales managers can have a positive impact on the performance of salespeople. In most cases high expectations lead to high performance.[6]
3. *Decisions are made promptly and firmly.* An effective sales manager is willing and able to make decisions in a timely way. An ineffective manager often postpones important decisions, hoping the problem will go away. Of course most decisions cannot be made until all the facts are available. A good sales manager keeps the lines of communication open and involves subordinates in making the truly important decisions.
4. *Performance of salespeople is appraised regularly.* All employees want to know "where they stand" with the manager. An effective sales manager provides regular feedback. When a salesperson is not performing up to established standards, the sales manager takes immediate action.

Although structure is an important aspect of sales management, too much structure can sometimes create problems. In an effort to become better organized and more systematic, some sales organizations have developed

An effective sales manager provides regular feedback. All employees want to know where they stand with the manager.

detailed policies and procedures that rob salespeople of time and energy. Filling out endless reports and forms, for example, can cause unnecessary frustration and may reduce productivity.[7]

CONSIDERATION

A sales manager who displays the leadership dimension of **consideration** is more likely to have relationships with salespeople that are characterized by mutual trust, respect for salespeople's ideas, and consideration for their feelings. A climate of good two-way communication usually exists between the manager and the employee. The following behaviours provide evidence of consideration:

consideration A leadership dimension displayed by sales managers who have relationships with salespeople that are characterized by mutual trust, respect for the salesperson's ideas, and consideration for their feelings.

1. *Regular and effective communication receives a high priority.* Whenever possible, the effective manager engages in face-to-face communication with salespeople. They do not rely entirely on e-mail, letters, or sales reports for information sharing but arrange for face-to-face meetings. John Morrone, vice-president of sales for Pitney Bowes Management Services, frequently travels with his salespeople. He says, "My claim to fame is reaching out and touching people."[8] The effective sales manager is a good listener, and creates an atmosphere of co-operation and understanding.
2. *Each salesperson is treated as an individual.* The sales manager takes a personal interest in each member of the sales force. No one is treated "like a number." The interest is genuine, not artificial. The effective sales manager does not endanger effectiveness by showing favouritism to anyone.
3. *Good performance is rewarded often.* Positive reinforcement is one of the strongest morale-building factors in the work environment. Ken Blanchard, co-author of *The One-Minute Manager*, says, "The key to developing people will always be to concentrate on catching them doing something right instead of blaming them for doing something wrong."[9] Recognition for a job well done is always appreciated.

SITUATIONAL LEADERSHIP

Mastery of consideration and structure skills is an important first step toward achieving success in sales management. The next step is to match your leadership style to the various situations that surface among members of your sales force. Paul Hershey is credited with development of **situational leadership**. This leadership approach is based on the theory that the most successful leadership occurs when the leader's style matches the situation.

situational leadership Matching your leadership style to the particular situation that you face with individual members of your sales force.

Let's assume that a member of your sales team has almost totally abandoned customer service and follow-up activities. She is devoting nearly all of her attention to calls on new customers. Many of her regular customers have complained about poor service, and a crisis is developing. At this point, the leadership dimension of structure will require the most time and attention.

Sales managers who develop consideration and structure skills and the flexibility required to be a situational leader must pass one additional test. If you fail the character test, you fail as a sales manager. Character is composed of your personal standards of behaviour, including your honesty and integrity. If you are seen as an honest broker of advice and assistance, as someone who always tells the truth, trust and respect will build. But building trust is a slow process and it can be irreparably destroyed by a single lie or deception.[10]

COACHING FOR PEAK PERFORMANCE

"When you die there is an express line at the Pearly Gates for coaches," jokes Canadian consultant, international speaker, and award-winning retailer Donald Cooper (**www.donaldcooper.com**). He recognizes that the ability to be a good coach—to improve the attitudes and skills of others—is both rare and important.[11] A sales manager who develops a leadership style that combines structure and consideration behaviours possesses the skills needed to be an effective coach. **Coaching** is an interpersonal process between the sales manager and the salesperson in which the manager helps the salesperson improve performance in a specific area. The coaching process has two primary areas of focus: helping the salesperson recognize the need to improve his or her performance, and developing the salesperson's commitment to improve performance.[12]

coaching An interpersonal process between a sales manager and a salesperson in which the manager helps the salesperson improve performance in a specific area.

Coaching is often used to correct a specific performance problem such as ineffective prospecting, poorly developed sales presentations, or failure to provide service after the sale. We will outline a four-step coaching strategy:[13]

Step one in the coaching process involves documentation of performance problems. In some cases the best approach is to observe and assess performance during actual sales calls.

Step two involves getting the salesperson to recognize and agree that there is a need to improve performance in a specific area. Sales managers should never assume the salesperson sees the problem in the same way they do.

Step three involves exploring solutions. At this point it's often best to let the salesperson suggest ways to improve performance.

Step four involves getting a commitment from the salesperson to take action. This step may involve development of a contract—written or verbal—that clarifies the coaching goals, approaches, and outcomes.

A major goal of coaching meetings is to improve performance while enabling sales managers and salespeople to maintain a relationship based on mutual respect and trust.

Recruitment and Selection of Salespeople

Careful recruitment and selection of salespeople is very important. This is one of the most significant tasks sales managers perform because sales organizations have been forced to become more sophisticated. Today's salesperson still needs to know how to prospect, make sales presentations, negotiate and close sales, and they must also be familiar with changing market conditions and understand how different companies operate.[14]

The authors of *How to Hire and Develop Your Next Top Performer: The Five Qualities That Make Salespeople Great* say that about half of the people working in sales should be doing something else. In addition, they say that about 20 to 25 percent of the salespeople currently employed are selling products or services not suited to their personality.[15] If the research reported by these authors is accurate, then it appears that sales managers are frequently hiring the wrong people.

Successful salespeople are often difficult to identify. The selection of sales personnel today is, however, more of a science and less of an art. Sales managers no longer need to rely on "gut feelings." The ability to identify sales aptitude accurately can be acquired. Many progressive sales organizations recognize the need to help sales managers develop the interviewing skills necessary to make profitable hiring decisions. It is impossible to avoid occasionally hiring a poor performer, but sales managers can improve their average by using some established recruitment and selection guidelines.

DETERMINE ACTUAL JOB REQUIREMENTS

To decide what type of applicant is needed, the manager should first outline the duties the person will perform. The sales manager must have a clear picture of the job requirements before beginning the recruitment process.

Some sales managers make every effort to discover the success factors that contribute to the achievements of their high-performance salespeople. Success factors are the skills, knowledge, abilities, and behaviours considered critical for successful performance.[16] This information may be collected through interviews with salespeople or customers, by observing the salesperson during sales calls, or by some other method.

After a careful study of the duties the salesperson will perform and identification of the success factors, the sales manager should prepare, or have human resources prepare, a job description. A job description is an explanation of what the salesperson will do and under what conditions the work will be performed. It is a good idea to spell out in as much detail as possible the abilities and qualities that the applicant needs to be successful. This can be accomplished by answering a few basic questions about the position.

1. Will the person be developing new sales territory or assuming responsibility for an established territory?
2. Is the product or service well established, or is it new to the marketplace?
3. Will the salesperson work under the sales manager's close supervision or independently?
4. What amount of travel is required? What is the likelihood of eventual transfer? promotion?

Positive reinforcement is one of the strongest ways to build morale. Effective managers reward their subordinates for good performance.

Once the job description is prepared, the foundation has been established to determine the type of person to be hired. There is no substitute for knowing what the job requires.

SEARCH OUT APPLICANTS FROM SEVERAL SOURCES

To identify the best possible person, sales managers usually seek applicants from more than one source. As a rule of thumb, they try to interview three or more applicants for each opening. Some suggested sources of new employees follow.

1. *Candidates within the company and employee referrals.* An important first place to consider is other departments within the company where someone might aspire to a sales position. Current employees are generally already familiar with some important aspects of the company: its history, operations, policies, products, competitors, and customers. Companies are also increasingly using referral programs because employees often know of people with similar skills in other organizations. Microsoft rewards employees who make referrals with a gift certificate to the company store, and this has become one of the top three sources of new employees for the company.[17]

2. *College and university students.* Many business firms are turning to college and university campuses to recruit salespeople. Placement offices are usually co-operative about publicizing openings. Procter & Gamble Canada president Tim Penner spends 10 days every year touring university campuses, visiting career centres, and talking to deans about potential prospects to try to build a culturally diverse workforce more reflective of the consumer base his company serves.[18]

3. *Trade and newspaper advertisements.* A carefully prepared newspaper advertisement will often attract well-qualified job applicants. A well-written ad should accurately describe the job requirements and spell out the opportunities. The ad should "sell" the position, but it should not exaggerate its benefits.

4. *Employment agencies and listings.* There are 375 public employment offices located throughout Canada. These offices will recruit applicants and screen them according to your specifications. There is no charge for this service. There are also many private employment agencies. These firms specialize in matching applicants to the job and usually do some initial screening for employers. A fee is assessed for the services these agencies provide.

5. *Internet.* Many companies now solicit applications on their Web sites. As well, Internet job boards are becoming increasingly popular. They can reach candidates in distant places and can locate talented salespeople who are not actively searching for jobs. Vancouver human

resources executive Shirley Quinn finds job boards convenient and cost-effective when hiring the best sales and management people.[19]

SELECT THE BEST-QUALIFIED APPLICANT

Once you have identified qualified applicants, the next step is to select the best person. This is becoming more difficult as products become more complex, customers become more sophisticated, and competitors become more aggressive. Selecting the best-qualified applicant will never be easy, but there are some qualifications and characteristics that all sales managers should look for. One of the most important qualities is a high level of interest in and enthusiasm for the job and a high degree of self-motivation. Salespeople have to be self-starters. Barry Farber, president of Farber Training Systems (**www.barryfarber.com**), says that he would hire a salesperson without experience or knowledge of the industry who is willing to give 110 percent versus someone who has experience and is highly skilled but who is not motivated.[20]

Some sales managers use a performance activity to identify the self-motivated person. For example, a potential candidate could be given a product ID and asked to make a presentation to one or more people during a subsequent meeting. The candidate's motivational level is measured by the efforts made to obtain enough information about the product and company to prepare a good presentation. Brian Jeffrey, president of Carp, Ontario–based SalesForce Training & Consulting (**www.salesforcetraining.com**), recommends that you not offer an interview to candidates who phone you for a sales position. He says, "Candidates who won't ask for an interview won't ask for an order either." He also suggests that you tell candidates you will get back to them after a few weeks, when you have interviewed other candidates. A "closer" will say, "Wait. You don't need to interview anyone else. I'm the person you need."[21]

Bruce Diamond, vice-president of sales for a large office equipment company, says, "Our salespeople now need to be much more professional, much more educated about the market, customers, products, and business in general."[22] His strategy for finding good salespeople includes discussions of business trends and developments. During the interview, he poses business situations and asks the candidate to come up with solutions. Diamond says he is impressed when a candidate displays an understanding of profitable revenues and finding the right customers to do business with.

Reliability is another quality to search for. Do not hesitate to check references to determine police records, problems at previous jobs, or patterns of instability. The applicant for a sales position must be able to earn your complete trust.

One of the greatest challenges is hiring salespeople who can develop a close, trusting, long-term relationship with customers. As we have noted previously, the manner in which salespeople establish, build, and maintain relationships is no longer an incidental aspect of personal selling. Mike Mitchell, vice-president of human resources for Tiffany & Company, says, "We look for people who feel a great sense of purpose in serving our customers. You can train people to be consultative in their approach to the point that they master the mechanics of the sales process, but you can't teach someone to care."[23]

Experts in the field of employment testing say that psychological tests can be helpful as an element of the hiring process. These tests can assess self-confidence, competitiveness, and even a candidate's overall suitability for specific sales positions. Test results should always be used in conjunction with information obtained from interviewing the candidate. Reference checks are another valuable source of information and should always be used to confirm a candidate's suitability.

Orientation and Training

Once you have selected the best-qualified salesperson, two things should be done to ensure that this person becomes a productive member of your staff. First, give the new employee a thorough orientation to your business operation. Provide the orientation before the person begins working. This will include a review of your company's history, philosophy of doing business, mission statement, business policies, and compensation plan, as well as other important information.

Second, initiate a training program that will help the person achieve success. Sales training that is carefully planned and executed can make a major contribution to the performance of every salesperson. Study results indicate that salespeople have a more positive view about their job, greater commitment, and improved performance when their sales managers clarify their job role, how to execute their tasks, and how their needs will be satisfied with successful job performance.[24]

Even salespeople with great potential are handicapped when the company fails to provide adequate training. Keep in mind that, in the absence of formal training, employees will develop their own approaches to performing tasks. Many sales managers believe that new salespeople (i.e., those with no prior sales experience) need special attention during the orientation and training period. One expert said, "They must be managed differently, compensated differently, and they must be gradually converted to the ranks of experienced sales professionals. It is often an eighteen-month process."[25]

The size of the firm should not dictate the scope of the training program. Even the smallest marketing organization should have a formal sales training program. This program should have three dimensions:

- knowledge of the product line, company marketing strategies, territory information, and related areas
- attitude toward the company, the company's products and services, and the customers to be served, and
- skill in applying personal selling principles and practices—the "doing" part of the sales training program

An important part of the sales training program is foundation-level instruction. This aspect of sales training focuses on the *basics.* If salespeople are to plan and execute a sales call successfully, they must first master certain fundamen-

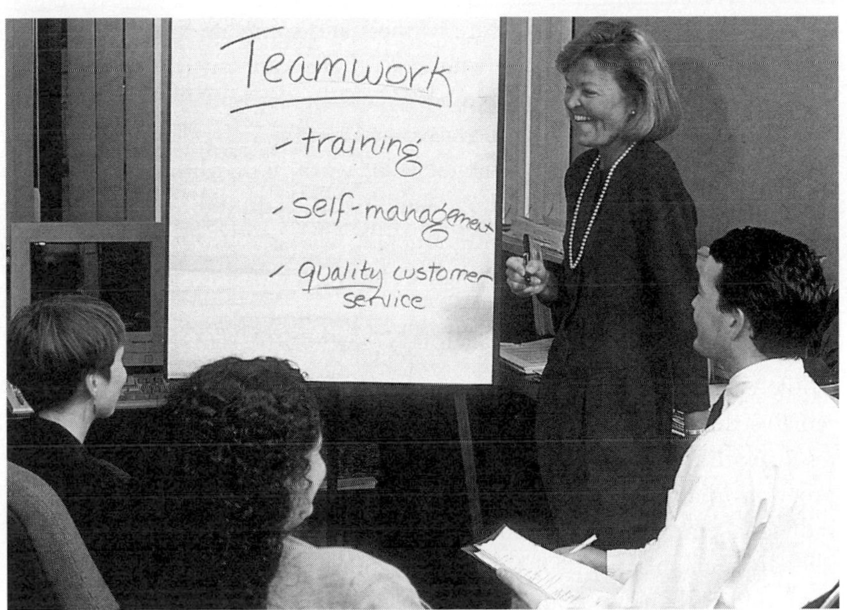

Orientation of new salespeople is one of the many duties performed by a sales manager. It's important that salespeople receive this early assistance.

tal selling skills—the skills that form the foundation for everything salespeople do in their careers. The steps that make up the Six-Step Presentation Plan (i.e., approach, presentation, demonstration, negotiation, close, and servicing the sale) represent fundamental selling skills (see Fig. 15.1).

Sales Force Motivation

It is helpful to note the difference between internal and external motivation. An **internal motivation** is an intrinsic reward that occurs when a duty or task is performed. If a salesperson enjoys calling on customers and solving their problems, this activity is in itself rewarding, and the salesperson is likely to be self-motivated.[26] Internal motivation is likely to be triggered when sales positions provide an opportunity for achievement and individual growth. **External motivation** is an action taken by another person involving rewards or other forms of reinforcement that cause the worker to behave in ways to ensure receipt of the award.[27] A cash bonus given to salespeople who achieve a sales goal provides an example of external motivation. Experts on motivation agree that organizations should attempt to provide a mix of internal satisfaction and external rewards.

internal motivation An intrinsic reward that occurs when a duty or task is performed.

external motivation Action taken by another person that involves rewards or other forms of reinforcement that cause the worker to behave in ways to ensure receipt of the reward.

A basic contention among too many sales managers has been that sales productivity can be improved by staging more elaborate sales contests, giving more expensive recognition awards, or picking exotic meeting locations. This point of view ignores the merits of internal motivation. One of the foremost critics of external rewards is Alfie Kohn, author of *No Contest: The Case against Competition* and *Punished by Rewards: The Trouble with Gold Stars, Incentive Plans, A's and Other Bribes.* Kohn states that a reward centre that forces people to compete for awards or recognition may undermine co-operation and teamwork. In addition, he says that reward plans can create a situation where some salespeople are winners and some are losers. Kohn further declares, "For each person who wins, there are many others who carry with them the feeling of having lost."[28]

In many cases, intrinsic motivators—achievement, challenge, responsibility, advancement, growth, enjoyment of work itself, and involvement—have a longer-term effect on employee attitudes than extrinsic motivators—contests, prizes, and money. A salesperson who is intrinsically satisfied in the job will work willingly at high-performance levels.

EFFECTIVE USE OF EXTERNAL REWARDS

While criticisms of external rewards have a great deal of merit, the fact remains that large numbers of organizations continue to achieve positive results with carefully developed incentive programs. It is possible to design programs that have long-range benefits for both the organization and the individual employee. Kirby Bonds, regional sales manager for the corporate sales division of Avis Rent-A-Car's corporate sales division has used sales contests to identify new accounts, build business within existing accounts, and generate endorsement letters from satisfied customers. Bonds keeps contest time frames short so more of his salespeople have an opportunity to win.[29]

Because people bring different interests, drives, and values to the workplace, they react differently to attempts at motivation. The owner of an incentive consulting company rewarded one of his highly productive employees with an attractive mink coat. She thanked him sincerely, took the coat home, but never wore it. When he asked her why, she explained that she didn't wear fur.[30]

If a salesperson is not making very much money, then a cash incentive may be an effective reward. An experienced salesperson who is earning a lot of money in salary and commission might be motivated by an exciting travel or merchandise incentive. High-performing salespeople employed by Hormel Foods Corporation were rewarded with a 1950s–themed road rally, complete with motorcycles and convertibles. People who are involved in a unique travel event often feel more valued and appreciated.[31]

EFFECTIVE COMMUNICATION

Some sales managers are finding that simply asking salespeople for their opinions and then following up on their suggestions, where appropriate, is an excellent way to motivate them. Effective communication is one of the most important qualities that salespeople desire from their sales manager.[32]

Many sales managers have discovered the value of communicating positive expectations to their salespeople. They recognize that most people can be greatly influenced by the expectations of others. Goethe gave some good advice that sales managers can use: "If you treat a man as he is, he will remain as he is; if you treat him as if he were what he could be, he will become what he could be." With the use of effective leadership practices and job enrichment, it is possible to release the motivation within each person.

Finally, an incentive premium that really hits home.

It seems most incentives lack one thing—incentive. That's why a gift card from The Home Depot makes so much sense. After all, what better way to reward someone who has helped improve your business than to help them improve their home? The gift cards are available in $10, $25, $50 and $100 amounts. Plus they'll be able to redeem their card at any Home Depot across Canada, making it the most practical gift of all. So to have an incentive program that really hits home, call your Home Depot incentive representative at (877) 423-3005.

Experts on motivation agree that organizations should provide salespeople with a mix of external rewards and internal satisfaction. Home Depot gift cards are redeemable across Canada and allow salespeople a choice of which products they wish to receive as external rewards.

Compensation Plans

A **compensation plan** for salespeople combines direct monetary payments (i.e., salary and commissions) and indirect monetary payments (such as paid vacations, pensions, and insurance plans). Compensation practices vary greatly throughout the field of selling. Furthermore, sales managers are constantly searching for the "perfect" sales force compensation plan. Of course, the perfect plan does not exist. Each plan must be chosen to suit the specific type of selling job, the objectives of the firm's marketing program, and the type of customer served.

compensation plan A pay plan for salespeople that combines direct monetary pay with indirect monetary payments such as paid vacations, pensions, and insurance plans.

As noted in Chapter 2, the highest amount of total compensation is earned by salespeople who practise value-added selling. Salespeople who use

EVERYONE SELLS

NBA Owner Motivates His Sales Team

Mark Cuban, owner of the National Basketball Association Dallas Mavericks, has been described as "probably the most involved owner in day-to-day activities that the pro basketball league has ever seen." When he bought the team, it had not been in the playoffs for 10 years. His mission, of course, was to improve the team's on-court performance, but also to dramatically increase its revenue from season ticket sales and sponsorships. Within one week, he added 30 new salespeople to the team's 5-member sales force. Cuban says, "I think the key to any business is to be able to connect with customers and prove to them that you can give better value than the next guy . . . . Too many companies, and too many teams in this league, are just praying companies. They pray that customers will respond to their ads and buy their products . . . . We take things into our own hands by selling and talking directly to customers." But, Mark Cuban is also careful to motivate his salespeople to superior performance. Most, but not all, incentives are cash. Many are given when specific goals are achieved, but there are surprises as well. George Killebrew, vice-president of corporate sponsorships, says, "It's the prize that you don't know is coming that is most motivating." In one year, paid attendance increased 60 percent; season ticket sales increased 25 percent; sponsorship revenue increased 30 percent; and the Mavericks made the playoffs.[a]

this approach realize that the solution to the customer's buying problem is more important than price. They are frequently involved in team selling and, in some cases, they are rewarded with a team compensation plan.

Increasingly, companies are abandoning compensation plans that are linked to a single target such as a sales quota. At Siebel Systems, an e-business software provider, 40 percent of each salesperson's incentive compensation is based on the customer's reported satisfaction with service and implementation of the products they have purchased. This plan encourages continual customer follow-up, which generates repeat business.[33]

In the field of selling there are five basic compensation plans. Here is a description of each:

1. *Straight commission plan.* The only direct monetary compensation comes from sales. No sales, no income. Salespeople under this plan are very conscious of their sales. Lack of job security can be a strong inducement to produce results. However, these people may also concentrate more on immediate sales than on long-term customer development.
2. *Commission plan with a draw provision or guaranteed salary.* This plan has about the same impact on salespeople as the straight commission plan. However, it gives them more financial security.
3. *Commission with a draw or guaranteed salary plus a bonus.* This plan offers more direct financial security than the first two plans. Therefore salespeople may adhere more to the company's objectives. The bonus may be based on sales or profits.

4. *Fixed salary plus bonus.* Salespeople functioning under this compensation plan tend to be more company centred and to have a fairly high degree of financial security if their salary is competitive. The bonus incentive helps motivate people under this plan.

5. *Straight salary.* Salespeople who work under this compensation plan are usually more company centred and have financial security.

According to the *Sales & Marketing Management*/Equation Research 2002 research study, most companies participating in the survey used some form of compensation plan that combined base salary and incentive.[34] The salary plus bonus and salary plus commission plans are both quite popular.

As might be expected, many companies are experimenting with some variation of these basic plans. In some situations, salespeople are rewarded for achieving a specific objective such as developing new accounts or improving the quality of customer service. Some awards take the form of cash or points that can be used to choose prizes. Award programs can be styled to suit a variety of sales objectives:

- *Specific product movement.* Bonus points can be given for the sale of selected items during a specified "push" period.
- *Percentage sales increase.* Sales levels can be established with points that are given only when those levels are reached.
- *Establish new accounts.* A block of points can be awarded for opening a new account, or for expansion selling to existing accounts.
- *Increase sales activity.* For each salesperson, points can be awarded based on the number of calls.[35]

There is no easy way to develop an effective compensation plan. There are, however, some important guidelines for your efforts to develop a good plan.

1. Be sure that your sales and marketing objectives are defined in detail. The plan should complement these goals. If sales and marketing objectives are in conflict with the compensation plan, problems will surely arise.

2. The compensation plan should be field tested before full implementation. Several questions should be answered: Will the new plan be easy to administer? How does the proposed plan differ in terms of payout compared with the existing plan?

3. Explain the compensation plan carefully to the sales force. Misunderstanding may generate distrust of the plan. Keep in mind that some salespeople may see change as a threat.

4. Change the compensation plan when conditions in the marketplace warrant change. One reason for the poor showing of many plans is

Recognition for success in sales can be an effective form of external motivation.

that firms fail to revise their plan as the business grows and market conditions change. Review the compensation plan at least annually to ensure that it's aligned with conditions in the market place and the company's overall marketing strategy.

Assessing Sales Force Productivity

As the cost of maintaining a sales force increases, sales managers must give more attention to measuring productivity. The goal is to analyze the profitability of each salesperson's sales volume. This task is complicated because sales territories, customers, and business conditions vary.

CUSTOMER RELATIONSHIP MANAGEMENT WITH TECHNOLOGY

Staying Informed

A key role of the sales manager is to provide a steady flow of information and advice to salespeople. Salespeople look to their managers for information about market trends, products, company policies, and assistance with their accounts. CRM software improves and enhances the flow of information between managers and the sales force. The same features that are used to enrich communications with customers also support the sales organization's internal communications. With direct access to a shared CRM database, for example, a sales manager can review relationships with accounts in "real" time by examining a salesperson's notes at any time. This makes it possible for the manager to enter advice about an account directly into that account's record. (See the exercise Receiving Advice through CRM on page 420 for more information.)

SELLING IN ACTION

Firing Customers and Firing Up the Sales Force

Today's sales managers are becoming more focused on profitability than sales. There is increasing recognition that a company can have too many or the wrong customers, or can focus on selling the wrong mix of products. Too many customers drain precious resources and endanger a company's ability to serve its most important accounts. Wrong customers often demand customized products and services at prices so low they cannot be served profitably. Selling the wrong products can damage profitability in both the short term and the long term if a company fails to recognize competitive changes and changing customer needs.

There are several things a sales manager can do to improve profitability. First, the sales manager needs to determine if the company is trying to serve too many customers. Jeff Multz, director of sales and marketing at FirstWave Technologies, relates an example that occurred when he owned his own consulting business. He realized that 80 percent of his customers were a drain on his business, so he called 3000 of them to explain he could no longer serve them. Partly as a result, his sales increased by 50 percent the next year, but his profit increased by 50 percent in just five months.

Second, the sales manager needs to determine if the company is trying to serve the wrong customers. David Sutcliffe, CEO of Richmond, B.C.–based Sierra Wireless, knows the value of not focusing on less price-sensitive customers who typically buy small quantities but demand special attention. He says, "I give them a competitor's name, phone number or e-mail address. I know they're thinking I'm out of my mind. But if your competitors are so busy choking on those small orders, you can focus on and win the more profitable opportunities."

Finally, the sales manager can focus salespeople on accounts and products that are profitable or strategically important by designing a compensation plan that rewards them for profitability rather than sales. KMC Telecom, for example, used to pay a flat commission rate on sales of all products. The company recently changed its commission structure to focus salespeople on more profitable products, and now pays commissions from 50 to 225 percent depending on the products sold.[b]

The problem of measuring sales force productivity is more complicated than it might appear at first glance. In most cases sales volume alone will not tell you how much profit or loss you are making on the sales of each member of the sales force. A small manufacturer was losing money until he analyzed the profitability of sales generated by each person. He found that one salesperson created a loss on almost every order. This salesperson was concentrating on a market that had become so competitive she had to reduce the markup to make sales.

Some sales managers view the frequency of calls as an indicator of success. This information is only helpful when compared with the profit earned on each account. The number of calls made on an account should bear some relationship to the sales and profit potential of that account. In some cases it is possible to maintain small accounts without frequent personal calls.

To compare a salesperson's current productivity with the past can also be misleading. Changes in products, prices, competition, and assignments make comparisons with the past unfair—sometimes to the salesperson, sometimes to the company. It is better to measure cumulative quarterly, semi-annual, or annual results in relation to established goals.

Some sales managers use performance evaluation criteria that communicate to the sales force which elements of their jobs are most important and how they are doing in each area. Evaluating salespeople involves defining the bases on which they will be evaluated, developing performance standards to determine the acceptable level of performance desired on each base, monitoring actual performance, and giving salespeople feedback on their performance.[36] Some of the most common criteria for assessing the productivity of salespeople are:

Quantitative Criteria

Sales volume in dollars or units

Sales volume compared with previous year's sales

Sales volume by product or product line

Number of new accounts opened or accounts lost

Amount of new account sales

Net profit dollars

Number of customer calls

Qualitative Criteria

Attitude

Product knowledge

Communication skills

Personal appearance

Customer goodwill generated

Selling skills

Initiative

In most cases it is best to emphasize assessment criteria that can be expressed in numbers (i.e., quantitative). The preceding quantitative items are especially significant when accompanied by target dates. For example, you might assess the number of new accounts opened during a six-month period. Of course a sales manager should not ignore the other criteria listed here. The other items can affect a salesperson's productivity, and deserve to be evaluated as well.

Some sales managers ask their salespeople to complete a self-evaluation as part of the overall evaluation process. Many salespeople feel that self-evaluation contributes to their personal development.[37]

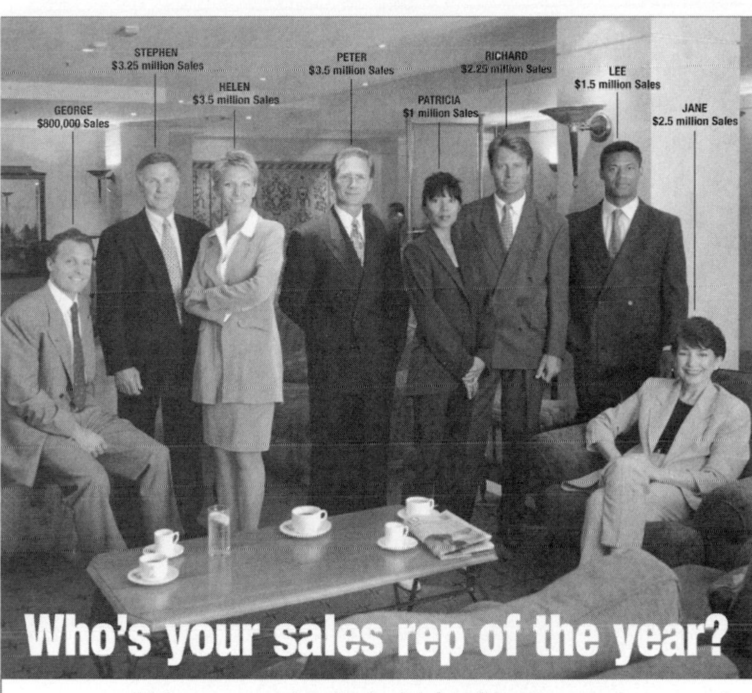

Cognos Business Intelligence helps sales managers quickly assess their salespeople's profitability performance.

SUMMARY

Many capable salespeople have advanced to the position of sales manager. This job involves such diverse duties as recruiting, selecting, training, and supervising salespeople. Some sales managers are concerned solely with the management of salespeople; others have responsibility for additional marketing functions such as advertising and market research.

The sales manager is part of the management team and therefore must be concerned with leadership. An effective sales manager is an effective leader. While the qualities of effective leaders are subject to debate, most research tells us that such people display two dimensions: structure and consideration. Sales managers who develop a leadership style that combines structure and consideration possess the skills needed to be an effective coach. The most effective leadership occurs when sales managers are able to match their leadership style to situations that surface among members of their sales force. They practise a leadership approach known as *situational leadership.*

Many sales managers are involved directly or indirectly in recruiting and selecting salespeople. This is an important responsibility, because mistakes can be costly. Each member of the sales force will influence a portion of the company's profit picture and the firm's image positively or negatively.

Training and motivating salespeople are almost daily concerns of the sales manager. Training should always be viewed as an investment in human resources. Training helps members of the sales force reach their fullest potential.

We discussed the difference between internal and external motivation. In many cases intrinsic motivators (e.g., achievement, challenge, responsibility, involvement, and enjoyment of work itself) have a longer-term effect on employee attitudes than extrinsic motivators (e.g., contests, prizes, and money). Sales managers need to discover the individual differences between salespeople in order to select the most effective motivation strategies.

The most common compensation plans were discussed. Compensation plans should be field tested before being fully implemented.

Assessing sales force productivity is a major responsibility of the sales manager. Sales managers use both quantitative and qualitative criteria.

Key Terms

Coaching **404**

Compensation Plan **411**

Consideration **403**

External Motivation **409**

Internal Motivation **409**

Sales Manager **401**

Situational Leadership **403**

Structure **401**

Review Questions

1. What are the sales manager's two main areas of responsibility?
2. Are all sales managers' duties the same? Explain.
3. What are the two main leadership qualities displayed by most successful sales managers? Define and explain each of these qualities.
4. List and describe the four basic steps involved in coaching.
5. What is a job description? Explain the importance of job descriptions when selecting salespeople.
6. What are four sources for recruiting new salespeople?
7. What should sales managers look for when selecting new salespeople? Describe at least three important qualities.
8. What are some common criticisms of external rewards?
9. List and describe the five basic compensation plans for salespeople.
10. What are the best criteria for measuring a salesperson's performance? List additional criteria that should be considered in evaluating individual performance.

Application Exercises

1. Assume that, as a new sales manager, you have been given the authority to hire the television or movie character of your choice for your sales team. Whom would you choose? Defend your choice.
2. You have been reviewing the performance of your sales force over the past year. You are very pleased that sales have increased by nearly 30 percent, but you are somewhat concerned that customer service complaints have increased by 50 percent over the same period. It appears that your salespeople are concentrating on closing sales, but are not following up with customers to ensure they are serviced properly. Explain how you would motivate your sales force to pay more attention to after-sale service?
3. Schedule an appointment with two sales managers. Interview each of them, using the following questions as a guide:
   a. What are your functions as a sales manager?
   b. How do the functions of a sales manager differ from those of a salesperson?
   c. What criteria do you use in selecting salespeople?
   d. What kinds of training program do you have for new salespeople?
   e. What method of compensation do you use for your salespeople?
   f. How do you evaluate the performance of your salespeople?
   g. What personal qualities are important for becoming a sales manager?

   Write the answers to these questions. Summarize the similarities and differences of the sales managers' responses.
4. Psychological testing is an important tool for selecting sales candidates. One of the most widely used is SalesAP (Sales Achievement Predictor). View information on this test at **www.careermotiv8.com**. Why might this tool be of value to sales managers? Also, view a complete SalesAP sample report via the link near the bottom of the page and evaluate the information on this particular candidate. How might a sales manager use this information if this particular candidate were hired?
5. SalesForce Training & Consulting has been providing sales training and consulting for nearly 20 years. What types of services does this company provide that would benefit sales managers? Visit its Web site (**www.salesforcetraining.com**) and hit "Resources." Be prepared to discuss in class one article relevant to sales managers and one article relevant to salespeople.

ROLE-PLAY EXERCISE

For the purpose of this role play, assume the role of a sales manager who is currently supervising a sales team made up of 22 salespeople. Your employer manufactures and sells radio equipment for private aircraft. You plan to open a new sales territory in a western Canadian province and need a self-motivated salesperson to assume the position. You have identified a person who seems to be a qualified applicant and you have scheduled a meeting to discuss the position. Using information in this chapter, prepare a list of questions you will ask during the interview. Use these questions to interview another class member who will assume the role of the applicant. After the role play, review the interview process.

CRM Application Exercise RECEIVING ADVICE THROUGH CRM

Becky Kemley, your sales manager at SimNet Systems, regularly reviews your progress with accounts by examining your notes. She recently entered into one of your records a note about an account's debt problems. Find her note and the two accounts she refers to by selecting Lookup, Keyword, type "debt," check Notes, and press Enter. Print the information contained in these records by selecting Report, Contact Report, Active Lookup, Printer, and Enter.

Case Problem

One of the more interesting developments in sales force management is the use of customer feedback to improve the performance of salespeople. Most of these programs are relatively new and go by a variety of names such as 360-degree feedback, customer-conscious compensation, and customer satisfaction rewards. Organizations that have adopted this assessment strategy believe salespeople can benefit from feedback collected from the customers they serve. Also, information collected can be used by the company to improve customer service.

The use of customer-driven evaluation programs is on the increase because of the rising regard for the role of sales at many companies. Tom Mott, a consultant with Hewitt Associates, says, "Salespeople who were volume pushers are now becoming the manager of their company's relationship with the customer." Tom points out that customer feedback is likely to reflect on the performance of the salesperson and the performance of the company. If problems surface in either area, customer dissatisfaction may surface.

Data collection methodology is not uniform at this point. Some companies use telephone surveys while others use mailed questionnaires. IBM has experimented with a series of in-person meetings that bring together corporate customers, their IBM sales representatives, and the salesperson's boss.

Some salespeople have not welcomed the use of customer evaluations. Maryann Cirenza, senior account executive at Teleport Communications Group (TCG) of New York, said that she felt betrayed when she saw the questionnaire the company was sending to her customers. One of the questions asked, "Does your sales rep know your industry?" Maryann said, "I thought the company was checking up on me." Later her anger subsided when she learned the survey was not simply a monitoring system but a trial run for a new compensation plan. After field testing the surveys, TCG used customer feedback to set bonuses. MaryAnn Cirenza was actually rewarded for good customer service by earning a bonus of about 20 percent of her base pay.

Greg Buseman, an IBM salesperson, believes the shift to compensation through customer feedback has improved personal selling at his company. He now spends more time understanding the customer's business and learning to be a problem solver for his clients.[38]

Questions

1. Should the customer be given a major voice in determining how salespeople are performing? Explain.
2. Should sales force compensation be linked to customer feedback? What are the advantages and disadvantages of this approach?
3. Assume you are a sales manager preparing to develop and implement a customer feedback system. How might you gain support for this system from members of your sales force? What data collection method would you use?
4. Research indicates that customers rank "understanding of our business" as an important criterion used to evaluate salespeople. Why is this criterion ranked so high?

APPENDIX

Software Installation

FOR SALES FORCE AUTOMATION (CRM) APPLICATIONS

A Special Note to the Student

USE OF ACT! CUSTOMER RELATIONSHIP MANAGEMENT (CRM) SOFTWARE

Selling Today now offers you a unique opportunity to learn why modern software is helping to redefine sales and marketing. You can install and use a scaled-down version of the popular ACT! software, which more than 3 million salespeople use to build relationships with their customers. The software is easy to use and includes information about more than 20 customers. You can experience first-hand how salespeople today gain the sales advantage with this new category of software.

Beginning in Chapter 1, you will find simple, easy-to-follow instructions on using this software to store and access a wide variety of business and personal information about your customers. You will discover the convenience of using this software to stay in touch with people. The ACT! software includes important customer information that you will use in your CRM case study assignments. You will access the information in your ACT! database to approach, present, demonstrate, negotiate, close, and service more than $1.2 million–worth of sales volume.

Effectively using information technology, especially CRM, will give you a career advantage in today's highly competitive workplace. After mastering the exercises provided, you can report your CRM experience on your résumé.

INSTRUCTIONS FOR INSTALLING AND USING THE CRM SOFTWARE

The software that you will be using is a demonstration version of ACT!, the leading Customer Relationship Management (CRM) software. This version is limited in that no more than 25 contacts may be entered. The ACT! 2000 program is much more robust, extensive, and powerful, and can manage thousands of contacts.

The software that you need is found on the CD-ROM that comes with this book. When you browse the CD-ROM on your computer you will see a large collection of files and folders. While it is possible to run the software directly from the CD-ROM, it is best to copy the files to your hard drive so that you can easily save changes to your data files.

COPYING FILES TO YOUR COMPUTER

Create a folder on your hard drive in which to save the files (e.g. C:\Program Files\Act).

Select all the files on the CD-ROM and copy them to the Act folder on your hard drive.

You should also make sure the Read-only attribute is removed from the files. Right-click the Act folder and select Properties from the Options menu. Make sure the check mark is cleared from the Read-only attributes box.

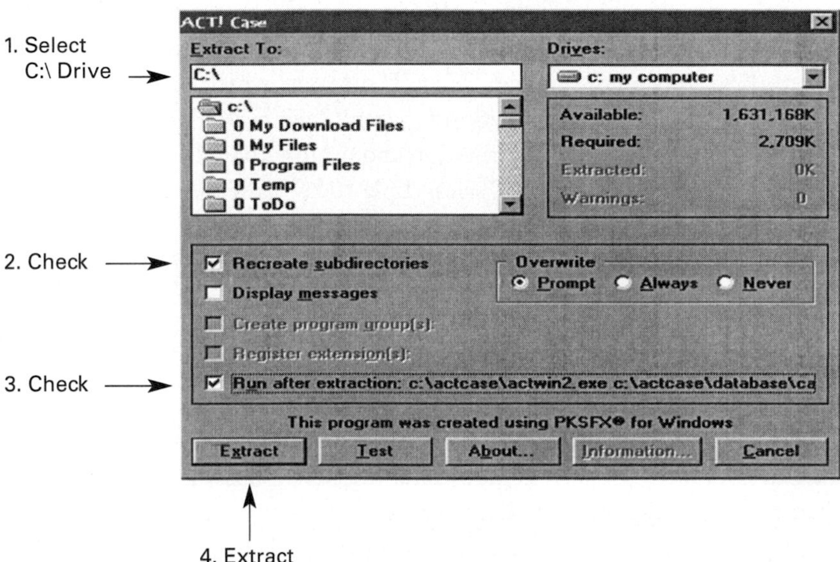

LAUNCHING THE SOFTWARE

Once you have copied the files to your drive you can launch the ACT! Software by double-clicking the "ACTWIN2.EXE" icon in the Act folder, or by using the Run command on the Windows Start menu (e.g., run "C:\Program Files\Act\ACTWIN2.EXE").

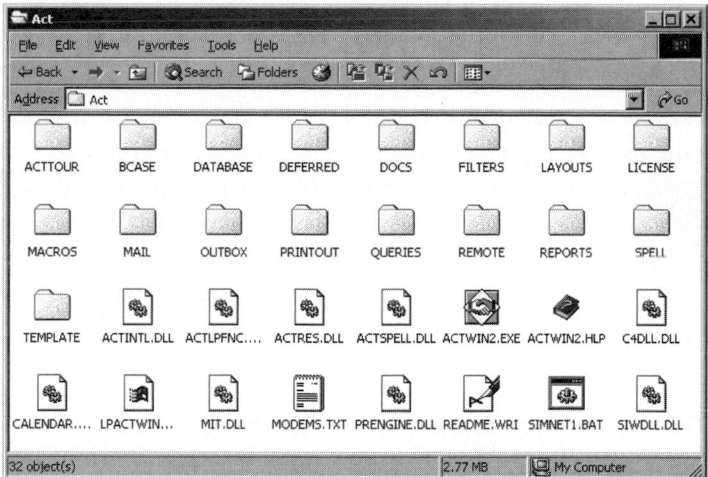

Note: there are two files called ACTWIN2. The second file is a Help file (ACTWIN2.hlp), and should appear with an icon of a small purple book. The icon with the two shaking hands is the one for executing the program.

The first window that you see should look similar to the following:

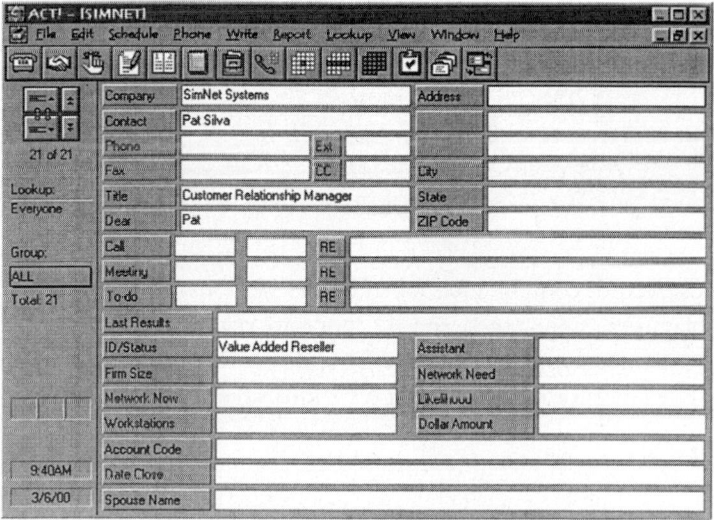

Software Status. The program on your hard drive can be run as many times as you need. After completing the CRM Case Study, you may choose to leave the demonstration software on your hard drive or you may remove it. You can reload the software from the CD-ROM at any time.

UNDERSTANDING THE SOFTWARE

ACT! is a Windows-based program and uses the standard Windows features. It is "menu driven," which means that you can operate the program by selecting from lists of choices. The main menu is displayed at the top of the screen.

The screen that displays the information about a customer is referred to as the Contact Screen. ACT! has two Contact Screens that can be toggled by pressing the F6 function key.

You can use the arrows on the Rolodex icon (see inset at left) to move among the records. A single arrow moves to the next record and a double arrow displays the first (up) or last (down) record in the database. You can also use the PageUp or PageDown key to move between records. The records are in alphabetical order, by company name. The first record (double arrow up) in the database is for Able Profit Machines, Inc.

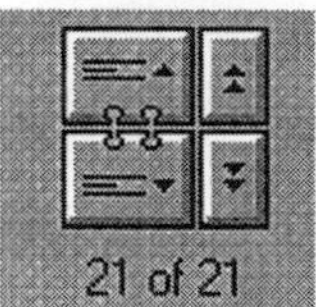

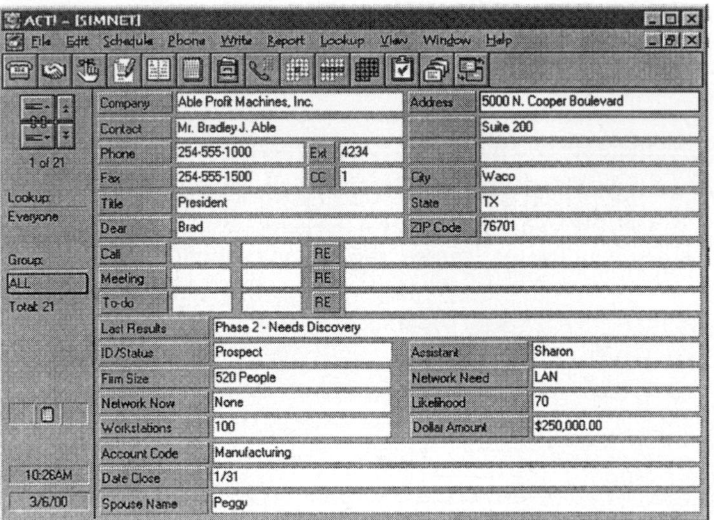

Most records contain notes taken by the previous salesperson, Pat Silva. To display these notes, press the F9 function key. When you are through examining a note, you can press the Escape key. To save changes, select File Close. The notes for the Able Profit Machines company follow.

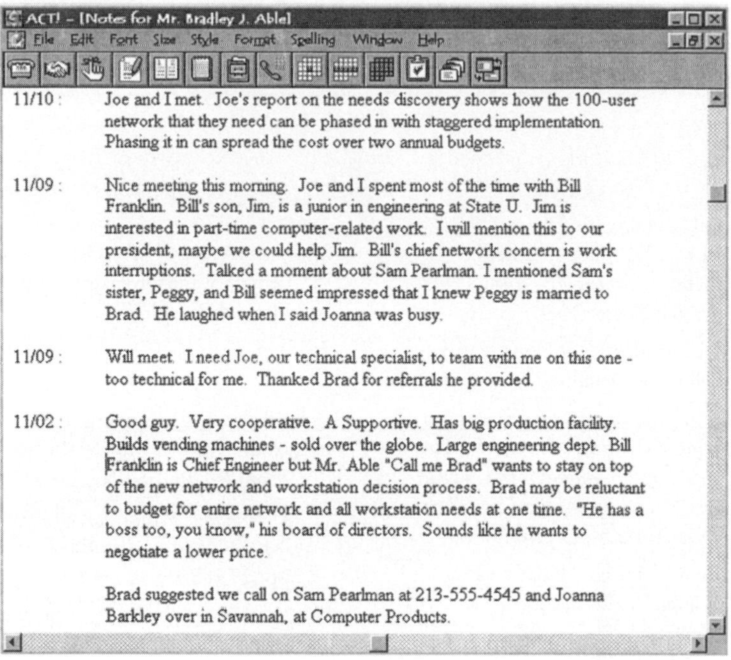

Using the ACT! Software with the CRM References throughout the Book

With the instructions provided above, you can complete any of the references to CRM located throughout the book. These references include the following:

Customer Relationship Management with Technology Features. These features, located within the chapter, describe how salespeople are using CRM software today to build relationships with customers.

CRM Application Exercises. These application exercises located at the end of the chapter provide you instructions for learning how to use the software, and gain expertise. Detailed instructions lead you through the important functions salespeople use to develop, build, and maintain relationships with customers.

CRM Case Study. The case study located at the end of most chapters provides you with a database of customers supplied by a previous salesperson. You assume the role of a newly hired salesperson and, with the information supplied, create relationship, product, customer, and presentation strategies to manage the sales activities in the territory you are assigned. Questions are supplied to help you plan your activities. The CRM case studies start in Chapter 9 and continue through Chapter 16.

Notes

Chapter 1

1. Interview with Joe Murphy, June 9, 1999.
2. John Naisbitt, *Megatrends* (New York: Warner Books, 1982), pp. 14–16.
3. Stan Davis and Christopher Meyer, *Blur: The Speed of Change in the Connected Economy* (New York: Addison-Wesley Publishers), 1998, p. 9.
4. David Shenk, *Data Smog: Surviving the Information Glut* (New York: HarperEdge, 1997), pp. 27–29.
5. Michael Hammer, *The Agenda* (New York: Random House, 2001), p. 6.
6. Greg Ip, "Why High-Flyers, Built on Big Ideas, Are Such Fast Fallers," *Wall Street Journal,* April 4, 2002, p. A1.
7. Pam Withers, "Rules of the Road," *Profit,* February/March 2002, p. 26.
8. Malcolm Fleschner, "World Wide Winner–The UPS Story," *Selling Power,* November/December 2001, p. 58.
9. "America's 25 Best Sales Forces," *Sales & Marketing Management,* July 2000, p. 59.
10. Dennis Fox, "Ringing Up Prospects," *Sales & Marketing Management,* March 1993, pp. 75–77.
11. Leslie Angello-Dean, "Converting Salespeople to Consultant/Advisors," *Sales & Marketing Training,* March/April 1990, p. 18.
12. William M. Pride, O. C. Ferrell, H. F. (Herb) MacKenzie, and Kim Snow, *Marketing: Concepts and Strategies,* Canadian Edition (Toronto, ON: Houghton Mifflin, 1998), p. 523.
13. Robert E. Miller and Stephen E. Heiman, *Strategic Selling* (New York: Warren Books, 1985), p. 26.
14. Jack Snader, "Is It Consultative Selling or Detailing?" *Newspost,* Fall 1999, pp. 21–32.
15. James G. Barnes, *Secrets of Customer Relationship Management: It's All about How You Make Them Feel* (New York: McGraw-Hill, 2001).
16. John Heinrich, "Relationship Selling," *Personal Selling Power,* May/June 1995, p. 32.
17. Robert M. Peterson, George H. Lucas, and Patrick L. Schul, "Forming Consultative Trade Alliances: Walking the Walk in the New Selling Environment," *NAMA Journal,* Spring 1998, p. 11; Beth Belton, "Technology Is Changing Face of U.S. Sales Force," *USA Today,* February 9, 1999, p. 2A; Neil Rackham and John DeVincentis, *Rethinking the Sales Force* (New York: McGraw-Hill, 1999), p. 25.
18. Geoffrey Brewer, "The Customer Stops Here," *Sales & Marketing Management,* March 1998, pp. 31–32.
19. Montrose S. Sommers and James G. Barnes, *Fundamentals of Marketing,* 10th Canadian ed. (Toronto, ON: McGraw-Hill Ryerson, 2004), p. 287.
20. Neil Rackham, "The Other Revolution in Sales," *Sales & Marketing Management,* March 2000, pp. 34–36.
21. Patricia Seybold, *The Customer Revolution* (New York: Random House, 2001), p. 1.
22. John O'Toole, "Get Inside Your Clients' Skin," *Selling,* May 1995, p. 77.
23. Interview with Wes Delnea, president of Windsor Factory Supply Limited, March 20, 1997.
24. Ibid.

SOURCES FOR BOXED FEATURES

a. Barbara Pachter and Marjorie Brody, *Complete Business Etiquette Handbook* (Upper Saddle River, NJ: Prentice Hall, 1995), pp. 279–80.

b. Dave Kahle, *The Six-Hat Salesperson: A Dynamic Approach to Producing Top Results in Every Selling Situation* (Toronto, ON: AMACOM, 1999).

Chapter 2

1. Susan Green, personal interview, July 18, 1999.
2. Laura Wood, personal interview, April 17, 2002.
3. Jim Carroll, "Getting Back to the Basics," *Contact,* November/December 2001, p. 53.
4. John Naisbitt, *Megatrends* (New York, NY: Warner Books, 1982), p. 18.
5. Julie Gordon, "Teaching Selling Skills to the Corporate World," *Denver Business World,* November 3–9, 2000, p. 10B.
6. Christopher Caggiano, "Sign of the Cross-Training Times," *Inc.,* December 1998, p. 105.
7. Harry Beckwith, *Selling the Invisible* (New York: Warner Books, 1997), p. 38.
8. Allan S. Boress, *The I Hate Selling Book* (New York: AMACOM, 1995), p. 8.
9. Linda Corman, "Look Who's Selling Now," *Selling,* July/August 1996, pp. 46–53.

10. Linda Corman, *ibid.*, p. 53.
11. Paul Grescoe, *The Mavericks* (Toronto, ON: McGraw-Hill Ryerson, 1999), p. 122.
12. Ibid.
13. Beth Belton, "Technology Is Changing Face of U.S. Sales Force." *USA Today*, February 9, 1999, p. A2.
14. Brian Tracy, *The 100 Absolutely Unbreakable Laws of Business Success* (San Francisco, CA: Berrett-Koehler Publishers, 2000), p. 192.
15. Mary Sykes Wylie, "Free," *Networker*, January/February 1998, p. 25.
16. "A Career in Sales," *Selling Power*, 1997, p. 12; "Selling Sales to Students," *Sales & Marketing Management*, January 1998, p. 15.
17. Gabrielle Birkner, "Who Says Titles Don't Matter," *Sales & Marketing Management*, July 2001, p. 14.
18. "The *Selling Power* 400," *Selling Power*, September 1998, p. 70.
19. Ken Liebeskind, "Sporting Chance," *Selling Power*, June 1998, pp. 14–16.
20. Brett Ruffell, "The 2004 Salary Report," *Contact*, December 2004, pp. 12–14.
21. Ibid.
22. Ibid.
23. "Help Wanted," *Sales & Marketing Management*, July 1998, p. 14.
24. Rhea Seymour, "Ms. versus Mr." *Profit*, October 2000, p. 53.
25. Eli Jones, Jesse N. Moore, Andrea J. S. Stanaland, and Rosalind A. J. Wyatt, "Salesperson Race and Gender and the Access and Legitimacy Paradigm: Does Difference Make a Difference?" *Journal of Personal Selling & Sales Management*, Fall 1998, p. 71.
26. Michael Davidson, personal correspondence, January 4, 2005.
27. Canadian Bankers Association, "Your Guide to Financial Services," **www.cba.ca/eng/Tools/Brochures /tools_financialservices2.htm** and **www.cba.ca/eng/Tools/Brochures /tools_financialservices2.htm** downloaded April 18, 2002.
28. "Young Entrepreneur Award Winners Have What It Takes," *Globe and Mail*, October 26, 1998, p. C13; "Seizing the Opportunity of a Lifetime," News Release, Business Development Bank of Canada, October 21, 1998; Interview with Ruth Bell Steinhauer, May 20, 1999.
29. "Delivering the Goods," *Profit*, December/January 1999, p. 42.
30. Alex Hays, "Wholesalers: A Key Link in Canada's Economy," Statistics Canada Cat. 11-621-MIE, available **www.statcan.ca**, accessed June 19, 2005.
31. Mark Stevenson, "The Lean, Mean Sales Machine," *Canadian Business*, January 1994, pp. 32–36.
32. Allan Lynch, "Secrets of a Super Salesman," *Atlantic Progress*, April 1999, pp. 5–52, 56.
33. Beth Belton, "Technology Is Changing the Face of U.S. Sales Force," *USA Today*, February 9, 1999, p. A2.
34. Michele Marchetti, "Sales Training Even a Rep Could Love," *Sales & Marketing Management*, June 1998, p. 70; *Field Sales Training: Postal Education*, CPC Certified Postal Consultant (Pitney Bowes Canada, Sales Programs & Operations, 1998); correspondence from David Munro, February 13, 2000.
35. "Industry Report 1998," *Training*, October 1998, p. 55.
36. Gerhard Gschwandtner, "Rendezvous with a Rainmaker," *Selling Power*, May 2001, pp. 98–100.
37. Interview with Trevor Adey, April 22, 2002.
38. Alex Pettes, correspondence and personal interviews, November 2004–January 2005.

SOURCES FOR BOXED FEATURES

a. CBC News, "A Criminal Mind: The Life and Times of Eddie Greenspan," aired January 20, 2005, **www.cbc.ca/lifeandtimes/greenspan.html**, accessed June 13, 2005; "My Greatest Sale," Eddie Greenspan, interviewed by Laura Pratt, *Profit*, May 2005, p. 36.

b. Betsy Cummings, "Selling Around the World," *Sales & Marketing Management*, May 2001, p. 70; Jan Yager, *Business Protocol* Second Edition (Stamford, CT: Hannacroix Books, 2001), pp. 120–21.

c. Douglas J. Dalrymple and William L. Cron, *Sales Management: Concepts and Cases* (New York: John Wiley & Sons, 1998), pp. 344–47; William Keenan, "Time Is Everything," *Sales & Marketing Management*, August 1993, p. 61.

Chapter 3

1. "Cold, Hard Cash," *Profit*, October/November 1997, pp. 13–14, 16, 21; **www.premdor.com/aboutpremdor/strip-abouttext.html**, May 13, 1999.
2. Daniel Goleman, *Working with Emotional Intelligence (*New York: Bantam Books, 1998), pp. 24–28, 317.
3. Daniel Goleman, *Emotional Intelligence* (New York: Bantam Books, 1995), p. 34; Cary Cherniss and Daniel Goleman (eds.), *The Emotionally Intelligent Workplace,* (San Francisco, CA: Jossey-Bass, 2001), pp. 22–24.
4. L. B. Gschwandtner and Gerhard Gschwandtner, "Balancing Act," *Selling Power*, June 1996, p. 24.
5. Ibid.
6. Denis Waitley, *Empires of the Mind* (New York: William Morrow, 1995), p. 3.
7. Ilan Mochari, "In a Former Life," *Inc.*, April 2001, p. 100.
8. J. D. Power Consumer Center, **www.jdpower.com**, accessed May 4, 2002.

9. *Partnering: The Heart of Selling Today.* VHS (Des Moines, IA: American Media Incorporated, 1990).
10. Paul S. Goldner, "How to Set the Playing Field," *Selling,* April 1998, p. 9.
11. Larry Wilson, *Selling in the 90s* (Chicago, IL: Nightingale Conant, 1988), p. 35.
12. William Keenan, Jr. "Customer Satisfaction Builds Business," *Selling,* March 1998, p. 12.
13. Tim Sanders, *Love Is the Killer App* (New York: Crown Business, 2002), p. 23.
14. Malcolm Fleschner, "World Wide Winner—The UPS Story," *Selling Power,* November/December 2001, p. 58.
15. Neil Rackham and John R. DeVincentis, *Rethinking the Sales Force* (New York: McGraw-Hill, 1999), pp. 79-83.
16. Maxwell Maltz, *Psycho-Cybernetics* (Englewood Cliffs, NJ: Prentice-Hall, 1960), p. 2.
17. Phillip C. McGraw, "Dr. Phil: Know Your Goal, Make a Plan, and Pull the Trigger," *The Oprah Magazine,* September 2001, pp. 60–61.
18. Nathaniel Branden, *Self-Esteem at Work* (San Francisco, CA: Jossey-Bass, 1998), pp. 20–21.
19. Robert B. Miller and Stephen E. Heiman, *Strategic Selling* (New York: Warner Books, 1985), p. 60.
20. Clifton Leaf, "Enough Is Enough," *Fortune,* March 18, 2002, pp. 60–76; Marcia Vickers and Mike France, "How Corrupt Is Wall Street?" *Business Week,* May 13, 2002, pp. 37–42.
21. Nathaniel Branden, *Self-Esteem at Work,* p. 35.
22. Eli Jones, Jesse N. Moore, Andrea J. S. Stanaland, and Rosalind A. J. Wyatt, "Salesperson Race and Gender and the Access and Legitimacy Paradigm: Does Difference Make a Difference?" *Journal of Personal Selling and Sales Management,* Fall 1998, p. 74.
23. Barry L. Reece and Rhonda Brandt, *Effective Human Relations—Personal and Organizational Applications* (Boston, MA: Houghton Mifflin, 2002), p. 37.
24. Ginger Trumfio, "More Than Words," *Sales & Marketing Management,* April 1994, p. 55.
25. "Get to the Truth of the Message," *The Pryor Report,* Vol. VI, No. 1A, p. 7.
26. Susan Bixler, *The Professional Image* (New York: Putnam Publishing Group, 1984), p. 216.
27. Barbara Pachter and Marjorie Brody, *Complete Business Etiquette Handbook* (New York: Prentice Hall, 1995), p. 14.
28. Adapted from Leonard Zunin, *Contact: The First Four Minutes* (New York: Nash Publishing, Ballantine Books, 1972), p. 109.
29. "Name That Customer," *Personal Selling Power,* January/February 1993, p. 48.
30. Deborah Blum, "Face It!" *Psychology Today,* September/October 1998, pp. 32–69.
31. Barbara Pachter and Mary Brody, *Complete Business Etiquette Handbook* (Englewood Cliffs, NJ: Prentice Hall, 1995), p. 27; "The Eyes Have It," *Sales & Marketing Management,* January 2002, p. 20.
32. Anne M. Phaneuf, "Decoding Dress Codes," *Sales & Marketing Management,* September 1995, p. 139.
33. Melinda Ligos, "Does Image Matter?" *Sales & Marketing Management,* March 2001, p. 52–55.
34. Susan Bixler, *Professional Presence* (New York: G. P. Putnam's Sons, 1991), p. 141.
35. Susan Bixler and Nancy Nix-Rice, *The New Professional Image* (Adams Media Corporation, 1997), p. 11–15; Barbara Pachter and Marjorie Brody, *Complete Business Etiquette Handbook,* p. 12.
36. Peter Urs Bender, *Secrets of Power Presentations,* Eighth Edition (Toronto, ON: The Achievement Group, 1999), pp. 188–89.
37. Susan Berkley, "Hone Your Sharpest Sales Weapon," *Sales & Field Force Automation,* July 1997, p. 24.
38. Tim Sanders, *Love Is the Killer App,* p. 18.
39. Steven Covey, *The 7 Habits of Highly Effective People* (New York: Simon & Schuster, 1989), pp. 240–41.
40. "Sales-Related Book Picked in Top Ten for Shaping America's Culture," *Des Moines Register,* April 3, 1985, p. 3.
41. L. B. Gschwandtner, "Mary Lou Retton," *Personal Selling Power,* Fifteenth Anniversary Issue, 1995, p. 99.
42. Arnold A. Lazarus and Clifford N. Lazarus, *The 60-Second Shrink* (San Luis Obispo, CA: Impact Publishers, 1979), pp. 1–2.

SOURCES FOR BOXED FEATURES

a. Steven J. Stein and Howard E. Book, *The EQ Edge* (Toronto, ON: Stoddart Publishing, 2000).

b. Brenda Lockyer, personal correspondence, January 4, 2005.

c. Gerald A. Michaelson, "Build Relationships by 'Making Deposits,'" *Selling,* August 1997, p. 7.

Chapter 4

1. Robert Kreitner, *Management,* Eighth Edition (Boston, MA: Houghton Mifflin, 2001), p. 293; "The Top 25 Managers of the Year," *Business Week,* January 14, 2002, p. 65.
2. Robert Bolton and Dorothy Grover Bolton, *People Styles at Work* (New York: AMACOM, 1996), p. 10.
3. David W. Merrill and Roger H. Reid, *Personal Styles and Effective Performance* (Radnor, PA: Chilton Books, 1981), p. 1.
4. Robert J. Sternberg, *Thinking Styles* (New York: Cambridge University Press, 1997), p. 8.

5. Robert Bolton and Dorothy Grover Bolton, *People Styles at Work.*
6. Robert M. Hecht, *Office Systems,* February 1990, p. 26.
7. The dominance factor was described in an early book by William M. Marston, *The Emotions of Normal People* (New York: Harcourt, 1928). Research conducted by Rolfe LaForge and Robert F. Suczek resulted in the development of the Interpersonal Checklist (ICL), which features a dominant–submissive scale. A person who receives a high score on the ICL tends to lead, persuade, and control others. The Interpersonal Identity Profile, developed by David W. Merrill and James W. Taylor, features a factor called "assertiveness." Persons classified as being high in assertiveness tend to have strong opinions, make quick decisions, and be directive when dealing with people. Persons classified as being low in assertiveness tend to voice moderate opinions, make thoughtful decisions, and be supportive when dealing with others.
8. David W. Johnson, *Reaching Out—Interpersonal Effectiveness and Self-Actualization,* Second Edition (Englewood Cliffs, NJ: Prentice-Hall, 1981), p. 44.
9. The research conducted by LaForge and Suczek resulted in identification of the *hostile–loving continuum,* which is similar to the *sociability continuum.* Their Interpersonal Checklist features this scale. L. L. Thurstone and T. G. Thurstone developed the Thurstone Temperament Schedule, which provides an assessment of a "sociable" factor. Persons with high scores in this area enjoy the company of others and make friends easily. The Interpersonal Identity Profile developed by Merrill and Taylor contains an objectivity continuum. A person with low objectivity is seen as attention seeking, involved with the feelings of others, informal, and casual in social relationships. A person who is high in objectivity appears to be somewhat indifferent toward the feelings of others. This person is formal in social relationships.
10. Charles Margerison, *How to Assess Your Managerial Style* (New York: AMACOM, 1979), p. 49.
11. Pierce J. Howard and Jane M. Howard, "Buddy, Can You Paradigm?" *Training & Development,* September 1995, p. 31.
12. Sam Deep and Lyle Sussman, *Close the Deal* (Reading, MA: Perseus Books, 1999), p. 157.
13. Len D'Innocenzo and Jack Cullen, "Chameleon Management," *Personal Selling Power,* January–February 1995, p. 61.
14. Rod Nichols, "How to Sell to Different Personality Types," *Personal Selling Power,* November/December 1992, p. 46.
15. Stuart Atkins, *How to Get the Most from Styles-Based Training* (Beverly Hills, CA: Stuart Atkins, 1996), p. 1.
16. Gary A. Williams and Robert B. Miller, "Change the Way You Persuade," *Harvard Business Review,* May 2002, p. 65.
17. Robert Bolton and Dorothy Grover Bolton, *People Styles at Work,* p. 65.
18. Tony Alessandra and Michael J. O'Connor, *People Smart* (LaJolla, CA: Keynote Publishing, 1990), p. 15.
19. Nina Munk, "How Levi's Trashed a Great American Brand," *Fortune,* April 12, 1999, p. 85.
20. Peter Verburg, "Jaws," *Canadian Business,* October 10, 1997, p. 52.
21. Stuart Atkins, *How to Get the Most from Styles-Based Training,* p. 3.
22. Ron Willingham, *Integrity Selling* (New York: Doubleday, 1987), pp. 21–23.
23. Eric F. Douglas, *Straight Talk* (Palo Alto, CA: 1998), p. 92.
24. Ron Willingham, *Integrity Selling,* pp. 21–23.
25. David W. Merrill and Roger H. Reid, *Personal Styles and Effective Performance,* pp. 134, 135.
26. Stuart Atkins, *The Name of Your Game* (Beverly Hills, CA: Ellis & Stewart, 1981), p. 51.
27. Chris Lee, "What's Your Style," *Training,* May 1991, p. 28.

SOURCES FOR BOXED FEATURES

a. Correspondence with Dr. Steve Bajura dated April 14, 2002.

b. Carey Toane, "Shake hands in 10 different languages," **www.profitguide.com** downloaded October 14, 2004; Michael Wynne, "Shake, Hug or Kiss?" *Global Cosmetic Industry,* May 2004, pp. 26–27.

c. Roger Wenschlag, *The Versatile Salesperson* (New York: John Wiley & Sons, 1989), pp. 165–71; Malcolm Fleschner, "The Adaptability Factor," *Selling Power,* January/ February 1997, pp. 54–56; Rod Nichols, "How to Sell to Different Personality Types," *Personal Selling Power,* November/ December 1992, pp. 46–47; David W. Merrill and Roger H. Reid, *Personal Styles and Effective Performance,* p. 2; Tony Alessandra, *People Smarts* (San Diego, CA: Pfeiffer & Company, 1994), p. 55.

Chapter 5

1. Leslie Scism, "Some Agents 'Churn' Life Insurance Policies, Hurt Their Customers," *Wall Street Journal,* January 3, 1995, p. 1.
2. "Can Art Ryan Move 'The Rock'?" *Business Week,* August 5, 1996, p. 70; Leslie Scism, "Prudential Cleanup in Wake of Scandals Hurts Insurance Sales," *Wall Street Journal,* November 17, 1997, p. A1; Deborah Lohse, "Suits Settled by Prudential for $62 Million," *Wall Street Journal,* February 16, 1999, p. C1; Ruth Simon, "Broker Complaints Vary by Firm," *Wall Street Journal,* May 14, 2002, p. D2.
3. Peter Schwartz and Blair Gibb, *When Good Companies Do Bad Things* (New York: John Wiley & Sons, 1999), pp. 1–10, 177–78.

4. Vivian Arnold, B. June Schmidt, and Randall L. Wells, "Ethics Instruction in the Classrooms of Business Educators," *Delta Pi Epsilon Journal,* vol. 38, no. 4, Fall 1996, p. 185.
5. Stephen R. Covey, *The 7 Habits of Highly Effective People* (New York: Simon & Schuster, 1989), p. 18.
6. Jan Yager, *Business Protocol* (Stamford, CT: Hannacroix Creek Books, 2001), pp. 199–200.
7. "Nearly Half of Workers Take Unethical Actions—Survey," *Des Moines Register,* April 7, 1997, p. 18B.
8. Sharon Begley, "A World of Their Own," *Newsweek,* May 8, 2000, pp. 53–56.
9. John A. Byrne, "How to Fix Corporate Governance," *Business Week,* May 6, 2002, pp. 69–78.
10. Josh Freed, "Investigators: Drug Salesman Foiled Pharmacist," *The News & Observer,* August 26, 2001, p. 12A.
11. Robert Simons, Henry Mintzburg, and Kunal Basu, "Memo to CEOs," *Fast Company,* June 2002, pp. 117–21.
12. Marjorie Kelly, "Waving Goodbye to the Invisible Hand," *Business Ethics,* March/April 2002, p. 4.
13. Yochi J. Dreazen, "Pressure for Sales Fostered Abuses at WorldCom," *Wall Street Journal,* May 16, 2002, p. B1.
14. Beth Schultz, "Ethics under Investigation," *Network World Framingham,* April 26, 2004, pp. 72–74.
15. Robert Simons, *et al.,* "Memo to CEOs," pp. 120–21.
16. Patrick Smith, "You Have a Job, But How About a Life?" *Business Week,* November 16, 1998, p. 30.
17. "Corporate Governance: The Road Back," *Business Week,* May 6, 2002, p. 116.
18. Michael Deck, "Good Intentions Aren't Enough," *Globe and Mail,* October 23, 1997, p. B2.
19. "Survey Reveals What Motivates Loyalty," *Selling,* September 2000, p. 2.
20. Brenda Bouw, "In praise of an ethical education," *Globe and Mail,* March 18, 2002, p. C1.
21. Corinne McLaughlin, "Workplace Spirituality Transforming Organizations from the Inside Out," *The Inner Edge,* August/September 1998, p. 26.
22. Michele Krebs, "All the Marketing Men," *Autoweek,* February 16, 1998, p. 11.
23. Melinda Ligos, "Gimme! Gimme!" *Sales & Marketing Management,* March 2002, pp. 33–40.
24. "GM's Gift Policy Covers the Bases—From Football to Prickly Plants," *Globe and Mail,* September 11, 1997, p. B17.
25. Fiona Gibb, "To Give or Not to Give," *Sales & Marketing Management,* September 1994, pp. 136–39.
26. Linda Corman, "The 13 Sins of Selling," *Selling,* September 1994, p. 77.
27. Steven Sack, "Watch the Words," *Sales & Marketing Management,* July 1, 1985, p. 56.
28. Ibid.
29. Rob Zeiger, "Sex, Sales & Stereotypes," *Sales & Marketing Management,* pp. 52, 53.
30. Barry L. Reece and Rhonda Brandt, *Effective Human Relations in Organization,* Seventh Edition (Boston, MA: Houghton Mifflin, 1999), p. 123.
31. Ron Willingham, *Integrity Selling* (New York, NY: Doubleday, 1987), p. xv.
32. Ron Willingham, "Four Traits All Highly Successful Salespeople Have in Common," Phoenix, AZ, 1998 (audiotape presentation).
33. Robert Kreitner, Barry Reece, and James P. O'Grady, *Business,* Second Edition (Boston, MA: Houghton Mifflin, 1990), pp. 647–48.
34. Karin Schill Rives, "Workers Find Clause Has Teeth," *News & Observer,* July 29, 2001, p. E1.
35. Dawn Marie Driscoll, "Don't Confuse Legal and Ethical Standards," *Business Week,* July/August 1996, p. 44.
36. Carol Wheeler, "Getting the Edge on Ethics," *Executive Female,* May/June 1996, p. 47.
37. Ron Willingham, *Integrity Selling,* p. xv.
38. Ibid.
39. Sharon Drew Morgan, *Selling with Integrity,* (San Francisco, CA: Berrett-Koehler Publishers, Inc., 1997), pp. 25–27.
40. Ibid., pp. 27–28.
41. Tom Peters, *Thriving on Chaos* (New York: Alfred A. Knopf, 1988), p. 521.
42. Gerhard Gschwandtner, "Lies and Deception in Selling," *Personal Selling Power,* Fifteenth Anniversary Issue, 1995, p. 62.
43. Price Pritchett, *The Ethics of Excellence* (Dallas, TX: Pritchett & Associates, Inc., [n.d.]), p. 18.
44. Neil Rackham and John R. DeVincentis, *Rethinking the Sales Force* (New York: McGraw-Hill, 1999), pp. 83–84.
45. Geoffrey Colvin, "The Verdict on Business: Presumed Guilty," *Fortune,* November 15, 2004, p. 78.

SOURCES FOR BOXED FEATURES

a. Beth Schultz, "Ethics under Investigation," *Network World,* April 26, 2004, pp. 72–73; "Living the Values: A Guide to Ethical Business Practices at Nortel Networks. **http://www.nortelnetworks.com/corporate/community/ethics/collateral/code_of_conduct_nolinks.pdf**, downloaded December 30, 2004.

b. Jeff Kemp, "Rules to Live by On and Off the Field," *Imprimis,* July 1998, p. 3.

Chapter 6

1. *In the Know: Acquiring Product Knowledge* (Pasadena, CA: Intelecom).

2. Erick Schonfeld, "The Customized, Digitized, Have-It-Your-Way Economy," *Fortune,* September 28, 1998, p. 116.

3. Michael R. Solomon and Elnora W. Stuart, *Marketing: Real People, Real Choices,* Second Edition (Upper Saddle River, NJ: Prentice Hall, 2000), p. 561.

4. "Strategic Vista International Inc. Introduces a Revolution in Safety and Security Protection to Consumers," Canada NewsWire, Ottawa, July 28, 2004, p. 1.

5. "Loki Management Systems Is Selected as Finalist in Microsoft 2004 Impact Awards," Canada NewsWire, Ottawa, October 29, 2004, p. 1.

6. Neil Rackham and John R. DeVincentis, *Rethinking the Sales Force* (New York: McGraw-Hill, 1999), p. 79.

7. Department of Finance Canada. **www.fin.gc.ca/toce/2002/cmfi_e.html**, accessed May 6, 2002.

8. Karen E. Starr, "Simple Solutions," *Selling Power,* July/August 2001, p. 22.

9. John Fellows, "A Decent Proposal," *Personal Selling Power,* November/December 1995, p. 56.

10. Adapted from John Fellows, "A Decent Proposal."

11. "Feeling under the Gun? Check Your Proposal," *Selling,* October 2001, p. 3.

12. "What Kind of Rep Is Most Trustworthy?" *Sales & Marketing Management,* February 2001, p. 90.

13. "Ontario Global Traders Awards," *Profit,* September 2001, Advertising Supplement.

14. Interview with Michelle A. Reece, Certified Medical Representative Institute, Inc., Roanoke, VA, July 19, 1996.

15. Sarah Lorge, "Can ISO Certification Boost Sales?" *Sales & Marketing Management,* April 1998, p. 19.

16. Betsy Cummings, "Welcome to the Real Whirled," *Sales & Marketing Management,* February 2001, pp. 87–88.

17. Ian Gelenter, "Build Satisfaction with a Service Contract," *Selling,* May 1998, p. 7.

18. Tom Reilly, "Should You Set Prices?" *Selling,* August 2000, pp. 1, 14.

19. Gerhard Gschwandtner, "ROI Selling," *Selling Power,* November/December 2004, p. 10.

20. William M. Pride, Robert J. Hughes, and Jack R. Kapoor, *Business,* Eighth Edition (Boston, MA: Houghton Mifflin, 2005), pp. 456–57.

21. "Pfizer Canada Consistently Chosen among the Best Companies to Work for in Canada," Canada NewsWire, Ottawa, December 31, 2004, p. 1.

22. Jennifer Myers, "Lessons from Canada's Fastest Growing Companies," *Profit,* June/August, 2001, pp. 22–32; "Letter from Growth Camp," *Profit,* November 2001, p. 26.

23. Michael R. Williams and Jill S. Attaway, "Exploring Salespersons' Customer Orientation as a Mediator of Organizational Culture's Influence on Buyer-Seller Relationships," *Journal of Personal Selling & Sales Management,* Fall 1996, pp. 33–52.

24. Jennifer Myers, "Lessons from Canada's Fastest Growing Companies," pp. 22–23.

25. Interview with Mike Urquhart, May 20, 1997.

26. Alan Test, "The Scoop on the Competition," *Personal Selling Power,* November/December 1995, p. 38.

27. Jim Dickie, "Lowest Price Isn't the Answer," *Selling,* August 2000, p. 14.

28. "Power Tools," *Sales & Marketing Management,* March 1999, p. 50; Matt Purdue, "Networked with . . . Chip Herbert," *Sales & Field Force Automation,* January 1998, p. 18.

29. Jill Rosenfeld, "Unit of One," *Fast Company,* April 2000, p. 98.

30. Neil Rackham, *The SPIN Selling Fieldbook* (New York: McGraw-Hill, 1996), pp. 149–52.

31. Gary Hamil, *Leading the Revolution* (Boston, MA: Harvard Business School Press, 2000), p. 87; Neil Rackham, "Improve This Skill and Boost Sales up to 27%," *Value-Added Selling 21,* March 2, 2004, p. 1.

32. Jerry Vass, "Ten Expensive Selling Errors," *Agency Sales Magazine,* July 1998, pp. 38–39.

33. Stephen E. Heiman and Diane Sanchez, *The New Conceptual Selling* (New York: Warner Books, 1999), pp. 83–85.

SOURCES FOR BOXED FEATURES

a. Rhea Seymour, "Ideas That Work," *Profit,* June 2002, p. 69.

b. Robert G. Cooper, *Product Leadership* (Reading, MA: Perseus Books, 1998), p. 12; Neil Rackham, "What's New," *Selling Power,* January/February 1999, pp. 90, 92–93.

Chapter 7

1. Peter Egan, "The Best of All Worlds Bunch," *Road & Track,* July 2002, pp. 52-78.

2. William M. Pride, O. C. Ferrell, H. F. (Herb) MacKenzie, and Kim Snow, *Marketing: Concepts and Strategies,* Canadian ed. (Toronto, ON: Houghton Mifflin, 1998), p. 217.

3. D. Lee Carpenter, "Return on Innovation—the Power of Being Different," *Retailing Issues Letter,* May 1998, p. 3.

4. Tom Reilly, "You Must Differentiate to Win," *Selling,* April 2001, pp. 1, 10.

5. Gary Armstrong and Philip Kotler, *Marketing: An Introduction,* Sixth Edition (Upper Saddle River, NJ: Prentice Hall, 2003), p. 263.

6. "Secrets of the Best Sellers," *Profit,* January/February 1999, p. 21.

7. Carl K. Clayton, "Sell Quality, Service, Your Company, Yourself," *Personal Selling Power,* January/February 1990, p. 47.

8. Elaine Parker, "How I Made the Sale," *Value-Added Selling 21,* June 17, 2003, pp. 1–2.

9. Suein L Hwang, "It Was a WOMBAT for the Meatware, But It Was a Good Sell," *Wall Street Journal,* May 15, 2002, p. B1.

10. J. Thomas Russell and W. Ronald Lane, *Kleppner's Advertising Procedure* (Englewood Cliffs, NJ: Prentice-Hall, 1996), pp. 46–47.

11. Alison Overholt, "New Leaders, New Agenda," *Fast Company,* May 2002, p. 52.

12. Andy Cohen, "Copy Cats," *Sales & Marketing Management,* August 2000, pp. 50–58.

13. Personal correspondence from Rick Winston, Sun Life Assurance Company of Canada, June 11, 1997.

14. Michael R. Solomon and Elnora W. Stuart, *Marketing: Real People, Real Choices,* Second Edition (Upper Saddle River, NJ: Prentice Hall, 2000), p. 362.

15. Michael Treacy, "You Need a Value Discipline—But Which One?" *Fortune,* April 17, 1995, p. 195.

16. Robert Shulman and Richard Miniter, "Discounting Is No Bargain," *Wall Street Journal,* December 7, 1998, p. A30.

17. Andy Cohen, "Survey Says: Service Beats Price Online," *Sales & Marketing Management,* July 2002, p. 18.

18. Derek DeCloet, "The Good, the Bad and the Ho-Hum," *Canadian Business,* September 24, 1999, p. 76; Joe Chidley, "Down and Out on Bay Street," *Canadian Business,* September 24, 1999, p. 115.

19. Adapted from a model described in "Marketing Success through Differentiation—of Anything," *Harvard Business Review,* January/February 1980.

20. Joanna Johnson, "A New Perspective on Marketing," *Construction Dimensions,* April 1990, p. 14.

21. Ted Levitt, *Marketing Imagination* (New York: Free Press, 1983), p. 80.

22. Chuck Salter, "On the Road Again," *Fast Company,* July 2002, pp. 50–58.

23. Thomas A. Stewart, "A Satisfied Customer Isn't Enough," *Fortune,* July 21, 1997, pp. 112–13.

24. "Business Bulletin," *Wall Street Journal,* September 24, 1998, p. A1.

25. Larry Wilson, *Changing the Game: The New Way to Sell* (New York: Simon & Schuster, 1987), p. 200.

26. Ted Levitt, *Marketing Imagination,* p. 82.

27. Francy Blackwood, "The Concept That Sells," *Selling,* March 1995, pp. 34–36.

28. Neil Rackham and John R. DeVincentis, *Rethinking the Sales Force* (New York: McGraw-Hill, 1999), p. 89.

29. Ibid., pp. 89–90.

30. Ibid., p. 90.

SOURCES FOR BOXED FEATURES

a. Susan Creco, "Sales: What Works Now," *Inc.,* February 2001, p. 56.

b. Personal interview with Gary Svoboda, June 3, 2002.

Chapter 8

1. Tom Peters, *Re-imagine! Business Excellence in a Disruptive Age* (London, UK: Dorling Kindersley, 2003), pp. 309–10.

2. Interview with Ron Trudel and Ike Vickar, March 5, 1997.

3. Michael Hammer and James Champy, *Reengineering the Corporation: A Manifesto for Business Revolution* (New York: Harper Business, 1993), p. 18.

4. Keith M. Eades, *The New Solution Selling* (New York: McGraw-Hill, 2004), pp. 32–33.

5. Tom Peters and Nancy Austin, *A Passion for Excellence* (New York: Random House, 1985), p. 71.

6. "How Well Do You Know Your Customers?" *Sales & Field Force Automation,* January 1999, p. 141.

7. Gary Armstrong and Philip Kotler, *Marketing: An Introduction,* Sixth Edition (Upper Saddle River, NJ: Prentice Hall, 2003), pp. 191–92, 215.

8. *Ibid.*, p. 215.

9. Michael R. Solomon and Elnora W. Stuart, *Marketing: Real People, Real Choices,* Third Edition (Upper Saddle River, NJ: Prentice Hall, 2003), pp. 200–202.

10. Gary Armstrong and Philip Kotler, *Marketing: An Introduction,* Seventh Edition (Upper Saddle River, NJ: Prentice Hall, 2005), p. 169.

11. Ibid.

12. **www.fedex.com**, accessed December 16, 2004.

13. Philip Kotler and Gary Armstrong, *Principles of Marketing,* Tenth Edition (Upper Saddle River, NJ: Prentice Hall, 2004), p. 198.

14. Ibid., p. 198.

15. Ibid., p. 197.

16. Keith M. Eades, *The New Solution Selling,* pp. 32–33.

17. Ibid., p. 31.

18. Stephen E. Heiman and Diane Sanchez, *The New Conceptual Selling* (New York: Warner Books, 1999), pp. 190–91.

19. Gary Armstrong and Philip Kotler, *Marketing,* Seventh Edition, p. 160.

20. Neil Rackham and John R. DeVincentis, *Rethinking the Sales Force* (New York: McGraw-Hill, 1999), p. 66.

21. Bill Stinnett, "Reverse-Engineer the Buying Process," *Selling,* December 2004, p. 16.

22. Neil Rackham and John DeVincentis, *Rethinking the Sales Force,* p. 68.

23. Ibid., p. 69.

24. Neil Rackham and John DeVincentis provide extensive coverage of these three selling modes in *Rethinking the Sales Force.* See also Neil Rackham and John R.

DeVincentis, "Let the Customer Define Value—and Sales Will Rise," *Value-Added Selling 21,* January 13, 2004, pp. 1–2.

25. Neil Rackham and John R. DeVincentis, "Let the Customer Define Value—and Sales Will Rise," pp. 1–2.
26. Ken Brown, "Little-Known Avaya Tackles Cisco in Internet Calling Gear," *Wall Street Journal,* October 26, 2004, p. B1.
27. Neil Rackham and John DeVincentis, *Rethinking the Sales Force,* p. 74.
28. "Commodity partnerships: saving time and money on MRO materials at Nortel Semiconductors," *Modern Purchasing,* November, 1996, accessed via *Proquest* search, May 3, 2004.
29. Stan Davis and Christopher Meyer, *Blur: The Speed of Change in the Connected Economy* (New York: Addison-Wesley Publishers, 1998), p. 16.
30. Barry L. Reece and Rhonda Brandt, *Effective Human Relations in Organizations,* 7th edition. (Boston: Houghton Mifflin, 1999), p. 180.
31. William M. Pride and O.C. Ferrell, *Marketing,* Fourth Edition (Boston, MA: Houghton Mifflin, 1985), pp. 84–92.
32. Douglas A. Bernstein, Alison Clark-Stewart, Edward J. Roy, and Christopher D. Wickens, *Psychology,* Fourth Edition (Boston, MA: Houghton Mifflin, 1997), p. 570.
33. William F. Schoell and Joseph P. Guillinan, *Marketing* (Boston, MA: Allyn & Bacon, 1992), p. 164.
34. Douglas A. Bernstein, et al., *Psychology,* Fourth Edition, p. 21.
35. Louis E. Boone and David L. Kurtz, *Contemporary Marketing,* Eleventh Edition (Mason, OH: Southwestern Publishing, 2004), p. 13.
36. Roger Hart, "Luxury, VW's Way," *AutoWeek,* December 27, 2004, p. 19.
37. Phil Kline, "Dominant Buying Motive Is the Result of Strong Emotions," *Marketing News,* May 24, 1993, p. 4.
38. Stan Davis and Christopher Meyer, *Blur,* p. 52.
39. Hal Lancaster, "It's Time to Stop Promoting Yourself and Start Listening," *Wall Street Journal,* June 10, p. B1.
40. Gary Armstrong and Philip Kotler, *Marketing,* Sixth Edition, p. 216; Sid Chadwick, "New Twists in Price vs. Perceived Value," *Sales and Marketing Advisory Magazine,* July/August 2001, p. 6.
41. Interview with Ron Trudel and Ike Vickar, "How Well Do You Know Your Customers?" *Sales and Field Force Automation,* January 1999 (Supplement to the January Issue).

SOURCES FOR BOXED FEATURES

a. Susan M. O'Dell and Joan A. Pajunen, *The Butterfly Customer* (Toronto, ON: J. Wiley & Sons Canada, 1997).

b. Adapted from discussion in Leonard L. Berry, A. Parasuraman, and Valerie A. Zeithaml, "The Service-Quality Puzzle," *Business Horizons,* September/October 1988, pp. 35–43; Robert Kreitner, *Management,* Fifth Edition (Boston, MA: Houghton Mifflin, 1992), pp. 613–14.

Chapter 9

1. **www.stevens.ca**, downloaded June 20, 2002; interview with Jeff Stevens, May 6, 1997.
2. Don Peppers, Martha Rogers, and Bob Dorf. "Is Your Company Ready for One-to-One Marketing?" *Harvard Business Review,* January/February 1999, pp. 151–54.
3. Gerhard Gschwandtner, "Thoughts to Sell By," *Personal Selling Power,* Fifteenth Anniversary Issue, 1995, p. 122.
4. Dorothy Leeds, "Where Are the Real Decision Makers?" *Personal Selling Power,* March 1993, p. 62; Gerhard Gschwandtner, "Getting Squeezed," *Selling Power,* May 2002, p. 10.
5. Gerhard Gschwandtner, "The Funnel Concept," *Personal Selling Power,* May/June 1993, p. 22.
6. Bob Donath, "Fire Your Big Customers? Maybe You Should." *Marketing News,* June 21, 1999, p. 9.
7. Ibid., p. 23.
8. Zig Ziglar, *Ziglar on Selling* (New York: Ballantine Books, 1991), pp. 70–71.
9. Ian Selbie, *If you were arrested for selling... would there be enough evidence to convict you?* (self-published, available from Power Marketing, **www.power.ca**).
10. "Harland Sanders," *Selling Power,* July/August 2001, p. 107.
11. Thomas Petzinger, Jr., "Selling a 'Killer App' Is a Far Tougher Job Than Dreaming It Up," *Wall Street Journal,* April 3, 1998, p. B1.
12. Pam Withers, "Rules of the Road," *Profit,* February/March 2002, pp. 24–35.
13. Ben Chapman, "The Trade Show Must Go On," *Sales & Marketing Management,* June 2001, p. 22.
14. Chad Kaydo, "How to Find New Customers," *Sales & Marketing Management,* February 2000, p. 100.
15. Mary Klonizakis, "Salespeople Have Staying Power," *Contact,* January 2000, p. 16.
16. Trish Rintels, "Use Avatars to Enhance Your Sales Message Online," *Selling,* September 2001, p. 3.
17. "PCs Make Selling More Personal," *Sales and Marketing Digest,* October 1987, p. 98.
18. Alan Test, "Cold Calls Are Hot," *Agency Sales Magazine,* September 1995, p. 28.
19. Steven J. Schwartz, *How to Make Hot Cold Calls,* revised edition (Toronto, ON: Stoddart Publishing, 2001).
20. Anne Baber and Lynne Waymon, "No-Nonsense Networking," *Your Company,* Summer 1993, p. 34.

21. Barry Siskind, *Making Contact* (Toronto: Macmillan Canada, 1995), pp. 1, 83.
22. Maxwell Maltz, Dan S. Kennedy, William T. Brooks, Matt Oechsli, Jeff Paul, and Pamela Yellen, *Zero-Resistance Selling* (Paramus, NJ: Prentice-Hall, 1998) pp. 179–180.
23. Interview with Gene Chahley, Polaroid Canada Inc., May 19, 1997.
24. Chad Kaydo, "Teach Your Clients Well," *Sales & Marketing Management,* April 1988, p. 83.
25. "A Company of Lead Generators," *Inc.,* September 1987, p. 111.
26. This example was adopted from "Skills Workshop" by William F. Kendy, *Selling Power,* January/February 2000, p. 26.
27. Mitchell Pacelle, "Former SEC Chairman Levitt Decries Business Ethics in the U.S.," *Wall Street Journal,* June 17, 2002, p. C7.
28. Rick Page, *Hope Is Not a Strategy* (Atlanta, GA: Nautilus Press, 2002), pp. 69–71.
29. "Senior Execs Share Insider Tips," *Selling,* March 2000, pp. 1, 14; Tom Reilly, "Selling to Mr. Big Is Tough, But . . . " *Selling,* February 2001, pp. 1, 12.
30. Harvey Mackay, *Swim with the Sharks* (New York: William Morrow, 1988), pp. 43, 44.
31. Tricia Campbell, "Managing Leads," *Sales & Marketing Management,* December 1998, p. 38.
32. Geoffrey Brewer, "Selling to Senior Executives," *Sales & Marketing Management,* July 1996, p. 43.
33. Gerald A. Michaelson, "Selling to the Top," *Selling,* October 1998, p. 7.
34. "Prospecting Is Where the Gold Is," *Institutional Distribution,* May 15, 1990, pp. 70–72.
35. Jack Stack, "A Passion for Forecasting," *Inc.,* 1997, pp. 37–38.
36. Paul Tindall, "Prospecting: It Separates the Best from the Rest," *Sales Exchange,* November 17–23, 2003.

SOURCES FOR BOXED FEATURES

a. Barbara Siskind, *Seminars to Build Your Business* (North Vancouver, BC: Self-Counsel Press, 1998), pp. 9–12; Sheldon Gordon, "Punch Up Your Profits," *Profit,* May 1999, pp. 17–22.

b. Debi Rosati, personal correspondence, October 27, 2004.

c. Kali Pearson, "The Good, the Bad and the Ugly," *Profit,* February–March 2002, pp. 48–50; Brian Ziegler, "Your Business Card Can Be a Powerful Tool," *Des Moines Register,* August 2, 1999, B17.

Chapter 10

1. Interview with Brenda Fisher, February 24, 1997.
2. Malcolm Fleschner, "Too Busy to Buy," *Selling Power,* March 1999, p. 36.
3. Bradford Agry, "Every Client Meeting Provides a Dynamic New Opportunity," *Selling,* April 2002, pp. 1, 4.
4. Malcolm Fleschner, "Anatomy of a Sale," *Selling Power,* April 1998, p. 76.
5. "Set the Agenda," *Personal Selling Power,* May/June 1995, p. 79.
6. Donna Fenn, "Because His Family Business Makes an Art of Customer Service," *Inc.,* April 2005, p. 94; Telephone interview with Pamela Miles, staff member at Mitchells/Richards, March 22, 2005.
7. Philip Kotler and Gary Armstrong, *Principles of Marketing,* Tenth Edition (Upper Saddle River, NJ: Prentice Hall, 2004), p. 531.
8. Rick Page, *Hope Is Not a Strategy* (Atlanta, GA: Nautilus Press, 2002), p. 25.
9. Henry Canaday, "Teaming with Sales," *Selling Power,* May 1998, pp. 94–102.
10. James F. O'Hara, "Successful Selling to Buying Committees," *Selling,* February 1998, p. 8.
11. Betty Cummings, "Do Customers Hate Salespeople?" *Sales & Marketing Management,* June 2001, p. 46.
12. Thomas A. Freese, *Secrets of Question Based Selling* (Naperville, IL: Sourcebooks, 2003), p. 144.
13. John Fellows, "Your Foot in the Door," *Selling Power,* March 1996, pp. 64–65.
14. Adapted from Art Sobczak, "Please, Call Me Back!" *Selling,* March 1999, p. 12.
15. *Ibid.*
16. Susan Bixler and Nancy Nix-Rice, *The New Professional Image* (Holbrook, MA: Adams Media Corporation, 1997), p. 3.
17. Dean A. Goettsch, "Make Your First Meeting Count," *Selling,* July 2004, pp. 1, 4.
18. Melissa Campanelli, "Sound the Alarm," *Sales & Marketing Management,* December 1994, pp. 20–25.
19. James E. Lukaszewski and Paul Ridgeway, "To Put Your Best Foot Forward, Start by Taking These 21 Simple Steps," *Sales & Marketing Management,* June 1990, p. 84.
20. Carolee Boyles, "Prewarm Cold Calls," *Selling Power,* July/August 2001, p. 30.
21. Abner Little, "Selling to Women Revs Up Car Sales," *Personal Selling Power,* July/August 1990, p. 50.
22. "Six Great Upselling Questions," *Personal Selling Power,* April 1993, p. 44.
23. Interview with Larry Short, June 9, 1997.
24. Alan Farnham, "Are You Smart Enough to Keep Your Job?" *Fortune,* January 15, 1996, pp. 34–42.
25. "The Disappointment Trap," *Selling Power,* January/February 1999, p. 14.
26. Roy Chitwood, "Still Trying to Slip Past Gatekeepers? Forget It!" *Value-Added Selling 21,* December 16, 2003, pp. 1–2.

SOURCES FOR BOXED FEATURES

a. Richard R. Gesteland, *Cross-Cultural Business Behavior* (Copenhagen: Handelshøjskolens Forlag, Copenhagen Business School Press, 1999), pp. 19–23; Canada, Departments of Foreign Affairs and International Trade, "What Is Team Canada?" **http://www.tcm-mec.gc.ca/what-e.asp**, downloaded March 25, 2002.

Chapter 11

1. Betsy Cummings, "Beating the Odds," *Sales & Marketing Management,* March 2002, pp. 24–28.
2. "97 Ways to Sell More in '96," *Selling,* January/February 1996, p. 50.
3. Rose A. Spinelli, "Listening: A Priority in Shopping for Others," *Chicago Tribune,* November 30, 2003, p. 55.
4. Ann Demarais and Valerie White, *First Impressions —What You Don't Know About How Others See You* (New York: Bantam Books, 2004), pp. 68–69.
5. Barry L. Reece and Rhonda Brandt, *Effective Human Relations: Personal and Organizational Applications* (Boston, MA: Houghton Mifflin, 2005), pp. 38–40.
6. Ibid., p. 40.
7. Demarais and White, *First Impressions,* p. 70.
8. Matthew McKay, Martha Davis, and Patrick Fanning, *The Communication Skills Book* (Oakland, CA: Harbinger, 1995), p. 15; Susan Scott, *Fierce Conversations* (New York: Viking Penguin, 2002), p. 157.
9. William F. Kendy, "How to Be a Good Listener," *Selling Power,* April 2004, p. 43.
10. Tom Riley, *Value-Added Selling* (New York: McGraw-Hill, 2003), p. 130.
11. "Presentation-Wise, We've Lost Our Tails," *Sales & Field Force Automation,* July 1999, p. 4.
12. Gary A. Williams and Robert B. Miller, "Change the Way You Persuade," *Harvard Business Review,* May 2002, p. 6.
13. Robert Frank, "Frito-Lay Devours Snack-Food Business," *Wall Street Journal,* October 27, 1995, p. B1.
14. Robert B. Cialdini, "Harnessing the Science of Persuasion," *Harvard Business Review,* October 2001, p. 74.
15. Stephanie G. Sherman and V. Clayton Sherman, *Make Yourself Memorable* (New York: AMACOM, 1996), pp. 58–59.
16. Art Sobczak, "How to Sell with Sizzle Stories," *Selling,* November 1998, p. 12.
17. Thomas A. Stewart, "The Cunning Plots of Leadership," *Fortune,* September 7, 1998, pp. 165–66.
18. "97 Ways to Sell More in '96," *Selling,* January/February 1996, p. 52.
19. Chad Kaydo, "Lights! Camera! Sales!" *Sales & Marketing Management,* February 1998, p. 111.
20. Neil Rackham and John DeVincentis, *Rethinking the Sales Force* (New York: McGraw-Hill, 1999), p. 17.

SOURCES FOR BOXED FEATURES

a. Judith C. Tingley and Lee E. Robert, *GenderSell: How to Sell to the Opposite Sex* (New York: Simon & Schuster, 1999).

b. Raizel Robin, "The Pitchman," *Canadian Business,* December 10, 2001, p. 57.

Chapter 12

1. *Show and Tell: Custom Fitting the Demonstration* (Pasadena, CA: Intelecom), "The World's Best Live Animation," **www.simg.com**, cited August 2, 2002.
2. Larry Tuck, "Presentations That Cut through the Information Clutter," *Sales & Field Force Automation,* June 1999, p. 86; Price Pritchett, *Carpe Manana* (Plano, TX: Pritchett Rummler-Brache, 2000), p. 3.
3. Ken Taylor, "Help Your Audience Visualize Your Message," *Selling,* April 1998, p. 10.
4. Lisa Gschwandtner, "Persuasive Presentation," *Selling Power,* July/August 2001, p. 92.
5. "Country-wide Creativity," *Selling Power,* April 1998, p. 58.
6. Douglas A. Bernstein, Alison Clarke-Stewart, Edward J. Roy, and Christopher D. Wilkens, *Psychology,* Fourth Edition (Boston, MA: Houghton Mifflin, 1997), p. 237.
7. Harold H. Bloomfield and Robert K. Cooper, *The Power of 5* (Emmaus, PA: Rodale Press, 1995), p. 196.
8. Lambeth Hochwald, "Simplify," *Sales & Marketing Management,* June 1998, pp. 66–67.
9. Corbin Ball Associates, "Avoiding Death by PowerPoint," **www.corbinball.com**, accessed April 12, 2005.
10. Personal correspondence from Christa Lee McWatters, May 22, 1997.
11. Merrie Spaeth, "Prop Up Your Speaking Skills," *Wall Street Journal,* July 1, 1996, p. A14.
12. Rick Page, *Hope Is Not a Strategy* (Atlanta, GA: Nautilus Press, 2002), pp. 114–15.
13. Dale Buss, "Sock It to 'Em!" *Sales & Marketing Management,* October 2001, pp. 57–64.
14. Rick Page, *Hope Is Not a Strategy,* p. 126.
15. Lambeth Hochwald, "Simplify," pp. 65–66.
16. Interview with Amir Hooda, May 29, 1997.
17. David Ranii, "Dermabond's Debut Disappoints," *News & Observer,* July 31, 1999, p. D1.

18. "Three Guides to Using Your Catalog as a Sales Tool," *Value-Added Selling 21,* June 17, 2003, p. 4.
19. Heather Baldwin, "Star Light Star Bright," *Selling Power Source Book 2002,* p. 55.
20. Heather Baldwin, "Up Your Powers," *Selling Power Source Book,* October 2001, pp. 88–92.
21. Kevin Ferguson, "Reinventing the PowerPoint," *Inc.,* March 2004, p. 42; Corbin Ball Associates, "Avoiding Death by PowerPoint."
22. Dana Ray, "Presentations," *Selling Power Source Book,* 1999, p. 66.
23. Gerald L. Manning and Jack W. Linge, *Selling-Today.com* (Upper Saddle River, NJ: Prentice Hall, 1998), p. 34.
24. Cindy Waxer, "Presenting the Power," *Selling Power Source Book* 2005, pp. 70–71.
25. Ibid., p. 71.
26. Malcolm Campbell, "All in a Day's Presentation," *Selling Power,* November/December 1998, pp. 91–93.

SOURCES FOR BOXED FEATURES

a. Personal interview with Susan Abramson and Rachel McGarry, April 6, 2002.

b. Michael Chylewski, "Memorable Sale," *Selling Power,* January/February 1999, p. 22.

c. Erin Strout, "The Show Must Go On," *Sales & Marketing Management,* November 2001, pp. 52–59; Ellen Neuborne, "Tag-Team Pitches," *Sales & Marketing Management,* March 2002, p. 57.

Chapter 13

1. Correspondence from Doug Macnamara, Vice-President, The Banff Centre, and General Manager, The Banff Centre for Management, September 30, 1999.
2. Geoff James, "The Art of Sales Negotiation," *Selling Power,* March 2004, pp. 25–28.
3. Tom Riley, *Value-Added Selling* (New York: McGraw-Hill, 2003), p. 17.
4. Hal Lancaster, "You Have to Negotiate for Everything in Life, So Get Good at It," *Wall Street Journal,* January 27, 1998, p. B1.
5. Ron Willingham, *Integrity Selling for the 21st Century* (New York: Currency Doubleday, 2003), p. 154.
6. Brian Tracy, *The 100 Absolutely Unbreakable Laws of Business Success* (San Francisco, CA: Berrett-Koehler Publishers, 2000), p. 235.
7. Ron Willingham, *Integrity Selling,* p. 153.
8. Gregg Crawford, "Let's Negotiate," *Sales & Marketing Management,* November 1995, pp. 28–29.
9. William F. Kendy, "Solving the 'Friendship Buying' Problem," *Selling Power,* November/December 2001, pp. 40–44.
10. Steven J. Schwartz, *How to Make Hot Cold Calls,* revised edition (Toronto, ON: Stoddart Publishing, 2001), p. 42.
11. Homer Smith, "How to Cope with Buyers Who Are Trained in Negotiation," *Personal Selling Power,* September 1988, p. 37.
12. Ibid.
13. Robert Adler, Benson Rosen, and Elliot Silverstein, "Thrust and Parry," *Training & Development,* March 1996, p. 47.
14. Homer Smith, "How to Cope with Buyers," p. 27.
15. Laura Pratt, "Everyone's a winner," *Profit,* November 2001, p. 47.
16. Tom Riley, *Value-Added Selling,* pp. 191–92.
17. Joseph Conlin, "Negotiating Their Way to the Top," *Sales & Marketing Management,* April 1996, p. 58.
18. Sam Deep and Lyle Sussman, *Close the Deal: Smart Moves for Selling* (Reading, MA: Perseus Books, 1999), p. 225.
19. Roland M. Sandell, "Five Sure-Fire Methods to Overcome Objections to Price," *American Salesman,* October 1976, p. 38.
20. Alex Taylor, "Little Jets Are Huge," *Fortune,* September 4, 2000, pp. 275–78.
21. Joseph Conlin, "Negotiating Their Way," p. 62; Neil Rackham, "Winning the Price War," *Sales & Marketing Management,* November 2001, p. 26.
22. David Stiebel, *When Talking Makes Things Worse!* (Dallas, TX: Whitehall & Norlton, 1997), p. 17.
23. Lain Ehman, "Not a Done Deal," *Selling Power,* November/December 2003, pp. 42–44; "Negotiate the Right Price Despite Customer Pressure," *Selling,* July 2004, p. 2.
24. Jeff Keller, "Objections? No Problem," *Selling Power,* September 1996, pp. 44–45.
25. Adapted from Nanci McCann, "Irate over Rates," *Selling,* July/August 1996, p. 25.
26. Rick Kang, "Management by Defiance," *Profit,* June 1999, pp. 63–64.
27. See Neil Rackham, *The New SPIN Selling Fieldbook,* (New York: McGraw-Hill, 1996), pp. 127–45.

SOURCES FOR BOXED FEATURES

a. Hal Lancaster, "You Have to Negotiate for Everything in Life, So Get Good At It," *The Wall Street Journal,* January 27, 1998, p. B1; Amy Lindgren, "Want a Raise? Don't Daydream; Polish Your Negotiating Skills," *Des Moines Register,* April 26, 1998, p. 1L.

b. Mary Klonizakis, "A Class Act," *Contact,* September 2000, p. 18.

c. "Getting to Yes, Chinese Style," *Sales & Marketing Management,* July 1996, pp. 44–45; Sam Deep and Lyle Sussman, *Close the Deal: Smart Moves for Selling* (Reading, MA: Perseus Books, 1999), pp. 279–81; James K. Sebenius, "Six Habits of Merely Effective Negotiators," *Harvard Business Review,* April 2001, p. 90.

Chapter 14

1. Linda Corman, "The Slow and Steady Ryder Race," *Selling,* January/February 1996, pp. 56–58.
2. Kristine Ellis, "Deal Maker or Breaker?" *Training,* April 2002, p. 37.
3. Gene Bedell, *3 Steps to Yes* (New York: Crown Business, 2000), pp. 72–80.
4. Tom Riley, *Value-Added Selling* (New York: McGraw-Hill, 2003), p. 176.
5. Dan Kennedy, *No B.S. Sales Success,* Second Edition (North Vancouver, BC: Self-Counsel Press, 1999), p. 113.
6. Andy Cohen, "Are Your Reps Afraid to Close?" *Sales & Marketing Management,* March 1996, p. 43.
7. Stephen E. Heiman and Dianne Sanchez, *The New Conceptual Selling* (New York: Warner Books, 1999), pp. 117–29.
8. Graham Denton, "The Single Biggest Closing Mistake," Graham Denton Skills Center (Web page) May 4, 1999, p. 1. Accessed Jan. 9, 2006 at http://members.fortunecity.com/salesman2/salescom/closing/thesingl.html.
9. "The Closing Moment," *Personal Selling,* October 1995, p. 48.
10. Ron Karr, "Expert Advice The Titan Principle," *Selling Power,* October 2001, p. 32.
11. Ron Willingham, *Integrity Selling for the 21st Century* (New York: Currency Doubleday, 2003), p. 184.
12. Kelley Robertson, *Stop, Ask, and Listen* (Toronto, ON: Stoddart Publishing, 2002), p. 128.
13. Tom Riley, *Value-Added Selling,* p. 179.
14. Jenny C. McCune, "The Brief Story of Underwear's Stupendous Success," *Selling,* March 2000, p. 15.
15. Joan Leotta, "The Management Close," *Selling Power,* November/December 2001, pp. 26–28.
16. "Salestalk," *Sales & Marketing Management,* May 1990, p. 116.
17. "Selling Tips," *Selling,* May 1999, p. 13.
18. Mel Siberman, *Active Training* (Toronto, ON: Maxwell Macmillan Canada, 1990), pp. 96–99.
19. T. J. Becker, "That Queasy Feeling," *Chicago Tribune,* July 21, 2002, p. W1.
20. Betsy Wiesendanger, "When a Sale Goes South," *Selling Power,* November/December 2003, pp. 65–67.

SOURCES FOR BOXED FEATURES

a. "Ask for the Order" (West Des Moines, IA: Video Learning, LLC, 2004).

b. Interview with Greg Brophy, February 19, 1997; correspondence from Judy Robson, August 26, 1999; correspondence from Bonnie Shettler, May 2005.

Chapter 15

1. Rick Kang, "Management 2000," *Profit,* June 2000, pp. 89–96.
2. Tim Connor, **www.timconnor.com/articles/article16.html**, downloaded July 2, 2002.
3. Bob Johnson, "Loyalty Lessons from the Pros," *Customer Support Management,* July/August 1999, p. 115.
4. Gary Armstrong and Philip Kotler, *Marketing: An Introduction,* Sixth Edition (Upper Saddle River, NJ: Prentice Hall, 2003), p. 553.
5. Theodore Levitt, *The Marketing Management* (New York: Macmillan, 1983), pp. 117–18; Tahl Raz, "The '4 + 2 Formula' for Success," *Inc.,* August 2003, p. 42.
6. Geoffrey Brewer, "The Customer Stops Here," *Sales & Marketing Management,* March 1998, pp. 31–32.
7. "Why Customers Leave," *Sales & Marketing Management,* May 1998, p. 86; Tom Peters, *The Circle of Innovation* (New York: Vintage Books, 1997), pp. 138–39.
8. Max Morden, "Service with a Smile," *In Touch* (Richard Ivey School of Business, Fall 1999), p. 37.
9. Bill Gates, *Business @ the Speed of Thought* (New York: Warner Books, 1999), p. 67.
10. Sarah Mahoney, "Look at Sales Through Your Customer's Eyes," *Selling,* March 1997, pp. 1–2.
11. Mack Hanan, *Consultative Selling,* 3rd ed. (New York: AMACOM, 1985), pp. 121–22.
12. Bob Johnson, "Loyalty Lesson from the Pros," p. 116.
13. Thomas A. Stewart, "A Satisfied Customer Isn't Enough," *Fortune,* July 21, 1997, p. 113.
14. Bill Gates, *Business @ the Speed of Thought,* p. 67.
15. Chad Kaydo, "An Unlikely Sales Ally," *Sales & Marketing Management,* January 1999, p. 69.
16. Sally J. Silberman, "An Eye for Finance," *Sales & Marketing Management,* April 1996, p. 26.
17. Benson P. Shapiro, V. Kasturi Rangon, and John Sviokla, *Harvard Business Review,* July/August 2004, p. 162.
18. Daryl Allen, "Relationship Selling Is Key to Success," *Selling,* March 2002, p. 12.
19. Tom Reilly, "Create Satisfied Customers: Always Be Sure to Exceed Their Expectations," *Selling,* January 2001, p. 3.
20. Tom Riley, *Value-Added Selling* (New York: McGraw-Hill, 2003), p. 117.
21. Andrea Nierenberg, "Eight Ways to Stay Top of Mind," *Selling,* April 1998, p. 7.
22. Melinda Ligos, "The Joys of Cross-Selling," *Sales & Marketing Management,* August 1998, p. 75.
23. Tom Riley, *Value-Added Selling,* pp. 124–25.
24. William F. Kendy, "Skills Workshop," *Selling Power,* June 2000, pp. 33–34.

25. Jo Ann Brezette, "Smart Answers to Clients' Questions," *Window Fashions Design & Education Magazine,* September 2001, p. 120.
26. "Inspirations from Michele," *Inspiring Solutions,* February 1999, p. 3.
27. Bob Johnson, "Loyalty Lessons from the Pros," *Customer Support Management,* July/August 1999, p. 115.
28. Bradley E. Wesner, "From Complaint to Opportunity," *Selling Power,* May 1996, p. 62
29. Sam Deep and Lyle Sussman, *Close the Deal: Smart Moves for Selling* (Reading, MA: Perseus Books, 1999), p. 252.
30. Bradley E. Wesner, "From Complaint to Opportunity," p. 62
31. Gerald A Michaelson, "When Things Go Wrong, Make It Right," *Selling,* March 1997, p. 12.
32. Michael Abrams and Matthew Paese, "Winning and Dining the Whiners," *Sales & Marketing Management,* February 1993, p. 73.
33. "How to Diffuse a Customer Problem," *Sales & Marketing Management,* May 2000, p. 14.
34. Interview with Garnet Kindervater, November 10, 1999.

SOURCES FOR BOXED FEATURES

a. Jeff Barbian, "It's Who You Know," *Training,* December 2001, p. 22.

b. "Relationships with Customers Must Be Job Number 1," *Food-Service Distributor,* July 1989, p. 74; Joan O. Fredericks and James M. Salter II, "Beyond Customer Satisfaction," *Management Review,* May 1995, pp. 29–32.

Chapter 16

1. Paula Shannon, personal correspondence, May 2005.
2. "Data Trends," *Selling,* June 1999, p. 1.
3. Laura Pratt, "Twenty-five Hours a Day," *Profit,* November 2001, p. 41.
4. Bob Urichuck, *Up Your Bottom Line* (Carp, ON: Creative Books, 2001), p. 57.
5. Ibid., pp. 58–59.
6. Cy Charney, *The Salesperson's Handbook* (Toronto, ON: Stoddart Publishing, 2002), p. 227.
7. Ibid., p. 228.
8. Laura Pratt, "Twenty-five Hours a Day," p. 41.
9. Ibid.
10. Michele Marchetti, "Territories: For Optimal Performance, Segment Your Customer Base by Industry," *Sales & Marketing Management,* December 1998, p. 35.
11. Erika Rasmusson, "Wanted: Profitable Customers," *Sales & Marketing Management,* May 1999, pp. 28–34.
12. Arnold A. Lazarus and Clifford N. Lazarus, *The 60-Second Shrink* (San Luis Obispo, CA: Impact Publishers, 1997), p. 86; Howard I. Glazer, *Getting in Touch with Stress Management* (American Telephone and Telegraph, 1988), p. 2.
13. Rhea Seymour, "Fighting the Pressure," *Profit,* November 2001, p. 43.
14. Ibid.
15. David Shenk, "Data Smog," *Perdid,* Spring 1999, pp. 5–7.
16. "More Useful Tips for Running Your Home Office," *Selling,* January 2001, p. 11; "Home Office Etiquette," *Sales & Marketing Management,* January 2000, p. 74.
17. "Canada's Fastest Growing Companies 2002," *Profit,* June 2002, p. 36.
18. Fiona Gibb, "To Give or Not to Give," *Sales & Marketing Management,* September 1994, pp. 136–39.
19. Betsy Cummings, "Sales Ruined My Personal Life," *Sales & Marketing Management,* November 2001, pp. 45–50.
20. "Canada's Fastest Growing Companies 2002," *Profit,* June 2002, p. 36.
21. Health Canada. **www.hc-sc.gc.ca/hppb/ fitness/work/case_template_e.html**, downloaded June 11, 2002.
22. Tavia Grant, "Husky Woos Workers with Unique Perks," *Globe and Mail,* August 20, 2001, p. M1.
23. Robert Hough, "A Make or Break Proposition," *Canadian Business,* February 1997, p. 18.

SOURCES FOR BOXED FEATURES

a. Kip Grant, "Saying 'I Do' to Lifelong Learning," *Contact,* January 2000, p. 9.

b. **www.jimpattison.com**, accessed June 20, 2002; Diane Francis, "What Makes Jim Pattison Run—and Whistle?" *Financial Post,* March 5–7, 1994, p. S3.

c. Mark Williams, *The Ten Lenses: Your Guide to Living and Working in a Multicultural World,* (Dulles, VA: Capital Books, 2002); Harvey Schachter, "The 21st Century CEO," *Profit,* April 1999, pp. 25–34.

d. Jim Carroll, "Too Much Technology?" *Contact,* April 2002, pp. 14–15; Cy Charney, *The Salesperson's Handbook* (Toronto, ON: Stoddart Publishing, 2002) pp. 242–45; Rhea Seymour, "Fighting the Pressure," *Profit,* November 2001, p. 43.

Chapter 17

1. Henry Canaday, "A New Vision of Change," *Power Selling,"* July/August 2001, pp. 62–64.
2. William Keenan Jr., "Death of the Sales Manager," pp. 72–79.
3. Sally J. Silberman, "Troubling Transitions," *Sales & Marketing Management,* February 1996, pp. 20–21.
4. These dimensions are described in Edwin A. Fleischman, *Manual for Leadership Questionnaire* (Chicago, IL: Science Research Associates, 1960), p. 3.
5. Phillip Gelman, "The Good Sales Manager," *Personal Selling Power,* January–February 1993, p. 56.

6. Alison Furnham, "Expect Good Work and You'll Get It," *Executive Female,* September/October 14, 1996, pp. 13–16.
7. Jack Falvey, "The Absolute Basics of Sales Force Management," *Sales & Marketing Management,* August 1990, p. 8.
8. Sarah Lorge, "In the Box," *Sales & Marketing Management,* April 1998, p. 15.
9. Ken Blanchard, "3 Secrets of the One-Minute Manager," *Personal Selling Power,* March 1993, p. 48.
10. Ron Zemke, "Trust Inspires Trust," *Training,* January 2002, p. 10; William F. Kendy, "Build Trust—Don't Destroy It," *Selling Power,* July/August 2001, p. 56.
11. Rhea Seymour, "The Mentor's Reward," *Profit,* November 2001, p. 35.
12. Kenneth R. Phillips, "The Achilles' Heel of Coaching," *Training & Development,* March 1998, p. 41.
13. Ibid., pp. 41–44.
14. Andy Cohen, "What Keeps You Up at Night?" *Sales & Marketing Management,* February 2000, pp. 47–48.
15. Anne Fisher, "Essential Employees Called Up to Serve," *Fortune,* October 2000, p. 210.
16. Richard J. Mirabile, "The Power of Job Analysis," *Training,* April 1990, p. 70.
17. Katharine Kaplan, "Help (Still) Wanted," *Sales & Marketing Management,* February 2002, pp. 38–43.
18. Virginia Galt, "Procter & Gamble Finds Loyalty Does Wash with Young Recruits," *Globe and Mail,* May 13, 2002, pp. B1, B4.
19. Paula Lima, "Talent shortage? That Was Yesterday," *Profit,* February/March 2002, pp. 65–66.
20. William Keenan, Jr., "Who Has the Right Stuff?" *Sales & Marketing Management,* August 1993, p. 28.
21. "Parting Company: The Right Time to Cut Bait and Run," *Personal Selling Power,* May–June 1995, p. 68.
22. Andy Cohen, "What Keeps You Up at Night?", pp. 44–52.
23. Gerhard Gschwandtner, "A Jewel of the Company," *Personal Selling Power,* March 1995, p. 17.
24. Alan J. Dubinsky, Francis J. Yammarino, Marvin A. Jolson, and William D. Spangler, "Transformational Leadership: An Initial Investigation in Sales Management," *Journal of Personal Selling & Sales Management,* Spring 1995, p. 27.
25. Jack Falvey, "The Care and Feeding of New Salespeople, *Sales & Marketing Management,* February 1992, p. 22.
26. Barry L. Reece and Rhonda Brandt, *Effective Human Relations in Organizations,* Sixth Edition (Boston, MA: Houghton Mifflin, 1996), p. 153.
27. Ibid.
28. Alfie Kohn, "Why Incentive Plans Cannot Work," *Harvard Business Review,* September/October 1993, pp. 58–59.
29. "Selling with Sales Contest," *Sales & Marketing Management,* June 1995, p. 35.
30. Audrey Bottjen, "Incentives Gone Awry," *Sales & Marketing Management,* May 2001, p. 72.
31. Nora Wood, "What Motivates Best," *Sales & Marketing Management,* September 1998, pp. 71–78.
32. Andy Cohen, "The Right Stuff," *Sales & Marketing Management,* January 1999, p. 15.
33. Eilene Zimmerman, "Quota Busters," *Sales & Marketing Management,* January 2001, pp. 59–63.
34. Christine Galea, "2002 Salary Survey," *Sales & Marketing Management,* May 2002, pp. 32–36.
35. "Point Incentive Sales Programs," *SBR Update,* Vol. 1, No. 4.
36. Donald W. Jackson, Jr., John L. Schlacter, and William G. Wolfe, "Examining the Bases Utilized for Evaluating Salespeople's Performance," *Journal of Personal Selling & Sales Management,* February 1995, p. 57.
37. "Survey of Sales Education Process —What Works, What Doesn't," *Selling Power,* September 1999, p. 115.
38. Lisa Holton, "Look Who's in on Your Performance Review," *Selling,* January/February 1995, pp. 47–55; Barry L. Reece and Rhonda Brandt, *Effective Human Relations: Personal and Organizational Applications* (Boston, MA: Houghton Mifflin, 2002), p. 203; "Customer Ratings Are Misleading," *Selling,* November 1996, p. 1.

SOURCES FOR BOXED FEATURES

a. Andy Cohen, "Is This Guy for Real?" *Sales & Marketing Management,* May 2001, pp. 36–44.

b. Betsy Cummings, "You're Outta Here, "*Sales & Marketing Management,* June 2001, pp. 65–66; Rhea Seymour, "Ideas That Work," *Profit,* June 2002, pp. 66–70; Betsey Cummings, "The Perfect Plan," *Sales & Marketing Management,* February 2002, p. 53.

Name Index

***Note:* Boldface page numbers indicate figures or photos.**

Subject Index

***Note:* Boldface page numbers indicate figures or tables.**

Credits

FIGURE CREDITS

Fig. 3.3, p. 64: From the book *The Double Win* by Dennis Waitley (Old Tappan, NJ: Fleming H. Revell Co., 1985). **Fig. 7.3, p. 163:** Adapted and reprinted by permission of *Harvard Business Review.* An exhibit from "Marketing Success through Differentiation of Anything" by Theodore Levitt (Jan/Feb 1980). Copyright © 1980 by the President and Fellows of Harvard College, all rights reserved. **Fig. 12.5, p. 298:** Screen shot reprinted with permission of Microsoft Corporation. **Fig. 16.1, p. 383:** Supplied by author. **Fig. 16.4, p. 391:** Used with the permission of 3M Corp.

ADVERTISEMENT CREDITS

p. 10: Courtesy Coast Hotels & Resorts. **p. 18:** Courtesy of Campbell's Soup Company. **p. 40:** Courtesy of Edward Jones Investment. **p. 45:** Courtesy Canadian Professional Sales Association. **p. 57:** Courtesy Clarica, a member of the Sun Life Financial Group of Companies. **p. 134:** Courtesy of BOC. **p. 138:** Courtesy BCBC. **p. 145:** Courtesy of Sensors & Software Inc. **p. 165:** Courtesy of Lexus. **p. 191** *(top)***:** Courtesy AIM Funds Management Inc. **p. 191** *(bottom)***:** Reprinted with permission of Samsung Electronics Canada. **p. 203:** Courtesy International Training and Management Company. **p. 204:** Courtesy Scott's Directories. **p. 209:** Reprinted with permission of infoCANADA. **p. 229:** Courtesy of Proxima, San Diego, CA. **p. 231:** Courtesy of The Complex Sale, Inc. **p. 274:** Microsoft. **p. 283:** Courtesy of SimGraphics. **p. 288:** Courtesy of Tone Brothers, Inc. **p. 289:** Courtesy of Bell Helicopter Textron. **p. 322:** Aramark. **p. 333:** ServiceMaster of Canada **p. 340:** Toshiba Corporation. **p. 353:** Courtesy of Quebecor Printing. **p. 387:** Courtesy of TerrAlign Group, Inc. **p. 411:** Courtesy of Home Depot. **p. 417:** Courtesy of Cognos Inc.

PHOTO CREDITS

***Note:** cartoon credits appear on page.*

p. 1: © Masterfile. **p. 12:** Getty Images. **p. 13:** David Graham. **p. 30:** Liaison/ Getty Images. **p. 34:** © Stewart Cohen/ Maxx Images. **p. 37:** Supplied by author. **p. 38:** Supplied by author. **p. 43:** Frank Siteman/Omni-Photo Communications, Inc. **p. 44:** Supplied by author. **p. 52:** Romily Lockver/The Image Bank. **p. 59:** Dick Hemingway. **p. 65** *(top)***:** Romily Lockver/The Image Bank. **p. 65** *(bottom)***:** Supplied by author. **p. 67:** Stone/Getty Images. **p. 68:** Robert Baumgardner, © 2000 Robert Baumgardner. All rights reserved. **p. 73:** David Madison/Stone/ Getty Images. **p. 79:** © CORBIS/ Sygma. **p. 81:** Stone/Getty Images. **p. 87:** AP/World Wide Photos. **p. 88:** © CORBIS/Outline. **p. 89:** CP Photo. **p. 90:** © The Copyright Group/ SuperStock. **p. 91:** © Superstock. **p. 96:** Stone/Getty Images. **p. 110:** Image Bank/ Getty Images. **p. 114:** © CORBIS. **p. 115:** © CORBIS. **p. 124:** David Frazier/The Image Works. **p. 131:** © CORBIS. **p. 132:** Jose L. Pelaez/The Stock Market. **p. 140:** Tony Freedman/ Photo Edit. **p. 141:** © Photodisc. **p. 154:** Supplied by author. **p. 172:** © Digital Vision. **p. 192:** Supplied by author. **p. 201:** © CORBIS. **p. 205:** Bentley Motors, Inc. **p. 207:** © Bill Varie/CORBIS. **p. 214:** Mackay Envelope Company. **p. 222:** © Digital Vision. **p. 230:** David Joel/Tony Stone Images. **p. 232:** Marc Romanelli/ Image Bank/Getty Images. **p. 236:** © Superstock. **p. 238:** Supplied by author. **p. 243:** Myrleen Ferguson Cate/ Photo Edit. **p. 255:** Jose L. Pelaez/ The Stock Market. **p. 264:** Jeffrey Shaw. **p. 265:** © CORBIS/Stock Market. **p. 286:** SMART Technologies, Inc. **p. 291:** © Lisette Le Bon/SuperStock **p. 295:** Uniphoto Pictor. **p. 307:** © Superstock. **p. 316:** © Digital Vision. **p. 331:** Taxi/Getty Images. **p. 339:** © CORBIS/Sharpshooters. **p. 344:** © Royalty-Free/CORBIS. **p. 355:** AP/World Wide Photos. **p. 358:** © Superstock. **p. 359:** © Superstock. **p. 376:** © Eyewire. **p. 379:** © Photodisc. **p. 285:** Michael Paras/Photographic Services. **p. 385:** Jose L. Pelaez/ The Stock Market. **p. 394:** Supplied by author. **p. 402:** Michael Newman/ Photo Edit. **p. 406:** Jonathan Nourak/ Photo Edit. **p. 409:** John Coletti/ Allyn & Bacon. **p. 414:** Jose L. Pelaez/ The Stock Market.

"AS IS" LICENSE AGREEMENT AND LIMITED WARRANTY

READ THIS LICENSE CAREFULLY BEFORE OPENING THIS PACKAGE. BY OPENING THIS PACKAGE, YOU ARE AGREEING TO THE TERMS AND CONDITIONS OF THIS LICENSE. IF YOU DO NOT AGREE, DO NOT OPEN THE PACKAGE. PROMPTLY RETURN THE UNOPENED PACKAGE AND ALL ACCOMPANYING ITEMS TO THE PLACE YOU OBTAINED THEM. *THESE TERMS APPLY TO ALL LICENSED SOFTWARE ON THE DISK EXCEPT THAT THE TERMS FOR USE OF ANY SHAREWARE OR FREEWARE ON THE DISKETTES ARE AS SET FORTH IN THE ELECTRONIC LICENSE LOCATED ON THE DISK:*

1. **GRANT OF LICENSE and OWNERSHIP:** The enclosed computer programs <<and any data>> ("Software") are licensed, not sold, to you by Pearson Education Canada Inc. ("We" or the "Company") in consideration of your adoption of the accompanying Company textbooks and/or other materials, and your agreement to these terms. You own only the disk(s) but we and/or our licensors own the Software itself. This license allows instructors and students enrolled in the course using the Company textbook that accompanies this Software (the "Course") to use and display the enclosed copy of the Software for academic use only, so long as you comply with the terms of this Agreement. You may make one copy for back up only. We reserve any rights not granted to you.

2. **USE RESTRICTIONS:** You may not sell or license copies of the Software or the Documentation to others. You may not transfer, distribute or make available the Software or the Documentation, except to instructors and students in your school who are users of the adopted Company textbook that accompanies this Software in connection with the course for which the textbook was adopted. You may not reverse engineer, disassemble, decompile, modify, adapt, translate or create derivative works based on the Software or the Documentation. You may be held legally responsible for any copying or copyright infringement which is caused by your failure to abide by the terms of these restrictions.

3. **TERMINATION:** This license is effective until terminated. This license will terminate automatically without notice from the Company if you fail to comply with any provisions or limitations of this license. Upon termination, you shall destroy the Documentation and all copies of the Software. All provisions of this Agreement as to limitation and disclaimer of warranties, limitation of liability, remedies or damages, and our ownership rights shall survive termination.

4. **DISCLAIMER OF WARRANTY: THE COMPANY AND ITS LICENSORS MAKE NO WARRANTIES ABOUT THE SOFTWARE, WHICH IS PROVIDED "AS-IS." IF THE DISK IS DEFECTIVE IN MATERIALS OR WORKMANSHIP, YOUR ONLY REMEDY IS TO RETURN IT TO THE COMPANY WITHIN 30 DAYS FOR REPLACEMENT UNLESS THE COMPANY DETERMINES IN GOOD FAITH THAT THE DISK HAS BEEN MISUSED OR IMPROPERLY INSTALLED, REPAIRED, ALTERED OR DAMAGED. THE COMPANY DISCLAIMS ALL WARRANTIES, EXPRESS OR IMPLIED, INCLUDING WITHOUT LIMITATION, THE IMPLIED WARRANTIES OF MERCHANTABILITY AND FITNESS FOR A PARTICULAR PURPOSE. THE COMPANY DOES NOT WARRANT, GUARANTEE OR MAKE ANY REPRESENTATION REGARDING THE ACCURACY, RELIABILITY, CURRENTNESS, USE, OR RESULTS OF USE, OF THE SOFTWARE.**

5. **LIMITATION OF REMEDIES AND DAMAGES: IN NO EVENT, SHALL THE COMPANY OR ITS EMPLOYEES, AGENTS, LICENSORS OR CONTRACTORS BE LIABLE FOR ANY INCIDENTAL, INDIRECT, SPECIAL OR CONSEQUENTIAL DAMAGES ARISING OUT OF OR IN CONNECTION WITH THIS LICENSE OR THE SOFTWARE, INCLUDING, WITHOUT LIMITATION, LOSS OF USE, LOSS OF DATA, LOSS OF INCOME OR PROFIT, OR OTHER LOSSES SUSTAINED AS A RESULT OF INJURY TO ANY PERSON, OR LOSS OF OR DAMAGE TO PROPERTY, OR CLAIMS OF THIRD PARTIES, EVEN IF THE COMPANY OR AN AUTHORIZED REPRESENTATIVE OF THE COMPANY HAS BEEN ADVISED OF THE POSSIBILITY OF SUCH DAMAGES.** SOME JURISDICTIONS DO NOT ALLOW THE LIMITATION OF DAMAGES IN CERTAIN CIRCUMSTANCES, SO THE ABOVE LIMITATIONS MAY NOT ALWAYS APPLY.

6. **GENERAL:** THIS AGREEMENT SHALL BE CONSTRUED AND INTERPRETED ACCORDING TO THE LAWS OF THE PROVINCE OF ONTARIO. This Agreement is the complete and exclusive statement of the agreement between you and the Company and supersedes all proposals, prior agreements, oral or written, and any other communications between you and the company or any of its representatives relating to the subject matter.

Should you have any questions concerning this agreement or if you wish to contact the Company for any reason, please contact in writing: Editorial Manager, Pearson Education Canada, 26 Prince Andrew Place, Don Mills, Ontario, M3C 2T8